YOUTH, EDUCATION, AND SEXUALITIES

YOUTH, EDUCATION, AND SEXUALITIES

AN INTERNATIONAL ENCYCLOPEDIA

Volume One
A–J

Edited by
James T. Sears

Greenwood Press
Westport, Connecticut • London

Library of Congress Cataloging-in-Publication Data

Youth, education, and sexualities : an international encyclopedia /
   edited by James T. Sears.
    2 v. cm.
   Includes bibliographical references and index.
   ISBN 0-313-32748-3 (set : alk. paper)—ISBN 0-313-32754-8 (v. 1 :
alk. paper)—ISBN 0-313-32755-6 (v. 2 : alk. paper)
   1. Homosexuality and education—Encyclopedias.   2. Sex differences
in education—Encyclopedias.   3. Gay youth—Education—Encyclopedias.
   4. Gay youth—Social conditions—Encyclopedias.   5. Sexual orientation—
Encyclopedias.   I. Sears, James T. (James Thomas), 1951–   .
   LC192.6.Y68   2005
   371.826′6′03—dc22   2005018961

British Library Cataloguing in Publication Data is available.

Library of Congress Catalog Card Number: 2005018961
ISBN: 0-313-32748-3 (set)
0-313-32754-8 (vol. I)
0-313-32755-6 (vol. II)

First published in 2005

Greenwood Press, 88 Post Road West, Westport, CT 06881
An imprint of Greenwood Publishing Group, Inc.
www.greenwood.com

Printed in the United States of America

The paper used in this book complies with the
Permanent Paper Standard issued by the National
Information Standards Organization (Z39.48-1984).

10   9   8   7   6   5   4   3   2   1

Table of Contents

Alphabetical List of Entries

Alphabetical List of Entries

Guide to Related Topics

Colleges and Universities

Administrators
College Age Students
College Campus Organizing
College Campus Programming
College Campus Resource Centers
Community and Technical Colleges
Counseling
Curriculum, Higher Education
Fraternities
Johns Committee
Lavender Graduation
Residence Life in Colleges
School Climate, College
Single-Sex Schools
Sororities
Women's Colleges

Communities

Community LGBT Youth Groups
HIV Education
Identity Politics
Internet, Gay Men and the
Internet, Lesbians and the
Queer Zines
Race and Racism Social Class

Curriculum and Pedagogy

Art, Teaching of
Australia, Sexualities Curriculum in
Biology, Teaching of
Campus Resource Centers
Career Counseling
Children of the Rainbow Curriculum
Cocurricular Activities
College Campus Organizing
College Campus Programming
Communication
Counseling
Counselor Education
Curriculum, Antibias
Curriculum, Early Childhood
Curriculum, Higher Education
Curriculum, Primary
Curriculum, Secondary
Dance, Teaching of
ESL, Teaching of Geography, Teaching of

History, Teaching of
HIV Education
Language Arts, Teaching of
LGBT Studies
Literature, College
Literature, Early Childhood
Literature, Middle School
Literature, Secondary School
Men's Studies
Multicultural Education
Music, Teaching of
New Zealand, Teaching of Sexualities in
Philosophy, Teaching of
Physical Education, Teaching of
Poetry, Teaching of
Political Science, Teaching of
Psychology, Teaching of
Queer Pedagogy
Queer Studies
Science, Teaching of
Sexuality Education
Social Work
Theater, Teaching of
Women's Studies

Educational Associations and Organizations

Gay, Lesbian, and Straight Education
  Network (GLSEN)
GLBT Educational Equity (GLEE)
Professional Educational Organizations Scouting

Educational Policies and Practices

Antidiscrimination Policy
Disabilities, Intellectual
Disabilities, Physical
Discrimination
Educational Administration
Educational Policies
Gay–Straight Alliances
Gifted Education, LGBT Youth in
Harassment
Heteronormativity
Heterosexism
Homophobia
Lavender Graduation
Multicultural Education

Project 10
School Safety and Safe School Zones
Secondary Schools, LGBT
Sexism
Sexual Harassment
Sexuality Education
Single-Sex Schools
Special Education, LGBT Youth in
Workplace Issues

Educators and Professionals

Activism, LGBT Teachers
Allies
Administrators Coming Out, Teachers
Counseling
Educational Administration
Films, Youth and Educators in
Licensure
Mentoring
Professionalism
Social Work
Teachers, LGBT and History
Workplace Issues

Elementary and Secondary Schools

Administration, Educational
Administrators
Catholic Education and Youth
Counseling
Curriculum, Early Childhood
Curriculum, Primary
Curriculum, Secondary
Gay–Straight Alliances
Project 10
Proms
Rural Youth and Schools
School Climate, K-12
Secondary Schools, LGBT
Single-Sex Schools
Urban Youth and Schools

Ethnicity and Ethnic Groups

African American Youth
Asian American Youth
ESL, Teaching of
Ethnic Identity
Latinos and Latinas
Native or Indigenous LGBT Youth
Race and Racism
Racial Identity
Rural Youth and Schools
Urban Youth and Schools
White Antiracism

Government Policies and Practices

Acquired Immune Deficiency Syndrome
  (AIDS)
Britain, Section 28
Colonialism and Homosexuality
Discrimination
Domestic and Relationship Violence
Hate Crimes
Licensure
Sexual Harassment
Workplace Issues
Youth, Homeless

Health

Acquired Immune Deficiency Syndrome
  (AIDS)
Adolescent Sexualities
Agency
Alcoholism
Behavior Disorders
Bullying
Canada, HIV/AIDS Education in
Counseling
Deaf LGBT Youth
*Diagnostic & Statistical Manual of Mental
  Disorders* (DSM)
Disabilities, Intellectual
Disabilities, Physical
Domestic and Relationship Violence
Drug Use
Eating Disorders and Body Image
Gender Identity Disorder
Homophobia
Identity Development
Japan, HIV/AIDS Education in
Mental Health
Pregnancy, Teenage
Prejudice
Prostitution or Sex Work
Religion and Psychological
  Development
Reparative Therapy
Resiliency
School Safety and Safe School Zones
Sexual Abuse and Assault
Sexual Health, Gay and Bisexual
Sexual Health, Lesbian and Bisexual
Substance Abuse and Use
Suicide
Transsexuality
Youth, At-Risk
Youth Risk Behavior Surveys

History

Activism, LGBT Teachers
Administrators
Feminism
Johns Committee
Lesbian Feminism
Pink Triangle
Rainbow Flag and Other Pride Symbols
Stonewall
Teachers, LGBT and History
Women's Colleges
Women's Movement

Legal Matters

Boy Scouts of America et al. v. Dale
Discrimination
Domestic and Relationship Violence
Harassment
Hate Crimes
Lawrence v. Texas
Legal Issues, Students
Sexual Abuse and Assault
Sexual Harassment
Teachers, LGBT and History
Workplace Issues

Parents

Adoption
Allies
Children of LGBT Parents Families, LGBT
Parents, LGBT
Parents, Responses to Homosexuality

People

Butler, Judith
Foucault, Michel
Freud, Sigmund
Hall, G. Stanley
Hirschfeld, Magnus Kinsey, Alfred
Lacan, Jacques
Shepard, Matthew

Popular Culture

Camp
Cartoons
Comics
Dating
Films, Youth and Educators in
Graffiti
Identity Politics
The L Word

Music, Popular
Popular Culture
Queer as Folk
Queer Zines
Sports, Gay Men in
Sports, Lesbians in
Stereotypes
Tong-zhi
Youth Culture

Regions and Countries

Africa, LGBT Youth and Issues in
Asia, LGBT Youth and Issues in
Australia, LGBT Issues in
Australia, LGBT Youth in
Australia, Research on Sexual Identities
Australia, Sexualities Curriculum in
Brazil, LGBT Youth in
Britain, Section 28
Bulgaria, LGBT Youth in
Canada, HIV/AIDS Education in
Canada, LGBT Issues in
Canada, LGBT Youth in
China, LGBT Issues in
China, LGBT Youth in
Egypt, LGBT Youth and Issues in
Europe, LGBT Youth and Issues in
France, LGBT Youth and Issues in
India, LGBT Youth and Issues in
Ireland, LGBT Youth and Issues in
Israel, LGBT Issues in
Israel, LGBT Youth in
Japan, Gay and Transgender Youth in
Japan, HIV/AIDS Education in
Japan, Lesbian and Bisexual Youth in
Japan, LGBT Issues in
Mexico, LGBT Youth and Issues in
New Zealand, LGBT Youth and Issues in
New Zealand, Teaching of Sexualities in
Russia, LGBT Youth in
South Africa, LGBT Issues in
South Africa, LGBT Youth in
South America, LGBT Youth and Issues in
United Kingdom, LGBT Youth in

Religion

Catholic Education and Youth
Christian Moral Instruction on Homosexuality
Jewish Moral Instruction on Homosexuality
Muslim Moral Instruction on Homosexuality
Religion and Psychological Development
Religious Fundamentalism
Spirituality

Guide to Related Topics

Sexuality and Gender

Australia, Research on Sexual Identities
Bisexuality
Compulsory Heterosexuality
Cross-Dressing
Crush
Dating
Desire
Gender Identity
Gender Roles
Intersex
Multiple Genders
Prostitution or Sex Work
Sexism
Sexual Abuse and Assault
Sexual Harassment
Sexual Identity
Sexual Orientation
Sissy Boy
Stereotypes
Tomboy
Transsexuality

Symbols and Celebrations

Day of Silence or Silencing
Lavender Graduation
National Coming Out Day
Pink Triangle
Rainbow Flag and Other Pride Symbols

Teachers

Activism, LGBT Teachers
Coming Out, Teachers
Teachers, LGBT and History

Technology

Internet, Gay Men and the
Internet, Lesbians and the
Queer Zines
Virtual Schooling

Theory and Philosophy

Critical Social Theory
Feminism
Heteronormativity
Lesbian Feminism
Poststructuralism
Psychoanalysis and Education

Psychoanalysis and Feminism
Queer and Queer Theory

Youth

Activism, LGBT Youth
Adolescence
Adolescent Sexualities
Agency
Bisexual Youth
Childhood
Children of LGBT Parents
College Age Students
Coming Out, Youth
Dating
Deaf LGBT Youth
Drug Use
Eating Disorders and Body Image
Families, LGBT
Films, Youth and Educators in
Gay Youth
Gender Identity Disorder
Gifted Education, LGBT Youth in
Identity Development
Intersex
Lesbian Youth
Mental Health
Mentoring
Passing
Pregnancy, Teenage
Prostitution or Sex Work
Research, Qualitative
Research, Quantitative
Racial Identity
Resiliency
Rural Youth and Schools
Scouting
Sexual Identity
Sexual Orientation
Sissy Boy
Special Education, LGBT Youth in
Substance Abuse and Use
Suicide
Tomboy
Tong-zhi
Transgender Youth
Urban Youth and Schools
Youth, At-Risk
Youth Culture
Youth, Homeless
Youth Risk Behavior Surveys

Preface

Although sexuality is one of the most meaningful and important aspects of the human condition, most people have inadequate understanding of it. What limited instruction exists generally is contoured by moral and political interests as well as techno-rational discourse, which have restricted its teaching to moral pronouncements and reduced it to biological study. This has resulted in the exclusion of or marginalization of non-heterosexual issues and topics in schools and other institutions serving youth. *Youth, Education, and Sexualities: An International Encyclopedia* queers the singular understanding of sexuality as heterosexual by detailing lesbian, gay, bisexual, and transgender (LGBTQ) sexualities as it relates to youth and education.

This authoritative two-volume international encyclopedia encompasses the extant knowledge on research, policy, and practice on queer sexualities, focusing specifically on its intersection with young people and their formal as well as informal schooling. Employing up-to-date disciplinary and cross-disciplinary scholarship, these volumes provide a worldview of the current state of LGBT educational policies, curricula, and teaching approaches as well as topics relevant to queer youth and their allies.

The nearly 250 entries collectively represent cutting edge scholarship in the bourgeoning fields of LGBT studies and queer theory within education and allied fields. These entries are written in a clear and cogent style for a general audience, but particularly with teachers, administrators, counselors, youth workers, as well as students and parents in mind. The twin volumes should be of particular interest to high school/undergraduate students and teachers at all grade levels who will find this a key sourcebook for class papers and projects, for speaking to practical issues, and in addressing personal interests. It, too, will be an important resource for scholars and graduate students in such fields as education, anthropology, health, history, psychology, literature, and sociology, as well as for courses in human sexuality that may be found in several departments, such as psychology, health, counseling, biology, and women's, gender, or queer studies.

For our purposes, education is characterized as either formal schooling (preschool through higher education) or nonformal instructive efforts, ranging from youth organizations and radio talk shows to ancient myths and the work of non-government organizations. Sexualities is understood as a ubiquitous yet ambiguous concept constructed from experiences, discourses, and understandings of the body, gender identities and gender relations, genital behavior, and the erotic. Youth is considered to fall in the period of adolescence and postadolescence (to mid-twenties), although entries related to children and primary education are included in this encyclopedia.

There are 242 entries, ranging from 1,000 to 2,500 words. Each entry includes an up-to-date bibliography, references, and one or more related annotated Web sites. Relevant and timely resources within most entries also include video documentaries, films, textbooks, novels, or popular culture of interest to the general reader and of special value to educators and students. Some entries include photographs or illustrations, and all are indexed and cross-referenced within and between the volumes.

(Each entry contains bold-faced words indicating topics of interest that can be found within the encyclopedia, as well as a cross-reference list.) These entries were written or revised during the second half of 2004 from contributors who were identified by the editor's professional networks, search and review of scholarship in this area, and recommendations from the encyclopedia's board of advisors.

Since our understanding about [homo]sexualities is affected largely by our unexamined assumptions regarding [hetero]sexualities, this encyclopedia includes entries that would commonly be found in any sourcebook on sexuality and youth (e.g., teen pregnancy, HIV education, gender roles). However, these topics are examined through a "queered reading," thus complicating our singular and essentialized notion of sexuality. It also includes entries which are found in more general reference books on LGBT culture and issues (e.g., Stonewall, homophobia, graffiti). Here, these topics are addressed specifically within the context of youth and education.

There, too, are entries directly relating to: youth (e.g., bullying, legal issues for students, adolescent sexuality, workplace issues, sororities); educators (e.g., deafness, teaching of biology, licensure, mentoring); concerned adults and parents (e.g., allies, adoption, parents responses to homosexuality); the general academic community of students and scholars (e.g., resiliency; qualitative and quantitative research, youth risk behavioral surveys, queer theory); and activists, social service providers, and youth leaders (e.g., *Lawrence & Garner v. Texas*; hate crimes; community LGBT youth groups; scouting). Queer youth's popular culture, too, is represented with entries such as queer zines, music, the Internet, comics, and the TV series *Queer as Folk* and *The L Word*.

Although there are common educational issues and challenges that LGBTQ youth face worldwide, there are also distinct challenges based on geographical location, whether it be rural–urban, East–West, or industrial versus developing countries. Thus, coverage—in both content and contributors—includes Africa, Asia, Europe, the Middle East, North and South America, Oceania, and the United Kingdom. Current issues related to queer youth from every region of the world are discussed; greater detail generally is provided through additional entries of one or more countries within a particular geographic region. Nonetheless, there is an emphasis on policy, practice, and research directly related to education and youth within the United States.

This encyclopedia, too, is inclusive of gender, racial, and ethnic concerns—in terms of both language and content. Coverage includes native and indigenous youth, African American youth, Latinos and Latinas, Asian American youth, concepts such as ethnic identity, multiple genders, and multicultural education, and concerns like racism and sexism. Throughout the entries are strands related to youth of color, historical and contemporary contributions of women and minorities, as well as unique concerns facing transgender and intersex persons.

Youth, Education, and Sexualities is wide-ranging in its coverage, featuring content never before presented in an encyclopedic format, organized alphabetically, and extensively cross-referenced and indexed. Although it can be employed as a standard reference text to look up specific words, events, persons, or concepts as needed, it is my hope that it will be used more often for brief but regular queries to learn about sexualities which our secondary and college teachers or professional education programs have been so remiss in providing.

Introduction

During the last quarter of the past century, remarkable progress has been made politically, culturally, and educationally with respect to lesbian, gay, bisexual, and transgender (LGBT) concerns. Research and scholarship on sexualities, youth, and education have exploded in North America, Oceania, and Europe. In schools, hundreds of gay–straight alliances operate in the United States, a growing number of court settlements have resulted in greater administrative sensibility to issues of anti-gay harassment and visibility, and the number of LGBT/Queer[1] college courses have increased along with efforts to meet the needs of these youth. In countries where there is a more supportive cultural climate and proactive governmental policies, like the Netherlands and New Zealand, the efforts to support queer youth and to address issues of [homo]sexualities in the schools has been significantly greater. And even where queer youth attend schools in lands that are less hospitable, like India and Mexico, there has been progress during the last ten years, including queer youth support groups and conferences on LGBT issues attended by youth.

Although disciplinary and interdisciplinary-based research and scholarship on queer youth, education, and sexualities now routinely appear in academic publications, there is no single, detailed, and authoritative source that encompasses current research, policy, and practice. This encyclopedia details such information. Here I provide an overview, beginning with brief comments regarding the background of the field and then following with a synoptic review of research on LGBT youth and education. I conclude with an analysis of global policies and practices.

BACKGROUND OF THE FIELD

Thirty-five years since the emergence of the modern homosexual movement, there is an emerging space for lesbian, bisexual, transgender, and gay studies. From "free university" classes and gay student organizations of the 1970s to college courses and programs during the 1980s, to campus resource centers and queer studies in the 1990s, public and private universities have embraced—to varying degrees—the sexual other. This, of course, has been part of a larger societal response to demands for equality and visibility among sexual minorities. Within the same time span, we have seen a queering of the professions—from the establishment of academic caucuses in psychology and sociology, to the Gay, Lesbian and Straight Educators Network (GLSEN) and its chapters in hundreds of high schools, from greater acceptance of gay students/faculty to the inclusion of LGBT issues in accreditation standards and professional studies.

Initial research into "homosexual" issues related to education (including youth and young adults) began during the early 1970s and was centered in psychology, benefiting from the reversal of the American Psychiatric Association's original classification of homosexuality as an illness, per se, in 1973 as well as a similar resolution passed by the American Psychological Association two years later. Also, in

---

[1]"Queer" is used here to confront this pejorative epitaph as heteronormative construct and to underscore the essential instability of sexualities.

1973, the newly formed Gay Academic Union hosted its first conference, entitled "Scholarship and the Gay Academic Experience," which was attended by more than 300 students and faculty. Scholars were disciplinary-based and, through the networking of these annual conferences, many were represented in the groundbreaking work, *The Gay Academic* (Crew 1978), in fields ranging from library sciences and psychology to linguistics and history—education was not represented. One year later, the *Journal of Homosexuality* was founded.

Gay research relating to education from the 1970s through the 1980s was conducted by researchers from other academic fields and generally focused on college-age students in a variety of areas, most notably in identity development (with some type of linear stage model predicated upon developmental tasks and data gathered from case study or small scale survey research), adjustment and risk behavior (employing a deficit model focusing on a range of mental health problems), and homophobia (with a particular focus on intercorrelated traits and demographic variables among homophobes). "Gay studies" paralleled disciplinary-based scholarship and research, as academics—mostly gay white males within psychology and the social sciences—worked within their respective fields and uncritically employed a biological and transhistorical understanding of sexuality and sexual orientation (known as "essentialism").

By the late 1970s and into the 1980s, some scholars working in "gay *and* lesbian studies" stressed the paramount importance of gender and social class, often employing feminist theory, lesbian feminism, and critical social theory. Challenging the discourse of essentialism, this far from monolithic academic group operated within the conceptual umbrella known as "constructionism." They situated sexuality within particular historical and cultural contexts, arguing that sexual identity was a social construction and that sexuality was inextricably intertwined with language and power. Social constructivists criticized the unexamined essentialist assumptions of earlier scholarship and the languid positivism of gay research.

Both essentialist and constructivist scholarship, however, remained marginal to their heteronormative parental research fields such as sociology, history, English, psychology, and political science; it was absent from the field of education. By the early 1990s, some subfields, like literary studies, more fully embraced sexualities scholarship. Research into LGBT studies was transformed to queer studies, at least within more elite academic locations. Applying poststructuralism (most notably the work of Jacques Lacan, Michel Foucault, Jacques Derrida, and Judith Butler), scholars interrogated not only the universal and transhistorical understandings of sexuality but also the definitional and binary representational codes of gender and sex. Challenging the singular "reading" of sexuality, queer theorists were interested in the performativity of gender and sexual practices as they questioned culturally accepted binaries (e.g., gay–straight, male–female), analyzed social texts (ranging from film and literature to cartoons and popular music), and examined the multiple intersections of racial, sexual, gender, and other social identities within the context of heteronormativity and desire. Queer theory entered the field of education in the late 1990s with the publication of *Queer Theory in Education* (Pinar 1998).

Queer studies is to gay studies what hip-hop is to disco. Born in resistance to the hegemony of heterosexual relationships, gay studies was much like disco, which rose out of the New York gay culture to challenge the prominence of FM rock. Conversely, hip-hop is a postmodern pastiche of samples and images ripped from one context and placed into another—precisely what queer theorists do with respect to cultural identities. Just as we would not have hip-hop without disco, we would not have queer theory without gay studies. Although theorizing about textual understandings is now the norm in queer academia, educators have just begun to grapple with multimedia textualities, multidimensional subjectivities, and multiplexed narratives as well as their translation into pedagogical practices.

Nineteen eighty-seven, however, was an earlier turning point within the field of educational research. Through the support of the Women's Special Interest Group (SIG) of the American Educational Research Association (AERA), the Lesbian and Gay Studies SIG was formed to foster scholarship in a professional field that had effectively ignored queer issues, and to develop a network of support among LGBT education faculty and students. Similar networking and support efforts were initiated in the Association for Supervision and Curriculum Development and the National Educational Association in this same year.[2] The first SIG-sponsored session was held at the AERA conference in San Francisco two years later, with presentations of research based on either essentialism or constructionism. These papers would form the core chapters for the first major research publication in the field of education, *Coming Out of the Classroom Closet* (Harbeck 1992).

Within a decade, a body of education-based scholarship and research was published in other edited books, peer-reviewed articles, doctoral dissertations and masters theses. These works, employing essentialist, constructivist, or poststructuralist analyses, were primarily from Australia, New Zealand, Canada, the United Kingdom, and the United States. These efforts have been fostered through: conferences; small gatherings of researchers supported by LGBT organizations; funded research from nonprofit organizations and government agencies; research conducted or supported by groups like GLSEN and the Australian Research Centre in Sex Health and Society at La Trobe University, and the Policy Institute of the National Gay and Lesbian Task Force; and the development of LGBT-designated book series and specialized journals like the *Journal of Gay and Lesbian Issues in Education*. A new generation of scholars as well as persons working in Africa, Asia, Europe, the Middle East, and South America are now advancing the field.

RESEARCH CONTOURS OF THE FIELD[3]

Research on education and sexualities generally falls into one of five major areas: youth; professionals; curriculum and pedagogy; families; and, educational policies. These form the bedrock of this encyclopedia whose entries detail the research summarized here.

Youth

Studies on LGBT issues focusing on adolescents and young adults constitute the largest body of research among these five areas. Until recently, most research was conducted with college age, generally Caucuasian, participants and has been dominated by psychology and conducted within a positivist research paradigm. These

---

[2]Regarding ASCD, see the first essay published under the auspices of this organization about gay issues in education (Sears 1987). For an overview of the emergence of educational research on gay and lesbian issues see: Szalacha, 2005; Tierney and Dilley 1998. A detailed discussion of the emergence of LGBT and queer studies in other fields can be found in *Lesbian and Gay Studies* (Sandfort et al. 2000).
[3]This section is an abbreviated and updated version of an earlier paper (Sears 2002).

studies were possible, given, paradoxically, the students' power to freely consent and their captive status in the classroom. Many psychology-based studies have focused on heterosexist and homophobic attitudes among heterosexuals and their correlation to other factors such as gender, gender roles, religiosity, sexism, LGBT friendships, college major, along with demographic and personality traits. High degrees of homophobia, low levels of knowledge, and reports of homophobic behavior have been generally reported. These are often associated with a rigid understanding of gender roles, little or no personal contact with LGBT persons, and conservative religious views. They, too, are more likely to be male and live in the South or Midwest.

A paradigmatically identical strand of research has focused on gay and lesbian youth (only occasionally including and rarely focusing on bisexual or transgender students), generally attending college. These studies have documented risk factors related to their sexual identity—including harassment, substance abuse, suicide, eating disorders, and depression—along with issues of identity development. Data from adolescents were also drawn from community-based samples of convenience such as youth groups and support services like the Hetrick-Martin Institute in New York City. Since the mid-1990s, researchers have accessed larger and more representative samples and have employed more sophisticated statistical analyses. Using anonymous youth risk behavior surveys administered in secondary schools by state officials or similar data sets gathered in countries other than the United States, they have compared the response of lesbian, bisexual, and gay adolescents (there are no questionnaire items used to identify transgender or intersex youth) to a comparable group of heterosexual students with a focus on sexual behavior, violence and victimization, discrimination, substance abuse, and mental health problems.

Based on this growing body of research, some generalized findings are warranted:

- Between three and nine percent of secondary school students can be identified as lesbian or gay youth.
- A young person is aware of her or his same sex orientation by midadolescence.
- Adolescent sexual identity does not closely correspond to youth sexual behaviors.
- On average, by age fifteen, gay males have more sexual partners than their heterosexual peers. Bisexuality may account for upwards of one-third of adolescents' sexual experiences.
- Twice as many lesbian and bisexual adolescents than heterosexual students who engage in sexual behavior report that they or their partner has become pregnant. This finding is consistent in population-based surveys within several countries.
- LGB youth are two to three times as likely to consider or attempt suicide and twice as likely to report substance use than their heterosexual peers. Bisexual and lesbian youth appear to be at highest risk for the latter. Similarly higher rates for suicidality and substance abuse have been found in other countries, such as Italy, France and Australia, for LGB youth.
- In grades seven through twelve, 69 percent of LGB youth reported feeling unsafe in their schools, and one-third reported that they missed at least one day of school in the past month because they felt unsafe.

- LGBT high school students are twice as likely to have been threatened or injured with a weapon, and 1.5 times more likely to have carried a weapon at school.

- Self-identified transgender youth attending secondary school are nearly twice as likely to fear for their safety as compared to LGB youth, of whom about 40 percent report such fears. Although the school climate is more favorable for all sexual minorities at the college level, a nearly two-to-one ratio of fear continues (41 to 28 percent).

- Gay males have significantly lower levels of body satisfaction and self-esteem than their heterosexual peers. Anorexia is most often associated with gay males (along with heterosexual females); lesbians are at greater risk for obesity.

Simply stated, the educational environment for many queer youth is a context of fear and harassment, often which is linked to heightened rates of substance abuse and mental health problems—all of which are associated with higher suicide risks.

The second area of study, influenced by sociological and anthropological research using qualitative methods, centers on youth voices. Here, studies are just as likely to have been drawn from school-based populations or community or school-based youth groups. Some qualitative research has captured the voices of heterosexual students such as textual comments on campus surveys or graffiti on restroom walls, which evidence themes of heterosexism and homophobia. Queer youth research often focuses on the college experience, although some studies document their experiences at elementary through secondary schools. Some of these are personal narratives or retrospective accounts; a smaller proportion is case study or ethnographic research contemporaneous with queer youth's experience. Generally, these studies chronicle the difficulties faced by queer youth, ranging from insult and assault, to heteronormative curricula and homophobic educators, to enforcement of gender codes and roles.

Researchers have only begun to look at LGBT youth who participate in special education or gifted programs or who have physical or mental disabilities. Given the greater control exercised by parents, teachers, and health providers for those youth who are intellectually or physically challenged, these queer youth face additional hardships, particularly where any sexual expression is viewed unfavorably. However, educational research detailing how homophobia impacts these youth—ranging from learning disabled students to deaf youth—is slim, as are studies evaluating the effectiveness of educational programs ranging from gay–straight alliances to anti-bullying programs.

Most recently, there has been a conceptual movement away from the sociology of victimhood and psychopathology of at-risk youth to the sociology of agency and the psychology of resiliency. Here, studies center on how queer youth effectively navigate through institutions such as school and social agencies while (re/de)constructing sexual identities. Other promising avenues include examining how masculinities and femininities and gender roles are constructed in schools, cocurricular activities, and among adolescent peer groups. Similarly, researchers seek an understanding of adolescent life from the vantage point of queer-identified youth as they intersect emerging queer youth culture, such as the Internet. This research, employing queer theory or challenging deficit models of queer youth, is just underway and represents less than 1 percent of all research studies conducted since 1987.

The overwhelming proportion of queer youth-related research is focused on white, mostly gay youth. However, just as mainstream young adult literature about gays and lesbians has changed, there has been slow but consistent movement, since the 1990s, to research youth of color. The impetus and focus for many of these studies have been AIDS and the efficacy of HIV education. Other areas for research within populations of color are "coming out," same-gender relationships, and sexual identity development, as well as the extent of homophobia within racial and ethnic communities and a concomitant challenge to the "minoritizing" Euro-American view. Within this thin body of work, some research has reported on African American and Latino(a) populations, though there is less research on Asian American or indigenous/native youth. One of the more surprising findings, based on comparative data analysis from the National Longitudinal Study of Adolescent Health, is the significant gender and racial differences regarding "romantic attraction," as males reported attraction to the same gender more often than females and Hispanics more often than non-Hispanics (Russell, Seif, and Truong 2001). Of equal interest is the finding that whites were more negative regarding their educational experiences than nonwhites, challenging the essentialist notion of "double" or "triple" oppression theory.

These studies are generally based on males living mainly in urban settings, further distorting our limited knowledge on youth of color. About a million LGBT youth attend schools in small towns in the United States. Reports are that harassment and bullying are particularly pervasive in these underserved rural communities, which have been largely unaffected by progress in urban school districts—although, even there, only 6 percent of these large districts include homosexuality in any depth in the school curriculum. Further, research studies exploring rural issues and contexts of queer youth are extremely limited, particularly outside North America. The little that has been produced can be largely attributed to Australian researchers who have documented the impact of geographic isolation, community conservatism, and limited access to LGBT-related resources. For example, among sexual minority males, the rates of suicide for Australian rural youth were twice that of their urban counterparts.

Despite the obvious economic disparities among racial groups and those living in rural areas, there has been a paucity of research examining the effect of social class. Clearly, this factors into the degree of access these youth have to resources from traveling to community youth groups to using the Internet superhighway. It also frames how sexual and gender identities are performed and are reacted to by others. And, certainly, it determines the type of schools available to attend, which may have very different approaches to LGBT issues and services for queer students. Further, most community activists and researchers believe that LGBT youth are an overrepresented population among street-based youth. These youth, many who have been tossed out of their homes or have departed due to a difficult home environment, are more likely to engage in substance abuse, experience violence, and to engage in sex work. Services provided for (and research conducted on) transgender street youth is particularly wanting.

A final trend on LGBT-youth related research is its downward focus during this fifteen-year period from college to secondary schools and, during the past few years, to middle schools and early adolescence. Elementary school research is more limited. For example, there is no empirical research on the school climate for students who fail to follow expected gender roles or heterosexual norms in elementary schools. Research on elementary and middle school age youth has examined how gender identities are based on heterosexist assumptions, manifested in everyday childhood language and behavior, and reinforced through the heteronormativity of the school curriculum.

A concomitant finding is that youth are coming out at an earlier age than in earlier generations—although even the cultural concept of "coming out," that is, disclosing one's sexual identity to others, has been found to be problematic in the differences found, for example, between African American and Euro American queer experiences. Even terms like "queer" have whiteness associated with them as some same-gender-loving African American youth prefer to describe their experiences as being "on the Down Low" or "in the life."

As the body of research on LGBT youth grows along with greater support for such research, which increasingly is using more sophisticated methodologies, there will likely be substantial advances in this sub-field during this decade.[4]

Professionals

There has been relatively substantial research on attitudes about homosexuals and homosexuality among those who work with children and young adults. Counselors are a particularly represented population, as are teachers. In contrast to teachers, recent research on counselor attitudes evidences a lower level of homophobia than is found in society. There have been fewer studies on other professional groups such as school nurses, administrators, social workers, psychologists and psychiatrists, and pediatricians.

A variety of studies, too, have been conducted on attitudes about homosexuals/homosexuality among groups of preprofessionals. These include nursing students, resident assistants, preservice teachers and those bound for social work, counseling psychology, and medicine. Generally, these have found negative attitudes toward gay men and, to a lesser degree, lesbians. One of the problems, perhaps symptomatic of the absence of comfort, confronted by these professionals is a general absence of disclosure from their LGBT patients. However, recent research among preservice teachers has found greater acceptance of homosexuality than earlier studies found and the recognition that issues of professionalism and school safety trump personal beliefs, possibly reflecting changes evidenced in the evolution of popular culture and, perhaps, education itself.

Studies of teachers' attitudes or knowledge have focused principally on public schools, although there is some research related to Catholic institutions with respect to guidance counselors' attitudes and gay, lesbian, and bisexual teachers. Little research exists on LGBT professionals who are associated in some way with education—with the exception of queer teachers, which has a substantial body of work. Areas of focus here include coming out experiences or strategies, psychological differences with heterosexual teachers, reports of harassment and homophobia, and the construction of queer identities within the school context.

Within this genre, there are a disproportionate number of studies on lesbian physical education teachers and few studies of queer administrators, perhaps reflecting (or challenging) various stereotypes. Most studies in this area use qualitative methodologies or seldom go beyond descriptive statistics. One of the more interesting

---

[4]For an array of essays on the future of conducting research on LGBT youth, see the special issue of *The Journal of Gay and Lesbian Issues in Education* (vol. 3, Nos. 2–3).

studies, however, documents an increase in positive attitudes among college students at the end of the school term following disclosure of the instructor's sexual orientation midway through the course (Waldo and Kemp 1997). The impact that openly queer teachers have on their students, particularly those who are LGBT and for whom they may serve as role models and mentors, has not been adequately studied.

Cutting-edge researchers now integrate critical and postmodern theories into design and analysis. Rather than looking at issues of coming out, for instance, a researcher may explore how these teachers resist heteronormative discourse in the school, the strategies they use to process the resultant tension, and how they negotiate their identities within this context.

Curriculum and Pedagogy

Unlike fifteen years ago, there is some coverage within professional schools on LGBT issues; its depth and breadth, however, varies and seldom matches accreditation expectations or even program descriptions. Within professional schools, researchers have examined the coverage of LGBT issues related to counseling and clinical psychology, in social work curriculum or journals, and in curricula and textbooks of psychology programs and pediatric medicine. Within education, there has been some examination of commonly used textbooks, graduate school catalogs, and integration into the teacher education curriculum, generally reporting only superficial coverage. Across the board, these curricula have been found wanting in preparing teachers, counselors, and social workers to both address LGBT issues and work with queer youth effectively.

Some studies, too, have been conducted on the impact of interventions in professional programs designed to reduce homophobia by increasing knowledge. The most effective strategies, however, have been found to be those that focus on professional attitudes and personal feelings, integrate a variety of pedagogical strategies including panel presentations, role playing, films, and small group discussions, and that are integrated throughout the curriculum, rather than placed in a single course as a brief unit.

Comparably few studies have focused below the college level and these have largely centered in secondary schools within the areas of sexuality education and health, where the triangulation of biologism, sexism, and heterosexism have been fortified by the growing use of "abstinence-based" approach and administrative fear of community controversy. Whether it is in these areas or in social studies and the arts, there is meager evidence of integration of queer-related content, knowledgeable and comfortable educators, or inclusive and queer pedagogy. Not surprisingly, the positive impact of such courses on high school students' knowledge and attitudes toward homosexuality and on opinions on LGBT issues has been minimal. Further, the connection between acquisition of knowledge and incumbent changes in attitudes and behaviors is even more tenuous.

Although there is an extensive amount of scholarship regarding queer pedagogy, how to teach queerly[5] on subjects ranging from art and history to science and biology at the K-12 level, *and* the impact of such pedagogy has been poorly documented

---

[5]As detailed in my introductory chapter to *Queering Elementary Education*, "Teaching queerly is not teaching sex. It embodies educators who model honesty, civility, authenticity, integrity, fairness, and respect. . . . [I]t is creating classrooms that challenges categorical thinking, promote interpersonal intelligence, and foster critical consciousness." (Sears, 1999, pp. 4–5)

and even less well-researched. There have been some examinations of more conventional teaching strategies and processes vis-à-vis the reduction of homophobia/heterosexism through exercises such as the Pink Triangle experiment. However, even here the research designs have been weak, as longitudinal or experimental studies of particular classroom interventions are rare.

Curriculum, however, is conceived more broadly than simply a course of study or textbooks, as it extends to cocurricular activities from intramural sports and Greek organizations to theater and band, library resources, in-school LGBT counseling programs and support groups, residence living, and the overall school climate. A positive climate within higher education is associated with the availability of student support services, LGBT campus resources centers, and mentoring relationships with faculty or staff members. The existence of student run queer groups, offering support, information, and leadership opportunities, are also important and widespread. However, they are less developed or less likely to be found in the South, particularly in smaller or private southern institutions, at historically black colleges and universities, or at community and technical colleges (about which there is very little research). These student groups, too, are much more common in North America than in Europe or other world regions.

At the secondary level, qualitative and quantitative research has documented a chillier school climate for queer students and educators. They routinely face harassment and bullying, confront heterosexism and homophobia, or experience isolation and ostracism while a smaller percentage experience physical and even sexual harassment in the school. There has been little research at the middle and primary school levels. From this body of work, there is meager evidence of progress regarding the development of safe and supportive educational settings for queer youth as typified in recent studies that report a hostile environment for high school students.

Community and school-based support groups for sexual minority youth began in the 1970s. Within a decade there were a few affirmative counseling programs in some public schools, most notably Project 10 in Los Angeles and Boston, and many more community-based youth outreach programs. At the turn of the twenty-first century, there were over 2,000 gay–straight alliances in public schools throughout the United States (with the exception of Mississippi). There, too, is an emerging body of quantitative and qualitative research regarding students' experiences in such programs and their effectiveness in enhancing their resiliency, increasing feelings of personal safety, reducing at-risk behaviors and suicidality, improving the quality of their school or community life, and improving school attendance. The limitations of these programs with respect to meeting the needs of queer youth of color have also been documented but, again, this research is only in its infancy.

Families

In the United States, lesbian and gay parents are estimated to range from six to ten million; six to fourteen million children in the U.S. have one or more parents who are lesbian, gay, or bisexual. The most recent census found that from the 600,000 same-sex couples, about one-third of lesbian and bisexual female-headed households and 22 percent of gay and bisexual male households had one or more children residing with them. Since the 1980s there has been consistent research related to gay and lesbian-headed families (research on transgender and bisexual parents is now underway). Most studies—based, like the early youth at-risk research, on a deficit model—have found no differences between parenting techniques of gay and nongays or the impact of same-sex parents on their children's sexual orientation or emotional development. Studies conducted in the 1990s, however, began to focus on the *strengths* brought to a gay or lesbian family or documented the positive long-term impact of living within such a nontraditional setting.

The vast majority of LGBT youth are raised by parents who do not share their minority status and only a minority of heterosexual-identified youth is raised by LGBT parents. Most research directly related to education have examined the impact of such families on the school, the experiences of children from those families who attend school, and teachers'/administrators' attitudes toward nontraditional families. Researchers have also explored the impact on heterosexual families of the coming out of their school-age child or sibling. Although the increase in the number of children in sexual minority-headed households (and greater publicity) has created an awareness among educators, educational policies (e.g., disclosure of student information to the second parent who does not have legal custody), curriculum (integration of diverse family stories in primary school), or pedagogy (not assuming all children have a mother and father) are far from inclusive.

Whereas LGBT parents do not negatively impact their children in terms of pscho-sexual development, schools create additional burdens for these youth who are mostly heterosexual. Reporting harassment at rates nearly those found among LGBT youth, it is not surprising that their parents are concerned about school safety and the degree to which they choose to be "out" in their child's school (particularly beyond elementary age). Neither is it remarkable (albeit disturbing) that many of these children go through a period of rejection or passing with respect to their parents' sexual orientation. Ultimately, most become supportive and some engage in activism in support of LGBT issues. There is, though, little research in this area (as there is, in general, on research on LGBT allies).

As in other areas, there are disparities between options available to LGBT families from urban areas (where LGBT support groups, generally more tolerant attitudes, and other institutional support systems, such as major universities, are more prevalent), and the more limited options afforded to families residing in small towns or rural areas. Access to the Internet has proven important to these more isolated families, although this, too, is limited by financial resources. Options for schooling are also limited and there is no research on the degree to which such alternative families make use of home schooling.

Educational Policies

A variety of legislative and institutional policies have been promulgated during the past two decades. As detailed in the next section, these include adoption statutes prohibiting discrimination on the basis of sexual orientation and the implementation of educational policies at the state and school district levels relating to LGBT teachers, harassment of students, and so forth. Studies included in this area generally focus on the history of educational policies discriminating against LGBT teachers, efforts to deny licensing or remove them from the profession, such as occurred in Florida with the infamous Johns Committee, or the self-imposed silencing of queer teachers.

There, too, has been research on the impact of policies related to LGBT youth and issues education. Initially, this work focused on legal issues in education. However, as courts, legislatures, school boards, and the public have influenced educational policy there is an emerging body of literature that assesses the impact of antidiscrimination and antibullying policies, safe school and inclusive counseling policies.

In the mid-1990s, Massachusetts began implementing a state safe schools plan for gay and lesbian youth. Research has focused on school districts' efforts to implement these policies and factors that lesbian and gay teachers feel are important in their self-disclosure and school activism. Similarly, in Los Angeles, despite the national attention to the longstanding Project 10, a survey of programs and services provided by the county school district found them to be less than accessible or supportive, documenting factors that have inhibited their development. In contrast, there is no research on the effectiveness of suicide prevention school-based intervention programs for sexual minority youth.

A few studies also have explicitly examined the effect of tenure, state laws, inclusive contracts, school district training or programs, and local ordinances on the openness and public identities of gay teachers or explored the relationship between such policies and school board adoption of school-based programs for queer youth. However, only one study has appropriated poststructural analysis and queer theory to examine school board policies and curriculum vis-à-vis experiences of students participating in board discussions.

EDUCATIONAL POLICIES THROUGHOUT THE WORLD

What are the various governmental and educational policies related to LGBT youth and issues of sexual diversity in education around the world? Generally, Europe, North America, and Oceania are the three regions of the world that have the most extensive educational policies related to LGBT issues, students, and educators. At best, however, these can be judged as weak to moderate in their coverage and impact. Further, the relationship between governmental policies on LGBT issues and formal/informal educational policies in a country is far from direct.

A Matrix of Governmental and Educational Policies

Governmental policies include legal protection (accorded by court, statute, or constitution) against discrimination (workplace, military, housing, family), criminal codes, enforced or unenforced, (sodomy, hate crimes) related to same-sex behavior; and budgetary support for LGBT persons, issues, and research. As a subset, educational policies can be categorized into two broad areas: Formal (budgetary allocations, executive orders, state department guidelines, federal education mandates, judicial decisions and consent decrees, accreditation and licensure standards, and local school board regulations); and, informal (staff training, student peer culture, hidden curriculum of values and beliefs, un/enforced regulations and procedures, inclusive health services, support for LGBT groups).

These policies are debated, enacted, and implemented within a cultural climate. Culture is reflected in and influenced by religion and religious beliefs related to cross-gender and same-sex behaviors, the degree and nature of media coverage (magazines, film, television, radio), the extent of technology (e.g., the Internet), the existence and value of indigenous legacies of multiple genders and sexual expressions, the importance of tradition in family, marriage, and children, grassroots and national LGBT activism, as well as the specific form of the political and economic system.

Within a cultural context, governmental policies on gender identity and sexual orientation and support for LGBT persons can range from persecutorial to proactive. These policies, in turn, provide the political context within which educational policies can be promulgated, having no, little, marginal, moderate, or significant *potential* impact on schools, educators, students, and parents. Just as removing sodomy statutes does not necessarily mean an end to persecutorial conduct by the state and deleting discriminatory provisions in criminal laws does not translate to nondiscriminatory practices, so too, the adoption of educational policies may have little impact on day-to-day school practices and on the lives of queer youth. Simply because a country enunciates constitutional or statutory protection of LGBT persons, does not mean that complementary educational policies will have been enacted across the country or enforced by local schools or educators. Conversely, the absence of such laws may not preclude communities, schools, or teachers from adopting policies supportive of queer youth. Even the most federalized educational ministry is loosely coupled and in those countries, such as Australia and the United States, that have a tradition of local control, national policy is, at best, an invitation to "do the right thing" on behalf of sexual minority youth. Thus, there are significant LGBT supportive educational policies and practices in Massachusetts and none in South Carolina.

The typology represented in Figure 1, The Queer Governmental and Educational Policy Matrix, allows us to consider broadly the overall cultural climate and type of state policies (proactive to persecutorial) vis-à-vis the existence and extent of educational policies and practices. For example, South Africa, whose 1996 constitution was the first in the world to recognize LGBT rights, has made little progress in enacting LGBT-inclusive educational policy, and the school climate for

State Policies / Cultural Climate

Persecutorial	Homophobic	Heteronormative	Supportive	Proactive		LGBT Educational Policies and Programs
Egypt	Russia		France		None	
	Bulgaria India	China	South Africa		Little	
	Mexico	Japan	Israel		Marginal	
	Brazil	United Kingdom	Australia	New Zealand	Moderate	
	United States		Canada	Netherlands	Significant	

Figure 1   Queer Governmental and Educational Policy Matrix

sexual minorities remains poor. And, in Egypt, same-sex behavior not only remains illegal, but the penalties meted out for violators can be severe.

In sharp contrast, New Zealand's *Homosexual Law Reform Act of 1986* decriminalized homosexuality, the *Bill of Rights Act of 1990* gave everyone the right to be free from discrimination, and the *Human Rights Act of 1993* outlawed discrimination against someone on the basis of sexual orientation. The Human Rights Amendment Act of 2001 advances human rights through education, the Ministry of Education has devoted substantial resources to a second phase of the Gender and Diversity project, and the Ministry of Youth Affairs has promulgated a Youth Development Strategy that includes fostering a "positive sexual identity" for LGBT youth. Nevertheless, inclusion of nonheterosexualities and gender identities remains limited in the formal school curriculum.

Although details about several countries are provided here to explicate this matrix, more importantly, this was the basis upon which various countries, representing each region of the world, have been included in this encyclopedia. Given the limitations of space, it was not possible to include most nations and, due to the uneven dispersion of LGBT scholarship, it was impossible to identify scholars able to write authoritatively about each of the 193 countries in the world. However, the 32 country and regional entries provide a reasonable understanding of the different faces of LGBT youth, as well as the global commonalities and diversities of educational policies.

Countries with Proactive Policies

In countries which traditionally have adopted more progressive governmental polices on LGBT issues, most notably those in Northern Europe, there has been traditionally more attention to queer youth and greater access to schools by advocacy groups.

Like New Zealand/Aotearoa, the Netherlands is a country where governmental policies are proactive. Article 1 of the Dutch Constitution, detailed in the Equal Treatment Act, mandates equality for its LGBT citizenry, estimated at one million. Dutch policy is further detailed in its Homosexual Emancipation Policy (2001), amendments to Dutch Family Law (2002), and in the report to Parliament submitted by the Ministry of Health, Welfare and Sport in 2004 (http://www.minvws.nl). Homosexuals have had access to the armed forces since 1974 and, in 1998, same-sex couples have been able to legally register as domestic partners (six other EU nations have domestic-partnership laws that grant most rights of marriage without that designation). More recently, the Netherlands (along with Belgium) has allowed same-sex couples to marry and has granted adoption rights—although, like all countries offering children for international adoption, this does not extend to noncitizens. The Dutch legislature has also recognized gender reassignment on civil status documents.

Government-funded population studies have been conducted on Dutch attitudes toward LGBT persons and issues as well on the attention given to local policies by municipal administrators (http://www.homo-emncipatie.nl). Further, the Knowledge Centre for Homosexual Emancipation and Local Policy project provides municipalities, along with private organizations, support and knowledge on legal and practical issues. Given the increased emigration into the Netherlands, the Dialogue Project, completed in 2004, breached communication across religious and cultural groups on issues related to homosexuality. *Behind Every Colour* portrays in cinematic and book form the narratives of six gay immigrant youth. A related pilot project, *Homosexuality and Islam*, provides a guide for teachers on how to address these issues with their secondary and college-age students.

Nongovernmental organizations like the Dutch Federation of Associations for the Integration of Homosexuality (known as COC Nederland and officially recognized by the government as the national advocate for LGBT persons) have assisted teachers to acquire the knowledge and skills to combat discrimination and homophobia. The Dutch Education Inspectorate is attentive to LGBT youth and issues in schools. It monitors safety and tolerance for LGBT students and recently published and distributed to all schools, including schools of education, *Everyone is Different*, which details the role of the Inspectorate and that of administrators to ensure nondiscrimination and provides specific strategies for equal treatment of LGBT persons. Schools, with the assistance of the National Centre for School Improvement and the COC Nederland, are responsible to ensure not only youth safety, but also the integration of LGBT content into the curriculum.

Even here, religious schools are allowed to discriminate against homosexual teachers if such discrimination is deemed necessary given their functions, such as teaching religion or ethics. Further, in this nation with the most significant educational policies on LGBT issues, a recent survey of Dutch students (nearly 500 respondents) still found that at many schools homosexuality remains "a taboo subject . . . lacking support from teachers and school boards. Pupils feel abandoned. Homosexual teachers feel isolated" (Tomas 2003, 16).

Countries with Supportive Policies

Although few countries have taken a proactive position on a wholesale range of LGBT issues, from workplace discrimination to same-sex marriage, many have become supportive of LGBT citizens, embedding their rights legally or constitutionally.

There has been widespread legislation to ensure LGBT French citizens rights in a country that has not prosecuted homosexual behavior for three centuries. In 1999, the *Pacte Civil de Solidarité* provided the same legal rights to couples wedding regardless of sexual or gender identities. Queer youth, however, are invisible from legislation, policy, or research. Very few organizations within the gay communities (none in the government sector) provide support for LGBT youth. There is no requirement for the schools to address any specific needs of LGBT youth, and in the very limited health education curriculum, there is no inclusion of LGBT issues or youth.

Israel's first LGB group, the Society for the Protection of Personal Rights (SPPR) was formed in 1975. Until 1988, male homosexuality was punishable by up to ten years imprisonment, even though the unofficial policy was nonprosecution. During the Labor Government (1992–1996), there was substantial progress on LGBT issues. In January 1992, the Knesset approved a nondiscrimination law in the workplace and ended discriminatory rules in the military the following year. In 1994, a Supreme Court judged in favor of domestic partner employment benefits. Further, gender reassignment surgery is facilitated by the Ministry of Health, which also helps transsexuals receive new identity papers. However, with the victory of the Likud party, there has been little further progress, albeit for the election or reelection of a handful of openly gay or lesbian politicians and the continued very low level of hate crimes perpetrated on LGBT citizens.

Unlike France, however, these changes are reflected, in part, within the educational system. The Ministry of Education, Culture, and Sport published two pamphlets during the 1990s. *Homosexual Orientation*, addressed to educators, provided both foundational information and classroom activities. An HIV education publication, *AIDS: A Question of Life*, employed a comprehensive, safe-sex approach for middle and secondary school students. Its use in the sexuality education classroom, however, has been sporadic. In higher education, however, courses on LGBT studies as well as student organizations are typical, including an annual conference on queer theory hosted by Tel Aviv University. There is, however, little research on LGBT youth and related educational issues. Although community-based groups provide speakers to high schools, there are no school-based LGBT support groups or significant integration of LGBT content into the curriculum.

Like Israel, Australia has made enormous strides in its governmental policies related to LGBT citizenry during the past two decades. Since 1997, homosexuality has been legal throughout the country. However, given the diversity of its territorial political climate and its decentralized system of governance, progress on LGBT issues has been uneven. Tasmania, at one time the most conservative of states, now allows the state to register "significant relationships" and has repealed the law forbidding "the promotion" of homosexuality in schools. Although LGBT people are protected under the broad banner of the Commonwealth Anti-Discrimination Act, the federal government does not include any reference to same-sex individuals, couples, or families in legislation. In recent years, the number of LGBT youth support groups have increased in urban areas, research on LGBT youth has begun, and networks of LGBT teachers have been initiated. Most state and territory education departments have implemented antibullying programs, which include same-sex bullying, and, in 2002, a National Safe Schools Framework was adopted. Homophobic harassment and discrimination continues, particularly outside metropolitan schools. The Queensland and Tasmanian Education Departments disseminate resources on homophobia, and the latter also sponsors the Gay, Lesbian, Bisexual, Transgender Reference Group. More substantive LGBT educational initiatives, such as curriculum integration, have not been forthcoming. Even when sexual diversity is included within the syllabus, as in the case for sex education, it is seldom consistently integrated into the classroom.

Canada has nationwide protection against discrimination on the basis of sexual orientation. Sexual practices between individuals of the same sex were decriminalized in 1969. As a result of a court challenge, the federal government, in 1992, removed the prohibition on lesbians and gays serving in the military. By the end of that decade, the Charter of Rights and Freedoms, which addresses the acts of government, and the Human Rights Act, which applies to individuals, protected persons from discrimination based on sexual orientation. And in 2003, by judicial decree, Canadians enjoyed the right to civil unions. Two years later Supreme Court Chief Justice Beverley McLachlin signed the legislation, drafted by Prime Minister Paul Martin's minority Liberal Party and passed by the House of Commons and the Senate, allowing gay couples to marry and enjoy the same rights as heterosexual couples. Canada became the fourth country (after The Netherlands, Belgium, and Spain) in the world to legally recognize same-sex marriage.

Like the United States, however, school governance issues are much more localized. Support from the ministries of education regarding LGBT issues and youth varies among provinces and territories as well as within particular school systems. In recent years, most provincial ministries have adopted some supportive LGBT policies, particularly in the areas of antigay harassment and suicide prevention. As in other industrial countries, there tends to be more support in metropolitan areas and in those regions that are more liberal in politics and religion. Religious conservatism still plays a significant role on issues related to sexualities and the schools, such as the long legal battle in British Columbia to remove LGBT-inclusive books from the school library.

Nevertheless, significant support has been forthcoming from professional teacher organizations, notably the Alberta Teachers' Association, which includes sexual orientation and gender identity as protected categories in its *Code of Professional Conduct*. The Canadian Teachers Federation has produced the handbook, *Seeing the Rainbow: Teachers Talk about Bisexual, Lesbian, Gay, Transgender and Two-Spirited Realities*. Gay–straight alliances operate throughout the school systems in Canada, and the longstanding Triangle Program, funded by the Toronto government, is a stand-alone classroom for LGBT youth. Most Canadian teacher education programs address LGBT issues, and the University of Regina and the University of Saskatchewan offer specific courses for preservice teachers and host conferences on this issue. Finally, there are a range of nongovermental programs for LGBT youth, primarily in urban areas, ranging from Vancouver's GAY Youth Services and British Columbia's *YouthQuest* to the Halifax Lesbian, Gay, and Bisexual Youth Project.

Countries with Heteronormative Policies

Much more common than the proactively supportive countries are countries which have never legally prohibited homosexuality or which have rescinded criminal statutes but, in either case, have taken little supportive action and, at times, have been restrictive in their policies. Many Asian countries such as Japan, Thailand, Vietnam, South Korea, the Philippines, and China have no official policies prohibiting homosexual behavior, but neither do they have laws protecting sexual minorities; some countries, too, have adopted policies that discriminate against its LGBT citizens. Japan, for example, prohibits homosexuals from serving in the military, and even in Thailand, certainly the world's most commercial sexual culture, there are pockets of intense homophobia within the government. Chinese policies preclude publications by LGBT groups. Consequently, there are no officially recognized queer organizations in mainland China (groups are organized around HIV education), and the only publication for gays and lesbians is a small "unofficial" magazine, *Friends*. Ironically, it was only with the departure of British rule, in 1997, that policies and activism related to LGBT issues in Hong Kong have advanced—and transsexuals have greater respect and rights on the mainland than in either Hong Kong or Taiwan. Violence against gays is rare in China; however, there remain dangers of blackmail and police harassment. Although, in 2000, the Chinese Psychiatric Association removed homosexuality from its list of mental disorders, there are no legal protections against discrimination.

The strong emphasis on the family, respect for elders, and concern for public propriety, particularly notable in Asian cultures, translate into expectations that young adults will marry and provide (preferably male) children. Thus, disclosing homosexuality to parents is difficult, and most queer youth get married, perhaps having a same-sex lover on the side. This situation is beginning to change, especially in the major cities, because globalization and technology are changing ideas of marriage and the family while connecting queer youth with others around the world.

Countries that lack policies on LGBT issues and persons are generally silent on LGBT issues in education. This silence results in a less than neutral educational experience as heterosexism and homophobia is manifested in institutional policies, curricula, and pedagogies. In most Asian countries, for instance, there is no protection against discrimination or harassment of sexual minority students (or educators), and there is seldom inclusion of LGBT topics, except occasionally in HIV education. In Japan, the Ministry of Education's guidelines on sexuality education have not included information on nonheterosexual topics, and governmental curriculum guidelines do not include discussion about or resources for LGBT youth. At the local level, however, the Osaka-City Board of Education issued its own sex education guidelines, including LGBT issues. No secondary school in Osaka-City (or in the entire country) has a transgender or gay student support group and, at those universities where such groups exist, they meet without formal administrative support. Perhaps because of the greater public visibility and acceptance of transgender persons, some schools have altered policies which have forced students to wear uniforms of one gender or the other.

Although laws and policies vary across England, Northern Ireland, Scotland, and Wales, the situation in the United Kingdom has improved markedly during the past few years. The age of consent has been equalized for queer adults (age 16 except 17 in Northern Ireland) and, as a member of the European Union, the UK does not discriminate on the basis of sexual orientation. Hate crime legislation and the increased involvement of the Crown Prosecution Service and local police in England and Wales have worked to reduce violence against LGBT persons. The Adoption and Children Act of 2002 allows gay couples to jointly apply for adoption (although this was not adopted in Scotland until mid-2005) and The Civil Partnerships Bill of 2004 allows same-sex couples to register in a procedure similar to a marriage. Although the government will insist it is not officially a "marriage," same-sex couples have rights to pensions, will not have to pay inheritance tax on property passed between them, and will have access to hospital records. The Royal Navy has become the first branch of the British military to welcome gay and lesbian personnel to stay in family quarters once they have registered (all services allow homosexuals to serve openly). Prisoners in England and Wales with gay partners are classified as close relatives allowing them to visit, while those in a relationship with another inmate at a different prison may apply for "interprison visits." Most importantly, in England and Wales, the debate on LGBT issues in education, which has been dominated for fifteen years by "Section 28" (prohibiting local authorities from "promoting" homosexuality and preventing councils from spending money on related educational materials and projects), ended with its repeal in 2003. In Scotland, its sister legislation (Clause 28) had been repealed in 2000.

Heterosexuality, however, remains the governing norm as evident in the maintenance of the fig leaf of heterosexual marriage and policies and practices in schools. Nevertheless, the Human Rights Act of 1998, the 1998 School Standards Act, and the 2003 Employment Equality (Sexual Orientation) Regulations, legally protect LGBT teachers and students from discrimination and harassment. Additionally, the High Court has indicated that teachers in faith schools are "likely" to have full protection from discrimination on grounds of sexual orientation (http://www.hmcourts-service. gov.uk/judgmentsfiles/j2478/amicus-v-ssti.htm). There has also been a national school effort to address homophobic bullying. *Stand Up for Us* (http://www.wired-forhealth.gov.uk/PDF/stand_up_for_ us_04.pdf), a guide for teachers produced by the National Healthy Schools Standard organization and launched by the School Minister, advises schools to teach about all types of relationships, and teachers to recommend that children keep a log of homophobic incidents. It also recommends that awareness of homophobia be included in school plans. Currently, only one in four secondary school teachers report that they are aware of physical homophobic bullying and just one in every twenty has policies that address it. Non-government organizations such as the National Union of Teachers and School's Out have played prominent roles in addressing LGBT issues in education.

Countries with Homophobic Policies

Many countries, ranging from Jamaica to Sudan, still criminalize homosexual behavior and others, like Russia, harass homosexuals or engage in state-sponsored homophobia despite the absence of criminalization. For instance, one-third of Russians recently surveyed viewed homosexuality as an illness, and 32 percent supported "isolation" or "liquidation." Although the younger generations are less homophobic, the twin legacy of Stalinism and Communism translates into a desire for secrecy, while the shortage of housing and importance of family leaves little room for privacy. The silencing of all expression (sexual and otherwise) during the Soviet era coupled to the emergence of religion and theological conservatism in the post-Soviet era has also contributed to a climate where LGBT activism is difficult and educational policies and programs for queer youth are nonexistent. Efforts to reinstate sodomy laws (removed in 1993), rising hate crimes against LGBT persons, and a genuine fear among some queer youth that parents may commit them to an asylum illustrate the difficult context of growing up queer in Russia.

Laws and homophobic institutions also undermine emerging gay youth organizations and HIV education efforts in India, which has a rich history of embracing sexualities from its Hindu culture: *Kama Sutra*, tantric rites, the temples of Kornark and Modhera, *Sanskrit* epics. Since the era of British colonialism, nonheterosexual behavior is punishable by up to ten years imprisonment. Section 377 of the Indian Penal Code provides justification for the lack of governmental support to LGBT issues, persons, and groups. In fact, the movement for LGBT rights in India is rooted in the efforts of Indian activists outside the country during the 1970s and 1980s. Since the early 1990s, however, there have been legal challenges to this sodomy statute, protests against police arrests and harassment, and efforts to network and educate queer Indian youth. The dozen or two existing Indian-based groups now provide an array of services, including support for LGBT youth and hosting of state, national, and regional conferences. Nevertheless, homophobic harassment and violence perpetrated by individuals and the government remain common. Gender nonconforming boys frequently are targeted for harassment and bullying by students and school employees, and reparative therapy is a popular option for more affluent families. At the national level, India's Information and Broadcasting Ministry removed the nation's first lesbian-themed and internationally-acclaimed film, *Fire*, returning it to the censor board. Members of Shiv Sena, a right-wing Hindu ally of the prime minister, organized violent protests and attacked theaters in New Delhi and Bombay, with little police intervention. Given a paucity of research on LGBT-related issues, educators and counselors are ill-prepared to work with sexual minority youth, and even traditional hijra communities have been relegated to charity work and begging.

In Mexico, where homosexuality is not criminalized, laws against public indecency are frequently used by corrupt police to harass or blackmail homosexuals. Although the district of Mexico City has banned discrimination on the basis of sexual orientation, parents have complete property ownership over their children, and schools can expel LGBT youth. It was only in the late 1980s that the first LGBT community youth group was formed, and there remain just a handful of such groups—all located in urban areas. Only one university-based LGBT group exists in the country, there are no LGBT courses taught in higher education, and research on LGBT issues and youth is, at best, meager. Nevertheless, a high school serving LGBT students was inaugurated in 2004, queer space is evident in major urban areas like the Zona Rosa in Mexico City, and two openly gay persons have been elected to Congress.

Although homosexual behavior is not criminalized in the country, Brazil has been ranked by UNESCO as the world's worst for violence perpetrated against its LGBT citizens. On the other hand, it has earned worldwide admiration for providing free drugs to all HIV-positive citizens. Like Mexico, in Brazil, a handful of states and municipalities have taken more supportive or even proactive positions on LGBT issues such as the extension of family rights to gays and lesbians, within a larger homophobic society. Even in these localities, the impact has been limited by the inaction or resistance of government officials and educators.

With substantial support from the federal government, Programa Brasil Sem Homofobia (Brazil without Homophobia) was implemented in 2004 to further the progress of LGBT activism in the country. Rio de Janeiro, Porto Alegre, and São Paulo have implemented this project as schools seek to reduce homophobia through seminars and discussions, usually inviting LGBT group members and scholars to participate in both their development and implementation. A year earlier, the São Paulo public schools inaugurated Orientação Sexual na Escola (Sexual Orientation in School) for every student in every grade. The program, which includes transgender issues and is designed to reduce sexual harassment and bullying, and requires teachers to work on antiprejudice while abandoning the understanding that sexuality is simply for procreation.

The United States, too, has eliminated its sodomy laws, but retains heterosexist laws and policies which countenance homophobia. The Bush administration and the Republican-controlled Congress, for example, have expressed a willingness to put forth a Constitutional Amendment banning gay marriage, and discriminatory Federal policies ranging from military to social services continue. Although one might expect few policies on LGBT issues in education within countries that routinely deny rights for its LGBT citizenry, in those countries—particularly the United States where schools are largely controlled at the state and local levels—there has been marked but uneven progress.

In the United States, every state constitution gives children the right to a free education and its benefits. LGBT students, therefore, cannot be dismissed from public school or be denied educational benefits, such as textbooks and transportation. In addition, "public accommodation" laws in California, Connecticut, Hawaii, Massachusetts, Minnesota, New Jersey, Wisconsin, and the District of Columbia prohibit discrimination on the basis of sexual orientation by agencies serving the public, such as schools. On the other hand, discussion of LGBT issues in classes and other school-sponsored activities are often restricted by school districts, and the courts have given schools wide latitude to dictate attire, thus creating problems for transgender youth.

Sexual minority students and LGBT issues in education within the United States have been generally supported in some states, such as Massachusetts and

New York, and met with opposition in others like Arizona and South Carolina. South Carolina bans discussion of "alternative sexual lifestyles," and Arizona prohibits instruction promoting "a homosexual lifestyle." Massachusetts, like seven other states, specifically prohibits sexual-orientation discrimination in any school activity or benefit. The Massachusetts Department of Education has administered a state-wide Safe Schools Program for Gay and Lesbian Youth. However, the program was eliminated in 2002 with state officials citing budgetary constraints.

Policies are not only subject to budgetary support, but to political backing. For instance, although the New York City Board of Education has had a policy since 1985 that includes sexual orientation as a protected class, the Children of the Rainbow curriculum, introduced in 1992, was a first grade teachers' guide to incorporating multicultural education that met an untimely end due to conservative protest after the curriculum was released and one district board president refused to implement any form of gay-inclusive multicultural curriculum.

In 1989, gay and heterosexual secondary school students began forming school-based alliances in Massachusetts. Fifteen years later, about one in every twenty-five secondary schools in the country has such a group on campus. Most of these, however, are located in urban areas or in more liberal regions of the country such as the upper Midwest. Further, the development of these groups was largely the result of judicial action which allowed for these groups due to an unintended Federal law. The "Equal Access Act," passed in 1984, allows student-initiated non-curricular clubs to meet during noninstructional time. Although conservative lawmakers wrote the law to protect groups of religious students, it now protects all student-initiated clubs and has been used to force school districts to allow gay student groups on campus.

In most school districts, there are few formal policies explicitly inclusive of LGBT students or LGBT issues such as bullying, and fewer that impact heterosexism and homophobia in informal policies and practices such as the invisibility of LGBT parents or teachers ignoring students' homophobic comments directed at other pupils. Studies of homophobic harassment in U.S. schools (like those in other countries) have reported that the overwhelming majority of LGBT students report hearing homophobic remarks throughout the school day and that many experience direct physical or verbal harassment. Such harassment is particularly pervasive in underserved rural communities, which have been largely unaffected by recent shifts in educational policies. Again, the role of the courts has been critical. Students can recover damages under Title IX (a federal gender equity law enacted in 1972) from schools that deliberately fail to control severe and pervasive same-sex harassment.

Countries with Persecutorial Policies

Homosexuality not only remains illegal in many countries, but the penalties meted out for violators can be severe, including death in Afghanistan, Arab Emirates, Chechnya, Iran, Mauritania, Pakistan, Saudi Arabia, Sudan, and Yemen. Afghan men have been executed by the toppling of a wall on the accused sodomites. Other countries such as Malaysia and Singapore routinely arrest and incarcerate sexual deviants. Even in countries where homosexuality is not explicitly outlawed, there can be state persecution. For example, Egyptian police arrested 52 men, in 2001, on the grounds of "debauchery," which was only the most public incident. Following international condemnation, President Mubarak ordered a retrial. Afterward the 21 defendants received *harsher* sentences of imprisonment and forced labor.

In countries where LGBT citizens are persecuted, it is not surprising that there is no education on sexualities or institutional support for LGBT youth. There are a few initiatives even at the private or underground sector, but most supportive LGBT groups are located outside of the country, operated by LGBT and allied expatriates. For example, the Al Fatiha Foundation, an organization dedicated to LGBT Muslims, is based in the United States while the Safra Project is in London.

There is little evidence to suggest a one-to-one relationship between countries that have (or do not have) a wide-range of laws and policies protecting LGBT persons and school systems that promulgate supportive educational policies on LGBT issues and for LGBT youth. This has much to do with the generally decentralized nature of many educational systems coupled to the logistical and political difficulties of effectively lobbying for passage and implementation of policies which directly impact local schools and communities. Federal policies, particularly those arising out of the court system, are generally a necessary, if not sufficient condition, for the enactment of educational policies. However, policy enactment, school implementation, and educational impact are also very loosely coupled. Thus, when one examines specific curricular and pedagogical interventions coupled to extant research on the quality of school life for LGBT students, it is difficult to identify any country in the world that truly could be categorized as fully meeting the needs of LGBT students and teachers or addressing LGBT issues in its schools.

CONCLUSION

A century has passed since the founding of the Scientific Humanitarian Institute and the groundbreaking work of Magnus Hirschfeld, who linked scientific research with policy reform. There has been progress in how professions such as law, medicine, education, and public health have addressed sexual minority issues and, in turn, how the public has begun to understand and accept nonheterosexuals. Nevertheless, a college student is beaten and left for dead on a windswept Wyoming field; the seven-year-old daughter of lesbian parents comes home in tears after learning she doesn't have a "normal family;" an adolescent and his parents successfully sue a Wisconsin school district for ignoring years of prolonged harassment; a North Carolina teenager comes out to her school as a lesbian, and is cautiously accepted, but a year later, when she identifies herself as a male, she is abandoned; a middle-school student participates in a sex education module, but there is no word spoken or materials provided that speaks to her same-sex desires; an African American youngster reads about the Harlem Renaissance in a textbook, but there is no mention of the prominence of lesbians and bisexuals of color. Meanwhile, a young man puts a handgun to his head, a lesbian has a baby proving her heterosexuality to family and friends, a star pupil buries herself in homework, denying her sexual feelings, and a youth engages in unprotected sex since "only druggies and fags get AIDS." And, as some well-meaning adults, supportive professional associations, and LGBT organizations provide training workshops, enact policies, develop curriculum materials, organize youth programs, and so on, there remains a void as to their effectiveness and impact.

Hopefully, this encyclopedia will help to fill that void.

Bibliography

Crew, Louie, ed. 1978. *The Gay Academic*. Palm Springs, CA: ETC Publications.

Harbeck, Karen, ed. 1992. *Coming Out of the Classroom Closet*. Binghamton, NY: Haworth Press.

Pinar, William, ed. 1998. *Queer Theory in Education*. Mahwah, NJ: Lawrence Erlbaum.

Russell, Stephen, Hinda Seif, and Nhan Truong. 2001. "School Experiences of Sexual Minority Youth in the United States: Evidence from a National Study," *Journal of Adolescence* 24, no. 1: 111–127.

Sandfort, Theo., Judith Schuyf, Jan Willem Duyvendak, and Jeffrey Weeks. 2000. *Lesbian and Gay Studies*. London & Thousand Oaks, CA: Sage.

Sears, James T. 1987. "Peering into the Well of Loneliness: The Responsibility of Educators to Gay and Lesbian Youth." Pp. 79–100 in *Social Issues and Education*. Edited by Alex Molar. Alexandria, VA: Association for Supervision and Curriculum Development.

———. 1999. "Teaching Queerly: Some Elementary Propositions." Pp. 3–14 in *Queering Elementary Education: Advancing the Dialogues about Sexualities and Schooling*. Edited by Will J. Letts and James T. Sears. Landham, MD: Rowman & Littlefield.

———. 2002. *Fifteen Years Later: The Draft Summary Report on the State of the Field of Lesbian, Gay, Bisexual and Transgender Issues in K-16 and Professional Education, A Research Review (1987–2001)*. Paper presented at the Annual meeting of the American Educational Research Association at Seattle, WA, April.

Szalacha, Laura. 2005. "The Research Terrain: A Brief Overview of the Historical Framework for LGBTQ Studies in Education." Pp. 77–87 in *Gay, Lesbian, and Transgender Issues in Education*. Edited by James T. Sears. Binghamton, NY: Haworth Press.

Tierney, William, and Patrick Dilley. 1998. "Constructing Knowledge: Educational Research and Gay and Lesbian Studies." Pp. 49–71 in *Queer Theory in Education*. Edited by William F. Pinar. Mahwah, NJ: Lawrence Erlbaum.

Tomas, J. 2003. "Dykes and Fags Out of Class." *IGLA Newsletter* 3, no. 3, pp. 16.

Waldo C., and J. Kemp. 1997. "Should I Come Out to My Students? An Empirical Investigation." *Journal of Homosexuality* 34, no. 2: 79–94.

Activism, LGBT Teachers

Jackie M. Blount

The last three decades of the twentieth century have witnessed unprecedented activism by LGBT (Lesbian, Gay, Bisexual, Transgender) school workers and students in the United States and abroad. Before this time, the increased visibility of **sexual identity** issues typically was met with public hostility, routine police **harassment**, and the ongoing threat of employment **discrimination**—especially against school workers, but also against students. Nonetheless, some teachers, such as Adolph Brand of Berlin, who edited a magazine "for masculine culture, art, and literature," assumed leadership in early homosexual movements before 1933. Although most teachers dismissed for suspicion of homosexuality acquiesced, a few defended themselves in court. However, as a larger gay liberation movement formed after the 1969 **Stonewall** rebellion, LGBT teachers enjoyed gradually improved legal and social support for their cases. LGBT school workers eventually organized their groups to resist the discrimination they experienced in schools. More recently, LGBT educators and **allies** have championed efforts to improve the rights and welfare of LGBT and questioning youth. They have formed chapters of the **Gay Lesbian Straight Education Network** (GLSEN), sponsored **gay–straight alliances**, pressed for reforms, and broadened the **curriculum** to include LGBT issues.

Before **Stonewall**, lesbian and gay teachers typically resigned quietly when they ran afoul of school **administrators**. Legal challenges cost more than they could afford. Although homophile organizations such as the Daughters of Bilitis and the Mattachine Society supported the employment rights of lesbians and gay men, they scarcely possessed the resources necessary to assist with protracted court battles. Teachers such as Elver Barker participated in these organizations nonetheless, sometimes assuming important leadership roles (Sears 2005). Matters shifted substantially in the 1960s, however, when the American Civil Liberties Union (ACLU) joined the case of fired California teacher, Mark Morrison. Morrison had engaged in a brief sexual relationship with another male teacher. Morrison later lost his life teaching credentials because of his supposedly immoral behavior. After lengthy proceedings, the California Supreme Court ruled (*Morrison v. State Board of Education*) that Morrison's "homosexual character" per se did not interfere with his ability to teach; however, it held that the school district could keep him away from impressionable children (Harbeck 1997). Although Morrison could not resume his teaching career, his case softened the legal logic that homosexuality necessarily meant unfitness for educational service.

In 1971, Peggy Burton's principal dismissed her from her teaching position because of rumors that she was a lesbian. Burton brought a lawsuit against the district with the support of the ACLU (American Civil Liberties Union). Eventually, the U.S. District Court (*Burton v. Cascade School District*) decided that the Oregon

See also Activism, LGBT Youth; Administration, Educational; Coming Out, Teachers; Johns Committee; Licensure; Professional Educational Organizations; Professionalism; Teachers, LGBT and History; Transsexuality; Workplace Issues.

statute granting school districts power to dismiss teachers for immorality was too vague (Harbeck 1997).

The next year, three different teachers faced dismissal because they were gay. Teachers unions provided legal support for each. John Gish, a New Jersey high school teacher, formed the Gay Teachers Caucus of the National Education Association (NEA) in 1972. His district then transferred him out of the classroom. Joseph Acanfora, a Maryland teacher, had been active in a college homophile organization, which nearly prevented him from getting his teaching license. When his school district learned in a *New York Times* story about the difficulties Acanfora had faced in getting his license, they similarly dismissed him from the classroom. And, when Tacoma school officials learned that high school teacher James Gaylord was gay, they immediately terminated his job even though they had no evidence that he had engaged in sexual activities. All three of these cases (*Acanfora v. Board of Education of Montgomery County*; *Gaylord v. Tacoma School District*; *Gish v. Board of Education*) resulted in high-level court decisions that made more difficult the dismissal of lesbian, gay, and bisexual teachers for status. However, none of the three retained their jobs.

As the larger gay liberation movement gained strength, some teachers organized groups to fight for employment rights. In 1969, Morgan Pinney and students at San Francisco State University successfully encouraged the California Federation of Teachers to pass an ambitious resolution supporting the rights of homosexual teachers. The delegates decreed that they would work for "the abolition of all laws or other governmental policy which involves nonvictim sexual practice" ("Teachers Favor Freedom for Gays" 1970, 7). Two years later, a group of lesbian and gay teachers in New York City picketed the Board of Education to protest job discrimination. The group instigated a sit-in at the State Board of Examiners office, resulting in arrests for five of the protesters. Then, in 1974, the NEA added **sexual orientation** to its **antidiscrimination policy**, which committed the vast legal resources of the organization to fighting such discrimination ("Job Protection" 1974).

Also in 1974, several teachers formed the Gay Teachers Association of New York City, perhaps the first local organization of LGBT teachers. The group eventually won the support of the American Federation of Teachers (AFT), successfully lobbied against discriminatory employment practices in the city, educated school workers throughout the enormous system about conditions for LGBT educators, marched in annual "Christopher Street" parades, and also hosted social events. In 1975, teachers in San Francisco similarly organized the Gay Teachers and School Workers Coalition. The first actions of the Coalition included demonstrations and behind-the-scenes lobbying that resulted in the inclusion of sexual orientation in the nondiscrimination policy of the San Francisco Schools. Other LGBT school workers organizations followed in Los Angeles, Boston, Philadelphia, Denver, Oregon, Texas, and Maryland. Many of these groups increased the visibility of LGBT teachers through their newsletters, political activism, and appearances in gay pride parades. In higher education, a small group of professors organized the Gay Academic Union in 1972. This organization published scholarly journals on LGBT issues and spurred the creation of discipline-specific coalitions within academic associations and organizations.

Then, in 1977, Anita Bryant and her followers successfully campaigned against a Miami–Dade nondiscrimination ordinance that included sexual orientation. The centerpiece of their efforts was to "Save Our Children" from increasingly visible and "militant homosexual teachers," an appeal that drew active supporters from around the country. California Senator John Briggs, hoping to capitalize on this sentiment, introduced a referendum in 1978 making it easy for school officials to dismiss visible LGBT school workers and their allies. LGBT activists and organized school workers responded by forging strong ties with a wide variety of grassroots coalitions, individuals, media, and other organizations around the state. In the end, the state's voters soundly defeated the Briggs Initiative.

During the 1990s, local and state organizations of LGBT school workers gave way to other kinds of activist groups. Some organizations have become affiliates of GLSEN, a national group dedicated to improving the school climate for all LGBT and **allies,** particularly students. Hundreds of high schools have started gay–straight alliances, with the support of organized LGBT and allied school workers.

Meanwhile, transgender and transsexual school workers have been waging legal battles to win protection from employment discrimination. In the late 1990s, a California teacher unsuccessfully battled to regain his position after he revealed a planned sex-change operation. However, an Illinois principal who transitioned from man to woman enjoyed the support of her school board (Golab 2001).

Beyond these legal cases and the activism of organizations of LGBT and allied school workers, as the twenty-first century opens, LGBT issues now fall solidly within the mainstream of school activities. Every school now confronts a range of LGBT issues such as: the inclusion of the topic in the curriculum; how students and school workers will respond to gay–straight alliances; whether students may embrace, kiss, or attend school dances and **proms** with others of the same sex; how dress codes should accommodate persons with unconventional gender presentation; and how to handle students and workers who harass or contribute to a hostile school climate for LGBT persons. LGBT activism is no longer the exclusive province of such school workers, but instead is shared by growing numbers of persons and **allies** committed to creating schools that are welcoming and supportive of all their students and workers.

Bibliography

Blount, Jackie. 2004. *Fit to Teach: Same-Sex Desire, Gender, and School Work in the Twentieth Century.* Albany: State University of New York Press.

Golab, Art. 2001. "Sex Change Ignites Debate." *Chicago Sun-Times* (August 29): 4.

Harbeck, Karen. 1997. *Gay and Lesbian Educators: Personal Freedoms, Public Constraints.* Maulden, MA: Amethyst Press.

"Job Protection for Gays: Teachers Union Votes Rights Stand." 1974. *The Advocate* (August 28): 3.

Rofes, Eric. 1985. *Socrates, Plato, and Guys Like Me.* Boston: Alyson.

Sears, James. 2005. *Behind the Mask of the Mattachine: The Early Movement for Homosexual Emancipation.* Binghamton, NY: Haworth Press.

"Teachers Favor Freedom for Gays." 1970. *The Advocate* (March): 7.

Web Sites

AERA: Queer Studies SIG. August, 2004. Accessed August 12, 2004. http://www. education.ua.edu/queersig/ The Queer Studies SIG Web site offers opportunities for LGBT and allied scholars in education to connect and share research.

The Rights of Lesbian and Gay Teachers and Education Personnel: 2001–2004 Triennial Report. July 2004. Accessed August 12, 2004. http://www.ei-ie.org/congress2004/documents/07E_GLBT_Rep_FINAL.pdf. This report outlines the rights of LGBT educators around the world. It places conditions of LGBT educators and students within the larger scope of global human rights.

Activism, LGBT Youth

Kevin C. Franck

Young people who publicly acknowledge their queerness and seek understanding company are committing, in the simple pursuit of happiness, an act of opposition to the regime of normalcy. LGBT youth activism is spurred by the desires of youth who do not fit neatly within the confines of a "normal" identity to socialize with each other, attend school, and experience life with the same ease and lack of restrictions enjoyed by their straight peers. As the modern LGBT community developed, young people organized groups and undertook direct action. And, as time has progressed, queer youth activists have developed their agenda to overcome a sense of isolation and abnormality and to create safer spaces.

After World War II, the Mattachine Society, ONE, and the Daughters of Bilitis breathed life into the homophile movement. Following the lead of **Magnus Hirschfeld** in Germany and a failed attempt by gay men to organize in Chicago before the American Great Depression, this movement sought to involve homosexuals and their **allies** to bring about political, legal, and social reform as well as to enlarge the social space within which gays and lesbians can interact. Until the late 1960s, membership in these organizations was limited to persons twenty-one years of age or older, although some young people joined these groups by lying about their age. In 1967, the first student homophile group formed at Columbia University, creating the first queer youth activist organization. By the fall of that year, other New York colleges formed chapters of the new Student Homophile League (SHL). One year later, arguably the first organized direct action by queer youth occurred when SHL members seized control of a medical school symposium, featuring scholars who viewed homosexuality as a disease. That evening activists from a variety of movements led a series of protests during which Columbia students occupied several buildings on the Upper West Side campus.

In 1969, the patrons of the **Stonewall** Inn marked the beginning of a new activist era for gays and lesbians in the United States. Within the crowd of protesters and rioters was the founder of the Homophile Youth Movement (HYMN), Craig Rodwell, who would later open the first gay bookstore in the country. He immediately began organizing other queer youth. Several days after the Stonewall rebellion, when members of East Coast Homophile groups met in Philadelphia for a protest at Independence Hall, Rodwell broke ranks with the event's older organizers who insisted on conservative dress and heterosexual decorum. The tension between the two generations of leadership exploded that night at a New York Mattachine meeting. In its aftermath arose the Gay Liberation Front (GLF).

See also Activism, LGBT Teachers; College Campus Organizing; Films, Youth and Educators in; Identity Politics; Legal Issues, Students; Resiliency; Youth Culture.

Representatives of the GLF attended the North American Conference of Homophile Organizations' (NACHO) annual meeting two months later. The NACHO Committee on Youth adopted a twelve-point mission statement, "A Radical Manifesto," linking the emerging Gay Liberation Front with other movements fighting against the oppression of people of color, women, and the poor, and calling upon the homosexual community to divorce itself from heterosexual ways of thinking.

Not only did it fail to achieve support from the older generation of leadership but, mirroring divisions within other student movements, the group splintered. One group, the Gay Activists Alliance (GAA), was solely concerned with advocating for the rights of homosexuals. Another, Gay Youth, began publishing a periodical, *Gay Journal*, with news, social announcements, and discussions on sexuality. More radical groups such as Youth Liberation Front, based in Ann Arbor, San Francisco's Vanguard Youth, and New York's Street Transvestite Action Revolutionaries, led by Silvia Riveria, published newsletters espousing manifestos, presenting **research**, and provoking debate. While members of the homophile movement wrote and edited newsletters, often under pseudonyms, and mailed them discreetly to their members, gay liberation youth were not as secretive. **Gay** and **lesbian youth** activists also pushed many underground newspapers to cover gay and lesbian issues. Although the *Daily Texan* (Austin), *Great Speckled Bird* (Atlanta), and *Protean Radish* (Raleigh) were slow to devote space, these and others eventually provided a public forum for discussion of gay liberation politics within the context of other youth movements.

Gay Lib Comes to High School. *GAY*, April 9, 1973. Courtesy of Gay, published by Four Swords, Inc.

The spread of queer student groups to more college campuses in the United States and Canada met with resistance from school administrators. Students, for example, at the University of Kansas, Oklahoma, New Hampshire, and Missouri filed law suits claiming discrimination (*Gay Student Organization of the University of New Hampshire v. Bono*, and *Student Coalition for Gay Rights v Austin Peay State University*). Even though some of those cases were lost, mainstream newspapers carried the stories, as the 1970s was marked by significant legal, political, and social change.

During this unprecedented era of acceptance and visibility for gay citizens in the United States, there were more realistic and positive portrayals of gays and lesbians in film and on television, there was expansion of gay clubs and bars (notably discos), there was the removal of homosexuality from the **Diagnostic and Statistical Manual of Mental Disorders**, and there were elections of the first openly gay and lesbian politicians. It is not entirely clear whether queer youth activism was tepid for most of the decade because of this increased visibility and tolerance or in spite of it. Surely, though, toward the decade's end, the assassination of Harvey Milk, the emergence of conservative religious groups such as the "Moral Majority," and Anita Bryant's "Save Our Children" campaign reinvigorated activism and sharpened the distinction between organizations aligned with the assimilation tendencies of the homophile movement and those which espoused the radical ideology of Gay Liberation.

Under the dark cloud of an unknown killer and amid the deafening silence of a government and nation that did not seem to care, radicalized queer youth activists worked throughout the 1980s to focus the world's attention on HIV/**AIDS**. Their efforts congealed when the AIDS Coalition to Unleash Power (ACT-UP) formed in March 1987. Its Youth Brigade was known for its aggressive and sometimes comical tactics, such as distributing condoms and safer sex information outside of New York City public schools, which often resulted in arrests.

Queer Nation gained prominence around 1990. Never a tightly structured organization, it has been effective in planning and executing direct action campaigns targeting antigay businesses and groups. Best known for the slogan "We're Here. We're Queer. Get Used to It," Queer Nation mimicked much of ACT-UP's aggressive style. Perhaps its most notorious action were sit-ins at the Cracker Barrel, a restaurant chain located mostly in the South and Midwest, which had begun to purge its gay and lesbian employees. Activists stayed at a dining table for stretches of twelve to fifteen hours without ordering anything more than soda or coffee, but tipped servers for their missed income. The radical strain of ACT-UP and Queer Nation began to wane during the 1990s as new drug therapies and prevention programs lessened the impact of AIDS on the queer community.

Three major trends impact today's queer youth activism. First, youth are **coming out** at a younger age. Queer activists are now high school students confronting **discrimination** and hatred as they avail themselves of the legal system. Jamie Nabozny effectively sued his Wisconsin school system for failing to stop other students from years of assault and **harassment** for being gay. James Dale, an Eagle Scout and Assistant Scoutmaster from New Jersey brought the **Boy Scouts of America** (BSA) to court after he was banned when his homosexuality was discovered. In **sports**, high school star athletes such Dan Bozzuto and Cory Johnson have come out, forcing their peers as well as coaches and the community to rethink their **prejudice**s.

New and accessible **communication** technologies have also had a major impact on activism among queer youth. The **Internet** and the relatively low cost of printing has allowed individual queer activists and small groups to access startling amounts of information, to network across the globe, and to reach the public at large. During the 1990s, youth activists began publishing **queer zines**, photocopied or mimeographed booklets proliferated by the punk rock scene in the United States and Britain, that served as alternatives to the mainstream press. More recently, activists also are engaging queer youth issues through "blogs," online journals.

As technologies have become more accessible, queer youth publications have become much more diverse and varied in terms of content, style, and distribution. This evidences the third trend in queer youth activism: fragmentation. As in past queer activist generations, queer youth today are mainly organized into those seeking an expansion of what is considered "normal" along with assimilation into society, such as Human Right's Campaign's Youth College; and others who form gay and lesbian specific sections within nonqueer causes. For instance, the movement to free convicted murder and alleged political prisoner Mumia AbuJamal from death row in Pennsylvania enjoys support from well-organized groups of queer youth activists. The emergence of **bisexual, transgender,** and **transsexual** youth activists along with a resistance to fixed sexual identities has challenged the queer youth movement to reconsider its modernist origins in favor of a postmodern understanding of **sexual identity** and **gender identity** that embraces ambiguity and fluidity while still advocating for concrete political and social change.

Bibliography

Cohen, Stephan. 2005. "Dances of Identities: An Examination of Queer Youth Program Praxis." *Journal of Gay and Lesbian Issues in Education* 2, no. 3: 67–86.

Kumashiro, Kevin. 2002. *Troubling Education: Queer Activism and Anti-Oppressive Pedagogy*. New York: RoutledgeFalmer.

Rodriguez, Nelson. 1998. "(Queer) Youth as Political and Pedagogical." Pp. 173–188 in *Queer Theory and Education*. Edited by William F. Pinar. Mahwah, NJ: Lawrence Erlbaum.

Sears, James T. 2001. *Rebels, Rubyfruit and Rhinestones*. New Brunswick: Rutgers University Press.

Web Sites

International Queer Zines Around the World. Mike Paré. Accessed May 26, 2005. http://digitalqueeries.905host.net/files/international_queer_zines.htm. Links to queer activist zines in various countries.

Youth.org. April 15, 2001. Youth Assistance Organization. Accessed May 26, 2005. http://www.youth.org. Material for young people just coming out, links to activist organizations and profiles of notable queer youth activists.

Administration, Educational

Catherine A. Lugg

Educational administration is the profession concerned with the operation of public primary and secondary schools. The administration of public schools involves: monitoring and evaluating teacher instruction, enforcing student discipline codes, complying with all local, state and federal regulations, planning and budgeting for a school's operations, hiring and firing instructional and noninstructional staff, maintaining strong school–community relations, networking with other administrators within the immediate area and the state, and maintaining strong labor relations with the district's unions. Additionally, public school administrators have a measure of what is called "police power." That is, not only are they required to enforce state and federal laws, as well as the dictates of their local school board, but they can fire and sanction school personnel and expel students who may run afoul of various regulations—including morality clauses that cover adult personnel and sodomy laws that cover both students and adults. Consequently, educational administration has been fiercely homophobic regarding **lesbian, gay, bisexual,** and **transgender** (LGBT) youth, educators, and issues.

See also Antidiscrimination Policy; Discrimination; Educational Policies; Johns Committee; Passing; Professional Educational Organizations; Professionalism; Workplace Issues.

Given the high degree of managerial tasks involved with operating public schools, the profession in the United States has modeled itself after business and industry. Embracing a business model has also served to reinforce traditional **gender roles** because the ideal administrator has been a business*man*. In fact, during educational administration's early history, possessing teaching experience was seen as an impediment to being an effective public school administrator. Since the overwhelming majority of teachers were women at this time, the bias against teaching experience and university limits on women entering administration preparation programs, coupled with the long bias against women working in leadership positions, helped curtail their numbers in administration. Furthermore, school boards have long been dominated by businessmen, who tend to hire people looking and acting like themselves. Although the number of women has increased since the 1990s, today, educational administration remains a male profession.

During the Cold War, the constant equating of homosexuality with communism by both the mass media and politicians triggered witch hunts in the federal government—the U.S. State Department in particular—to purge any suspected "**queers**" from its ranks. This paranoia quickly spread to the public schools. Educational administrators were under significant legal and political pressure to ensure their schools were free of LGBT people as well as any LGBT related **curriculum** or library material. As a result, principals and superintendents largely had carte blanche to remove any suspected homosexuals in their midst. During this era, the mere rumor of homosexuality could be enough for school workers—whether they were LGBT or not—to be fired. Similarly, LGBT students who were discovered could be either expelled or strongly counseled to drop out or hide their **sexual orientation**.

Furthermore, aspiring educational **administrators** were compelled to demonstrate their own "straight credentials" to both the local school board and larger community. To be considered for a leadership position, every principal and/or superintendent candidate would almost always have to be a married man. Fledgling male administrators could further buff their straight credentials if they had served as a boys' athletic coach at some point in their career. Many school districts sought to hire "manly men" for leadership positions so that generations of young men would not be unduly "sissified" by the overwhelmingly female workforce within the schools (Blount 1999; Blount 2003). The assumption was that by having "real men" lead schools, young men and women (although this was a lesser concern) would not come into contact with or be contaminated by "pernicious influences."

The legacy of **homophobia** and **sexism** has shaped the administration of public schools in profound ways. First, the profession itself is defined by homophobia. Historically, educational administrators working in public schools have been both the exemplars and enforcers of **compulsory heterosexuality** (Blount 1998; Blount 2003; Lugg 2003a). Consequently, there is a reluctance to acknowledge—much less embrace—LGBT persons who either work or learn within the public school's walls. One contemporary example of this reluctance is the numerous battles across the United States to institute **gay/straight alliances**—a gay positive club for all students. Additionally, some administrators are more likely than not to blame LGBT personnel and students for any **harassment** they might encounter: this is true even in states that maintain nondiscrimination clauses that protect LGBT people (Lugg 2003b). Educational administrators generally *minimize* the verbal and physical abuse that LGBT students, and those students suspected of being LGBT, receive (Fraynd and Capper 2003; Lugg 2003b).

LGBT public school administrators tend to remain closeted to their colleagues and to the larger community in which they work. These individuals employ various identity maintenance strategies to protect their patinas of "straightness." They are sure to wear gender-appropriate clothing, and they might bring an appropriate gender colleague or friend to public functions. When asked about their personal life, they tend to respond by changing the pronouns of their significant other or claim that they are "married to their job" (Fraynd and Capper 2003).

The state of LGBT awareness is much the same with the professional public school leadership organizations. AASA, NASSP, and NAESP (American Association of School Administrators, National Association of Secondary School Principals, and National Association of Elementary School Principals, respectively), have all posted little information regarding LGBT people posted on their Web sites. AASA—the superintendents' association—has the least, NAESP—the elementary principals' association—has the most. None acknowledge the possibility of LGBT public school administrators. In 1999, AASA was the only one of these organizations to cosponsor the booklet *Just the Facts*, which addressed LGBT issues and public schools. Nevertheless, AASA has since removed this from its Web site, although it does continue to post older information regarding other topics. Furthermore, none of these organizations' Web sites have links to LGBT organizations, nor do they (or any accrediting body for university-based licensure programs) require knowledge and/or sensitivity regarding LGBT issues for membership or **licensure**.

There are numerous actions required to better prepare aspiring administrators to work in public school settings. First, educational administration professors need to acknowledge the possibility that not all of the students in preparation programs are "straight." Students, faculty, staff, and their partners and/or spouses should be welcomed at social events and formal ceremonies. Sheer visibility of LGBT people is known to reduce homophobia and build LGBT-friendly consciousness (Herek and Glunt 1993). Second, there must be an infusion in educational administration preparation programs with LGBT issues as part of a broader multicultural/antiracist/antioppressive curriculum. Educational administration students need to know how LGBT issues shape the more traditional areas of the program (foundations, organizational theory, education law, educational politics, personnel, leadership, and school finance). Third, aspiring administrators need to learn how to take the initiative in promoting LGBT-friendly policies and procedures within their public school districts. At times, this may call for a form of "policy subversion" or looking for the existing wiggle room in long-established policies and procedures to move them in admittedly novel directions. Finally, educational administration programs should encourage both students and faculty to conduct more **research** on LGBT issues. At this point, the extant research on LGBT public school administrators is fairly scanty, as serious study has only recently begun (Lugg and Koschoreck 2003).

Bibliography

Blount, Jackie M. 1998. *Destined to Rule the Schools: Women and the Superintendency, 1873–1995*. Albany: State University of New York Press.

———. 1999. "Manliness and the Construction of Men's and Women's Work in Schools, 1865–1941." *International Journal of Leadership in Education* 2, no. 2: 55–68.

———. 2003. "Homosexuality and School Superintendents: A Brief History." *Journal of School Leadership* 13: 7–26.

Callahan, Raymond E. 1962. *Education and the Cult of Efficiency*. Chicago: University of Chicago Press.

Fraynd, Donald J., and Colleen A. Capper. 2003. "Do You Have Any Idea Who You Just Hired?!?!" A Study of Open and Closeted Sexual Minority K-12 Administrators." *Journal of School Leadership* 2: 86–124.

Herek, Gregory M., and Eric K. Glunt. 1993. "Interpersonal Contact and Heterosexuals' Attitudes Toward Gay Men: Results From a National Survey." *The Journal of Sex Research* 30, no. 3: 239–244.

Lugg, Catherine A. 2003a. "Our Straitlaced [sic] Administrators: The Law, Lesbian, Gay, Bisexual and Transgendered Educational Administrators, and the Assimilationist Imperative." *Journal of School Leadership* 13: 51–85.

————2003b. "Sissies, Faggots, Lezzies and Dykes: Gender, Sexual Orientation and the New Politics of Education?" *Educational Administration Quarterly* 39, no. 1: 95–134.

Lugg, Catherine A., and James W. Koschoreck, 2003. "Introduction—The Final Closet: Lesbian, Gay, Bisexual, and Transgendered Educational Leaders." *Journal of School Leadership* 13: 4–6.

Administrators

Jackie M. Blount

Over the past century, administrators have been centrally involved in regulating the gender and sexuality of students and workers in the schools they have supervised. First, the work of school administration, in and of itself, has been configured to match the role of father/husband in traditional married relationships—in opposition to teachers in wife/mother roles. Second, male school administrators largely have been expected to demonstrate extreme masculinity and heterosexuality. Finally, principals, superintendents, personnel directors, and other administrators have been charged with normalizing the gender presentation and sexuality of students and teachers. In recent years, however, despite widespread general resistance, some administrators have begun fostering climates in their schools that support sexual and gender diversity. A very small number of administrators have claimed LGBT status openly and kept their jobs. The status and function of educational administrators, then, reveal much about the permissible range of genders and sexualities among students and school workers. Because of the significant regulatory functions of school administrators, they are uniquely well positioned to improve conditions for LGBT youth.

When school districts began hiring school administrators in significant numbers during the mid- to late-1800s, the persons holding these positions existed in relationship with teachers much as husbands did with wives. Husbands managed financial resources and served as the legal figurehead for family units just as school administrators handled fiscal affairs and represented their schools in community business. Wives governed household matters, especially including childrearing, as they deferred to their husbands—much as teachers directed the daily work of the classroom while submitting to administrative authority. Not surprisingly, then,

See also Administration, Educational; Coming Out, Teachers; Educational Policies; Licensure; Professional Educational Organizations; Professionalism.

from the mid- to late-1800s, women quickly moved into the overwhelming majority of teaching positions while men filled virtually all the positions in school administration.

In earlier days, men had held all teaching positions. Only a few school districts saw fit to hire administrators then because local lay school board members handled routine duties not already performed by teachers. However, as women entered teaching in notable numbers, which coincided with a rapid expansion of tax-supported schooling across the country, districts hired school administrators. This new class of school workers assumed responsibilities formerly held by teachers and school board members, such as hiring teachers, maintaining school facilities, purchasing materials, and handling payroll. They also visited schools on a rotating basis to oversee teachers' work as well as to dictate curriculum and pedagogical practice. Many of these early school administrators had little preparation for their work. What they invariably brought to their duties, though, was the fact that they were men. As such, they were thought eligible to oversee the growing cadre of single women, who, for the first time in U.S. history, could live respectably on their own and not necessarily with husbands or their families.

Women's movement into the classroom accelerated until they accounted for over 70 percent of all teachers in 1900. Simultaneously, teaching became configured all the more to align with gendered expectations for women. Gradually, teachers lost autonomy and authority to the extent that administrators gained in these areas. Teacher salaries decreased relative to the cost of living, which further discouraged males who enjoyed opportunities elsewhere. Administrative positions paid increasingly well in comparison, a shift thought necessary to attract men with families. Principals and superintendents became high-profile community figures who typically exerted influence in civic and business affairs (Blount 1998). Consequently, schoolwork not only had become deeply polarized by sex, but also by gender.

When superintendencies and principalships were created, then, they were structured to resemble the institution of marriage with men assuming roles and duties much like those of husbands. Similarly, the unmarried cadre of women who taught in schools was expected to submit to administrators much as wives deferred to their husbands. Though this arrangement largely concerned preserving idealized gender roles of the time, it was grounded in the socially approved institution for regulating sexuality: marriage.

From the early- to mid-twentieth century, school administration, particularly the superintendency, became not only male-identified, but also hypermasculine work. Not just any man would do. Men who aspired to the superintendency increasingly needed to demonstrate their physical vigor, authority, and status as married men with families. Through such overt displays, men in the larger field of education—which generally had become known as "women's work—could avoid questions about their masculinity and heterosexuality. Margaret Mead explained, in 1962, that teaching was work that men entered on peril of accusations of effeminacy, unless they entered administrative or fiscal roles.

Public demands for stereotypically or hypermasculine school administrators soared during the Cold War as panics erupted around the country about the possible presence of homosexuals in the military, government, and then schools. Because the public typically conflated homosexuality with gender nonconformity, persons wishing to avoid accusations of homosexuality needed to display appropriate or even exaggerated gender behaviors and characteristics. School officials in one district, in 1946, described the kind of school administrator they sought: "The man selected could not be labeled as an effeminate being. He was a former collegiate athletic hero. His physique was comparable to any of the mythical Greek gods. He was truly the ultimate in manliness. The last but not least in importance of his personal characteristics was the fact that he was married" (Leonard 1946, 21–22). Those who refrained from marriage were considered to be "odd," or "peculiar," possibly even deviant. Not surprisingly, marriage rates for male school administrators, especially superintendents, were substantially higher than those for men in the general workforce (Tyack 1976). Marriage had become a means by which men demonstrated their masculinity, which was especially important for men in women's work, men whose masculinity—and therefore sexuality—otherwise might be questioned.

Women who aspired to school leadership positions contended with a different set of shifting expectations. In the decades before WWII, thousands of women attained principalships, especially at the elementary level, and superintendencies, particularly the lower-paid, less-esteemed county superintendency. They did so in schools and districts composed mostly or entirely of female workers. Most women school administrators were unmarried, just as were most women teachers. Some maintained long-term companionships with other women. Among college administrators, women such as Mary Woolley, Jeannette Marks, and M. Carey Thomas also maintained such relationships. However, as Cold War fears of homosexuals in schools galvanized communities around the country, women's gender and sexual identities were called into question if they remained in high-level administrative positions. Increasingly, women who aspired to such positions were thought manly, which necessarily raised suspicions of lesbianism in a climate that equated gender nonconformity with homosexuality. Married women, who enjoyed some protection from such suspicions, found that the increasing demands of school administration required the active assistance of a partner. At the time, few men were willing to acquiesce to the needs of their wives' careers. Women who resolved the dilemma by having female partners put their positions at risk. Not surprisingly, women's representation in school leadership positions plummeted during these years.

School administrators not only needed to demonstrate obvious gender conformity then, but they also assumed growing responsibility for assuring the gender conformity and heterosexuality of school workers. Because homosexuality was thought at the time to spread easily, communities called on school officials to keep homosexual teachers away from children. Administrators were urged to scrutinize teaching candidates carefully for signs of gender nonconformity, which was thought to indicate homosexuality.

In the 1950s and 1960s, California and Florida instituted formal programs for assuring that homosexuals did not teach. Postwar changes in California law required law enforcement officials to notify school districts when teachers were arrested on "morals" charges such as those resulting from frequent undercover operations in public rest rooms. More informally, a climate of such fear pervaded schools around the state that teachers knew any allegation of homosexuality, whether proven or not, was sufficient for dismissal. Max Rafferty, who for years had served as state superintendent, maintained that, "School principals and superintendents should refuse to rehire probationary teachers who turn out to be abnormal despite the efforts of preliminary screening. . . . Don't tell me it can't be done. I've been a school administrator for 30 years and I know darnned well it can" (Rafferty 1977, 91–92).

In Florida, the legislature took up the work of identifying homosexuals in public schools and universities. Using tactics developed by the likes of Senator Joseph McCarthy, legislative officials followed up on police tips about possible homosexual teachers. After years of work, the **Johns Committee**, as the legislative investigation committee was known, reported that the state's teaching force had been scrutinized carefully and that the number of homosexual teachers was lower than in other states. The public universities of the state also faced intensive investigation. Wayne Reitz, then-president of the University of Florida, encouraged the Florida Legislative Investigation Committee to probe the alleged homosexuality of some faculty members. Although the much-publicized proceedings netted few dismissals, campus administrators maintained a chilly climate for LGBT persons during subsequent decades.

From these years through the waning days of the Cold War, many school administrators took active roles in policing the ranks of teachers to ensure gender conformity and apparent heterosexuality. More recently, however, a few school administrators have reversed course by laboring to foster school climates supportive of LGBT school workers and students. Some have welcomed the efforts of **Gay Lesbian Straight Education Network** (GLSEN) members and a few have become active members themselves. More than a thousand high schools around the country now also have **gay–straight alliances** where students and school workers endeavor to support one another and generally improve **school climate** for LGBT persons. High school principals have been instrumental in the establishment of some of these groups. And in Massachusetts, which in 1993 passed a law requiring schools to eliminate student discrimination or harassment on account of sexual orientation, school administrators across ranks have been mandated to comply.

However, school administrators who identify as LGBT themselves continue to face great professional risk, and as such, few claim their identities openly. First, traditional curriculum for the preparation of educational administrators generally lacks content about the unique experiences of LGBT persons. Second, in many communities around the country, LGBT school administrators who come out face contentious parents and school board members, many of whom demand resignation. Third, most do not enjoy legal support from their organizations of fellow school administrators. Relatively few belong to the National Education Association or the American Federation of Teachers, which have gone on record in support of LGBT school workers and therefore provide legal representation for members faced with employment discrimination on account of sexual orientation or gender presentation. Organizations such as the American Association of School Administrators and the National School Boards Association have devoted little, if any, resources to supporting the employment rights of LGBT administrators. Finally, because school administrators serve at the pleasure of their school boards, employment security is reduced further still (Blount 2004).

Bibliography

Blount, J. 1998. *Destined to Rule the Schools: Women and the Superintendency, 1873–1995.* Albany: State University of New York Press.

———. 2004. *Fit to Teach: Same-Sex Desire, Gender, and School Work in the Twentieth Century.* Albany: State University of New York Press.

Leonard, V. 1946, September. "No Man's Land." *American School Board Journal* (September): 21–22.

Lugg, Catherine A., and James W. Koschoreck, eds. 2003. "The Final Closet: Lesbian, Gay, Bisexual, and Transgendered Educational Leaders." Special Issue. *Journal of School Leadership*.

Rafferty, Max. 1977. "Should Gays Teach School?" *Phi Delta Kappan* (October): 91–92.

Tyack, David. 1976. "Pilgrim's Progress: Toward a Social History of the School Superintendency, 1860–1960." *History of Education Quarterly* 16: 257–300.

Web Sites

American Civil Liberties Union, Lesbian & Gay Rights: Youth and Schools. November 2004. Accessed November 27, 2004. http://www.aclu.org/LesbianGayRights/ LesbianGayRightslist.cfm?c=106 The ACLU maintains current information about legal action supporting the rights of LGBT students and school workers.

National Education Association. November 2004. Accessed November 27, 2004. http://www.nea.org. The NEA has supported the employment rights of lesbian, gay, and bisexual employees since 1974. Their current reports and policies on LGBT issues regarding both students and school workers can be found here.

Adolescence

Laura A. Szalacha

Adolescence is defined differently in each society and era. In North America, it denotes the period of individual maturation (physical, emotional, psychological, intellectual, and social) and the transitions that shape our lives between puberty and adulthood. For LGBTQQI youth—those who self-identify with the social categories of **lesbian, gay, bisexual, transgender, queer,** questioning or **intersex** or whose emerging sexual attractions or behavior are directed toward same-sex partners— there are additional unique challenges (such as **coming out** processes) that must be met within varying cultural contexts. While the readiness for growth is set by biological maturation, the main developmental tasks (the psycho–social challenges of integrating growth as we mature, interacting with others) that comprise the transition of adolescence to adulthood is not only physical change. It includes accepting one's physique and establishing a positive body image, achieving emotional independence from parents and other adults and developing close and healthy relationships with peers. Other development tasks are social, such as acquiring a set of values or an ethical system; intellectual progression, moving from concrete to abstract thought; and psychological, such as establishing a gender role, a sexual self-concept, a sense of worth as a person and, ultimately, a personal identity that encompasses all of these developments. Although rooted in biological, social, and psychological development, the concept of adolescence is socially constructed. It is intimately tied to culture and situated in a particular time and geography.

Posited by **G. Stanley Hall** (1904) and later developed by Peter Blos (1962) and **Sigmund Freud** (1958), adolescence was first conceived as a time of great

See also Adolescent Sexualities; Films, Youth and Educators in; Identity Development; Mental Health; Queer Zines; Racial Identity; Religion and Psychological Development; Resiliency; Sexual Orientation; Youth, At-Risk; Youth, Homeless.

upheaval and emotional tumult. More recent research, however, suggests that the transitions in adolescence are less a harsh break from **childhood** and more a series of renegotiations of human roles and expectations. However, understanding adolescence as a tumultuous transition for LGBTQQI youth underlies **qualitative** and **quantitative research** conducted from a "lens of deficit," that is, focused on what was unhealthy or absent from their lives rather than their resilience and their potential contributions to society. Social science research of the late 1990s witnessed a transition to a focus on both the **resiliency** and strengths of LGBTTQI teenagers and attention to the social contexts of and interactions between multiple contexts (such as interconnections among home, peer group, school, and community) in which youth development occurs. These studies document that many LGBTQQI youth enjoy their adolescence and transition successfully into adulthood. While some queer teenagers become overwhelmed by the obstacles in their lives, most encounter barriers but manage to overcome them and succeed.

LGBTQQI youth negotiate the same developmental tasks as do heterosexual youth; that is, all adolescents must establish a stable identity and become complete and productive adults. Within a North American cultural context, these youth develop a sense of themselves that endures and encompasses many changes in experiences and roles. In early adolescence (ages eleven to fourteen), the processes of redefining their sources of personal strength, moving toward self-reliance, and developing their definitions of what it means to be male or female begins. While these processes continue throughout adolescence, from ages fifteen through seventeen young people begin acquiring an ethical system to guide behavior and become comfortable with their bodies. Finally, in late adolescence (ages eighteen to twenty-one), there are the tasks of preparing for economic careers, mutually fulfilling adult relationships, and socially responsible behavior.

LGBTQQI youth must also integrate these developmental tasks coupled with the unique challenge of coming out (to oneself and to others). Identified by many theorists, these challenges, include transforming a societally stigmatized identity into a positive identity; exploring and socializing in queer communities, disclosing to others, managing one's **sexual identity** in heterosexist environments, and building families and communities for support (Garnets and Kimmel 1991). Despite these common developmental tasks, the experience varies considerably depending on **social class** and religiosity, acceptance of family members and social milieu, concurrent developmental tasks of adulthood, as well as **ethnic identity** and **gender identity** development.

Adolescents who occupy racially, ethnically, and sexually discriminated against "social categories" and ecologies, for example, may face higher levels of **discrimination** than those who do not experience multiple oppressions. These "categories" are never experienced singly or in a simple additive manner, but are experientially interconnected with gender, class, age, physical ability, and others. These intersecting oppressions exist within economic and historical contexts that bestow benefits to some and stigma to others based on their location within this matrix of identities and behaviors. Traditionally, research on sexual identity development among ethnic minorities, however, (Chan 1989; Morales 1990; Rotheram-Borus, Rosario, and Koopman 1991) has delineated how many LGBTQQI people of color often establish a "dual identity." The ability to straddle multiple worlds wherein they are, at times, the minority, the majority, and both constitutes another type of biculturalism which these adolescents, in spite of external threats, most often negotiate successfully.

Lorde (1984) described a fundamental dilemma with which many racial/ethnic and LGBTQQI adolescents must struggle: the conflict of the fear of stigmatization in the ethnic or racial community as queer versus the loss of support for their identity as a person of color in the mainstream queer community. More recent scholarship in **queer studies** focusing on youth of color has explored the paradoxes and troubling intersections of these multiple identities (Davis 1999; Kumashiro 2001).

One primary arena for all adolescent development in the Western hemisphere is secondary education. Schools and school-related activities comprise a major portion of adolescents' lives, and it is within these environments that most LGBTQQI youth and youth perceived to belong to these groups confront **harassment** and victimization. Numerous studies conducted in the United States, **Canada, Australia, New Zealand,** and Western **Europe** have documented that queer students are far more likely to have been physically or verbally threatened or otherwise victimized, to abuse substances, to become **sex work**ers, to attempt **suicide**, and to be homeless than are heterosexual youth.

Concurrently there are also both educators and students in various cities and states worldwide who are committed to enhancing the **school climate** for LGBTQQI students. Led by social movements, and many times by the very students they are committed to serving, **teachers** and **administrators** are establishing **educational policies** specifically citing intolerance of harassment based on sexual identity. They are establishing appropriate faculty and staff training to prepare school personnel for working with LGBTQQI students and to educate with antioppressive agenda. Most importantly, there has been the development of school-based programs such as **gay–straight alliances**.

Outside of school, queer adolescents are constructing sexual and gender identities differently just as our psychological understanding of adolescence, in general, and LGBTQQI youth, in particular, have changed. One example is "zines" (Knobel and Lankshear 2002). These self-made, independent, and **Internet**-based magazines are a worldwide phenomenon. This modern version of the homophile publications during the 1950s and gay liberation press of the 1960s has exploded as the genre for alternative sexual expression and "Distros," their means of distribution. Believing the mainstream queer press is primarily for adults, many queer youth express themselves and raise consciousness through zines, reflecting a diversity in queer communities (bear-zines, dyke-zines, bi-zines, porn-zines, trans-zines).

Bibliography

Chan, Connie. 1989. "Issues of Identity Development among Asian American Lesbians and Gay Men." *Journal of Counselling and Development* 68:16–20.

D'Augelli, Anthony. 1998. "Lesbian and Gay Male Development: Steps Toward an Analysis of Lesbians' and Gay Men's Lives." Pp. 118–132 in *Lesbian and Gay Psychology: Theory, Research, and Clinical Applications. Psychological Perspectives on Lesbian and Gay Issues, Vol. 1*, ed. Beverley Greene and Gregory Herek. Thousand Oaks, CA: Sage.

Davis, James. 1999. "Forbidden Fruit: Black Males' Construction of Transgressive Sexualities in Middle School." Pp. 49–59 in *Queering Elementary Education: Advancing the Dialogue about Sexualities and Schooling*. Edited by William J. Letts IV and James T. Sears. Lanham, MD: Rowan and Littlefield Publishers.

Flos, Peter. 1962. *On Adolescence*. New York: Free Press.

Freud, Sigmund. 1958. *Adolescence: The Psychoanalytic Study of the Child*, 13:255–278. New York: International Universities Press.

Garnets, Linda, and Douglas C. Kimmel. 1991. "Lesbian and Gay Male Dimensions in the Psychological Study of Human Diversity." Pp. 143–192 in *Psychological Perspectives on Human Diversity in America*, ed. Jacqueline D. Goodchilds. Washington, DC: American Psychological Association.

Hall, G. Stanley. 1904. *Adolescence: Its Psychology and Its Relations to Physiology, Anthropology, Sociology, Sex, Crime, Religion and Education.* 2 vols. New York: Appleton.

Knobel, Michele, and Colin Lankshear. 2002. "Cut, Paste, Publish: The Production and Consumption of Zines." Pp. 147–163 in *New Literacies and Digital Epistemologies: A Focus on Adolescent Learners*, ed. Donna Alvermann. New York: Peter Lang.

Kumashiro, Kevin, ed. 2001. *Troubling Intersections of Race and Sexuality: Queer Students of Color and Anti-Oppressive Education.* Lanham, MD: Rowman and Littlefield.

Lorde, Audre. 1984. *Sister Outsider.* Trumansburg, NY: Crossing Press.

Morales, Edward S. 1990. "Ethnic Minority Families and Minority Gays and Lesbians. Pp. 217–239 in *Homosexuality and Family Relations, ed.* Frederick Bozett and Marvin Sussman. Binghamton, NY: Harrington Park Press.

Rotheram-Borus, Mary Jane, Margaret Rosario, and Cheryl Koopman. 1991. "Minority Youths at High Risk: Gay Males and Runaways." Pp. 181–200 in *Adolescents and Stress: Causes and Consequences, ed.* Susan Gore and Mary Ellen Colten. Hawthorne, NY: Aldine de Gruyter.

Web Site

GRRR Zine Network. 2004. Accessed November 14, 2004. http://grrrlzines.net/resources/artandmusic.htm. A place where lesbian, queer, and transgender youth from around the globe express their voices without being censored or ridiculed.

Adolescent Sexualities

John C. Spurlock

The adolescent period involves a variety of physical changes that will confront growing youth with challenges related to sexual feelings, behaviors, and roles. The years from ten to twenty are considered the most important for the development of **sexual identity. Lesbian, gay, bisexual**, and **transgender youth** (LGBT) confront a wide range of challenges, often including discoveries about **sexual orientation.** The period following puberty generally includes experiences of sexual arousal, masturbation, and sex play. One's feelings about and responses to these experiences become part of the more general struggle of **adolescence**: achieving a sense of an autonomous self. Both the general physical changes and the development of sexual behavior will take on specific meanings depending on the individual's gender, culture, sexual orientation, and family situation. Although many generalizations about

See also AIDS: Australia, Sexualities Curriculum in; Biology, Teaching of; Compulsory Heterosexuality; Cross-Dressing; Identity Development; Intersex; Native and Indigenous LGBT Youth; New Zealand, Teaching of Sexualities in; Parents, Responses to Homosexuality; Prostitution or Sex Work; Sexual Abuse and Assault; Sexual Health, Lesbian and Bisexual Women; Sexual Health, Gay and Bisexual Men; Transsexuality; Youth, at At-Risk.

adolescent sexuality apply to youth of all sexual orientations, the struggle to develop a sexual identity is almost inevitably more serious for sexual minority youth. While most adolescents embrace the essential features of heterosexuality that family and peers already assume they possess, LGBT youth must work out an identity that is stigmatized in the wider culture.

Feelings of arousal probably depend on physical changes that take place before and during puberty. For both girls and boys adrenal androgen increases sharply around age ten, the age that many adults recall as the time of their first attraction for someone else or fantasies with sexual content. (McClintock and Herdt 1996) The usual physiological marker for puberty is gonadarche, the maturation of the ovaries in girls (on average, around age twelve) and the testes in boys (around age fourteen). Long before puberty, children find themselves immersed in messages about sexual behaviors and roles. Early adolescents, while they have a widening sense of themselves as sexual beings, are generally satisfied with noncoital behaviors (Rice 1996). Young adolescents frequently have a mix of heterosexual and homosexual desires, fantasies, and even sexual experiences. In early to midadolescence **desire** and experience tend to solidify into a clearer sexual identity, and experimentation increases with age. The majority of adolescents in the United States will have sex before the end of their teenage years (Rice 1996). But teenagers become sexually active in many other ways. Masturbation typically begins during adolescence, and other types of sex play will become more common and more intense for older adolescents. Sexual behaviors become linked to the individual's search for intimacy and emotional attachment. Adolescents must negotiate all of these changes in intimate behaviors and expectations with only partially developed social skills and probably with a poor sense of self and self-worth.

The experience of sexuality will differ by gender, **social class**, sexual orientation, **race**, and **ethnicity**. Even though girls develop physically more rapidly than boys, girls begin to masturbate later, and only about half as many girls as boys masturbate. Girls also delay other forms of becoming sexually active. One study found that the reason given for the first intercourse by 51 percent of men was curiosity and readiness for sex, while only 25 percent of women gave this reason. But about half of women reported that affection for their partner motivated the first intercourse, whereas only one-fourth of men gave that response (Hyde and Jaffe 2000). Race also makes a difference in sexual activity. In the mid-1990s, half of **African American** males had heterosexual intercourse by age fifteen. For **Latinos** the comparable age was a year later, and for white males it was eighteen. In each group, adolescent females reached the same rates at later ages (age seventeen for African American women, eighteen for white and Latina women). Social class is also an important consideration. Although whites and blacks have significantly different ages for first intercourse, when the groups are compared by class, the racial differences diminish. Similarly, white, Latino, and African American gay males show little difference in the timing of their first sexual experiences.

The challenges of adolescent sexuality are generally much greater for LGBT youth because they develop desires that are marginalized, stigmatized, or invisible in the wider culture. Sexual minority youth typically grow up with parents and siblings who assume they will marry someone of the other gender and become parents themselves. Teenagers are surrounded by messages about heterosexual desire and romance, and typically heterosexual activities such as **dating** and having steadies are important elements of social status and acceptance in high school. LGBT youth find few positive messages in the media about their sexualities, and their families will generally have little understanding or sympathy for nonheterosexual desire or experimentation.

Today most school systems offer **sexuality education**, and a majority of large districts offer it from elementary through senior high. Most of these programs, however, run for only a few hours each school year. All types of sex education suffer from the marginalization of homosexual experience. The clear message of these curricula is that heterosexuality is the normal goal of sexuality. Only 6.3 percent of large school districts studied in the mid-1990s provided "in-depth" discussion of homosexuality (Rice, 1996). The only topic given less attention was masturbation.

Consequently, a gay, lesbian, or bisexual teenager will suffer from the invisibility of homosexual culture and may know few, if any, homosexual peers. Transgender youth, even when they are heterosexual, often exhibit behaviors that defy gender roles. Consequently, these adolescents experience the same marginalization as lesbian, gay, and bisexual teenagers, and will often seek out homosexual peers as their reference group. Sexual minority teenagers will also be aware of the fear and hostility of homosexuality (**homophobia**) that exists throughout society. Verbal and physical **harassment** of adolescents who do not conform to typical **gender roles** occurs quite commonly, with a majority of gay male adolescents reporting some harassment. Homophobia will often cause sexual minority youth to hide their desires until later in life.

Because of the marginalization of the experiences of lesbian, gay, bisexual, and transgender desires in contemporary culture, the process of **coming out** is a distinctive and important experience for a growing number of North American youth. In spite of generalized homophobia and the continuing possibility of harassment, the average age of coming out has declined in recent decades, with some estimates placing it in the mid-teens (Raymond 1994). The process begins with desires in late childhood and early adolescence that young people quickly recognize are not socially acceptable. Many sexual minority youth will have internalized negative ideas about nonheterosexual behavior. This internalized homophobia can lengthen the struggle around sexual identity. Gay and lesbian youth often use heterosexual activity as a means of exploring sexuality or even of attempting to overcome homosexual desire. Transgender youth, who have desires and often display behavior outside typical gender roles, may adopt homosexual behaviors as a means of finding a reference group. An important step in this process comes when the young person recognizes sexual desire as part of his or her identity. There may be a long gap in time before a young person acts on this recognition, with lesbians taking as many as five years more than gay males to move to an important sexual act with another individual of the same gender. Sexual minority youth recognize the importance of claiming nonheterosexual identities, and also realize the danger of rejection. As many as three-fourths of youth come out first to friends before family (Ryan and Futterman 1998). Although parents may be accepting of the adolescent's sexual orientation, there exists a significant possibility of rejection and even expulsion from the family home. Coming out has less importance in other cultures. Some western European countries have greater acceptance for sexual minorities, so embracing a nonheterosexual identity may not provoke a crisis.

Rejecting a heterosexual identity may hold even greater risk for youth in ethnic-minority communities. LGBT youth who are **Latino**, **Asian American**, or **African American** commonly feel pressure to remain invisible within the ethnic group, and they experience their ethnic communities as more homophobic than dominant United States culture. Within these ethnic groups, however, sexual activity with a same gender partner may carry less stigma than in mainstream Anglo culture. In Latino culture, for instance, girls and women develop close emotional relations, and physical relations may become part of this. Young Latino males often experiment sexually with other males. For all of these groups, however, embracing an identity as gay or lesbian creates conflict between the individual and the ethnic community (Greene 1994).

Adolescents face diverse problems regarding sexuality. One of the most important is unwanted **pregnancy**. The United States has one of the highest fertility rates and abortion rates for teenagers among developed countries. An unwanted pregnancy can be a crisis for any woman, particularly for an unmarried teenager, and 41 percent of pregnant teens responded by aborting their pregnancies during the 1990s. A substantial proportion, however, decide to give birth and about 95 percent of these mothers keep their children (Luker 1996). Homosexuality has been identified as a risk factor for pregnancy. Sexual experimentation prior to self-identification as lesbian will generally come at earlier ages, and younger teens are less likely to use contraceptives. But lesbians also try to **pass** by having sex with males. This behavior may be complicated by confusion over sexual identity and internalized homophobia, leading to nonprotected sex.

Sexually transmitted infections (STIs) remain a major problem. The group most affected by STIs is twenty to twenty-four-year olds, followed by fifteen to nineteen-year olds. Teenagers have one-fourth of all cases of gonorrhea. Sexually active teenagers are also at high risk for contracting HIV because of the lower frequency of protected sex among younger populations. By the early 1990s, the average age for persons infected with HIV had dropped to twenty-five, with one-fourth of all cases occurring in those age twenty-two or younger (Rice 1996). Because HIV may remain latent up to ten years, a huge proportion of transmission of the disease takes place among teenagers. Infection rates are higher for African American adolescents than for Latino or white. Studies consistently show high rates of infection for gay male adolescents. Sexual minority youth may engage in high risk sexual activities for a variety of reasons. Sexual or **gender identity** confusion, compounded by homophobia, may lead to unprotected sex as part of sexual exploration. On average, by age fifteen, gay males have had more sexual partners than their heterosexual peers (Rotheram-Borus and Langabeer 2001). By seeking environments where their sexual orientation is not stigmatized, sexual minority youth can place themselves at high risk for exploitation.

Bibliography

Greene, Beverly. 1994. "Ethnic-Minority Lesbians and Gay Men: Mental Health and Treatment Issues." *Journal of Consulting and Clinical Psychology* 62: 243–251.

Hyde, Janet Shelby, and Sara R. Jaffee. 2000. "Becoming a Heterosexual Adult: The Experience of Young Women." *Journal of Social Issues* 56: 283–296.

Luker, Kristin. 1996. *Dubious Conceptions: The Politics of Teenage Pregnancy*. Cambridge, MA: Harvard University Press.

McClintock, Martha K., and Gilbert Herdt. 1996. "Rethinking Puberty: The Development of Sexual Attraction." *Current Directions in Psychological Science* 5: 178–183.

Raymond, Diane. 1994. "Homophobia, Identity, and the Meanings of Desire: Reflections on the Cultural Construction of Gay and Lesbian Adolescent Sexuality." Pp. 115–150 in *Sexual Cultures and the Construction of Adolescent Identities, ed.* Janice M. Irvine. Philadelphia: Temple University Press.

Rice, F. Philip. 1996. *The Adolescent: Development, Relationships, and Culture.* 8th ed. Boston: Allyn and Bacon.

Rotheram-Borus, Mary Jane, and Kris A. Langabeer. 2001. "Developmental Trajectories of Gay, Lesbian, and Bisexual Youth." Pp. 97–128 in *Lesbian, Gay, and Bisexual Identities and Youth: Psychological Perspectives.* Edited by Anthony R. D'Augelli and Charlotte J. Patterson. New York: Oxford.

Ryan, Caitlin, and Donna Futterman. 1998. *Lesbian & Gay Youth: Care & Counseling.* New York: Columbia University Press.

Web Sites

LGBTQ Youth Statistics. 2002. Hetrick-Martin Institute. Accessed December 5, 2004. http://www.hmi.org/Community/LGBTQYouthStatistics/default.aspx This is a summary of statistics on LGBT youth from the Hetrick-Martin Institute, the home of the Harvey Milk School for gay, lesbian, bisexual, and transgendered youth.

National Center for HIV, STD, and TB Prevention. December 2004. Center for Disease Control. Accessed December 5, 2004. http://www.cdc.gov/nchstp/od/hiv_plan/Young%20people.htm Statistics with charts, from the Centers for Disease Control on HIV infection among youth.

Adoption

Eric M. Richardson

Throughout the world there is a critical shortage of adoptive parents, and in many countries people have acknowledged that unless lesbian, gay, transgender, and bisexual adults are permitted to adopt, either individually or as couples, an exceedingly high number of children will remain in foster care or children's homes. Given the **research** suggesting that children raised in homes with LGBT parents develop in much the same way as children of heterosexual parents, many **professional organizations** support adoption of children, regardless of **sexual orientation** or **gender identity**. Unlike heterosexual parents, however, same-sex couples might not be able to hide the fact that their child is adopted. Since adoption remains stigmatized, even when the parents are heterosexual, adopted children raised by homosexual partners are likely to be mocked for not having "real" parents or a "real" family. Consequently, **educational policies** addressing the **harassment, bullying,** or rejection by their peers that these children are likely to suffer are critical. Teachers also need to consider the needs of adoptees with transgender parents, and the needs of LGBT children of straight adopted parents.

See also Children of LGBT Parents; Heteosexism; Homophobia; Identity Development; Parents, LGBT; Youth, Homeless.

Studies involving lesbian or gay parents have focussed on the parents' child-rearing abilities and practices, and the children's development and **gender role** identity. Most of the studies have focussed on second-parent adoptions, where one of the parents is raising a child or children from a previous heterosexual relationship. Comparisons have then been made with straight parents and their children, using a variety of measures. A substantial body of research has generally reached positive conclusions about gay and lesbian parenting:

- The sexual identity of parents has no impact on the sexual identity of the child.
- The development and psychological well-being of children with gay or lesbian parents is much the same as children with heterosexual parents. However, when children perceive their community to be homophobic or antigay, having a gay father may result in them feeling stress.
- Children of lesbian or gay parents appear to adopt "appropriate" gender roles and behaviors. However, "children with lesbigay parents appear less traditionally gender-typed and more likely to be open to homoerotic relationships" than children with straight parents (Fisher 2003, 349).
- Lesbian and gay parents are aware of, and make attempts to negate, the negative effects of the stigmatization of having homosexual parents. This may result in homosexual parents becoming better parents than heterosexual people.

Although some research has been criticized for using relatively small samples, major professional organizations support eligibility of LGBT adults to become adoptive and foster parents. In the United States, the National Association of Social Workers, the National Conference of Commissioners on Uniform State Laws, the Child Welfare League of America, the American Psychological Association, the American Academy of Pediatrics, and the American Psychiatric Association all maintain that sexual orientation is irrelevant to a person's capacity to be a good parent. According to the National Association of Social Workers: "two decades of scientific investigation have in fact, provided considerable evidence . . . that children who retain regular and unrestricted contact with a gay or lesbian parent are as healthy psychologically and socially as children raised by heterosexual parents, and that the parenting skills of gay fathers and lesbian mothers are comparable to their heterosexual counterparts" (ACLU 2002, 31).

In **South Africa**, permanent same-sex couples are permitted to adopt children. Although the HIV/**AIDS** pandemic has resulted in thousands of children being orphaned, the impetus of the change in law occurred in May 2002 when a lesbian couple, Suzanne du Toit and Anna-Marie de Vos, challenged the constitutional validity of certain sections of the Child Care Act 74 and the Guardianship Act 192 of 1993. These acts provided for the joint guardianship of children by married persons only, and did not provide for the joint adoption or second-parent adoption of children by partners in a permanent same-sex life partnership. Thus, although only De Vos was the legal parent of the two children who had been adopted into the family; the couple wanted Du Toit to be declared the second-parent. Second-parent adoptions legally protect the inheritance rights of the child, ensures custody rights and responsibilities should the couple separate, and if one of the parents dies, the child is able to remain with the second-parent.

Although same-sex marriage was not yet legal in South Africa, the Constitution prohibited **discrimination** on the basis of sexual orientation and marital status, thus allowing du Toit and de Vos to challenge provisions in the Child Care and Guardianship Acts. They also argued in court that in the event of De Vos's death, the children would become wards of the state. This would deny them a loving and stable family life, which, the couple claimed, would conflict with the Constitution's principle of serving the best interests of the child. South Africa's High Court upheld the application and declared the impugned provisions unconstitutional. The judge of the Constitutional Court agreed with the High Court's order, mandated a non-heterosexist reading of the acts, and declared that a lesbian or gay man should be permitted to adopt his or her partner's child without the partner giving up any of his or her rights and responsibilities (resulting in the legalization of second-parent adoptions by same-sex partners), and that prospective adoptive couples should be evaluated on a case-by-case basis, regardless of their sexual orientation (resulting in joint adoptions by permanent same-sex couples). A year later, in December 2004, South Africa's Supreme Court of Appeal ruled that the marriage ban was in conflict with the Constitution.

Throughout the world, there is a shortage of potential adoptive parents. In the United States, for example, an estimated half million children are in foster care; only 20,000 will be adopted by qualified adoptive parents (ACLU 1998). Recently, a number of state supreme courts, intermediate appellate courts, and lower courts have changed their laws to enable lesbian and gay adults to adopt. These include courts in New York, New Mexico, Utah, and Washington; at least twenty-one states have granted second-parent adoptions by lesbian or gay partners. But in some states such as Florida, lesbians and gay men are not permitted to adopt children even when homosexuality is legal.

Three separate lawsuits have challenged Florida state courts to overturn the 1977 law prohibiting any homosexual person from adopting; these have been un-successful (ACLU 1998). Although single heterosexuals can adopt and homosexuals can foster children, this state justifies the ban because of its disapproval of homosexuality and because "children are better off in homes with a mother and a father who are married" (ACLU 2002, 11). The research suggests, however, that children would be better off in permanent homes with loving parents of any sexual orientation or gender identity (Tye 2003)

As adoptions by same-sex parents become more numerous and more visible, teachers will have to respond in ways which support all their pupils, including those children who are subjected to harassment, rejection, or bullying because their parents are lesbian or gay. This requires familiarity with professional literature re-garding gay and lesbian parents and their children, some understanding of adop-tion, nontraditional families, and an LGBT-inclusive **curriculum**. There should be no assumptions about the child's sexuality or gender identity.

In Massachusetts, the Department of Social Services (DSS) has developed a set of **social work** standards to meet the needs of the LGBT youth and their families. DSS social workers are trained to create an LGBT-friendly environment where all involved—employees, youth, and foster or adoptive parents-are free from **prejudice** and discrimination. As a result of this training, it is hoped that homophobic families will not adopt LGBT homeless youth.

Bibliography

American Academy of Pediatrics. 2002. "Coparent or Second Parent Adoption by Same-Sex Parents." *Pediatrics* 109, no. 2: 339–340.

American Civil Liberties Union. 1998. *In the Child's Best Interests: Defending Fair and Sensible Adoption Policies*. Available at http://www.aclu.org/LesbianGayRights/LesbianGayRights.cfm?ID=9185&c=104.

———. 2002. *Too High a Price: The Case against Restricting Gay Parenting*. New York: Author.

Bigner, Jerry, J., and R. Brooke Jacobsen. 1989. "Parenting Behaviours of Homosexual and Heterosexual Fathers." *Journal of Homosexuality* 18: 173–186.

Bozett, Frederick W., ed. 1987. *Gay and Lesbian Parents*. New York: Praeger.

———. 1988. "Social Control of Identity by Children of Gay Fathers." *Western Journal of Nursing Research* 10: 550–565.

Constitutional Court of South Africa. 2002. *Suzanne du Toit and Anna-Marie de Vos versus The Minister for Welfare and Population Development and Others*. Case CCT 40/01.

Evan B. Donaldson Adopt. Inst. 1997. *Adoption by Lesbians and Gays: A National Survey of Adoption Agency Policies, Practices, and Attitudes*. New York: Author.

Fisher, Allen P. 2003. "Still 'Not quite as good as having your own?' Toward a Sociology of Adoption." *Annual Review of Sociology* 29:335–361.

Flaks, David K., Ilda Ficher, Frank Masterpasqua, and Gregory Joseph. 1995. "Lesbians Choosing Motherhood: A Comparative Study of Lesbian and Heterosexual Parents and their Children." *Developmental Psychology* 31, no. 1: 105–114.

Hoeffer, Beverly. 1981. "Children's Acquisition of Sex-Role Behaviour in Lesbian-Mother Families." *American Journal of Orthopsychiatry* 51: 536–544.

Lambda Legal. August 2004. Mediapolis. Accessed August 13, 2004. http://www.lambdalegal.org.

Patterson, Charlotte J. 1992. "Children of Lesbian and Gay Parents." *Child Development* 63: 1025–1042.

Stacey, Judith, and Timorthy Biblarz. 2001. "(How) Does the Sexual Orientation of Parents Matter?" *American Sociological Review* 66 (April): 159–183.

Tye, Marus C. 2003. "Lesbian, Gay, Bisexual, and Transgender Parents: Special Considerations for the Custody and Adoption Evaluator." Family Court Review 41, no. 1: 92–103.

Web Sites

Adoptions.com. 2000. R&C Communications. Accessed August 13, 2004. http://www.adoptions.com/aecgaylez.html. Offers advice for gay and lesbian adoptive parents.

The Family Pride Coalition. 2004. Accessed December 2, 2004. http://www.familypride.org. Services to LGBT parents and families.

Lambda Legal. 2004. Accessed August 13, 2004. http://www.lambdalegal.org. An American organization concerned with the rights of LGBT people.

National Adoption Information Clearinghouse. August 2004. U.S. Department of Health & Human Services. Accessed August 13, 2004. http://naic.acf.hhs.gov. Provides general information and research findings to prospective and adoptive LGBT parents.

National Center for Lesbian Rights. August 2004. Lucille Design. Accessed August 13, 2004. http://www.nclrights.org. Legal resource center involved in litigation, counseling, resources for the LGBT community, and public education.

Africa, LGBT Youth and Issues in

Eric M. Richardson

Although homosexual practices in Africa predate Arab and European **colonialism**, people did not identify as "gay" or "lesbian." Only in more recent years have adult homosexual identities been embraced, leading to the formation of LGBT organizations on the continent. For the most part homosexuality in Africa is demonized and seen as immoral, foreign, and the cause of the **AIDS** pandemic. Given these extremely homophobic contexts, adolescents **coming out** as LGBT youth or who are suspected of being homosexual because of nonconforming gender behaviors may be scorned, harassed, imprisoned, threatened with deportation, raped, or abandoned by their families or communities. Consequently, LGBT youth and youth who do not adopt the label but who are in same-sex relationships remain largely invisible; very little is known about them, even in **South Africa** where the constitution protects sexual minorities.

Africa is a continent diverse in history and the size of its countries, in ethnicity, in religions, in languages (French, Portuguese, and English included), in natural resources, and in development. In any one country, people may find themselves with considerable differences in cultures, customs, and languages. In addition, **rural** and **urban** Africans in the same country may have very different life experiences.

Nevertheless, throughout the fifty-four countries, elders maintain a strong belief in "traditional" African ethics, which emphasize the importance of family, conformity of the individual to the social group, and the preservation of social cohesion and harmony. Patriarchal leaders assert that "black" people need to be ever vigilant for that which is un-African and a threat to "the African way of life" (Human Rights Watch 2003). In Kenya, for example, the Office of the President approves all survey **research** designs to ensure that these are "appropriate" in an African context.

The idea that men who have sex with men are **"gay"** and that women who have sex with women are **"lesbian"** is a Western construct. Although homosexual experiences have been shown to have existed in Africa before colonialism (Murray and Roscoe 1998), people seldom embraced a homosexual identity. Nowadays, only Africans comfortable with more Westernized connotations seem to claim such an essentialized **sexual identity** or **sexual orientation**.

In Zaire, for instance, Evans-Pritchard's research, in the 1920s, found numerous examples of youth serving as "boy-wives" to older men—a practice where younger men have sex with older men before marriage to prepare them for married life. Yet they were not called "gay." In addition, "homosexual or transgendered males have had a role as spiritual functionaries among a number of African cultures—the Lango people of Uganda, Murus of Kenya, Ilas of southern Zambia and Zulu people of South Africa" (Baird 2001, 50). In Burkina Faso, "gatekeepers," like Two-Spirit people in **Native American** cultures, are believed to be the mediators between the world of the village and the spirit world. They also stand on the threshold of the gender line: in some sense neither male nor female in spirit.

In Dakar, Senegal, research has found that many men who have sex with men (MSM) do not view themselves as gay. Even so, gender norms and **gender roles** do

See also Adolescent Sexualities; Bisexuality; Compulsory Heterosexuality; Identity Politics; Multiple Genders.

influence their interactions (The Population Council 2002). Men who adopt "masculine" mannerisms are generally the ones who penetrate the "feminine" men during sex. In Tanzania, the penetrator is called the *basha*; the other is the *msenge; basha* do not get involved sexually with other *basha*. As in other cultures, the man being penetrated is stigmatized more than the man penetrating.

Although such "indigenous homosexualities" are real, they have often been rendered invisible (Epprecht 1998). Despite claiming not to be gay or bisexual, the men in the Senegal research wish to keep their homosexual acts secret. Exposure could result in violence, rejection, bribery, and rape, even by policemen. Marc Epprecht (1998) found in his Zimbabwe research that even gay men and lesbians who have "come out" continue to marry and have families; in this way these men and women fulfill customary obligations and ensure that in times of economic hardship members of the extended family can support each other.

Women who have sex with women are also understood differently in many African societies. In Namibia, same-sex oriented women may adopt socially accepted gender roles and mannerisms of men, dress as men, and work as men. These self-described "lesbian men," have relationships with "heterosexual women" (Morgan 2003). Additionally, young girls growing up in Nigeria engage in activities which Westerners might label as "lesbian" (Emecheta 1989). However, since sex is socially defined in Nigeria as male vaginal penetration, girls "playing" with girls are seldom considered to be doing something wrong.

In Nigeria, women have been known to marry other women. These marriages, however, are understood as social not sexual: The younger woman is encouraged to take a male lover and have a son, who is then the older woman's or female husband's heir.

Research conducted in Zimbabwe, Namibia, Zambia, Botswana, and South Africa suggests that historically Africans have adopted a "don't ask, don't tell" attitude (Human Rights Watch 2003). So long as people conform to gender norms, do not challenge the dominant gender relations, and reject labels such as "gay" or "lesbian," many communities have been, and still are, willing to accommodate their homosexual behaviors. Ironically, communities have also tolerated cross-dressers or transvestic people who play the role of the other sex (Murray & Roscoe, 1998).

It is difficult to find out about the experiences of LGBT youth since many do not adopt these particular labels even though they are involved in same-sex relationships. Even when youth do identify as LGBT, it may be too dangerous for them to participate in research about youth. In most instances, researchers have had to ask adult lesbians and gay men to reflect on their adolescent years in order to learn more about the experiences of LGBT youth in Africa. For example, researchers in Senegal found that the average age for the first homosexual encounter of the 250 MSM surveyed was at age 15 and with an adult (The Population Council 2002).

Laws introducing stiffer penalties for "gay sex" and people celebrating gay "marriages," such as the one passed, in May 2004, in Zanzibar, off the Tanzanian coast, are intended to keep homosexual couples from becoming public about their lives. Throughout much of the continent, state-sanctioned homophobia and **heterosexism** result in gays, lesbians, and bisexuals being subjected to interrogation, beatings, and harassment. In Uganda, homosexuals can be sentenced to life imprisonment. In Botswana, the sodomy law has been broadened to ensure that sexual conduct between women is also a criminal offense. In Sudan, the death penalty applies. In Zambia a person can be arrested for supporting LGBT people, and in Togo, homosexual acts are often prosecuted as assault or rape. It is only in South Africa that sexual minorities are constitutionally protected.

With more people opting to "flaunt" their sexuality and to challenge traditional gender relations and stereotypes that gays are always "feminine" and lesbians "masculine," it is no wonder that many indigenous Africans are threatened by the changes, resulting in an upsurge of intolerance and violence against LGBT people and what Epprecht (1998) calls "invented homophobic traditions." In public, boys who appear "feminine" and girls who are "masculine" are assumed to be homosexual. In schools, these gender nonconformists may encounter persistent **harassment** and **discrimination, homophobia** is not challenged, and the teachers do not teach tolerance. Isaiah, a young man interviewed by the Human Rights Watch, tells how the male students would physically attack him and call him *moffie* while his teachers looked on.

With few exceptions, it is the political leaders who are most vocal in their opposition to "gayism." For example, Sam Nujoma, president of Namibia, has claimed that "most of ardent supporters of this perverts [sic] are Europeans who imagine themselves to be the bulwark of civilisation and enlightenment . . . we made sacrifices for the liberation of this country and we are not going to allow individuals with alien practices such as homosexuality to destroy the social fabric of our society" (Human Rights Watch 2003, 1). Autocratic leaders like Robert Mugabe, president of Zimbabwe, also help to vilify homosexuality. Paradoxically, by rejecting the notion that lesbians and gays deserve human rights, he has created a context in which queer youth who did not label themselves as such now do (Human Rights Watch 2003, 169).

Homosexuals, as defined by the West, are seen by most African leaders to be unnatural, immoral, against African norms and traditions, traitors, and deserving of abuse. Referencing **Christian** and **Muslim** fundamentalist teachings, their rhetoric perpetuates the notion that homosexuality is not only a threat to the family but also to the nation, justifying harsh penalties. In Morocco, Libya, and other Islamic African countries, same-sex relationships and gender nonconformists are severely punished.

Some religious leaders, most notably Bishop Desmond Tutu of South Africa, have spoken against the "immorality" of violence against homosexuals. Lesbian and gay organizations concerned with the rights of sexual minorities have also formed. These include: Lesbians, Gays, Bisexuals and Transgender Association (LEGATRA) in Zambia, the Rainbow Project in Namibia, Sexual Minorities of Uganda (SMUG), and Sierre Leone Lesbian and Gay Association (SLLAGA). One organization that specifically works with **queer** youth is the Durban Lesbian and Gay Community and Health Center in South Africa. Such groups seek to challenge state-sanctioned homophobia, repressive laws, negative representation in the media, and poverty. These groups, which enable queer youth to socialize with each other, also attempt to compensate for those HIV/AIDS organizations which neglect the needs of those engaged in same-sex relations.

In February 2004, over sixty-five representatives from lesbian and gay organizations in seventeen African countries met in Johannesburg, South Africa. Organized by Gays and Lesbians of Zimbabwe (GALZ) and a poverty alleviation program in Uganda, the All Africa Programme provided an opportunity for activists to consider how they could help fight HIV/AIDS among LGBT people, men who have sex with men (MSM), and women who have sex with women (WSW). For security reasons, the conference received little publicity and the participants refused to have their photographs taken. By the end of the Conference the "All Africa Rights Initiative" (AARI) was established, with the steering committee being tasked with the creation of a constitution and the organizing of further meetings of this type. It remains to be seen whether or not these organizations will also have an impact on the African Union and the future of LGBT youth on the continent.

Bibliography

Baird, Vanessa. 2001. *The No-Nonsense Guide to Sexual Diversity*. Oxford: New Internationalist Publications.

Emecheta, Buchi. 1989. "Natural Gestures." *New Internationalist*. Accessed July 14, 2004. http://www.newint.org/issue201/gestures.htm.

Epprecht, Marc. 1998. "The 'Unsaying' of Indigenous Homosexualities in Zimbabwe: Mapping a Blindspot in an African Masculinity." *Journal of Southern African Studies* 24, no. 4: 631–651.

Human Rights Watch. 2003. *State Sponsored Homophobia and its Consequences in Southern Africa*. New York: Author.

Morgan, Ruth. 2003. *Newsletter of the Gay and Lesbian Archives of South Africa* (GALA).

Murray, Stephen O., and Will Roscoe. 1998. *Boy-Wives and Female Husbands: Studies of African Homosexualities*. New York: St Martin's Press.

The Population Council. 2002. *Meeting the Sexual Needs of Men who have Sex with Men in Senegal*. Accessed July 14, 2004. http://www.popcouncil.org/pdfs/horizons/msmsenegal.pdf.

Web Sites

Behind the Mask. November 2004. Accessed November 14, 2004. http://www.mask.org.za. Useful Web site for people interested in tracking developments in gay and lesbian issues in Africa.

Gayscape. 2004. Accessed November 14, 2004. http://www.gayscape.com. Offers a list of entries that one can browse, and a search tool on lesbian, gay, bisexual, and queer issues.

Q-online. August 2004. Accessed November 14, 2004. http://www.q.co.za/homosaurus/a. htm. Search directory for anything related to queer Africa.

Virtual City. August 2004. http://www.virtualcity.com/youthsuicide/links5a-1.htm. Award-winning site with many links to other Web sites dealing with LGBTQ issues in Africa and elsewhere.

African American Youth

Brett Genny Beemyn

Black same-gender loving (SGL) youth in the United States at the turn of the twenty-first century have more role models and resources available to them than ever before. However, they still often feel isolated and marginalized within the larger black and LGBT communities. As a result, many black SGL youth do not disclose their sexual and gender identities, making it more difficult, at times, for them to meet other same-gender loving African Americans. But while relatively few

See also Activism, LGBT Youth; Africa, LGBT Youth and Issues in; College Campus Organizing; Cocurricular Activities; College Age Students; Music, Teaching of; Passing; Racial Identity; School Safety and Safe School Zones.

African American or people of color SGL groups have been established in secondary schools, at historically black colleges and universities (HBCUs), and at predominantly white higher education institutions, black SGL people have been able to find support through informal social networks and the **Internet**.

People of African descent who engaged in same-sex sexual activities existed in traditional African societies and throughout U.S. history, but rarely has this aspect of their lives been included in school curricula. For example, same-sex sexual behavior and relationships among young men and women were often an accepted and institutionalized practice in African cultures, and some African societies allowed for a wider range of sexual activities and gender possibilities in the sixteenth and seventeenth centuries than did many European countries (Murray and Roscoe 1988).

In recent years, though, some college and high school courses have discussed the sexual and gender identities of SGL African Americans, including Harlem Renaissance luminaries such as Bessie Smith, Ma Rainey, Countee Cullen, and Claude McKay; civil rights leader Bayard Rustin; and writers James Baldwin, Alice Walker, Audre Lorde, and June Jordan. While there are relatively few out SGL African Americans in **popular culture**, black SGL youth can find role models in the entertainer RuPaul, novelist E. Lynn Harris, musician Méshell Ndegéocello, and Sophia Pasquis of *Road Rules*.

The lack of well-known openly SGL African Americans points to the difficulties experienced by out black SGL people. Despite many black families and communities being aware of their SGL members and some predominantly white LGBT organizations taking steps to address racism, black SGL youth are rarely completely accepted by either group. In black settings, particularly in black cultural and religious institutions, they often feel pressured to deny their **sexual** or **gender identity**; whereas, in LGBT social and political spaces, they often feel compelled to downplay their **race** (Wall and Washington 1991).

African American students often attend historically black colleges and universities to develop stronger ties to black culture and other black people. But instead of finding a supportive environment, students who are perceived as same-gender loving or gender nonconforming have often faced hostility and rejection. The severe beating of a student at Morehouse College, in 2002, by another student who thought the victim was looking at him in the shower is an extreme example of the anti-SGL **school climate** that has existed at many HBCUs. Of the more than 100 historically black colleges and universities, only a handful (e.g., Howard University, Spelman College, and Johnson C. Smith University) host SGL student organizations. These groups have traditionally been small and isolated. For example, "Sapphrodykie" (2000, 132, 141) found that Howard University's SGL group "was the only welcoming and safe place on campus for gay, lesbian, bisexual, transgender, and questioning students." Although she persevered to graduate, "[her] undergraduate experience was everything but nurturing" because of "the general intolerant attitude toward homosexuality."

But students at HBCUs are making important strides to improve their campus climates. When the Lambda Student Alliance, the first SGL group to be founded at a HBCU, was established at Howard in 1979, the student government refused to recognize the organization and the administration only granted it a charter when the group threatened to bring a lawsuit. In contrast, Howard's new SGL group was selected by students and school officials as the university's "Student Organization of the Year" in 2003. At Johnson C. Smith University, Jonathan Perry founded the school's SGL education group, in 2002, and appealed to the administration for help after repeatedly being threatened and harassed because of his sexuality. His efforts led the university to provide LGBT awareness training to staff members, develop a campus **allies** program, and seek inclusion of LGBT issues in the **curriculum**.

Although LGBT organizations exist at most predominantly white colleges and universities, many of these groups have not been inclusive of black SGL students. Typically, few African Americans and other students of color serve in leadership positions, even fewer white members have addressed their own racism and racial privilege, and groups tend to have a narrow LGBT focus, ignoring the multiple identities and concerns of SGL people. For many SGL African Americans, who have grown up in largely black communities and who understand their sexuality within the context of their blackness, mainly white LGBT organizations are alien and often alienating environments. These groups rarely integrate sexuality and race, consider the many forms of oppression that black SGL people daily experience, or promote **white antiracism**.

The cultural gap between African Americans and whites who are attracted to others of the same sex is demonstrated by the language that members of each group often use to describe themselves. A significant number of African Americans and other youth of color use phrases such as "same-gender loving," "in the life," or "on the Down Low" to refer to their sexual identities. They feel that the terms "lesbian, gay, bisexual, and transgender" and "**queer**" are primarily associated with whiteness and do not adequately reflect their cultural experiences.

Not finding a welcoming environment or having their needs met in many campus LGBT organizations, black students and other students of color began to found their groups at some large universities and progressive liberal arts colleges in the mid- to late 1970s. Today, SGL groups exist at more than twenty institutions with a significant number of students of color and/or a more supportive atmosphere for LGBT students. The organizations founded by students of color are similar to primarily white groups in that they provide support, offer social opportunities, and sponsor educational programs, but their activities reflect the specific racial and cultural needs of members. For example, SGL organizations have held discussions on the intersections of race and sexuality, the particular difficulties of **coming out** in communities of color, and the experiences of SGL African Americans in the black church.

One of the more active SGL organizations, Queer People of Color (QPOC) at the University of California-San Diego, was established in 1999. According to the leader of the group, it serves as "a safe space for students who are both a person of color and queer to address issues pertaining specifically to their own needs." He joined QPOC because "as a 'minority of the minority,'" he felt that the organization "provided an outlet to discuss issues regarding race and **ethnicity** in a queer context that has long been overlooked" (personal communication 2003). Other schools with active SGL organizations include Brown University, Carleton College, Colorado State University, Cornell University, Michigan State University, New York University, and Swarthmore College.

The boundaries between African Americans and whites who are attracted to others of the same gender is perhaps most pronounced in secondary schools, as students establish individual and group identities and often seek to differentiate and separate themselves from members of other social groups. Like students in general, same-gender loving and gender nonconforming youth tend to be defined and divided by race. Among many African American students, openly identifying as LGBT or being involved in an LGBT organization such as a **gay–straight alliance** is considered "a white thing" and contrary to what it means to be a black woman or man. As a result, black SGL youth often have to de-emphasize their sexuality and conform to traditional gender expectations in order to avoid ridicule and rejection from their black peers. For example, "Jamal," a black SGL student at a multiracial California high school, was not involved in an extracurricular LGBT support group because it would have subjected him to verbal and physical **harassment**. "David," another black student at the school, also did not feel comfortable joining the group, even though other students knew he was gay, because he perceived it as an organization for whites (McCready 2001). Given this association between same-sex sexuality and whiteness, it is not surprising that only a small number of gay–straight alliances exist at predominantly black high schools.

While relatively few black same-gender loving youth have joined or established extracurricular SGL organizations, many belong to small, private social networks consisting primarily of students of color away from school. Some of these are organized youth groups facilitated by a **community LGBT group**, center, or social service agency, while others involve informal gatherings at member's homes or in other safe spaces. By meeting outside of school, participants in these networks do not have to disclose their sexuality to classmates; most are not known as SGL beyond their immediate circle of friends. They are thus able to feel less isolated and develop a positive, integrated self-identity, even if their lives do not correspond with traditional sexual **identity development** models, which see coming out to oneself and others as a necessary final stage of development.

J. P. Demornay, Mr. Teen Iowa Unltd., 2001. Courtesy of Gay Youth Unlimited, http://www.youth-unlimited.org

Like other LGBT youth, same-gender loving and gender nonconforming black youth have also been able to meet and share experiences anonymously through Web sites, Internet chat rooms and message boards, and blogs. These online forums are particularly valuable for SGL students who are questioning or struggling with their sexual or gender identity and have no other place to turn for support. With more and more African American youth gaining Internet access, virtual SGL communities will continue to grow in importance.

Bibliography

Dumas, Michael J. 1998. "Coming Out/Coming Home: Black Gay Men on Campus." Pp. 79–85 in *Working with Lesbian, Gay, Bisexual, and Transgender College Students: A Handbook for Faculty and Administrators*. Edited by Ronni L. Sanlo. Westport, CT: Greenwood Press.

McCready, Lance. 2001. "When Fitting In Isn't an Option, or, Why Black Queer Males at a California High School Stay Away from Project 10." Pp. 37–53 in *Troubling Intersections of Race and Sexuality: Queer Students of Color and Anti-Oppressive Education*. Edited by Kevin K. Kumashiro. Lanham, MD: Rowman and Littlefield.

Murray, Stephen O., and Will Roscoe, eds. 1988. *Boy-Wives and Female Husbands: Studies of African Homosexualities*. New York: St. Martin's Press.

Sapphrodykie. 2000. "The Iconoclast." Pp. 131–41 in *Out and About Campus: Personal Accounts by Lesbian, Gay, Bisexual, and Transgendered College Students*. Edited by Kim Howard and Annie Stevens. Los Angeles: Alyson.

Sears, James T. 1995. "Black-Gay or Gay-Black?: Choosing Identities and Identifying Choices." Pp. 135–57 in *The Gay Teen: Educational Practice and Theory for Lesbian, Gay, and Bisexual Adolescents*. Edited by Gerald Unks. New York: Routledge.

Wall, Vernon A., and Jamie Washington. 1991. "Understanding Gay and Lesbian Students of Color." Pp. 67–78 in *Beyond Tolerance: Gay, Lesbians, and Bisexuals on Campus*. Edited by Nancy J. Evans and Vernon A. Wall. Alexandria, VA: American College Personnel Association.

Web Sites

African American Youth. 2004. Advocates for Youth. Accessed December 5, 2004. http://www.youthresource.com/community/youth_of_color/african_american/index.htm Provides information and resources specifically for black LGBT and same-gender loving youth, including Web resources and personal stories.

Keith Boykin. November 2004. Accessed December 4, 2004. http://www.keithboykin.com An author, activist, and educator, Boykin provides news stories, commentaries, and message boards focused on the experiences of LGBT African Americans, including many posts related to and by black youth.

A Resource Guide to Coming Out for African Americans. March 2004. Human Rights Campaign. Accessed December 4, 2004. http://www.hrc.org/Content/ContentGroups/Publications1/AfricanAmericanResourceGuide.pdf. Recognizing the unique challenges faced by African Americans who come out, the HRC site has numerous resources, easily found by using the search engine. The resource guide is a useful overview of issues and sources of information.

Agency

Greg Curran

Agency refers to the ability of individuals to act autonomously—to have control over their lives, to make choices, and to actively pursue their interests and **desires**. Young queers are generally not considered as having, or exercising agency, within the fields of education, health, and welfare in Australia, the United States, or the United Kingdom. Workers and researchers in these fields have tended to de-emphasize queer youth's agency, placing much greater emphasis on the "problems" faced by queer youth, than on the ways in which they pursue their social and sexual interests and desires, and overcome any difficulties that may arise in their lives. A small number of contemporary researchers, however, have critiqued this narrow representation of young queers, documenting how agency is manifested among them.

Queer youth are often represented as unable to deal with, or overcome, the range of troubles posed by living in a homophobic society. They are regularly referred to as being at much "higher risk" (than young heterosexuals) of **suicide**, **drug use**, unsafe sex, and homelessness in education and health-related literature (Kosciw and Cullen 2001; Thurlow 2001). The practice of highlighting the problems

See also Activism, LGBT Youth; Australia, LGBT Youth in; Critical Social Theory; Day of Silence or Silencing; Gay–Straight Alliances; Identity Development; Resiliency; Social Work; Youth, at At-Risk.

of young queers, in a way that renders them as passive, powerless victims of homophobic **discrimination** and **bullying**, has contributed to the notion that queer youth are lacking in agency and requiring the assistance and support of others—usually meaning youth workers, counselors and teachers—in order to avoid, overcome, or cope with these problems.

Some educational researchers are highlighting the limits of this "problem-focused" approach to queer youth (Martino and Pallotta-Chiarolli 2003; Quinlivan 2002). They point out that the sexuality of young queers is often constructed as an individual or personal problem by school authorities, whereas those aspects of school culture that contribute to inequity remain unexamined. This occurs, for example, whenever heterosexuality is taken for granted.

In addition, these researchers are describing and analyzing queer youth lives that don't fit the harassed, abused **stereotype**. This shift toward recognizing young queers as having agency, affords us a glimpse at the knowledge and experiences of young queers who have gained confidence in their queerness (Hillier et al. 2005). Agency, in this respect, encompasses queer youth living more expansively as queers; being more open and less self-regulating in terms of how they talk, walk, move, and dress.

Agency among queer youth takes many forms; resisting and challenging **homophobia** and **heterosexism** (in their various manifestations), and interrogating and questioning taken-for-granted assumptions that serve to stifle or deny agency. These assumptions include the notion that young queers must hide their sexuality in order to reduce the risk of reprisal or must rely on others to act on their behalf. Young queers are, for example, participating in pride marches/rallies and are organizing and operating support/social groups.

Agency also involves young queers recognizing that they have skills, knowledge, and experiences that are valuable to other young queers. This can be seen in **community LGBT support groups,** where they share strategies for dealing with homophobia and **"coming out,"** and take on leadership positions, **mentoring** their peers.

Two corelated factors contribute to and support agency among queer youth. First, visibility; that is, the extent to which queer sexualities and cultures are visible to others. Socialization, or more particularly the opportunity to socialize with other queers, is the second factor. Visibility comes about through young queers being "out." It enables queer youth to connect, and socialize with, others who have similar interests and sexual desires. This provides opportunities for affirmation and support in respect to their sexual desires, feelings, and experiences. Young queers are also able to gain first-hand knowledge about how to resist and challenge homophobia and heterosexism, as well as the stigma and shame associated with homosexual feelings and desires.

For young queers who have previously felt alone and isolated, or who have understood themselves and their desires as "unnatural," "wrong," or "dirty," having access to **queer** worlds, language, and cultures can be tremendously empowering—allowing them to imagine, and experience, being, doing, or living queer, in more positive and expansive ways.

Social changes reflecting agency among queer youth have mostly occurred in youth settings. By contrast, school systems generally maintain a conservative position, where the recognition of queer youth, beyond the homophobia/victim paradigm, remains the exception, not the norm. Those few schools that encourage agency, support queer youth who wish to be "out," as well as the presence and participation of queer staff and students in school life. Key here are **educational policies** that specifically name **"sexual orientation"** and "homophobia," the facilitation of socialization between queer youth, visible queer resources—including information about queer youth support groups, queer space within the **curriculum** and school, and links to queer youth support agencies.

Bibliography

Curran, Greg. 2003. *Young Queers Getting Together: Moving Beyond Isolation and Loneliness.* (Unpublished) Doctoral Dissertation, Department of Education Policy and Management, The University of Melbourne. Online at: http://eprints.unimelb.edu. au/archive/00000428.

Hillier, Lynne, Alina Turner, and Anne Mitchell. 2005. *Writing Themselves In Again: 6 Years On, The 2nd National Report on the Sexuality, Health and Well-Being of Same-Sex Attracted Young People in Australia,* Melbourne: Australian Research Centre in Sex, Health and Society, La Trobe University.

Kosciw, Joseph G., and M. Cullen. 2001. *The School-Related Experiences of Our Nation's Lesbian, Gay, Bisexual and Transgender Youth.* New York: Gay, Lesbian and Straight Education Network.

Martino, Wayne, and Maria Pallotta-Chiarolli. 2003. *So What's a Boy: Addressing Issues of Masculinity and Schooling.* Buckingham: Open University Press.

Quinlivan, Kathleen. 2002. "Whose Problem Is This? Queerying the Framing of Lesbian and Gay Secondary School Students within 'At-Risk' Discourses." Pp. 17–31 in *From Here to Diversity: The Social Impact of Lesbian and Gay Issues in Education in Australia and New Zealand.* Edited by Robinson, Kerry. H., Jude Irwin, and Tania Ferfolja. Binghamton, NY: Haworth Press.

Thurlow, Crispin. 2001. "Naming the 'Outsider Within': Homophobic Pejoratives and the Verbal Abuse of Lesbian, Gay and Bisexual High-School Pupils." *Journal of Adolescence*, 24: 25–38.

Web Sites

Minus18. 2003. Accessed May 23, 2005. http://www.minus18.org.

The Queer Youth Alliance. 2003. Accessed May 23, 2005. http://www.queeryouth.org.uk. Both of the above Web sites are created by, and for, queer youth. The first is based in Melbourne, Australia, and the second in the United Kingdom. Both have news, advice, projects, message boards, and support group listings.

Young Gay America 2003. Accessed May 23, 2005. http://www.younggayamerica.com. This site documents young queers' voices, predominantly focusing on agency among them.

Acquired Immune Deficiency Syndrome (AIDS)

Francisco Ibáñez-Carrasco

Since the early 1980s, the Acquired Immune Deficiency Syndrome (AIDS) has been a public health disaster and a human tragedy. By the end of 2002, approximately 42 million people were living with HIV and more than 20 million people worldwide had perished (Joint United Nations Programme 2004). The Human

See also Adolescent Sexualities; Africa, LGBT Youth and Issues in; Asia, LGBT Youth and Issues in; Canada, HIV/AIDS Education in; Discrimination; Drug Use; Japan, HIV/AIDS Education in; Mental Health; Prostitution or Sex Work; Sexual Health, Lesbians and Bisexual Women; Sexual Health, Gay and Bisexual Men; Sexuality Education; South America, LGBT Youth and Issues in; Youth, At-Risk.

Immunodeficiency Virus (HIV) is the biomedical cause of a "syndrome," that is to say a set of "disorders" that extend from the individual and purely biomedical to the person as a whole (psycho–social aspects), and to the sociocultural life of the communities it affects. The early perceptions that HIV would affect only specific social groups based on a perceived moral outlook such as gay men has been proven wrong as HIV presently affects all social groups across the globe—it is a pandemic—but most poignantly, it affects the vulnerable and underserved in all societies. Even though "youth" has been constructed as a commercial consumer in capitalistic Western societies, the same attention and care is not always placed on this generational segment at a time when sexuality and health are of paramount importance.

Although there is no cure for HIV/AIDS, the profile of HIV disease has changed. At one time, HIV infection caused imminent decline in health and death. Today, new drugs can slow disease progression and help people to live longer. In first world countries, living longer with HIV often means dealing with side-effects (e.g., cardiovascular disease, liver dysfunction) and opportunistic infections that may result in impairments, disabilities, and handicaps that range from moderate and inconvenient to severe and debilitating. In contrast, in third world countries, the challenges lie on basic prevention of infection, access to universal medications, and treatment options. Whether the emphasis is on those who are *infected* and their quality of life or those who are *affected* by virtue of their risk of infection, two effective social tools continue to be *care* and *prevention*. Care refers to direct compassionate services to those at risk of HIV or to those living with the virus, and prevention can include a range from *abstinence* to the understandings of social and sexual lives of persons observed in *harm reduction* approaches.

Historically, AIDS has manifested in a number of interrelated facets: biomedical, technological (including services), epidemiological, environmental (geography and demographics), and sociocultural (that range from aesthetic response to activism and legal action). Much of the basic functioning of HIV was described early in the epidemic: It is a blood-borne pathogen, a virus that seeks a host cell. Once it enters the bloodstream directly, it attaches to CD4 cells, creating an efficient replication factory. The entry into the bloodstream is called "seroconversion," which is often followed by five to ten years in which the body more or less effectively counteracts the replication of the virus. In untested and untreated persons, following this latency period, there is the onset of opportunistic illnesses due to a compromised immune system that cannot repel many types of infections.

Today, HIV is detected through two blood tests (ELISA and Western Blot). Although by no means a generality, it is expected that the HIV tests are offered to all individuals with pre- and post-counseling and with legal protection of their confidentiality (and sometimes their anonymity). In infected individuals, the "CD4 cell count" measures the number of CD4 in the blood and the "viral load" measures the amount of HIV viral material in the blood. Current guidelines recommend that people start treatment when their CD4 count is under 350. In 1996, highly active antiretroviral therapies (HAART) revolutionized the lives of people living with HIV by suppressing effectively HIV replication within the CD4 cells. Under optimal sociocultural conditions, HAART increases life expectancy.

HIV can only be transmitted and acquired through a) unprotected sexual intercourse among individuals of any gender and **sexual orientation**, b) the use and sharing of contaminated drug paraphernalia such as disposable syringes and snorting straws, c) perinatal transmission from an HIV positive mother to her child at the time of birth, and d) transfusion of HIV infected blood (now uncommon in most regions of the world). **Workplace** risks of health care workers in direct contact with HIV infected blood or even sex trade work are subcategories of infection. Although educators, health care providers, and agencies often rank "risk of infection" by levels, there is latitude in their interpretation by professionals and individuals at large.

In epidemiological terms, AIDS progresses along two vectors: "vulnerable populations" and environments/regions. AIDS occurs in populations rendered vulnerable to HIV by sexual exposure, workplace hazards, and **drug use**. In addition, epidemiologists look at a set of variables called "determinants of health" that may range from day-to-day challenges such as housing and nutrition to psycho–social that includes depression, social isolation and stigmatization for reasons of gender (e.g. male to female **transgender** people, Aboriginal women), sexual orientation (e.g. gay men, **bisexual** women), and religious belief.

Technology has shaped the ways in which HIV disease is contained within human organizations and deployed across the world through health and informal services. Male and female condoms are a prevention technology targeted at men that has remained rudimentary throughout the AIDS epidemic. In contrast, the testing and treatment of HIV disease technology have evolved into a lucrative international industry. In addition to the ELISA and Western Blot tests, which are administered in a health care setting, there is investigation on the adoption of rapid test kits to be used in the privacy of one's home. However, the impact of this self-diagnosis technology is not known. Once diagnosed, those individuals who have access to antiretroviral treatments (HAART) need favorable social conditions to follow costly and rigid medication regimens. The long-term effects of HAART are not fully understood yet and they may be biomedical (e.g., abnormal redistribution of fat in the body, toxicity of the liver) to psycho–social (e.g., clinical depression). The full biomedical impact of HIV strains' resistance, mutations, and HIV reinoculation is still under investigation.

Silence = Death. *GAY*, April 9, 1973

In 20 years, there has been an accelerated medicalization of the epidemic and a professionalization of services that once sprouted as temporary measures. In many regions of the world, the prevalence of an individualistic attitude toward well-being and neoliberal economic models regarding health care has fostered the development of an AIDS service industry of legal advocates, treatment activists, rehabilitation professionals and alternative medicine practitioners that provide services ranging from legal assistance in legal cases involving HIV transmission to Reiki or acupuncture.

AIDS has progressed through populations and regions, often with great negative impact in vulnerable social groups. The decades of the 1980s and 1990s were underlined by sensationalistic media coverage and fruitless debate about the origins of HIV. It was first detected as an epidemic among gay men in North America, followed by bisexual and heterosexual men and women in marginalized populations, and injection drug users. Today, all individuals are at risk of contracting HIV, but we know that individuals in social networks weakened by poverty, **homophobia**, stigma, and other damaging cultural norms are particularly vulnerable to contracting HIV. In those networks, HIV often precedes or follows other health conditions such as Hepatitis C and sexually transmitted infections (STIs).

Geographically, HIV has traveled steadily through all continents, and both **urban** and **rural** areas. Regions affected by social maladies such as poverty and malnutrition, lack of health and social services (and even political and civil unrest) are often vulnerable to HIV and other health risks. HIV has even poignantly brought into relief underserved and underdeveloped regions and populations even within first world countries such as aboriginal peoples in rural **Canada**, and injection drug users in most Western societies. Hence the current educational efforts concentrate on harm reduction and strengthening of social networks and environments.

Educational efforts related to HIV and AIDS typically range from providing biomedical information on the basic modes of transmission to exploring the ethical issues that underpin them; for example, what motivates and sustains drug use among young **gay youth** that puts them at risk of contracting HIV? Most **HIV education** strategies can be said to be deep-rooted in either abstinence (from illicit substances and sexual intercourse) which can be interventionist and paternalistic or "harm reduction," which intends to leave the agency and rights of individuals intact. Also, HIV/AIDS education is often confused with "primary prevention" of infections. Gradually, educators have introduced the notion of "secondary prevention" (from opportunistic illness due to HIV) and "positive prevention" based on the premise that for each infection to occur, a positive individual must be present. The "positive prevention" approach includes HIV positive persons in educational processes without victimizing or overburdening them with unrealistic and individualistic expectations of acting as educators for the community at large.

Despite much biomedical certainty around HIV—its modes of transmission, prevention, care and treatment—our understandings of HIV continuously shift between what is individual and what is collective in relation to HIV. Nowhere is this constant shift and ambivalence manifested more strongly than in the cultural responses to AIDS. Thus, it has been called "an epidemic of signification" (Treichler 1999). AIDS, like other health "issues" is socially and culturally constructed through the deployment of our practices and ideas (beliefs, motivations, fears). HIV/AIDS has different meanings for individuals or social groups. For example, it may be the case that people with orthodox religious beliefs feel that drug use or consenting sex among adults of the same gender are moral aberrations with poor sexual health and HIV infection as the consequence. Researchers, health providers, and educators see a rise in HIV incidence and other sexually transmitted infections (STIs) as the possible consequence of individual or collective neglect.

The social–cultural response of HIV/AIDS includes areas as diverse as ethics, social justice and activism, sexual liberation, philanthropy, and multisectoral approach to restorative health care. We all face many *ethical issues* in relation to HIV that include disclosure of one's (negative or positive) HIV status to others (especially potential sexual or IDU partners) and requests for assisted **suicide** by those affected by HIV/AIDS whose health and autonomy is in severe decline. Living with HIV/AIDS disrupts moral absolutes regarding harm and care. There has been much social **activism** and leadership for *social justice* to access treatment and care that are antiracist, affordable, and low-threshold (gives access to services to persons who are not "clean and sober"). Living with HIV has compelled much direct social action regarding illness, disability, and health. At all levels of health service, medicine, and research, AIDS activism has contributed to changing the traditional relations between doctors and "patients" who used to be expected to voluntarily adhere to and comply with prevention and treatments. Thus, some HIV-positive mothers may decide to become pregnant, people living with HIV decide to go on medication holidays to minimize harm to the body, and HIVpositive individuals negotiate unprotected sex in "closed relationships."

The ethical and cultural response to HIV/AIDS includes *activism toward a liberated sexuality* from homophobia, erotophobia, and the stigmatization of individuals. HIV has been a factor in the erosion of our certainty of a pure **heteronormative** sexuality. In HIV/AIDS education, we accept "gray areas" in the sexuality of individuals as "men who have sex with men" (MSM). Thus, radical thinking about sexuality is integrated into collaborative interventions such as negotiating safe(r) sex, and into socialization approaches such as harm reduction and "Positive Prevention" that involves HIV-positive peers. In many countries, legal changes regarding disclosure and infection are being implemented that will affect HIV/AIDS education and prevention and the very sexual practices of individuals (e.g., disclosure of one's HIV status may be enforced). It is expected that sexual activism in the context of HIV will blaze new trails in this area.

Bibliography

Treichler, Paula. 1999. "AIDS, Homophobia, and Biomedical Discourse: An Epidemic of Signification" Pp. 11–41 in *How to Have Theory in an Epidemic*. Edited by in Paula A. Treichler. Durham and London: Duke University Press.

Web Sites

The Centre for Infectious Disease Prevention and Control, Division of HIV/AIDS.
Health Canada: AIDS. September 2004. Accessed November 16, 2004. http://www.hc-sc.gc.ca/english/diseases/aids.html. Official Canadian source of HIV/AIDS related medical and scientific information.
Joint United Nations Programme on HIV/AIDS (UNAIDS). November 2004. Accessed November 16, 2004. http://www.unaids.org. Official source of HIV-related global issues.
National Center for HIV, STD, and TB Prevention: Divisions of HIV/AIDS Prevention. November 2004. Centers for Disease Control. Accessed November 16, 2004. http://www.cdc.gov/hiv/dhap.htm. Official American source of HIV/AIDS related information.

Alcoholism

Connie R. Matthews

Alcohol use and abuse is a serious concern among **lesbian, gay, bisexual,** and **transgender** (LGBT) youth, as it is among young people in the general population. Although information about alcohol use in this population is limited, **research** suggests that a large percentage of LGB adolescents use alcohol and that many of them

See also African American Youth; Counseling; Drug Use; Identity Development; Latinos and Latinas; Mental Health; Mentoring; School Safety and Safe School Zones; Substance Abuse and Use; Youth, At-Risk.

are experiencing problems as a result. Where comparisons with heterosexual youth and/or general national samples have been made, percentages of LGB youth who use alcohol are greater than percentages of comparison groups. Gender differences have also been reported, suggesting that young lesbians, as is the case with adult lesbians, may be at particular risk for problems related to alcohol. There is less information available about use of alcohol among ethnic minority LGB youth and less still about use among transgender individuals. However some evidence suggests that use among these populations is also high and that they face unique concerns related to their further marginalized status.

Rates of alcohol use among adult gay males have gone down and do not differ significantly from those of heterosexual males; however, the rate of use among lesbians is higher than among heterosexual women (Bux 1996). Among adolescents, the rate of use is higher for both gay males and females (Rosario, Hunter, and Gwadz 1997), although the difference is greater between lesbian/bisexual and heterosexual female adolescents than between gay/bisexual male and heterosexual male adolescents. Additionally, lesbian/bisexual females' use of alcohol is greater than gay/bisexual males', whereas the reverse is true among heterosexual males and females (Orenstein 2001; Rosario, Hunter, and Gwadz 1997).

Rosario, Hunter, and Gwadz (1997) examined the patterns and correlates of substance use of 154 youth recruited from gay organizations in New York City. Alcohol use was prevalent among both males (78 percent lifetime use) and females (88 percent lifetime use), making it the most popular drug among both genders. No significant differences were found among ethnic groups, nor were there differences between those who self-identified as gay or lesbian versus those who identified as bisexual. Orenstein (2001) found similar results in a study of high school students in Massachusetts. Rather than ask students to identify as gay or lesbian, he asked questions which would be indicators (e.g., "During the past 12 months, how much did you worry about the following problems? . . . being gay or lesbian"), then examined differences between those students reporting no indicators and those reporting multiple indicators. Forty-seven percent of the youth who most consistently identified as gay or lesbian (multiple indicators of gay/lesbian involvement) reported using alcohol in the month prior to the study, compared to 31 percent of the heterosexual youth, although there were no differences in reported lifetime use. In addition, gay and lesbian youth were more likely to report drinking to get drunk (30 percent of gay and lesbian youth; 20 percent of heterosexual youth). These results are similar to the Rosario study with respect to gender. Among those most consistently identifying as gay or lesbian, 53 percent of the females reported drinking in the last month compared to 37 percent of the males; no differences were found between male and female heterosexual youth.

The above studies either did not address **ethnicity** or consisted primarily of white adolescents. In samples in which the majority of the respondents were black or Hispanic, Rotheram-Borus and colleagues (Rotheram-Borus, et al. 1994; Rotheram-Borus et al. 1995) found high rates of alcohol use among gay and bisexual male youth. In one study, 76 percent reported lifetime use, with 22 percent indicating alcohol use weekly or more often. In the other study, two-thirds reported using alcohol in the past month, with one-quarter indicating use weekly or more often. In both instances, rates of use were higher than those reported in large national studies of adolescents. Although information on alcohol use among transgender adolescents is scarce, studies of use among transgender adults indicates the seriousness of this problem (Finnegan and McNally 2002). Given the additional strains of **adolescence**, it seems likely that these patterns would apply to youth as well.

Why are many gay, lesbian, and bisexual adolescents using alcohol? In addition to the developmental issues faced by all adolescents, LGB teens face a number of concerns, making adolescence even more challenging (Johnson and Johnson 2000). These include myths about homosexuality, social isolation, and lack of support. Social myths about the "problems" with homosexuality are rampant, often predicting a life of promiscuity, loneliness, misery, and lack of salvation. Cutting across all of these myths is the social presentation of heterosexuality as normal and anything else as abnormal (Rivers and D'Augelli 2001). This is exacerbated by the social isolation created by a minority status that is not immediately evident. Due to "cultural invisibility," it is difficult for LGB teens to find role models to counteract these myths and **stereotypes** and often difficult to find each other (Johnson and Johnson 2000). Furthermore, family and religious institutions that could offer support and teach coping skills to LGB young people often create additional stress within them. In addition, sexual minority youth who are more visible are often subject to **harassment** and violence directly related to their **sexual orientation,** and those who are less visible live in fear of such acts (Johnson and Johnson 2000; Rivers and D'Augelli 2001).

It is not surprising that some LGBT teens turn to alcohol for self-medication as a means of coping with these stresses (Olson 2000). This is exacerbated by the presence of the gay bar, which has historically been one of the few places where sexual minority adults could find each other, socialize, and be themselves. Although, there are now many more varied opportunities, the gay bar is still one of the most visible and accessible entrances into the community (Gay and Lesbian Medical Association 2001). Without other venues, many teens questioning their sexual orientation often turn to the bars.

Reducing the risk of alcoholism among LGB youth requires addressing the stressors that they face and improving sources of support. Providing safe space within schools, such as **gay–straight alliances,** as well as in the community, for them to develop healthy nonheterosexual identities and to celebrate their lives with others like themselves is one important strategy. However, making the larger social contexts that they inhabit, for instance schools, neighborhoods, and workplaces, safe and accepting is equally important. And mentors, who can support them in the process and model healthy and empowering rather than self-destructive behaviors, require that these schools, neighborhoods, and workplaces must be safe for LGBT adults. Equally important are heterosexual allies.

Bibliography

Bux, Donald A., Jr. 1996. "The Epidemiology of Problem Drinking in Gay Men and Lesbians: A Critical Review." *Clinical Psychology Review* 16: 277–298.

Finnegan, Dana G., and Emily B. McNally. 2002. *Counseling Lesbian, Gay, Bisexual, and Transgender Substance Abusers: Dual Identities*. New York: Plenum.

Gay and Lesbian Medical Association and LGBT Health Experts. 2001. *Healthy People 2010: Companion Document for Lesbian, Gay, Bisexual, and Transgender (LGBT) Health*. San Francisco, CA: Author.

Johnson, Cheri C., and Kirk A. Johnson. 2000. "High-Risk Behavior among Gay Adolescents: Implications for Treatment and Support." *Adolescence* 35: 619–637.

Olson, Eva D. 2000. "Gay Teens and Substance Use Disorders: Assessment and Treatment."
Pp. 69–80 in *Addiction in the Gay and Lesbian Community*. Edited by Jeffrey R. Gus
and Jack Drescher. New York: Haworth Press.

Orenstein, Alan. 2001. "Substance Use among Gay and Lesbian Adolescents." *Journal of
Homosexuality* 41, no. 2: 1–15.

Rivers, Ian, and Anthony R. D'Augelli. 2001. "The Victimization of Gay, Lesbian, and
Bisexual Youths." Pp. 199–223 in *Lesbian, Gay, and Bisexual Identities and Youth*.
Edited by Anthony R. D'Augelli and Charlotte J. Patterson. New York: Oxford
University Press.

Rosario, Margaret, Joyce Hunter, and Marya Gwadz. 1997. "Exploration of Substance
Use among Lesbian, Gay, and Bisexual Youth: Prevalence and Correlates." *Journal of
Adolescent Research* 12: 454–476.

Rotheram-Borus, Mary Jane, Margaret Rosario, Heino F. L. Meyer-Bahlburg, Cheryl
Koopman, Steven C. Dopkins, and Mark Davies. 1994. "Sexual and Substance
Use Acts of Gay and Bisexual Male Adolescents in New York City." *Journal of Sex
Research* 31: 47–57.

Rotheram-Borus, Mary Jane, Margaret Rosario, Ronan Van Rossem, Helen Reid, and Roy
Gillis. 1995. "Prevalence, Course, and Predictors of Multiple Problem Behaviors among
Gay and Bisexual Male Adolescents." *Developmental Psychology* 31: 75–85.

Web Sites

Gay and Lesbian Medical Association (GLMA). 2004. Accessed December 5, 2004.
http://www.glma.org. GLMA works to address a variety of health issues for GLBT
people, including substance alcoholism. They provide education and information,
advocacy, and referrals to GLBT affirmative health care providers.

National Association of Lesbian and Gay Addiction Counselors (NALGAP). 2004. Accessed
December 4, 2004. http://www.nalgap.org. NALGAP works to promote affirmative,
nonheterosexist, nonhomophobic addiction prevention and treatment services for
LGBT people. This organization also provides information, training, advocacy, networking, and support for individuals in recovery and addiction professionals; the Web
site provides information about treatment programs targeting the LGBT population.

Allies

Allison J. Kelaher Young and *Toby Daspit*

Allies are people who work toward ending the oppression of any minority group, in
this case sexual minorities. Allies for **gay, lesbian, gay, bisexual, transgender**, and
questioning (LGBTQ) youth can include heterosexual and sexual minority peers,
teachers, counselors and other school staff, as well as community members. Most
research has focused on heterosexual allies and their important role as liaisons with
the dominant culture. Sexual minority allies develop out of a sense of personal connection with a LGBTQ person or group, or they may be led to ally status out of a
sense of social justice. As with LGBTQ people, allies go through a process of developing an ally identity. Allies support sexual diversity by challenging heteronormative statements, thoughts, feelings, and behaviors through intrapersonal integration

See also Agency; Communication; Mentoring; School Safety and Safe School Zones.

(i.e., self-identification and education) and interpersonal integration (i.e., networking with and participating in LGBTQ groups and events).

LGBTQ ally models have generally been adapted from more general models of ally development. Jackson and Hardiman's Social **Identity Development** Model (Broido 2000), for example, is derived from the development of white people as antiracists. It specifically describes the changes in attitudes and behaviors as people become allies. This five-stage model describes the process of learning and unlearning oppression:

1. Naïve—notices differences , but does not evaluate them.
2. Acceptance—accepts the dominant cultural norm (**heteronormativity**).
3. Resistance—recognizes oppression and oppressive cultural structures, such as language, **discrimination**.
4. Redefinition—reassesses one's identity.
5. Internalization—stabilizes identity; integrates both dominant and anti-heterosexist identities.

In each stage, allies must navigate their thoughts and feelings. For example, as an ally begins to recognize oppression, he or she may feel overwhelmed and incapacitated (passive) or angered and enraged (active). This recognition, accompanied by the motivating emotions, eventually leads the person to redefine him or herself as an ally.

Another model is based on Prochaska, Norcross, and DiClemente's (1994) transtheoretical model of change. This model, developed to raise awareness of LGB issues for **counseling** graduate students, describes the statements, thoughts, feelings, and behaviors of individuals at each of four stages (Tyler et al. 1997):

1. Precontemplation—unaware of the need for change
2. Contemplation—reevaluation of beliefs and values
3. Action—practice with new behaviors, attitudes, beliefs, and strategies
4. Maintenance—commitment to the changes made in the first three stages

This model is similar to the Social Identity Development Model in that both describe a process of moving from a place of unawareness of the experiences of LGBTQ people toward recognizing the situations that need to change in order to effectively support LGBTQ people. The transtheoretical model is more parsimonious and demonstrates the need for reevaluating old behaviors and beliefs while practicing new strategies for working with LGBTQ issues. Strategies are an important emphasis since they focus on specific actions that can be taken rather than a more general process.

Allies for **queer** youth employ several strategies. The first set of strategies focuses on intrapersonal integration, such as self-identification and education. The second set of strategies focuses on interpersonal integration, starting with networking and participating with LGBTQ groups and events. These sets of strategies require increasing visibility in demonstrating one's ally status.

Intrapersonal integration strategies involve the ally examining one's assumptions as well as learning more about the experiences of sexual minority individuals.

Self-identification and education are fundamental. The former involves adopting the label of ally and subsequently being visible about the ally status. This may involve displaying LGTBQ positive artifacts such as posters, pins, or magazines. Some college and high school campuses have signs for faculty and staff that indicate "safe space/safe zone" for LGTBQ students.

Coupled with these artifacts, the use of inclusive language enhances an ally's visibility. Making references with words like "partner" or "significant other" rather than "boyfriend/girlfriend" indicate that an ally questions dominant heteronormative assumptions. Using current identifiers, such as "gay," "lesbian," "bisexual," "transgender," and "**sexual orientation**" demonstrates an ally's understanding of how sexual minority people identify themselves and that sexual minority status is not a "preference" or a "lifestyle."

Education involves an ally's active participation in LGBTQ cultural events rather than a reliance on learning from LGBTQ individuals. For example, attending or participating in events around a Gay Pride celebration, **Day of Silence, National Coming Out Day** or a queer film festival would allow an ally to gain firsthand knowledge of the experiences of sexual minority people. Reading **literature** by and about sexual minority people or attending comedy shows or concerts featuring LGBTQ performers can shed further light on their experiences.

A second set of strategies relate to interpersonal integration. These include challenging heteronormative comments and actions, participating in LGBTQ groups and events, and finally, including sexual minority cultures in presentations and curricula. These activities allow an ally to question the assumptions of others. Allies can correct pejorative languages use and misinformation. Phrases like "This assignment is just so gay" or "That test was so fruit" require immediate correction. Intervention strategies range from reminding the student that such language is unacceptable to having an in-depth discussion about how language usage affects others. One approach might be to ask, "Do you mean to say that this assignment is stupid or that it is homosexual?" Often, asking students to publicly clarify their language usage sets a tone for the classroom culture. Other students will understand that such phrases are inappropriate and will adapt accordingly.

A number of organizations and groups, like Parents, Families, and Friends of Lesbians and Gays (PFLAG), the **Gay, Lesbian, and Straight Education Network** (GLSEN), **gay–straight alliances** (GSA), and **college campus resources centers** are designed for or are welcoming to allies. Here they can learn about LGBTQ issues as well as provide opportunities for networking with other allies. In addition, allies can have an impact in the role of advisor to LGBTQ youth groups. In all, these groups support allies in their work toward equity for sexual minority people at a social–organizational level. Participation in such groups can also support the internalization or maintenance of an ally identity.

The implications of being an ally are both personal and sociopolitical; however, Broido (2000) reports little, if any, research on the consequences of being an ally. As with any issue imbued with a guilt-by-association mechanism, allies may expect to experience consequences similar to those experienced by open sexual minority individuals. At an interpersonal level, allies might be more likely to experience social exclusion, scorn, or verbal or physical **harassment** by peers, family, students, and school **administrators**. For example, student allies in a GSA might experience name-calling and **bullying** in similar ways as LGBTQ students. At a social organizational level, an ally might be labeled as radical or liberal. In some instances, this might jeopardize an ally's employment status or professional connections. An ally who is a teacher might be excluded from faculty gatherings, thus restricting professional and personal connections.

Allies can give voice to queer issues where these issues might not otherwise be heard. Because of their "insider" status, allies play a pivotal role in changing the social norms for many people who might not be able to consider the same ideas from a LGBTQ person. Thus, an ally teacher who is safely considered heterosexual (i.e., married) might be taken more seriously on such issues than a LGBT teacher. Ultimately, the positive consequences to being an ally are intrinsically altruistic in that allies are agents of social change furthering the cause of social justice.

Bibliography

Bott, C. 2000. "Fighting the Silence: How to Support Your Gay and Straight Students." *Voice of Youth Advocates* 23, no. 1: 22, 24, 26.

Broido, Ellen M. 2000. "Ways of Being an Ally to Lesbian, Gay, and Bisexual Students." Pp.345–369 in *Toward Acceptance: Sexual Orientation Issues on Campus*. Edited by Vernon A. Wall and Nancy J. Evans. Lanham, MD: University Press of America.

DeGeneres, Betty. 2001. *Just a Mom*. Los Angeles: Alyson.

DiStefano, Teresa M., James M. Croteau, Mary Z. Anderson, Sheila Kampa-Kokesch, and Melissa A. Bullard. 2000. "Experiences of Being Heterosexual Allies to Lesbian, Gay, and Bisexual People: A Qualitative Exploration." *Journal of College Counseling* 50, no. 2: 131–141.

Marcus, Eric, and Jane O'Connor. 2000. *What If Someone I Know Is Gay?: Answers to Questions about Gay and Lesbian People*. New York: Price Stern Sloan.

Powers, Bob, and Allan Ellis. 1996. *A Family and Friends Guide to Sexual Orientation: Bridge the Divide Between Gay and Straight*. New York: Routledge. Prochaska, J., J. Norcross, and C. DiClemente. 1994. *Changing for Good*. New York: Avon.

Tyler, J. Michael, Leah Jackman-Wheitner, Scott Strader, and Rich Lenox. 1997. "A Change-Model Approach to Raising Awareness of Gay, Lesbian, and Bisexual Issues among Graduate Students in Counseling." *Journal of Sex Education and Therapy* 22, no. 2: 37–43.

Woog, Dan.1999. *Friends and Family: True Stories of Gay America's Straight Allies*. Los Angeles: Alyson.

———. 2000. "Friends, Families, and the Importance of Straight Allies." *Voice of Youth Advocates* 23, no. 1: 23, 25–26.

Web Sites

American Friends Service Committee. November 2004. Accessed December 5, 2004. http://www.afsc.org/lgbt/Default.htm. This Quaker organization has historically supported GLBTQ people and provides up–to-date information for allies interested in learning about contemporary policy issues regarding the rights of GLBTQ individuals.

Gay Lesbian Straight Education Network. November 2004. Accessed December 5, 2004. http://www.glsen.org. An effective resource for allies in education, particularly straight ally teachers who are asked to sponsor or advise a GSA.

Human Rights Campaign Foundation. 2003. Accessed May 26, 2005. http://www.hrc.org. HRC Web site is a guide to resources for a variety of allies, from parents, children, educators, and counselors with links to such topics as "how to come out as a straight ally."

National Consortium of Directors of LBBT Resources in Higher Education. January 2003. Accessed December 5, 2004. http://www.lgbtcampus.org/faq/safe_zone.html. Describes the development and maintenance of college-aged heterosexual allies with an emphasis on campus-wide "safe zone" programs.

Unitarian Universalist Association. 2003. Accessed December 5, 2004. http://www.uua.org/cde/handbook/conghand-16b.html. Details how to form a welcoming congregation. This might be a useful resource for youth group leaders at churches, meetings, synagogues, mosques, and other religious affiliated groups that have a commitment to human rights.

Antidiscrimination Policy

Ian K. MacGillivray

Antidiscrimination policy prohibits **discrimination** in employment, housing, and public accommodations based on certain protected classes such as **race, ethnicity,** gender, age, disability, and religion. Increasingly, state and local governments as well as public school districts and universities are adopting antidiscrimination policies that further ban discrimination based on **sexual orientation** and **gender identity**. The courts, too, are increasingly ruling in favor of LGBT plaintiffs seeking equal treatment under the law. Advocates of including sexual orientation and gender identity in school antidiscrimination policy contend that these **educational policies** help educate teachers, students, and parents about the prevalence and severity of antigay abuse in the schools. Another effect of the policies is to help prevent discrimination in employment against LGBT teachers and **administrators** who choose to disclose their sexual orientations and gender identities.

When school districts add sexual orientation and gender identity to their antidiscrimination policies, heated debates often erupt over the presumed effects the policies will have. Such was the case in the High Plains School District, a pseudonym given to a school district described in a case study that looked at how parents, students, and employees of the school district reacted to and were affected by the inclusion of sexual orientation in the district's antidiscrimination policy (Macgillivray 2004). The district's policy reads, "The High Plains School District will not tolerate discrimination, **harassment**, or violence against anyone, including students and staff members, regardless of race, ethnicity, gender, sexual orientation, age, disability, or religion." Though this policy does not include gender identity, it puts sexual orientation on the same level as other protected classes, such as religion, and prohibits discrimination against anyone simply for being hetero-, homo- or bisexual. The policy came about largely because students perceived to be LGBT are often the victims of antigay **bullying** and harassment in school. Nationally, the 2001 **Gay, Lesbian, Straight Education Network** (GLSEN) School Climate Survey found that over 80 percent of LGBT students experience verbal, physical, or **sexual harassment** while in school. Antigay abuse was a problem in High Plains, too, and one way the district enforced the new policy was with an educational campaign letting students know that antigay harassment would not be tolerated.

Opposition arose by conservative parents in the community who felt the district was sending a "progay" message to students. One of their concerns was

See also Activism, LGBT Youth; Administration, Educational; Africa, LGBT Youth and Issues in; Asia, LGBT Youth and Issues in; College Campus Organizing; Europe, LGBT Youth and Issues in; Legal Issues, Students; School Safety and Safe School Zones; South America, LGBT Youth and Issues in; Workplace Issues.

that the policy would open the door for teaching about homosexuality in the **curriculum**. These parents felt the inclusion of sexual orientation in the district's policy, as well as the discussions about homosexuality that the policy sparked in the classrooms, would legitimize homosexuality as an acceptable lifestyle and promote homosexuality as being as good as or equal to heterosexuality. The end result, they felt, would be that the policies would send the message to students that, "It's okay to be gay."

While advocates maintained that the policy was needed to make the schools safe for students perceived to be LGBT, opponents claimed that the policy violated their right to teach their children that homosexuality is wrong. A conclusion of this study, however, was that while conservative parents have the right to teach their children that homosexuality is wrong, that right does not extend into the public school class-room. LGBT students and parents have rights, too, and the public schools must protect the rights of all students. The awareness raised by the district's policy and the class discussions it motivated helped students, teachers, and administrators to be proactive in reducing levels of antigay violence, bullying, and harassment in their schools.

After including sexual orientation and gender identity in their antidiscrimination policies, districts may follow the U.S. Department of Education Office of Civil Right's (1999) guide, *Protecting Students from Harassment and **Hate Crime***, in enforcing their new policy. A community's local chapter of the American Civil Liberties Union (ACLU) can also help the district word the policy so that everyone's rights are protected to the fullest extent possible. If the policy is worded too broadly it risks violating First Amendment rights to freedom of speech. In this case it can easily be struck down if challenged in a court of law, as was the case with one district's policy in *Saxe v. State College Area School District* (2001).

These policies assist LGBT students by raising awareness, creating support, and possibly giving students some legal foundation to form **gay–straight alliances** (GSAs). Several recent high profile cases have helped define the rights of LGBT students and their supporters. With the case of *East High Gay/Straight Alliance v. Board of Education* (2000) in Salt Lake City, Utah and, more recently, in Boyd County, Kentucky, district and state officials banned all noncurricular student clubs to prevent students from forming GSAs. In both cases, like *Colin v. Orange Unified School District* (2003), the courts ruled that this administrative strategy is a violation of the federal Equal Access Act as well as students' constitutional rights to free speech, association, and equal protection.

Congress enacted the Federal Equal Access Act in 1984, largely at the request of religious parents who wanted student clubs with religious themes to be able to meet on school property. The intent of this legislation was to give all noncurricular student groups, including religious student clubs, the right to meet on school property. Ironically, this law now benefits students who want to form GSAs. Similarly, a famous court ruling that has benefited advocates of LGBT equality is *Romer v. Evans* (1996); a U.S. Supreme Court decision that overturned a ballot measure passed by the voters of Colorado in 1992 that sought to deny legal protections based on the categories of gay, lesbian, or bisexual identity. The U.S. Supreme Court declared that people could not be denied access to due political process simply because of their sexual orientation. This landmark case represented a positive shift in the way American courts have ruled in related cases involving LGBT people seeking equal rights—most recently *Lawrence v. Texas*.

A generation earlier, in the 1970s and early 1980s, similar social and legal battles were taking place at the university level. "Gay Liberation Fronts," composed of student and community activists, sponsored gay studies courses, LGBT theater programs, and gay and lesbian conferences, such as the West Coast Lesbian Conference, in 1973, at the University of California Los Angeles. LGBT students and faculty organized, resulting in the formation of the first university-sanctioned LGBT student organizations and LGBT inclusive policies. Currently, university faculty and staff continue to petition the governing bodies of their universities for domestic partner benefits and the inclusion of sexual orientation and gender identity in their university's antidiscrimination policies. Domestic partner benefits would allow university faculty and staff with same-sex partners to receive health insurance and other employment benefits similar to those of their married coworkers. Opponents claim, however, that extending domestic partner benefits, especially to same-sex couples, would cost too much money and would weaken the institution of marriage.

Other countries, such as **Canada**, **Australia**, and the European Union, have adopted similar policy approaches and are ahead of the United States in granting equality to LGBT people. For instance, LGBT people have full marriage rights in The **Netherlands**, Belgium, and several provinces in Canada. For a country to become part of the European Union it must eliminate any laws which criminalize sex between consenting same-sex adult partners and prohibit discrimination based on sexual orientation, in accordance with Article 13 of the European Community Treaty as amended by the Treaty of Amsterdam. An example of the European Union's commitment to ending antigay bias in schools is the creation of the **GLBT Educational Equity** (GLEE) Project, which trains educators, develops curricula, and conducts research.

Bibliography

Ball, Carlos. 2002. *The Morality of Gay Rights: An Exploration in Political Philosophy.* New York: Routledge.

Harbeck, Karen. 1997. *Gay and Lesbian Educators: Personal Freedoms, Public Constraints.* Malden, MA: Amethyst Press.

Hills, Jr., Roderick. 1997. "You Say You Want a Revolution? The Case against the Transformation of Culture Through Antidiscrimination Laws." Review of the book *Antidiscrimination Law and Social Equality. Michigan Law Review* 95:1588–1635.

Koppelman, Andrew. 1996. *Antidiscrimination Law & Social Equality.* New Haven, CT: Yale University Press.

MacGillivray, Ian. 2004. *Sexual Orientation and School Policy: A Practical Guide for Teachers, Administrators and Community Activists.* Lanham, MD: Rowman and Littlefield.

Web Sites

American Civil Liberties Union (ACLU). December 2004. American Civil Liberties Union. Accessed December 3, 2004. http://www.aclu.org. The ACLU's mission is to fight civil liberties violations wherever they occur. This site contains many resources on Constitutional rights and LGBT court cases.

Lambda Legal Defense and Education Fund. December 2004. Lambda Legal Defense and Education Fund. Accessed December 3, 2004. http://www.lambdalegal.org. News on legal cases and policy involving discrimination against LGBT people.

Protecting Students from Harassment and Hate Crime. January 1999. United States
Department of Education Office of Civil Rights. Accessed December 3, 2004.
http://www.ed.gov/offices/OCR/archives/Harassment/index.html.

Art, Teaching of

Donovan R. Walling

Today's visual arts curriculum for elementary and secondary schools provides greater opportunities for the inclusion of sexual-minority information, viewpoints, and sensibilities than ever before. Several education "movements" have been influential in changing the content and pedagogy of art education in ways that more fully address the needs and interests of **lesbian, gay, bisexual**, and **transgender** (LGBT) students and teachers. Prominent among these movements are postmodernism, discipline-based art education (DBAE), and constructivist teaching.

Postmodernism has altered the "what" of the art curriculum: What art is universal? What aesthetic or whose? DBAE has moved art education beyond the nearly exclusive focus on art making, which once dominated school art, by drawing attention to art history, criticism, and aesthetics. And constructivist teaching has expanded traditional viewpoints and enlarged the art canon. Thus, art educators are more aware of lesbian, gay, bisexual, and transgender issues and influences in art. Postmodernism, discipline-based art education, and constructivist teaching have also stimulated many art educators to offer LGBT students not only expanded opportunities for self-expression through art making but also avenues to explore art and artists in ways heretofore either inaccessible or taboo. Accessibility has been aided by educators' increasing use of **Internet** resources.

As this convergence of influences has changed the content and pedagogy of the art classroom, it also has contributed to the emergence of greater acceptance in schools and society generally of faculty and staff openness about **sexual orientation**. Gay and lesbian teachers, for example, are now permitted to be more candid regarding their sexual identities, at least in some schools. This openness, many educators believe, better allows them to relate to their students and to connect the lives and works of studied artists to the artistic and identity struggles of the students.

The key attributes of postmodernism, first stated by Charles Jencks in his 1977 book, *The Language of Post-Modern Architecture*, are pluralism and complexity. These have been amplified and extended to other disciplines as the postmodern perspective has fundamentally altered definitions of universality, worth, and aesthetics, not only in visual arts but in the arts writ large. For LGBT students and educators, this is important because postmodernism is anticanonical. Therefore, teaching that proceeds from a postmodern viewpoint can more readily accommodate works, philosophies, and sensibilities that previously were outside the canon and the **curriculum**. The first step outside the canon of Western art was the embrace of cultural diversity. "Cultural" soon was enlarged beyond the initial, narrow idea of foreign, however. Consequently, art content in general has become broadly inclusive—of sexual orientation, **gender, race**, and **ethnicity**—as it has become more geographically multicultural.

See also Agency; Coming Out, Teachers; Poststructuralism.

DBAE developed in the 1980s to return art education to the core of schooling. This philosophy is now widely integrated into art curriculum guides and textbooks and is reflected in the national arts standards. DBAE focuses on four art disciplines: art history, criticism, aesthetics, and art making (also called studio art). The last of these had been emphasized mostly in isolation before the advent of DBAE. For LGBT students and educators, this new, expanded view of the essential art curriculum, particularly coupled with postmodernism, provides revitalized avenues for entry into art that is expressive of LGBT sensibilities, cultures, and concerns. **Queer** youth not only can explore avenues of self-expression but are encouraged to seek models and information related to their **sexual identity**.

Constructivist teaching offers ways for teachers and students to manage pluralism and complexity because it requires classroom approaches that encourage students to "construct" their understandings through action and reflection. Orchestrating constructivist teaching is a complex challenge. At times, teachers have difficulty relinquishing the directorial role for a facilitative one that such teaching requires. The approach has particular value for LGBT students, however, because it places them in control of their learning. A constructivist teacher may be unfamiliar, for example, with gay artists in **history**, but can readily support the inquiring student's search for information, rather than impose a narrower viewpoint or traditional canon.

Finally, for all students, but especially LGBT students (and teachers), the Internet is a trove of resource information about artists, art movements, works, exhibitions, and related topics. As connectivity extends into more individual classrooms, art educators are finding many ways to use this resource, from accessing lesson plans and encouraging independent inquiry by students to taking their classes on virtual field trips. Internet research and exploration is particularly valuable for LGBT students, who may be on their own in seeking out sexual-minority artists, for example. Web sites range from those of little known artists, working solely in virtual space, to well known figures such as gay Pop artist Andy Warhol, whose seven-story museum in his hometown of Pittsburgh, Pennsylvania, can be "toured" online.

For LGBT students the postmodern construction of art education has opened doors to self-knowledge. Teachers are beginning to recognize, for example, that teaching about gay artists, whether Michelangelo or David Hockney, without acknowledging the artists' sexual orientation, robs students of key information. This information is needed not only for students to understand fully the artists, their motivations, and their artworks, but also for students to form their self-identity as individuals and artists in their own rights.

Exploration related to sexual identity, facilitated by access to Internet sites and mediated by greater openness in the art classroom, is becoming increasingly possible for LGBT and questioning students. This is a significant development, although access is hardly universal as yet for a number of reasons. Simple lack of available computer equipment, Internet access, or time can be factors. Many educators, parents, and communities also struggle with issues of sexuality and the schools, often voicing the question: "What does sexuality have to do with art?" (The answer, most artists and art educators would aver, is "a great deal."). And Internet blocking protocols designed to keep students out of online pornography sometimes block access to valuable sites that contain words such as "gay," "lesbian," and "homosexual."

LGBT students engaged in visual arts education, more than in most school subjects, have opportunities to explore identity in terms ranging from **body image** to

Quilt and outtake panel, produced by Triangle Students. Courtesy of Triangle Program, Toronto

sexual awareness and orientation. A postmodern, noncanonical approach to teaching art offers diverse images, philosophies, and critical viewpoints. LGBT and questioning youth now have unprecedented opportunities not merely to consider artists such as Francis Bacon, Louise Nevelson, and Frida Kahlo in their historical contexts but also from the perspectives of their respective gay, lesbian, and bisexual identities. Such perspectives enrich dialogue about art images and the ideas behind them because artistic expression is most often representative of the artist in toto. Intellect, emotion, cultural heritage, sexuality, and other components intermingle to inform artistic expression.

Accessibility and the more open postmodern pedagogy also mean that classroom teachers can facilitate students' explorations of new art and artists, both historical figures new to the curriculum (such as relatively little known lesbian painter Romaine Brooks, 1874–1970) and living artists now at work. As important, teachers who are sensitive to the identity needs of their students are becoming more open in addressing—and allowing students to address—their informational needs in areas that formerly were taboo, such as nudity, sexual orientation as a theme in created images, or the frank inclusion of concerns about everything from homophobic violence to HIV/**AIDS**.

Bibliography

Cooper, Gail, and Garry Cooper. 1997. *Virtual Field Trips*. Englewood, CO: Libraries Unlimited.

Greene, Maxine. 1995. *Releasing the Imagination: Essays on Education, the Arts, and Social Change*. San Francisco: Jossey-Bass.

Horne, Peter, and Reina Lewis, eds. 1996. *Outlooks: Lesbian and Gay Sexualities and Visual Culture*. New York: Routledge.

Lampela, Laurel, and Ed Check, eds. 2003. *From Our Voices: Art Educators and Artists Speak Out About Lesbian, Gay, Bisexual, and Transgendered Issues*. Dubuque, IA: Kendall/Hunt.

Saslow, James M. 1999. *Pictures and Passions: A History of Homosexuality in the Visual Arts*. New York: Viking.

Walling, Donovan R. 2000. *Rethinking How Art Is Taught: A Critical Convergence*. Thousand Oaks, CA: Corwin.

———. 2005. *Visual Knowing: Connecting Art and Ideas Across the Curriculum*. Thousand Oaks, CA: Corwin.

Wilson, Brent. 1997. *The Quiet Evolution: Changing the Face of Arts Education*. Los Angeles: Getty Education Institute for the Arts.

Web Sites

Queer Arts Resource. December 2003. Accessed November 28, 2004. http://www.queer-arts.org. Gallery, archive, bookshop, and membership opportunity.

Queer Culture Center. November 2004. Accessed November 28, 2004. http://www. queerculturalcenter.org. San Francisco center for LGBT art and culture with extensive galleries.

World Wide Arts Resources. November 2004. Accessed November 28, 2004. http://www.wwar.com. Information and links on artists, museums, and materials.

Asia, LGBT Youth and Issues in

Yin-Kun Chang

LGBT adolescents or youth in Asia often choose to hide their sexual identities for the sake of acceptance within their family, community, and peer group. In the everyday lives of Asian LGBT youth, school fosters this invisibility, thus contributing to negative **stereotypes** about queerness. Further, Asian schools, as in all modern societies, produce and reproduce sex/gender subjectivities, where youth conform, deviate, challenge, participate, and engage with gendered and heterosexual regimes. Moreover, schooling promotes **heterosexism** and **homophobia** at both formal and hidden levels. In Asian countries where schools are controlled by a central state authority, this is especially pernicious. School textbooks in these countries, for example, must comply with nationally standardized curricular guidelines and publishers become state-certified through its censorship system. Thus texts distort and omit certain content, including **queer** or emancipatory themes. When textbooks include LGBT issues or persons in Asia, these are frequently identified primarily as a high-risk group for HIV or **AIDS**. Given the scant information in schools or the mass media about LGBT issues and the connection of homosexuality with either AIDS or crime, queer youth in Asia must first tackle the pervasive ignorance about AIDS and homosexuality to help prevent sexual transmission of the deadly disease and to reduce sexual and gender stereotypes.

On high school campuses in **China**, male youth lacking strong "masculine" characteristics are often seen as "niang-niang-chiang" or "niang-pei" (**sissy boys**). Regularly labeled as gay, they often are attacked by other youth. On Taiwanese campuses, the practice of "aluba" separates the sissy boy's legs and presses his penis against a tree or a building pillar. Symbolic violence is also used. Students as well as teachers often devalue sissy boys with negative language and spoken codes, viewing them as carriers of a moral disease. For instance, girls and masculine boys giggle at the effeminate boy's attempt to play **sports** with bitter comments like, "I never saw anyone so faggy before in my life!" This kind of stereotype also sets up standards for boys' gender performance in academic work. If the boys with "sissy" temperaments stand out in traditionally male-dominated subjects such as sport and **science**, the teacher may describe his behavior and temper positively as gentle or elegant. On the contrary, if the sissy boy's academic performance is poor, the teacher negatively grumbles at his soft temper, saying that this boy lacks a penis or has a sick dick.

This atmosphere of moral panic functions in Asian society at large as it does within the school. Recently, at a Taiwanese government hearing entitled "Who Cares about Gay Rights?," a Ministry of Education (MOE) official compared

See also Activism, LGBT Teachers; Activism, LGBT Youth; Asian American Youth; College Age Students; College Campus Organizing; Colonialism and Homosexuality; Compulsory Heterosexuality; India, LGBT Youth and Issues in; Mental Health; Parents, Responses to Homosexuality; Queer and Queer Theory; Race and Racism.

homosexuals to drug addicts and questioned whether they should be granted basic human rights. "Homosexuals should not pollute others with their relationships," the official declared, adding that education authorities "do not know how to handle this problem" (Chiang 1998, 9–10).

LGBT issues lack legitimacy in the eyes of Taiwanese educational authorities. The phrase "visible and invisible hierarchical supervision in schooling" aptly describes Chinese superintendents, administrators, and parents who keep a watchful eye, in visible and invisible ways, to insure "moral" orders and rules are maintained. Auditing students' diaries is one powerful monitoring system. For example, when school **administrators** found one gay teacher's response to a **gay youth**'s concern about his sexuality, administrators promptly informed the student's parents, who then sent their son to professional therapy. This teacher was forced to transfer to a different school due to parental anger about the teacher's supposed "gay bias." These conflicts between traditional cultural structure and the expression of homosexual **desire** illuminate the **heteronormativity** of schooling itself. Even in **Japan**, which receives and assimilates Western culture, LGBT issues and homosexuality are seen as a threat to school culture.

Government authorities in China show little hesitancy in dispersing LGBT youth in public places. Homosexuality is labeled "tu-liu" (poison tumor), which is usually a reference to problems or conflicts easily spread within society. For instance, Taipei City police have assaulted homosexual youths in various incidents at Taipei New Park, which at night becomes a predominantly gay park like Beijing's Dongdan Park and Shanghai's People's Park. In China, as in other Asian countries which have no formal **LGBT community groups** or other support organizations and where few queer youth can afford to meet in the handful of gay clubs, **harassment** by police in public places is especially rampant.

Given the political structure of China, it is perhaps not surprising that it is particularly unwelcoming to queer youth; but generally, educational representations of LGBT issues and support for queer youth throughout Asia are homophobic and voyeuristic. Opposition to inclusion of LGBT issues in textbooks and the **curriculum** along with the association of HIV/AIDS with homosexuality is widespread. **Homophobia** remains the most respectable of **prejudices**, although it is often invisible because in many Asian societies people ignore homosexuality—unless it comes close to them. Thus, LGBT youth in Asia who may be "out" with their friends seldom disclose their **sexual identity** to their families; indeed, **coming out** publicly would be a disaster for a typical youth, as it would ostracize both himself and his family within the community. Thus, many Asian queer youth, burdened with ignorance, **discrimination**, and fear, are unable to comprehend their homosexual yearnings and, therefore, close themselves off from society, tormented by self-hate. Other LGBT youth strive to keep their secret from all but a close circle of gay friends.

Teaching based on certain stereotypes—in elementary and high school **sexuality education** or moral education classes—is also the norm in Asia. However, some queer teachers use underground textbooks, edited by progressive groups, as their teaching material; these underground textbooks define homosexuality more objectively. Like the classic feminist movement slogan, "the personal is political," real life experiences such as personal stories or collective oral histories are much more effective in teaching than are official texts. For instance, sexual minorities may use **literature** to contest unequal relations of power in their schools and everyday lives. Queer romance fiction or autobiographies become useful resources. The best example is the Japanese women's comic book, which includes many details about "shōnen'ai" (boy-love) or "doseiai" (same-sex love). Although these loves have never been accepted openly in school curricula, queer romances or **comics** offer imaginative ways to integrate LGBT issues into schools and reflect multiple voices and the negotiation of sexual and gender meanings.

LGBT youth in Asian colleges often have access to a more tolerant space than their high school peers. LGBT student groups are one reason for this. These students sometimes adopt a euphemistic strategy to deal with school authorities such as calling their group a "jazz music fan club" or "queer literature study group," as opposed to the popular LGBT **college campus resources centers** in the United States. Thus, LGBT youth are more likely to experience solidarity in college since it is more difficult for college officials to censor the real goal of such groups. In addition, some feminist professors offer their support to these student groups, often acting as advisors or offering relevant courses. This kind of faculty support is the key difference between colleges and high schools. Once these clandestine LGBT groups are able to establish a kind of legitimacy, they can then develop alliances with different social movement groups, thus gradually creating a new cultural space for LGBT issues. Additionally, some groups hold LGBT film festivals, which also impact the heterosexual-centered culture. Some important Asia queer youth **films** such as the South Korean movie *Bungee Jumping of Their Own* (2001), the Chinese film *Lan Yu* (2001), and the Taiwanese film *Murmur of Youth* (1997) influence Asian audiences to rethink LGBT issues.

LGBT issues, however, emerge against different cultural backgrounds in various parts of Asia. For instance, the Philippines is a most un-Asian country, reflecting nearly five hundred years of Spanish influence and a century of dominance by the United States. Values are more Latin, especially in definitions of masculinity, and religious influence (except in the southern island of Mindanao) is Catholic. Similarly, Vietnam, which was colonized by the French before the World War II and experienced significant U.S. influence from the 1950s through the 1970s, represents different cultural formations of Asian queerness than neighboring Thailand, Cambodia, and Malaysia. Nevertheless, the most common situation for LGBT youth across Asia is formulating a positive self-identity. This is compounded by the lack of positive queer role models and by discriminatory and incorrect information on LGBT issues.

Coming out has been at once the most simple and the most fundamental activity of the new sexual **identity politics** in Western societies. However, it is quite difficult in Asia and, perhaps, problematic, given the history and cultures of the East. To be young and queer in Asia is to be constantly aware that one bears a stigma with relatively little social or institutional support. Further, unlike the United States' emphasis on individualism, the prominence of the family and community weighs heavily on many LGBT youth in Asia. Even in the United States, for Asian–American LGBT youth coming out into a queer community dominated by white Anglo culture can be both a liberating and a painful experience. The queer community provides a space where Asian LGBT youth can affirm their sexuality. However, it is, at the same time, a site of pain and humiliation where the contradictions of being queer and Asian are exposed. The slang term "rice queen," for example, refers to white men who fetishize Asian men (Cho 1998). Rice conveys the idea of sexual interaction as a form of consumption and imperialism for the past several hundred years. The task of the new identity politics is to understand why queer youth are stigmatized and how to fight that oppression within an Asian context.

Bibliography

Chu, Wei-Cheng Raymond. 1997. "Some Ethic Gays are Coming Home; or The Trouble with Interraciality." Textual Practice 11, no. 2: 219–235.

Garcia, Neil C. 1996. *Philippine Gay Culture*. Quezon City: University of the Philippines Press.

Huang Has. 1996. *Be(com)ing Gay: Sexual Dissidence and Cultural Change in Contemporary Taiwan*. Unpublished Master Thesis, Sussex University.

Jackson, Peter A., and Gerard Sullivan, eds. 1999. *Lady Boys, Tom Boys, Rent Boys: Male and Female Homosexualities in Contemporary Thailand*. Binghamton, NY: Harrington Park Press.

Kumashiro, Kevin. K. 1999. "Barbie, Big Dicks, and Faggots: Paradox, Performativity, and Anti-Oppressive Pedagogy." *Journal of Curriculum Theorizing* 15, no. 1: 27–42.

McLelland, Mark, J. 2000. *Male Homosexual in Modern Japan: Cultural Myths and Social Realities*. Richmond, Surrey: Curzon.

Parekh, Suresh. 2003. "Homosexuality in India: The Light at the End of the Tunnel." *Journal of Gay and Lesbian Psychotherapy* 7, nos. 1/2: 145–163.

Song Cho. 1998. *Rice: Explorations into Gay Asian Culture + Politics*. Toronto: Queer Press.

Chiang Su-Ming. 1998. *We Are Homosexual Teachers*. Unpublished Master Thesis, National Tai-Tung Teacher College.

Summerhawk, Barbara, Cheiron McMahill, and Darren McDonald.1998. *Queer Japan: Personal Stories of Japanese Lesbians, Gays, Bisexuals and Transexuals*. Norwich, VT: New Victoria.

Chang Yin-Kun. 2001. "Restoring the Mutilated Text: Gender Issue on Production and Censorship of Taiwan's Textbook." *Journal of Women and Gender Studies* 12: 139–165.

Web Sites

Queer Asian Youth. November 2004. Accessed December 5, 2004. http://www.acas.org/QAY. The surfing point to access to queer Asian youth, including AIDS/HIV, queer campus group, coming out resources, queer youth sites, and so on.

Queer Samurai Japan for Gay Youth. Accessed Oct 16, 2004. http://www.geocities.co.jp/Berkeley/3508/start.html. This gateway to Japanese queer mostly for gay youth material also offers some information about queer Japan today and the history of Japanese gay men.

Taiwan Tongzhi Hotline Association. Accessed December 5, 2004. http://www.hotline.org.tw/. Offers important recourses for queer youth in Taiwan and has some of the latest information about queer Taiwanese events. TTHA provides peer counseling, support networks, and a community resource center as well as trains peer counselors to use their personal life histories as reference points in counseling others and enhancing their understanding of queer history and culture.

Asian American Youth

Nina Asher

Typecast as the academically hyperachieving and economically successful "model minority" (Kumashiro 1999; Lee 1996), Asian Americans and their diverse cultures, histories, and struggles as immigrants and racial/ethnic minorities have remained largely absent even from **multicultural education**. In that sense, **lesbian, gay, bisexual, transgender/transsexual** (LGBT) Asian American youth may be considered to be "doubly marginalized." However, in effect, there are multiple forms of oppression which intersect and play out differently in different cultural

See also Asia, LGBT Youth and Issues in; Parents, Responses to Homosexuality; Passing.

spaces, rendering Asian American **queer** youth invisible at multiple levels, including within Asian American communities which may reject homosexuality as un-Asian. Ultimately, deconstructing **stereotypes** and oppressive forces of othering requires a rethinking of what any community identifies as "normal." Therefore, transforming practices of representation in the larger context and the discourse of multicultural-ism also requires a rethinking of the Asian American self/identity.

The Asian American population in the United States will increase from seven million in 1990 to twenty million in 2020 (Leong 1996), comprising a vast and dis-parate group in terms of location, national origin, language, culture, and religion. Queer Asian Americans may have their roots in East Asian, South Asian, and South-east Asian countries such as Bangladesh, Cambodia, **China, India**, Indonesia, **Japan**, Korea, Laos, Malaysia, Nepal, Pakistan, Sri Lanka, The Philippines, Thailand, and Vietnam. They represent such diverse religious backgrounds as Buddhism, Catholi-cism, Christianity, Hinduism, Islam, Judaism, Sikhism, Zoroastrianism, among others. Queer youth of Asian descent may be first (or immigrant), second, third, or fourth generation Americans. Educators need to be aware of this range of cultural, historical, and geographic differences, moving beyond stereotypes to recognize the particular identifications and context-specific struggles of each LGBT student.

Historically, Asian Americans have been concentrated on the two coasts (California, New York, and New Jersey being key states). In recent years, their communities have be-come visible in other regions of the country. However, in more established **urban** areas, organizations and resources for LGBT Asian American youth are more likely to be found. "Pan-Asian" organizations, such as Gay Asian/Pacific Islander Men of New York (GAPIMNY), provide general support and information to diverse Asian Americans Other **community LGBT support groups**, such as Asian & Pacific Islander Wellness Cen-ter, focus on issues related to **HIV education** and **AIDS**. Asian Pacific Islander Queer Women and Transgender Coalition (APIQWTC) is a San Francisco area organization

"Asian Pacific Lesbians" is the title of this picture by renowned lesbian photographer Theresa Thadani, born in San Francisco to a South Asian father and Japanese mother. Thadani's photos have appeared in a variety of books and magazines, including *The Femme Mystique, The China Girls, Fillipinas*, and *Deneuve: The Lesbian Magazine*. © Theresa Thadani

which facilitates networking and communication for Asian and Pacific Islander queer women and transgender people. It has a link to AQU²⁵A (Asian and Pacific Islander, Queer and Questioning, Under 25 and Under, All Together)—a group for and run by young queer (lesbian, gay, bi, and trans) and questioning Asians and Pacific Islanders. AQU²⁵A offers drop-in hours, workshops, individual counseling, a peer leadership program, youth scholarships, socials, and retreats throughout the year.

The greater number of organizations for gay men of Asian descent may be a reflection of gendered differences in expectations regarding compliance to community norms and limitations in terms of self-representation. For example, Asian American girls may have less leeway in deviating from community gender and sexual norms. LGBT organizations serving specific Asian groups, such as Chinese Rainbow Association (a gay Chinese organization of Los Angeles) and SALGA (South Asian Lesbian and Gay Association) in New York provide social support to community members. For instance, SALGA offers a monthly meeting for queers of South Asian descent who are 25 years or younger (Eng and Hom 1998).

Within the context of Orientalism—the Western doctrine which has construed the East as mysterious, feminine, and exotic—Asian American males are stereotyped as effeminate, slender, submissive, and, ultimately, objects of homoerotic fantasy. By contrast, Asian American lesbian and bisexuals remain largely invisible. At the same time, given the "model minority" stereotype of the hardworking, obedient, high achieving Asian American student, school personnel and peers may not typically associate either male or female Asian Americans with queer identifications, which, after all, are seen as "deviant" in the **heteronormative** contexts of school and society. Hence Asian American queer youth may be objectified and/or rendered invisible based on racial and ethnic stereotypes prevailing in the popular imagination in the United States.

Located at the intersections of **race, ethnicity**, culture, language, **social class**, and immigration, Asian American queers are particularly vulnerable to the effects of commonly occurring conservative political reactions such as backlash against affirmative action, anti-immigration, and antigay movements. Experiences range from physical violence to verbal abuse (racist and homophobic) to silencing at home, within their particular community and the larger social context. Furthermore, Asian American queers may internalize the violence and respond by overcompensating (hyperperforming in academics, **cocurricular activities**, and/or (heterosexual activity), self-denial, depression, and even **suicide** (Kumashiro 1999). In a study about the differences in the ages at which LGB ethnic minority male youth became aware of their same-sex attraction, Russell and Truong (2001) found Asian Americans first had sex with other males an average of three years later than men in other racial/ethnic groups.

LGBT Asian American youth may also encounter struggles within their families and communities. Immigrant peoples' efforts to keep intact their sense of their cultural heritage, to remain connected to their home country, and to be perceived and accepted as "good" citizens in their host country can contribute to homophobic sentiment. This, for example, may lead them to shun their LGBT children or for their children to remain in the closet. Witness the struggles around issues of culture, gender, and sexuality experienced by young South Asians from immigrant families as illustrated in the highly popular British **film**, *Bend It Like Beckham* (USA 2003).

The presence of **homophobia** and the internalization of the model minority stereotype within Asian American communities may also result in queer youth focusing on academic achievement and career goals rather than addressing their sexuality. Furthermore, immigrant parents may find themselves handicapped in terms of race, culture, language, and the security of their immigration status in seeking ways of meeting the needs of and supporting their LGBT offspring. Thus, cultural clashes and lacunae may compound the climate of **heterosexism** and homophobia for Asian American youth.

There are a number of implications in terms of education at various levels. Educators and mental health providers (such as those in school **counseling**, psychotherapy, and **social work**) who work with LGBT Asian American youth need an understanding of their diverse histories, struggles, and needs. School personnel can draw on local community organizations as well as access the **Internet**. Schools can organize in-service education sessions and teacher educators can engage critical, self-reflexive perspectives on understanding and accepting sexual difference vis-à-vis the intersections of race, class, gender, and culture. That is, multicultural education can prepare teachers to recognize that the identities and cultures—of Asian American students or those from any other racial/ethnic background—are not static and prefixed. Through case studies and self-reflexive inquiry, teachers can learn to engage each individual student's negotiation of identity in relation to her/his particular context, without boxing the student in on the basis of ethnicity and sexual orientation. Asian American communities themselves need to have information about LGBT youth—their identities, the struggles and issues they confront, and the resources available to them. Asian American organizations providing support and resources to Asian American queers can serve as a link at these various levels—with educators and other professionals who work with Asian American youth, with other LGBT organizations, and with Asian American communities.

Bibliography

Amerasia Journal. 1994. "Special Issue: Dimensions of Desire: Other Asian & Pacific American Sexualities: Gay, Lesbian, and Bisexual Identities and Orientations." 20, no. 1.

Eng, David L., and Alice Y. Hom, eds. 1998. *Q & A: Queer in Asian America*. Philadelphia: Temple University Press.

Kumashiro, Kevin K. 1999. "Supplementing Normalcy and Otherness: Queer Asian American Men Reflect on Stereotypes, Identity, and Oppression." *International Journal of Qualitative Studies in Education* 12: 491–508.

———, ed. 2001. *Troubling Intersections of Race and Sexuality: Queer Students of Color and Anti-Oppressive Education*. Lanham, MD: Rowman and Littlefield.

Lee, Stacey J. 1996. *Unraveling the "Model Minority" Stereotype: Listening to Asian American Youth*. New York: Teachers College Press.

Leong, Russell, ed. 1996. *Asian American Sexualities: Dimensions of the Gay and Lesbian Experience*. New York: Routledge.

Nayar, Deepak, and Gurinder Chadha (Producers), and Gurinder Chadha (Director). (2003). *Bend It Like Beckham* [Motion Picture]. USA: Twentieth Century Fox.

Russell, Stephen T., and Nhan L. Truong. 2001. "Adolescent Sexual Orientation, Race and Ethnicity, and School Environments: A National Study of Sexual Minority Youth of Color." Pp. 113–130 in *Troubling Intersections of Race and Sexuality: Queer Students of Color and Anti-Oppressive Education*. Edited by Kevin K. Kumashiro. Lanham, MD: Rowman and Littlefield.

Web Sites

Asian Pacific Islander Queer Women & Transgender Coalition May 11, 2004. Accessed May 26, 2005. http://www.apiqwtc.org/index.html. Active in the Bay Area since 1999,

APIQWTC offers Asian American queer women and transgender peoples resources and opportunities to network. Links to Web sites for support groups for queer women from different ethnic backgrounds, including Filipino, Mandarin-speaking, Japanese, Korean, Singaporean and Malaysian, and Vietnamese. Information regarding different support groups for queer women of Asian descent who are cancer survivors, twenty-five years or younger in age, and thirty-five years or older is also available.

Asian & Pacific Islander Wellness Center: Community HIV/AIDS Services. December 2004. Accessed December 2, 2004. http://www.apiwellness.org. Extensive information about this San Francisco-based organization's services (case work, mental health counseling, HIV testing, etc.) related to HIV and AIDS for LGBT Asian Americans. Links to several other organizations/groups for Asian American queers are on this site.

Gay Asian Pacific Alliance (GAPA). November 2004. Accessed December 2, 2004. http://www.gapa.org. A San Francisco Bay area group focused on promoting a positive, collective identity and a supportive community for gay and bisexual Asian and Pacific Islander men. Links for social/cultural events, participation in political events, and for a scholarship for LGBT Asian Americans pursuing higher education are available.

Gay Asian/Pacific Islander Men of New York (GAPIMNY). October 2004. Accessed December 2, 2004. http://www.gapimny.org/. Web site provides information about social events and also links other LGBT of color organizations and health-related organizations in the New York area. Links for legal and advocacy organizations as well as arts-based community groups for Asian Americans are also available.

Australia, LGBT Issues in

Mahoney Archer

The Australian LGBT Rights and Law Reform movements have made enormous advances in the recognition of legal rights and protection. The closet, however, continues to be pervasive, concealing LGBT Australians. Within Australia's schools, several factors impact LGBT teachers and students: conservatism of the Federal and State governments; surveillance, policing, and punishment of sexual difference; and, invisibility in school communities and curricula. LGBT issues in **Australia** are politically fraught. There have been advances made with regard to age of consent laws and property rights across Australia's states and territories. However, these and other issues are far from a satisfactory resolution for LGBT youth.

Australian state and territory politics are diverse. Age of consent laws, with the exception of Queensland (age eighteen), are virtually uniform and equal to those of heterosexuals (age sixteen). Property rights, however, vary across the nation, and the political climate lacks a general preparedness to put LGBT issues on the agenda. Tasmania once laid claim to the most draconian, antihomosexual laws in the country. After an intense, vigorously pursued challenge, which was eventually brought before the United Nations, this southernmost state is now widely regarded as a model for relationships legislation. Tasmanian law recognizes and honors the different kinds of relationships through a state register of "significant relationships."

See also Activism, LGBT Teachers; Administration, Educational; Antidiscrimination Policy; Families, LGBT; Hate Crimes; Identity Politics; Licensure; Mentoring; Passing; Professionalism; School Safety and Safe School Zones; Teachers, LGBT and History; Workplace Issues.

Western Australia, Queensland, and the Northern Territory also have reformed their legal system in recent years wherein the age of consent, property rights, and the elimination of exemptions under the Anti-Discrimination Act have improved. LGBT law reform in New South Wales, South Australia, Victoria, and the Nation's Territories has moved more slowly. South Australia, home of Australia's Parliament, continues to explore legislative reform through great political debate because an audit identified fifty-four laws that entrench legal inequality of LGBT citizens. New South Wales also is widely criticized for its lack of reform. Although the Labor government has made some effort to alter or remove discriminatory provisions, LGBT citizens maintain that the nation's oldest state should lead in reforming laws such as same-sex couples' **adoption** rights.

While state and territorial (predominantly more left-wing Labor) governments have implemented or amended legislation, as recently as 2003, the federal government indicated that it would not accept any reference to same-sex individuals, couples, or families in legislation. However, in Australia, LGBT people are protected under the broad banner of the Commonwealth Anti-Discrimination Act. Nevertheless, the conservative government of Prime Minister John Howard has outlawed gay marriage, refused to recognize LGBT people at the federal level, limited access to fertility services for same-sex and single women, and promised to reward "traditional" family units. Earlier, under the more progressive Labor governments of Robert J. Hawke and Paul Keating (1983–1996), Australian society underwent a social justice "revolution." Systemic policy was radicalized to include and acknowledge **race**, gender, sexuality, and **social class** that had been invisible earlier. Howard's coalition government has buttressed the voices of privilege across a variety of racial, gender, class, and family issues. This is evident by Howard refusing to say "Sorry" to the Indigenous Stolen Generation, creating social furor and anti-asylum seeker sentiment over the "Children Overboard" scandal (illegal immigrants), and the systematic attack of unions and elimination of unfair dismissal provisions through amended Industrial Relations legislation.

Throughout the Federal political campaign of 2004, many LGBT citizens supported Labor Party leader Mark Latham. Elected as his party's leader in 2003, Latham underscored his lack of distinction between same-sex or different sex relationships. With the reelection of John Howard, however, conservative and ultra-conservative Australian voices and influence grows, as evident in the election of Assemblies of God Church-affiliated party representatives to the Australian Senate who denounce lesbians as witches who should be burned at the stake.

It is within this political context that LGBT youth attend school and LGBT teachers consider **coming out**. Australian schools are administered by state or territorial governments and are classified as either public (free, government funded and staffed) or private (government-funded, privately levied and staffed). Many private schools are denominational, embracing specific religious beliefs; it follows that children of Catholic families, for example, attend **Catholic** schools. Since the 1970s, private school enrollments have risen (rapidly during the Howard administration) from one in five to one in three Australian school children; two-thirds of Australian first year university students attended a private school.

Public schools are extensions of the state and as such the state's social charter becomes that of the school—directly and indirectly. Schools are places where heterosexuality is not only taught, but promoted as positive and moral. School staff, students, and parents are presumed heterosexual, from the common presumption that a male and female will attend the school formal or **prom** to the silence/shame surrounding homosexuality in school yard conversations and classroom experiences. The conventional belief is that recognition of LGBT people means advocating alternate sexual behavior. Consequently, LGBT students represent an explicit challenge to heterosexual dominance and LGBT teachers are not presented as viable models. Though their existence is acknowledged, they are marginalized and punished. "The closet" is the primary means through which this is achieved.

This is not to say that mention of LGBT people or issues are absent from **curriculum** documents, which still reflect the more liberal spirit of an earlier period in Australian history. The inclusion of anything "**queer**" occurs only as it is mandated in syllabus documents. For example, in Health and **Physical Education**, LGBT sexuality is included within the parameters of sex and sexuality discussions. However, due to the current climate of conservatism, the push to recognize difference has been weakened and many schools lack consistent translation of these documents to practical applications in classrooms. Ultimately, it is the determination of individual teachers as to what they believe is appropriate material and the measure of visibility the LGBT model is afforded in the classroom. Generally, LGBT people or sexuality is not freely mentioned in classroom contexts and the conventional curriculum does not consistently reflect sexual diversity.

Punishment often accompanies marginalization. There is a climate of hatred and **discrimination** in Australian schools and in the wider social context (Dolan 1994). This is commonly experienced through physical violence, name-calling, **bullying**, exclusion, and deprivation of opportunity and in some cases, liberty. Visible LGBT teachers and students are often targets of punishment or the subject of ridicule in the classroom and schoolyard.

In an effort to address homophobic bullying, **educational policy**, resource kits, and staff professional development experiences have focused upon recognizing it, minimizing it, and building safe and supportive school environments. Specific groups also have introduced initiatives. In New South Wales, "Skool's Out" Mardi Gras Forum raises community awareness of homophobic bullying, harassment, violence, discrimination, and vilification in and around public and private schools.

Despite these efforts, violence and harassment perpetuated on LGBT students continue. This is compounded for indigenous queer youth and others of non-European ethnicity whose sexuality and race are visible. In some closed **native** communities, as well as in the wider context, queer youth have been targets of physical violence and commonly subjects of community hatred and mockery.

Through marginalization and punishment, "the closet" is given form. Surveillance and policing of sexual or gender difference by teachers and peers are active deterrents to visible homosexuality. The "safety" of the closet presents for many LGBT teachers and students the opportunity to be considered heterosexual.

For numerous LGBT teachers, the closet is regarded as one of the conditions of their employment. The fear that one will/could be perceived as a risk to children and, subsequently, be exposed/vulnerable or considered inappropriate for employment is the predominant means by which LGBT staff are "encouraged" to remain closeted, irrespective of legal or professional standards. Many LGBT teachers maintain that closeted behavior enables them to address the "anti-education" (Appleby 1997; Sanders and Burke 1994) of youth within schools. These teachers believe they can "re-educate" within the closet such as challenging homophobic comments or integrating LGBT issues while maintaining their role as "allies." Nevertheless, others maintain working within the closet simply reinforces "anti-education," since it renders LGBT teachers invisible and maintains the closet.

For many LGBT teachers, a lack of authenticity in the classroom and potentially adverse effects in their general professional practice are concerns. Educational and **professional organizations** have acknowledged these. For example, as a condition of teacher employment, a teacher agrees to be appointed to any school within their state or territory. However, LGBT teachers may contest appointments to locations (remote, **rural**) that may pose an unreasonable risk to their professional success and personal safety. And, once they are in a school, teachers are protected by antidiscrimination and antibullying legislation/policy. However, in practice, the options for an "out" teacher in a school are limited in that one needs the support of **administrators**, colleagues, and the continued tolerance of the school community for their tenure to remain viable in that setting. Recognizing such problems, queer teacher networks have been launched in various states and territories, as well as within Education Departments, and the Australian Education Union and its state/territory subsidiaries have developed LGBT school teacher support groups.

Much of the continued violence perpetuated against LGBT people in Australian society stems from the absence of LGBT models of difference. "Out" teachers provide collegial support to closeted workmates and may well be the first, positive example of a "homosexual" that many queer youth (and nonqueer) might encounter. Their impact, however, is difficult to measure beyond anecdotal accounts since little research has been completed. Nevertheless, anecdotal evidence suggests that for queer youth the presence of, or interaction with, an "out" or "obvious" LGBT teacher reduces feelings of isolation, and for some closeted teachers the presence of an "out" teacher creates a sense of community and solidarity.

Bibliography

Appleby, Yvonne. 1997. *Negotiating the Narrow Straits of Education*. Pp. 24–38 in *Straight Studies Modified: Lesbian Interventions in the Academy*: Edited by Gabriele Griffin and Sonya Andermahr. London: Cassell.

Croome, Rodney. 2004, March 25. "Human Rights versus Human Values." *Sydney Star Observer*. Accessed December 4, 2004. http://www.ssonet.com.au/display.asp?ArticleID=2817.

Dolan, Jill. 1994. "Gay and Lesbian Professors — Out on Campus." *Academe* 85 no. 5: 40–45.

Robinson, Kerry, Jude Irwin, and Tania Ferfolja, eds. 2002. *From Here to Diversity: The Social Impact of Lesbian and Gay Issues in Education in Australia and New Zealand*. New York: Harrington Press.

Sanders, Susan, and Helena Burke. 1994. "Are You a Lesbian, Miss?" Pp. 65–77 in Debbie Epstein, ed. *Challenging Lesbian and Gay Inequalities in Education*. Buckingham: Open University Press.

Skool's Out. 2003. *A Report Based on a NSW Mardi Gras Forum on Homophobic Bullying and Harassment*. Sydney: Mardi Gras Association.

Web Site

Buranda State School. http://www.burandass.qld.edu.au. Accessed November 27, 2004. Details the work of this multiage Queensland-based school with a literature-based program, which has been effective in eliminating bullying and harassment.

Australia, LGBT Youth in

Greg Curran

Lesbian, gay, bisexual and **transgender youth** have only recently become a visible group within the Australian queer community. This has been achieved, in part, through the work of youth services in major cities such as Melbourne and Sydney. Since the late 1990s there has been an increase in the number and variety of support and social groups for young queers, offered by the youth services sector. This follows the release of the first national study of queer youth, which draws attention to the discrimination, harassment, and isolation they often experience (Hillier et al. 1998).

Historically, it has been very difficult for LGBT youth in Australia to meet one another. Although this is still the case in **rural** areas, in the past five years queer youth in metropolitan areas have found and created new ways to connect and socialize with each other. They have done so through recreation, **theater**, writing/publishing, artistic, and other interest-based groups catering to young queers, along with ethnic-based LGBT groups, as well as **Internet** chat rooms and Web sites.

Australian **queer** youth reflect a diversity of cultures, views, interests, and needs. Through their active participation, collaboration with each other, and leadership, they have influenced the structure, scope, purpose, and direction of initiatives (programs, services, and activities) for queer youth across Australia. "Minus18" dance parties for LGBT youth 14–17 years in Melbourne, for example, have youth conveners and youth comprise the majority of the management committee. Growing numbers of young Australian queers are attending LGBT dance parties for under eighteen-year-olds in Melbourne, Perth, and Sydney. Here, they can be open about their sexuality, dancing, socializing, watching drag and talent shows, playing amusement games, performing and watching karaoke, "chilling out," meeting and "checking out" others.

Australia has a range of queer community shops, venues, and events in all capital cities. Although these commercial areas have existed since the mid- to late 1970s, only in recent years have young queers gained visibility at these places. Queer youth support groups organize trips to queer community spaces and events such as pride marches or Mardi Gras. They also run information stalls and provide entertainment at queer community events such as Melbourne's "Midsumma Festival."

Little **research** has been undertaken into the informal social gatherings, groups, and recreational pursuits of queer youth in Australia. At an organizational level, however, there are numerous health and well-being related programs for them, which take a variety of forms. **AIDS** Councils, which are located in capital cities, offer peer-education groups for same-sex attracted young men that focus on sexual and social health. Community health and family planning centers, local councils, and AIDS councils in larger regional or capital cities provide a range of services for young queers. The most common initiative is support/social groups, which offer combinations of social outings, education, and a space to chat and receive support. Other services include queer youth drop-in centers such as The Freedom Centre in Perth, Western Australia and Open Doors in Brisbane, Queensland, a **mentoring**

See also Activism, LGBT Youth; Adolescent Sexualities; Agency; Community LGBT Youth Groups; Educational Policies; Passing; Racial Identity; Sissy Boy; Tomboy.

program for people of all ages who are **coming out,** Working It Out in Tasmania, and a homeless center, Twenty Ten, for queer youth in Sydney, New South Wales. There are also a number of interest-based initiatives such as YGLAM, a performing arts project, which is based in Melbourne, Victoria.

Major Australian studies on queer youth have predominantly focused on those identifying as gay, lesbian, and bisexual. These studies provide the first empirical data on this population, although queer youth with **disabilities,** along with transgender and **intersex** queer youth, have been underrepresented or absent. In a national survey of 1749 same-sex attracted young people (fourteen to twenty-one years), 61 percent identified as "gay/lesbian," 19 percent "bisexual," 18 percent chose "no label," 2 percent chose "other," and 1 percent identified as "heterosexual" (Hillier et al. 2005). Bisexual identification was found to be much more common among young women than young men. They were also more likely to choose 'no label'. Differences also existed between age groups where more nineteen- to twenty-one-year-olds identified as "gay/lesbian" than did fourteen to eighteen-year-olds. Youth in the latter age group were more likely to identify as "bisexual" than those youth in the older age group.

Australian bisexual youth are often pressured to assume either a heterosexual or homosexual identity, with their peers often dismissing their **bisexuality** as experimentation (Martino and Pallotta-Chiarolli 2003; McLean 2001). This leads many to hide their bisexuality, or refer to themselves as gay, lesbian, or heterosexual. A small number of bisexual youth are unpacking, challenging, and resisting mainstream assumptions about sexual identity. They are articulating limitations in taken-for-granted ways of thinking about sexuality, and are devising strategies to affirm their sexual identities while also challenging conventional norms. Martino and Pallotta-Chiarolli (2003, 94) for example, discuss a young man who styles himself in ways he considers symbolic of bisexuality through "bright pink shoulder-length hair" and shoes of differing colors (red and blue).

Little is known about the specifics of queer youth's sexual behaviors in Australia. This is due, in part, to the taboo nature of such research. National surveys on same-sex attracted young people have not until relatively recently inquired into sexual practices in any detail vis-à-vis the broader surveys of Australian youth (Smith et al. 2003). The second national study on same-sex attracted youth (Hillier et al. 2005, 30) found that 77 percent had sex, 90 percent had "experienced deep kissing," 89 percent had engaged in "genital fondling," 81 percent had given and received oral sex, and 70 percent had "experienced penetrative sex."

Three predominant themes in Australian research on young queers at school are loneliness, isolation and alienation (Hillier et al. 2005, Martino and Pallotta-Chiarolli 2003). As in other countries, these youth often feel excluded and not valued. There are generally few, if any, openly queer people in their schools; the same can be said for queer representations in the curriculum. Given the high levels of homophobic abuse occurring in Australian schools, queer youth are wary of being open about their sexuality at school for fear of being harassed, abused, or discriminated against. In addition, they generally do not confide in teachers or school-welfare counselors.

Despite educational policies and frameworks at the federal, state and territory levels, boys who don't fit the dominant male **stereotype** continue to be targeted for abuse and **harassment** in Australian schools and in male peer cultures (Hillier et al. 2005). "Suspect" behaviors include having an interest in reading, being a "good student," showing emotion, dressing and moving in ways considered "feminine," and disliking or not being good at sports. To be recognized as "normal," a boy must talk, walk, stand, gesture, dress, and relate to others in the "normal" (hetero-sexual) way (Plummer 1999). This involves a high degree of self-censorship and self-monitoring in order to avoid being labeled gay.

By the late 1990s most state/territory education departments across Australia had adopted policies requiring public (government) schools to implement policies, programs, and processes to minimize or eliminate **bullying**, violence, **discrimination**, and disruptive behavior. In 2002, a National Safe Schools Framework (including nongovernment schools) along the same lines was implemented. There has also been an increase in antihomophobia initiatives targeting schools and community service/health organizations, along with an increased number of support groups for same-sex attracted youth, which often encompass strategies to challenge **homophobia**. In addition, the Queensland and Tasmanian Education Departments provide information and resources relating to homophobia. The Tasmanian Education Department also has a Gay, Lesbian, Bisexual, Transgender Reference Group.

The release of the second national study on same-sex attracted youth (Hillier et al. 2005, 40, 37) provides the first opportunity to assess trends or changes in re-spect to homophobic bullying, violence and abuse in Australian schools. It reports that there is "no evidence that [homophobia-related] interventions have made a dif-ference," with "little change in levels of reported abuse." Though higher numbers of same-sex attracted young people felt safe in school and more had learnt about same-sex relationships, safe sex, discrimination and homophobia in school the number of schools involved in such work remained "quite small" (Hillier et al. 2005, 83).

Recent research (Hillier et al. 2005, 75) has provided some of the first substan-tive data on young queers from culturally and linguistically diverse backgrounds. They are less likely to have spoken to their parents about their sexuality and less likely to have received support from them. This lack of disclosure may, according to Hillier et al. (2005, 75), be a means of maintaining a "positive" relationship with parents. Young people from culturally and linguistically diverse backgrounds are also less likely to have gained information about gay, lesbian and heterosexual safe sex from their parents, and are less likely to have felt safe at home. They are, however, gaining support from a range of sources outside the 'family' unit, and do not score worse on any health outcomes. Here, in line with earlier Australian re-search, (Martino and Pallotta-Chiarolli, 2003), cultural identity is understood as being "one part of the multiple layers that make them who they are" (Hillier et al. 2005, 75).

Martino and Pallotta-Chiarolli's (2003) research on Australian boys and mas-culinity, devotes significant attention to same-sex attracted boys from culturally and linguistically diverse backgrounds. They characterize these boys as "border dwellers" who reject the notion of having to choose between the varying socio-cultural groups they participate in—ethnic/racial, gay, school—along with con-ventional notions of **ethnicity** or sexuality as being fixed and unchanging. With cultures being sites of "acceptance, mediation, and active support," as well as "reg-ulation, exclusion, and omission," these boys instead negotiate the values, prac-tices, and customs of the cultures they inhabit and move between, determining what does and does not "work for them" (Martino and Pallotta-Chiarolli 2003, 112).

Another key issue for same-sex attracted boys from culturally and linguistically diverse backgrounds is that of marginality. These boys, it is argued, experience being "sexually marginal" within already marginalized and misunderstood ethnic/racial Australian communities (Martino and Pallotta-Chiarolli 2003, 113). It could be argued that they also experience being ethnically/racially marginalized within some gay communities. This marginalization is a consequence of many factors. The most significant factors identified in research are: normative cultural expectations and the privileging/subordinating of particular identities (or forms of identity), values and practices; **prejudice**s, discrimination, and assumptions based on stereotypes; and a lack of visibility of same-sex attracted people of ethnic and **native/indigenous** backgrounds within their ethnic, native/indigenous, and/or gay communities (Martino and Pallotta-Chiarolli 2003, Ridge, Hee, and Minichiello 1999). In regard to the latter factor, **queer** ethnic and indigenous social/support groups, which have increased in number over the past five years, have been particularly important because they provide a setting where ethnicity, indigeneity, and sexuality need not be hidden.

By 1997, homosexuality had been decriminalized in all Australian states and territories. Since that time, perhaps the most significant area of law reform to affect queer youth is the achievement of equal age of consent laws. All Australian states and territories have reformed their respective age of consent laws to remove discrimination on the basis of sexual preference, with the exception of Queensland, which has a higher age of consent for anal sex (eighteen years) than for other sexual activity (sixteen years). Another significant piece of reform, in recent times, is the repeal of laws forbidding the promotion and encouragement of homosexuality in schools in Western Australia and Tasmania.

Isolation, as previously stated, is a key issue confronting queer youth in Australia. Nowhere is this more apparent than in the rural areas. According to the 2001 Census, 13 percent of Australia's total population (18.8 million) lived in outer regional, remote, and very remote areas. Many queer youth living in these areas are afraid of being "out," or to seek support or advice relating to homosexuality in schools or health services (Frere, Jukes, and Crowhurst 2001). They fear that word will get out and soon everyone will know about their sexuality, potentially making life very difficult, and unsafe, in a small country town. Furthermore, education institutions and health services, which are limited in rural areas, are not seen as being open to, or supportive of, same-sex attracted young people. Consequently, many rural queer youth seek queer social networks and venues located in the capital cities.

A number of Australian research projects, along with rural-focused initiatives, have made links between the isolation, loneliness, and alienation of queer youth, and suicide/suicide ideation, especially in rural areas. Rural male youth **suicide** rates were twice that of male youth in **urban** areas (Quinn 2003). Initiatives launched to address the high youth suicide rates include the training of local service providers (schools, community health centers, libraries) to better cater to queer youth, antihomophobia programs in schools, support groups/services for queer youth in some regional centers, and queer youth-related theater and **art** projects (Frere, Jukes, and Crowhurst 2001).

The Internet plays a significant role in the health and well-being of queer youth in rural and metropolitan Australia, according to the first national study of Internet use among same-sex attracted youth (Hillier et al. 2001; Hillier et al. 2005). The most common reasons given for the use of the Internet were, in order of importance: to visit sex information Web sites; to contact other same-sex attracted youth; to e-mail friends; to download pornography; to participate in sex related chat rooms; to help deal with isolation; to access **sexual health** information; and to gain support away from the Internet.

Queer youth, however, are largely absent from cultural media in Australia. Australian **films** have only occasionally focused on, or included, young queer characters. Two films devoted to queer youth experiences are *Only the Brave* (1994) and *Head On* (1998). In both, the lead character is a young Greek–Australian queer. A small number of youth-related documentaries have also been produced over the past decade. They include *Out in the Bush* (1997), which deals with the experiences of queer youth in rural Australia, and *China Dolls* (1998), which examines issues involving identity, **desire**, racial stereotyping, and discrimination for Gay Asian Australians. Queer Film Festivals in Melbourne, Adelaide, and Sydney include a youth program. These programs have, on occasions, featured short Australian films about queer youth, some produced by young Australian queers.

Queer themed books are more prevalent in Australian schools and local libraries than films. There are, however, relatively few Australian titles with queer youth characters. Sydney's 2004 Gay and Lesbian Mardi Gras Festival had a forum specifically devoted to this issue. Recent Australian **literature** includes *Tumble Turn* (MacLeod 2003) and *Sushi Central* (Duncan 2003), both of which focus on the life of a queer male teenager.

Queer youth also receive little attention in other forms of Australian media. Gay newspapers, in major capital cities, carry occasional coverage on youth social initiatives such as Minus18, and the school-related problems experienced by queer youth, but generally, little is written about queer **youth culture**s. A small number of Australia's community radio stations provide a weekly slot—usually half to one hour—hosted by queer youth. One of these stations "JOYFM," is a full-time gay and lesbian station in Melbourne.

It is only in recent years that queer youth have gained some visibility on Australian television. Shows such as "Sweat" (1996), "Raw FM" (1997–1998), "Breakers" (1998–1999), and "Always Greener" (2001–2003) have included school-age queer youth characters on an ongoing basis. These characters have been predominantly gay male teenagers, with the exception of "Breakers" and "Raw FM," which also included bisexual and lesbian youth. Of the current popular teenage drama serials, "Home and Away" (1988–) has featured occasional young queer characters. Television shows targeting the young adult audience, such as "The Secret Life of Us" (2001–2004), and reality TV shows such as "Big Brother" (2001–) and "Australian Idol" (2003–) have included gay, lesbian and bisexual queer youth characters or participants. *Queer as Folk* and *The L Word* have also aired nationally.

Young queers on Australian-made television shows have mostly been white, middle class, and male. The representations have, however, broadened beyond the traditional **"camp"** and "butch" characters to reflect a greater degree of diversity. Story lines and topics explored in these television shows have included the familiar themes of "coming out," homophobia, the questioning of one's **sexual identity**, and **drug use**. Some television shows have also broached topics or issues rarely given attention on mainstream television. "The Secret Life of Us," a drama revolving around youth in their twenties, had story lines exploring the use of beats (public locations such as toilets and parks) for sex, a nonmonogamous gay relationship, and the fluidity of sexual attraction.

Bibliography

Curran, Greg. 2003. *Young Queers Getting Together: Moving Beyond Isolation and Loneliness.* Unpublished Doctoral Dissertation, Department of Education Policy and Management, The University of Melbourne. Accessed May 23, 2005. http://eprints. unimelb.edu.au/archive/00000428/.

Duncan, Alasdair. 2003. *Sushi Central.* Brisbane: University of Queensland Press.

Frere, Marion, Janet Jukes, and Michael Crowhurst. 2001. *Our Town: Working with Same-Sex Attracted Young People in Rural Communities. Key Learnings from the Sexual Diversity Grants Scheme.* Carlton South: Vichealth.

Hillier, Lynne, Deborah Dempsey, Lyn Harrison, Lisa Beale, Lesley Matthews, and Doreen Rosenthal. 1998. *Writing Themselves In: A National Report on the Sexuality, Health and Well-Being of Same-Sex Attracted Young People,* Melbourne: Australian Research Centre in Sex, Health and Society, La Trobe University. Accessed May 23, 2005. http:// www.latrobe.edu.au/ssay/publications.htm.

Hillier, Lynne, Chyloe Kurdas, and Philomena Horsley. 2001. *It's Just Easier: The Internet as a Safety-Net for Same Sex Attracted Young People,* Melbourne: Australian Research Centre in Sex, Health and Society, La Trobe University. Accessed May 23, 2005. http:// www.latrobe.edu.au/ssay/publications.htm.

Hillier, Lynne, Alina Turner, and Anne Mitchell. 2005. *Writing Themselves In Again: 6 Years On, The 2nd National Report on the Sexuality, Health and Well-Being of Same-Sex Attracted Young People in Australia,* Melbourne: Australian Research Centre in Sex, Health and Society, La Trobe University. Accessed May 26, 2005. http://www.latrobe.edu.au/ssay/publications.htm.

MacLeod, Doug. 2003. *Tumble Turn.* Camberwell, Victoria: Puffin.

Martino, Wayne, and Maria Pallotta-Chiarolli. 2003. *So What's a Boy: Addressing Issues of Masculinity and Schooling.* Buckingham: Open University Press.

McLean, Kirsten. 2001. "Living Life in the Double Closet: Bisexual Youth Speak Out." *Hecate* 27, no. 1: 109–119.

Plummer, David. 1999. *One of the Boys: Masculinity, Homophobia and Modern Manhood.* Binghamton, NY: Haworth Press.

Quinn, Karolynne. 2003. "Establishing an Association between Rural Youth Suicide and Same-Sex Attraction." *The International Electronic Journal of Rural and Remote Health Research, Education, Practice and Policy.* Accessed May 23, 2005. http://e-jrh.deakin.edu.au/articles/showarticlenew.asp?ArticleID=222.

Ridge, Damien, Amos Hee, and Victor Minichiello. 1999. "Asian Men on the Scene: Challenges to 'Gay Communities.'" Pp. 43–68 in *Multicultural Queer Australian Narratives.* Edited by Peter A. Jackson and Gerard Sullivan. New York: Haworth Press.

Smith, Anthony, Paul Agius, Sue Dyson, Anne Mitchell, and Marian Pitts. 2003. *Secondary Students & Sexual Health: Results of the 3rd National Secondary Students, HIV/AIDS and Sexual Health.* Melbourne: Australian Research Centre in Sex, Health and Society, La Trobe University.

Web Site

Minus18. October 2004. Accessed May 23, 2005. http://www.minus18.org. This Melbourne-based site is created by, and for queer youth. It has news, advice, a message board, events and support group listings.

Australia, Research on Sexual Identities

Jane Mitchell and *lisahunter*

There is a small yet growing body of educational **research** concerned with young people's sexual identities in the context of schooling in **Australia**. Much of this recent research, connected to research conducted elsewhere, particularly from the **United Kingdom** and North America, challenges stereotypical and deficit conceptions of (homo)sexuality and young people and charts its implications for **curriculum** and pedagogy. This recent research often is focused on the intersection between masculinity, sexuality, and schooling, with antecedents in a strong line of Australian feminist theorizing broadly concerned with gender and education. As well it reflects a more recent intersection of lesbian/gay/**queer theory** and **feminist theory** and its application to schooling.

There have been several broad studies documenting sexual diversity among young people in Australia. Of a national survey of 3500 senior students, 8 to 9 percent reported feelings that were not "exclusively heterosexual" (Lindsay, Smith, and Rosenthal 1997). Another national study of 750 same-sex attracted young (SSAY) people documented considerable diversity in terms of attractions, behaviors, and identities (Hillier, et al. 1998). The study also documents how this sexual diversity intersects gender, geographic locations, family, and school experience.

Accompanying these broad studies of young people's sexualities has been research specifically focused on schooling and its relationship to the formation and expression of sexual and gendered subjectivities and identities. Sexual diversity notwithstanding, this research documents both a pervasive heteronormative and homophobic culture in Australian schools evidenced, for example, through sex-based **bullying** (Hillier, et al. 1998; Martino 1999; Mills 2001).

Recent research has drawn on the concept of "hegemonic masculinity" and "emphasized femininity" to explain ways in which particular gender and sex-based forms of power and privilege are manifest in Australian school cultures. Hegemonic masculinity, which in Australia is unambiguously heterosexual, is defined in opposition to femininity, represented by women and those men who do not conform to the heterosexual norm. Forms of hegemonic masculinity in schools in Australia are sporting prowess, the gendered nature of work in many schools (for teachers and students), and power over women and other men (Mills 2001). Emphasized femininity, on the other hand, is underpinned by discourses of compliance, care, and empathy. Studies of classroom interactions have illustrated ways in which teachers position girls as helpers and supports (Kamler et al. 1994).

Interview and survey data conducted with Australian youth document ways in which homophobic and heteronormative attitudes are expressed in the school context. A series of interviews with young men in one middle-class **Catholic** high school, for example, details their hierarchy of masculinities: "cool boys," "party animals," "squids," and "poofters" (Martino 1999). Cool boys and party animals, played out particularly through sports and alcohol consumption, were the dominant forms of masculinity. Nonconforming boys, particularly those associated with subjects like English, **art** or **dance**, were labeled poofters or gays, while the "squids" were the high academic achievers. Many researchers have documented the

See also Adolescence; Gender Roles; Heteronormativity; Homophobia; Mental Health; School Safety and Safe School Zones; Sexism; Youth, At-Risk.

actions drawn on by young men, in particular, to create and maintain heterosexual boundaries. Mills (2001), for instance, demonstrates ways in which current patterns of violence and bullying seen in schools are gendered and sexualized and represents ways in which certain males can assert heterosexual dominance. Mills suggests that this manifests itself in both homophobic and antilesbian **harassment**.

In Australian schools, SSAY respondents report homophobic abuse from peers and teachers. For example, nearly one-half of participants in one study reported some verbal abuse and about one-in-ten reported physical abuse related to their sexuality (Hillier et al. 1998). Of these reports of abuse, 70 percent took place in schools. This abuse at school was more prevalent among the young male respondents than among the young female respondents. One-quarter of respondents also reported some form of discrimination while at school, such as not being able to take a partner to the school dance or not being allowed in the changing rooms. The effect of this **school climate** meant that some of these students chose to keep their **sexual identity** invisible and/or reported loneliness, depression, and alienation.

Ways in which school cultures can sanction homophobic and heteronormative practices have been identified in the research (Martino and Pallotta-Chiarolli 2003; Mills 2001). These may be in the form of teachers doing little to support SSAY people or failing to stop homophobic bullying. SSAY students are unlikely to disclose matters pertaining to their sexuality to teachers or other workers in their school (Dyson et al. 2003). Butler (1995) notes that there is little by way of pastoral care in the curriculum more generally that might recognize, if not value, homosexualities. Students also typically have access to information about heterosexual sex and heterosexual safe sex at school, yet little access to information about gay and lesbian sex and relationships (Hillier, et al. 1998). Moreover, young people in **rural** areas have more difficulty accessing information about gay and lesbian safe sex than young people in metropolitan areas. Hence, SSAY people are discriminated for two contradictory reasons: if homosexuality is invisible it doesn't have to be dealt with, and if it is visible it can be rejected (Mission 1995).

Numerous reports document ways in which sexuality intersects with other identity markers in the context of school and comment on ways in which dominant constructions of masculinity and femininity impact on the understandings and practices among same-sex attracted youth. For SSAY males there is a clearer construction of sexuality in terms of a hetero–homo binary, and the "battleground" of the school environment which rigidly enforces hegemonic masculinity is crucial to this (Dempsey, et al. 2001).

Research conducted by Martino and Pallotta-Chiarolli (2003) provides examples of ways in which the sexuality of young gay men intersects with other identity markers such as **ethnicity**, gender, and **social class. Gay youth** in their study talked about how they negotiate the multiple and sometimes conflicting expectations associated with being part of an Italian or Filipino community, the gay community, the school community, and the broader Australian community. Documenting how these intersections played out in these participants' schooling is indicative of multiple, fluid, and complex ways in which sexual subjectivities are understood and expressed.

For SSAY females the social scripts linking femininity to homosexuality are less clear (Dempsey, Hillier, and Harrison 2001). An evaluation of a **sexuality education** program in the state of Victoria found that students had little knowledge of homosexual (especially lesbian) sexual practice, and that the representations of homosexuality in schools were typically about male homosexuality (Harrison 2000). This lack of social script has particular problems in relation to a lack of clarity and visibility for forms of lesbian identity, making it difficult for young women to, for example, name and legitimate feelings.

Bibliography

Butler, James. 1995. "The Poof Paradox: Homonegativity and Silencing in Three Hobart High Schools." Pp. 131–149 in *Schooling and Sexualities*. Edited by Louise Laskey and Catherine Beavis. Geelong, Vic: Deakin Centre for Education and Change.

Davies, Bronwyn. 1989. *Frogs and Snails and Feminist Tails: Preschool Children and Gender*. Sydney: Allen and Unwin.

Dempsey, Deborah, Lynne Hillier, and Lyn Harrison. 2001. "Gendered (S)explorations Among Same-Sex Attracted Young People in Australia." *Journal of Adolescence* 24: 67–81.

Dyson, Sue, Anne Mitchell, Anthony Smith, Gary Dowsett, Marian Pitts, and Lynne Hillier. 2003. *Don't Ask Don't Tell — Hidden in the Crowd: The Need for Documenting Links between Sexuality and Suicidal Behaviours Among Young People*. Monograph series No.45 Australian Research Centre in Sex Health and Society: La Trobe University, Melbourne Australia.

Harrison, Lyn. 2000. "Gender Relations and the Production of Difference in School-based Sexuality and HIV/AIDS Education in Australia." *Gender and Education* 12, no. 1: 5–19.

Hillier, Lynne, Deborah Dempsey, Lyn Harrison, Lisa Beale, Lesley Matthews, and Doreen Rosenthal. 1998. *Writing Themselves In: A National Report on the Sexuality, Health and Well-Being of Same-Sex Attracted Young People*, Carlton South: Australian Research Centre in Sex, Health and Society, La Trobe University.

Kamler, Barbara, Rod Maclean, Jo-Anne Reid, and Alyson Simpson. 1994. *Shaping Up Nicely: The Formation of Schoolgirls and Schoolboys in the First Month of School*. Canberra: Australian Government Printing Service.

Lindsay, Jo, Anthony Smith, and Doreen Rosenthal. 1997. *Secondary Students, HIV/AIDS and Sexual Health*. Monograph No. 3, Centre for the Study of Sexually Transmitted Diseases: La Trobe University, Melbourne, Australia.

Martino, Wayne. 1999. "Cool Boys, Party Animals, Squids and Poofters: Interrogating the Dynamics and Politics of Adolescent Masculinities in Schools." *British Journal of Sociology of Education* 20, no. 2: 239–263.

Martino, Wayne, and Maria Pallotta-Chiarolli. 2003. *So What's a Boy?* Maidenhead, UK: Open University Press.

Mills, Martin 2001. *Challenging Violence in Schools: An Issue of masculinities*. Buckingham, UK: Open University Press.

Mission, Ray. 1995. "What's in It for Me? Teaching Against Homophobic Discourse." Pp. 117–129 in *Schooling and Sexualities*. Edited by Louise Laskey and Catherine Beavis. Geelong, Vic: Deakin Centre for Education and Change.

Australia, Sexualities Curriculum in

lisahunter and *Jane Mitchell*

There is a mandate in Australian schools to provide a safe environment for students and to build **sexuality education** into the **curriculum**. Ways in which **educational policy** and practice has responded to these mandates has been the subject of considerable discussion in the **research** literature (Connell 1994). Public debate about the

See also Adolescence; Adolescent Sexualities; Biology, Teaching of; Curriculum, Antibias; Educational Policies; HIV Education; New Zealand, Teaching of Sexualities in; Queer Pedagogy.

nature and place of sex and sexuality education in **Australia**'s curriculum has generally been framed by a binary opposition between so-called conservative and progressive discourses—on the one hand religious and moral concern over the inclusion of sex education in the school curriculum, and on the other a concern to emancipate the sexual self and enable sexual diversity (McLeod 1999). However, a national educational response to the HIV/**AIDS** pandemic in the 1980s served not only to raise questions about new ways in which sex, sexualities, and homosexualities could be represented in the curriculum, but also served to further justify the place of sexuality education in the curriculum (Harrison 2000). This—coupled with greater recognition of homophobic **bullying** in schools and, paradoxically, greater public legitimacy attached to homosexualities—has meant that "**sexual orientation**" is at least mentioned in many state syllabi, and antiviolence/**antidiscrimination** (if not explicitly antihomophobia) policies and practices have been invoked in Australian schools.

National curriculum statements targeting Grades 1–10 (developed in the late 1980s and early 1990s) typically located sex and sexuality topics in the subject areas of health, **physical education,** and social science. These statements act as guidelines for the development of specific state-based syllabi in the government and nongovernment school sectors. Included in the documents were strands associated with human development, sex, sexual health, safety, and human relations. These curriculum statements and syllabi extended previous curricula founded on biologism and developmental psychology in which the focus had been on reproductive sex, anatomy, heterosexual relationships, and age-stage theories of sexual development. Learning outcomes stated typically assume that students will identify factors that shape understandings of sex, sexuality, and gender. In theory, this opens a space for critical discussion in relation to, for example, the social construction of sex, sexuality, and gender, and how particular constructions are legitimated.

There has also been a range of other formal and informal curriculum interventions by educational authorities, youth advocacy groups, health workers, researchers and so on that exists both inside and outside the mandates of specific health and physical education syllabi. These interventions have included various pedagogies and support materials designed to provide information for SSAY people, extend knowledge about a range of sexualities, and address **homophobia.** These also include whole-school approaches to the development of safe environments, antibullying programs, and integration of sexualities into various curriculum areas. Whole-school approaches, for example, attend to the gendered and sexualized reasons for **harassment** and do not pathologize victims' sexualities (Beckett 1998; Martino and Pallotta-Chiarolli 2003). Activities that enable students to critically examine their assumptions about masculinity, femininity, and sexualities in the whole-school approach include, for example, undertaking a "gender audit" in which students are anonymously able to document their gender experiences at school. There have been a range of analyses on the ways in which homosexualities have been represented in the curriculum. These vary from a consideration of students' responses to programs, to critical analyses of how knowledge about sexualities should be represented in curriculum and pedagogy, to the preparation of teachers. Some of these assessments and responses include:

- Program Evaluations: There is little by way of large-scale or longitudinal evaluations of particular interventions. Further, there is little evidence to support significant large-scale changes to the practice of sexuality education that might go beyond discussions of future adult (typically heterosexual) sex, its biological and procreative functions and associated risks. Nevertheless, evaluative data pertaining to interventions that specifically concern antihomophobia interventions or activities that require analysis of assumptions about gender and sexualities report some success in at least raising awareness (Martino and Pallotta-Chiarolli 2003). Not surprisingly cautions have been noted with respect to the potential for creating more opportunities for hostility or for "we're all the same" forms of tolerance (Harrison 2000).

- Conceptions and Views of Young People: Young people are often missing from the negotiation and construction of the sex and sexuality education curriculum. Curricula and pedagogies serve to censor and sanitize much of this education. The real experiences and thoughts of young people in relation to, for example, masturbation, same-sex partnerships, **desire**, love, pleasure, "pashing," intimacy, **sexual harassment**, **sexism**, and bodily exposure in changing rooms remain largely ignored (Davies 1999).

- Representations of Homosexualities: Whether the sexualities curriculum and pedagogy take account of diverse homosexualities is debatable. Harrison (2000) argues that the dominant representation of homosexuality in schools is male homosexuality. Rasmussen (2003), arguing for more attention to **queer theory** in conceptualizing a pedagogy of sexualities, observes that **bisexual**, **transgender**, and **intersex** people are typically ignored in the pedagogical literature and that some school programs serve to pathologize these students, reproducing homo–hetero binaries.

- Teacher Preparation: Research documents ways in which teachers and preservice teachers may feel unwilling, unable, or underprepared to engage with syllabi that are explicitly focused on diverse beliefs and values pertaining to sex, sexuality, and gender (Robinson and Ferfolja 2001). Lesbian or gay preservice teachers may fear being "outed," while heterosexual **allies** supportive of different sexualities risk conflict through peer reluctance to discuss ideas.

Bibliography

Beckett, Lori, ed. 1998. *Everyone Is Special! A Handbook for Teachers on Sexuality Education.* Sandgate, Qld: Association of Women Educators.

Connell, Robert. W. 1994. "Poverty and Education." *Harvard Educational Review* 64, no. 2: 125–149.

Davies, Bronwyn. 1999. "The Discourses of Love." *Melbourne Studies in Education* 40, no. 2: 41–57.

Harrison, Lyn. 2000. "Gender Relations and the Production of Difference in School-based Sexuality and HIV/AIDS Education in Australia." *Gender and Education* 12, no. 1: 5–19.

Martino, Wayne, and Maria Pallotta-Chiarolli. 2003. *So What's a Boy?* Maidenhead, UK: Open University Press.

McLeod, Julie. 1999. "Incitement or Education? Contesting Sex, Curriculum and Identity in Schools." *Melbourne Studies in Education* 40, no. 2: 7–39.

Rasmussen, Mary Louise. 2003. "Queer Trepidations and the Art of Inclusion." *Melbourne Studies in Education* 44, no. 1: 87–107.

Robinson, Kerry and Tania Ferfolja. 2001. "'What Are We Doing This for?' Dealing with Lesbian and Gay Issues in Teacher Education." *British Journal of Sociology of Education* 22, no. 1: 121–132.

Web Site

Same Sex Attracted Youth Web Site. Australian Research Centre in Sex, Health and Society. November 2004. Accessed December 1, 2004. http://www.latrobe.edu.au/ssay. Research, questionnaire, reports on same-sex attracted young people including the report about young people who are attracted to their own sex. This is part of a larger comprehensive site.

B

Behavior Disorders and LGBT Youth

Valerie Harwood

The term "behavior disorders" is largely linked in popular and educational discourse to the *Diagnostic and Statistical Manual of Disorders*, produced by the American Psychiatric Association. Behavior disorders of youth are often considered to be prevalent and an issue of concern. Common use of the term is reflected in its popularity across a range of sites, including schools and the media (television chat shows current affairs shows, and Web sites for parents). Yet, there is debate over these disorders and what they represent. For **lesbian, gay, bisexual, transgender,** and questioning youth, the use of the term needs to be assessed critically since these "disorders of behavior" are arguably more to do with contravening normative societal conceptualizations of behavior than of representing some type of innate mental dysfunction.

In the *DSM-IV-TR*, behavior disorders are situated under the section "Disorders Usually First Diagnosed in Infancy, Childhood, or Adolescence." Mental disorders listed in this section include "Attention-Deficit/Hyperactivity Disorder (ADHD)," "Attention-Deficit/Hyperactivity Disorder Not Otherwise Specified," "Conduct Disorder," "Oppositional Defiant Disorder," and "Disruptive Behavior Disorder Not Otherwise Specified" (APA 2002). Each behavior disorder has a description and a checklist of criteria from which the disorder is defined. For example, "conduct disorder" is "characterized by a pattern of behavior in which the basic rights of others or major age-appropriate societal norms or rules are violated" (APA 2002 68).

Because of the association with the *DSM-IV-TR* (APA 2000), the use of the term behavior disorder in education makes a connection to an authoritative form of psychopathology. LGBTQ young people who are diagnosed with a behavior disorder are thus connected to a convincing scientific truth and arguably one that can speak authoritatively about their identity. A student diagnosed with a behavior disorder such as ADHD is thus inserted into a powerful discourse that is persuasive and very difficult to counter.

The issue with conceptualizing LGBTQ youth in terms of models of behavior disorder is evident in this statement by one group of frequently cited researchers who claim "some youths who identify as gay or bisexual do engage in problem behaviors from an early age" (Rotheram-Borus et al. 1995, 75). These authors list "substance use" and "delinquent acts" as problems, and also claim that a young person's running away from home could be indicative of conduct problems. The notion of listing running away as a behavior problem may seem unusual. However, running away was specifically included in *DSM-II* (APA 1968, 50). Listed as "Runaway Reaction of Childhood" (308.3) this mental disorder was defined as:

> Individuals with this disorder characteristically escape from threatening situations by running away from home for a day or more without permission. Typically they are immature and timid, and feel rejected at home, inadequate, and friendless. They often steal furtively.

See also Disabilities, Intellectual; Mental Health; Queer and Queer Theory; Substance Abuse and Use; Youth, At-Risk; Youth, Homeless.

The notion of running away was incorporated into subsequent versions of the DSM, including, the *DSM-III*, published in 1980. In this version, it was included under "312.10 Conduct Disorder, Undersocialized, Nonaggressive," criteria 2, "repeated running away from home overnight" (APA 1980, 48). In the next edition, *DSM-III-R*, running away is included in the list of thirteen items of diagnostic criteria in conduct disorder. In *DSM-IV-TR* running away fits into the diagnostic criteria for conduct disorder under the category "Serious Violations of Rules" (APA 2002).

To continually include running away as part of the diagnostic criteria for a behavior disorder such as conduct disorder means that it is possible that the contextual issues that may be associated with running away could be largely ignored, if not trivialized. For a LGBTQ young person, running away could be a response to an array of factors—and not necessarily a symptom of mental dysfunction on the part of the individual. Using running away as an example draws attention to the serious issues involved in the application of behavior disorders to LGBTQ youth—and moreover, the potential for a lack of understanding of the complex social and cultural issues they face (Hart and Heimberg 2001). And, even those researchers who do address this complexity too often neglect **intersex**, transgender, or **queer** and questioning youth.

Bibliography

American Psychiatric Association. 1968. *Diagnostic and Statistical Manual of Mental Disorders Second Edition (DSM-II)*. Washington DC: Author.

American Psychiatric Association. 1980. *Diagnostic and Statistical Manual of Mental Disorders Third Edition (DSM-III)*. Washington DC: Author.

American Psychiatric Association. 2000. *Diagnostic and Statistical Manual of Mental Disorders Fourth Edition, Text Revision (DSM-IV-TR)*. Washington DC: Author.

American Psychiatric Association. 2002. *Desk Reference to the Diagnostic Criteria from the DSM-IV-TR*. Washington DC: Author.

Breggin, Peter, and Ginger R. Breggin. 1994. *The War against Children: How Drugs, Programs and Theories of the Psychiatric Establishment are Threatening America's Children with Medical "Cure" for Violence*. New York: St Martin's Press.

Harwood, Valerie. 2003. "Methodological Insurrections: The Strategic Value of Subjugated Knowledges for Disrupting Conduct Disorder." *Melbourne Studies in Education* 44, no. 1: 45–61.

———. 2004. "Subject to Scrutiny: Taking Foucauldian Genealogy to Narratives of Youth Oppression." Pp. 85–107 in *Youth and Sexualities: Pleasure, Subversion, and Insubordination In and Out of Schools*. Edited by Mary Lou Rasmussen, Susan Talburt, and Eric Rofes. New York: Palgrave.

Harwood, Valerie, and Mary Lou Rasmussen. 2004. "Problematising Gender and Sexual Identities." Pp. 413–437 in *Gay and Lesbian Psychology: Australasian Perspectives*. Edited by Damien Riggs and Gordon Walker. Perth: Brightfire Press.

Hart, Trevor A., and Richard G. Heimberg. 2001. "Presenting Problems among Treatment-Seeking Gay, Lesbian, and Bisexual Youth." *Journal of Clinical Psychology: In Session, Psychotherapy in Practice* 57, no. 5: 615–627.

Rotheram-Borus, Mary J., Margaret Rosario, Ronan Van Rossem, Helen Reid, and Roy Gillis. 1995. "Prevalence, Course, and Predictors of Multiple Problem Behaviors among Gay and Bisexual Male Adolescents." *Developmental Psychology* 75, no. 150: 75–85.

Web Sites

Critica, Ronald Gonsalves. Accessed August 14, 2004. http://www.critica.com. A page for critical psychology with a good range of links.

Medical Abuse of GLBT Youth. Nancy Sharp. Parents and Friends of Lesbians and Gays. Accessed August 14, 2004. http://www.critpath.org/pflag-talk/gid.htm. Discusses the issues of the psychiatric diagnosis of Gender Identity Disorder (GID) and the effects on gay, lesbian and transgender youth.

Psychiatric Drug Facts. July 7, 2004. Peter. R. Breggin. Accessed August 14, 2004. http://www.breggin.com/index.html. Critical information on psychiatric drugs, including material directly related to youth.

Biology, Teaching of

Michael J. Reiss

School and college biology typically examines issues of sexuality through the lens of human reproduction. This immediately tends to assume heterosexuality. Biology is all too often presumed to be a neutral subject so that many biology teachers and lecturers continue to teach it as unquestioned fact. In particular, differences between females and males are often presented as clear-cut and inevitable, and the study of school biology textbooks shows that they are often sexist and typically ignore lesbian and gay issues (Reiss 1998). For example, they often omit all mention of the clitoris and, when they do refer to it, describe it as the female's equivalent of a penis. When homosexuality is addressed, it is generally portrayed as a sort of second-best option, which the reader may well grow out of. At the same time, homosexuality is generally equated with feelings, omitting any discussion as to the expression of those feelings. However, closer examination of sex in human biology provides plenty of space for critical reflection and allows for a richer understanding of what it is to be a sexual person.

Emily Martin (1991) has shown that while menstruation is sometimes viewed in scientific textbooks as a failure (because it is a process that results when the body does not become pregnant), sperm maturation is viewed as an achievement in which countless millions of sperm are manufactured each day. Furthermore, sperm are pictured as active and streamlined whereas the egg is large and passive, drifting along or waiting. Nearly fifty years earlier, Ruth Herschberger (1948) argued that the female reproductive organs are viewed as somehow being less autonomous than those of the male. The way the egg is portrayed in science textbooks has been likened to that of the fairy tale *Sleeping Beauty*, in which a dormant, virginal bride awaits a male's magical kiss. However, for well over a decade, biologists have considered the egg and sperm as *active* partners. Just as sperm seek out the egg, so the vagina discriminates between sperm and the egg, seeking out sperm to catch. Nevertheless, as Martin points out, even when acknowledged, such biological equality is still generally described in a language which gives precedence to the sperm. When the egg is presented in an active role, the image is one of a dangerous aggressor "rather like a spider laying in wait in her web" (498).

See also Identity Politics; Poststructuralism; Queer and Queer Theory; Science, Teaching of; Sexism; Sexual Health, Lesbian and Bisexual Women; Sexual Health, Gay and Bisexual Men.

Social historical **research** on sex hormones documents that textbooks and scientific papers give messages that go well beyond what the data indicate. For example, since the 1920s it has been known that each sex contains the "other's" hormone (i.e., males contain estrogen and females testosterone). Nevertheless, school textbooks typically ignore both this fact and the close chemical similarity between estrogen and testosterone (Roberts 2002). Indeed, school textbooks more in line with the scientific evidence about the working of sex hormones would present femaleness and maleness on a continuum (a model common among academic endocrinologists since the 1940s). While this model can lead to an essentialist understanding of sexuality and **sexual orientation**—and it correlates with a rise in the number of studies of the presumed femininity of gay men (Oudshoorn 1994)—it can also be seen as allowing a far more fluid understanding of sexuality, accommodating, for example, some forms of **intersex**uality.

The principle of intersexuality dates largely from **Magnus Hirschfeld**'s pioneering work in the first three decades of the twentieth century on sexual difference. By rejecting the discrete categories of male and female, arguing instead that each of us uniquely sits on a continuum, Hirschfeld did not so much give rise to the notion of "the third sex" as radically deconstruct the sexual binary (Bauer 2003).

Biological indicators of sexual orientation have long been sought and reports about discoveries of such indicators frequently surface. Precisely which indicator is identified (e.g., a hormone, a gene, parental upbringing, relative finger length) may tell us more about research fashions than sexual orientation. Around the middle of the twentieth century, hormones were widely thought to be responsible for our sexuality. Hormones are chemicals made in glands which then circulate in the body and reach target organs where they have their effects. Toward the end of the century, the focus shifted to genes, the building blocks of our chromosomes. Genes are responsible for the chemicals, including hormones, made in the body and, from a reductionist perspective, they determine not just sex and sexuality but almost all of what it is to be ourselves.

Much of the literature about the "causes" of sexuality concentrates on gayness. Lynda Birke (1997, 58), a biologist as well as a feminist and a lesbian has "spent much time and energy refuting the allegations that any social categories (of gender, race, or sexuality) are fixed by biology." However, she hesitates in rejecting entirely biological explanations of sexual orientation. For one reason, some have effectively used such biological notions politically to argue for gay rights, in a manner similar to ethnicity, **race**, or gender. Although this approach has gained some measure of civil rights, it is hotly contested (Schüklenk and Brookey 1998); more prosaically, it may well yet turn out that there are biological bases to at least some people's sexuality.

How might biology be taught better in schools and colleges? Much biology teaching is focused around the use of textbooks yet "Teachers can read subtextually and resistantly and can help their students to do likewise. Too rarely are students encouraged to critique their science textbooks; too often are textbooks used as if they contained only unquestionable truths" (Reiss 1998, 148). This simple message provides teachers and their students with a powerful tool. It challenges the general assumption of teacher (and text) as the expert repository of facts. Sitting more comfortably with emancipatory understandings of education, this also fits well with an information society, which provides students with plenty of opportunities to obtain many of the facts they want/need to know at their pace.

A fuller account of what biology teachers can do is provided by Anne-Marie Scholer. She describes her teaching program for a two-semester intermediate-level college course in anatomy and physiology, required for first-year students in nursing, athletic training, and physical therapy majors. Scholer (2002) begins with the idea that male/female is not a dichotomy. Here she draws on the various causes of indeterminate gender in humans, the sex hormone story outlined above, the existence of breast cancer in men, and transgender concerns. As she says, "While the foregoing material is undoubtedly familiar to individuals in the fields of sexuality education, it is quite new to most of my students and peers. I have found such examples to work well in class, creating vocal displays of cognitive dissonance" (78). As every teacher knows, cognitive dissonance, if well-handled, can be a powerful incentive to learning. Scholer challenges the prevailing **stereotype** of eggs as passive objects, to discuss how sex is not just anatomy and hormones, to avoid **heteronormativity**, and generally to "create an inclusive environment in my classroom" (p. 82).

There may be some who think that the teaching of biology is not an important battleground, even that to fight **discrimination** and injustice on this front is to risk allowing the discourse to be predetermined by the other side. However, as Mariamne Whatley (1999, 238) points out: "Using science to attack comprehensive **sexuality education** and to support abstinence-only education is one strategy being used currently." Similarly, Will Letts (2001) explores how school **science** structures and is structured by norms of heterosexual masculinity. Focusing on classroom examples of primary school science (where some might assume that at this age science is fairly neutral), Letts argues that science, including school science, functions as a grand narrative that seduces students and teachers. He concludes: "As a plan of action, I advocate that school science becomes an active and generative site for critical science literacy. The words 'science literacy' in this phrase are intended quite differently than popular utterances of them have come to mean. 'Science literacy' does not simply mean an intake and consumption of science texts and 'facts,' either purposefully or through acts of seduction. I am using critical science literacy to denote something akin to critical media literacy" (270).

A school/college science classroom/lab for critical science literacy, at any age, would be one in which the traditional virtues of science—its open-mindedness and refusal to accept tradition on trust—were more widely (reflexively) applied. It would allow young people to think about themselves and their sexuality more meaningfully. It would help those uncomfortable with traditional descriptions of masculinity and femininity to realize that they are not alone in their rejection of such simple dichotomies. All this can be achieved without harming those students who are comfortable with such conventional descriptions.

Bibliography

Bauer, J. Edgar. 2003. *Magnus Hirschfeld's Doctrine of Sexual Intermediaries and the Transgender Politics of Identity*. Paper presented at the Past and Present of Radical Sexual Politics Conference, Amsterdam, October 3–4, 2003. Accessed September 17, 2004. http://www.iisg.nl/~womhist/bauer.doc.

Birke, Lynda. 1997. "Born Queer? Lesbians Interrogate Biology." Pp. 57–70 in *Straight Studies Modified: Lesbian Interventions in the Academy*. Edited by Gabrielle Griffin and Sonya Andermahr. London: Cassell.

Epstein, Debbie, and James T. Sears, eds. 1999. *A Dangerous Knowing: Sexuality, Pedagogy and Popular Culture*. London: Cassell.

Herschberger, Ruth. 1948. *Adam's Rib*. New York: Pelligrini and Cudaby.

Letts, Will. 2001. "When Science is Strangely Alluring: Interrogating the Masculinist and Heternormative Nature of Primary School Science." *Gender and Education* 13: 261–274.

Martin, Emily. 1991. "The Egg and the Sperm: How Science Has Constructed a Romance Based on Stereotypical Male-Female Roles." *Signs: Journal of Women in Culture and Society* 16: 485–501.

Miller, Jane. 1991. *Seductions: Studies in Reading and Culture*. Cambridge, MA: Harvard University Press.

Oudshoorn, Nelly. 1994. *Beyond the Natural Body: An Archeology of Sex Hormones*. London: Routledge.

Reiss, Michael J. 1998. "The Representation of Human Sexuality in Some Science Textbooks for 14–16 Year-Olds." *Research in Science & Technological Education* 16: 137–149.

Roberts, Celia. 2002. "'A Matter of Embodied Fact': Sex Hormones and the History of Bodies." *Feminist Theory* 3: 7–26.

Scholer, Anne-Marie. 2002. "Sexuality in the Science Classroom: One Teacher's Methods in a College Biology Course." *Sex Education* 2: 75–86.

Schüklenk, Udo, and Robert A. Brookey, 1998. "Biomedical Research on Sexual Orientation: Researchers Taking Our Chances in Homophobic Societies." *Journal of the Gay and Lesbian Medical Association* 2, no 2: 79–84.

Whatley, Mariamne H. 1999. "The 'Homosexual Agenda' Goes to School." Pp. 229–241 in *A Dangerous Knowing: Sexuality, Pedagogy and Popular Culture*. Edited by Debbie Epstein and James T. Sears. London: Cassell.

Web Sites

The Council for Responsible Genetics. Accessed May 26, 2005. http://www.gene-watch.org/programs/privacy/gene-sexuality.html. Position paper that discusses whether genes determine sexual orientation, concluding that "The scientific argument for a biological basis for sexual orientation remains weak. The political argument that it will bolster gay pride or prevent homophobic bigotry runs counter to experience."

Inside Intersexuality. Accessed March 9, 2004. http://www.healthyplace.com/communities/gender/intersexuals. One of the growing number of Web sites about intersexuality, this discusses the meaning of "intersexuality," considers how common the condition is, provides answers to frequently asked questions, discusses gender assignment surgery, and gives electronic access to a number of pertinent articles.

Bisexual Youth

Maria Pallotta-Chiarolli

Bisexual people have the capacity to love people of either gender. This can include physical, sexual, and emotional attraction to and/or relationships with men and women. **Bisexuality** cuts across distinctions of **race, ethnicity**, gender, age, **social class**, ability, and religious affiliation. Young people often feel pressure to self-identify as either heterosexual or homosexual. They might feel that they do not fit either of

See also Adolescent Sexualities; Children of LGBT Parents; Films, Youth and Educators in; Japan, Lesbian and Bisexual Youth; Multiple Genders; Queer and Queer Theory; Sexual Orientation; Stereotypes; Youth, at At-Risk; Youth Culture.

these categories and might wish to identify as bisexual. However, bisexual youth often experience biphobia from both heterosexual and homosexual peers and adults in schools and in communities. This includes **prejudice, discrimination, harassment,** and acts of violence, which can result in **substance abuse** and other risk-taking behaviors.

There has been minimal **research** into bisexual young people (Fox 1996; McLean 2001; Pallotta-Chiarolli 2005). The exact number of bisexual youth is difficult to determine for two main reasons. First, due to the label itself being stigmatized, many young people may feel coerced to identify as either heterosexual or homosexual. Second, the figures vary depending upon whether the research has been conducted using **sexual identity** and/or sexual behavior as the defining criteria (Fox 1996). For example, many heterosexual identifying young people do have one or more same-sex experiences. Taking these complicating factors into account, Owens (1998) estimates lesbians and gays at 6 to 10 percent of the adolescent population and bisexuals at less than 3 percent.

Bisexuality is subjected to one or more of four types of problematic representations in sexual and emotional adolescent health research as well as in the wider **popular culture**. First, underrepresentation makes bisexual young people invisible. For example, very rarely do we hear positive stories about bisexual young people's strategies of negotiating their sexual practices and emotional relationships with their female and male partners. Youth and **identity development** theories are generally modeled on lesbian and gay identities. And although many education and health organizations focusing on same-sex attraction appear to be inclusive of bisexual young people by including bisexuality in their project outlines and funding proposals, they seldom provide bisexually-specific recommendations, outcomes, and services for youth (Russell and Seif 2002).

Second, misrepresentation occurs in popular culture through stereotypical constructions, societal presumptions, and prejudices. "Bisexual Men as **AIDS** Carriers," for example, has been a dominant misrepresentation in young women's magazines wherein female readers, presumed to be heterosexual, are advised: that all bisexually active "boys" are secretly engaging in sexual relations with other boys; that a bisexual boyfriend is "dangerous" and "risky;" that women in relationships with bisexually active men are unaware of or have no say in their partner's sexual identity and sexual practices; that most girls who experiment sexually with other girls do so for the "normal" titillation of their heterosexual boyfriends and often under the influence of alcohol or drugs before returning to or restoring one's true "normal" heterosexuality (McLean 2001; Russell and Seif 2002).

Third, outdated representation is also evident. Many young people reject what they consider to be an outdated "tripartite system of stable identities" (Russell and Seif 2002, 76). In other words, they find all three labels—gay, lesbian, and bisexual—limiting and concretizing their more fluid and unfixed sexualities. Jack, an Australian young man who identifies as bisexual and polyamorous, recalls the fear and anxiety he experienced in high school, realizing he was bisexual and wanting both a male and female partner. He perceives the either/or categorization of sexuality and the possessiveness of monogamous relationships:

> [I remember] developing a very strong fear. I never really got any education
> about it [bisexuality and polyamory]. You have these feelings and everything
> else [monogamous heterosexuality and homosexuality] you have resources

for . . . there was no one to talk to . . . It's like there's all these boxes out in the school field and you have to be in one of them. You can't be out in the open air, you can't be yourself, because to be an individual as opposed to part of the group is just too terrifying and traumatic at school, the competition and the pressure that we breed into our children at a very early age. They're put in teams to compete against each other. (Pallotta-Chiarolli 2005)

Finally, homogenized representation is apparent. Here the sexual diversity within youth groups, youth subcultures, and categories is seldom acknowledged or explored. Rarely do we read of class, ethnicity, geographical location, gendered expectations, **disabilities,** and other factors that impact upon a bisexual young person's decisions, negotiations, and experiences. Bisexual young people are often not just sexual border-dwellers but also border other forms of community and culture such as ethnic and religious affiliations. For example, Gianna, a young bisexual woman, grew up referring to herself as "Bob, a Bit of Both" since not only was she aware of her bisexuality but her cultural and class backgrounds were also mixed:

My father's from a working class migrant, Italian family, where the only books in the house were the Bible. My mother's from a French intellectual class, and so I come from quite a strange mix. You know most people are brought up with two working-class parents or two middle-class parents. I've got one of both. . . . So I guess when I think about my culture [and sexuality], that's often what I think about . . . I started off very young calling myself "Bob" and that stood for "A bit of both" and that summed up what I felt. (Pallotta-Chiarolli 2005)

In an effort to numb the effects of such societal stigma and stereotyping, bisexual youth may turn to drugs and alcohol or attempt **suicide.** Recent studies are pointing to higher rates of anxiety, depression, and other **mental health** concerns among bisexual-identifying young people as compared to homosexual and heterosexual young people (Jorm et al. 2002). Other research has found that bisexually active adolescent males report especially high levels of AIDS risk behavior (Goodenow, Netherland, and Szalacha 2002). There appears to be a link between these findings and the four above mentioned problematic representations in schools, ethnic, gay and lesbian communities, and the wider society (Pallotta-Chiarolli 2004). Most bisexual young people try to hide their bisexuality in both heterosexual and homosexual social settings (Russell and Seif 2002). As a bisexual adolescent, Marita, explains:

It's like we're the X-files or something. We're not straight A files or gay B files. It's like we mess up their tidy sex files. But that means they make you feel like you're messed up yourself, as if there's no way their filing system is what's really fucked. (Pallotta-Chiarolli 2005)

The limited research on the experiences of bisexual young people in schools points to several concerns. First, most of the antihomophobic and sexuality pedagogy and policy currently in schools is framed by Western discourses of sexual duality. For example, gay and lesbian youth workers and other members of the gay and lesbian communities who work and liaise with schools in antihomophobic education can be biphobic in silencing bisexual young people's realities

(Pallotta-Chiarolli 2005; Russell and Seif 2002). The rigid binary of sexual categorization, where everyone is supposed to slot into either heterosexuality or homosexuality, is a Western late nineteenth-century medical construction when scientific systems of classification gained prominence. This included classifying human sexuality into a duality even though cross-cultural, historical, and anthropological research illustrated and continues to show that human sexuality is far more fluid, multiple, and context-specific. Human sexuality is universally polymorphous. Different cultures and different times have classified, ritualized, ostracized, and promoted various forms of sexual behaviors, identities, and relationships (Fox 1996).

Second, framed by dominant sociocultural and historical discourses outside the school—the absence of healthy and happy bisexual people in popular culture, historical texts, and the media—education has largely left bisexuals hidden between heterosexuals and homosexuals (McLean 2005). Young people often report consciously and privately seeking out information about bisexuality and bisexual people while still at school as it was not forthcoming as part of the official **curriculum** or public school culture (Fox 1996; McLean 2001). Many people in history who were bisexual in their behaviors, relationships, or identities are hidden or have been reclassified as heterosexual, thereby upholding a heterosexual relationship as the "real" one and ignoring any same-sex attracted relationship. Likewise, bisexual people have been subsumed into the categories of gay and lesbian based on same-sex relationships. These include Alexander the Great, Michelangelo, Leonardo Da Vinci, Eleanor Roosevelt, Oscar Wilde, Margaret Mead, Frida Kahlo, Laurence Olivier, David Bowie, Vita Sackville-West, Yukio Mishima, Marlene Dietrich (Fox 1996).

Third, where bisexual young people are given space in research, they talk about negative school experiences based upon biphobia or bisexual invisibility, including verbal and physical harassment and feelings of isolation (McLean 2001; Pallotta-Chiarolli 2005). Bisexual youth are subsumed into the category of same-sex attracted or are nominally "tacked on" in the LGBT acronym. However, the specific experiences of bisexual young people are often ignored in schools, youth services, social and mental health services as well as in schools' **educational policies**, programs, and practices.

Fourth, when sexually diverse young people speak about their multisexual families or bisexual parents, they report negative experiences if they "out" their families or feeling coerced not to talk about their families. Multisexual or "queerly mixed" family structures and realities fall between the polarities of families with normative heterosexual monogamous married parents and the increasingly prominent gay and lesbian families; bisexual parents are generally invisible in schools (Arden 1996). For example, an adolescent male, Trent, who refuses to apply sexual labels to himself, and whose father is bisexual and in a loving twenty-year nonmonogamous marriage with his mother, feels disillusioned with and resistant to schooling:

> There's a lot more bisexual people out there and I'm more happy to know that instead of it hidden away from me . . . [At school] all you hear about is the basic mother, father and child. You don't hear father and father and mother and child. There's not all varieties, and that's not the way it works . . . I feel lucky because I'm blessed that I've got such an open family and I look around and see all these people at school who are living with this very small mind, very narrow minded, and I can look around with this wide open view and see the real world and how other people are going about life. (Pallotta-Chiarolli 2005)

Bibliography

Arden, Karen. 1996. "Dwelling in the House of Tomorrow: Children, Young People and Their Bisexual Parents." Pp. 247–257 in *Bisexual Horizons: Politics, Histories, Lives*. Edited by Sharon Rose and Cris Stevens. London: Lawrence and Wishart.

Firestein, Beth, ed. 1996. *Bisexuality: The Psychology and Politics of an Invisible Minority*. Thousand Oaks, CA: Sage.

Fox, Ronald C. 1996. "Bisexuality in Perspective: A Review of Theory and Research." Pp. 3–50 in *Bisexuality: The Psychology and Politics of an Invisible Minority*. Edited by Beth A. Firestein. Thousand Oaks, CA: Sage.

Goodenow, Carol, Julie Netherland, and Laura Szalacha. 2002. "AIDS-Related Risk Among Adolescent Males Who Have Sex With Males, Females or Both: Evidence from a Statewide Survey." *American Journal of Public Health* 92, no. 2: 203–210.

Jorm, Anthony F., Alisa Korten, Bryan Rodgers, Patricia Jacomb, and Helen Christensen. 2002. "Sexual Orientation and Mental Health: Results from a Community Survey of Young and Middle-Aged Adults." *British Journal of Psychiatry* 180: 423–427.

McLean, Kirsten. 2001. "Living Life in the Double Closet: Young Bisexuals Speak Out." *Hecate* 27, no. 1: 109–118.

———. 2005. "Out of the Shadows: Talking Bisexuality in the Classroom." Pp. 126–131 in *When Our Children Come Out: How to Support Gay, Lesbian, Bisexual and Transgendered Young People*. Edited by Maria Pallotta-Chiarolli. Sydney: Finch Publishing.

Owens, Robert E. 1998. *Queer Kids: The Challenges and Promise for Lesbian, Gay, and Bisexual Youth*. New York: Harrington Park Press.

Pallotta-Chiarolli, Maria. 2005. "We're the X-Files:" Bisexual Students 'Messing Up Tidy Sex Files'" Pp. 21–39 in *Seminal Fluid: The Underbelly of Youth Culture*. Edited by Keith Gilbert. Aachen, Germany: Meyer and Meyer.

Russell, Stephen T., and Hinda Seif. 2002. "Bisexual Female Adolescents: A Critical Analysis of Past Research, and Results from a National Survey." *Journal of Bisexuality* 2, nos. 2/3: 73–94.

Web Site

Bryant, Wayne, Kim Ward, and Bobbi Keppel. Bisexual Resource Center. December 2000. http://www.biresource.org/pamphlets/mightbebi.html. Accessed December 12, 2004. List of questions and answers for young people who think they may be bisexual. Topics covered include what it means to be bisexual, decisions about "coming out," sexual health information, how to meet other bisexual people, and a list of resource organizations.

Bisexuality

Victor J. Raymond

Bisexuality may be defined as the capacity for sexual attraction to both male and female genders. It is difficult to estimate the number of people who identify as bisexual; although a fairly large number of people may have some bisexual experience, only a small percentage of the population actually identifies as bisexual.

See also Bisexual Youth; Films, Youth and Educators in; Identity Development; Identity Politics; Latinos and Latinas; Multiple Genders; Native and Indigenous LGBT Youth; South America, LGBT Youth and Issues in.

Distinct from heterosexuality and homosexuality, bisexuality is often misunderstood and even considered by many people to not be a "real" sexual orientation, even though historically there have been many examples of bisexual behavior being tolerated or accepted in different cultures and places. A growing body of **research** indicates that bisexuality is a legitimate **sexual orientation**, which is matched by a small but growing bisexual political movement in the United States and Europe.

Defining bisexuality as "being attracted to both genders," however, is not necessarily accurate, as bisexuals themselves often offer alternative definitions of what bisexuality means. Some even reject gender as a determining factor in their attractions and identify other factors as the basis for their sexual orientation. This "fluidity" of definition is both a strength and weakness, as it recognizes the complexity of human sexual relations but is often challenged as lacking focus. Many bisexual activists reject attempts to come up with a single definition of bisexuality, as they believe this would simply create another category "in-between" hetero- and homosexuality, which they reject in favor of a more complex view of human sexuality and sexual orientation.

It is important to distinguish between bisexual behavior and bisexual identity. While it is difficult to estimate the number of people who have had bisexual experiences, only a small number (2 to 3 percent of the population) actually identifies as bisexual. Many bisexuals previously identified themselves as heterosexual; however, some have also identified as **gay** or **lesbian** prior to becoming bisexual.

Self-identified bisexuals often face **discrimination** from the broader society as well as from gays and lesbians. Within the gay and lesbian communities there has been and remains a considerable amount of irrational fear of bisexuals, often duplicating patterns of discrimination against gays and lesbians themselves, including the claim that bisexuality is merely a phase in the development of "**coming out**" as gay or lesbian. Within the mainstream United States society there has been a fascination with bisexuality, alternating with sometimes irrational concern about the potential for bisexuals to act as a "bridge" for the transmission of **AIDS** and other sexually transmitted diseases from primarily the gay men's community (the so-called "Typhoid Mary" syndrome). This all has the unfortunate result of simultaneously affirming the existence of bisexual behavior while denying the legitimacy of bisexual identity.

Several misconceptions exist about bisexuality. One prevalent misconception is the notion that a person is bisexual only if he or she is romantically involved with a man and a woman at the same time. Another misconception is that bisexuals are incapable of monogamy and have many more sexual partners than either hetero- or homosexuals (an argument also made about homosexuals by heterosexuals). While many bisexuals are nonmonogamous or polyamorous, there is also evidence that suggests many bisexuals are monogamous (Rust 1996).

These and similar misconceptions contribute to the invisibility of bisexuality and the maintenance of biphobia (the irrational fear of and discrimination against bisexuals), and are a constant source of frustration for many self-identified bisexuals. Mainstream films such as *Basic Instinct* (USA 1992) or *Blue Velvet* (USA 1986) portrayed bisexuals as villains with sinister motives toward heterosexuals, whereas movies such as *Go Fish* (USA 1994) or television shows such as ***Queer as Folk*** underscored the ambivalence and hostility felt by many gays and lesbians toward bisexual men and women. In addition to negative portrayals of bisexuals, a recurring phenomenon in both visual and print media has been the avoidance of using "bisexual" as a label to identify positive characters or behavior. Thus, in *Kissing Jessica Stein* (USA 2001) or *Chasing Amy* (USA 1997) clearly bisexual characters are often labeled as lesbians in **popular culture** reviews and discussions. Possibly the only place in popular media where there have been a relatively large number of positive portrayals of bisexuals has been in the science fiction/fantasy literary genre (science fiction/fantasy films and video, however, are not as accepting).

The recognition of bisexual behavior has a long history, dating back to ancient Greece and Rome. These examples show the differences between older and more modern definitions of bisexuality, however. In ancient Greece, for example, social norms were such that adult men could have sex with adolescent boys and younger men, as well as with women—but not with men of their age. Even in the past, however, there were exceptions to the rule—Alexander the Great had both male and female lovers. Having married several wives, he maintained a close relationship with his male companion and cavalry commander, Hephaistion. More recently, different historical periods are associated with the visibility of bisexual behavior, including early modern England in the seventeenth and early eighteenth centuries, or the Weimar Republic in Germany (1919–1933), though this latter example was also accepting of gay and lesbian behavior.

The first scholarly consideration of bisexuality may be traced to the late nineteenth century. Perhaps the most influential interpretation of bisexuality during this period was Freud's characterization of bisexuality as a form of *polymorphous perversity* (a form of unfocused, infantile sexuality). **Sigmund Freud** argued that there was a universal predisposition to bisexuality. However, he saw this as a precursor stage to either heterosexuality or homosexuality whereas his associate Wilhelm Stekel maintained that heterosexuality or homosexuality were symptoms of a self-denying neurosis. Havelock Ellis and R. v. Kraft-Ebbing also believed that bisexuality preceded homosexuality.

It was not until the groundbreaking publication of **Alfred C. Kinsey**'s *Sexual Behavior in the Human Male* (1948) that ideas about bisexuality began to change. Kinsey's research revealed a much larger percentage of same-sex desire than had been hitherto predicted, and also a large percentage of the population he studied who either had responded erotically or who were sexually active with both men and women. His findings, while controversial, have served as the basis for further scientific investigation of sexuality, in general, and bisexuality, in particular. Current research has recognized bisexuality as its own **sexual identity**, but there is considerable work to be done on numbers of self-identified bisexuals and their behaviors.

Outside of the United States, bisexuality has received relatively more acceptance within many European countries, but is not well understood elsewhere. In many places, bisexuality is conflated with a general sense of homosexual orientation as well as with alternative gender identities and presentations. In many European countries, the acknowledgment of bisexuality has been part of a larger social acceptance of homosexuality and tolerance for a diverse range of sexual orientations and gender identifications. This is particularly true in the Netherlands and the Scandinavian countries, while somewhat less so in southern Europe.

Outside of Europe, cultural understandings of bisexuality vary widely. In many Spanish-speaking countries, for example, a man who engages in penetrative sex with another man is considered "*activo*" (active), while the man who is being penetrated is considered "*pasivo*" (passive). The "active" man may behave bisexually, but would be considered heterosexual, while the "passive" man would be considered a homosexual, regardless of the gender of his other sexual partners. In North America, many Native American tribes recognize more than two genders, as well as different sexual orientations; a contemporary term for gay, lesbian, bisexual, and transgender Native Americans is *two-spirited*. In Thailand, the term *kathoey* refers to men whose gender presentation includes female characteristics, whereas other terms refer to gay and lesbians—but there is little recognition of bisexuality as distinct from these other categories. These examples suggest that **gender identity** and sexual orientation are interpreted differently in other cultures, making the definition of bisexuality much more culturally dependent.

There is an increasing amount of research on bisexuality, which suggests that there is greater recognition of bisexuality as distinct from homosexuality or heterosexuality, in terms of behavior and identity. In particular, books such as *Bisexuality: The Psychology and Politics of an Invisible Minority* (Firestein 1996), *Bisexuality and the Challenge to Lesbian Politics: Sex, Loyalty, and Revolution* (Rust 1995), and *The Bisexual Option* (Klein 1993) have added to academic understandings of bisexuality, along with more popular works as *Vice Versa: Bisexuality and Eroticism in Everyday Life* (Garber 1995). In addition, the *Journal of Bisexuality* provides a venue for further scholarly inquiry. Topics have included: bisexual identities, bisexual histories in San Francisco, bisexual issues in sex therapy, bisexual AIDS and safer sex activism, bi-negativity, coming out in the Netherlands, bisexuality and religion, and bisexuality and biracial identity.

Bibliography

Angelides, Steven. 2001. *A History of Bisexuality*. Chicago: University of Chicago Press.

Cantarella, Eva. 1992. *Bisexuality in the Ancient World*. New Haven, CT: Yale University Press.

Firestein, Beth A. 1996. *Bisexuality: The Psychology and Politics of an Invisible Minority*. Thousand Oaks, CA: Sage.

Garber, Marjorie. 1995. *Vice Versa: Bisexuality and Eroticism in Everyday Life*. New York: Simon and Schuster.

Hall, Donald T., and Maria Pramaggiore. 1996. *Representing Bisexualities: Subjects and Cultures of Fluid Desire*. New York: New York University Press.

Hemmings, Clare. 2002. *Bisexual Spaces: A Geography of Sexuality and Gender*. New York: Routledge.

Ka'ahumanu, Lani, and Loraine Hutchins. 1991. *Bi Any Other Name: Bisexual People Speak Out*. Boston: Alyson.

Klein, Fred. 1993. *The Bisexual Option/Fritz Klein*. Binghamton, NY: Haworth Press.

Ochs, Robyn. 2003. *Bisexual Resource Guide*. Boston: Bisexual Resource Center.

Rodriguez Rust, Paula C. 2000. *Bisexuality in the United States: A Social Science Reader*. New York: Columbia University Press.

Rust, Paula C. 1995. *Bisexuality and the Challenge to Lesbian Politics: Sex, Loyalty, and Revolution*. New York: New York University Press.

———. 1996. "Monogamy and Polyamory: Relationship Issues for Bisexuals." Pp. 127–148 in *Bisexuality: The Psychology and Politics of an Invisible Minority*. Edited by Beth A. Firestein. Thousand Oaks, CA: Sage.

Tucker, Naomi, ed. 1996. *Bisexual Politics: Theories, Queries, and Visions*. Binghamton, NY: Haworth Press.

Weinberg, Martin S., Collins J. Williams, and Douglas W. Pryor. 1994. *Dual Attraction: Understanding Bisexuality*. New York: Oxford University Press.

Web Sites

The Bisexual Foundation. August 2004. Bisexual.Org – Bringing Bisexuals Together. Accessed September 4, 2004. http://www.bisexual.org. Averaging more than 700 visitors each day, the site includes current news, chat forums and personals, catalogs for music, video, and books as well as FAQs and details on the Klein Sexual Orientation Grid.

Bisexual Resource Center. June 2004. BRC home page. Accessed September 4, 2004. http://www.biresource.org. The most active bisexual advocacy and resource group in the United States (originally the East Coast Bisexual Network), this site has a wide range of resources, listings of support groups, job opportunities, and events, as well as links to other useful sites.

Boy Scouts of America v. Dale

James Anthony Whitson

In *BSA v. Dale* (2000), the Supreme Court of the United States ruled that state **antidiscrimination** laws cannot be used to limit the rights that are guaranteed by the United States Constitution to the Boy Scouts and other private associations to enforce their membership policies—even if those policies use **sexual orientation** or other criteria that would be outlawed as a basis for **discrimination** by a public group, or by private entities (like restaurants or other businesses) that are generally open to the public. The *Dale* case did not require the Court to issue a decision on youth membership policies, since this was a case involving only an adult leader who was kicked out by the Boy Scouts because of his sexual orientation. Therefore, the *Dale* decision is not, strictly speaking, a precedent that would preclude courts from considering arguments for a different decision on matters of youth membership in Scouting or in other groups; but the reasoning used by the Supreme Court as the basis for deciding this case supports a general rule that private groups do have the right to discriminate against **lesbian, gay, bisexual**, and **transgender youth** (LGBT), and that the Constitution does not allow state laws, school board policies, and so forth to interfere with those groups' freedom to exercise that right.

James Dale entered the Cub Scouts as an eight-year-old, and achieved the rank of Eagle Scout before turning eighteen and becoming an assistant scoutmaster. Dale first acknowledged his homosexuality to himself and others when he attended Rutgers University. After he was interviewed by a local newspaper about the importance of gay role models for lesbian and gay teenagers, he received a letter from the local Boy Scout Council informing him that his membership had been revoked. Dale then filed a lawsuit in the New Jersey Superior Court, alleging that the Boy Scouts' action was a violation of the state's laws against discrimination in "public accommodations."

The New Jersey Supreme Court upheld this application of the state's antidiscrimination law, ruling in favor of Dale's reinstatement as a Boy Scout leader. However, the United States Supreme Court overturned the New Jersey court's decision and ruled, in a 5–4 decision, that the First Amendment gives the Boy Scouts of

See also Discrimination; *Lawrence v. Texas*; Legal Issues, Students; Scouting; Workplace Issues.

America a right to exclude gay men from leadership positions. The majority concluded that "a state requirement that the Boy Scouts retain Dale as an assistant scoutmaster would significantly burden the organization's right to oppose or disfavor homosexual conduct," and that the state's interests "do not justify such a severe intrusion on the Boy Scouts' rights to freedom of expressive association" (659).

The Boy Scouts argued that instilling values is essential to its mission. Among the values that it seeks to instill are those expressed in the "Scout Law" that "A Scout is . . . Clean," and in the "Scout Oath" to "do my best . . . [t]o keep myself . . . morally straight" (649). They maintained that their purpose includes teaching the lesson that homosexuals, as such, are not "clean" or "morally straight," and that the association's efforts to have scouts learn this lesson would be undermined if the scouts actually know any gay men working as Scoutmasters or in other leadership roles. In the case of James Dale, himself, Rehnquist noted that "by all accounts, Dale was an exemplary Scout" (644); so, allowing him to continue serving as assistant scoutmaster could plausibly be seen as interfering with the scouts' ability to learn the lesson that homosexuals are not clean and morally straight.

Joined by three other Justices, Justice Stevens noted in his dissent that "unfavorable opinions about homosexuals" are like "equally atavistic" racial **prejudices**. He argued that, although such prejudices have historically been nourished by sectarian doctrine (which people in this country are free to espouse under the First Amendment), "interaction with real people" has, over the years, served as a corrective antidote (699–700).

The job of the U.S. Supreme Court was not, however, to pass judgment on the wisdom of the Boy Scouts' policy of excluding homosexuals from adult leadership roles. The Court's job was to decide whether the First Amendment gives the Boy Scouts a right to implement such a policy. In this case, the Court ruled that the Boy Scouts' First Amendment right to "expressive association" includes the right to express negative views of homosexuality by excluding homosexuals from adult leadership.

In his dissenting opinion, Justice Stevens argued that the BSA had failed to demonstrate that the Association did, in fact, have a unified position condemning homosexuality. For example, it had not shown that the terms "morally straight" and "clean" in the Scout Oath and Law actually had established meanings that excluded homosexuals. In his majority opinion, Rehnquist countered that expressive associations have a First Amendment right to determine for themselves the meaning of their messages. Although different people may disagree about the meaning of the terms "clean" or "morally straight," it is not the role of courts to dispute the association's definition of those terms (651). Moreover, Rehnquist argued that increasing acceptance of homosexuality by the public is not a reason for ruling against the Boy Scouts, since "the fact that an idea may be embraced and advocated by increasing numbers of people is all the more reason to protect the First Amendment rights of those who wish to voice a different view" (660).

Such arguments in favor of First Amendment protection for the Boy Scouts' exclusion of homosexuals were supported in a "friend of the Court" brief by Gays and Lesbians in Support of Individual Liberty (2000). This organization argued that First Amendment protection for groups with unpopular ideas, and for the freedom of such groups to decide who will be admitted as members in their associations, is no less important for minorities, including homosexuals, than for more mainstream groups such as the Boy Scouts.

Instead of arguments about whether private groups should enjoy freedom of expressive association, and the related right to determine their membership, reactions to the Court's decision have been more concerned with whether the Boy Scouts' claim to exercise such rights, as a private association, are consistent with the status and special treatment they have traditionally received from public bodies at the national, state, local, and school district and school building levels.

Following the Court's decision, eleven Congress members sent a letter to President Clinton calling for his resignation as honorary head of the Boy Scouts—a position held by every U.S. President since the founding of the BSA in 1910. More consequentially, local school authorities across the United States began reviewing their policies of providing meeting space on public property for use by local Boy Scout troops.

As an amendment to the No Child Left Behind legislation in 2001, Congress passed the Boy Scouts of America Equal Access Act, purportedly to make sure that the Boy Scouts would not be given less access to public facilities compared with other private groups. Ironically, this act, which expressly bans "discriminating for reasons based on the membership or leadership criteria or oath of allegiance to God and country of the Boy Scouts of America," covers the BSA on the basis of its status as a "patriotic society" specially chartered by the U.S. Congress. Although the Supreme Court upheld the Boy Scouts' right *as a private association* to discriminate against homosexuals on the basis of its own interpretation of its Oath and Law, subsequent legislation by the Congress arguably attenuates the "private" character of these very practices.

At some point, such incongruities could be pursued in future legislative and judicial action, especially after *Lawrence v. Texas* (2003). For the time being, more productive efforts to assure equal opportunities for young people of all sexualities are being pursued by activist groups including Scouting for All, which has grown from efforts starting in 1997 by a then twelve-year-old Boy Scout named Steven Cozza to oppose the Boy Scouts' policies of discriminating against LGBT youth, atheists, and girls.

Protesting BSA's policies, Steven Cozza, cofounder of Scouting for All. Courtesy of Scouting for All.

Bibliography

Boy Scouts of America, et al., v. James Dale, 530 U.S. 640 (2000).
Boy Scouts of America Equal Access Act, 20 USCS § 7905 (2003).
Gays and Lesbians in Support of Individual Liberty. Brief Amicus Curiae of Gays and Lesbians in Support of Individual Liberty in Support of Petitioners, *BSA v. Dale* (2000). Available at http://supreme.lp.findlaw.com/supreme_court/briefs/99-699/99-699fo19/brief.pdf. Accessed December 18, 2004.

Lawrence v. Texas, 123 S.Ct. 2472 (2003).

Mechling, Jay. 2001. *On My Honor: Boy Scouts and The Making of American Youth*. Chicago: University of Chicago Press.

Web Site

Scouting for All. 2004. Accessed December 18, 2004. http://www.scoutingforall.org. This constantly updated site has news about developments and background information on the Scouting movement. It also provides information about a wide variety of ongoing efforts and events to fight against discrimination and to promote diversity within the Scouting movement.

Brazil, LGBT Youth and Issues in

Anibal Ribeiro Guimarães, Jr

Lesbian, gay, bisexual, and transgender youth (LGBT) in Brazil, though not yet well-organized and deprived of economic status, have made some meaningful achievements. A better understanding of sexuality and LGBT issues in education is contributing decisively to that result. In several instances, adolescents have shown pride and awareness, despite strong opposition and the fact that Brazil ranks number one in the world for violence against sexual minorities. Although homosexuality is not a crime in Brazil, LGBT people may be charged for "public offenses," an amorphous term commonly used for extortion by the very law enforcement officers charged with protecting them (Green 1999; Trevisan 1986). Only during Carnival is one fully allowed to live his/her sexuality in public; inequality and invisibility are the rule throughout the year. The absence of geographically-defined gay communities and the primacy of gender role over sexual identity when engaging in sexual behavior have complicated organizational and educational efforts.

Brazil is two countries within the same boundaries: a rich, well-developed and progressive South; a poor, underdeveloped North. In both regions, there is social injustice and extremely uneven income distribution. To some, Brazil is an example of racial integration: a mix of blacks, whites, and native/indigenous people. Racism and discrimination, which is a little more subtle than the former, still exist. James Green (1999), an American gay Brazilianist, argues that homosexuality offers an opportunity for an interaction among people from different backgrounds, notwithstanding these tensions.

Unlike Europe and North America, where homosexuality is generally a lesser issue for those "out of the closet" and where there is a greater focus on sexual identity and a gay community, Brazilians observe boundaries between sexual identity and behavior. Among many men, there is a dichotomy between active and passive sexual roles, which, at least in less-educated and poorer classes, defines one's identity as a "real man" or "gay" (Mott 1997; Trevisan 1986). Power, roughness, and

See also Adolescent Sexualities; Parents, Responses to Homosexuality; Prostitution or Sex Work; Sexism; South America, LGBT Youth and Issues in; Youth, At-Risk; Youth, Homeless.

dominance in same-sex behavior define identity, and this belief often rules relations among Brazilian men who have sex with men (MSM). This has significant implications for HIV transmission and LGBT **activism**.

Brazil is praised worldwide for its provision of free antiretroviral drugs to every HIV positive citizen through its public health system since 1996. This intervention strategy also includes **HIV education**, prevention, and monitoring efforts. The government has argued that providing the drugs improves the quality of life of HIV-positive individuals, reduces the number of AIDS-related deaths, and lowers the cost of hospital admissions and treatment for opportunistic infections among people with HIV (Galvão 2002). Adolescents, ranging from fifteen to twenty-four years old, represent one of the most vulnerable groups to HIV/AIDS in Brazil. More young women, ranging from thirteen to nineteen years old, have been found HIV-positive compared to males in the same range. From twenty to twenty-four years old, both genders share the same vulnerability (Ministry of Health, STD/AIDS National Program 2004). Lately, more than 50 percent of the new HIV-positive cases in Brazil are detected among adolescents. Moreover, since the first **AIDS** cases in the early 1980s and eight years after the beginning of the distribution of the antiretroviral drugs, the first generation of HIV-positive babies are entering **adolescence**.

The lack of a self-identified homosexual community delayed the response to HIV/AIDS related illnesses. Instead of a defined community, there is a spectrum of sexual identities and behaviors. De Sousa (2000), for instance, in a study with 103 Brazilian street youths, reports that these adolescents engage in high-risk sexual activity not only for money, but also as a rite of passage for men (sexual experimentation), as birth control for women (anal intercourse) and for both genders, as a means to get affection. Then, there is the typical "michê"—a poorly-educated sex worker who engages in same-sex behavior but denies that he is a homosexual. He frequently lives a double life, split between his poor suburban heterosexual lifestyle and a somewhat profitable career as an **urban** sex worker. Frequently sought for his youth, masculine and tough appearance, at the age of twenty, a "michê" is considered "old" for the standards of the "career" (Mendès-Leité 1995). And, as part of the Brazilian gay scene, he is sometimes involved in homophobic violence as may happen when a "michê" is trapped into an "unwanted" homosexual lifestyle and believes that by murdering his male sex partner he rids himself of the "threatening" behavior.

The "travesti"—a transgender person who has not been submitted to a sex-reassignment surgery—due to her sexual status, is seldom able to find employment other than prostitution (Green 1999). She has likely left home as an adolescent, due to her unwanted gendered and sexual behavior, and is desperately looking for a place to live. Most men who engage in sex with travestis, according to the latter report, are married men who seem to need the female façade of a travesti to not feel sexually threatened.

Like the travesti, lesbians face additional obstacles in a society which privileges heterosexuality and maleness. Given that Brazilian sexual roles in this area are not particularly rigid, lesbians may engage in heterosexual sex for money. However, there are no available data on the frequency or extent of this behavior.

Although a wide range of sexual behaviors may be tolerated, there is less tolerance for sexual minorities, including LGBT youth. A newly-released report by UNESCO documents the pervasive **discrimination** against homosexuals in Brazil. The largest and most comprehensive study to date, led by Miriam Abramovay (2004), shows the serious situation of LGBT youth and education as reported by heterosexual-identified students and teachers. Researching 16,422 students—ranging from 10 to 24 years old—3,099 teachers and 4,532 parents in private and public schools in 13 most important Brazilian state capitals, the study covered students from the fifth to eleventh grades. On average, one in four students is unwilling to have homosexuals as their schoolmates, though girls are more welcoming than boys. LGBT students in Brazil also face **bullying** and **sexual harassment** at schools, however, educators perceive such violence and threats of violence as isolated cases. Dismissed by teachers and school staff as "unimportant stuff," their attitudes reinforce the isolation and humiliation experienced by queer youth. This is not lost on the students as **harassment** against homosexuals is ranked by boys (in sixth position) and girls (in third position) as the most "unbearable" form of violence.

In 2003, an innovative program concerning sexual orientation was launched in São Paulo public schools by the Secretariat of Education. Covering children and adolescents in every grade, Orientação Sexual na Escola (Sexual Orientation in School) sets aside the view of sexuality as solely reproduction, calling on teachers to eliminate all **prejudice** and to embrace diversity at school—mainly racial and sexual—in order to reduce bullying and sexual harassment. This **curriculum** includes transgender persons. In CIEJA Cambuci, a central school, one nineteen-year-old male student "felt so comfortable with the support found, that he decided to live his sexuality full time, cross-**dressing**, adopting a 'new' name, thus leaving years of anxiety and suffering behind," according to Cambuci's Director and Pedagogical Coordinator.

The importance of this program is underscored by the UNESCO study. For example, in Fortaleza—a northern state capital—48 percent of students' parents were unwilling for their children to have homosexuals as schoolmates; in the southernmost state capital, Porto Alegre, one-quarter of the parents were so inclined. Further, although teachers affirm that homosexual prejudice and discrimination are major problems among students, few admit to holding such views. In Brasilia, the nation's capital, only 6 percent acknowledged such prejudice and in Porto Alegre only 2 percent. These data, however, are contradicted by many students, who report the opposite concerning teachers' homophobic behaviors.

Greater acceptance can be found in Brazil's **popular culture**. There are very popular and well-respected "out" lesbian, bisexual, and gay men singers—although most actors remain closeted (Trevisan 1986). When the late deep-voice pop singer Cássia Eller (http://www.brazzil.com/pages/p06jan02.htm) died in 2001, for example, her lesbian partner, gained legal custody of her eight-year old son, Chicao, which helped to build support for gay foster **parents** and **adoption**s. Cazuza, the rock poet of his generation (http://www.vidaurbana.hpg.ig.com.br/cazuza.htm) died in 1990 from AIDS. A foundation caring for HIV-positive children bears his name and is chaired by his activist mother. Angela RoRo and Ney Matogrosso, who both came out in the beginning of their careers, in the 1970s during a harsh military regime, still remain popular today.

In contrast, most gay television characters are **stereotypes**. In soap operas, lesbian couples have become more visible, though no explicit kisses are allowed. The 2002 Brazilian **film**, *Madame Satã*, (http://mongrelmedia.com/films/MadameSata. html) perhaps best explores the intersection of **homophobia**, popular culture, and **race**. Inspired by the extraordinary life of vagabond João Francisco dos Santos, through a series of theatrical guises he turned his sexuality, race, and **social class**

Brazilian Youth Kissing. © Ennio Brauns

into statements of resistance and strength in early and mid-twentieth century Brazil.

Each June, São Paulo, the nation's biggest city with 18 million inhabitants, hosts the world's largest gay pride parade. In 2004, 1.8 million people gathered to celebrate past events and to show their strength. During the previous year, some young gay people were targeted by shopping center security officers because they were cuddling each other. A few days later, hundreds of gays gathered at that same place to kiss each other with major media coverage, in an episode later called *beijaço* ("a big and noisy kiss"). On Valentine's Day, a Brazilian mobile phone company created a campaign to photograph and award prizes to "the most beautiful couples." Depicted same-sex couples were dismissed from consideration. Following a huge protest and a threatened boycott from gay people, there were apologies from the company.

Achieving important and positive visibility and attention to their demands, LGBT activists have found AIDS to be an important issue around which to organize and garner financial resources. In the early 1980s, two important nongovernmental organizations were founded in Rio de Janeiro: AIDS Interdisciplinary Brazilian Association (ABIA) and Grupo Atobá. These contributed to raising awareness of implementing public health policies concerning HIV/AIDS and to developing a sense of community and identity.

The struggle to reduce prejudice and discrimination, end homophobic violence, support LGBT youth, and integrate issues into the schools has only begun in Brazil. Unequivocal and essential support has been found among some heterosexual **allies**. Maria Berenice Dias, President of the Seventh Panel of Judges of the Court of Appeals of the State of Rio Grande do Sul, with a specialty in Family Law, is a good example (http://www.mariaberenicedias.com.br.). Through her innovative attitude and despite all social prejudice, her rulings have extended family rights to lesbian and gay men in Brazil. Contributing a feminist progressive voice inclusive and human understanding at LGBT issues, Dias has put forth a judicial doctrine regarding homosexual unions. In her book, *União Homossexual—O Preconceito e a Justiça* (Homosexual Unions: Prejudice and Justice), she calls for "homoaffective unions," adoptions by both same-sex partners, and the rights of **transsexuals** to alter their legal identities.

Other initiatives are also underway. In 2004, after intense lobbying efforts by LGBT activists, the federal government released its campaign, Programa Brasil Sem Homofobia (Brazil without Homophobia). This initiative helps to consolidate advances in political, social, and legal fields regarding LGBT people because substantial financial support from the federal government will be provided toward this goal. As part of this effort, the Brazilian delegation to the United Nations Commission on Human Rights (UNCHR) introduced a historic resolution on "human rights and **sexual orientation**." This resolution, to be considered in its 2005 session, affirms the universality of human rights and the basic principle that lesbians, gays and bisexuals are entitled to the same human rights protection as other human beings.

Bibliography

Abramovay, Miriam. 2004. *Juventudes e Sexualidade* (Youth and Sexuality). Brasília: UNESCO, MEC, Ministério da Saúde/DST/Aids, Secretaria Especial de Políticas para as Mulheres, Instituto Ayrton Senna.

Caminha, Adolfo. 1982. *Bom-Crioulo: The Black Man and the Cabin Boy.* San Francisco: Gay Sunshine Press.

De Sousa, Isabela Cabral Félix. 2000. "Deadly Education: The Spread of HIV/AIDS— Conceptual and Practical Approaches to HIV/AIDS: The Brazilian Experience." *Current Issues in Comparative Education* 3, no. 1. Accessed May 26, 2005. http://www.tc.columbia.edu/cice/articles/if131.htm.

Galvão, Jane. 2002. "Access to Antiretroviral Drugs in Brazil." *The Lancet* 360: 1862–1865. Accessed October 4, 2004. http://www.thelancet.com/journal/vol360/iss9348/full/llan.360.9348.editorial_and_review.23488.1.

Green, James N. 1999. *Beyond Carnival: Male Homosexuality in Twentieth-Century Brazil.* Chicago: University of Chicago Press.

Inter-Church Committee on Human Rights in Latin America. 1996. *Violence Unveiled: Repression against Lesbians and Gay Men in Latin America.* Accessed May 26, 2005. http://www.choike.org/documentos/gays_violence.pdf.

International Gay and Lesbian Human Rights Commission. 2003. "2003: Couple among 132 Women Murdered in Brazilian Province." *Gay Today* 8, no. 167. Accessed May 26, 2005. http://gaytoday.com/world/110503wo.asp.

Kulick, Don. 1998. *Travesti: Sex, Gender, and Culture among Brazilian Transgendered Prostitutes.* Chicago: University of Chicago Press.

Mendès-Leité, Rommel. 1995. *Michê: La Masculinité au Marché ou Les Aléas de la 'Prostitution Virile' au Brésil.* (Michê: Masculinity on the Market or The Chances of "Virile Prostitution" in Brazil) . Accessed May 26, 2005. http://semgai.free.fr/contenu/textes/RML/rML_Miche.html. Originally published in *Un Sujet Inclassable? Approches Sociologiques, Littéraires et Juridiques des Homosexualités.* Edited by Rommel Mendès-Leité. Lille: Cahiers GKC.

Mott, Luiz. 1997. *Epidemic of Hate: Violations of the Human Rights of Gay Men, Lesbians, and Transvestites in Brazil.* New York: International Gay and Lesbian Human Rights Commission.

Trevisan, João Silvério. 1986. *Perverts in Paradise.* Boston: Alyson.

Web Sites

Brazilian Resolution. Accessed October 17, 2004. Updated information on LGBT world coalition's efforts toward a resolution on human rights at UNCHR. http:// www.brazilianresolution.com.

International Gay and Lesbian Human Rights Commission. October 2004. Accessed May 26, 2005. http://www.iglhrc.org. Good source of information (including Brazil), through its reports, fact sheets and links. Its action-alerts have helped relieve and improve LGBT people's condition.

International Lesbian and Gay Association. October 2004. Accessed May 26, 2005. http://www.ilga.org. Founded in 1978, this 400-member organization is a federation of local and national groups. The site includes news and information on current political events in specific countries.

Lesbian and Gay Rights. 2004. Human Rights Watch. Accessed May 26, 2005. http://hrw.org/doc/?t=lgbt. Along with Amnesty International, one of the best LGBT-friendly NGOs; a rich source for Brazilian LGBT human rights issues.

Love Sees No Borders. 2004. Marta Donayre and Leslie Bulbuk. Accessed May 26, 2005. http://www.loveseesnoborders.org. Cofounded by a Brazilian lesbian and her American partner, this is "a site dedicated to disseminating information about the injustices suffered by gay Americans and their foreign born partners."

Britain Section 28

Akihiko Komiya

Section 28 of the Local Government Act 1988 prohibited local authorities in Great Britain from "promoting" homosexuality in state-maintained schools. During the fifteen years it was in effect, this law often hampered the **lesbian, gay, bisexual**, and **transgender** (LGBT) youth from getting help and information on homosexuality from teachers. Though the Section didn't prohibit teachers or school governors from objectively discussing homosexuality in classrooms or **counseling** pupils about their sexuality, many misunderstood or chose to misunderstand its application. Consequently, fueled by tabloid journalism and within the context of **homophobia** and **AIDS**, LGBT issues were neglected and homophobic **bullying** was ignored in schools. Section 28, however, also served as an effective organizing issue for LGBT activists.

Section 28 had its origins in a bill proposed in 1986. The AIDS crisis accelerated the homophobic climate in Great Britain, and the mass media played a pivotal role throughout the two-year debate on this legislation. Great emphasis was placed on the presence, in an Inner London Education Authority teachers' center (where only teachers had access to materials), of *Jenny Lives with Eric and Martin*. This children's picture book tells a story of an ordinary day in the life of a Danish girl being raised by her gay father Martin and his partner, Eric. In one illustration, the little girl is shown, like countless other children within conventional heterosexual families, enjoying breakfast with her father and his partner. This image was seized upon with prurient and salacious outrage by the British tabloids, which went on to falsely report the Inner London Education Authority was distributing copies of this book to young children. In fact, the Chief Education Officer of ILEA had ruled that it *not* be made available in school libraries.

Even before Section 28 took effect, it was evoked in an educational context. For example, East Sussex County council banned from its schools a booklet produced by the National Youth Bureau because of an entry on the London Lesbian and Gay Centre, asking that volunteers (ages 14 and up) should have a "positively expressed sexuality" (Davies 1988). Once in effect, the impact of Section 28 was both real and symbolic. In September 1988, a production of *Trapped in Time*, due to be performed by the Avon Touring Theatre Company in a secondary school, was cancelled by the school's head teacher. The play, examining the way different people

See also Children of the Rainbow Curriculum; Educational Policies; Identity Politics; Literature, Early Childhood; United Kingdom, LGBT Youth and Issues in.

have been represented in history, was a serious educational effort challenging young people to think about issues of **racism, sexism,** and sexuality. In one short scene, "Queen Victoria's Coming Out," a character tells his friends that he is gay.

Interviews with teachers found a large majority either believed that they could not intervene in the area of homosexuality because of Section 28, were nervous about these issues and did not know how best to deal with them, or expressed **prejudice** and used the Section as an excuse for failing to intervene when encountering homophobic **harassment** (Epstein 2000).

Although Section 28 attempted to police homosexuality in schools, it was more effective in politicizing homosexuals whose leaders seized on the Section to push for its repeal and related reforms. For instance, Stonewall, The National Steering Group on Lesbian and Gay Policing Issues, emerged in 1988 at a time when there were no professional lobbying groups of this kind (Wise 2000). The largest gay rights march ever in Britain occurred in Manchester to protest Section 28, and many LGBT societies in colleges held rallies against the section, further encouraging **activism** among a younger generation of LGBT students and their **allies.** Older persons also were galvanized to action. Most notably, actor Sir Ian McKellen came out on a radio talk show, following the host's antigay remarks, and became one of the founding lobbyists in Stonewall.

In Scotland, after the executive ministers agreed to accept a compromise by emphasizing the value of marriage in sex education in schools, Section 28 (known there as Clause 28) was finally repealed in 2000. In 2003, following several failed attempts to repeal Section 28 due to opposition by "family value" proponents in the House of Lords, the law was abolished in England and Wales.

Despite these repeals, Kent County Council maintains a "son of Section 28," having an effect on that English county's 600 schools. Also, a parliamentary candidate sparked controversy by calling for a county-by-county introduction of Section 28. LGBT people, including Queer Youth Alliance, a nationwide LGBT youth federation, continues to fight such challenges.

Bibliography

Colvin, Madeleine, and Jane Hawksley, eds. 1989. *Section 28: A Practical Guide to the Law and Its Implications.* London: National Council for Civil Liberties.
Davies, Paul. 1988, May 26. "Sexuality: A New Minefield in Schools." *The Independent.*
Epstein, Debbie. 2000. "Sexualities and Education: Catch 28" *Sexualities* 3, no. 4: 387–394.
Jivani, Alkarim. 1997. *It's Not Unusual: A History of Lesbian and Gay Britain in the Twentieth Century.* Bloomington: Indiana University Press.
Jones, Carol, and Pat Mahony, eds. 1989. *Learning Our Lines: Sexuality and Social Control in Education.* London: Woman's Press.
Wise, Sue. 2000. "'New Right' or 'Backlash'? Section 28, Moral Panic and 'Promoting Homosexuality'." *Sociological Research Online* 5, no. 1: 1–13. Accessed December 5, 2004. http://www.socresonline.org.uk/5/1/wise.html.

Web Sites

Schools Out. December 2004. Accessed December 4, 2004. http://www.schools-out.org.uk/. A group working for LGBT equality in education to network all LGBT people in education, to research curriculum development on sexuality, and to campaign on LGBT issues in education. The Web site provides very useful information and materials such as a directory of books and videos, and lesson plans.

Stonewall: Equality and Social Justice for Lesbians, Gay Men, and Bisexuals. November 2004. Accessed November 23, 2004. http://www.stonewall.org.uk/stonewall. This professionalized lobbying group is active inside and outside the Parliament. Site includes a searchable database, current UK news, and ongoing projects.

Bulgaria, LGBT Youth and Issues in

Monika Pisankaneva

The lives of **lesbian, gay, bisexual,** and **transgender** (LGBT) people in Bulgaria still remain largely hidden from the public sphere, affecting LGBT youth development. Nevertheless, these youth enjoy more freedom than the last generation and are no longer subject to legal persecution and social censure. The discriminatory provision in the Bulgarian Penal Code (article 157, paragraph 4) that defined homosexuality as a perversion and criminalized its display in public was abolished in June 2002 as part of the accession process to the European Union. The age of consent (currently fourteen) was equalized for hetero- and homosexual people. Furthermore, since 2004 a new **antidiscrimination** law includes **sexual orientation**. Though legal improvement of the human rights status of LGBT people did not automatically produce a transformation in social attitudes, it created the ground for gradual increase of their visibility. LGBT youth born after the demise of communism are in the forefront of this social change. Nevertheless, the socialization problems of LGBT youth have been effectively ignored or neglected by public sector policy while institutional **homophobia** and **heterosexism** prevail.

Bulgaria is a country of about 8 million people consisting mainly of ethnic Bulgarians (83.9 percent), and two sizable minorities, Turks (9.4 percent) and Roma (4.7 percent). The communist regime (1944 to 1989) suppressed the pluralism of identities. The democratization of the country at the beginning of the 1990s brought improved freedoms for many people, especially the previously repressed ethnic minorities. At the same time, the new movement for political, economic, and social transformation was rather conservative. Drawing upon traditional patriarchal values embedded in Eastern Orthodox Christianity (the dominant religion in the country), liberal social theories that inspired the sexual emancipation in the West were not embraced. Although the majority of Bulgarians are not very religious, most people prefer to adhere outwardly to **Christian** norms of gender and sexuality, and this affects sexual identities construction. Nonheterosexual people are still marginalized, although open **discrimination** is rare. These factors affect sexual **identity development,** and internalized homophobia is the main challenge facing LGBT youth. Self-hatred for being homosexual and disapproval of the ones who are flamboyantly gay, lesbian, or trans are common reactions.

The increased access to information about LGBT lifestyles, which are becoming commonplace in the more advanced democracies, encourages greater autonomy in identifying as a LGBT Bulgarian youth. Support, however, is very limited. Since

See also Coming Out, Youth; Community LGBT Youth Groups; Cross-Dressing; Heteronormativity; Parents, Responses to Homosexuality; Passing; Popular Culture; Russia, LGBT Youth and Issues in; Youth, At-Risk.

access to the gay night club scene is limited to people above eighteen, **Internet** forums and chat rooms are the main sources of information and contacts for LGBT youth. A small number of LGBT nongovernmental organizations (NGO), such as the Queer Bulgaria Foundation and the Bilitis Lesbian and Bi-women Resource Center, work predominantly in the capital. Queer meeting places and commercial infrastructures exist only in a few cities besides Sofia, such as Varna, Plovdiv, and Bourgas. Outward LGBT identification happens only in **urban** centers because they allow for greater anonymity and noncompliance with traditional norms. Family and social pressure in the smaller towns and **rural** areas contribute to urban migration.

Peer support for LGBT adolescents remains weak due to the difficulty of the Bulgarian LGBT community to organize. Despite availability of international assistance and funding after 1990, lesbian and gay **activism** did not reach many people and inspire a strong movement. The lack of open **discrimination** and **harassment** combined with a social standard allowing for considerable sexual freedom as long it is secretly consumed is the probable explanation of this reluctance to form self-support structures. For more than ten years after 1990, there was only one NGO officially registered as a gay organization. The Bulgarian Gay Organization, Gemini, experienced considerable difficulties in attracting and retaining members. The formalization of other openly identified LGBT organizations is a fairly recent phenomenon, whose impact on the LGBT community is yet to be seen.

There are promising recent developments which will eventually improve the situation of LGBT youth. Queer Bulgaria Foundation supports initiatives promoting the diversity of sexual identities in mass culture. One example is the youth campaign, Izrazi se ("Express Yourself"). Organized by the Club of Young Journalists, it consists of a series of performances fostering youth's freedom of expression. Other pending projects of Queer Bulgaria aim to increase the sensitivity of medial workers and school personnel to the specific needs of LGBT youth. Bilitis Lesbian and Bi-Women Resource Center, paying special attention to the needs of young lesbian and bisexual women, works at the grassroots level to start self-support groups, **sports** clubs, and libraries of lesbian **literature**. Finally, the Bulgarian Gay Organization Gemini hosted the annual conference of the International Lesbian and Gay Youth Organization (IGLYO) in 2004, which generated useful ideas for future activities targeting LGBT youth in Bulgaria. Transgender youth, however, are still underrepresented in these organizations, and there is no organization dedicated specifically to transgender Bulgarians.

Ursula began as a club dancer in 1996 at the age of 16. She is widely known throughout Bulgaria, appearing on popular TV shows as well as popular web sites like www.dir.bg. © Ursula

Military service is compulsory for eighteen-year-old males. Although gay men may serve, they can also skip military service by disclosing their **sexual orientation** to the recruiting commission. Military psychologists still consider gay men "inapt for military service," according to an outdated medical standard no longer accepted by civilian doctors. The new antidiscrimination law, which includes sexual orientation, gives special attention to preventing discrimination at the **workplace** and within educational institutions. In practice, institutions which are most unprepared to prevent **bullying** of LGBT youth are schools, the military, and youth penitentiary institutions. Here, bullying can take place without any consequences for the offender. In most cases the psychological and physical abuse happens in secrecy and the victim is unwilling to report it, fearing escalation of the torture or public disgrace. The issue of harassment of young gay males in the army was made public in 2002, when a young cross-dresser appeared in the popular television show "Iskrenno i lichno" (Sincere and Private) to tell his story. He had deserted the obligatory military service and was hiding from the military police for six months to avoid the verbal and physical abuse that he had been subjected to in the military.

Education is highly valued in Bulgaria and parents do their best to keep their children in school as long as possible. School is the place where the majority of adolescents spend most of their time, with the exception of Roma youth who usually leave school at about age fifteen or earlier to start work or get married. The Bulgarian education system seems to be a much more slowly liberalizing sphere compared to the mass media and the legal system. The state-approved core **curriculum** does not provide any information concerning sexual identities. An exception was an NGO-piloted alternative civic education program for secondary school students, which contained some, though very meager, analysis of **sexual identity**. These were implemented only at a few schools and continued only as long as the international funding lasted. Human sexuality is still discussed only within the natural sciences or in relation to sexually transmitted diseases. The psychological **counseling** services, which every school offers to students, are not adjusted to accommodate the needs of LGBT youth. Further, peer isolation and ridicule of more effeminate teenage boys is common. Schools are obliged to adopt internal regulations that prohibit harassment and bullying, but these do not effectively prevent the occurrence of incidents. The increased rate of violence in society negatively affects the behavior of young people and LGBT youth are among the most common targets of harassment at school.

Higher education institutions in Bulgaria have more freedom and autonomy with respect to curriculum development than secondary schools. The social aspects of sexuality are discussed today within **psychology** and anthropology at the New Bulgarian University and in gender studies at Sofia University. At the same time, homosexuality is classified as a mental disorder in outdated psychiatry textbooks, some of which are still being used by medical students. There are no services and support groups for LGBT **college students**.

In the absence of **educational policies** and guidelines about whether or how the concept of sexual identities should be introduced at school, it is largely based on the teacher's belief system. Educators are generally unprepared to acknowledge and discuss sexual identities. Teacher training programs do not include any information about the needs of LGBT students and there are no openly LGBT **teachers** in the primary and secondary schools. Thus, many of the schools' heterosexual "rites of passage" such as classroom romances, coupled to the absence of knowledgeable and supportive adults, LGBT role models, and a heteronormative curriculum, negatively affect the socialization of young LGBT people and make it more difficult to come out.

Lack of public role models who are "out" is another disadvantage for LGBT youth. Popular Bulgarian television stars and singers, whose sexual orientation is a public secret, argue that sexuality is a personal matter. Recently teenage lesbian relationships received huge attention due to the music video clips of the Russian teen duo "tATu," which topped the charts on MTV as well as on Bulgarian television. Their performances in Bulgaria inspired many teenagers to live their lives as they choose. Although standards of masculinity still dominate self-identification and relationships for men, a higher degree of intimacy between teenage girls has always been considered allowable as part of the preparation for intimate relationships with men. This, however, discourages the continuation of such relationships after entering adulthood.

Although ridiculed at school, young cross-dressers are very popular in the artistic circles and have become the most visible part of the LGBT community, topping the hierarchy (Brooks 2000). Transvestites have gained recognition for their aesthetic tastes and fashion in the mainstream culture, and it is not uncommon for wealthy businessmen and political leaders to choose entertainment places where drag is performed. Although they can afford to cross-dress in public, many trans youth are not out to their family.

Parental pressure is a concern since most young people in Bulgaria live with their parents until marriage, which occurs after age twenty-five for those attending universities and somewhat earlier for those who work after high school. Leading a double life is the most common way of avoiding conflicts at home. Even LGBT people, who are "out" at work and among heterosexual friends, seldom disclose their sexuality to their family. Fake marriages are still a common way of avoiding suspicion. Though nonconforming lifestyles are today considered allowable during **adolescence**, many LGBT people discard them when they enter adulthood and start a career.

Conflicts with nonunderstanding parents are a common concern for LGBT youth that often results in self-destructive behavior. The challenges that these youth face often lead to general dissatisfaction with life and to suicide attempts, although there is no **research** in Bulgaria about their frequency of occurrence. When the joint **suicide** of two teenage girls from the town of Pleven, in the summer of 2003, was reported by the mass media, sexual orientation was not suggested as a possible reason, although one of the girls had left **poetry** featuring her desired female lover.

Risky sexual behavior and **substance abuse** are not unusual among LGBT youth in Bulgaria, though their rate in this specific group has not been researched. Similarly to other postcommunist countries, Bulgaria experienced a rise of HIV infection and drug addiction in recent years. **HIV education** programs, implemented by the Bulgarian Gay Organization Gemini, primarily addresses gay men, not encompassing other segments of the LGBT population.

Bibliography

Ammon, Richard. 2003. "Gay Bulgaria." Accessed July 30, 2004. http://www.globalgayz.com/g-bulgaria.html.

Brooks, Robin S. 2000. "Cross-Dressing in Bulgaria: Gay-Identity, Post-Communist Fear, and Magical Love." *Bad Subjects* no. 50. Accessed May 26, 2005. http://eserver.org/bs/50/brooks.html.

Pisankaneva, Monika. 2002. "Reflections on Butch-Femme and the Emerging Lesbian Community in Bulgaria." Pp. 135–145 in *Femme/Butch: New Considerations of the Way We Want to Go*. Edited by Michelle Gibson and Deborah T. Meem. Binghamton, NY: Harrington Park Press.

Web Sites

Bulgarian Lesbian Community Site. August 2004. Patricia Vassileva-Elia. Accessed May 26, 2005. http://www.bg-lesbian.com. FAQs, news, lesbian profiles, photo gallery, articles, forums, culture information.

Queer Bulgaria Foundation. August 2004. Accessed May 26, 2005. http://www.queer-bulgaria.org. Analysis of the situation of LGBT people in Bulgaria.

Bullying

Pamela K. Autrey

Bullying is a long-term relationship built on escalating acts of repeated aggression performed by a more powerful subject against a victim who is somehow helpless and which is intended to harm. Possible victims of sexual bullying are those who violate heterosexual expectations or do not perform according to conventional gender norms. Bullying differs from other forms of **harassment** in schools because the conditions for its emergence are the organizational structures and hidden **curriculum** of middle and high schools which promote heterosexuality and seldom police antigay harassment. **Lesbian, gay, bisexual, transgender,** and questioning (LGBTQ) youth cross all racial, cultural and subcultural groups, and socioeconomic levels, yet little is known about how these youth manage bullying. Mainstream articles are largely silent on the intersection of sexuality with bullying and ignore the further impact of **sexism**, classism, and **racism** on bullying (Jiwani et al. 1999).

The **school climate** is important not only in the development of academic and occupational skills, but also the personal and social skills that shape the first twenty years of life. However, schools and educators are typically ill-equipped to meet the needs of sexual minority youth. LGBTQ students often enter middle schools without familial or institutional supports, without access to informal peer social groups, unsure of spiritual support, and often without supportive **educational policies,** curricula, or faculty. Gay and lesbian issues and people remain largely invisible, particularly in primary through secondary schools where same-sex lives are underrepresented in curricula, teachers remain silent about same-sex sexuality, and many sexual minority teachers remain in the closet. A study on the development of adult **homophobia** found patterns of **prejudice** were established during **adolescence** (Baker and Fishbein 1998). Researchers have concluded that victims *and* bullies are at-risk for maladjustment in their adult lives (French et al. 1998). Policies, therefore, that are enforced and that explicitly prohibit bullying on the basis of **sexual orientation** or **gender identity** are important for both victims and victimizers.

Two major categories of bullying are overt or direct aggression, and covert or indirect aggression; males prefer the former and females the latter. Overt aggression is verbal and physical harassment or abuse in public situations with nonintimate peers; covert aggression involves a panoply of secret strategies, such as rumor-spreading, designed to stigmatize and, therefore, isolate, victims from social groups.

See also Antidiscrimination Policy; Legal Issues, Students; Mental Health; Sexual Abuse and Assault; Sexual Harassment; Workplace Issues; Youth, At-Risk; Youth, Homeless.

The preference for covert forms of bullying by females is seen as early as preschool (Pellegrini and Long 2002). Males typically show greater intolerance toward gender nonconformity than females, and victims of overt bullying are predominantly male (Taywaditep 2001).

It has been suggested that males, with their gender privilege, have much more to lose in a patriarchal culture and become threatened when heteronormative boundaries are crossed (Baker and Fishbein 1998). Masculinity is an asset highly valued by both males and females and gender-nonconforming youth are the most vulnerable to victimization by a bully (Taywaditep 2001). In the United States, lesbians are victimized for violating imperatives to be subordinate to men, and gay youth for being effeminate (Human Rights Watch 2001).

Middle school **administrators** sometimes police these boundaries and often ignore the importance of the construction of **sexual identity** for young adolescents, as expectations of **gender role** conformity intensify during this time. Two ninth-grade girls, for example, were approached by five middle-school boys who called them "**queer**," "faggots," and "dykes" and began to harass them sexually by rubbing against them and making sexually explicit suggestions (Safe Schools Coalition 2004 Web site). While the girls did not identify as lesbians, they were both vocal about standing up for gay rights in the junior high school they attended. At another middle school, a young male gave an account of his victimization in a game called "Smear the Queer"—played out while students were in class (Safe Schools Coalition). When the incident turned physical and he fought back, this boy was the only one suspended.

Bullying generally is subtler in areas under the direct supervision of faculty. Savin-Williams (1994) found that many LGBTQ youth are indirectly victimized through social commentary among their peer group, including cruel references, jokes, and name-calling. In one study that found that youth may hear more than two dozen antigay comments each day in school, it also found that, when teachers hear these remarks, they fail to respond to them 97 percent of the time (Callahan 2001).

Bullying, however, often occurs outside of the classroom or in space more directly controlled by students. Playgrounds are *gender schools* where isolation means stigmatization (Taywaditep 2001). Olweus (1993) measured this hidden form through responses to a survey item—"being alone at break time." Although a British study challenged this item as too broad, it also found most isolation occurs on the playground and more often than not indicates victims of indirect bullying (Rivers and Smith 1994).

Stigmatization works by targeting victims not because of *who* they are but rather for *what* they are. The cleverness of the bully lies in his or her choice of a victim who exhibits "any nonheterosexual form of behavior, identity, relationship, or community" and using these behaviors to create cultural capital (Herek 1992, 89). Young adolescents are particularly at risk for sexual bullying due to perceived or actual sexual orientation (Duncan 1999). This bullying can begin as verbal aggression but, because it is a long-term relationship, the aggression tends to escalate.

Bully and victim have a relationship that is public but also personal. Like any long-term relationship, the bully and victim know each other in a unique way and, though motivated by homophobia, the pairing of the bully and the victim sometimes has a homoerotic dimension. Sexual bullying reinforces **heterosexism** and the masculinity of the bully, while it resists authorities' efforts at containment of sexuality. Bullying also contributes to a gender identity hierarchy. The emergence of gay masculinity has been marked by antieffeminacy prejudice within gay communities and there is the possibility this parallels the sex typing and gender schema of the larger society in which females and femininity are devalued. While bullying requires three actors—the bully, the victim, and the bystander—the extreme and violent defamation of the victim by the bully gives the bully power over the victim. For heterosexual males, this show of sexual power reinforces the heterosexist and patriarchal right to such power—over heterosexual girls and more satisfyingly, because the victim is male, over gay youth.

Bullying, on the basis of perceived sexual orientation or gender nonconformity, is a human rights issue. Human Rights Watch (2001) issued the findings of a two-year study, concluding that gay students endure verbal harassment on a daily basis and, when teachers and administrators fail to intervene, verbal abuse often turns physical. A study of over 230,000 seventh through twelfth grade California students found 7.5 percent of all students reported being bullied on the basis of sexual orientation (California Safe Schools Coalition & 4-H Center for Youth Development 2004). Transgender youth may be particularly vulnerable to bullying by both their peers and adults and yet there is no definitive data on the prevalence of people who identify as transgender.

This hostile environment has significant educational and social implications. Although adults most often attempt suicide during January, for LGB youth it is September—the beginning of the school year (Oregon Department of Human Resources 1998). Further, a comparison of homosexual and heterosexual adolescents who are homeless found that LGBT youth leave home more often than their heterosexual counterparts and face the same heightened risk for victimization on the street as they do in schools, suggesting the generalization of victimhood to other life situations (Cochran et al. 2002). The harassment and violence experienced by LGBTQ youth in schools make them twice as likely to have skipped school because of fear, 1.5 times more likely to report being in a physical fight at school, twice as likely to have been threatened or injured with a weapon, and 1.5 times more likely to have carried a weapon at school in the thirty days prior to the survey (DuRant, Krowchuk, and Sinal 1998; Faulkner and Cranston 1998).

Intersections with race, gender, and socioeconomic status produce heightened risks for victimization because of a compounding effect (Jiwani et al. 1999). Compared to 1 percent of their heterosexual counterparts, 10 percent of the lesbian, bisexual, or questioning females in one study were victimized 10 or more times in the preceding year, and 23 percent of lesbian and bisexual girls indicated that their peers had attempted to hurt them in a sexual way, compared to 6 percent of their heterosexual counterparts (Bontempo and D'Augelli 2002). Forty-eight percent of the LGBT youth of color surveyed in one study experienced verbal harassment based on *both* their sexual orientation and their race/ethnicity (Kosciw and Cullen 2003). Ninety percent of self-identified transgender youth reported feeling unsafe in their school because of their gender, as compared to less than half of male (46 percent) or female (41 percent) students in the same study (Kosciw and Cullen 2003).

Research has emerged on suicide that examines the experiences of sexual minorities in their school contexts, including bullying and harassment. An analysis of Oregon's 1997 **Youth Risk Behavior Survey** (Oregon Department of Human Resources 1998) found boys harassed because of perceived sexual orientation in the thirty days prior to the survey to be six times more like to commit **suicide**. A comparison with heterosexual counterparts, based on Massachusetts' 1995 Youth Risk Behavior Survey data, found LGB youth more than three times as likely to have attempted suicide in the preceding twelve months, nearly five times as likely to have missed school because of fear about their **school safety**, and four times as likely to have been threatened with a weapon at school (Garofalo et al. 1998).

The two national teachers' unions and a gay rights organization have urged the United States Department of Education to step up its enforcement of laws aimed at such abuse, but only eight states have laws that forbid **discrimination** on the grounds of sexual orientation: Connecticut, Massachusetts, Vermont, Washington, Wisconsin, and three others—California, Minnesota, and New Jersey—that also offer protections based on gender identity and expression (Browman 2001). There is no federal law aimed specifically at protecting homosexual students.

Increasing the visibility of sexual minority youth can alter the sociopolitical climate of schools, resulting in an increased acceptance (Jordan 2000). **Gay–straight alliances** and similar support groups, events such as **National Coming Out Day** and the **Day of Silence** together with supportive **allies** and the enforcement of anti-harassment school policies can ameliorate LGBTQ youth's sense of alienation while challenging **heteronormativity**.

Bibliography

Baker, Janet G., and Harold D. Fishbein. 1998. "The Development of Prejudice towards Gays and Lesbians by Adolescents." *Journal of Homosexuality* 36, no. 1: 89–100.

Bontempo, Daniel E., and Anthony R. D'Augelli. 2002. "Effects of At-School Victimization and Sexual Orientation on Lesbian, Gay, or Bisexual Youths' Health Risk Behavior." *Journal of Adolescent Health* 30: 364–374.

Browman, Darcia Harris. 2001. "Report Says Schools Ignore Harassment of Gay Students." *Education Week* 20, no. 39: 5.

Brown, Brett V., and Sharon Bzostek. 2003. "Violence in the Lives of Children." *Cross Currents 1*. Accessed December 5, 2004. http://childtrendsdatabank.org/.

California Safe Schools Coalition and 4-H Center for Youth Development. 2004. *Safe Place to Learn: Consequences of Harassment Based on Actual or Perceived Sexual Orientation and Gender Nonconformity and Steps for Making Schools Safer*. Accessed July 8, 2004. http://www.casafeschools.org/SafePlacetoLearnLow.pdf.

Callahan, C. J. 2001. "Protecting and Counseling Gay and Lesbian Students." *Journal of Humanistic Counseling, Education & Development* 40, no. 1: 5–10.

Cochran, Bryan N., Angela J. Stewart, Joshua A. Ginzler, and Ana Mari Cauce. 2002. "Challenges Faced by Homeless Sexual Minorities: Comparison of Gay, Lesbian, Bisexual, and Transgender Homeless Adolescents With Their Heterosexual Counterparts." *American Journal of Public Health* 92, no. 5: 773–777.

Duncan, Neil. 1999. *Sexual Bullying: Gender Conflict and Pupil Culture*. New York: Routledge.

DuRant, Robert H., Daniel P. Krowchuk, and Sara H. Sinal. 1998. "Victimization, Use of Violence, and Drug Use at School among Male Adolescents Who Engage in Same-Sex Sexual Behavior." *Journal of Pediatrics* 133, no. 1: 113–118.

Faulkner, Anne H., and Kevin Cranston. 1998. "Correlates of Same-Sex Sexual Behavior in a Random Sample of Massachusetts High School Students." *American Journal of Public Health* 88, no. 2: 262–266.

French, Simone, Mary Story, Michael D. Resnick, Gary Remafedi, and Robert Blum. 1998. "The Relationship between Suicide Risk and Sexual Orientation: Results of a Population-Based Study." *American Journal of Public Health* 88, no. 1: 57–63.

Garofalo, Robert, R. Cameron Wolf, Shari Kessel, Judith Palfrey, and Robert H. DuRant. 1998. "The Association between Health Risk Behaviors and Sexual Orientation among a School-Based Sample of Adolescents." *Pediatrics* 101, no. 5: 895–902.

Henning-Stout, Mary, Steve James, Samantha Macintosh. 2000. "Reducing Harassment of Lesbian, Gay, Bisexual, Transgender, and Questioning Youth in Schools." *School Psychology Review* 29, no. 2: 180–191.

Herek, Gregory M. 1992. "The Social Context of Hate Crimes: Notes on Cultural Heterosexism." Pp. 89–104 in *Hate Crimes: Confronting Violence Against Lesbians and Gay Men*, Edited by Gregory M. Herek, and Kevin T. Berrill. Newbury Park, CA: Sage Publications.

Human Rights Watch. 2001. *Hatred in the Hallways: Violence and Discrimination Against Lesbian, Gay, Bisexual, and Transgender Students in U.S. Schools*. Accessed August 21, 2004. http://hrw.org/reports/2001/uslgbt.

Jiwani, Yasmin, Kelly Gorkoff, Helene Berman, Gail Taylor, Glenda Vardy-Dell, Muriel McQueen Fergusson. 1999. "Violence Prevention and the Girl Child: Phase One Report." Alliance of Five Research Centres on Violence. Accessed September 19, 2004. http://www.harbour.sfu.ca/freda/reports.

Jordan, Karen M. 2000. "Substance Abuse among Gay, Lesbian, Bisexual, Transgender and Questioning Adolescents." *School Psychology Review* 29, no. 2: 201–206.

Kosciw, Joseph, and M. K. Cullen. 2003. *The GLSEN 2001 National School Climate Survey: The School-Related Experiences of Our Nation's Lesbian, Gay, Bisexual, and Transgender Youth*. New York: Gay, Lesbian, and Straight Education Network.

Nansel, Tanja R., Mary Overpeck, Ramani S. Pilla, W. June Ruan, Bruce Simons-Morton, and Peter Scheidt. 2001. "Bullying Behaviors among US Youth: Prevalence and Association with Psychosocial Adjustment." *The Journal of the American Medical Association* 285, no. 16:1–16.

Olweus, Daniel. 1993. *Bullying at School: What We Know and What We Can Do*. Oxford, England: Blackwell.

Oregon Department of Human Resources. 1998. *Suicidal Behavior: A Survey of Oregon High School Students 1997* (prepared by David Hopkins). Portland: Author.

Pellegrini, Anthony D., and Jeffrey D. Long. 2002. "A Longitudinal Study of Bullying, Dominance, and Victimization during the Transition from Primary School Through Secondary School." *British Journal of Developmental Psychology* 20, no. 2: 259–280.

Rivers, Ian, and Peter K. Smith. 1994. "Types of Bullying Behavior and Their Correlates." *Aggressive Behavior* 20: 359–368.

Savin-Williams, Ritch. 1994. "Verbal and Physical Abuse as Stressors in the Lives of Lesbian, Gay Male, and Bisexual Youths: Associations with School Problems, Running Away, Substance Abuse, Prostitution, and Suicide." *Journal of Consulting and Clinical Psychology* 62: 261–269.

Solberg, Mona E., and Dan Olweus. 2003. "Prevalence Estimation of School Bullying with the Olweus Bully/Victim Questionnaire." *Aggressive Behavior* 29, no. 3: 239–268.

Taywaditep, Kittiwut Jod. 2001. "Marginalization among the Marginalized: Gay Men's Anti-Effeminacy Attitudes." *Journal of Homosexuality* 42, no. 1: 1–28.

Walton, Gerald. 2003. "Bullying and Homophobia in Canadian Schools: The Politics of Policies, Programs, and Educational Leadership." *Journal of Gay and Lesbian Issues in Education* 1, no. 4: 23–36.

Web Sites

The Empower Program. January 2004. Accessed January, 16, 2004. http://www. empowered.org/svpi.htm. This site, particularly aimed at empowering adolescent females, expands the definition of violence to include root causes such as cliques, gossip, harassment, and bullying.

The National Center for Victims of Crime. November 2004. Accessed December 6, 2004. http://www.ncvc.org. Assistance on violence against gays and lesbians, including reports of homophobic violence.

The National Latino/a Lesbian, Gay, Bisexual & Transgender Organization. October 2004. Accessed December 6, 2004. http://www.llego.org. Devoted to representing Latino/a LGBT communities and addressing their growing needs regarding social issues ranging from civil rights and social justice to health and human services.

Parents, Families and Friends of Lesbian, Gay, Bisexual and Transgendered Persons. 2004. Accessed December 6, 2004. http://www.pflag.org. In 2000, this organization launched a multiyear project, "From Our Home to the Schoolhome" safe schools campaign, because it recognizes schools as the "ground zero" of homophobia in the United States.

The Safe Schools Coalition. December 2004. Accessed December 6, 2004. http://www. safeschoolscoalition.org/. There are 111 stories of antigay harassment and violence in elementary, middle school, and high schools collected by the Coalition in the 1990s, which provide a rich resource for the different forms LGBT bullying takes.

Butler, Judith (1956–)

Mary Lou Rasmussen

Judith Butler is the Chancellor's Professor of Comparative Literature and Rhetoric at the University of California, Berkeley. Butler received her B.A. and Ph.D. in philosophy from Yale University, but she was first exposed to philosophy at her hometown synagogue in Cleveland. Butler, who is considered one of the principal figures in **queer theory**, has written extensively on questions of **identity politics**, gender, and sexuality. Drawing on a dense mix of philosophy, postmodernism, and feminism, her most influential contribution in this area of scholarship is her book *Gender Trouble*. For Butler, sex (male, female), gender (masculine, feminine), and sexuality (lesbian, gay, bisexual, heterosexual) are not fixed, nor are they dependent upon one another. The ideas formulated by Judith Butler are especially relevant to those working with young people on **lesbian, gay, bisexual**, and **transgender** (LGBT) issues because they provide one mechanism by which people can challenge fixed ideas about identity; ideas that can inadvertently contribute to young people's disengagement from schooling.

According to Butler, sex does not equal gender or **desire**. A female may perform a masculine **gender identity** yet engage in sexual relations with men and women. This is not to argue that people may assume any sex, gender, or desire they choose on any given morning, but rather to emphasize the "regulatory fictions" that exist within society in order to reinforce the interests of various power regimes.

An example Butler uses to illustrate the operation of these "regulatory fictions" is the power of specific speech acts to have meaning in specific cultural contexts. For instance, the act of pronouncing a couple man and wife undeniably has power as a "regulatory fiction"; it is a speech act recognized by the law, and it has cultural and religious significance as well. However, the power of this "regulatory fiction"

See also Communication; Foucault, Michel; Lacan, Jacques; Poststructuralism; Queer Pedagogy; Queer Studies.

changes according to the context. When children act out the wedding ceremony in play, or when we see it on television, we do not assume that the words uttered have the same meaning as they do when they are uttered by a Catholic priest standing at the altar. Similarly, the words will have a different effect if the same priest standing in front of a same-sex couple utters them because the **Catholic** Church doesn't recognize same-sex marriages. In short, these "regulatory fictions" are hard to pin down because they are constantly shifting as they are challenged, parodied, resisted, and reinscribed.

Butler's notion of performativity makes it possible to see how struggles related to "regulatory fictions" are not specifically related to individuals, but to techniques of power that endeavor to control or classify individuals through specific discourses. It doesn't make sense to declare that you are "gay" unless there is some broader understanding about what "gayness" refers to as an identity category. Relatedly, it is possible to see how "regulatory fictions" relating to **native/indigenous** people have changed markedly throughout the course of the twentieth century, often according to racist systems of classification devised by colonial powers. Looking back, it is possible to see how these "regulatory fictions" can be used to rationalize and reinforce discrimination.

Although these labels may come to be seen as "real," it is precisely because they are constituted through processes of repetition that disruption of these labels can occur. Education is potentially an important institutional site for engaging in such disruption, although it has generally been employed to maintain the illusion of these "regulatory fictions."

Essentializing identity categories abound in education, such as when people predicate tolerance on the possession of innate characteristics (race, gender), setting up boundaries about who is and is not worthy of protection. Thus, **sexual identity** issues and LGBT persons may be excluded from **multicultural education** because it is thought to reflect "a lifestyle" or choice rather than an immutable human trait. It is a "regulatory fiction" that racial and gender identities are fundamental. Where does this leave people who adopt gender and sexual identities that aren't perceived as somehow fundamental? Whose identities are defined as illegitimate or somehow deviant? And, whose business does it become to determine which identities are worthy of protection?

Butler acknowledges the political necessity of laying claim to terms such as "women," "queer," "gay," and "lesbian." There is no doubt that deploying these terms can be a valuable strategy within educational contexts. But it is necessary to ask who is represented by the use of identity terms and who is excluded? For instance, schools might endeavor to focus on the perceived needs of gay and lesbian youth while, simultaneously, heterosexual youth remain unmarked, and those who are transgender or resist an either/or label are ignored. Such practices may provide useful support to gay and lesbian students, but they also demonstrate the pervasiveness of normative notions of sexuality within educational contexts.

How might it be possible to support young people who are exploring their sexual and gender identifications without asking them to label themselves in a particular way? Drawing on Butler, we may be mindful of essentialist school support programs, such as **gay–straight alliances** and **Project 10**, that are identity-based because they may present impossible conflicts between racial, ethnic, or religious affiliation, and sexual politics. As an alternative, students and teachers might turn their focus to developing alliances that were based on protecting human rights, rather than gay rights, or Jewish rights, or the rights of people with disabilities. In the absence of such a system a students might, conceivably, find themselves having to choose between identity groups.

It is also useful to consider those school practices and **educational policies** which reinscribe specific gender and sexual identities while erasing others from view. For example, unisex bathrooms are rarely at the forefront of struggles for equality in schools, yet for some students access to such facilities within the school can provide respite from frequent **harassment** in sex specific toilets and changing rooms. In these ways we can draw on Butler's concept of "performativity" to construct alternative practices and policies which disrupt essentialist understanding of identity.

Performativity is one means whereby we can also analyze the relationships queer youth form with themselves, their peers, and their teachers, perhaps explaining why gay–straight alliances are less likely to attract students of color. It provides a structure for questioning how members of school communities are implicated in the negotiation of "truths." Butler helps us to map the chains of signification that lead from students being called "poofter" or "dyke" to students believing that they are abnormal or deficient and in need of help.

Using Butler, these powerful chains can be disrupted as teachers and students make more strategic use of powerful identity terms such as "lesbian," "gay," "queer," and "straight." At best, she offers us more say in defining who we are, and recognizes that the labels we use to describe ourselves, within and outside the school, are not fixed. Butler also helps us to recognize the significance of labels; they can wound, but they can also be politically useful, playful and offer comfort.

Bibliography

Butler, Judith. 1990. *Gender Trouble: Feminism and the Subversion of Identity*, New York: Routledge.
———. 1993. *Bodies that Matter: On the Discursive Limits of "Sex."* New York: Routledge.
———. 1994. "Gender as Performance." *Radical Philosophy* 67 (Summer): 32–39.
———. 1997a. "Critically Queer." Pp. 11–29 in *Playing with Fire: Queer Politics, Queer Theories*. Edited by Shane Phelan. New York: Routledge.
———. 1997b. *Excitable Speech: A Politics of the Performative*. New York: Routledge.
———. 1999. *Gender Trouble: Feminism and the Subversion of Identity*. New York: Routledge.
Failler, Angela. 2001. "Excitable Speech: Judith Butler, Mae West and Sexual Innuendo." *International Journal of Sexuality and Gender Studies* 6, nos. 1/2: 49–62.
Salih, Sara. 2002. *Judith Butler*. New York: Routledge.
Rasmussen, Mary Lou, and Valerie Harwood. 2003. "Performativity, Youth, and Injurious Speech." *Teaching Education Journal* 14, no. 1: 25–36.

Web Sites

Judith Butler. 2001. David Gauntlett. Accessed December 15, 2004. http://www.theory. org.uk/ctr-butl.htm. Provides a great introduction to some key theorists that inform studies of culture and identity, including Butler.
Judith Butler: A Bibliography. 2001. Eddie Yeghiayan. Accessed December 15, 2004. http://sun3.lib.uci.edu/%7Escctr/Wellek/butler/. A comprehensive list of Butler's works.

C

Camp

Elizabeth Whitney

Camp is an integral part of contemporary **lesbian, gay, bisexual,** and **transgender youth culture** because it is a means of revealing the façade of seemingly sedimented **gender roles** through exaggerated performances. Camp has been particularly equated with gay males, although some lesbian researchers have argued that many women have also engaged in camp behaviors (Davy 1995; Halberstam 1998; Robertson 1996), and it continues to be important for queer youth who wish to explore the rich history of camp. Camp performance, in particular, is marked by excessive gesture and imagery. It is always purposefully "big" and "over the top," and this purposeful exaggeration of subject matter calls attention to the shaky structure of that which is being imitated. Thus, camp has the power to challenge the notion of gender performance as an imitation and suggests instead that there is no original. Camp performance also employs the logic of failure; that is, camp performances must fail or be in some way transparent in order to successfully display the artificiality of that from which they draw. LGBT youth demonstrate an increasing interest in exploring historical meanings of camp by pushing boundaries of gender identification through both staged performance and in everyday life.

Chicago Kings, Gay Pride Parade, Chicago, 2003. © Spencer

Having been a leading signifier of "gay" performance throughout the twentieth century, camp has been a subject of intense interest for many queer theorists, who are interested in the possibilities that camp offers to examine gender as a social construction. Moe Meyer (1995, 265) suggests that the term "camp" first appeared in *Passing English of the Victorian Era*, J. Redding Ware's 1909 dictionary of Victorian slang. Here, camp was defined as "actions and gestures of exaggerated emphasis. Probably from the French. Used chiefly by persons of exceptional want of character." The concept of excessive and exaggerated behaviors, when engaged in by gay men—for example, a limp wrist, a noticeable lisp, or swaying hips—led to the equation of camp with homosexuality, resulting in the idea that homosexuals "camp it up." Camp was formally introduced into Western popular culture in 1964, when Susan Sontag displaced the concept of camp from a generalized gay male body and repositioned it in her essay about urban style. Suddenly, to be camp was to be chic.

While camp does indeed exist in forms that vary from garage sale art to stylized staged performances of gender, such as performances of masculinity by drag kings, for most consumers drag queens are the most accessible prototype of camp in popular culture. **Film**s like *The Birdcage* (USA 1996) and *Priscilla: Queen of the Desert*

See also Cross-Dressing; Gender Identity; Popular Culture; Queer and Queer Theory; Sissy Boy; Tomboy; Stereotypes.

(Australia 1994) exemplify not only drag queen camp, but also signify its growing presence in mainstream media. Drag queen camp is a marker of our cultural acknowledgment of the artificiality of gender, as well as a marker of gender essentialism: If gendered behaviors weren't believed to be particular to biological sex, male bodies parading as female bodies wouldn't be such a point of interest and humor in popular culture. And, drag queen camp is perhaps the most recognizable form of camp in queer culture—a form that is steadily migrating into mainstream heterosexual culture.

In addition to being recognizable, for many LGBT youth, drag performance is an accessible means of exploring the rich history of camp. Youth Unlimited (http://www.youth-unlimited.org.), for example, is an Iowa-based group run by and for youth that offers drag pageants and a drag summer camp (both male and female impersonation)—an ironic double play on the concept of camping it up. While drag performance has been given the most mainstream attention when it is done by drag queens—biological men who perform as women—it also has an important place in history as performed by drag kings—biological women who perform as men. It is important to note that some scholars (e.g., Davy 1995; Halberstam 1998) argue that drag kings are not necessarily performance camp, but rather, are recuperating masculinity in a unique way. And in fact, drag is not limited to such binaries; drag is an exemplar of camp performance because it allows the performer to play with gender in imaginative ways beyond male/female binaries— for example, in the film, *Hedwig and the Angry Inch* (USA 2001).

Because camp's historical presence lies in its coded nature, what possibilities for subversion does camp continue to offer? In the past, many LGBT individuals used camp as a means of coding their actions, only recognizable to those "in the know." As LGBTQ communities have become more visible and continue to make political gains, camp will inevitably continue to develop different implications from its original meaning. Though **discrimination** against LGBT individuals is by no means ended, contemporary youth have infinitely more opportunities for support than were available even twenty years ago. It is important to ask, then, in what ways are today's queer youth employing camp as either a heuristic or a performance style? Which is to say, what aspects of dominant culture are youth reappropriating in subversive and coded ways?

Cultural trends popular especially with youth, might include "grrrl power (feminist reclaiming of "girl" as a pejorative term for women)," "knitting (feminist reclaiming of knitting as "women's work")," and "boi culture ("boyish" gay males or females with "boyish" presentation)." However, capitalist marketing precludes any of these from being too coded. It is difficult to argue that something is intended as camp, for instance, when it can initially be bought in the form of a T-shirt. However, camp as a heuristic is always readily available, and as LGBT communities continue to merge with heterosexual mainstream cultures, camp, as well, becomes less coded and more available for use by anyone who wants to be in on the wink.

Bibliography

Butler, Judith. 1989. *Gender Trouble: Feminism and Subversion of Identity*. New York: Routledge.

Case, Sue-Ellen. 1989. "Toward a Butch-Femme Aesthetic." Pp. 282–299 in *Making a Spectacle: Feminist Essays on Contemporary Women's Theatre*. Edited by Lynda Hart. Ann Arbor: University of Michigan Press.

Cleto, Fabio. 1999. *Camp: Queer Aesthetics and the Performing Subject a Reader*. Ann Arbor: University of Michigan Press.

Davy, Kate. 1995. "Fe/male Impersonation: The Discourse of Camp." Pp. 231–247 in *Critical Theory and Performance*. Edited by Janelle G. Reineldt and Joseph R. Roach. Ann Arbor: University of Michigan Press.

Halberstam, Judith. 1998. *Female Masculinity*. Durham, NC: Duke University Press.

Meyer, Moe. 1995. "The Signifying Invert: Camp and the Performance of Nineteenth Century Sexology." *Text and Performance Quarterly* 15: 265–281.

Robertson, Pamela. 1996. *Guilty Pleasures: Feminist Camp from Mae West to Madonna*. Durham, NC: Duke University Press.

Russo, Vito. 1987. *The Celluloid Closet: Homosexuality in the Movies*. New York: Harper and Row.

Sontag, Susan. 1990. *Against Interpretation*. Garden City, NY: Anchor Books.

Canada, HIV/AIDS Education in

Francisco Ibáñez-Carrasco

In Canada, since the early 1980s, the implementation of HIV/AIDS education has been sporadic. Most educational efforts have been attached to primary prevention interventions and recently to more complex understandings of the social determinants of the biomedical epidemic such as social status, **sexual orientation, gender identity, race,** and **ethnicity**. For youth, in general, it is important to understand that HIV/AIDS prevention works well when embedded within a larger context of health education that includes physical and psychosocial issues. For **lesbian, gay, bisexual, transgender,** and questioning youth (LGBTQ), in particular, HIV/AIDS education and health education must be placed within a historical context of political and human rights issues. So far, teachers and researchers in Canada's formal educational system have given insufficient attention to this necessary conceptualization. In contrast, **AIDS** service organizations, out of sheer necessity, have included these issues in their programming and policy. Yet, a great deal of the focus lies on young men who have sex with men (MSM) in detriment of the social, sexual, and health conditions of bisexual, lesbian, queer, or questioning young women.

Out of 18,332 AIDS cases with age information reported to the Centre for Infectious Disease Prevention and Control (CIDPC), 627 (3.4 percent) were of youth aged ten to twenty-four years (Health Canada 2004). In the twenty and older segment almost half of the new infections are attributed to homosexual sex. These are the cases known to health authorities; a number of untested young HIV-positive individuals often come to the health authorities' attention at the onset of opportunistic illness, STDs, or other health problems. Canadian youth begins to have sexual intercourse with multiple sexual partners at age fifteen. Males tend to have more sexual partners than females in the same periods of time. Sexual activity is often unprotected, which has increased the incidence of chlamydia and gonorrhea, and often takes place in a complex sociocultural and economic scenario.

See also Adolescent Sexualities; Agency; Biology, Teaching of; Canada, LGBT Youth in; Community LGBT Youth Groups; HIV Education; Japan, HIV/AIDS Education in; Mental Health; Prostitution or Sex Work; Sexuality Education.

A 2001 Vancouver study, for example, found that young gay and bisexual men, ages fifteen to thirty, sell sex for money, drugs, or a place to live (de Castell and Jenson 2002; Weber et al. 2001). Community-based **research** has confirmed that dysfunctional family background, traumatic school experience, and a nonhetero-sexual orientation are some of the confounding factors in the sexual lives and **sexual health** of these youth (de Castell and Jenson 2002). Those under thirty have more "unmet prevention needs and thus more HIV vulnerabilities than older [gay] men" (Trussler, Marchand, and Barker 2003, 69).

Younger generations, especially LGBTQ youth, are at greater risk for several reasons. There are perceptions of low risk when engaging in sexual and drug activities, which are fostered by feelings of invincibility compounded by optimistic treatment reports particularly in youth-targeted media. Contradictory perceptions of self-identity, **sexual identity**, and self-image may result in low self-esteem. Lack of power to negotiate emotional and sexual relationships, and even physical relationships impact such things as **eating disorders** to maintain "cool" images. Vulnerability to poverty, homelessness, physical and **sexual abuse**, recruitment into the sex or drug trades, and lack of spaces to socialize (other than bars or bathhouses) also contribute to the greater HIV risk of **queer** youth. Ostensibly, these issues may also be present differently by regional location, be it **rural** or **urban**, inner city or suburban.

Canadian HIV/AIDS education efforts take place in the schooling system, the AIDS service organizations (ASOs), which include peer-driven organizations by people living with HIV, and in federal and provincial health facilities. At the public nondenominational school level, HIV/AIDS education, as part of sexual health education, is implemented in cursory ways. The Ministry of Health maintains an arm's length relationship with the **curriculum** implemented. Decision-making powers rest in the hands of district School Advisory Boards in provinces and territories.

Effective HIV/AIDS education is tied to a myriad of factors that need to be in place in order to "teach" and "learn" about sexual health. Traditional pedagogical practices need to provide greater specificity in HIV/AIDS education, and sexual orientation needs to be addressed in the schools as in the efforts of the Toronto Board of Education (Campey et al. 1994).

In Canada, there are a number of community and school-based initiatives to approach LGBTQ youth with messages that may indirectly contain HIV/AIDS prevention messages (messages for those youth already living with HIV/HCV are less frequent) such as Youth Understanding Youth in Alberta (http://members.shaw.ca/yuy), YouthQuest (http://www.youthquest.bc.ca) which provides safe and supporting drop-in sites, a toll free support line, community education, and social support in rural areas of British Columbia, and Gab, in Vancouver, which sponsors drop-ins, workshops, and social events (http://www.lgtbcentrevancouver.com/Gab%20Youth.htm). And there are gay–straight alliances (http://www.pinktriangle.org/pts_site/Eng/gsaguide.pdf) across Canada. Of these groups Condomania, funded by the Vancouver Coastal Health Authority (http://www.planetahead.ca), and YouthCo AIDS Society (http://www.youthco.org) are primarily devoted to HIV/AIDS prevention. Currently, there are no permanent provincial or federal networks of these initiatives.

Although the government has a Canadian Strategy on HIV/AIDS and a set of Canadian Guidelines for Sexual Health Education (http://www.hc-sc.gc.ca/pphb-dgspsp/publicat/cgshe-ldnemss/cgshe_2e.htm), there have been no national campaigns specifically targeted at LGBTQ youth. The efforts at specific HIV/AIDS education are strongest within the voluntary sector, mainly in ASOs. In rural and urban settings, ASOs act as educational sentinels and intermediaries between local health authorities, school system, other nonprofit organizations and the community at large. A cadre of grassroots educators implement programs, ranging from conventional information delivery on sexually transmitted diseases (STDs) and infection by blood borne pathogens (e.g., HIV and Hepatitis C), to complex modules that include contents on drug use, global aspects of AIDS, antihomophobia, **heterosexism**, antiracism, and local concerns. The sophistication of HIV prevention education can be largely attributed to the pioneering efforts of gay and lesbian AIDS activists.

Understanding individual and collective vulnerabilities to poverty and other problems empowers youth to make healthy choices when engaging in sexual behavior, using street drugs, and planning **pregnancy** (by positive mothers). In Canada, the information, motivation, behavioral skills model (IMB) and a harm reduction approach underlie current prevention efforts. IMB is derived from a Health Belief model (Strecher and Rosenstock 1997). Initially developed to understand why people did not participate in disease detection programs, it has since been used to determine why patients do not always comply with treatment regimens. The harm reduction approach intends to reduce harmful behaviors, like **drug use,** to the individual, the community, and society. Understanding the consequences of risky behaviors rather than focusing on their elimination is the focus of this approach.

Following the prevention model of **United Kingdom** organizations such as the Terrence Higgins Trust, some Canadian ASOs such as the BC Persons With AIDS Society (http://www.bcpwa.org/index.php) are implementing a strategy of "Positive Prevention." This strategy places the HIV-positive individual (*and those who behave as if they were HIV-positive*) at the center of all educational, research, and evaluative endeavors in order to maximize their physical, mental, and sexual health. It seeks to dismantle the narratives of HIV "villains" (the Canadian patient zero of Randy Shilts' *And the Band Played On*), "heroes," "celebrities," or "victims," in practical ways.

Positive Prevention seeks to turn the institutional idea of what needs to be prevented—often judged by persons in positions of power and authority to be beneficial to both individuals and society—on its head. For example, what is labeled unsafe and unprotected sex within safer sex guidelines can be enacted as "barebacking" by the person living with AIDS through an organic decision-making process that involves affects (**desire**, trust), information, sociality (e.g., belonging to a leather **queer** subculture), and ethics. Hence, an HIV-positive/HIV-negative couple can voluntarily negotiate "unprotected" penetrative sex. Positive prevention, in its harm reduction approach, includes risk and usefully assesses the many issues faced by LGBQ youth.

Positive Prevention also poses challenges. It might mask further victimization of those who are already vulnerable (including legal risks associated with not disclosing one's "infectious" status to others and carrying the burden of **social work** around treatment and self-care (Bresalier et al. 2002). Also, positive prevention grapples with what Adams et al. (2003) identified as "semiotic snarls" and a "neoliberal" and individualistic approach to one's sexual health; that is, the belief that one is responsible for one's health alone or one's promise of sexual monogamy in a cultural environment where promiscuity may be the norm. Here, the challenge is to enhance communication between those who may be taking risks and to strengthen social networks in order to support individuals.

Bibliography

Adam, Barry, Winston Husbands, James Murray, and John Maxwell. 2003. *Renewing HIV Prevention for Gay and Bisexual Men.* AIDS Committee of Torornto (ACT) and Department of Sociology and Anthropology, University of Windsor, Ontario. Accessed December 4, 2004. http://www.actoronto.org/website/research.nsf/pages/renewinghiv prevention.

Bresalier, Michael, Loralee Gillis, Craigh McLure, Liza McCoy, Eric Mykhalovskiy, Darien Taylor, and Michelle Webber. 2002. *Making Care Visible: Antiretroviral Therapy and the Health Work of People Living with HIV/AIDS.* Making the Care Visible Group. Canadian HIV/AIDS Clearinghouse, Canadian Public Health Association. Accessed December 4, 2004. http://www.clearinghouse.cpha.ca.

Campey, John, Tim McCaskell, John Miller, and Vanessa Russell. 1994. "Opening the Classroom Closet: Dealing with Sexual Orientation at the Toronto Board of Education." Pp. 82–100 in *Sex in Schools: Canadian Education and Sexual Regulation.* Edited by Susan Prentice. Toronto: Our Schools / Our Selves Education Foundation.

de Castell, Suzanne, and Jennifer Jenson. 2002. "No Place Like Home: Final Research Report on the Pridehouse Project." Vancouver: Human Resources Development Canada and the PrideCare Society. Accessed December 4, 2004. http://www.sfu.ca/pridehouse.

Stretcher V.J., and Irvin Rosenstock. 1997. "The Health Belief Model." Pp. 41–59 in *Health Behavior and Health Education.* Edited by Karent Glanz, Barbara K. Rimer, and Frances M. Lewis. San Francisco: Jossey-Bass.

Trussler, Terry, Rick Marchand, and Andrew Barker. 2003. "Sex Now by the Numbers: A Statistical Guide to Health Planning for Gay Men." Vancouver: Community Based Research Centre. Accessed December 4, 2004. http://www.sexnowsurvey.com/index_2002.html.

Weber E. Amy, Kevin J. P. Craib , Keith Chan, Steve L. Martindale, Mary Lou Miller, Martin T. Schechter, and Robert Hogg. 2001. "Sex Trade Involvement and Rates of Human Immunodeficiency Virus Positivity among Young Gay and Bisexual Men." *International Journal of Epidemiology* 30: 1449–1454.

Web Sites

Health Canada: AIDS. September 2004. Accessed November 16, 2004. http://www.hc-sc.gc.ca/english/diseases/aids.html. Official Canadian source of HIV/AIDS related medical and scientific information.

YouthCO AIDS Society. November 2004. Youth Community Outreach. Accessed November 16, 2004. http://www.Youthco.org. Prime example of harm reduction HIV education from a well-established community based AIDS service organization.

Canada, LGBT Issues in

André P. Grace

Sexual orientation and gender identity are very much in the Canadian consciousness. Despite this visibility, and perhaps because of it, homophobia remains pervasive. It is exacerbated in intersections with classism, sexism, and white supremacy.

See also Antidiscrimination Policy; Canada, HIV/AIDS Education in; Canada, LGBT Youth in; Coming Out, Teachers; Identity Politics; Lesbian Feminism; Native and Indigenous LGBT Youth; Parents, LGBT; Professional Educational Organizations; Professionalism.

For example, "Two-Spirited" males often speak about the double oppression of being aboriginal and gay, which is something they can experience both inside and outside of LGBTQ (lesbian, gay, bisexual, trans [transgender and transsexual], and queer) communities (Warner 2002).

In Canada, citizens across sex, sexual, and gender differences have substantial legal and legislative protections ensuring their human and civil rights. Overarching and absolute protection is provided by the *Canadian Charter of Rights and Freedoms*. Specifically, in Section 15.1, **discrimination** on the ground of sexual orientation is prohibited. This protection is reiterated in Section 3 of the *Canadian Human Rights Act*. Furthermore, this protection is enforced in those sections of the *Criminal Code of Canada* dealing with **hates crimes** involving physical violence as well as symbolic violence such as verbal defamation of LGBTQ character in **graffiti** and talk-show rhetoric. However, LGBTQ Canadians still lack constitutional personhood (Lahey 1999). Moreover, legal and legislative progress has not sufficiently resulted in significant cultural change respecting and accommodating LGBTQ diversity and inclusion.

A recent study conducted with LGBTQ **teachers** in the province of Alberta reveals that while some teachers choose to be out in their classrooms, many, particularly those over thirty-five years old, remain closeted (Grace et al. 2004). Those closeted—that is, hiding their sex, sexual, and gender differences—fear for their personal safety and worry about the professional consequences of being out despite all the protections, including LGBTQ-supportive policy from the Alberta Teachers' Association. In Alberta, as in the rest of Canada, conservative religious groups and politicians still have sway, significantly reducing the possibility of inclusive education.

Nevertheless, Canada has come a long way since December 22, 1967, when then Justice Minister Pierre Elliott Trudeau proposed amendments to the *Criminal Code of Canada* that resulted in the decriminalization of homosexuality in 1969. As Trudeau spearheaded this law reform and moved Canada away from state control of individual freedoms, like those embodied and embedded in sexuality, he poignantly asserted: "The State has no business in the bedrooms of the nation" (Goldie 2001, 18).

Prior to this liberating historical event, a Canadian citizen could be jailed simply for being a homosexual. This was made clear, in 1965, when George Everett Klippert was sentenced to jail for acknowledging that he was gay, was unlikely to change, and had had sex with men over a twenty-four year period (Warner 2002). He was confined to prison for an indefinite time period and the Supreme Court of Canada labeled him a "dangerous sex offender." His incarceration incited further debate about Canada's treatment of homosexuals under the *Criminal Code*. Klippert was finally released from prison in 1971.

The threat or reality of incarceration is just one example of the historical abuse, mistreatment, and exclusion of LGBTQ Canadians (Warner 2002). In 1953, Canada's *Immigration Act* was amended to declare homosexuals a prohibited class whose entry into the country could be denied. As well, in its own expression of McCarthyism, the Canadian government prohibited homosexuals from holding positions in foreign affairs, the military, and the Royal Canadian Mounted Police. Indeed, until the early 1960s, the federal department of External Affairs summarily dismissed homosexual employees. In light of the historical compulsion to eradicate homosexuality from the mainstream educational consciousness, which has generally focused on the moral and political in heterosexual and procreative terms, teachers in this period (and indeed until 1995) could be fired simply for publicly acknowledging that they were homosexual (MacDougall 2000). This was particularly true of teachers in **Catholic** and other religious schools that have traditionally been hostile toward homosexuality.

The Canadian gay community started organizing in Canada with the formation of the Association for Social Knowledge in Vancouver in April 1964. During its five-year struggle to survive economically, this groundbreaking advocacy group engaged in building public awareness through public forums and newsletters as it fought for reform of criminal laws regarding homosexual activity. A number of homophile groups such as the University of Toronto Homophile Association cropped up in the late 1960s only to be displaced in the early 1970s, as a new international militancy and radical lesbian and gay consciousness took hold in the face of post-1969 gay liberation. However, most Canadian lesbian and gay groups emerging in the early 1970s were not particularly militant or political, expending their energies on social interaction and creating safe spaces. Nevertheless, work did begin to change provincial human rights legislation to include sexual orientation. As the 1970s unfolded, lesbian separatism took hold as lesbians felt disenfranchised by straight women's and gay men's groups. The early 1980s were marked by backlash, dissent, and crisis in lesbian and gay arenas and Canadian culture, society, and even the Courts continued to see homosexuals as a "menacing 'other'" (Warren 2002, 100). During this time period, lesbian and gay bookstores and organizations as well as hundreds of gay men charged in various bathhouse and bar raids found themselves involved in court proceedings. The calamitous early 1980s also saw the rise of community **activism** on **AIDS** in Canada's larger cities. Warner recounts that, by the late 1980s, Canada's lesbian and gay movement appeared divided in purposes. One contingent focused exclusively on human and civil rights, and another contingent focused on transgressing heteronormative sexual expression and community standards in efforts to overcome the notion of homosexual as victim and to insert visibility and pride as the markers of lesbian and gay presence in Canadian society.

Since legislators can be swayed by popular opinion that can be variously biased, prejudicial, and exclusionary, it is the responsibility of the courts to respect and foster inclusion of society's disenfranchised, including marginalized LGBTQ citizens. Canadian courts have generally accepted this responsibility, especially since 1982 when the *Canadian Charter of Rights and Freedoms* was entrenched in the Constitution, which was patriated from Britain in that year. Since then Canadian courts have protected the Charter and the individual rights of Canadians. Key decisions by the Supreme Court of Canada accommodating sexual orientation have proliferated since the mid-1990s. In Canada, when cases are insufficiently resolved at the provincial or territorial Court of Queen's Bench or the Court of Appeal they can move through a usually protracted process to be heard by the Supreme Court of Canada. In terms of LGBTQ cases, decisions under the Charter are binding on all provinces and territories. Three very significant Supreme Court decisions have been rendered regarding LGBTQ rights (MacDougall 2000).

In 1995, *Egan and Nesbit v. Canada* was the first case to deal directly with sexual orientation under Section 15 of the *Canadian Charter of Rights and Freedoms*. While J. Egan and his partner J. Nesbit lost their lawsuit against the Government of Canada for the right to claim a spousal pension under the *Old Age Security Act*, the Supreme Court of Canada was unanimous in its agreement that sexual orientation was a protected category under the Charter. Since then, sexual orientation has been *read in* to the Charter, and the Supreme Court has declared that a heterosexual definition of partnerships contravenes Section 15 of the Charter. In education, this decision resulted in Canadian teachers' federations and associations amending their codes of professional conduct and statements of teachers' rights and responsibilities to include sexual orientation as a character of person to be protected against discrimination in keeping with the law of the land.

In 1991, Delwin Vriend, an educator at Kings College, Edmonton, Alberta, had been dismissed on the pretext that his employment violated that conservative Christian institution's religious policy. He responded with a legal challenge to have sexual orientation read into Alberta's human rights legislation. The Supreme Court of Canada handed down its long-awaited decision in *Vriend v. Alberta* on April 2, 1998, declaring Alberta's human rights legislation unconstitutional. This decision made it clear that Section 15 of the Charter prohibits legislative omission of sexual orientation (Lahey 1999). Most significantly, the decision confirmed equality rights for lesbian and gay Canadians.

Vriend had repercussions for Canadian provinces and territories that had not yet moved on their own to include sexual orientation as a prohibited ground of discrimination in their human rights legislation. It also had a deep impact on education. For example, in the wake of *Vriend*, the Alberta Teachers' Association (ATA) moved quickly to protect LGBTQ students, passing a resolution at its 1999 annual general meeting (AGM) to include sexual orientation as a protected category in its *Code of Professional Conduct*. Then, at its 2000 AGM, ATA members provided the same protection to LGBTQ teachers by voting to include sexual orientation as a category of person protected by equality provisions in its *Declaration of Rights and Responsibilities for Teachers*. At its 2003 AGM, the ATA became the first teachers' association in Canada to include gender identity in its *Code of Professional Conduct*, thus protecting trans students.

Perhaps, the most widely noted case is *M v. H*, which led to legal recognition of same-sex relationships in 1999. M and H had been a lesbian couple for over ten years. In 1992, upon dissolution of their partnership, M sued H for spousal support under the Ontario *Family Law Act*. The Act defined spouse in terms of heterosexual partners. The Ontario Court of Queen's Bench ruled that the definition violated the *Canadian Charter of Rights and Freedoms* and that the phrase "a man and a woman" should be replaced with "two persons." H appealed but the Ontario Court of Appeal upheld the decision. Neither M nor H continued with the case, but the Ontario Attorney General appealed the decision to the Supreme Court of Canada.

Since the 1999 Supreme Court ruling, Ontario, British Columbia, Québec, Manitoba, Nova Scotia, Saskatchewan, Newfoundland and Labrador, and the Yukon Territory have moved to sanction gay marriages. This has a number of implications for schooling. With greater recognition and legitimacy given to same-sex couples, the onus is on schools to accommodate their families through inclusive representations in the **curriculum** and inclusive involvement in school social and cultural contexts. Moreover, there must be attention to their needs in **educational policies** and practices dealing with relationships and interactions with parents or guardians.

Bibliography

Canadian Teachers' Federation, ed. 2003. *Seeing the Rainbow: Teachers Talk about Bisexual, Gay, Lesbian, Transgender and Two-Spirited Realities*. Ottawa and Toronto: Canadian Teachers' Federation and the Elementary Teachers' Federation of Ontario.

Goldie, Terry, ed. 2001. *In a Queer Country: Gay & Lesbian Studies in the Canadian Context*. Vancouver: Arsenal Pulp Press.

Grace, Andre P., Robert J. Hill, Corey W. Johnson, and Jamie B. Lewis. 2004. "In Other Words: Queer Voices/Dissident Subjectivities Impelling Social Change." *International Journal of Qualitative Studies in Education* 17, no 3: 301–323.

Lahey, Kathleen A. 1999. *Are We Persons Yet? Law and Sexuality in Canada*. Toronto: University of Toronto Press.

MacDougall, Bruce. 2000. *Queer Judgments: Homosexuality, Expression, and the Courts in Canada*. Toronto: University of Toronto Press.

Warner, Tom. 2002. *Never Going Back: A History of Queer Activism in Canada*. Toronto: University of Toronto Press.

Web Sites

Alberta Teachers' Association's Sexual Orientation and Gender Identity Educational Web site. 2004. Last updated May 2005. Kristopher Wells. Accessed May 26, 2005. http://www.teachers.ab.ca/Issues+In+Education/Diversity+and+Human+Rights/Sexual+Orientation/Index.htm. Provides resources and guidelines to help teachers address homophobia and heterosexism in their school, classroom, and community environments.

Canadian Broadcasting Corporation (CBC) Archives. 2002. *The Charter at 20*. P. Saunders. Accessed December 2, 2002. http://cbc.ca/news/features/constitution. CBC Archives. 2003. *B.C. Court Backs Same-Sex Marriages*. Accessed May 26, 2005. http://www.cbc.ca/storyview/CBC/2003/05/01/samesex_bc030501. The CBC keeps archives that include a rich database on historical and contemporary aspects of gay liberation in Canada.

Equality for Gay and Lesbians Everywhere (EGALE Canada). 2004. Updated regularly. Accessed May 26, 2005. http://www.egale.ca. EGALE Canada engages in political action to achieve more equitable laws for LGBTQ Canadians; intervenes in legal cases that have an impact on LGBTQ human rights and equality; and increases public education and awareness by providing information to individuals, groups, and the media. The site has rich archives.

Canada, LGBT Youth in

S. Anthony Thompson and Gerald Walton

Canadian **lesbian, gay, bisexual,** and **transgender youth** (LGBT) represent a wide expanse of ethnic, linguistic, and geographical diversity. Canada, a large country with approximately thirty million people in twelve provinces and three territories, officially declares itself as multicultural, which shapes the experiences of these

See also Activism, LGBT Teachers; Activism, LGBT Youth; Canada, HIV/AIDS Education in; Canada, LGBT Youth in; College Campus Organizing; Community LGBT Youth Groups; Legal Issues, Students; Native and Indigenous LGBT Youth; Professional Educational Organizations; Religious Fundamentalism; School Climate, K-12; Secondary Schools, LGBT; Social Class; Youth, At -Risk; Youth, Homeless.

youth. Within educational structures, support for LGBT youth fluctuates as a function of the commitments of provincial and territorial ministries of education, the official government bodies that regulate curricula and school-related initiatives. Most ministries make some efforts to assist LGBT students, often within antibullying, antiviolence, or **suicide** prevention programs. At the same time, as there are inconsistent and often nonspecific educational and social supports for LGBT youth within Canada, there are high rates of suicidal behavior among LGBT Canadian youth. Bagely and Tremblay (1997, 24) conducted a study of 750 young men in Calgary, Alberta; "homosexually oriented males" accounted for two-thirds of "suicide attempters." Filax (2002) focused on the ways in which **queer** youth in Alberta are routinely disenfranchised. LGBT Canadian youth may also be more likely than heterosexual counterparts to become drug and/or alcohol addicted, drop out of school, or engage in prostitution (McCreary Centre Society 1999). According to the Ottawa-Carleton LGBT Health Task Group, 25 to 40 percent of Canadian homeless youth are LGBT. Wolfman (1996) reported that queer youth respondents found their high schools in Ottawa bred **homophobia** through explicit physical and verbal means, but also through the **curriculum**. EGALE Canada (2004) maintains that LGBT youth continue to be routinely disenfranchised despite increased visibility in **popular culture**.

For LGBT youth, Canada's vast geography sometimes presents an obstacle. In provinces such as Saskatchewan, there are many **rural** and isolated communities. These have significantly fewer resources—ranging from safe sex information to support groups for LGBT youth—than metropolitan areas. Within Canada's Atlantic region, there is now a push to provide more support. The AIDS Committee of Newfoundland and Labrador is conducting a project entitled *Reaching Out to Young Gay Men* as part of the Canadian strategy on HIV/**AIDS**. Other services cater to LGBT youth, such as *YouthQuest* Canada's largest such organization. Although specific to British Columbia, *YouthQuest* staff and volunteers organize drop-ins for LGBT youth in urban and rural areas, as well as provide a 24-hour toll-free support line and Web site (http://www.youthquest.bc.ca.), community education, and peer support. GaBaLoT (http://gabalot.ca) provides similar services for youth in rural southern Ontario. These are exceptions, but generally for Canadian youth to identify as LGBT, it is necessary to identify as urban.

First Nations or Metis persons represent a significant population within the multicultural mix. In the 1950s and 1960s, the Canadian government created residential schools, removing aboriginal children from their families. Effects upon First Nations communities have been disastrous—and most saliently here—upon LGBT youth of aboriginal cultural backgrounds. Gil Lerat, a counselor from the Two-Spirited Youth Program (TSYP), based in Vancouver, laments: "Just look at the number of teen suicides on reserves. It's really hard for two-spirited youth to come out and the statistics show that approximately 70 percent of the Aboriginal teen suicides that are happening on reserves today is by two-spirited youth. That's startling!" (Wilson 2000). Consequently, TSYP promotes healing for these youth while integrating aboriginal notions of spirituality and [homo]sexuality. There are other organizations for LGBT youth of different ethnic heritages, such as QAY (Queer Asian Youth), and *Association des Jeunes Gais, Lesbiennes et Bisexuelles de l'Estrie* for francophone youth in Quebec. There are also pockets of efforts to help youth who identify as trans such as *Trans Youth Toronto* and those LGBT youth who have developmental **disabilities**. There are even clubs/organizations that cater to particular aspects of queer culture, such as the GEN X Bears, a club for male youth who have significant amounts of body and / or facial hair. The term "bear" also has connotations with being "cuddly."

In support of LGBT youth, the Canadian Teachers Federation (CTF) has produced the handbook, *Seeing the Rainbow: Teachers Talk about Bisexual, Lesbian, Gay, Transgender and Two-Spirited Realities*. Although the CTF is a national private organization, most public education institutions operate on a provincial and/or municipal basis. Public education is also structured by culture and language (French and English), by religion (most commonly **Catholic**), and by students/curricula (elementary/secondary). Each of these impacts the kinds of support offered to LGBT youth. For example, the Ontario English Catholic Teachers' Association produces and/or endorses few materials supportive of LGBT youth, in contrast to the Elementary Teachers' Federation of Ontario (EFTO) and The Alberta Teachers' Federation (ATF). EFTO has a LGBT standing committee; the ATF has authored a *Safe and Caring Schools* guide specifically for queer youth. Unlike public schools, private schools are often channels for religions such as **Muslim**, Mennonite, and evangelical **Christian** and, as such, oppose recognizing and providing educational and social support for sexual minority youth.

The ATFs commitment is noteworthy since the province of Alberta is politically very conservative; its government has attempted and/or threatened to thwart almost any supportive LGBT legislation via an often misused constitutional "notwithstanding" clause. Alberta shares its border with British Columbia (BC), parts of which also shares its social conservatism. Consequently, the Gay and Lesbian Educators of BC (GALE-BC) have been active since 1993. Recently, it proposed School's Out Day, a national day of solidarity for the equality rights of LGBT youth.

A prominent GALE-BC member and elementary school teacher, James Chamberlain, was embroiled within a sustained legal battle with the Surrey School Board. In 1997, the trustees, supported by several Christian organizations, banned three books for children depicting same-gender couples and/or families that Chamberlain used within his classroom. Such a ban privileged these Surrey parents' brand of religious beliefs above others. In opposition, certain teachers, parents, and students filed human rights complaints against the Board, alleging the action discriminated against LGBT youth and created a "hostile environment" for LGBT students, teachers, and staff. Six years later, the Supreme Court of Canada ordered the Board to reevaluate. Its position on the three books remains unchanged, although two other picture books featuring same-gender parents were eventually approved (Walton 2004).

Other legal implications and battles impacting LGBT youth emerged in Canada throughout the 1990s. In 2000, the British Columbia College of Teachers (BCCT) discontinued the certification of teacher candidates from Trinity Western University (TWU), a private Christian University in BC. TWU students are required to sign a code of conduct that they will not engage in activities that are seen as incompatible with Christian values, such as homosexuality. Neither the Supreme Court of Canada or the BC Civil Liberties Association ruled in BCCT's favor, on grounds that private institutions are exempt from charges of discrimination in the BC Human Rights Code and can limit membership to those who share their views.

Canadian students, too, have entered the legal fray, but not always with successful results. In 2002, siblings David and Katherine Knight of Burlington, Ontario, launched a $500,000 lawsuit against their former school board for not protecting them against years of **bullying**, much of which was homophobic in nature (Kresowaty 2003). The case has not been settled, although after protracted negotiations the family was able to get Yahoo to remove a hateful Web site about David. Sometimes, LGBT youth are victorious. In 1996, an eleventh-grade student, Azmi Jubran, filed a human rights complaint against the North Vancouver School District, claiming he was the victim of unrelenting homophobic slurs. Although Jubran does not identify as gay, he won on appeal. Twelfth-grade Ontario student Marc Hall took his Catholic public school board to court for not allowing him to attend the high school **prom** with his boyfriend. In 2002, an Ontario Superior Court ruled in his favor. Hall has become a national symbol of the pride, inspiring queer teens, especially those living in rural areas.

Within this political context, several social-service programs have been created to address social, emotional, and educational developmental needs of queer and questioning youth, mostly in urban areas. GAB Youth Services, for example, is a drop-in center for LGBT youth in Vancouver. Rainbow Youth Talk, located in Ottawa, Ontario, provides educational and social resources for queer youth. The Youth Outreach Project in Calgary, Alberta, is a joint project between Parents, Families, and Friends of Lesbians and Gays and Planned Parenthood Alberta. The Halifax Lesbian, Gay, and Bisexual Youth Project provides support, advocacy, and a safe place for Nova Scotia's LGBT youth. Canada's largest city, Toronto, has several diverse programs for LGBT youth, including Pink Ink, Teens Educating and Confronting Homophobia, Supporting Our Youth, and the Toronto Coalition for Lesbian, Gay and Bisexual Youth. The degree to which these programs successfully address issues of **race**, language, **social class**, and physical/mental ability is uncertain and varied.

The McCreary survey (1999) identified the need for support in schools for queer students and **allies**. To meet this need, **gay–straight alliances** (GSAs) operate in schools throughout the country, although they are more common in urban areas. Of particular note in Toronto is the Triangle Program, Canada's only classroom that specifically serves the educational needs of LGBT youth and those affected by homophobia. Students in the Triangle program are diverse in economic circumstance, race and **ethnicity**, ability, home life, **gender identity** and **sexual orientation**, yet all have experienced acute and chronic homophobia, which this program seeks to overcome. Nevertheless, it is not without its critics. Snyder (1996), for example, identified several problems, including a gay-inclusive curriculum still shaped by Eurocentric perspectives and a school board that is less than supportive of students of color.

Programs for LGBT youth usually include information and resources on the **Internet**. Potentially, Web-based resources overcome geographical limitations of rural LGBT living. Nevertheless, not all LGBT youth have Internet access. Financial constraints and lack of privacy at home, school, and the local library are significant barriers. Further, access to information and resources through Web sites is not an adequate substitute for social interaction with peers.

Most teacher education programs within Canada address LGBT issues, usually as one of many groups of labeled students. The University of Regina and the

University of Saskatchewan, among others, have specific courses for preservice teachers, "Schooling and Sexual Difference" and "Gay and Lesbian Issues in Education," respectively. Additionally, the University of Saskatchewan annually hosts the international conference, "Breaking the Silence: Gays and Lesbian in Our Schools." Agape, a sexual orientation and schooling focus group at the University of Alberta, hosts a similar albeit smaller forum, Sex-and-Gender Differences: Education and Culture. Organizations for LGBT students, especially undergraduates, are also available at most Canadian universities and colleges. Such organizations are usually funded by student societies and promote safety, social activities, and visibility on campus for young queer students and straight supporters.

There are some Canadian LGBT publications such as the quarterly online news magazine *Subculture*, produced by the Canadian Alliance Linking Young People around Sexual Orientation (CALYPSO). *Shameless: For Girls Who Get It*, is a magazine for teenage girls, often with queer content. On television, portrayals of LGBT youth have appeared in various youth-centered serials, such as *Degrassi Jr. High* (Canadian Broadcasting Corporation CBC 1987–1989), *Liberty Street* (CBC, 1995–1996) and *Riverdale* (CBC, 1997–2000) with a gay character George Patillo. More recently, on *Degrassi: The Next Generation* (2004, Canadian Television Network) two characters, Marco and Dylan, shared the series first on-screen teen-on-teen, gay kiss. Also, the reality series *The Lofters* (2001), following the lives of eight young people living together, includes an out-gay youth, Mathieu.

Bibliography

Bagley, Chris, and Pierre Tremblay. 1997. "Suicidal Behaviors on Homosexual and Bisexual Males." *Crisis* 18 no. 1: 24–34.

Canadian Teachers Federation. 2003. *Seeing the Rainbow: Teachers Talk about Bisexual, Lesbian, Gay, Transgender and Two-spirited Realities*. Ottawa, Ontario: Canadian Teachers Federation.

Filax, Gloria. 2002. *Queer Youth and Strange Representations in the Province of the "Severely Normal."* Unpublished Dissertation. University of Alberta.

EGALE Canada. 2004, August 12. "LGBT Young People Deserve Better: Egale Canada highlights U.N. International Day of Youth." Accessed September 19, 2004. http://www.egale.ca.

Kresowaty, Lija. 2003. "Young Activists Share Personal Struggles." *The Strand.ca*. Accessed September 19, 2004. http://www.thestrand.ca/news/2003/02/05/News/Young.Activists. Share.Personal.Struggles-362209.shtml.

McCreary Centre Society. 1999. *Being Out: Lesbian, Gay, Bisexual and Transgender Youth in BC, An Adolescent Health Survey*. Burnaby, BC: Author.

Pink Triangle Services and Ottawa-Carleton GLBT Health Task Group. 1999, November. *A Proposal for a GLBT Health/Wellness Needs Assessment and Community Resource Mapping Project*. Accessed September 19, 2004. http://www.pinktriangle.org/wellness/proposal.pdf.

Snyder, Kathryn. 1996. "Race and Sexual Orientation: The (Im)possibility of These Intersections in Educational Policy. *Harvard Educational Review* 66, no. 2: 294–302.

Walton, Gerald. 2004. "Bullying and Homophobia in Canadian Schools: The Politics of Policies, Programs, and Educational Leadership." *Journal of Gay and Lesbian Issues in Education* 1, no. 4: 23–36.

Wilson, Julian. 2000. Two-Spirited Youth Program. 2002, December 29. Accessed December 3, 2004. http://www.ainc-inac.gc.ca/nr/nwltr/drm/su2000/tsny_e.html.

Wolfman, Oscar. 1996. "Homophobia in/as Education." *Alternate Routes: A Journal of Critical Social Research* 13: 101–117.

Web Sites

Alberta Teachers' Federation. 2004. Diversity and Human Rights. Kris Wells. Accessed December 5, 2004. http://www.teachers.ab.ca/Issues+In+Education/Diversity+and+Human+Rights/Sexual+Orientation/Index.htm. An extensive resource to help create safe and caring learning environments for LGBT students. Includes many of their publications.

Gay and Lesbian Educators of BC. November 2004. Accessed December 4, 2004. http://www.galebc.org. Probably the most comprehensive Web site for LGBT youth resources within Canada.

Career Counseling

Kathleen J. Bieschke and *Jodi A. Boita*

Affirmative career counseling involves creating a context that invites lesbian, gay, bisexual, and transgender (LGBT) clients to feel free to seek services, disclose their **sexual identity** and/or **gender identity**, discuss common career concerns, as well as explore LGBT-unique career concerns. Counselor behaviors as well as an organizational climate that demonstrates support for LGBT clients facilitates the delivery of affirmative counseling. Unique concerns of LGBT career clients include the interaction between societal views and vocational interests and choices, vocational and sexual/gender **identity development**, **workplace** discrimination and climate, and managing sexual identity in the workplace. In addition, each subgroup of the LGBT population has unique career concerns. For example, lesbians frequently cope with multiple role concerns such as balancing work and family concerns. Transgender individuals who transition must often attend to **workplace issues**, ranging from deciding which restroom to use to being out in the workplace. Career decision-making is particularly complicated for LGBT youth as they are often faced with these decisions while simultaneously exploring and negotiating issues relative to their sexual identity. Career exploration is often disrupted or derailed as they attend to issues of **coming out**, identifying LGBT career role models, and considering how out to be in the workplace.

Career counselors may not be aware of clients' **sexual orientation** or level of disclosure status in various life realms. Therefore, it is important for counselors to behave affirmatively with all clients as clients' decisions about whether to be forthcoming about sexual identity issues may be dependent on such behaviors. Counselors should engage in professional development activities designed to illuminate and challenge heterosexist assumptions and behaviors. Further, professional development focused on activities designed to enhance knowledge about the unique career concerns of the LGBT population is essential. Affirmative in-session behaviors include displaying affirmative symbols, using language inclusive of same-sex

See also Antidiscrimination Policy; College Age Students; College Campus Resource Centers; Counselor Education; Mentoring; Parents, Responses to Homosexuality; Professionalism.

relationships (e.g., using the term "partner" rather than "husband" or "wife"), and not making the assumption that all clients are heterosexual.

Once a career counselor is aware that the client is LGB or T, engaging in strong, positive, affirming **counseling** behaviors is essential. Chung (2003) discussed the importance of counselors serving as advocates for LGBT clients in career services, particularly because of the oppression and **discrimination** these clients encounter. Further, career counselors must use traditional career inventories (e.g., Myers-Briggs Type Indicator, Strong Interest Inventory, Self-Directed Search) carefully with LGBT clients since they were not explicitly designed for use with this population nor have they been validated using a norm group of LGBT individuals. Other affirmative counselor behaviors include discussing the costs and benefits of **"passing"** as a heterosexual or appearing in the "appropriate" gender, finding LGBT career role models (e.g., employed individuals who are willing to discuss their sexual and/or gender identity management strategies in the workplace), discussing partnership and dual career issues, and having awareness of or access to information about company policies pertaining to LGBT workers.

Career counseling organizational climates that are nonheterosexist and broadly affirming of LGB career clients are related to counselors' LGB-affirmative behaviors (Bieschke and Matthews 1996). Creating an affirmative environment can take many forms, including hiring LGBT counselors, having visible affirmative indicators (e.g., advertising, subscribing to LGBT-affirmative publications), and providing professional development relative to the LGBT population.

Counselors must attend to the stage of identity development of the client in order to deliver effective career counseling. Multiple authors postulate that career and sexual identity development work together differently for heterosexual and nonheterosexual individuals. Heterosexual individuals are thought to be much more settled in identity development during the initial phases of career development, whereas lesbian and gay individuals may begin to explore sexual identity simultaneously with or after career development processes (exploration and planning) have begun, thus complicating both the career development process and the sexual identity development process. Such complications can result in the career development of **lesbian** and **gay youth** being delayed or misdirected (Croteau et al. 2000). In addition, other salient identities (e.g., **racial identity** or **ethnic identity**) serve to further complicate the career development of sexual minority individuals. Moreover, it is important to attend to issues of sexual identity development in relationship to environmental **heterosexism** present in the workplace (Gelberg and Chojnacki 1996). Knowledge of and attention to sexual identity theories can facilitate career counselors' ability to understand the vocational concerns of LGBT clients across the life span.

LGBT youth should be mindful that sexual and career identity exploration often occur simultaneously. For instance, as youth come out to central figures in their life, temporary or permanent conflicts may arise, which, in turn, may have a negative impact on career development. Lack of support from family members or absence of time to reflect on longer term life decisions can result. Further, although high school counselors are principally responsible for career guidance, they may not be in a position to discuss career issues related to sexual orientation or gender identity due to school district **educational policy** or their lack of knowledge. LGBT individuals may need to consider finding an affirmative counselor who is competent to work with career issues. In particular, youth should be advised of the difficulties associated with career choice amidst resolving other central identity issues, as well as the problems attendant in certain career choices, such as the military, or localities which do not ban discrimination on the basis of sexual orientation or gender choice.

Exposure to role models in a variety of occupations may be helpful prior to making decisions about a career's openness to individuals with marginalized sexual identities. Traditionally, this is accomplished through summer jobs and college apprenticeships. Youth may choose to use these opportunities to explore different occupations while perhaps exploring and experimenting with different identity management strategies in the workplace. Workplace identity management strategies include passing, covering, implicitly out, and explicitly out. Choice of an identity management strategy is complex and reflects not only occupational and workplace norms, but also personal factors such as culture, one's comfort level, and partner considerations.

Career counselors must attend to vocational issues that are unique to this population, including workplace discrimination, workplace climate, and identity management. Numerous empirical studies confirm that discrimination against LGB workers is common. Discrimination can be either formal (i.e., adverse decisions made on the basis of an employee's sexual orientation in relationship to hiring, wages, and benefits) or informal (i.e., adversity encountered in the workplace environment or climate such as verbal **harassment** or lack of respect by coworkers and supervisors). The likelihood of encountering both formal and informal discrimination makes the decision regarding disclosure of sexual identity at work a central task for LGBT workers. Career counselors must carefully attend to the tension between the desire for disclosure and the fear of discrimination by assessing the likelihood of negative job consequences and the importance of being out to the client. In addition, personal considerations such as past experiences with job discrimination and the impact such a decision would have on the individual's partner must also be taken into account.

Less well-examined in the theoretical or empirical literature is the extent to which social messages about gender and sexual orientation influence the career interests and choices of LGBT clients. In particular, given that LGBT individuals tend to express more androgynous career interests and demonstrate less conformity to **gender role**-related expectations than their heterosexual peers, it is difficult to ascertain how societal-based messages about gender affect career choice. Thus lesbians, for example, may be more willing to consider careers traditionally dominated by men (e.g., engineering, computer software design) than heterosexual women. Furthermore, perceptions of what occupations are and are not appropriate for LGBT individuals may influence LGBT clients' willingness to entertain entering some occupations. For example, some LGBT individuals may avoid careers that involve working with children perhaps, at least in part, because openness about one's sexual orientation may be limited due to the reaction of parents and school boards, or they may wish to avoid careers **stereotypically** associated with sexual minorities. Some LGBT individuals may be drawn to careers in fields such as telecommunications, financial/banking services, and computers because of their often affirmative stance toward LGBT individuals.

While counselors competent to provide career counseling to LGBT clients may not advertise as such, often career counselors have received training that would allow them to work effectively with this population. LGBT-affirmative career counselors and career centers in many colleges often use subtle means to communicate their affirmation and create a safe space, including displaying signs and symbols that evidence gay pride (e.g., **rainbow flags** or **pink triangles**), or displaying materials pertinent to the LGBT community. Further, college youth participation in LGBT school and community activities and organizations, such as the local gay business guild or specific gay interest or hobby groups, can lead to the identification of career role models.

The **Internet** can also be an excellent source for LGBT youth and adults to explore career options. There is a wide range of information available including: career planning and financial aid issues (http://www.nyu.edu/careerservices/students/diversity/page_four.html); links to LGBT professional societies as well as national and international LGBT business groups (http://webapps.acs.carleton.edu/campus/career/populations/lgbt/); legal issues pertaining to partner benefits and workplace discrimination issues (http://www.cbel.com/gay_workplace); support groups for individuals in a wide variety of careers groups (http://www.cbel.com/gay_workplace/); information on LGBT workplace policies for a wide range of careers and corporations (http://www.GayWork.com); and information pertinent to specific subgroups within the LGBT population such as transitioning and employment issues for transgender individuals (http://www.firelily.com/gender/sstgfaq/tstg.html#transatwork). At a minimum, the Internet provides LGBT individuals with the opportunity to gather information not available in any other medium.

Bibliography

Bieschke, Kathleen J., and Connie R. Matthews. 1996. "Career Counselor Attitudes and Behaviors toward Gay, Lesbian, and Bisexual Clients." *Journal of Vocational Behavior* 48: 243–255.

Chung, Y. Barry. 2001. "Work Discrimination and Coping Strategies: Conceptual Frameworks for Counseling Lesbian, Gay, and Bisexual Clients." *The Career Development Quarterly* 50: 33–44.

———. 2003. "Career Counseling with Lesbian, Gay, Bisexual, and Transgendered Persons: The Next Decade." *The Career Development Quarterly* 52:78–86.

Croteau, James M., Mary Z. Anderson, Theresa M. Distefano, and Sheila Kampa-Kokesch. 2000. "Lesbian, Gay, and Bisexual Vocational Psychology: Reviewing Foundations and Planning Construction." Pp. 383–408 in *Handbook of Counseling and Therapy with Lesbian, Gay, and Bisexual Clients*. Edited by Ruperto M. Perez, Kurt A. DeBord, and Kathleen J. Bieschke. Washington, DC: American Psychological Association.

Ellis, Alan L., and Ellen D. B. Riggle, eds. 1996. *Sexual Identity on the Job: Issues and Services*. Binghamton, NY: Harrington Park Press.

Gelberg, Susan, and Joseph T. Chojnacki, 1996. *Career and Life Planning with Gay, Lesbian, & Bisexual Persons*. Alexandria, VA: American Counseling Association.

Herring, Roger D. 1998. *Career Counseling in Schools: Multicultural and Developmental Perspectives*. Alexandria, VA: American Counseling Association.

Web Sites

Human Rights Campaign. December 2004. Accessed December 20, 2004. http://www.hrc.org. Current information about workplace issues such as domestic partnership benefits, employers with LGBT-related policies, and other legal issues pertaining to LGBT workers.

Walworth, Janie and Kammerer, Michele. Center for Gender Sanity. December 2003. Accessed December 20, 2004. http://www.gendersanity.com/. Information pertaining to workplace issues for transgender individuals; all provides information directed toward employers and human resource personnel.

Cartoons

Jeffery P. Dennis

Animated cartoons, or simply "cartoons," are films produced by projecting drawings in rapid sequence to give the illusion of motion, and usually marketed to children and youth. While many animated cartoons aggressively promote **compulsory heterosexuality**, their freedom in plot, characterization, and setting makes them unusually amenable to subtexts that hint at or even celebrate same-sex **desire**.

Through the first half of the twentieth century, cartoons generally appeared among the short subjects displayed before feature films, and thus they were intended for audiences of all ages. After World War II, when theater attendance decreased dramatically due to suburbanization, the baby boom, and competition from television, theatrical cartoons became virtually extinct. Warner Brothers and other studios began releasing their old theatrical cartoons for a television market, and soon original television cartoons were being produced. Usually they appeared in early evening or Saturday morning time slots popular among children and teenagers. By the 1960s, with the exceptions of independent animation and an occasional foray into prime time, animated cartoons were permanently associated with youth.

Cartoons are not popular tools for formal classroom instruction; indeed, teachers and parents tend to regard them as harmless trash and a waste of time with neither positive merit nor potential for permanent psychological damage. Thus, before the proliferation of network-based cartoons in the 1990s, animators enjoyed an enormous amount of conceptual freedom; their cartoons managed to subvert normative expectations concerning gender polarization and universal heterosexuality more successfully than most other products of youth culture. Indeed, the fluidity of the cartoon universe, in which there is no need for continuity in setting, character, social situation, or plot convention, often produces a tacit validation of same-sex romantic or domestic relationships, even when the animators most likely have no such intent.

Warner Brothers theatrical cartoons, produced in the 1940s and 1950s but perennial favorites on television, have been extensively mined for queer moments such as Bugs Bunny in drag, Porky Pig and Daffy Duck behaving as domestic partners, and Pepe Le Pew making amorous advances to a male cat (Abel 1995). Disney theatrical cartoons, however, tend toward a conservative, heterosexist ideology, making Mickey Mouse and Donald Duck suburban single parents with girlfriends rather than the rugged adventurers in all-male domains they were in the **comics**.

See also Cross-Dressing; Homophobia; Popular Culture; Queer and Queer Studies; Youth Culture.

Similarly, feature length Disney animation almost invariably promotes heterosexual romance as the meaning of life and gives villains gay-stereotyped mannerisms to accentuate their creepiness (e.g., Captain Hook in *Peter Pan*, Jafar in *Aladdin*), although sometimes same-sex partners appear as comic relief (e.g., Gus and Jacques in *Cinderella*, Timon and Pumbaa in *The Lion King*).

Scooby Doo, Where Are You! (1969 CBS Animated Series). Shown: Daphne Blake (Voice: Stefanianna Christopherson), Velma Dinkley (Voice: Nicole Jaffe). Hanna-Barbera Productions/CBS/Photofest. © Hanna-Barbera Productions

Among television cartoons, the famous Hanna Barbera duos of the 1960s (Yogi Bear and Boo Boo, Quick Draw McGraw and Baba Looie) are easily subject to queering as prototypic same-sex romantic partners, sharing domestic situations, ignoring girls, and bonding with an arguably erotic intensity. Baby-boomer message boards on the **Internet** are full of speculations about other "suspicious" cartoon couples, such as *Jonny Quest* (1963) and Hadji, ghost-chasers Daphne and Velma of *Scooby-Doo* (1969), or secret agent *Danger Mouse* (UK, 1981–87) and his prissy sidekick Penfold, but often queer **sexual identity** is ascribed even in the absence of same-sex pairing: in *He-Man and the Masters of the Universe* (1983), for instance, because He-Man was muscular and never dated girls.

Heterosexual and lesbian, gay, bisexual, and transgender youth (LGBT) may not differ significantly in their ability to locate same-sex desire in animated cartoons. In their memoir, brothers Timothy and Kevin Burke (1999), one gay, one heterosexual, grow up avidly watching Saturday morning cartoons, and neither seems more proficient than the other in speculating about why Fred and Barney on *The Flintstones* spent so much time together, or what the *Smurfs* were up to in their village of 99 men and one woman. However, heterosexual youth may approach such speculation as scandalous, naughty, or even frightening; a correspondent on *TV Party* (http://www.tvparty.com) recalls being "very disturbed" by the gay subtext in *The Mighty Hercules* (1963). LGBT youth, conversely, may find it a source of hope, providing perhaps the only hint of same-sex love in a **childhood** otherwise informed by near-hysterical indoctrination into compulsory heterosexuality.

Since the early 1990s, cable and satellite networks have produced an unprecedented number of new animated cartoon series for the global market, mostly aimed at children and teenagers. *Doug* (1991), *Pepper Ann* (1997), *La Classe en délire* (France, 1999), and many others are simply animated sitcoms, starring more or less realistically-drawn youth, with scripts that could be performed by live actors except for an occasional whimsical touch, like a semi-articulate pet dog on *Doug* or the autocratic King of the Playground on *Recess* (1997). These animated sitcoms may resist gender polarization—including tough, mechanically-inclined girls and sensitive, artistic boys in their casts—but they usually fail to resist the discourse of universal heterosexual desire; indeed, the more "realistic" the cartoon, the more often are viewers told that heterosexual desire is universal, that their only purpose in life is to find a heterosexual partner, and that they should begin in early childhood. The plots of *Doug* centered on a handholding romance between junior-high Doug and girl-next-door Patty Mayonnaise, and *Hey, Arnold* (1996) was primarily about a romantic triangle among twelve-year olds, Arnold, brassy Helga, and flirtatious Lila. Even the *Rugrats* (1991), babes-in-arms drawn realistically except for their ability to speak and their penchant for adventures, occasionally enjoyed heterosexual romances at the ages of one or two.

A smaller number of contemporary television cartoons are fantastic rather than realistic: set in magical kingdoms rather than middle schools, starring anthropomorphic animals rather than humans, or at least featuring non-naturalistic plotlines, as in *Fairly Oddparents* (2001), which regularly zaps ten-year old Timmy Turner into outer space, the distant past, or weird parallel worlds. Since these programs are not concerned with reflecting "real life," they are often lax about promoting compulsory heterosexuality, and sometimes same-sex relationships are subtly or not so subtly validated.

Spongebob Squarepants (1999) expresses his affection with starfish-next-door Patrick so aggressively that his creator, Stephen Hillenburg, felt it necessary to announce that he is "not gay," Hollywood code for "gay but not willing to admit it." The Australian series *Yakity Yak* (2003) pairs a teenage yak and an anthropomorphic pineapple. A *Lord of the Rings* spoof on *The Grim Adventures of Billy and Mandy* (2001) has a fey elf nearly overcome by desire as he praises a dwarf's muscular physique. As a result, these programs have a strong following among LGBT youth. *The Powerpuff Girls* (1998), kindergarten-age superheroes, have become veritable lesbian icons.

However, these programs are always extremely subtle in their portrayal of same-sex desire, reducing it to momentary jokes or sight gags easily missed by anti-gay pundits, who are more likely to look for flaming-queen **stereotypes** (such as Jerry Falwell's insistence that United Kingdom's *Teletubbies* promoted "the gay agenda" because the character Tinky Winky carried a handbag). In the end, the main characters usually promote heterosexual romance as assiduously as Disney movies, leaving the subtle hints to minor characters and villains. Dexter, the boy-mad scientist on *Dexter's Laboratory* (1996), develops frequent **crush**es on female babysitters, teachers, and science whizzes, leaving his nemesis, boy-mad scientist Mandark, to walk off into the sunset arm-in-arm with a new boy friend (in the 1998 episode "Sun, Surf, and Science"). For all their girl-power, the Powerpuff Girls often giggle at boys, and their chief nemesis is a demonic falsetto-voiced transvestite known only as *Him*. The implication is clear: youth must never know that same-sex desire exists, except among the inconsequential and the monstrous, but some references can be included for savvy adult viewers. Thus, a 2002 episode of *Fairly Oddparents*, in which two male characters express a longing for teen idol Chip Skylark, is entitled "Boys in the Band," but few children or teenagers are likely to catch the reference to the 1968 gay-themed movie.

Animated cartoons aired in primetime for all audiences, or late night for adults and older teenagers, began their renaissance in the early 1990s with a similarly skittish attitude toward expressions of same-sex desire. *Ren and Stimpy* (1991), a dog and a cat parodying the Hanna-Barbera cartoon duos of the 1960s, often expressed romantic interests; in one episode, Ren tries to coax Stimpy into bed, and Stimpy snipes "Is that all you think about?" Yet their creator John Kricfalusi still felt obligated to insist that they were not gay (at least until a revised version appeared late night on the heterosexual-male-oriented Spike network). *Pinky and the Brain* (1995), two laboratory rats plotting to take over the world, behave precisely as gay domestic partners without anyone ever saying that they are. No continuing character on Fox's *The Simpsons* (1989) has self-identified as LGBT to date, though Waylon Smithers hints at it constantly and, in one episode, makes a vague and old-fashioned allusion to his "chosen lifestyle."

Soon, however, gay jokes and even occasional gay characters began to appear. *The Simpsons* was most prolific, with throwaway jokes denigrating LGBT persons in almost every episode. In the 2003 episode "Special Edna," which is "about" a Teacher of the Year contest, there are three: neighbor Ned Flanders thinks that a man is asking him to dance; teenage boys at a lover's lane are forced to kiss each other (and comply with looks of utter disgust); and the Simpsons try out a talking car that tries to dissuade them from purchase by saying: "If you drive me, people will think that you're gay." Virtually every male character has expressed same-sex interest in comments meant to seem absurd, and the many gay walk-on characters, including steel mill workers, pride parade marchers, Log Cabin Republicans, and Homer's roommates (in an episode in which he leaves Marge), are all extremely flamboyant stereotypes.

Other prime-time animated cartoons are less obsessive about denigrating LGBT persons, but lesbians are rare (a few appear on *Clerks*, where they have crew-cuts and male voices), and the gay men invariably lisp and mince. On Fox's *King of the Hill* (1997), obtuse Hank Hill elicits laughs with his skittish fear of gender transgressions and his insistence that a gay couple he met must be brothers, yet he has no qualms about attending a gay rodeo (full of mincing, lisping cowboys, of course). *South Park* (1997), the Comedy Central series about foulmouthed fourth-graders who use the word "gay" to describe anything bad (e.g., "War is gay"), paradoxically displays flamboyant stereotypes and then preaches tolerance. There are three recurring nonheterosexual characters, all reminiscent of Edgar Pangborn's "pansy" characters in 1930s screwball comedies: Big Gay Al, the swishy owner of a refuge for gay pets; teacher Mr. Garrison, a psychopath who speaks through a hand puppet; and Satan.

While *South Park* and *King of the Hill* are extremely popular among heterosexual youth worldwide, they do not seem to have a major fan base among LGBT youth, since the gay men they present are far removed from everyday LGBT experience, and the pleas for tolerance, therefore, somewhat empty. It is in the cartoons intended for children and teenagers, the hints and in-jokes in *Fairly Oddparents*, *Spongebob Squarepants*, and *The Powerpuff Girls*, that LGBT youth might find validation, and freedom from the insistence on universal heterosexual desire that otherwise oppresses them.

Bibliography

Abel, Sam. 1995. "The Rabbit in Drag: Camp and Gender Construction in the American Animated Cartoon." *Journal of Popular Culture* 29, no. 3: 183–202.

Burke, Timothy, and Kevin Burke. 1999. *Saturday Morning Fever: Growing Up with Cartoon Culture*. New York: St. Martin's Press.

Griffin, Sean. 2000. *Tinker Belles and Evil Queens: The Walt Disney Company from the Inside Out*. New York: New York UP.

Hall, Donald E. 1997. "Introduction: Queer Works." *College Literature* 24, no. 1: 2–10.

Lenberg, Jeff. 1991. *The Encyclopedia of Animated Cartoons*. New York: Facts on File.

Stabile, Carole, and Mark Harrison. 2003. *Prime Time Animation: Television Animation and American Culture*. New York: Routledge.

Web Sites

The Big Cartoon Database. 2004. Accessed May 26, 2005. http://www.bcdb.com. Searchable database along with news, forum posts, and extensive lists of cartoons by studios.
Cartoon Research. 2004. Jerry Beck. Accessed May 26, 2005.
http://www.cartoonresearch.com. Comments, news and reviews, classic shorts and
intriguing trailers.

Catholic Education and Youth

Michael J. Maher

Catholic education refers to schools that are organized and administrated by bodies
of the Catholic Church, as a service to society and as a way to promote the
Catholic understanding of academic topics. As one example of its scope, in 2004, in
the United States, there were around 8,400 Catholic primary schools, secondary
schools, colleges and universities educating 7.6 million students. Worldwide there
are more than 40 million students enrolled in Catholic schools. The Catholic
Church makes a distinction between homosexual sexual activity (which it condemns) and people who are homosexual (who should be protected from **discrimination** and who should be welcomed in the Church). With this distinction, the
Catholic Church has instructed its schools' leaders and **administrators** to address
the topic of homosexuality. Catholics themselves tend to show more tolerant attitudes toward homosexuality than their Protestant counterparts, and graduates of
Catholic secondary schools tend to be less homophobic than graduates of public
high schools. Nevertheless, **lesbian, gay, bisexual** and **transgender youth** (LGBT) in
Catholic schools still experience isolation and silence while **harassment** and even
violence by students and teachers against LGBT students in Catholic secondary
schools have been reported. Catholic schools have only begun to address this issue.
In some instances, LGBT students in Catholic colleges and universities have had to
bring court cases to be allowed to have LGBT organizations. As a response to
recent **sexual abuse** scandals involving Catholic priests, the Church has actively
tried to prevent gay students from enrolling in or continuing at its seminaries.

In the 1970s, official bodies of the Catholic Church began to address the issue
of homosexuality, which had been neglected for several centuries. This was addressed both by the worldwide Catholic Church through official bodies in Rome
and by national bodies of Catholic bishops in some countries, especially English-
speaking countries and the Netherlands. LGBT Catholic support organizations,
such as Dignity in the United States, also began forming throughout the world.
Some important distinctions were articulated in these documents, reflecting general
Catholic thinking. One major distinction was a division between homosexual
orientation and homosexual activity; although *being homosexual* is not a sin,
according to the Church, *having sex* with a person of the same gender is. The
Church emphasized that LGBT people should not be discriminated against and that

See also Christian Moral Instruction on Homosexuality; College Campus Organizing; Legal
Issues, Students; Religion and Psychological Development; School Climate, K-12; Single-Sex
Schools.

Church institutions must protect their rights and provide them with ministry, or pastoral care. Another important distinction was between "transitory" homosexuality and "constitutional" homosexuality; according to the Church, some adolescents might go through a homosexual phase, whereas for many people their homosexuality is unchangeable. Because the Church recognizes that **sexual orientation** is most often unchangeable, "x-gay" movements have not been strong in Catholic circles. Finally, the Church made a distinction between doctrinal approaches and pastoral approaches to the topic of homosexuality. In regard to doctrine, the Church emphasized the official rules about what is right and wrong, whereas in regard to pastoral issues, the Church emphasized addressing peoples' spiritual needs without **prejudice**.

These distinctions have been the source of tension within the Church. Official statements from the Vatican generally have emphasized the sinfulness of homosexual acts, the correcting of an adolescent homosexual phase, and the importance of doctrinal beliefs. In contrast, statements from official national bodies of Catholic bishops, such as the United States Catholic Conference and the Roman Catholic Church of the Netherlands, have emphasized the dignity and rights of LGBT people, the permanence of constitutional homosexual orientation, and the pastoral needs of LGBT people. Two documents clearly demonstrate these approaches. The Sacred Congregation for the Doctrine of the Faith, the Vatican committee of bishops and cardinals responsible for interpreting Catholic doctrine, in Rome, issued, in 1986, *Letter to the Bishops of the Catholic Church on the Pastoral Care of Homosexual Persons*. A decade later, the United States Catholic Conference issued *Always Our Children: Pastoral Message to Parents of Homosexual Children and Suggestions for Pastoral Ministers*. Despite their different emphases, all official bodies of the Catholic Church state clearly that the topic of homosexuality must be addressed in Catholic education.

In the United States and in Great Britain, Catholics express more tolerant attitudes toward homosexuality than their Protestant counterparts. Even Catholics who have more conservative views about homosexual activity tend to support legal protection for the civil rights of LGBT people, and U.S. Catholics may be adopting more liberal attitudes toward homosexuality (D'Antonio et al. 2001; Smith 1999). There is some evidence that graduates of Catholic high schools have more liberal attitudes toward homosexuality than public high school graduates (Maher 2001).

At the level of secondary education, some Catholic secondary schools and associations have begun to address the issue of homosexuality, usually in the form of educating teachers and professional staff to be more sensitive to LGBT issues, but also in forming LGBT student organizations. School administrators who have taken these steps have typically promoted it as a matter of social justice. The Archdiocese of Saint Paul and Minneapolis has trained Catholic secondary school teachers and staff, allowed LGBT students to tell their stories in school newspapers, and created a support group for students (Gevelinger and Zimmerman 1997). The diocese provided several in-services for teachers, which focused on what life is like for LGBT students in their schools. The diocese also used PFLAG (Parents, Families, and Friends of Lesbian and Gays) as a resource for establishing its support groups for students.

In the **United Kingdom**, the Scottish Catholic Education Commission produced *Relationships & Moral Education*, a textbook teaching that homosexual behavior is morally wrong, but also promoted acceptance, respect, and compassion for LGBT people (Catholic World News 2000). In **Canada**, the Alberta Catholic School Trustees Association published *A Resource for an Inclusive Community: A Teacher's Guide for and about Persons with Same Sex Attractions*, in 2001, which placed overwhelming emphasis on ending discrimination of LGBT students in Catholic education. It also argued that while homosexual sexual acts could be judged, those who commit them could not. However, in 2002, a Canadian Catholic high school student had to sue his high school for the right to take a male date to his senior **prom**, and in **Australia** Catholic bishops sought exemption from a 1996 bill designed to prevent hate speech against gays and lesbians (Maher 2003).

In the United States, some LGBT student organizations at Catholic colleges and universities have had to take their schools to court in order simply to assure their right to exist and to meet on campus. Further, recent concerns about sexual misbehavior by Catholic priests has caused the Catholic Church more actively to try to "weed out" gay seminarians, estimated to number over 50 percent (Maher 2002; Nugent 1989). An in-depth study of one U.S. Catholic college found several barriers to dealing with the issue of homosexuality, including fear of reactions of Catholic authorities, parents, and alumni (Love 1997; 1998). Another barrier was misperceptions of what official Catholic teaching really said about homosexuality. Although Catholicism did not cause **homophobia** in the culture of the Catholic college, Catholicism was used to justify homophobia that existed there. Invisibility had marked the experiences of LGBT students at the college. Many of the LGBT students and their **allies** were very religious Catholics, understanding their work on LGBT inclusion as a calling from God. Support for LGBT students came from the department of campus ministry and the department of religious studies.

Catholic educational philosophy states that integration is a major goal of Catholic schools: integration of sexuality with **spirituality** and identity, integration of students of different backgrounds into one community, integration of lived experience with faith and with the **curriculum**, integration of the home with school. Nevertheless, LGBT students in Catholic schools have had an overall experience of exclusion, and a lack of harmony in their lives, which has been termed "dis-integration" (Maher 2001). It is not clear if this disharmony is greater than or less than that experienced by LGBT students in other schools, but those attending Catholic schools experience dis-integration from their families by not sharing important issues they are facing and, in some cases, by dealing with parents who are openly homophobic and even abusive. They experience dis-integration from their peers because they are usually not honest about who they are, fearing ostracism, harassment, or violence. They experience dis-integration from their schools due to their silence on homosexuality, enforcement of rigid ideas of gender conformity, and, in some cases, employment of homophobic teachers. They experience dis-integration from their faith because the Church is often perceived as unwelcoming to sexual minorities, because some priests and nuns appear to be self-hating gays and lesbians and because adolescent faith is so tied to social relationships, which are strained for them. They experience dis-integration from their **sexual identities** due to the inability of reconciling internal **desire** with external social and sexual expectations as well as **stereotypes** of LGBT people. Although most research has come from the United States, other researchers have noted similar poor experiences of gay men in Catholic schools in other countries (Maher 2003).

Bibliography

Catholic World News. 2000, January 14. "Catholic Students to be Taught about Homosexuality."

D'Antonio, William V., James D. Davidson, Dean R. Hoge, and Katherine Meyer. 2001. *American Catholics: Gender, Generation, and Commitment.* Walnut Creek, CA: AltaMira Press.

Gevelinger, Mary Ellen, and Laurel Zimmerman. 1997. "How Catholic Schools Are Creating a Safe Climate for Gay and Lesbian Students." *Educational Leadership* 55, no. 2: 66–68.

Love, Patrick G. 1997. "Contradiction and Paradox: Attempting to Change the Culture of Sexual Orientation at a Small Catholic College." *The Review of Higher Education* 20, no. 4: 381–398.

———. 1998. "Cultural Barriers Facing Lesbian, Gay, and Bisexual Students at a Catholic College." *Journal of Higher Education* 69, no. 3: 298–323.

Maher, Michael J. 2001. *Being Gay and Lesbian in a Catholic High School: Beyond the Uniform.* Binghamton, NY: Haworth Press.

———. 2002. "Openly Addressing the Reality: Homosexuality and Catholic Seminary Policies." *Religion & Education* 29, no. 2: 49–68.

———. 2003. "Review of Research: Some Background on Addressing the Topic of Homosexuality in Catholic Education." *Catholic Education: A Journal of Inquiry and Practice* 6, no. 4: 498–515.

Mattingly, Robert. 2004. "Gay Adolescents in Catholic Schools: Avoiding the Topic Won't Make It Go Away." *Momentum* (September/October): 42–46. Available at http://www.glsen.org/binary-data/GLSEN_ATTACHMENTS/file/413-1.pdf

Nugent, Robert. 1989. "Homosexuality and Seminary Candidates." Pp. 200–218 in *Homosexuality in the Priesthood and Religious Life.* Edited by Jeannine Gramick. New York: Crossroad.

Smith, Tom W. 1999, January. *American Catholics* (National Opinion Research Center Report). Chicago: University of Chicago.

Web Sites

The Catholic International Education Office. September 2000. Accessed May 26, 2005. http://www3.planalfa.es/oiec/oiecing.htm. Provides organizational details, including a newsletter and member contacts in various countries.

Dignity USA. 2004. Dignity USA. Accessed May 26, 2005. http://www.dignityusa.org. Catholic LGBT organization with a site that provides resources and links, sample liturgy, and FAQs are being gay and Catholic.

The Holy See. May 14, 2004. Congregation for the Doctrine of the Faith. Accessed May 26, 2005. http://www.vatican.va/roman_curia/congregations/cfaith/index.htm. An official Web site of the Catholic Church providing information on doctrinal questions.

Childhood

Stacy Otto

Childhood begins at birth and continues until human sexual organs mature, puberty is negotiated, and sexual reproduction becomes possible. But, this is a physiological definition. How our culture defines what it means to be a child and the presumptions

See also Bullying; Children of LGBT Parents; Children of the Rainbow Curriculum; Curriculum, Early Childhood; Curriculum, Primary; Foucault, Michel; Gender Identity; Gender Roles; Heteronormativity; Literature, Early Childhood; Psychoanalysis and Education.

that are made surrounding gender and the development of a person's **sexual identity** are major points of cultural contention, especially when it comes to the sexual identities of **lesbian, gay, bisexual**, and **transgender youth** (LGBT). There are several grand narratives that are central to our culture's notion of what it means to be a child. The first of these is the presumption of heterosexuality. The child is assumed to think and behave within the gender conventions of his or her physiologically-assigned sex and that there are only two possibilities: male/female (note that in this pair of terms "male" is privileged above "female"). Secondly, childhood is assumed to be a time of "innocence." The child is not sexual in thought or deed, any variation in this defiles the body of the child, their innocence is lost.

The meaning of the word "child" has undergone drastic revision in just the last one hundred or so years with a total transformation over the last two hundred. The concept of childhood as a stage of life separate from the rest gained acceptance during the beginning of the eighteenth century (the imposition of innocence was soon to follow), and, importantly, central to that concept was the power of childhood to mold and make the adult that child would become. Until the recent past, it was marriage that almost universally marked the ending of childhood. Since the Victorian era, the idea of **adolescence** has been "added on" to childhood, extending the time period that a person is considered a preadult by up to ten years.

Throughout childhood, especially within schools, heterosexuality is presumed at the individual level as well as at the institutional level. That is, children are invested with the social meanings of "boy" or "girl" on the basis of their physical sexual attributes. Presumed heterosexuality does not allow for any physical or cultural variation; rather a child is fit by the institutional practices of the school into either the category "boy" or the category "girl"—despite being considered a sexual innocent—and is correspondingly fit with the label "heterosexual." This development is also attributable to the rise of Freudian psychoanalytic theory, which pathologized homosexuality (identified as mental illness) and by extension, bisexual and transgender identities. When schools, as institutions, assume and promote students as exclusively heterosexual beings, the existence and validity of either alternative or multiple sexualities is firmly denied. Such a narrow definition of children's sexuality identifies the LGBT child as "other" and creates and supports the ideas and practices of **homophobia**. The identification within schools of heterosexuality as normal and desirable delivers social and cultural power to those children who appear to conform to the culture's notions of heterosexuality, leading LGBT youth to fear being "found out" as having sexual thoughts—and perhaps deeds—that are outside the strictly-enforced norms of heterosexuality.

Childhood negotiation of sexual identity formation is particularly problematic for LGBT youth because they must first challenge the overwhelming "presumption of heterosexuality" (Epstein 1994, 197) before they can begin to develop a personal sense of self. Given the cultural insistence on normalcy, to mount such a challenge to the authority of institutions, adults, the opinions of peers, and the staggering number of images that reinforce heterosexuality as normal and desirable, can be a truly daunting childhood task. A great number of researchers trace the effects of being made to feel different and "othered" by the dominant culture, and the corresponding **discrimination** and stigmatization, as the source of LGBT youth's tendencies toward **suicide, substance abuse**, and psychological illness. Recently, this view has been challenged by researchers who focus on the strength and **resiliency** of LGBT youth in the face of the many emotional and physical difficulties "sexual minority" youth face (Savin-Williams 2001). A strong multidisciplinary argument exists that children, and in particular LGBT youth, are sexual beings who embody an[other] sexuality than do adults: sexuality complete with **desire**.

But, this discussion of children as sexual beings is directly—and violently— opposed to the cultural assumption of children as perfectly innocent. This has been evidenced in schooling by the continuing uproar over **sexuality education** as well as the past practices of morality clauses resulting in the dismissal of teachers who became pregnant in an effort to shield schoolchildren from that visible proof of sexual intercourse. The cultural construction of children as innocent allows them to be dominated by adults—in fact, insists upon it. James Kincaid (1992) theorizes that by imposing an artificial innocence on the body and mind of the child, our culture creates the opposite of that innocence. This theory depends upon the notion that the identification of one term is largely defined by the term that opposes it: Light is defined as "not dark," for instance. Kincaid argues that to assume and therefore to imprint innocence upon the child is to create, as a culture, depravity against children. Were the [sexual] power relations between children and adults in our culture to be equalized, then depravity, or perverse thought and action against children, would not be prevalent. Furthermore, a romantic vision of childhood that paints the child as naturally innocent creates a number of impossible difficulties for the child who is not.

As a culture, we owe much of our knowledge of the perfect innocence of the child and childhood to the images that have established and reinforced such a notion, beginning with Sir Joshua Reynolds' painting *The Age of Innocence* in the late eighteenth century, and reinforced by the paintings of such artists as Kate Greenaway, Mary Cassatt, and Jessie Willcox Smith. But, it is through visual **art** that many of our cultural assumptions of the innocence and pleasures of childhood are being challenged. Sally Mann's modern-day photographs of her children are a provocative example, but the secreted Victorian-era photographs of Viscountess Clementina Hawarden's own children are just as challenging to the ideal innocence of the child given their day.

Same-sex play is culturally ubiquitous. But, the sexualized play of children is labeled (by the uncomfortable, uncertain teacher) as appropriate or inappropriate. These categories are dangerously confused and muddled together to include the behavior of children of LGBT orientations and the pathological behavior of victims of childhood **sexual abuse**. Most same-sex play research focuses on boys and the "all-boy" qualities of courage, stoicism (the suppression of fear and pain), loyalty, competition, and domination over the natural environment. It is the crybaby who is cruelly bullied by others and none more so than the **sissy boy**. Play evolves as boys "develop an interest" in girls (and vice versa) and failure to do so violates the Freudian stages of the normal child's sexual maturity.

There are some discussions of childhood in which LGBT youth are a part of the larger conversation of what it means to be a child—any child. Play is one of those areas that is terribly important to childhood, but is often conceptually invested with false innocence. Play defines childhood and is the means by which children navigate childhood, learn to bear loss, and are thus put on the pathway toward leading a psychologically happy and healthy adulthood (Winnicott 1982). There is quite a bit of **curriculum** theory that is centered around play in the classroom and outside it. But play can be dominated by children's efforts to seize power from one another and there is a great deal of anecdotal evidence of this phenomenon as well as that portrayed in images. Julie Zando's film *Let's Play Prisoners* (USA 1988) explores how same-sex play among female children is used to negotiate power between them. Her work, along with the photographs of Edward Steichen's *The Family of Man* 1956 exhibit at the Museum of Modern Art, are compelling evidence that children's play, and by extension childhood, is full of sadistic acts of taking power as children make their way toward sexual and emotional maturity. By turns delicious and terrifying, at once a mix of pleasure and pain, such evidence does not reflect the common conception of childhood, its innocence and perfect lack of sexuality; rather it delivers a perverse commentary on how children make sense of power relations within the secret worlds of childhood.

Bibliography

Epstein, Debbie, and Richard Johnson. 1994. "On the Straight and Narrow: The Heterosexual Presumption, Homophobias, and Schools." Pp. 197–230 in *Challenging Gay and Lesbian Inequalities in Education*. Edited by Debbie Epstein. Buckingham: Open University Press.
Jenkins, Henry, ed. 1998. *The Children's Culture Reader*. New York: New York University Press.
Kincaid, James R. 1992. *Child-Loving: The Erotic Child and Victorian Culture*. New York: Routledge.
Mavor, Carol. 1995. *Pleasures Taken: Performances of Sexuality and Loss in Victorian Photographs*. Durham, NC: Duke University Press.
Museum of Modern Art. 1955. *The Family of Man: The Photographic Exhibition Created by Edward Steichen for the Museum of Modern Art*. New York: Simon and Schuster.
Savin-Williams, Ritch C. 2001. "A Critique of Research on Sexual-Minority Youth." *Journal of Adolescence* 24, no. 1: 5–13.
Winnicott, Donald Woods. 1982. *Playing and Reality*. London: Routledge.

Web Site

Helping Adolescents Develop a Healthy Sexual Identity, San Francisco Medical Society. Accessed August 4, 2004. http://www.sfms.org/sfm/sfm503c.htm. Outlines the dilemma of how youth and their parents get questions answered about childhood and adult sexuality. This site articulates the cultural and physiological differences and relationships between sexual identity and sexual orientation.

Children of LGBT Parents

Pat Hulsebosch

There are an estimated six to fourteen million children in the United States who have one or more parents who are lesbian, gay, or bisexual. According to 2000 United States Census data, of the nearly 600,000 same-sex couples counted,

See also Adolescence; Allies; Curriculum, Antibias; Asian American Youth; Bullying; Childhood; Educational Policies; Ethnic Identity; Latinos and Latinas; Multicultural Education; Native and Indigenous LGBT Youth; Parents, LGBT; Passing; School Safety and Safe School Zones.

34 percent of the female households (i.e., lesbian and bisexual female couples) and 22 percent of the male households (i.e., gay or bisexual male couples) had at least one child under the age of eighteen living with them. Further, lesbians of color in same-sex relationships were more likely than white lesbians/bisexual women in same-sex relationships to give birth. Sixty percent of **African American** lesbians, 50 percent of Native American lesbians, 43 percent of Hispanic lesbians, 30 percent of Asian/Pacific Islander lesbians, and 23 percent of white non-Hispanic lesbians had given birth to at least one child.

Daughter with her gay father, a teacher. © Gigi Kaeser from the book and the touring photo-text exhibit LOVE MAKES A FAMILY: Portraits of Lesbian, Gay, Bisexual, and Transgender People and Their Families. For information, visit http://www.familydiv.org or e-mail info@familydiv.org

Children with LGBT parents vary widely in terms of the family structures in which they were conceived and currently live. Most were born to parents while in a heterosexual marriage before their biological parent came out. Some have parents who come out to their children when they divorce their heterosexual partner or when the child becomes an adolescent or an adult. A number of these children later became part of blended **families** with their birth parent's partner. Still other LGBT parents make a decision to never explicitly tell their children of their **sexual identity**. An increasing number of LGBT couples, particularly those with financial resources, have intentionally chosen to have children through new reproductive technologies, including donor insemination and surrogacy.

The recent rise in children with LGBT parents has led to a dramatic increase in public awareness of the existence of these children. As the current generation of children born into openly gay families has entered educational institutions, these institutions have been confronted with the need to acknowledge their presence and to determine how to be responsive to their strengths, interests, and needs. Family structures, as well as **race, social class**, gender, identity, political consciousness, and a variety of other factors, will also impact the extent to which children and their LGBT families are open and explicit about their families with educational institutions. Organizations such as Children of Lesbians and Gays Everywhere (COLAGE) and Children of Transexuals (COT), provide online support; and COLAGE and Family Pride Coalition sponsor national and local events and support groups for children.

Educators, influenced by society's **heterosexism**, often assume that growing up in a LGBT family negatively impacts children. Most existing **research** on children from queer families has been motivated by a need to disprove these heterosexist beliefs (Johnson and O'Connor 2002; Stacey and Biblarz 2001). All of the research that has been done has shown that there are no significant differences between children with lesbian, gay, or transgendered parents and children with straight parents on a variety of dimensions including intelligence, moral reasoning, personality, separation–individuation, gender role behavior, sexual identity, self-esteem, mental health or social relationships, either as children or in adulthood. Recent research that has begun to look at positive influences on children of growing up with LGBT parents indicates that children with gay or lesbian parents are more tolerant of diversity, more open to new points of view, and have increased empathy and understanding for others (Johnson and O'Connor 2002; Stacey and Biblarz 2001). As children raised in LGBT families get older, they may also adopt aspects of a queer cultural identity and, in doing so, become bicultural; that is, knowledgeable about queer cultural perspectives as well as heterosexual society. For example, they may become familiar with queer language, humor, political perspectives, and customs, and have a broader understanding of and appreciation for gender roles. While all of this research has explicitly focused on lesbian- and/or gay-headed families, it is likely that there are bisexuals in the same-sex couples included in the samples in many of these studies.

Children with queer parents share much in the way of context and, therefore, share common challenges. All have at least one parent with whom they have no biological tie; many of them also have no legal tie to at least one parent. Schools, like other societal institutions which have historically been most comfortable recognizing and affirming legally sanctioned family structures, often have difficulty accommodating children with LGBT parents. From the basic question of what term to use when discussing their same-sex parents ("Dad," "Papa," "Ema," "Mom"), to application forms with spaces only for "mother" and "father," teachers and administrators struggle with explicitly including children of LGBT families.

Although there are no significant developmental differences or negative effects on children of LGBT parents, these youth report facing more **prejudice** and **discrimination** because of societal **homophobia** and heterosexism (Brill 2001; Johnson and O'Connor 2002). School entry is often the first time that children of LGBT families encounter intolerance from peers, teachers, **administrators**, and staff. In fact, students who have LGBT parents experience harassment at the same rate as students who themselves are gay (Brill 2001). In order to learn effectively, children need safe schools to attend. Being teased or harassed, living in fear, hiding or feeling invisible because of one's family background is a detriment to learning. Adopting and implementing antibias policies and enacting inclusive curricula are essential.

Young children initially assume that all families are like theirs, but, as they get older, they begin to realize that there are differences among people and families. During the first few years of elementary school, children begin comparing their family to other families they know, including the families represented in the curriculum. When teachers incorporate depictions of diverse family structures, through discussions, visitors, books and other media, they allow all children to see LGBT families as part of our society. Similarly, teachers of older children can include explicitly "gay-" "lesbian-," "bisexual-," and "transgender-"related perspectives in their **curriculum**, particularly in young adult **literature**, whether or not they are aware of having students with LGBT families or LGBT students.

Children who have been brought up with a gay positive perspective initially expect to have themselves and their family accepted. As a result, young children seldom censor discussions about their families. The first time children experience negative consequences from talking about their family is the beginning of an awareness of the social stigma attached to LGBT families. This eventually brings the understanding that discussing family structure can have personal ramifications, and an initial understanding of oppression and **coming out**.

As children move through elementary school and beyond, they make daily decisions about if, when, and how to come out. Older children report that their decisions are based on how favorably they anticipate the response to be (Gottlieb 2003). These decisions may become more challenging as youth confront their own age-related identity issues. On the other hand, because adolescents don't often feel the need to discuss their parents, the sexual identity of their families may not come up as regularly.

At some point, youth may become aware of the political aspects of injustice and may take a role in educating their peers and teachers on heterosexist language and gay rights. Families and other educators can strengthen children's ability to handle bias-related slurs and other forms of prejudice when they teach children the skills to recognize and cope with oppression. The current climate of national debate on gay-related issues can also encourage youth in feeling part of a larger movement. As with other children raised by parents who are stigmatized in society (e.g., **deaf** parents) adolescents may struggle between a desire to support this movement and to fit into their mainstream peer culture.

Educators can create environments in which children of LGBT parents feel safe and respected by:

- Becoming aware of their heterosexism and homophobia and educating themselves about queer history and culture
- Asking questions when LGBT parents are willing to discuss their family life
- Including LGBT terminology, images, and information in and around the school setting in age-appropriate ways

Bibliography

Brill, Stephanie A. 2001. *The Queer Parent's Primer*. Oakland: New Harbinger.

Caspar, Virginia, and Stephen Schulz. 1999. *Gay Parents/Straight Schools*. New York: Teachers College Press.

Gottlieb, Andrew. J. 2003. *Sons Talk about Their Gay Fathers*. Binghamton, NY: Harrington Park Press.

Green, Richard. 1998. "Transexuals' Children." *International Journal of Transgenderism* 2, no. 3. Accessed August 23, 2004. http://www.symposion.com/ijt/ijtc0601.htm.

Howe, Noelle, Ellen Samuels, Margarethe Cammermeyer, and Dan Savage, eds. 2000. *Out of the Ordinary: Essays on Growing up With Gay, Lesbian, and Transgender Parents*. New York: St. Martin's Press.

Johnson, Suzanne M., and Elizabeth O'Connor. 2002. *The Gay Baby Boom: The Psychology of Gay Parenthood;* New York: New York University Press.

Patterson, Charlotte J. 1995. "Lesbian Mothers, Gay Fathers, and Their Children." Pp. 262–290 in *Lesbian, Gay and Bisexual Identities Across the Lifespan*. Edited by Anthony D'Augelli and Charlotte J. Patterson. New York: Oxford University Press.

Stacey, Judith, and Timorthy J. Biblarz. 2001. "(How) Does the Sexual Orientation of Parents Matter?" *American Sociological Review* 66: 159–183.

Tasker, Fiona L., and Susan Golombok. 1998. *Growing up in a Lesbian Family: Effects on Child Development*. New York: Guilford Press.

Web Sites

American Civil Liberties Union. Lesbian and Gay Rights Project. 1998. *In the Child's Best Interests: Defending Fair and Sensible Adoption Policies*. Accessed June 2, 2005. http://www.aclu.org/LesbianGayRights/LesbianGayRights.cfm?ID=9185&c=104.

Supporting the adoption by LGBT parents, Parts I and II include a Policy Memo and Legislative Strategies while Part III, *Responding To Proponents' Arguments*, has questions and answers about children raised by LGBT parents.

Children of Lesbians and Gays Everywhere (COLAGE). Accessed June 2, 2005. http://www.colage.org/. COLAGE is the only organization in the world specifically supporting young people with LGBT parents. The site has sections for youth, including children of transsexuals as well as local and national event listings, pen pals, and camps for youth.

Family Pride Coalition. Accessed June 2, 2005. http://www.familypride.org. Resources and event information LGBT families. The site also has a downloadable information booklet, *How to Talk to Children About Our Families*, as well as links to sections on LGBT family-related news, a library, advocacy, and parent groups.

Human Rights Campaign Foundation: HRC Focus on the Family-Parenting. Accessed June 2, 2005. http://www.hrc.org/Template.cfm?Section=Parenting&Template=/TaggedPage/TaggedPageDisplay.cfm&TPLID=26&ContentID=17907. Provides up-to-date news releases as well as links to resources on relevant state laws, adoption agencies, professional opinions, and HRC research reports such as *The Cost of Marriage Inequality to Children and Their Same-Sex Parents*.

United States Census Bureau. September, 2003. Simmons and O'Connell. *Married-Couple and Unmarried Partner Households: 2000*. Accessed June 2, 2005. http://www.census.gov/prod/2003pubs/censr-5.pdf. Data from the 2000 U. S. Census, including statistics about same-sex partner households with children.

Children of the Rainbow Curriculum

Cris Mayo

Introduced in New York City public schools in 1992, the Children of the Rainbow curriculum was a first grade teachers' guide to incorporating **multicultural education** in a wide range of subjects and classroom activities. Children of the Rainbow included lessons on **race** and **ethnicity**, and most controversially, lessons advocating respect for lesbian and gay families. The controversy over Children of the Rainbow was among the issues most publicized in the "culture wars" of the early 1990s. While some of the antihomophobia lessons weathered curricular revisions, three of the four gay- and lesbian-themed books that had been listed as age-appropriate teachers' resources—*Daddy's Roommate, Heather Has Two Mommies*, and *Gloria Goes to Gay Pride*—were removed.

Since 1985, the New York City Board of Education has had a policy that included **sexual orientation** as a protected class. This curriculum guide, however, was the first official effort to make gay and lesbian issues part of multiculturalism. Children of the Rainbow was also notable for situating lessons about diversity within traditional curricular areas, using culturally specific songs and stories within mathematics, for instance. Rather than having cultural diversity stand alone, Children of

See also Activism, LGBT Teachers; Curriculum, Antibias; Families, LGBT; Identity Politics; Literature, Early Childhood; Prejudice; Urban Youth and Schools.

the Rainbow encouraged students to see the variety of ways in which culture was a part of school. By including gay- and lesbian-headed families, this curriculum invited students to value and respect diverse families, although it did not address **bisexuality** or **transgender** issues.

LGBT educators had sought to become part of the development of multicultural education since the school board policy was instituted in 1985. Seven years later, and very late in the review process of Children of the Rainbow, the curriculum committee invited a lesbian teacher to add material that addressed sexual orientation. These additions, however, were not given to reviewers and at least some of the objections came from people who had worked on the review and were surprised to see controversial material in the final draft.

This gaffe does not seem to have been behind the vast majority of protests; there was already a precedent for removing even seemingly mundane references to gay relationships in New York City's **AIDS** curriculum, which had been implemented in 1987. A lesson discouraging **drug use** began: "Michael and Bill have been going together for one year" but was changed to "Michael and Bill are very good friends." The AIDS curriculum had already raised public outcry over the incursion of public education into matters previously considered private, like sex and condoms. Conservatives were still angry and organized.

Protests began shortly after the curriculum was released. Protestors objected to passages in the curriculum like, "children need actual experiences via creative play, books, visitors, etc. in order for them to view lesbians/gays as real people to be respected and appreciated." Additional objections were lodged against the four children's books included in the bibliography. Like the rest of the curriculum, these books were only intended as a guide for the teacher. Of the four books originally included in the teacher's bibliography (*Daddy's Roommate*, *Heather Has Two Mommies*, *Gloria Goes to Gay Pride*, and *Asha's Mums*) only the last one was not criticized; it remained on the teachers' reading list after the curriculum revision. *Asha's Mums* is also the only book of the four that deals directly with the difficulties a child might have having two mothers and that has substantial representation of people of color, including the main character and her mothers. Asha's teacher won't accept a permission slip for a field trip signed by two women. Although Asha's friends accept her two mothers, the teacher never actually endorses her mothers' relationship, nor is the word "lesbian" ever mentioned. Institutional acceptance remains questionable for Asha's mums, but it is clear that Asha's friends are very supportive.

The protests and the rebellion of Queens District 24's Board President Mary Cummins, who refused to implement any form of gay-inclusive multicultural curriculum, also began a trend in conservative organizing. Where only a short time before, during the revision of the New York State social studies curricula, conservatives had railed against people of color, they now demanded that gays and lesbians not be given the kind of attention that "legitimate minorities" rightfully deserved. This objection to the Rainbow curriculum suggested that gays and lesbians were white and people of color were heterosexual, a strategy that continues to be used by conservatives in other issues as well. The controversy over Children of the Rainbow, despite the eventual revision of most of the gay-inclusive content and the absence of funds to implement it, publicized the existence of gay- and lesbian-headed families and sexual minority students in schools.

Bibliography

Irvine, Janice M. 1997. "One Generation Post-Stonewall: Political Contests over Lesbian and Gay School Reform." Pp. 572–589 in *A Queer World: The Center for Lesbian and Gay Studies Reader*. Edited by Martin Duberman. New York: New York University Press.

Lee, N'Tanya, Don Murphy, and Juliet Ucelli. 1993, March. "Whose Kids? Our Kids! Race, Sexuality and the Right in New York City's Curriculum Battles." *Radical America* 25 no. 1, 9–21.

Phariss, Tracy. 1997. "Public Schools: A Battleground in the Cultural War." Pp. 75–79 in *Gay/Lesbian/Bisexual/Transgender Public Policy Issues: A Citizen's and Administrator's Guide to the New Cultural Struggle*. Edited by Wallace K. Swan. Binghamton, NY: Harrington Park Press.

Web Site

"The History of Heather." Accessed Dec. 6, 2004. http://www.alyson.com/html/00_files/00_ednote/0400/0400heather10_03_int.html. This commercial site is notable for its collection of excerpts from media coverage of the controversy about *Heather Has Two Mommies* and quotes from the Children of the Rainbow curriculum.

China, LGBT Issues in

Rodney Jones

Homosexuality in China has a long history, but it is only recently that it has been widely recognized as a legitimate social identity. This has to do both with political conditions and cultural factors, most importantly traditional Chinese conceptions of social identity itself, which tends to be seen more collectively, based primarily on kinship, rather than individualistically, based on social behavior or individual preferences. With the recent economic and political reforms and the influx of Western ideas, sexual minority identities are receiving increased social recognition; communities based on sexualities are growing in strength, especially in **urban** areas. The issues facing **lesbian, gay, bisexual** and **transgender youth** (LGBT) in contemporary China are in some ways similar to those in other countries, including **homophobia** and stigmatization, getting along with and **coming out** to family members, political recognition and legal protection, and gender and **social class** issues. How these are played out and understood, however, are often quite different because they are affected by China's unique cultural traditions and political circumstances.

The mention of homosexual behavior and same-sex love can be found in numerous historical annals, poems, and novels of ancient China. A number of emperors were purported to have kept male concubines, some of whom wielded enormous influence in the court. By most accounts, homosexual behavior enjoyed varying

See also Asia, LGBT Youth and Issues in; Bisexuality; China, LGBT Youth in; College Campus Organizing; Colonialism and Homosexuality; Identity Politics; LGBT Studies; Parents, Responses to Homosexuality; Passing; Popular Culture; Sexual Identity; Transsexuality.

degrees of acceptance in the dynastic period, especially among the upper classes (Hinsch 1992). The term "homosexuality," however, did not exist in China until the later part of the Qing Dynasty (1644–1911). The first widespread explicit representations of the "homosexual person" in China probably occurred during the Republican Period (1911–1949). Then, under the influence of the traditional conceptual link between sex and reproduction, the new nationalism, and a growing interest in eugenics, "homosexuality" was portrayed by government and academic voices as a foreign and "uncivilized perversion" which endangered familial and social order, "deteriorated the racial spirit," and threatened the "quality of the population."

Since the establishment of the People's Republic in 1949, official portrayals of homosexuality have undergone considerable revision. In the early Revolutionary Period, racist constructions of homosexuality from the Republican Period were reconceptualized in political and economic terms: Homosexuality was considered a symptom of bourgeois decadence and the homosexual person viewed as a kind of criminal or "class enemy." Although there have never been specific laws prohibiting homosexual behavior in China, during this period (and up until the mid-1990s) homosexuals were regularly arrested under article 106 of Chinese Criminal Law which prohibited "hooliganism."

In the Reform Period (starting in 1979), moral and political models of homosexuality were gradually replaced with medical models in which it was seen as a disease. Government clinics offered treatments such as "hate therapy" to "cure" citizens of their **desire** for same-sex behavior. In one account of this **reparative therapy** approach, patients were given electric shocks while viewing erotic images. Despite this medicalization of homosexuality, however, its association with hooliganism and foreigners still persisted. This association was particularly salient in early representations of **HIV/AIDS**, which portrayed the disease as a result of the moral bankruptcy and "sexual chaos" of the West epitomized by the image of the diseased homosexual body. Even though official reports of HIV prevalence among homosexuals in China are much lower than other traditional "risk groups" (such as IV drug users and sex workers), gay men are often associated with AIDS in public discourse. In many respects, AIDS-related stigmatization of homosexuality actually fuels the growth of the epidemic among gay men (Pilcher 2003).

More recently, Chinese officials, academics, and clinicians have been revising these medical and moral models and embracing social scientific constructions of homosexuality as a social identity rather than a mental disorder or a social problem. Sociologists, psychologists, and medical doctors from institutions with close links to the state (like the Chinese Academy of Social Sciences) have declared that homosexuality is just as prevalent in China as it is in the West. Gays and lesbians are beginning to be viewed as members of legitimate "communities" or "subcultures." In the spring of 2000, the Chinese Psychiatric Association announced the removal of homosexuality per se from its diagnostic list of mental disorders (**gender identity** disorders have been recognized by the association since the early 1980s and sexual reassignment surgery is recognized as a legitimate treatment). This opening has been accompanied by increased social opportunities for members of sexual minorities.

Nearly every major city in China has several commercial venues catering to gays and lesbians, including bars, discos, and bathhouses. One of the most important avenues for **communication** and community building among LGBT persons in China is the **Internet**. There are literally hundreds of Web sites in China devoted to the concerns of gays and lesbians (though fewer for bisexuals and transgender people), which include domestic and international news, personal ads, and chat rooms for users to meet friends and potential sexual partners. So far, the government has shown little interest in interfering with such Web sites. Actually there is quite a lot of political discussion on all kinds of Web sites in China—in particular, university bulletin boards have a lot of material that is very critical of the government.

Perhaps the overriding issues in the lives of LGBT in China are those of identity and community. The concept of "sexuality" itself is rather new to Chinese culture, and terms denoting homosexuality have traditionally been used to describe certain social practices rather than distinct social identities. In fact, the Chinese term for homosexual (*tong xing lian zhe*) is rarely used and little understood by many people outside of China's urban centers, and the term for bisexual (*shuang xing lian zhe*) is simply incomprehensible to most Chinese, not yet having made it's way into the vocabulary of everyday conversation. Some urban Chinese gay men and lesbians have appropriated Western terms like "gay" and "**queer**" to describe themselves, but many prefer using the Chinese word ***tong-zhi***, which means "comrade." This usage of the word "comrade" began in Hong Kong and Taiwan and is now widespread on the mainland, even in mainstream media. Borrowing of one of the Party-State's most sacred identity labels has multiple implications. On the one hand, it reflects a "dissident irony" and solidarity with Chinese gays and lesbians in Hong Kong and Taiwan (as well as those living in Western countries); on the other hand, it evidences a desire to distinguish themselves from the dominant Western models of queer culture.

Some scholars and activists consider gay and lesbian identity in China to be fundamentally different from that in the West, based more on collectivistic values, and eschew Western models of **activism** and gay liberation rhetoric, which they consider too confrontational (Chou 2000). Others, however, believe Chinese gays and lesbians can learn much from the West. This is one of the central debates in LGBT politics in China. In any case, dealing with an authoritarian government still wary of civil society and activist organizations is tricky; many believe that the best way to make progress is to work quietly and incrementally. There are no officially recognized LGBT organizations in China and the only publication for gays and lesbians is a small magazine, "Friends," published in Qingdao by Zhang Bei-Chuan, but distributed nationally with the sanction of the government given that it focuses primarily on **HIV education** for gay men.

One of the main reasons that the face of LGBT liberation in China is different from that in the West is that the face of homophobia is different. The widespread physical violence against sexual minorities and the association of homosexuality with "sin," common in the United States, are rare in China due to differences in cultural and religious norms and traditions. Rather, **discrimination** takes the form of silence and social invisibility. This is particularly true in the Chinese family, governed by Confucian values, which dictate a strict hierarchical relationship between parents and children, emphasizing children's duty to get married and produce (preferably male) offspring. Most Chinese gays and lesbians find "coming out" to their parents extremely difficult, if not impossible; the vast majority still get married. This situation is beginning to change, especially in the major cities, as Chinese ideas of marriage and family are being transformed by changing economic and social conditions as well as exposure to Western values. Although "gay bashing" and other **hate crimes** are rare in China, Chinese gays and lesbians must still contend

153

with blackmail and other dangers. Further, there are no legal protections against discrimination, nor are same-sex couples eligible for public housing, **adoption**, or other benefits enjoyed by heterosexuals.

The spread of HIV is another important issue facing Chinese sexual minorities, especially Chinese gay men. Measuring the extent of the epidemic among gay men in China is difficult since most men who have sex with men are married and reluctant to report their sexual activities in the context of an HIV test. Most official and unofficial estimates (3 to 5 percent in 2003) are quite low compared to gay communities in other countries (Choi 2003). At the same time, however, rates of condom use and knowledge about safer sex are also low, and some fear that the epidemic which has mushroomed among IV drug users and recipients of unhygienic blood donation schemes will soon take off among China's urban gay men (Wan 1999; Zhang, Xiufang, and Zhuzhong 2000). The danger seems particularly acute among older, married men. One recent study found that gay men over the age of thirty-nine are nearly five times more likely to be infected than younger gay men (Choi 2003).

Since the early 1990s, the government has made some efforts, though limited, to educate gay men about AIDS with published materials and outreach programs. There also have been important efforts among gay men themselves to educate their peers, especially in the urban centers of Beijing, Shanghai, and Guangzhou. These include hotlines, public forums, publications, and outreach activities in parks, bars, and other venues. Most of these activities have been permitted, and in some cases even encouraged, by the government. To some degree, these activities have helped to mobilize gay activists around a cause which is more acceptable to the government than "gay rights." Nevertheless, there have been numerous cases of gay/AIDS activists being investigated or detained by authorities, most notably the week long detention in 2002 of Wan Yan Hai, perhaps China's most famous AIDS activist, for distributing internal documents from the Ministry of Health through the Internet. While **sexuality education** in Chinese secondary schools includes information on HIV/AIDS, it usually does not specifically address the needs of LGBT youth. Several universities, however, including Shanghai's prestigious Fudan University, have opened courses addressing LGBT issues.

Ironically for "socialist" China, class issues are also central to Chinese queer life. There is a significant gap in access to gay and lesbian resources and lifestyles between more affluent urban gays and lesbians and less affluent men and women from the countryside. The recent influx of poor **rural** migrant workers into the major cities has resulted in a large "gay underclass," many of whom engage in **sex work** or blackmail. Currently, to be gay or lesbian in China means also to be urban and educated. Rural queer youth face numerous problems of discrimination, lack of access to community resources (including those available via the Internet), and increased vulnerability to HIV.

Surprisingly for such a sexually conservative culture, transsexuals in China seem to enjoy a large measure of acceptance, perhaps related to a dynastic history in which both eunuchs and cross-**dressing** opera singers enjoyed important status in the court and the society. In the Qing Dynasty, for example, *dans*, young men trained to play female parts in Chinese Opera, were expected to continue their feminine identity off-stage, and transgender characters appear in much classic Chinese literature, including the famous eighteenth century novel, *Dream of the Red Chamber*. China's first sex change operation was performed in 1983, and hospitals in major cities performing such operations follow guidelines and provide psychological counseling comparable to many places in the West. The country's most famous transsexual is probably Jin Xing, a former army colonel and famous choreographer. Trangender people in China have little difficulty in changing the **gender identity** on ID cards and official documents. In December 2004, the first transsexual wedding was announced in Chengdu and, in March, a male-to-female transsexual was also married in Sichuan province. According to official reports, as of 2004, there were about 1,000 postoperative transsexuals in China.

While Taiwan and Hong Kong are also officially part of China, the situation for sexual minorities there differs significantly from that on the mainland. In Hong Kong, under British colonial rule, homosexual acts were prohibited by law until 1991, and during the early 1990s gay and lesbian life was rather subdued, apart from the work of a few Western activists. Since the return to Chinese sovereignty in 1997, there has been a marked increase of gay publications and commercial entertainment venues and organizations. Gays and lesbians have become increasingly vocal, lobbying the government for equal rights and equal protection under the law. Sexual minorities have also become more visible in the media and entertainment worlds. Wong Kar Wai's award winning gay themed **film** *Happy Together* (1997), received both critical and popular acclaim, and when canto-pop superstar Leslie Cheung died in 2003, the local press positively and sympathetically reported the mourning of his male partner.

Ironically, transgender people in mainland China have more rights than they do in Hong Kong. Along with fierce social stigmatization, transgender people are not permitted to change their gender on their birth certificate and, though their identity cards show their new gender, a special code in the card marks them as trangendered.

Taiwan boasts probably the most open social environment for gays and lesbians despite a strong undercurrent of conservative Confucian thought. Along with numerous commercial publications and entertainment venues for gay men, lesbians, and transgender persons, most large universities have gay and lesbian student organizations, on mainstream networks there are gay-themed television shows such as *Nian Zi*, the tale of a young gay man in Taipei during the 1980s, and political candidates openly court the gay and lesbian vote. There has even been talk of granting marriage rights to same-sex couples. Since 1996, Chinese gays and lesbians have periodically organized global tong-zhi conferences, events for sharing social experiences and planning political strategies.

Nevertheless, there are still incidents of police raids of gay parties and saunas as well as sensationalistic stories in the press linking homosexuality to promiscuity and AIDS. Transgender people in Taiwan tend to face more social discrimination and stigmatization than gays and lesbians, although they are beginning to organize. The Center for the Study of Sexualities at National Center University has been important in advancing transgender **research**.

Bibliography

Choi, K. et al. 2003. "Emerging HIV-1 Epidemic in China in Men Who Have Sex with Men." *The Lancet* 361: 2125–2126.

Chou Wah-Shan. 2000. *Tongzhi: Politics of Same-Sex Eroticism in Chinese Societies.* Binghamton, NY: Harrington Park Press.

Fang Gang. 1995. *Tongxinglian zai Zhongguo.* (Homosexuality in China). Beijing: Jilin Publishing House.

Hinsch, Bret. 1992. *Passions of the Cut Sleeve: The Male Homosexual Tradition in China*. Berkeley: University of California Press.

Li Yinhe. 1998. *Tongxinglian Ya Wehua*. (The Homosexual Subculture). Beijing: China Today Publishing House.

Pilcher, Helen R. 2003. "Stigmatization Fueling Chinese HIV." *Nature*, June 20. Accessed December 4, 2004. http://www.nature.com/nsu/030616/030616–19.html.

Sang, Tze-Lan D. 2003. *The Emerging Lesbian: Female Same-Sex Desire in Modern China*. Chicago: University of Chicago Press.

Sullivan, Gerard, and Peter A. Jackson, eds. 2001. *Gay and Lesbian Asia: Culture, Identity and Community*. Binghamton, NY: Harrington Park Press.

Wan, Y. H. 1999. *Report on MSM and HIV/AIDS in China*. Report for UNAIDS/ASAP Regional Workshop of Policy and Programmatic Issues for Men who have Sex with Men, February. Hong Kong.

Zhang Beichuan, Li Xiufang, and Hu Zhuzhong. 2000. *Interventions among Men Who Have Sex with Men*. A paper presented at the 2nd AIDS Prevention and Control NGO Working Meeting/4th Hong Kong-China AIDS Joint Planning Meeting, 26–30 March, 2000, Zhuhai, PRC.

Web Sites

Aizhi Action. 2004. Accessed May 26, 2005. http://www.aizhi.net. AIDS education organization founded and operated by Wan Yan Hai, China's most famous AIDS activist.

Chi Heng Foundation. Accessed May 26, 2005. http://www.chihengfoundation.com. Hong Kong based organization that works for the rights of gays and lesbians in China as well as children orphaned by the AIDS epidemic.

Gay China. August 2004. Accessed May 26, 2005. http://www.gaychina.com. Bilingual Web site for Chinese and Asian men with personal ads, gallery, and an active BBS.

GTZ.org. Accessed May 26, 2005. http://www.gztz.org. The homepage of *Guangzhou Tongzhi*, one example of the hundreds of Web sites for Chinese gays and lesbians.

China, LGBT Youth in

Qiuxi Fann, James T. Sears, and *Denise Tse Shang Tang*

Lesbian, gay, bisexual, and **transgender** (LGBT) youth in China generally face more challenges than those in Western societies. Although homosexuality has been a gray area for centuries, five thousand years of Chinese culture and tradition has made it even harder for **queer** youth to handle issues related to **coming out,** family, and schooling. The open-door economic policy, the **Internet,** and the recent removal of homosexuality from mental disorders have positively contributed to the development of sexual and gender identities of Chinese youth and to the coming out process. Nevertheless, most Chinese still regard homosexuality as abnormal. Traditional

See also Activism, LGBT Youth; Adolescent Sexualities; Asia, LGBT Youth and Issues in; Bisexuality; China, LGBT Issues in; Compulsory Heterosexuality; Discrimination; LGBT Studies; Mental Health; Parents, Responses to Homosexuality; Passing; Popular Culture; Prejudice; Prostitution or Sex Work; Social Class; Transsexuality; Tong-zhi; Youth, At-Risk.

values and the enormous pressure of continuing the family line (for males) and getting married place additional burdens on LGBT youth, particularly those living in **rural** or remote areas. At school, outstanding academic records are often the best shield for students to avoid prying questions from family or peers and expectations for early marriage. Unlike Hong Kong and Taiwan, few official organizations/ groups serving LGBT youth exist in mainland China. There are some **HIV education** programs such as AiZhi Group and **AIDS** hotlines in large cities, such as Beijing, Shanghai, and Guangzhou, which target sexually active LGBT people. Web sites spread news for local activities, and most gay-theme poetry, essays, and stories are also published on the Internet, which remains largely uncensored from queer content.

Historically, Chinese have never viewed homosexuality as abnormal or criminal. From emperors to laypersons, homosexual behavior can be found in every historic period. Anal sex with a lower status young man was common; most heterosexuals did not pay attention to or care about homosexual activity. There are also homosexual accounts in some popular classical **literature** such as *Hong Lou Meng* (Red Mansion Dream), *Jing Pin Mei* (Golden Vase Plum), and *Pin Hua Bao Jian* (Guide to Appreciating Flowers).

Homophobia has become a new "tradition" in contemporary China as a result of decades of educational and political propaganda by the Chinese communist government. In Maoist China, for instance, there was no concept of individuality; diversity of any type was against "nature." Each citizen wore the same clothes, bought the same groceries, and read from the same newspapers. Despite the open-door policy and economic reforms begun a generation ago, this socialization against individuality has not been reversed completely.

As part of these reforms, the emergence of technology, and the **AIDS** pandemic, gay issues have entered public consciousness. In 1998, a survey by a leading Chinese researcher, Zhang Beichuan, was published in the *Southern Daily* newspaper (Wu 1998). In the weekend article, "If Society Was Tolerant," this study of gay men in China's 30 provinces found that loving relationships are not uncommon and that homosexual subcultures exist throughout the country. Television talk shows, novels, Internet chat rooms and Web sites, AIDS hotlines and NGOs coupled to the influence of Western media, tourism, and gay organizations are creating a new context for LGBT youth. Nevertheless, these young people must still deal with traditional views within their families and schools.

Most Chinese adolescents spend their pubescence in school. There is a little formal **sexuality education** provided except for physiology high school courses, which few teachers carry out effectively. Within a heterosexually dominant environment, there is a paucity of information on LGBT issues. Most queer youth, then, are "self-taught: acquiring as much LGBT information as possible" from books, Q&A in magazines, or friends, and later on television shows and the Internet (Li 1998, 63).

In July 2003, "You and Me" was established for Chinese young people to get knowledge of sexual and reproductive health. This semiofficial Web site, created by Marie Stopes' International (MSI) and the Chinese government and funded by UNFPA, is the first sex education to target youth. It covers many sensitive topics never appearing in textbooks, including masturbation (and how to do it), sexual harassment, safer sex, and homosexuality. In the sex knowledge column for boys, there is a connection called "Love between the Same Sex—Confusion of Homosexuality."

Reflecting official ambiguity on this subject, no substantial content is provided. Therefore, for many young people confused about their sexualities, there is still no official information. On the other hand, unofficial gay Web sites and publications such as *Peng You Tong xin* (Friends), operated by sex researcher Zhang Beichuan with the support of the Ford Foundation, and *AIZHI Jian Bao* (AIZHI newsletter), created by Chinese gay activist Wan Yanhai and sponsored by HIV/AIDS related groups, play an important educational role.

For Chinese boys, being different invites ridicule, isolation, **bullying**, and intimidation by fellow students. Name-calling such as *niang niang qiang* (**sissy boy**), *tong xing lian* (homo/fag), and *jia ya tou* (fake girl) are common scorn and mimicry. Although more straight-looking and acting gay students can remain closeted, their more effeminate appearing counterparts, irrespective of their **sexual orientation**, usually experience **harassment**. *Niang niang qiang* can avoid bullying if they earn excellent grades, garnering praise and compliments from teachers. But a "sissy" student with a poor or mediocre academic record faces a different fate.

Young Chinese lesbians are accorded different treatment. Those who display "**tomboy**" traits may not be perceived as weak or too mannish, and there are many accounts of young women experiencing same-sex intimacy and relationships in school settings (Li 2002). In addition, the popularity of sex studies in universities such as Shanghai University, Fudan University, Jiao Tong University, and Shanghai Teachers University has increased discussion on gender and sexualities. In recent years, the academic linkages between mainland China universities and Hong Kong universities have also provided many opportunities for lesbian youth, in both regions, to gather for emotional support via the Internet, bars, and student gatherings. A 2002 Web survey, conducted by Lesworld.Net, reported that 14 percent were between the ages of fifteen and eighteen, and 23 percent were in high school; 56 percent of its users were between the ages of nineteen and twenty-five, and 67 percent were attending universities.

Scholarship on transgender youth issues has not been easy to locate even though sex reassignment surgery has been available in mainland China since the early 1980s. Twenty year-old Zhang Ke Sha was the first person to have a successful male-to-female (MTF), in 1982. With her new name, Sha Sha, she struggled as an entrepreneur and moved to Taiwan where she worked in a nightclub. Sha Sha returned to mainland China, in 2002, where her biography was published (Deng 2003). Another account of a MTF is Shanghai's principal dancer, Jin Xing. A video documentary *L'étrange Destin du Colonel Jin Xing* (The Strange Destiny of Colonel Jin Xing, France 2001) was made about her journey from military colonel to fighting with the government to perform outside of China to the **adoption** of her baby.

Economic reforms, the Internet, and open gay bars and dance clubs have made it easier for this generation of LGBT youth. With the broad implementation of the open-door policy, more Western culture is available through **films** (both legal and pirated DVD copies), such as *Boys Don't Cry* (USA 1999), *Birdcage* (USA 1996), *Maurice* (UK 1987), television shows like **Queer as Folk**, *Sex and the City*, and *Friends*, as well as books, music, and art work. Hong Kong-produced films such as *Happy Together*, Taiwanese films like *Lan Yu* (2001) and *East Palace/West Palace* (1997), as well as other China-produced gay movies are never publicly showed, but are obtainable unofficially.

By either a phone line or broad band fiber connections available through Internet cafes, many LGBT youth in China search for friends, access information from sexual skills to public gay movements in developed countries, view erotica, and even publish essays, poems, and novels online. Popular Web sites include *Yang Guang Di Dai* (Sunshine Zone) and *Guangzhou Tong Zhi* (Guangzhou Comrades). These update global news, supply e-mail accounts, offer chat-room service, and provide access to personal profiles. Most of these are gay-oriented; LBT minorities and content are often absent (Heinz et al. 2002). Other Web sites, based on spreading safe sex knowledge and HIV/AIDS information, are less trafficked.

In major cities like Beijing and Shanghai, commercial gay bars are no longer underground and are gathering places for some gay and lesbian youth. Age and money are usually two major factors. Only white-collar gays can afford entry into discos or the high drink prices. However, attractive-looking youth can enter into this bar culture if they work informally with the bar owners as a "money boy" (Li 1998).

For LGBT youth in the countryside, access to the Internet, films, and gay bars is more problematic. The small population, geographic isolation, and economic lag time coupled to more traditional values of family, and the social pressure to continue the family line through marriage make it almost impossible to be openly gay.

Compared to those in the West, about one-fifth of gay men and one-third of the lesbians marry (Li 1998). In addition to pressure from family, fear of disclosing their sexual identities due to public shame, internalized **homophobia**, or loss of career options contribute to this phenomenon. For bisexual youth, marriage is a good option, allowing them to explore the "furtive" half of their lives. Further, a study of 2,000 gay men by Zhang Beichuan found two-thirds wanted children with women and only one-fourth had acknowledged their homosexuality to anybody—fewer still had told their families (Barillas 2000). In another revealing study, conducted by sociologist Liu Da Lin in the early 1990s, 2.3 percent identified as LGBT out of 20,000 Chinese surveyed; however, only one-in-twenty sexual minority respondents considered homosexuality as "good or beneficial;" more than one-half did not want to be gay (Barillas 2000).

In the fall of 1997, the *Zhejiang Province Mental Health Institute* journal sparked a debate on depathologizing homosexuality, marking the first time **sexual orientation** was discussed in such a forum. In April 2001, the third edition of the *Chinese Classification of Mental Disorders* (CCMD-III) removed the diagnosis of homosexuality per se (while a diagnosis of ego-dystonic homosexuality was added). Like earlier changes to the ***Diagnostic and Statistical Manual***, this is a significant step for LGBT youth.

The proportion of HIV infection among men who have sex with men has been officially as low as 0.2 percent (China Ministry of Health 2003). Many Chinese LGBT youth are largely unaware or ignore safer-sex practices, as evidenced in a 2001 homosexual behavior study (Liu, Liu, and Xiao 2001). Among those engaged in anal sex, less than one-third used a condom each time, and only about four-in-ten "receptors" reported condom usage.

Living as a sexual minority in China remains mostly an underground life, although there have not been laws or decrees against homosexuality. As Zhang Beichuan observed: "In China, we really don't have the radical conservatives and the radical liberation activists that you do in the West. We don't see gays being beaten to death in our country because of their sexuality. At the same time, we don't have gay and lesbian parades" (Pomfret 2000, A01).

Bibliography

Barillas, C. 2000. Gay Positive Attitudes Accelerating in China. Data Lounge. Accessed December 3, 2004. http://www.datalounge.com/datalounge/news/record. html? record=13625.

China Ministry of Health, UN Theme Group on HIV/AIDS in China (UNAIDS). 2003. December 1. "A Joint Assessment of HIV/AIDS Prevention, Treatment and Care in China." 12–14.

Fann, Rodge Q. 2003. "Growing up Gay in China." *Journal of Gay & Lesbian Issues in Education* 1, no. 2: 35–42.

Heinz, Bettina, Li Gu, Ako Inuzuka, and Roger Zender. 2002. "Under the Rainbow Flag: Webbing Global Gay Identities." *International Journal of Sexuality and Gender Studies* 7, nos. 2/3: 107–124.

Hui He. 2001, September. "*Zhong Guo Tong Xing Lian Nei Mu*" (Inside Story of Gay Chinese). *Mu Yu.*

Hui Liu, Ying Liu, Ya Xiao. 2001. "The KABP Investigation of Some Male Homosexual HIV/AIDS Patients in Beijing." *Zhongguo Xingbing Aizibing Fangzhi* (Chinese Journal of Prevention and Control of STD & AIDS) 7, no. 5: 289–291.

Jin Wu. 1998. Voices of Gay Men in China. April 27, 1998. Chinese Society for the Study of Sexual Minorities. Accessed June 13, 2005. http://www.csssm.org/English/e2.htm.

———. 2003. "From '*Long Yang*' and '*Dui Shi*' to Tongzhi: Homosexuality in China." *The Mental Health Professions and Homosexuality: International Perspectives* 7, nos. 1/2: 117–143.

Langfitt, Frank. 2000, February 27. "Out of Closet, Onto Internet." *Baltimore Sun.*

Li Yinhe. 1998. *The Homosexual Subculture*. Beijing: Jin Ri Zhong Guo Chu Ban She (China Today Press).

———. 2002. *Love and Sexuality of the Chinese Women*. Beijing: Zhong Guo You Yi Chu Ban Gong Shi.

Pomfret, John. 2000. "Among Chinese, a Low-Key Gay Liberation Openness Replacing Ostracism as Homosexuality Gains Some Acceptance." *Washington Post*, January

Samshasha (1984). *History of Homosexuality in China*. Hong Kong: Pink Triangle Press.

"Students Favor Sex Studies." March 3, 2004. Accessed October 26, 2004. http://www. chinadaily.com.cn/english/doc/2004–03/03/content_311257.htm.

Winter, Sam. 2002. "'Country Report': Hong Kong: Social and Cultural Issues." Accessed October 24, 2004. http://web.hku.hk/~sjwinter/TransgenderASIA/country_report_hk_ social.htm.

Ying Ru Deng. 2003. *Nu Ren Meng: Zhong Guo Bian Xin Di Yi Ren*. Hunan: Hunan Wen Yi Chu Ban She.

Zhang Beichuan. 1994. *Tongxing Ai* (Homosexuality). Jinan: Shandong Science and Technology Press.

Web Sites

AiZhi Group. Accessed December 2, 2004. http://www.aizhi.org. HIV/AIDS prevention Web site serving the LGBT community.

Guangzhou Tong Zhi (Guangzhou Comrades). December 28, 2003. Accessed December 2, 2004. http://www.gztz.org. Started in 1998, this was the first Internet domain for Chinese LGBT community.

Lesworld.Net. Accessed May 26, 2005. http://lesworld.nease.net/bbs/diaocha.htm. A high traffic Web site providing information for lesbians living in Mainland China.

Marie Stopes China. Accessed December 3, 2004. http://www.youandme.net.cn. Semiofficial Web site of sexual education directly for teenagers in China.

Yang Guang Di Dai (Sunshine Zone). December 29, 2003. A Yang. Accessed May 26, 2005. http://www.boysky.com. Largest online chatting Web site among LGBT youth in China, updated daily.

Christian Moral Instruction on Homosexuality

Linda L. Gaither

The historically dominant trend in Christian moral teaching rejects homosexual behavior, declaring the sin of homosexuality as immoral while calling the sinner to repentance, forgiveness, and a new life imbued with a spirit of self-control. This teaching advocates celibacy as the acceptable lifestyle for homosexuals and indeed all nonmarried believers. Christian moral instruction appeals to Scripture, tradition, and natural law for its justification. It has been used against sexual minority individuals as an instrument of spiritual violence, questioning their basic identity as children of God. This is especially destructive to **lesbian, gay, bisexual,** and **transgender youth** (LGBT) who are at a vulnerable moment in the process of **identity development**. It affects the relationship between Christian parents and their LGBT children. Some denominations are proactive in forming support and accountability groups for individuals who struggle with sexual sins and wish to be free from homosexuality. However, the plurality of viewpoints on homosexuality in most of the mainline denominations in North America means that LGBT youth may find their greatest source of support within the Christian community.

Christianity has historically justified its teaching on homosexuality by appeals to Scripture, tradition, and natural law. What is the biblical position on homosexuality? Traditional interpretations find outright prohibitions of homosexual behavior in frequently cited texts, such as Genesis 9:1–11; Leviticus 18:22 and 20:13; 1 Corinthians 6:9–10; 1 Timothy 1:9–10. The point of conflict between conservatives and progressives centers on how these texts are to be interpreted and applied to the contemporary exercise of church leadership. Conservatives apply the scriptures literally, saying no church leader shall practice any sin without repentance, whether it is homosexuality, greed, lying, or otherwise. Progressives weigh the Bible's authority with personal experience, church tradition, and reason. For example, progressives point out that homosexuality, as that term is used today, was an unknown category for the biblical writers at the time when the texts were written. A nuanced interpretation of the texts of prohibition is therefore necessary to determine the actual behavioral referent of the Greek words employed by the writers. Conservative interpreters reject these "revisionist" strategies as advocacy scholarship in the political struggle to change the structures of exclusion and oppression operative in Christian denominations. The texts have become contested ground, both within denominations as well as between denominations. The same tension exists for those scholars who question the claim for an unbroken negative tradition of moral instruction on homosexuality by providing evidence of tolerance in early Christian communities (Boswell 1980).

Other factors may influence both the way that texts are interpreted as well as a denomination's attitude to homosexual behavior. For example, "while the Black church and community share the logic of others who denounce homosexuality, their particular history of White racist oppression and sexual exploitation makes

See also Community LGBT Youth Groups; Families, LGBT; Jewish Moral Instruction on Homosexuality; Men's Studies; Parents, Responses to Homosexuality; Religion and Psychological Development; Religious Fundamentalism; Spirituality.

Black homophobia appear even more passionate, trenchant and unyielding" (Douglas 1999, 89). Like white conservatives, blacks appeal to the Bible when they condemn homosexuality. But in the **African American** community, homophobic **prejudice** has driven the interpretation of the Bible, as opposed to the Bible shaping **homophobia**. Negative responses to homosexuality in this context are linked to attempts to protect black manhood, womanhood, and the family. A community that is labeled "deviant" by the dominant white culture cannot support a deviant sexuality. For black LGBT youth, the faith community generally offers a paradoxical and painful experience: affirmation in blackness but condemnation for a **sexual identity** that appears to threaten a regulated and "normalized" black sexuality.

In the closing decades of the twentieth century, LGBT advocates in several mainline denominations brought organized pressure to bear for full inclusion in the decision-making structures of the denominations, as well as for the development of liturgies for the blessing of same-sex unions. Founded in 1974, Integrity in the Episcopal Church, for instance, sought to raise up and support the ministries of LGBT individuals. This advocacy work offered a ray of hope to young LGBT church members for a future of tolerance, full participation in the ministries of the church, and the possibility of the community's witness and support of committed, covenanted relationships. The existence of Integrity and similar organizations, such as Dignity within the Roman Catholic Church, gave courage to young people in the difficult decisions surrounding **coming out**, in what often seemed to be a hostile family and parish environment. In some more congregational denominations, blessing liturgies were a common practice as early as the 1970s, as seen in the Metropolitan Community Church in San Francisco, founded by Troy Perry, an ordained minister from an Evangelical denomination. Formed to speak and minister to LGBT Christians, it became a haven of fellowship and encouragement for **queer** youth as well as LGBT believers of all age groups. The development of liturgies to bless gay unions offered a deep affirmation to young people of the validity of their hopes for love and family and commitment. Progressive Quaker meetings were conducting blessing ceremonies in the 1970s as well. And the first large religious organization in North America to welcome homosexuals as full members, eligible to become clergy, was the Unitarian Universalists. At their 1996 annual convention, resolutions were ratified that called for celebration of marriage between any two consenting adults.

For hierarchical denominations with international accountability, forward movement has been slower and more deliberate. A good example is the Episcopal Church, a self-governing member of the worldwide Anglican Communion. To address issues connected with human sexuality, a complex process of study, dialogue, and reflection was initiated in the 1970s. A 1977 pastoral letter by the bishops of the Episcopal Church affirmed that the church rightly confines its nuptial blessing to the union of male and female, on the basis of scriptural authority and tradition. Advocates for full inclusion put forward the principle of congruence for interpreting Scripture: A valid interpretation must be congruent with the central and unifying message of God's healing, empowering, and liberating love, which by its very nature extends itself to all people. This dynamic and "revisionist" interpretive strategy proved persuasive to the General Convention of the Episcopal Church 2004 meeting in Minneapolis. There the deputies confirmed the election of a noncelibate gay priest to be Bishop of the Diocese of New Hampshire, and affirmed a "local option" for dioceses in the matter of blessing gay unions. The response from the wider Anglican Communion as well as from conservatives within the Episcopal Church has been highly critical. Cultural and contextual differences, such as the pressure of **Muslim** or Roman **Catholic** moral teaching on homosexuality, led a number of African, Southeast Asian, and South American dioceses to declare a state of impaired communion with the Episcopal Church. Bishops in the Congo, Kenya, Nigeria, Rwanda, Tanzania, and Uganda condemn homosexual behavior, and their LGBT members and clergy have been marginalized and closeted. Queer youth in **Africa** face a severe social stigma and the danger of physical violence for "coming out" in this context.

Evangelical Christians reject outright homosexuality and the possibility of same-sex unions on the basis not only of Scriptural prohibition but also the arguments of natural law. The "natural design" of marriage is seen as fulfilling three essential purposes: a biological purpose in procreation; an erotic purpose as a remedy for the sin of promiscuity; and a social purpose of mutual society, help, and comfort. Matthew 19:5 and Genesis 2:24 are cited as defining the essential nature of marriage: two-sexes-in-one-flesh communion of man and woman. Advocates of same-sex unions counter that lesbian and gays in committed relationships can fulfill these essential purposes in same-sex unions.

Electing to "love the sinner, cure the sin," some Evangelicals promote support groups such as Harvest USA and Stephen Bennett Ministries for persons who struggle with their sexual orientation. The stated goal of such groups is to deal biblically with the root causes of same-sex attraction in order to move on to healthy heterosexuality. **Reparative therapy** often functions to encourage denial and self-hatred, in some instances contributing to **suicide**. These therapies place tremendous pressure on LGBT youth to be transformed into "healthy" heterosexuals. The pressure may come not only from the church but from family as well. Family support networks provide a place for parents, friends, and other relatives to turn to upon learning that someone close to them is gay and assist them in returning the person back to the heterosexual norm. Reparative therapies raise the hope of a God-given spiritual cure, a cure offering complete fulfillment. Yet for many vulnerable young people, this so-called therapeutic process can be more damaging than helpful to identity-formation and **mental health**.

Bibliography

Boswell, John. 1980. *Christianity, Social Tolerance, and Homosexuality*. Chicago: University of Chicago Press.

Brawley, Robert L., ed. 1996. *Biblical Ethics and Homosexuality: Listening to Scripture*. Louisville, KY: Westminster John Knox Press.

Cohen, Richard. 2001. *Coming Out Straight: Understanding and Healing Homosexuality*. Winchester, VA: Oakhill Press.

Countryman, Louis William. 2003. *Dirt, Greed and Sex: Sexual Ethics in the New Testament and their Implications for Today*. Minneapolis: Fortress Press.

Douglas, Kelly Brown. 1999. *Sexuality and the Black Church: A Womanist Perspective*. Maryknoll, NY: Orbis Books.

Heyward, Carter. 1984. *Our Passion for Justice: Images of Power, Sexuality and Liberation*. Cleveland, OH: Pilgrim Press.

Noll, Stephen F. 1997. *Two Sexes, One Flesh: Why the Church Cannot Bless Same-Sex Marriage*. Solon, OH: Latimer Press.

Perry, Troy D., and Thomas L. P. Swicegood. 1992. *Don't be Afraid Anymore: The Story of Reverend Troy Perry and the Metropolitan Community Churches*. New York: St. Martin's Press.

Spong, John Shelby. 1990. *Living in Sin? A Bishop Rethinks Human Sexuality*. San Francisco: Harper.

Web Sites

Friends for Lesbian, Gay, Bisexual, Transgender and Queer Concerns. 2004. Accessed December 18, 2004. http://www.quaker.org/flgbtqc. This site collects marriage minutes written by participating Quaker Meetings, affirming same-sex Quaker marriages.

HARVEST USA. 2004. Accessed December 18, 2004. http://www.harvestusa.org. This non-profit organization stated goal is to partner with and equip the Church in bringing the power of the gospel of Jesus Christ to transform the lives of those affected by sexual sin.

Integrity. December 2004. A Network of Lesbian, Gay, Bisexual, and Transgender Ministry and Advocacy in the Episcopal Church. Accessed December 18, 2004. http://www. integrityusa.org. Integrity's mission is to be a witness of lesbian, gay, bisexual, and transgender persons in the Episcopal Church and to the world. They engage in a ministry of worship, education, advocacy, fellowship, and service.

Religious Tolerance. January 12, 2003. Accessed December 18, 2004. http://www. religioustolerance.org/hom_chur2.htm. Lists the policies of forty-four Christian denominations on homosexuality.

Unitarian Universalist Association. Accessed December 18, 2004. http://www.uua.org/owl/ uuares.html. Provides a list of all UUA resolutions on human sexuality from 1963 to the present.

Cocurricular Activities

Laura E. Strimpel

Cocurricular activities, an alternate term for extracurricular and used by many student affairs practitioners in the United States, take place outside the classroom and are diverse. Areas of cocurricular activities that are significant for the development of lesbian, gay, bisexual, and transgender (LGBT) students include **sports**, intramural athletics, Greek letter organizations, various student organizations, student activities boards, student governments, and residence hall councils. Involvement in cocurricular activities is influential in the development of LGBT undergraduates. Research suggests that students who are involved with cocurricular activities develop stronger psychosocial skills related to their confidence, sense of purpose, and interpersonal relationships (Evans, Forney, and Guido-DiBrito 1998). However, the likelihood of LGBT students actively engaging in cocurricular activities on their campus depends on the support and services offered to them by the institution and other students. Many times LGBT student involvement in cocurricular activities is limited as a result of not having institutional support.

Intercollegiate athletic teams are cocurricular activities in which students, reflecting diversity in terms of **race, ethnicity, social class**, and gender are integrated. Athletic teams create a sense of community among its members despite their

See also College Campus Organizing; College Campus Programming; Passing; School Safety and Safe School Zones.

differences. However, acts of **discrimination** aimed toward **lesbian, gay, bisexual,** and **transgender youth** are prevalent on teams. LGBT students who encounter discrimination might attempt to conceal their sexuality and continue to participate, whereas others will quit. Although LGBT students encounter verbal and physical **harassment** from teammates, opposing players, and coaches, transgender students face additional challenges. Few institutions, for instance, support gender-neutral restrooms let alone fund separate locker room facilities for transgender players.

Intramural athletic teams can be welcoming to LGBT players. Most intramural teams allow students to form teams. Students at the University of California in Los Angeles began an LGBT league in 2004. Less welcoming can be **fraternities** and **sororities**. LGBT students, like others, join Greek letter organizations to increase friendships, support, and a sense of belonging but often remain closeted or confront **homophobia** (Case 1998).

LGBT student organizations provide a variety of roles for LGBT students on campuses. There are LGBT organizations that focus on being support groups whereas others take political and activist roles. Involvement in these cocurricular organizations is beneficial for both LGBT students and campuses. Students work either directly or indirectly with campus administration to promote positive **school climates** regarding LGBT issues. Students might seek out LGBT organizations as a form of support that will help them work through their **identity development**. Students who are comfortable with their **sexual identity** might concentrate more on **activism** and education. For example, many students encourage the LGBT group(s) to sponsor speakers or performance artists to visit campus. There are also students who are unsure of their **sexual orientation** or who are not comfortable **coming out**. For many of these students, knowing that student organizations aimed at LGBT issues exist gives them comfort.

Institutions of higher education vary in size, public and private status, religious affiliation, and geographical location. A multi-institutional survey project, conducted within the United States focusing on southeastern institutions, assessed the available support services for lesbian, gay, and bisexual students (McRee and Cooper 1998). Student-run LGB organizations were found more often at larger, public institutions.

Theater, choral, band, and other performance arts activities also are important activities for LGBT students. Students who are unable or who simply do not desire to participate in LGBT student organizations often engage in these activities as outlets to express their feelings and to meet others. Activities like drama and choral productions that have LGBT-related themes may allow performances by queer students without making their lifestyles public.

Student activities boards (SABs) are cocurricular organizations with direct connections to all students on campus. The SABs make decisions on entertainment for campuses. LGBT students involved with SABs can lobby for funds to be allocated toward LGBT-focused presenters, artists, and films. Also, the presence of LGBT students helps to remind others that those activities traditionally aimed at heterosexual students, such as homecoming dances, can be more inclusive. In effect, LGBT students involved in SABs act as spokespeople for the LGBT communities within a campus. Although they are not representative of all LGBT students, their visibility and voices increase positive campus climates for LGBT students.

Just as student activities boards provide a direct connection to all students on campus, student government organizations (SGOs) provide this link. SGOs have significant influence on campus due to control over some university funds, which are dispersed to student organizations and constitute their budgets. Students who are members of SGOs can lobby for more funds to be aimed at those organizations supportive of LGBT issues. Student government organizations' meetings also provide forums to announce upcoming projects and concerns as well as opportunities to build alliances and foster **allies**.

Lesbian, gay, bisexual, and transgender students who live in residence halls face the challenge of deciding whether or not to disclose their sexual orientation to their roommates and other residents. LGBT students might feel isolated, uncomfortable, and even physically unsafe given their living conditions. At residence hall council meetings, students discuss rules and regulations of their buildings and offer suggestions for programs and activities such as educational programming to increase awareness of LGBT issues, particularly coinciding with events such as **National Coming Out Day, Day of Silence,** and Gay and Lesbian Pride Month.

College campus resource centers and offices for lesbian, gay, bisexual, and transgender concerns are extremely important support services for LGBT students. These provide physical and emotional safe space for LGBT students, collect data on campus climate, and inquire about and lobby for available on and off campus resources. These offices also become the hub from which students become more involved in campus life.

Many institutions of higher education provide environments that are inclusive and encourage the participation of LGBT student involvement in cocurricular activities. There is research on antigay sentiment on four-year institution campuses. Although there are community colleges that support the formation of LGBT student organizations, there is scant research regarding sexual orientation **discrimination** on **community college** campuses. One study, conducted across six community college campuses throughout the San Francisco Bay area, focused on antigay violence and harassment; more than one in three students had participated in such activities (Franklin 1998).

Few institutions of higher education encourage LGBT individuals to apply for high-level positions, such as presidents and deans. This "lavender ceiling" sends a clear message as does the presence of few out LGBT top-level administrators **mentoring** LGBT students. One way institutions demonstrate their inclusive dispositions is to hire qualified LGBT individuals in top level administrative positions. At Roosevelt University, Charles R. Middleton was hired, in March 2003, as its president. Also, Fred P. Hochberg, the former cochair of the Human Rights Campaign, has been appointed dean of New School University's Robert J. Milano Graduate School of Management and Urban Policy. Institutions also confirm their support of LGBT students, faculty, and staff by including sexual orientation in their nondiscrimination clauses, and implementing Safe Zone and Allies programs.

Lesbian, gay, bisexual, and transgender students need support that is different than that needed by other students (Carmona 1994). Furthermore, LGBT students of color need additional support. **African American** LGBT students face several issues, including those within the black church, family, and the increasing cases of HIV and **AIDS**. LGBT students of color participate less in cocurricular activities, particularly in student LGBT organizations. LGBT students of color do not always feel welcomed or comfortable joining LGBT organizations where the membership primarily consists of Caucasian students. Although white LGBT students generally do not consider the impact of their **race** on their sexual orientation, those of color do and are likely to focus on addressing their racial and ethnic identities prior to other areas of identity development (Taub and McEwen 1992).

Although the support for addressing lesbian, gay, bisexual, and transgender issues in historically white institutions has fluctuated over time, **administrators** of historically black colleges and universities (HBCUs) are generally hesitant to address LGBT issues on their campuses. Student affairs offices at HBCUs have been less than supportive of lesbian, gay, bisexual, and transgender students who wish to meet formally and establish organizations. Thus, due to the lack of institutional support and fear of physical assault, many LGBT students who attend HBCUs meet off campus (Braud 2003).

Nevertheless, acknowledging and openly supporting LGBT students, faculty, and staff at HBCUs has progressed. Johnson C. Smith University, with the assistance of the Human Rights Campaign, established a dialogue among students, administration, and the local community about being black and LGBT. More forums have been held in Atlanta, too, where there is a concentration of HBCUs. Local task forces were also established to address lesbian, gay, bisexual, and transgender concerns in the communities that surround the HBCUs. Speakers and artists from Black Lavender Resources visit various institutions, including HBCUs, and have had a positive impact on students, faculty, and staff.

Bibliography

Astin, Alexander W. 1993. "An Empirical Typology of College Students." *Journal of College Student Personnel* 34, no.1: 36–46.

Braud, Brandon. 2003. "LGBT Issues on Historically Black Colleges & Universities." Campus Pride.net. (February). Accessed May 26, 2005. http://www.campuspride.net/hbcu.asp.

Carmona, Jeff. 1994. "Anti-Gay Initiatives Cause Anxiety on State Campuses." *Chronicle of Higher Education* (March): A32.

Case, Douglas N. 1998. "Lesbian, Gay, Bisexual Issues within the Greek Community." Pp. 68–78 in *Working with Lesbian, Gay, Bisexual, and Transgender College Students: A Handbook for Faculty and Administrators*. Edited by Ronni L. Sanlo. Westport, CT: Greenwood.

Evans, Nancy, J., Deanna S. Forney, and Florence Guido-DiBrito. 1998. *Student Development in College: Theory, Research, and Practice*. San Francisco: Jossey-Bass.

Franklin, K. 1998. *Psychosocial Motivations of Hate Crimes Perpetrators: Implications for Educational Intervention*.(August) Paper presented at the 106th Annual Convention of the American Psychological Association, San Francisco, CA.

Malaney, Gary D., Elizabeth A. Williams, and William W. Geller. 1997. "Assessing Campus Climate for Gays, Lesbians, and Bisexuals at Two Institutions." *Journal of College Student Development* 38: 365–375.

McRee, Tina K., and Diana L. Cooper. 1998. "Campus Environments for Gay, Lesbian, and Bisexual Students at Southeastern Institutions of Higher Education." *NASPA Journal* 36: 48–60.

Taub, Deborah J., and Marylu K. McEwen. 1992. "The Relationship of Racial Identity Attitudes to Autonomy and Mature Interpersonal Relationships in Black and White Undergraduate Women." *Journal of College Student Development*, 32: 439–446.

Wolf-Wendel, Lisa E., J. Douglas Toma, and Christopher C. Morphew. 2001. "How Much Difference is Too Much Difference? Perceptions of Gay Men and Lesbians in Intercollegiate Athletics." *Journal of College Student Development* 42: 465–479.

Web Sites

Delta V. September 2004. Accessed December 3, 2004. http://www.dv8.com/resources/us/
local/campus.html. Directory of LGBT student and community organizations
by state.

National Consortium of Directors of Lesbian, Gay, Bisexual, and Transgender Resources in
Higher Education. July 2004. Accessed December 1, 2004. http://www.lgbtcampus.org/.
The combined vision and mission on the Consortium is to achieve higher education
environments in which lesbian, gay, bisexual, and transgender students, faculty, staff,
administrators, and alumni have equity in every respect.

College Age Students

Patrick Dilley

Traditionally, college-age students were those in their late teens and early twenties; today's undergraduate students include older students as well as young adults. Nonheterosexual college students today are one of the most visible and recognized campus populations, but this was not always the case. Over the past thirty-five years, college campus organizing among LGBT students has produced unique campus events and opportunities. These on- and off-campus experiences affect how LGBT students develop as adults and come to understand their sexual identities. Coming to terms with an identity that is not heterosexual poses many challenges to college-age youth, including coming to understand and acknowledge their **sexual orientation**. These challenges are heightened in college settings, where peer attention and pressure can provide both encouragement and approbation. Concepts of identity (and how it is formed) are central to many student development theories. One line of research on LGBT college student development emphasizes the similarities of their experiences, whereas another focuses on the differences among them.

Drawing initially from psychosocial identity theorists such as Arthur W. Chickering (1969), who conceptualized identity as a set of progressive stages or levels of development, researchers seeking similarities in nonheterosexual student development are concerned particularly with how LGBT students come to understand and define their identities, as well as the social, academic, and **cocurricular activities** and attitudes that influence those understandings.

In his extensive **quantitative research**, Ritch C. Savin-Williams (1990) outlines several important steps for many LGBT college students during college, including labeling self as LBG or T, disclosing that self-labeling to others, experiencing a romantic relationship with a person of the same gender, and integrating their self-concepts and experiences into positive self-identities as nonheterosexual. It appears that these activities are occurring at increasingly younger ages, allowing for further interpersonal development during college (Savin-Williams, 1998).

See also College Campus Organizing; College Campus Programming; College Campus Resource Centers; Coming Out, Youth; Community and Technical Colleges; Fraternities; Sororities.

Like Savin-Williams, Anthony D'Augelli (2001) examines how LGBT students' self-concepts, emotions, and **desires** are reflected into a personal identity as gay/lesbian/bisexual. One important task for LGBT students is developing a social, increasingly public nonheterosexual identity. Disclosing one's nonheterosexual identity to parents and redefining familial relationships is a second significant marker of LGBT identity development. Developing the skills—and the emotional capabilities—to have intimate nonheterosexual relationships (either with someone of the same gender or involving a transgender person) are also considered vital. Finally, D'Augelli suggests that becoming a member of a nonheterosexual community (on or off campus) is a culminating event in the lives of college-age LGBT youth.

D'Augelli posits these processes of **identity development** as nonlinear, but a progression from one sense of self to another is evident in his model. Savin-Williams theorizes differential developmental trajectories, or paths of development, to account for diversity in the experiences and self-ideations of LGB youth. These paths are influenced by the student's individual characteristics, their environmental contexts (including home and school), and the opportunities and constraints within those contexts to express a same-sex attraction, to label those feelings and attractions as nonheterosexual, to have sexual and/or emotional relationships with members of the same gender, and to disclose these facts to others. Although both models imply universality to the identity development process, these theories are descriptive, not prescriptive: Not everyone does (or has to) experience **coming out**-or nonheterosexual identity—in exactly the same way.

Differences on how LGBT college students understand and experience nonheterosexual identity is the second major line of research. This often uses a cultural analysis perspective. From his ethnographic study of nonheterosexual college men at Penn State, Robert Rhoads (1994) proposes a theory of gay male student "contraculture," a set of socialized communities that reflected differing values, interests, and ideologies of nonheterosexual students. Many such communities can exist, on a single campus or even within a student organization. In part, these conform to differences in how the students conceived of their identities; some students in a campus' LGBT group might view their nonheterosexual identity as mainly social, or mainly political, or particularly private, yet all view themselves as having some relationship to an LGBT minority community and to the group.

Based on historical research, Patrick Dilley (2002) presents seven possible forms of identity for nonheterosexual male collegians, including homosexual, gay, closeted, queer, "normal," parallel, and denying. These are shaped by seven common factors: campus environments; involvement (or not) in student LGBT organizations; involvement (or not) in Greek-letter life; attitudes toward sex and sexuality; concepts on if, how, and when to display nonheterosexual emotions; national and local media; and their relationship to the concept of what it means to be "normal." Dilley's research shows how the types developed contextually over time and in relation to changing ideas about being nonheterosexual. Although the concepts of identity based on a notion of privacy (i.e., closeted or denying) remained constant, public presentations of nonheterosexual identity changed. From the 1940s to the 1960s, a "homosexual" identity was most evident, but by the late 1960s a more radical, political "gay" identity emerged and became the dominant public campus identity. A generation later, an even more radical identity, "queer," represented yet another variation of how nonheterosexual students conceived of the relationship of their identities to society.

Socialization is a key factor of student development in both lines of research. Until the 1960s, socializing for LGBT students was usually relegated to off-campus, private, nonpublicized parties, strictly limited to small gay and/or lesbian social sets. College students were always at risk of being disciplined, expelled, or even arrested if "caught" socializing with other suspected or confirmed LGBT people, as is evident in Florida under the infamous **Johns Committee**. Starting in the late 1960s, nonheterosexual students began organizing on campus to provide themselves with spaces and opportunities where they could socialize without fear of discrimination or harassment. Gay and lesbian dances in the 1970s became a focal point of campus life. Historians (Chauncey 1994; Dilley 2002) have noted that gay and lesbian dances fostered a collective common identity among the attendees, provided typical collegiate social opportunities that previously were denied many LGBT students, and presented university **administrators** with empirical evidence of the existence of LGBT students on their campuses. Although dances have become less popular, due in part to many other social opportunities and the **Internet**, these events are still important at schools without a large concentration of LGBT students or without other off-campus venues.

In the late 1980s and early 1990s, a number of colleges and universities undertook studies of the **school climate**s for their LGBT populations. The most influential of these reports were done at Rutgers University and the University of Massachusetts at Amherst. Several consistent findings highlight important aspects of being LGB or T on campus. Nonheterosexual students struggle with invisibility on campus and ostracism when they are out. In and out of the classroom, they can often be victims of antigay **prejudice**, including verbal abuse, **sexual harassment**, and physical violence, which leads them to conceal who they are and potentially experience extreme feelings of isolation.

Institutions responded to the studies in varying levels of effectiveness. Several notable institutions eventually included sexual orientation in their nondiscrimination policies; a smaller number have extended specific domestic partnership benefits to students. Some U.S. universities and larger colleges created offices for LGBT concerns and advisory committees, providing a formal avenue of redress and advocacy for LGBT student issues. Courses in **LGBT Studies** as well as entire programs are also offered at a host of institutions.

For those "out" collegians today there are a variety of public expressions of identity and nonheterosexual life: queer student organizations; traditional protest marches; queer promenades and kiss-ins; parades proclaiming queer pride.

Many LGBT college students do not feel compelled to seek out similarly-oriented youth in campus groups; more students find heterosexual friendships and socialization opportunities that are open to their different sexualities—a spectrum of identities that go beyond gay–straight binaries. Still other students enter Internet chat rooms to explore identity issues, to find connections with other LGBT students that are not geographically bound, and to understand and express their identities. In addition, many LGBT students who do not become part of such identity-based organizations are active in their campus groups, ranging from sports to Greek-letter organizations. Further, today's college students are aware of a wider diversity of LGBT lived experiences and expressions, having grown up exposed to an increasingly wider array of sexual issues and nonheterosexual identities, in popular culture, politics, legal issues, and definitions of diversity. Consequently, what "being"

LGB or T "means" for students has changed much more quickly than it did a generation ago.

However, just as in generations past, for students who are not out, hiding (or keeping their LGBT lives separate from their daily campus lives) often takes a toll on their **mental health** and the quality of their friendships; this is particularly true for men and women involved in Greek-letter organizations. Fraternity and sorority members, from the 1940s to today, have reported feeling unable to be honest about their lives, experiencing more stress due to their approbation of LGBT sexuality within Greek-letter communities, and higher rates of suicidal impulses than straight peers. **Transgender youth** also face similar issues during their college years. The nonheterosexual student development models often reflect the issues and challenges these collegians—and others who are not able to be open about their sexuality or their gender identity—face as they struggle to come to terms with their identity.

Nevertheless, more students appear to feel more comfortable coming out publicly at earlier ages and in scholastic contexts; in part, this is due to changes in larger social contexts regarding homosexuality and gender identity. Because of these developments, many heterosexual and nonheterosexual college students today do not seem to fit within, or express the markers of, the student development markers of earlier sexual identity studies. For these students, finding comfort about their sexuality and identity is not quite so problematic as it was for LGBT students of the past. They work to change campus climates, institutional norms, and peer perceptions that they find discriminatory and heterosexist. In this regard, "out" students in college today often more closely fit within more traditional models of student development theory

Bibliography

Chauncey, George. 1994. *Gay New York: Gender, Urban Culture, and the Making of the Gay Male World, 1890–1940*. New York: Basic Books.

Chickering, Arthur W. 1969. *Education and Identity*. San Francisco: Jossey-Bass.

D'Augelli, Anthony R., and Charlotte J. Patterson, eds. 2001. *Lesbian, Gay, and Bisexual Identities and Youth: Psychological Perspectives*. New York: Oxford University Press.

Dilley, Patrick. 2002. *Queer Man on Campus: A History of Non-Heterosexual Men in College, 1495–2000*. New York: RoutledgeFalmer.

Howard, Kim, and Annie Stevens, eds. 2000. *Out & About on Campus: Personal Accounts by Lesbian, Gay, Bisexual, and Transgendered College Students*. Los Angeles: Alyson.

Rhoads, Robert A. 1994. *Coming Out In College: The Struggle for a Queer Identity*. Westport, CT: Bergin and Garvey.

Sanlo, Ronni L. 1998. *Working with Lesbian, Gay, Bisexual, and Transgender College Students: A Handbook for Faculty and Administrators*. Westport, CT: Greenwood.

Savin-Williams, Ritch C. 1990. *Gay and Lesbian Youth: Expressions of Identity*. New York: Hemisphere.

———. 1998. *". . . And Then I Became Gay": Young Men's Stories*. New York: Routledge.

Windmeyer, Shane L., and Pamela W. Freeman, eds. 1998. *Out on Fraternity Row: Personal Accounts of Being Gay in a College Fraternity*. Los Angeles: Alyson.

Windmeyer, Shane L., and Pamela W. Freeman, eds. 2000. *Secret Sisters: Stories of Being Lesbian and Bisexual in a College Sorority*. Los Angeles: Alyson.

Web Sites

Delta V., Ltd. College & University Campus GLBT Organizations. September 2004. Accessed November 25, 2004. http://www.dv-8.com/resources/us/local/campus.html. An extensive listing of LGBT student organizations in the U.S., by state, with links.
Delta V, Ltd. Local GLBT College & University Organizations. September 2004. Accessed November 25, 2004. http://www.dv-8.com/resources/canada/local/campus.html. A similar listing of LGBT campus student organizations in Canada, by province, with links.
Gay and Lesbian Humanist Association. Lesbian, Gay and Bisexual Student Societies, United Kingdom and Ireland. November 2004. Accessed November 25, 2004. http://www.galha.org. Listing of LGBT student associations and societies in the United Kingdom and Ireland, with links.

College Campus Organizing

Patrick Dilley

Campus organizing, rooted in social change and acceptance of nonnormative sexualities, is a hallmark of LGBT collegiate organizations and the students who comprise them. LGBT campus organizations have four central functions: activism; socialization; service; and visibility and awareness. The earliest campus gay groups often identified with New Left student politics, which variously appropriated **feminism, lesbian–feminism, critical social theory,** and were largely critical of an earlier generation of activists associated with groups like the Mattachine Society. Prior to 1967, no recognized LGBT campus organization existed; by 1996, the *Chronicle of Higher Education* estimated that over 2000 such groups were operating in the United States alone. During this time, campus organizing has changed or emphasized different missions and has adopted various names. Recognized LGBT campus organizations also exist in Canada, Australia, and Europe. The first non-heterosexual college organization was the Student Homophile League at Columbia University; founded in 1966 and officially recognized on April 19, 1967. Within a few years, others formed at universities, ranging from University of California at Berkeley and New York University to the University of Oklahoma and the University of Kansas. In 1968, the earliest documented European gay student organization, the Comite Pederastique de la Sorbonne, formed during student uprisings that spring.

In the United Kingdom, two types of LGBT organizations exist: societies and student associations. The societies and student unions are usually private, require dues, and focus on social and "welfare" activities (i.e., services) for their members; associations are usually open to all students within the institution, do not require dues, and are reformist in their activism. On October 13, 1970, the London Gay Liberation Front was founded, first meeting in the London School of Economics. Cambridge University's LGBT organization dates back at least to 1971, and by the 1990s Oxford University and University of Manchester also had similar organizations. Australia's political activist organization Gay Liberation was formed in 1972

See also College Age Students; College Campus Programming.

at Sydney University, and soon had chapters on campuses throughout Australia. Today major Canadian universities, including the University of Manitoba and the University of British Columbia in Vancouver, also have LGBT associations as do most larger public colleges and universities in the United States.

The impulse for creating these early LGBT associations echoed the social protest and change movements of the 1960s and early 1970s. Many of the founders viewed themselves as trying to remake society—or at least trying to make the higher education corner of it more hospitable and responsive to nonheterosexual students. Initially, nonheterosexual student alliances followed the lead of larger student protest and social change movements. Many LGBT activists were organizing both on campus and in local communities for a variety of causes. These early groups reflected their New Left ideology through names like FREE (Fight Repression of Erotic Expression) and Gay Liberation Front. Membership between campus political organizations and early LGBT campus groups often overlapped with those of women's liberation, African-American empowerment, and peace movement organizations. Within a few years, however, as the New Left student movement dwindled in infuence, United States campus LGBT organizations became more differentiated from organized American social movements. In contrast, many campus organizations in other countries remain affiliated with national social equality organizations, including the National Union of Students (which includes LGBT issues and campaigns) and Stonewall (an LGBT-specific organization) in Great Britain.

The majority of postsecondary educational **administrators**, however, were reluctant to allow homosexuals to congregate for any reason on campus, let alone be recognized as an official organization. Many of the original LGBT student groups resorted to litigation to force institutions to allow the organizations to operate on campuses, setting precedence for future rights of student groups at public institutions, including nondiscrimination, equality of access, and funding opportunities. *Gay Students Organization of the University of New Hampshire v. Bonner* (1974) affirmed LGBT organizations' rights of assembly and expression on campuses. *Gay Lib v. University of Missouri* (1977), after being overturned in appeal, provided the legal basis for LGBT student organizations to register on campuses despite state laws against homosexuality, for not allowing so would penalize the groups' members based on their status rather than their conduct.

The transformation of these campus organizations' ideology and goals were often reflected in the modified names of their organizations. At the University of Kansas, the Gay Liberation Front or Gay Lib changed into Gay Services of Kansas in the early 1970s, followed by Gay and Lesbian Services of Kansas; in the 1980s, it became Gay, Lesbian and Bisexual Services of Kansas before finally changing its name to Q&A (Queers & Allies) in 1995, a progression toward a more inclusive, encompassing vision of nonheterosexuality.

Reflected in their changing names, LGBT student groups incorporated other foci—apart from or in addition to politics—as central to their mission. Campus organizations for nonheterosexuals generally serve one or more of four basic functions for the students: socialization; service; visibility and awareness; and activism. As students matriculate and graduate, and with little formal codification, LGBT organizations go through alternating periods of activity and dormancy, where they emphasize one of the functions. When students feel their social or service needs are being met (or are not an issue), campus organizations are generally dormant; when students identify issues or problems to address, the groups become active again.

Socialization—providing LGBT students with regular opportunities to meet and interact with their peers without pressure to conform or confront heterosexual campus climates and cultures—is one reason why LGBT youth seek out LGBT college groups. Starting in the early 1970s, gay campus dances were a common staple of annual collegiate activity; some became large social events extending beyond the campus and into the surrounding communities. Other events, such as movie nights and the annual "Tea and Croquet" day at Michigan State, emphasized a playful, not so openly political aspect of gay campus life. Also during this time, **lesbian youth** on some campuses began activities limited to women, including dances, small musical concerts, and potluck dinners.

Providing services to campuses, which also increases visibility of LGBT students and awareness of LGBT issues, continues to be a mission for many LGBT collegiate organizations. In the early 1970s, gay and lesbian (and, later, bisexual and transgender) students felt that their campuses were not providing assistance to non-heterosexual students. To correct that, the initial gay organizations focused on outreach, including staffing hotlines, to provide information about queer activities on and off campus, as well as referrals for professional counseling. Students also developed training and staffing for peer counseling programs, as well as support groups (often called "rap groups") for students to discuss coming out issues. Many LGBT campus organizations initiated sexual orientation speakers bureaus, where students go to classes or groups on campus to answer questions about their experiences and LGBT life and safe zone programs, which provide for nonthreatening campus spaces and personnel in which LGBT students can be open about their sexuality.

Early efforts at service also included establishing LGBT lending libraries, particularly in the late 1960s and early 1970s, when many libraries would not purchase (or allow to be checked out) materials that dealt with nonnormative sexuality. In the decades prior to the Internet, LGBT student organizations often produced regular newsletters, which allowed for ongoing visibility and communication about events and activities for people who did not feel comfortable coming to an LGBT office or meeting. The newsletters often reflected, along with news and gossip, the life cycle of the campus organizations. Many of these newsletters are now housed in various archives that specialize in LGBT collections.

Early campus visibility included staffing information tables during student orientation and other events. The original LGBT student organizations also lobbied for permanent office space to demonstrate their parity with other student groups and to provide stable visibility of their efforts. In addition, many LGBT student organizations struggled—and continue to strive—to prompt their campus administrations to fund and staff an office devoted to serving the needs of nonheterosexual collegians. The first such center was created in 1971 at the University of Michigan when two graduate students, James Toy and Cynthia Gair, were hired as the first staff assigned to gay and lesbian students. In 2000, eighty-five LGBT campus resources centers existed.

By the late 1980s, LGBT student organizations began to return to their activist roots. Spurred by the actions of social movements Queer Nation and AIDS Coalition to Unleash Power (ACT-UP), LGBT students fought against personal discrimination on campus and general discrimination in society at large. Many protests in the late 1980s and early 1990s centered on Reserve Officer Training Corps (ROTC) programs, which LGBT students argued violated nondiscrimination statements, since ROTC would not accept any nonheterosexual student or recruits into its program. Student protests and petitions were often the impetus for campus-wide reviews of quality of life for LGBT students, faculty, and staff. These climate studies and their resulting reports (with varying degrees of institutional response), dominated much LGBT campus activism in the early 1990s.

New, less traditional forms of visibility and activism emerged in the early 1990s. Collegians embraced **National Coming Out Day** events, which stress the personal and political importance of being vocal and visible as a nonheterosexual person. Other campus events include celebrating National Gay, Lesbian and Bisexual History Month in October, Gay Pride celebrations, and the National Day of Silence, which highlights, through the public performance of not speaking, the daily student experiences of being silenced by **homophobia** and **heterosexism**. Many LGBT campus groups also present drag shows—once considered stereotypical, now viewed as a critique of sexuality and gender—which often attract heterosexual students as well. Other performance-based activities sponsored by LGBT student organizations include kiss-ins (pointing out the double standard of heterosexuals' unquestioned and accepted public displays of affection) and speak-outs (the telling or reading of coming out stories).

Not all LGBT campus activities seek to point out the differences between heterosexual and nonheterosexual students; some are based on campus traditions, including "Rainbow Graduation" (referring to the **rainbow flag** that is commonly used to symbolize the LGBT community) and "**Lavender Graduation**" ceremonies. LGBT alumni organizations, which began to form in the early 1990s, host homecoming receptions and sports tailgate parties. By the 2000, larger campuses boasted multiple LGBT groups; the University of Michigan had over twenty, including individual groups based on ethnic origin, religious affiliation, and academic major.

Despite the positive changes in LGBT college student organizing in the United States, failure to be inclusive to diverse populations remains a recurring criticism. In the 1970s, lesbians often cited the attitudes of gay men in the student organizations as fostering a nonaccepting environment. Many lesbian youth left to form their campus and community organizations, although many women returned to the original student groups in the 1980s. **Bisexual youth** began publicly proclaiming not being understood or included in lesbian and gay student groups of the 1980s and early 1990s; many of the campus organizations changed their names and philosophies to become more inclusive of that population. More recently, **transgender youth** have struggled to connect with and be included by campus groups, which appear to be changing to LGBT in focus. LGBT students of color, along with international LGBT students studying in the United States, continue to find difficulty fitting into campus LGBT organizations, for their multiple issues of identity and oppression are not always understood or addressed by their Caucasian LGBT peers.

Such a range in organizations reflects the diversity of LGBT students on college campuses, as well as the range of their interests and activities—not all of which might be organized exclusively for nonheterosexual students. LGBT students can be found in mainstream campus politics, **residence life** staffs, campus programming, **fraternities** and **sororities**, and other interest groups. From the activist beginnings of campus LGBT organizing, often LGBT students have been very involved in student governance and local politics during their collegiate careers. In 1971, Jack Baker was elected by the president of the Minnesota Student Association by the student body of the University of Minnesota. Baker withstood impeachment attacks and was reelected in 1972. Baker's sexuality was a part of his campaigning, deployed in what critics would now call a queer sensibility. In 1990, Suzanne Denevan at the University of Minnesota was the first out lesbian in the United States to hold such an office.

Bibliography

Dilley, Patrick. 2002. *Queer Man on Campus: A History of Non-Heterosexual Men in College, 1945–2000*. New York: RoutledgeFalmer.

Renn, Kristen A. 2002. "Lesbians, Gay Men, Bisexuals, and Transgender People in Higher Education." Pp. 398–401 in *Higher Education in the United States: An Encyclopedia*. Edited by James J.F. Forest and K. Kinser. Santa Barbara, CA: ABC-CLIO.

Sanlo, Ronni L., ed. 1998. *Working with Lesbian, Gay, Bisexual, and Transgender College Students: A Handbook for Faculty and Administrators*. Westport, CT: Greenwood.

Sanlo, Ronni L., Sue Rankin, and Robert Schoenberg, eds. 2002. *Our Place on Campus: Lesbian, Gay, Bisexual, Transgender Services and Programs in Higher Education*. Westport, CT: Greenwood.

Shepard, Curtis, Felice Yeskel, and Charles Outcalt. 1995. *Lesbian, Gay, Bisexual and Transgender Campus Organizing: A Comprehensive Manual*. Washington, DC: National Gay and Lesbian Task Force Policy Institute.

College Campus Programming

Nancy J. Evans

Programming refers to planned activities on college campuses designed to enhance the personal development and learning of individuals and student groups (Saunders and Cooper 2001, 310). Although educational programming has been a part of student affairs work in the United States almost from the beginning of the profession in the early twentieth century, only recently have American colleges and universities taken into account the needs of lesbian, gay, bisexual, and transgender students when planning programming; many campuses still ignore this population in their programming efforts. The first book in the student affairs literature focused on the needs of **lesbian, gay, bisexual**, and **transgender** (LGBT) students, *Beyond Tolerance*, edited by Nancy Evans and Vernon Wall, did not appear until 1991. Yet encouraging and much needed initiatives are being developed in U.S. colleges and universities, both to educate the campus community about LGBT issues and to provide support for LGBT students. In other countries, student services are much more basic, and programming for LGBT students tends to be initiated by student-run organizations rather than student affairs professionals.

LGBT-related programming can take the form of workshops, speaker series, training sessions for student organization officers, or other formal efforts to directly provide specific information, attitudes, or skills to an audience. It can also

See also College Age Students; College Campus Organizing; College Campus Resource Centers; National Coming Out Day; School Safety and Safe School Zones.

occur indirectly by offering opportunities for students to take part in LGBT-focused activities, clubs and organizations, or recognition programs. Programming can also be passive, such as the creation of bulletin boards, display cases, or posters.

LGBT programming has two purposes and targets: supportive programming for LGBT students and educational programming for heterosexual students. Some of the major programming initiatives designed to enhance the educational experience of LGBT students are LGBT student organizations, recognition programs, and Safe Zone programs. Programming for heterosexual students has as its main purpose building awareness and sensitivity to the issues facing LGBT individuals. Workshops and speakers bureaus, as well as passive educational approaches, are used to achieve these goals.

The first LGBT college student organization, the Student Homophile League, was founded at Columbia University in 1967, two years before the **Stonewall** riots that marked the beginning of the modern gay rights movement. This movement spurred the development of activist gay and lesbian groups on numerous college campuses. Today, the majority of major universities in the United States have at least one such organization and they can be found on many private college campuses as well. LGBT student organizations can also be found on campuses in many other countries, including **Canada**, the **United Kingdom**, Norway, Belgium, the Netherlands, Spain, and **South Africa**.

LGBT student organizations have a variety of purposes. They provide social activities where LGBT students can meet each other, develop friendships, and be open about their identities. They also serve as political action groups on many campuses, advocating for campus programs and policies that are inclusive of LGBT students. An LGBT student organization is often the first place on campus where students come out to others and seek validation of their **sexual identity**, support for **coming out** to family, and assistance in determining what being lesbian, gay, bisexual, or transgender will mean for their lives. Services provided by LGBT student organizations might include providing confidential hotlines, referral services, resource centers, and speaker panels. LGBT student organizations often play a major role in educating the campus community about **sexual orientation** and **gender identity** issues. They frequently sponsor workshops, speakers, and programs such as awareness weeks, pride weeks, and coming out days. Participating in LGBT student organizations can contribute significantly to the development of students' identity, leadership skills, and self-confidence. Often one student organization will attempt to achieve all of these goals. It is usually more effective, particularly if the LGBT student population is reasonably large, to establish several smaller groups with one or two specific goals. In any case, student organizations must address the challenge of being sensitive to gender differences and issues related to race and ethnicity to insure that all students feel welcome and supported.

Recognition programs are programs designed to celebrate the achievements of LGBT students. **Lavender graduation**, a special ceremony for graduating LGBT students, is a good example. The first such event was held in 1995 at the University of Michigan. By 1999, eighteen institutions were holding lavender graduations. Surveys completed at the lavender graduation held at UCLA indicated that the event was a positive experience for the graduating students, encouraged students still enrolled, and resulted in positive reactions from family and friends who attended (Sanlo 2000). Other recognition ceremonies include programs such as the "small victories" celebration at Iowa State University, held yearly to recognize the achievements of LGBT students, allies, and LGBT organizations on campus. Since LGBT students rarely receive validation on campus and succeed despite the many challenges they face, special recognition events are an important acknowledgement of their efforts.

Safe zone programs have become an important mechanism for visibly indicating that LGBT students and staff are welcome on campus. Through display of a sticker, button, or other visible symbol, faculty, staff, and students demonstrate that they are accepting of LGBT individuals. Often an ally training program is provided for individuals who wish to become safe zones. Such programs familiarize potential **allies** with the issues facing LGBT students, resources for referral, basic listening skills, and specific ways allies can assist LGBT students. An evaluation of the safe zone program at Iowa State University (Evans 2002) found evidence that the program increased visibility of LGBT issues and people, altered perceptions of the amount of support available to LGBT students, changed the image of campus to one that was more accepting, and increased the awareness level of faculty, students, and staff about LGBT people. LGBT students and staff felt more affirmed. Honest **communication** and networking among students and staff increased.

Intervening to change the campus climate is another important way of providing support to LGBT students. Educational programming targeting heterosexual students is critical for accomplishing this goal. Workshops on LGBT issues are often designed to raise awareness among various campus populations. To be successful, workshops must be based on a careful assessment of the campus climate and the audience. Ground rules will reduce anxiety and insure that respectful discussion occurs. The content of effective workshops must address development of (1) awareness, including participants' personal beliefs and biases as well as the issues facing LGBT individuals; (2) knowledge, including LGBT terminology, history, **identity development** models, and **school climate** issues; (3) skills, such as how to identify and interrupt **homophobia** and **heterosexism**; and (4) action, including how to be an ally to LGBT students and how to make a difference in one's setting. A closure activity should be included that sends participants away feeling positive about what they have learned. Finally, an evaluation is important to gather feedback on aspects of the program that worked and those that were less successful. Awareness programming can be designed to address the needs of specific populations on campus such as members of **fraternities** and **sororities**, student leaders, resident assistants, or campus police.

LGBT speaker bureaus, often sponsored by LGBT student organizations, provide panels of openly lesbian, gay, bisexual, and transgender speakers for classes, residence hall programs, Greek chapters, and other student and staff groups that request them. The purpose of these panels is to raise awareness of the issues that LGBT people face by providing opportunities for audience members to learn from and interact with individuals like themselves. Panelists usually start by sharing their personal experiences and then respond to questions from the audience. Speaker bureaus are generally staffed by students but may include faculty, staff, and alumni as well. Speakers usually go through a training program where they practice sharing their stories in a nonthreatening and honest manner and receive feedback from more experienced presenters, counselors, or student affairs staff. Training is important since speakers may face hostile audiences and challenging questions that require tact and carefully phrased responses. Speakers often find it helpful to process engagements with other members of the bureau either immediately after a presentation or later in a larger group. Research indicates that LGBT speaker bureaus are effective in changing attitudes and raising awareness (Croteau and Kusek 1992). They are also affirming to LGBT individuals who may be in the audience.

In 1971, the University of Michigan became the first major university to establish support services for LGBT students. Over sixty-five colleges and universities in the United States now have Lesbian, Gay, Bisexual, and Transgender student services offices, most of which have been established since 1995. The majority of offices are located on the campuses of large public universities, although several private colleges also provide this type of service. LGBT offices provide a number of services including: (1) library materials, speakers, and other informational materials on LGBT topics; (2) short-term counseling and referral services; (3) programming for LGBT students and the campus community; (4) sponsorship of student support groups; and (5) advocacy on behalf of LGBT students and staff.

Bibliography

Croteau, James M., and Mark T. Kusek. 1992. "Gay and Lesbian Speaker Panels: Implementation and Research." *Journal of Counseling and Development* 70: 396–401.

Evans, Nancy J. 2002. "The Impact of an LGBT Safe Zone Project on Campus Climate." *Journal of College Student Development* 43: 522–539.

Evans, Nancy J., and Vernon A. Wall. 1991. *Beyond Tolerance: Gays, Lesbians and Bisexuals on Campus*. Alexandria, VA: American College Personnel Association.

Lucksted, Alicia. 1998. "Sexual Orientation Speakers Bureaus." Pp. 351–362 in *Working with Lesbian, Gay, Bisexual, and Transgender College Students: A Handbook for Faculty and Administrators*. Edited by Ronni L. Sanlo. Westport, CT: Greenwood.

Mallory, Sherry L. 1998. "Lesbian, Gay, Bisexual, and Transgender Student Organizations: An Overview." Pp. 321–328 in *Working with Lesbian, Gay, Bisexual, and Transgender College Students: A Handbook for Faculty and Administrators*. Edited by Ronni L. Sanlo. Westport, CT: Greenwood.

Roberts, Dennis C. 2003. "Community Building and Programming." Pp. 539–554 in *Student Services: A Handbook for the Profession*. 4th ed. Edited by Susan R. Komives and Dudley B. Woodard, Jr. San Francisco, CA: Jossey-Bass.

Sanlo, Ronni. 2000. "Lavender Graduation: Acknowledging the Lives and Achievement of Lesbian, Gay, Bisexual, and Transgender College Students." *Journal of College Student Development* 41: 643–647.

Saunders, Susan A., and Diane L. Cooper. 2001. "Programmatic Interventions: Translating Theory to Practice." Pp. 309–340 in *The Student Affairs Administrator: Educator, Leader, and Manager*. Edited by Roger B. Winston, Don G. Creamer, and Ted K. Miller. New York: Brunner-Routledge.

Wall, Vernon A., Jamie Washington, Nancy Evans, and Ross Papish. 2000. "From the Trenches: Strategies for Facilitating Lesbian, Gay, and Bisexual Awareness Programs for College Students." Pp. 157–189 in *Toward Acceptance: Sexual Orientation Issues on Campus*. Edited by Vernon A. Wall and Nancy J. Evans. Lanham, MD: American College Personnel Association.

Web Sites

CampusPrideNet. 2004. Accessed December 14, 2004. http://www.campuspride.net. Provides information about a national online community and resource network for student leaders and campus organizations who want to create safer campus environments free from homophobia and heterosexism.

National Association of Directors of Lesbian, Gay, Bisexual, and Transgender Resources in Higher Education. July 2004. Accessed November 11, 2004. http://www.lgbtcampus. org. Designed to help college and university student affairs staff create environments in which lesbian, gay, bisexual, and transgender students, faculty, staff, administrators, and alumni have equity in every respect.

College Campus Resource Centers

Ronni Sanlo

Lesbian Gay Bisexual Transgender (LGBT) campus resource centers are departments within the student affairs division of colleges and universities. These provide education, information, referral, support, and advocacy for and about issues of **sexual orientation** and gender identity for students, faculty, staff, alumni, and the community. LGBT centers were created on many campuses as a response to a horrific **hate crime** such as the murder of **Matthew Shepard**, because of harassment by peers, or due to discriminatory policies that prohibited equality on a campus. While advocacy is much of the work of an LGBT campus resource center, its greatest value is helping a campus create a safe and welcoming learning environment so that LGBT students may achieve both personal and academic success.

The first LGBT center was established as a quarter-time office at the University of Michigan in 1971, as a response to the demands of the Black Action Movement to offer service centers for specific populations (Beemyn 2002). By 1994, there were six centers nationally that had full-time professional staff. Curt Shepard, campus organizer for the National Gay and Lesbian Task Force (NGLTF), traveled to the few campuses that had LGBT centers and assisted with their organization and needs. In 1995, these professionals gathered at the NGLTF Creating Change Conference. By 1996 there were thirty LGBT centers. As more institutions created LGBT centers, the directors began to organize. In 1997, Sue Rankin from The Pennsylvania State University, Robert Schoenberg from the University of Pennsylvania, and Ronni Sanlo then from the University of Michigan, met to create the founding bylaws of what has become the National Consortium for Directors of LGBT Resources in Higher Education (Sanlo, Rankin, and Schonberg 2002). In 2003, there were nearly 100 such centers on college and university campuses in the United States and a professional association to support the directors' development and work. In Canada, the University of Saskatchewan, York University, and the University of Toronto in Canada have established LGBT centers.

Generally, LGBT campus resource centers were created for three reasons. The first is a result of an institution's response to homophobic incidents which often spawn a **school climate** survey for quantifiable data. The second is administrative reaction to the demands of students, faculty, and staff to create a place of safety and provide resources to teach the university community about LGBT issues and concerns. The third and most uncommon is an understanding by an

See also College Campus Organizing; College Campus Programming; Coming Out, Youth.

institution's administration that the LGBT center is yet another way to foster diversity and to create a welcoming campus atmosphere (Sanlo, Rankin, and Schoenberg 2002). Most centers focus in each of these areas regardless of their original impetus.

Like the LGBT civil rights movement, LGBT campus centers have evolved. The first centers were the "gay" offices—the only word used to describe nonheterosexual people on college campuses. The University of Michigan experience illustrates the progression of name changes. In 1971, it was site for the Office for Human Sexuality, though often referred to as the "gay office." With the growth of the **women's movement**, lesbians demanded inclusion and participation, and, in the early 1980s, it became the Lesbian and Gay Programs Office. In 1994, the name was expanded to include bisexuals due to the patience and training of a bisexual staff person. When a transgender-identified graduate student began to work for the office, the name was changed to the Office of Lesbian, Gay, Bisexual, and Transgender Affairs.

Recently, students have used a wide variety of terminology to identify their nonheterosexual statues, from gay to **queer** to same-gender-loving to heteroflexible. As a result, there is a trend to be as inclusive as possible with campus office names such as the Stonewall Center (University of Massachusetts-Amherst), the Rainbow Center (University of Connecticut), and the Pride Center (California State Polytechnic University at Pomona). There is also a trend to merge with campus women's centers such as the Center for Sexual and Gender Equity at the University of California Santa Barbara. As names of campus offices have changed so, too, has its focus broadened. Many offices include the words, lesbian, gay, bisexual, transgender, intersex, queer, and questioning in their titles, and maintain a conscious effort to offer programming in each of these identity areas. Other areas of programming include ally or safe zone training, guest speakers, leadership workshops and retreats, and library and research services.

Today, the mission of many LGBT centers is similar. They provide information and referral both on campus and at off-campus entities. They also act as an advocate on behalf of a student faced with harassment by peers or by professors, or in times of financial hardship due to their sexual minority status (e.g., parents withdrew funding after learning their child's sexual orientation). These offices provide "safe space" when a student simply needs to talk with a knowledgeable person about LGBT campus issues or when experiencing an emotional crisis. Most LGBT centers offer individual counseling, speakers bureaus, support/rap groups, education and sensitivity training to departments on campus, and support for the campus LGBT organizations. Some centers, such as the one at UCLA, have lending and research libraries, large gathering spaces, and opportunities for internships.

The first twenty or so LGBT center directors were specifically hired to develop and maintain these centers. Most held masters or doctoral degrees in counseling, psychology, or some area of educational leadership. In addition, many were veterans of local LGBT community activism. Staff who are hired to direct LGBT programs are more likely than their predecessors to have masters level degrees in student affairs, higher education administration, or college student personnel programs, and less likely to have a history of community LGBT activism. These directors or coordinators reported directly to the dean of students or the vice president for student affairs. A few of the early centers, like the University of

Minnesota, were established as and continue to be part of an academic area of their institution.

Because of the growing demand by students, faculty, and staff for LGBT campus centers in the midst of tremendous budget cuts in higher education, new centers are being created in one of two new ways. Some, such as at DePauw, are housed within the institution's multicultural or cross-culture center. Integration provides both a forum and many opportunities for students to explore not just their sexual identities but also their racial/ethnic/cultural identities in a more holistic manner. Others, like the Queer Resource Center at the University of California Santa Barbara, merged with the campus women's center to become the Resource Center for Sexual and Gender Diversity, although each office maintains separate space for privacy. This arrangement allows for the consideration of gender and **sexual identity** simultaneously through their appropriate connection as well as a resource savings for the institution. Another trend is the growing inclusion of **allies** and non-LGBT students as users of an LGBT center. Many of these students have family members or friends who are LGBT or students who are conducting research or wishing to learn more about LGBT people. At UCLA, for example, a variety of non-LGBT student organizations meet at the Center in order to gain a greater understanding and to create collaborative programming with the LGBT student organizations. In addition, allies, that is, supportive heterosexual friends of LGBT people, are actively participating at the centers and within the LGBT student and faculty/staff organizations.

Lesbian, gay, and bisexual students are **coming out** at earlier ages than their predecessors, in high school or even middle school. They are coming to college campuses with the expectation of receiving the same excellent services as all other students (Sanlo 2000). **Transgender youth** are also becoming more visible at younger ages (FTM Alliance of Los Angeles 2003). Together they are creating more inclusive communities on college campuses. And, with the growing popularity of LGBT centers at colleges and universities, LGBT alumni are also becoming more visible and more willing to give back to their alma maters to help in the work of creating the safety they could not have experienced in their days as students (Sanlo, Rankin, and Schoenberg 2002).

Bibliography

Beemyn, Brett. 2002. "The Development and Administration of Campus LGBT Centers and Offices." Pp. 25–32 in *Our Place on Campus: Lesbian, Gay, Bisexual, and Transgender Services and Programs in Higher Education*. Edited by Ronni Sanlo, Sue Rankin, and Robert Schoenberg. Westport, CT: Greenwood Press.

National Gay and Lesbian Task Force (NGLTF). 2003. *The NGLTF Campus Organizing Manual*. Edited by Curtis Shepard, Felice Yeskel, and Charles Outcalt. Accessed September 1, 2003. http://www.ngltf.org/library/index.cfm

Outcalt, Charles. 1995. "Establishing a LGBT Resource Center." Pp. 213–217 in *The NGLTF Campus Organizing Manual*. Edited by Curtis Shepard, Felice Yeskel, and Charles Outcalt. New York: NGLTF Policy Institute.

Sanlo, Ronni L. 2000. "The LGBT Campus Resource Center Director: The New Profession in Student Affairs." *NASPA Journal* 37, no. 3: 485–495.

Sanlo, Ronni L., Sue Rankin, and Robert Schoenberg, eds. 2002. *Our Place on Campus: Lesbian, Gay, Bisexual, and Transgender Services and Programs in Higher Education*. Westport, CT: Greenwood Press.

Web Sites

FTM Alliance of Los Angeles. 2004. Accessed November 27, 2004. http://ftmalliance.org. Offers information regarding local and national resources for transgender people and their families and friends as well as medical and educational resources.

National Consortium for Directors of LGBT Resources in Higher Education. July 2004. Accessed November 27, 2004. http://www.lgbtcampus.org. Provides resources and information regarding the work of LGBT campus resources centers as well as contact information for the current offices or centers in the United States and Canada.

Colonialism and Homosexuality

Didi Khayatt

Almost every child in North America has come across the word "gay" and uses it, if only pejoratively. This is not the case around the world. While it is difficult to see the connection between colonialism and LGBT issues, the relation becomes clearer if one knows that, for instance, "homosexuality" is a term brought into being in **Europe** during the late nineteenth century as a concept describing same-sex practices; as an identity, rather than a set of sexual practices, it does not exist in many other cultures. If a language does not include a word for "homosexuality" (or any variation thereof), there is little hope that the other (more current) terms, such as **"lesbian," "gay," "bisexual,"** and **"transsexual/transgender,"** would exist. Given, however, the influence of Euro-North-American cultures on the rest of the world, such words as "gay" and **"queer"** have surfaced in a number of languages—always maintaining the English articulation. For this to happen, a certain cultural colonialism, or, more appropriately, imperialism is at work.

Ania Loomba (1998, 2) defines colonialism as "the conquest and control of other people's land and goods." Colonialism should be distinguished from another term, often used interchangeably with colonialism yet distinctly different from it: imperialism. Modern imperialism, Loomba reminds us, is a global system that is not necessarily tied to direct colonial rule. Thus, where the imperial country is the center from where the power emanates, the colony is the place that it penetrates and controls. Loomba summarizes: "Imperialism can function without formal colonies but colonialism cannot" (7).

Most critical scholars who have recently written about colonialism have insisted that neither term can be discussed outside of specific historical context. In other words, no colonial history of a particular people at a particular time in history can be generalized, and each instance of colonialism or imperialism should be discussed separately. Thus, European colonialism is substantively different from the Mongolian invasions of Gengis Khan, or the Ottoman expansions of nineteenth century, or the fabled empire of **China**. Modern European colonialism is considered within an historical context of these earlier histories of contact, while keeping in mind that it "ushered in new and different kinds of colonial practices which altered

See also Communication; Egypt, LGBT Youth and Issues in; ESL, Teaching of; Films, Youth and Educators in; Multiple Genders; Native and Indigenous LGBT Youth; Poststructuralism; Queer and Queer Theory; South America, LGBT Youth and Issues in.

the whole globe in a way that these other colonialisms did not." Loomba (1998, 7) also argues that modern European colonialism did more than extract the wealth of the lands it conquered; "it restructured the economies of the latter, drawing them into a complex relationship with their own, so that there was a flow of human and natural resources between colonized and colonial countries." Furthermore, one of the major consequences of colonialism is the influence of the colonizer's technologies and ideas on the colonized. This is precisely the point of entry through which "homosexuality," as a modern European colonizing concept, can be understood.

While eighteenth- and nineteenth-century Western Europe saw an intensification of colonial exploits, it also witnessed an era of scientific classification of its ever expanding universe. Nothing escaped this ordering: From Linnaeus' taxonomy to the Social Darwinists' hierarchies of races, every aspect of nature was classified and ranked. During this era, sexuality came under a different kind of scrutiny than previous religious condemnations. Sexual acts were named, classified, and ranked in order of deviance from what was perceived as "natural," that is, sex between a man and a woman for procreation. Sexual acts ceased to exist as discreet acts but were, conversely, ascribed to individual profiles; hence for the first time in European history, sexual acts were linked to a **sexual identity**: A man did not merely commit a perversion, he became perverse; he did not just engage in "homosexual" behavior, he became a homosexual (women's sexualities, of course, were seldom contemplated).

"Homosexuality"—a term coined by Karl Maria Benkert, in 1869, and popularized by Gustav Jaeger in the 1880s—is, to this day, the most recognized term that describes same-sex behavior (Dynes 1985, 67). According to a number of sources, the binary opposite term, "heterosexuality," became part of everyday discourse at a much later time in history, probably around the 1920s.

A relation between homosexuality and colonization began from the moment the term became current in describing same-sex behavior. The connection is a complicated one. Although the term allowed the possibility of naming of the specific behavior for which it was coined, it was precise enough to overlook many cultural practices that deviated even slightly from its imagined meaning. Thus, on the one hand, the French-named *berdache* of North American Aboriginal peoples (now known as Two Spirit people), the *mukhannath* (effeminate men) of the Arab Umayyad (661–750 CE) era, or the Hijra of **India** were not detected historically as incidences of "homosexuality." On the other hand, there was a tendency for nineteenth-century European travelers to imagine "homosexuality" in cultural practices that may not necessarily have been perceived as sexual by the culture itself. For instance, the intimate fondling that occurred between women as they washed each other in Turkish baths was perceived by nineteenth-century British women travelers as evidence of lesbianism. Furthermore, there was a tendency by colonizers and travelers of the time to connect deviant sexualities with cultures that were other than their own. As Anne McClintock (1995, 23) states: "Renaissance travelers found an eager and lascivious audience for their spicy tales, so that, long before the era of high Victorian imperialism, Africa and the Americas had become what can be called a porno-tropics for the European imagination—a fantastic magic lantern of the mind onto which Europe projected its forbidden sexual desires and fears."

Although most nations became independent of colonial rule during the twentieth century, the influence on the previously colonized subjects did not end when the colonizers departed. For one, some invaders remained: Witness the Americas and parts of **Africa** and **Asia**. Second, for those who had been previously occupied, the influence of the colonizers is still a factor that creates tensions in such areas as education, and second and third language acquisition (for instance, English or French are taught in schools in many parts of the world), in addition to the continued economic and political dependencies that seem inevitable for some nations. Third, a newer form of discursive colonization that requires no land occupation has been in effect, spreading its influence through satellite television and the **Internet**, not to mention through the power of multinational corporations and advertising. For instance, McClintock (1995, 13) argues that: "The power of U.S. finance capital and huge multinational corporations to command the flow of capital, research, consumer goods, and media information around the world can exert a coercive power as great as any colonial gunboat." These "postcolonial" influences are evident in the area of sexuality, where authors of books and articles in learned journals or those in other media are always looking for "lesbians" or "gays" in parts of the world where such terms do not exist. Information technology is flattening and standardizing language and images in previously unknown ways.

Homosexuality, as an identity, cannot easily be transposed onto languages lacking an equivalent term or to cultures where the concept is absent. This is not to say that same-sex practices are not universal, but to emphasize that the meanings people give to these practices depend upon their cultural contexts because these intersect with social class, religion, and gender, and so on. Searching for "lesbians" or "gays" transnationally imposes a European concept onto cultures that may not have an equivalent term and that would have to adopt the specific word (homosexual) to conceptualize local behavior. For instance, there is no equivalent term for "queer" in French and, therefore, to use this concept is to force the English term onto French speakers. Such languages as Chinese, Arabic, and Hindu lack comparable terms for "homosexuality," even though the concept itself may be understood and same-sex practices existed long before the coining of the European term. Imposing Euro-American terms and laws, social and religious attitudes, as well as **research** and scholarship, inflicts on these language speakers "the coercive power [that is] as great as any colonial gunboat" (McClintock 1995, 13).

Current international access to satellite television and to the Internet is allowing exchanges among peoples never before witnessed. North American television programs, newscasts, and documentaries are broadcast to the Middle East. Although satellite access remains the benefit of a privileged few, mostly in **urban** centers, and although such programs require a certain level of literacy, in time these will be accessible to all. Consequently, there is also no doubt that such terms as "homosexuality" will be absorbed, resisted, negated, appropriated, or accepted depending on the social, political, and religious contexts at hand in each particular cultural context.

In the Middle East, formal education rarely deals with issues of **desire** unless these are normative and under the rubric of marriage and family responsibilities. All nonnormative sexual practices would be condemned as abominations and only mentioned negatively. No sexual activities are permitted to girls. For boys, "experimenting" with other boys might be overlooked as long as they are young and not of age for marriage. For youth who have access to the Internet, sites dealing with "homosexuality" are monitored and it might be dangerous to investigate these. Consequently, youth might resort to hiding and silence, unless they are able to travel to Western countries.

185

Bibliography

AbuKhalil, As'ad. 1997. "Gender Boundaries and Sexual Categories in the Arab World." *Feminist Issues* 15, nos. 1/2: 92–104.

Dynes, Wayne. 1985. *Homolexis: A Historical and Cultural Lexicon of Homosexuality.* New York: Gai Saber Monograph no. 4.

Loomba, Ania. 1998. *Colonialism/Postcolonialism.* London and New York: Routledge.

McClintock, Anne. 1995. *Imperial Leather: Race, Gender and Sexuality in the Colonial Contest.* New York and London: Routledge.

Ng, Vivian. 1997. "Looking for Lesbians in Chinese History." Pp. 199–204 in *A Queer World: The Center for Lesbian and Gay Studies Reader.* Edited by Martin Duberman. New York and London: Routledge.

Thadani, Giti. 1996. *Sakhiyani: Lesbian Desire in Ancient and Modern India.* New York: Cassell.

Comics

Allison J. Kelaher Young

Comics are narratives that use pictures and words to simultaneously reinforce and critique ideas about the dominant culture. Because of their less formal nature and their place in **popular culture**, comics are a medium that are most often consumed by youth, and as such, adults may not take comic narratives seriously. However, this allows comics to challenge social norms and values, including traditional views on homosexuality. Sexual minorities are represented in comics that are drawn for mainstream audiences as well as in those drawn for **lesbian, gay, bisexual** and **transgender youth** (LGBT). Because of their less formal and graphic nature, queer youth may identify with various strips and their various characters. As such, comics present a potentially useful resource for educators and others working with these youth. Because comics are both graphic and textual, they have an immediate appeal to young people. Engaging in discussions at a level different from typical textual narrative, comics incorporated into the **curriculum** allow for critical discourse of issues of gender and sexuality. Mainstream comics can be categorized in terms of two major strands: homonormative and integrationist. The former have, or are perceived to have, a homonormative subtext; the inseparable pair of Batman and Robin is an example. Integrationist comics, like Lynn Johnston's *For Better or Worse*, and Matt Groening's *Akbar and Jeff*, incorporate sexual minority characters into the plot line.

In 1953, during an era where public condemnation of homosexuality was the norm, psychotherapist Frederic Wertham wrote a treatise on the dangers of comics. One of his arguments was the implicit homosexuality of the Marvel *Batman* duo, Batman and Robin. Additional evidence of this comic narrative's homonormative subtext is Robert Smigel's satire on the popular television show *Saturday Night Live*. This portrayal of superheroes Gary and Ace in *The Ambiguously Gay Duo* features obvious symbols and dialogue meant to draw explicit connection to

See also Cartoons; Queer Studies; Sexual Identity; Youth Culture.

homoerotic elements of the *Batman* narrative. Smigel's overt symbology leaves little room for interpretation as the car that the superheroes drive is shaped like male genitalia.

Most recently, mainstream comics publishers like Marvel and DC Comics have begun to capitalize on these ideas by integrating openly gay characters. In one issue of the DC publication *Green Lantern*, Terry Berg, the personal assistant of the Green Lantern's alter ego, is the victim of gay bashing. In late 2002, Marvel re-released a character called the Rawhide Kid, who in this incarnation is openly gay. Other Marvel publications have added or introduced gay characters, including Destiny and Mystique of *X-Men* and Phat and Vivisector of *X-Statix*. LGBT characters have been integrated to such an extent that, in 1997, an online site, The Gay League, was formed by and for gay fans, artists, and writers (http://www.gayleague.com/home.php).

For Better or For Worse is another example of gay integration into mainstream comics. Centering on the Patterson family, Johnston's strip unfolds the friendship between Michael Patterson and Lawrence, whose teenage **coming out** story involved a four-week set of strips in 1993. The immediate negative response from newspaper editors and readers came predominantly from United States audiences rather than those in Johnston's native **Canada**. In the end, though, Johnston reported that over 70 percent of the letters sent to her were positive.

The distance traveled from the homonormative *Batman* comics to the integrationist strips of the 1990s can be seen in the evolution of comics, beginning in the 1970s when social issues of **ethnicity** and gender appeared. Feminist comics like *It Ain't Me Babe* (1970) and *Wimmin's Comix* (1972) raised issues of lesbian rights within the women's liberation movement. Gay and lesbian newspapers and magazines in the late 1970s often carried strips by Howard Cruse and Allison Bechdel, which were later published as collections.

There, too, were gay male comics, such as Tom of Finland drawn by Tuoko Laaksonen, which explicitly objectified the male physique and portrayed a wide variety of homoerotic activities. This erotic art mirrored the overt sexuality of the gay men's communities during this era. It also changed the self-image and identity options for gay youth by providing images of hard-bodied men at a time when the vast majority of portrayals of gay males were effeminate. This strand is evidenced a generation later as the young gay character, Justin, in the television series **Queer as Folk** develops a best selling comic series featuring the unabashedly sexual character, Rage. Because of the feminist politic that birthed lesbian comics, the majority of comics during the 1980s tended to focus more on issues of identity (i.e., coming out, socializing with others, etc.) rather than of **desire** (Dean 1997). For example, independent Gay Comix, founded in 1980, focused on the issues confronting the gay and lesbian characters who played important roles in the strips as opposed to those who made cameo appearances.

In the 1990s, the evolution from homonormative to integrationist was complete. Pulitzer prize cartoonist Gary Troudeau's (who also received a 1995 GLAAD Media Award) longtime character Andy Lippincott died of **AIDS** on May 24, 1990. More recently, *Doonesbury*'s plot has featured the commitment ceremony and pending marriage of regular characters, Mark Slackmeyer, an FM disc jockey, to his partner, conservative commentator Chase Talbott.

There were also shifts in the narratives of gay and lesbian comics as animators navigated issues of identity and desire more equitably. For example, Howard

Within the first 9 panels of this Bechdel Strip (No. 321—"Mother Wit"), in this segment Clarice and Toni are talking to Raffi's new teacher. From *Post—Dykes to Watch Out For* (2000). Courtesy of Firebrand Books. © Alison Bechdel, Ann Arbor

Cruse's (1995, 2000) first person narrative *Stuck Rubber Baby* chronicles the main character's emotional life as identity and desire become interwoven in this graphic novel. Similarly, Alison Bechdel's work weaves these issues together throughout the now ten collections of her comic strip, *Dykes To Watch Out For*.

This strip uses a third-person narrative in the social context of a bi/lesbian community. Bechdel draws an ensemble of characters, each representing an aspect of the bi/lesbian community. For example, Mo is the thirty-something vegetarian, politically active lesbian who reacts vehemently to the political landscape, while her friend, Lois is the quintessential Don Juanita. Anjali, a youth working at Madwimmin Books, who appeared in a few cameos in the late 1990s. Rafael, son of Toni and Clarice, has been in the strip since he was conceived, and several other children have been featured, including the M-to-F transgender child, Jonah. **College age students** make regular cameo appearances in classroom instructed by Sydney and Ginger. Sydney's students, Scooter and Alex, helped her during her recent cancer treatment.

Bechdel is one of the first artists to draw lesbian sex scenes. The characters operate at the intersection of queer issues and what most would consider mainstream issues—getting and keeping a job, planning and maintaining a family, getting together and breaking up, engaging in socio-political activities. Other artists followed Bechdel with LGBT main characters or ensembles, including: Diane DiMassa (*Hothead Paisan*), Eric Orner (*The Mostly Unfabulous Social Life of Ethan Greene*), Dave Brousseau (*Couple of Guys*), Joan Hilty (*Bitter Girl*), Paige Braddock (*Jane's World*), and Glen Hanson and Allan Neuwirth (*Chelsea Boys*).

LGBTQ themes also appear in comics outside the United States. In **Japan**, for instance, there is an entire genre, Yaoi, devoted to romance between two boys (*Trip, Boku-no Sukina Sensei*). Other comics portray gender transforming characters (*Ranma 1/2, Hibarikun*) or have lesbian themes (*Love My Life, Indigo Blue*).

While much of the comic work was gay positive in terms of stories and characters, there has been negative reaction and controversy. In 1999, Jerry Falwell observed that one of the characters of a popular children's television show, Tinky Winky, was intended as a gay role model. His purple color (often used by the gay community), triangle-shaped antenna (a gay symbol), and red purse made him "suspect." Falwell's attack prompted satirical responses published in gay newspapers, which featured other "suspect" children's television and cartoon characters: Bert and Ernie from *Sesame Street*, Velma from *Scooby Doo*, Smithers from *The Simpsons*, Peppermint Patty from *Peanuts*, and Elmer Fudd from *Loony Tunes*. Conservative critics of popular comics from *Batman* to *Doonesbury* recognize the influence of such icons of popular culture, underscoring their potential for educational use.

Bibliography

Bechdel, Alison. 1998. *The Indelible Alison Bechdel: Confessions, Comix, and Miscellaneous Dykes to Watch Out For.* Ithaca, NY: Firebrand Books.
Dean, Gabrielle N. 1997. "The 'Phallacies' of Dyke Comic Strips." Pp. 199–223 in *The Gay 90's: Disciplinary and Interdisciplinary Formations in Queer Studies.* Edited by Thomas Foster, Carol Siegel, and Ellen E. Berry. New York: New York University Press.
Lafky, Sue A., and Bonnie Brennen. 1995. "For Better or For Worse: Coming Out in the Funny Pages." *Studies in Popular Culture* 18, no. 1: 23–47.
Martindale, Kathleen. 1997. *Unpopular Culture: Lesbian Writing After the Sex Wars.* Albany: State University of New York Press.
McCloud, Scott. 2000. *Reinventing Comics: How Imagination and Technology are Revolutionizing an Art Form.* New York: HarperCollins.
Medhurst, Andy. 2003. "Batman, Deviance, and Camp." Pp. 686–702 in *Signs of Life in the USA: Readings in Popular Culture for Writers,* 4th ed. Edited by Sonia Maasik and Fisher Solomon. Boston: Bedford.
Sabin, Roger. 1996. *Comics, Comix & Graphic Novels: A History of Comic Art.* Boston: Phaidon Press.
Wertham, Frederic. 1953. *Seduction of the Innocent.* New York: Rinehart.
Wiater, Stanley, and Stephen R. Bissette. 1993. *Comic Book Rebels: Conversations with the Creators of the New Comics.* New York: Penguin.

Web Sites

For Better or Worse. June 2005. Lynn Johnston. Accessed May 28, 2005. http://www.fborfw.com/char_pgs/lawrence/. Johnston described her experience with the backlash created by the story of the gay teen, Lawrence. Site includes scenes of the Pattersons, news of Johnston's forthcoming events, and archives of different strips.
Gay League. April 2005. Joe Palmer. Accessed May 28, 2005. http://www.gayleague.com/home.php. Group of AOL users targeting comic artists, writers, and fans.
Planetout. 2005. Beth Callaghan. Accessed May 28, 2005. http://www.planetout.com/entertainment/comics/superheroes/comics.html. Jim Provenzo presents a brief history of LGBT comic superheroes with a focus on Marvel and DC comics.
Queer Comics on the Web. July 2001. Accessed May 28, 2005. http://home.earthlink.net/~cfmdesigns/Comics/queer/strips.html. Links to queer comic strips and cartoon panels from both mainstream and queer sources.

Coming Out, Teachers

Susan Talburt

Teachers' coming out, or publicly declaring their nonheterosexuality, raises questions about teachers' rights and roles in educating youth. Coming out is a phenomenon made possible by the late nineteenth-century formulation of homosexuality as an identity or status, rather than an act or behavior. However, due to **discrimination**, it was not until the gay and lesbian movement of the 1970s that United States' teachers began to come out in significant numbers. Opponents of coming out, or of the presence of lesbian, gay, bisexual, and transgender (LGBT) teachers generally, argue that discussion of homosexuality is inappropriate in schools and that homosexual teachers are negative role models. Advocates argue that teachers' coming out is imperative to counter negative **stereotypes** and educate youth about [homo]sexualities in positive ways. Others question whether teachers' declaring a **sexual orientation** fixes categories that educators should instead question. The meanings of coming out vary according to educational level (K-12 or postsecondary), geography, history, and interpersonal relations.

In his 1932 *The Sociology of Teaching*, Willard Waller wrote of the dangers of homosexual teachers: "The real risk is that he may, by presenting himself as a love object to certain members of his own sex at a time when their sex attitudes have not been deeply canalized, develop in them attitudes similar to his own. For nothing seems more certain than that homosexuality is contagious" (Lipkin 1999, 196). Fears of adult influences on children often continue to define possibilities for LGBT teachers to come out. Although public discourse has focused on lesbians and gay men, the positions of bisexual and transgender individuals are also affected by gender and sexual norms. Opposition to openly LGBT teachers includes claims that they offer poor role models, recruit youth to homosexuality, and sexually molest young people.

Systematic efforts to exclude gay and lesbian teachers from public schools and universities began in significant form during the McCarthy era in the 1950s, and resulted in intimidation, loss of licensure, and firing for many teachers and university faculty, as in the campaign by the so-called **Johns Committee** of the Florida legislature. Two movements in the 1970s attempted to institutionalize heterosexuality in the teaching force. The unsuccessful 1978 Briggs Initiative sought a law declaring that California would refuse to hire or would dismiss school workers who engaged in homosexual activity or conduct in such a way that it came to the attention of schoolchildren or school employees. A year earlier Anita Bryant had waged the "Save Our Children" campaign to oppose a Dade County, Florida, employment nondiscrimination ordinance that included lesbians and gay men. The campaign centered on the threat of hiring homosexual teachers who would recruit youth.

With the defeat of the Employment Nondiscrimination Act, which sought to prohibit dismissal on the grounds of sexuality, there are no federal protections for LGBT teachers in the United States. Yet two 1998 federal court victories, *Glover v. Williamsburg Local School District*, in which Glover asserted discrimination as a basis of nonrenewal of his teaching contract, and *Weaver v. Nebo School District*, in which Weaver was admonished not to discuss her **sexual orientation** and was

See also Activism, LGBT Teachers; Antidiscrimination Policy; National Coming Out Day; Professionalism; Race and Racism; Teachers, LGBT and History; Workplace Issues.

removed as volleyball coach after coming out, offer federal precedents that uphold LGBT teachers' rights. In addition, some municipalities and school boards have passed nondiscrimination laws and clauses that protect LGBT teachers' rights; however, most have not. And private schools, particularly religious schools, are often exempted from nondiscrimination laws. Reluctance to pass nondiscrimination laws has been justified by state sodomy laws that criminalize consensual private behavior and thus define LGBT individuals as criminals. The effects of the Supreme Court's overturning of these sodomy laws in *Lawrence v. Texas*, in 2003, is yet to be seen.

Countries that have nationwide protection against discrimination on the basis of sexual orientation include **Canada**, Ecuador, **Ireland, Mexico, New Zealand, South Africa,** and Switzerland. The penal codes of Denmark, Finland, **France,** Iceland, Lithuania, Luxembourg, the Netherlands, Norway, Slovenia, Spain, and Sweden prohibit discrimination. Although Article 13 of the 1999 Treaty of Amsterdam gives the European Union authority to adopt measures against discrimination based on sexual orientation, education is outside its sphere of governance. In the **United Kingdom,** an effort to repeal **Section 28** of the Local Government Act of 1988, which prohibited "promotion of homosexuality" in schools, was defeated in 2000, but was finally repealed three years later. **Australia**'s federal government offers no protections; some states have regulations similar to Section 28, while others, such as New South Wales, prohibit discrimination. Countries on record as actively persecuting homosexuals include **Egypt**, Iran, Libya, Malaysia, Morocco, Namibia, Pakistan, Saudi Arabia, Sudan, and Syria. Some postcolonial nations, such as **India** and Zimbabwe, which have inherited discriminatory laws from their former rulers, frame homosexuality as a "problem" brought by foreigners and thus as irrelevant to education. Nonetheless, some openly LGBT university faculty in countries such as India, have begun to integrate lesbian and gay content into the **curriculum**, despite national criminalization of same-sex activity.

Even with legal protections, local norms often discourage teachers from declaring their sexuality. Many public K-12 teachers conceal their sexual orientation to avoid parent, student, or colleagues' complaints; harassment; limited possibilities for advancement; transfer; or dismissal. A tacit agreement of "don't ask–don't tell" defines many teachers' interactions. Researchers such as Griffin (1992) have identified strategies of "identity management" that range from total concealment, or "**passing**," to complete openness. Educators employ these strategies selectively according to context.

In response to silencing, organizations, such as the **Gay, Lesbian, and Straight Education Network** in the United States and **GLBT Educational Equity** (GLEE) in **Europe,** advocate for the rights of LGBT school workers and students. Unions such as the National Education Association and the American Federation of Teachers have active gay and lesbian caucuses and have issued statements supporting nondiscrimination clauses. Advocates for teachers to come out argue that they can gain a sense of integrity and self-respect, counter heterosexist stereotypes, offer LGBT youth positive role models, and work for curricular inclusion.

At the postsecondary level in the United States, faculty did not begin coming out in significant numbers until after the 1969 **Stonewall** uprisings. Spurred by gay liberationists, gay and lesbian faculty founded the Gay Academic Union (GAU) in New York in 1973. By 1975, the organization formed chapters in cities including Philadelphia, Ann Arbor, Boston, and Chicago. The GAU emphasized connections between personal liberation and social change, opposed discrimination against women and gay people, supported faculty and students coming out, and promoted the development of gay and lesbian studies. Coming out was thought to enable personal and disciplinary legitimation within the academy, as gay and lesbian faculty pursued the constitution of a visible history, literature, and culture.

Although university faculty do not face the same level of public opposition and hysteria over recruitment of youth and negative role modeling that K-12 educators do, some openly LGBT faculty have suffered discrimination in hiring procedures and tenure and promotion reviews, exclusion from collegial and professional networks, **harassment**, and intimidation. Some faculty members remain "closeted" until receiving tenure, if not afterward as well, in order to maintain credibility and to protect opportunities for their advancement. Faculty whose scholarship or teaching centers on gay and lesbian topics can face heightened **homophobia**. Some have lost access to prestigious research grants and peer-reviewed journals and have had their work devalued as politicized or trivial.

There are increasing numbers of openly LGBT university faculty. This openness varies according to gender, geography, institutional conservatism or religious affiliation, disciplinary location, and interpersonal departmental relations. Whether or not they engage in scholarship pertaining to LGBT issues, many LGBT academics struggle with issues of coming out in terms specific to their roles as educators. Many perceive a responsibility to come out in order to offer students role models, support and **mentoring**, and to use their presence in classrooms to foreground the personal and political relevance of subjects of study. Beyond the classroom, faculty who believe that invisibility allows homophobia and **heterosexism** to continue unaddressed come out in order to work against institutional and social discrimination on campuses and in **professional educational organizations**. At the same time, some "out" faculty face tokenization, as they may be called upon to be spokespersons for "the LGBT community."

Change that has encouraged LGBT faculty to come out has to some extent been made possible by social and campus movements' contributions to the creation of equitable campus policies, support services and organizations, and the increasing legitimacy of **LGBT studies**. For example, in postapartheid South Africa, following passage of the 1996 Constitution, whose "equality clause" prohibits discrimination on the basis of sexual orientation, faculty are increasingly incorporating courses in LGBT studies into the curriculum. Nondiscrimination clauses inclusive of sexual orientation and domestic partnership benefits offer LGBT faculty legal protection and resources on many campuses, although fewer than two dozen campuses acknowledge transgender issues by including **gender identity** in their nondiscrimination clauses. However, as in the case of K-12 teachers, legal protections do not always provide security, as discrimination can be disguised or subtle. Often, local, everyday relations at the departmental level form a basis for faculty members' decisions to come out, regardless of official policies. Thus, for educators, being "out" can have multiple meanings across contexts.

Despite commonsense beliefs that coming out is both a sign and a means of progress for K-12 and university faculty, some educators question the importance and efficacy of coming out. Advocates for coming out assert a right to authenticity and the potential for educators to effect social change by challenging heterosexuality as the norm. An unquestioned assumption underlying this logic is that coming out leads to acceptance and tolerance. Some educators point out that naming reinforces the norm of heterosexuality by upholding the dualistic, hierarchical categories of homosexual/heterosexual that naming seeks to challenge. Others point out that coming out is largely a phenomenon associated with white, male privilege in a patriarchal and racialized society. A mandate to come out not only imposes a fixing of self in a category that is not fully representative, but also assumes a responsibility to act on identifications that are not central to teachers' understandings of self or their educational priorities. For some educators, naming oneself as LGBT constitutes less an authentic representation of self than a performance that takes on different meanings in different contexts.

Bibliography

Blount, Jackie. 2005. *Fit To Teach: Same-Sex Desire, Gender, and School Work in the Twentieth Century.* Albany: State University of New York Press.

D'Emilio, John. 1992. *Making Trouble: Essays on Gay History, Politics, and the University.* New York: Routledge.

Garber, Linda, ed. 1994. *Tilting the Tower: Lesbians Teaching Queer Subjects.* New York: Routledge.

Griffin, Pat. 1992. "Identity Management Strategies among Lesbian and Gay Educators." *International Journal of Qualitative Studies in Education* 4, no. 3: 189–202.

Khayatt, Madiha Didi. 1992. *Lesbian Teachers: An Invisible Presence.* Albany: State University of New York Press.

Lipkin, Arthur. 1999. *Understanding Homosexuality, Changing Schools: A Text for Teachers, Counselors, and Administrators.* Boulder, CO: Westview Press.

Talburt, Susan. 2000. *Subject to Identity: Knowledge, Sexuality, and Academic Practices in Higher Education.* Albany: State University of New York Press.

Web Sites

Gay, Lesbian, Straight Educators Network. May 2005. Accessed May 28, 2005. http://www.glsen.org. Web site includes news reports, classroom resources, and announcements of events and conferences for teachers.

GLBT Educational Equity. February 2003. Accessed May 28, 2005. http://glee.oulu.fi. Numerous educational resources for teachers.

National Education Association–Gay, Lesbian, Bisexual, Transgender Caucus. May 2004. Accessed May 28, 2005. http://www.nea-glc.org. Web site includes guides to relevant issues and a legal response protocol.

Coming Out, Youth

Elizabeth Whitney

Motivated by the notion that individual visibility leads to community strength, **lesbian, gay, bisexual, transgender**, and questioning (LGBTQ) youth are encouraged to publicly narrate their sexual and gender identities as such and "come out of the closet." Coming out is integral to developing a healthy sense of self. The

See also Coming Out, Teachers; Community LGBT Youth Groups; Deaf LGBT Youth; Ethnic Identity; Heterosexism; Identity Politics; Mentoring; National Coming Out Day; Parents, Responses to Homosexuality; Queer and Queer Theory; Racial Identity; Rainbow Flag and Other Pride Symbols; Resiliency; Youth, At Risk.

process of coming out may not follow a sequential model, as it varies for each individual. For example, the acceptability of LGBTQ identity varies greatly across racial, ethnic, religious, and other socio–cultural categories; many youth may practice nonheterosexual behaviors without ever declaring LGBTQ identity. Young persons may come out to themselves long before they make a public declaration; some individuals may never come out publicly. Youth are able to come out earlier than previous generations, and the availability of support networks for LGBTQ youth are greater than perhaps could have been imagined even ten years ago. Regardless of public or private declaration, or both, coming out narratives are particularly important in light of the cultural phenomenon of **compulsory heterosexuality**. If silence is complicity, then coming out narratives are an essential tool for combating heterosexist assumptions. When adolescents are exposed to adults modeling LGBTQ identity through positive public behaviors, they are more comfortably able to express their identities through coming out narratives (Alexander 1999). Similarly, knowing someone who is LGBTQ consistently correlates with low levels of **homophobia** among heterosexuals.

The coming out narrative is one story we tell about ourselves and, due to the pressures of homophobia, it often becomes a primary narrative in defining existence. Storytelling is endemic to human existence (Beardslee 1990; Plummer 1995). We tell stories to make sense of ourselves and to give organizational meaning to our world. The coming out story has become increasingly common in personal narrative or self-identification through storytelling because it is crucial to the social construction of LGBTQ identity as the act by which one calls oneself into being as a sexual subject. In heterosexist or homophobic cultures, the coming out narrative plays a necessarily important role and is often enmeshed with adolescent development of sexuality and/or **gender identity**. Kenneth Plummer (1995, 52) writes that the coming out story "finds a crisis, a turning point, an epiphany; and then it enters a new world—a new identity, born again, metamorphosis. . . ."

However, coming out once, twice, or even multiple times does not ensure "being out." In a society where **heteronormativity** is presumed, as in most Western societies, if not most of the industrialized world, LGBTQ youth are placed in a sort of double bind. They must choose between a constant pressure to publicly announce their sexual identities, resulting in the frequent heterosexist response that they are "flaunting" it, or submit to compulsory heterosexuality and remain closeted, resulting in internalized homophobia. Coming out over and over again takes energy and it is often easier for youth to remain silent. "**Passing**," though perhaps understandable, may result in the forfeiture of the process of telling their stories and, thus, (re)constructing their sexual identities as closeted.

In order to be "out," there must be an "in" one has left behind, for only in an ideal world would there be no closet to leave. In fact, it is almost impossible to grasp a reality in which we would not need to come out, because it would require a complete lack of **prejudice** against sexual identification of any sort. The only way one can prove that one is "out" of the closet is to acknowledge that it does indeed exist. Thus, coming out is not a disavowal of the closet, but rather, a reaffirmation that there is something that one has indeed come out of.

Though the politics of coming out are confusing, those who come out in **adolescence** face an even more complex set of issues. The fear of being rejected by peer groups at school, in religious communities, or in a variety of social groups is intensely prohibitive of many youth coming out. In addition, the possibility of parental rejection, punishment, or at worse, complete alienation is a grave concern.

For scholars, adolescence also is a particularly contested site of LGBTQ identity. There are arguments over whether an individual's **sexual identity** is biologically determined or socially constructed. Many nonheterosexuals defend their sexual object choice by stating they were born that way and their **sexual orientation** cannot be changed. Today's youth, however, are more likely to believe than previous generations that sexuality and gender are fluid, choosing their identities from a cultural menu. Many youth resist categories such as lesbian, gay, bisexual, male, female, transgender, or transsexual by using more ambiguous labels such as "**queer**," "genderqueer," "pomosexual," or "omnisexual."

The possibility that youth may exercise such choices is particularly threatening to those who moralize against nonheterosexual **desire**. A complicating factor is that throughout history individuals have begun engaging in (arguably) consensual sexual activities at ages that many contemporary cultures consider inappropriate. For many, youth are not expected or encouraged to act on their desires, especially before reaching what is considered an age of consent—which, again, varies widely depending on the cultural context. This belief ties into homophobic fears that youth may be manipulated in their choices, or, as the **popular culture** saying goes, "recruited." To acknowledge that youth have the **agency** to make choices based on their desires is to acknowledge that they may make nonheterosexual choices.

Coming out is not necessarily a sequential process, though earlier studies had assumed so (Cass 1979; McCarn and Fassinger 1996; Troiden 1989). In fact, the concept of coming out presupposes a linear progression to an eventual staid identity. For example, both Cass's six-stage and Troiden's four-stage models of **identity development** stress a linear movement from confusion to acceptance, always with the assumption that an individual's development comes to a logical conclusion. Vera Whisman (1996), however, differentiates between "determined" and "chosen" accounts of sexual identity formation, the former tending to follow a linear pattern of development, with the latter being nonlinear. Many youth experience their sexuality, and hence, their coming out, as mutable.

As LGBTQ identities becomes more publicly accepted (and fluid), at least in certain cultures, youth may feel less pressure to "come out" and more desire/permission to just "be out." In the U.S. television show *Ellen*, the title character "accidentally" proclaims herself as a lesbian over an airport loudspeaker as the actress, Ellen Degeneress, chose to publicly come out on national television. This was the first time the leading character (and a Hollywood star) had declared her lesbianism on television. Although the comedy series lost audience share and was eventually cancelled, *Ellen* paved the way for the current spate of (at least, white middle-class) gay, lesbian, and bisexual characters on a range

MUM, DAD, I'VE GOT SOMETHING TO TELL YOU — I'M BICYCLE !

"Coming Out." Artist, John Landers. www.CartoonStock.com

television shows from the network comedy *Will and Grace* to cable drama series *Queer as Folk* and *The L Word*, to the Comedy Central **cartoon** *South Park*. As the media normalizes nonheterosexual images, the more awkward it may seem for LGBTQ youth to make a big deal about coming out. After all, who wants to stage the big performance of sitting friends and family members down to explain themselves in one shocking moment, when it would be far more comfortable to have one's identity accepted as "normal" all along? While such mundane acceptance might lead to the assimilation of LGBTQ identities, at the least, it would afford a more comfortable lifestyle for LGBTQ individuals. It would also evidence the end of heteronormativity, although it is very difficult to imagine a near-future society in which heterosexuality is not the norm.

Ultimately, the struggle over choice is a struggle to legitimate same-sex desire. Basing desire in **biology** rather than narrated lived experience is seen by mainstream activists as the most politically expedient approach for LGBTQ individuals to have a comfortable lifestyle. But, as Vera Whisman (1996, 7) points out, choice and the coming out narrative are inherently heterosexist, in that they "force us to explain ourselves, for ours is not the unquestioned, the unmarked, the center."

Despite the contested nature of the concept and process of coming out, the practice continues to be a foundation LGBTQ rights. During **National Coming Out Day** in the United States and **Canada** at many colleges and universities, students are encouraged to come out; those already out are encouraged to assume mentoring roles. Pride festivals are also an important part of the coming out ritual. Worldwide, many cities have Pride celebrations, with events ranging from parades to picnics to dances, some particularly geared toward youth, racial and/or ethnic groups, or center around issues of gender identity. Thus, youth who are coming out as transidentified can participate in a transpride celebration, and youth who are struggling with homophobia within their particular community will have the support of, say, a black pride celebration.

LGBTQ youth groups are also often rooted on the coming out process. One visible and important support network is the gay–straight alliance (GSA), which is increasingly found in high schools and even middle schools. Largely student organized and run (with some assistance from a faculty or staff sponsor), these groups have faced a gauntlet of **legal** and political challenges from conservative groups. City or region-based LGBTQ community centers also facilitate drop-in groups for youth that offer various activities ranging from social events (such as dances, queer-related entertainment and speakers, and movie nights), to opportunities to engage in political activism (lobbying elected officials, speaking to classes, **Day of Silence**, Day of Remembrance, and canvassing). In addition, **college students**, at least in the United States and Canada, will likely find a student run LGBTQ organization, **college campus resource center**, and/or recognition of related issues within student government, in **residence life, fraternities** or **sororities**, student services, and various **college campus programming**. Here youth can join and create peer mentoring networks that affirm their identities and perhaps make up for "traditional" adolescent opportunities denied by mainstream culture through activities such as **Lavender Graduation** and **proms**.

As these organizations and activities become more widespread, it becomes easier for youth to "be out" rather than repeatedly having to explain themselves by "coming out." Paradoxically, this presents challenges to those engaged in **activism**, as youth are sometimes able to exist almost entirely in queer space.

Bibliography

Alexander, Christopher J. 1999. "Mentoring for Gay and Lesbian Youth." *Journal of Gay and Lesbian Social Services* 10, no. 2: 89–92.

Beardslee, William A. 1990. "Stories in the Postmodern World." Pp: 163–75 in *Sacred Interconnections: Postmodern Spirituality, Political Economy, and Art*. Edited by David Ray Griffin. Albany: State University of New York Press.

Cass, Vivienne C. 1979. "Homosexual Identity Formation: A Theoretical Model." *Journal of Homosexuality* 4: 219–235.

McCarn, Susan R., and Ruth E. Fasinger. 1996. "Revisioning Sexual Minority Identity Formation: A New Model of Lesbian Identity and Its Implications." *Counseling Psychologist* 24, no. 3: 508–534.

Plummer, Ken. 1995. *Telling Sexual Stories: Power, Change and Social Worlds*. New York: Routledge.

Troiden, Richard R. 1989. "The Formation of Homosexual Identities." *Journal of Homosexuality* 17, nos. 1–2: 43–73.

Whisman, Vera. 1996. *Queer by Choice: Lesbians, Gay Men, and the Politics of Identity*. New York: Routledge.

Web Sites

Gay: Stories: Coming Out. Accessed May 28, 2005. http://www.bibble.org/gay/stories/comingout.html. A collection of coming out narratives from a variety of perspectives.

Lesbian and Gay Youth and Coming Out. November 2001. National Capital Freenet Services. Accessed May 28, 2005. http://www.ncf.ca/freeport/sigs/life/gay/out/menu. Useful links and information on a wide range of topics related to coming out.

Outpath Coming Out Archive. 2005. Accessed May 28, 2005. http://www.outpath.com. An archive of youth coming out stories with searchable database.

Read This Before Coming Out to Your Parents. 2005. Thomas Sauerman. OutProud. Accessed May 28, 2005. http://www.outproud.org/brochure_coming_out.html. Detailed essay of what to anticipate before coming out.

Communication

Gust A. Yep

Communication is the symbolic process whereby social reality is created, maintained, contested, repaired, and transformed. In Western cultures, this social reality is distinctively heterosexual as evidenced in queer youth's experiences in schools. Everywhere we look—from interpersonal interactions and group relationships to social institutions, cultural practices, knowledge systems, politics and the law, social policy, and the media—the social world is presented in heteronormative terms. In school texts, for example, romantic relationships are presented as heterosexual, often without question or hesitation. This heteronormative mindset is simultaneously everywhere and deeply buried in our personal psyches, collective consciousness, and modes of social organization. This hostile environment profoundly affects

See also Graffiti; Mental Health; Queer Pedagogy; Rainbow Flag and Other Pride Symbols.

the social realities of **lesbian**, **gay**, **bisexual**, **transgender**, and questioning (LGBTQ) youth and young adults, leading to social isolation, self-destructive behaviors, verbal, psychological and physical abuse, assault by others, and **suicide**. The heterosexual mindset is so powerful that it constantly regulates and controls the thoughts, feelings, and actions of everyone, including queer youth (Wittig 1992). In schools, LGBTQ students are unceasingly monitoring their affect and behavior to conform to heterosexual expectations in order to avoid **harassment**, isolation, and violence from peers, parents, and school personnel (Baker 2002; Unks 1995). However, just as communication can create and maintain **heteronormativity** in society, communication can also be used to contest and transform social reality. It is here that critically-minded educators can play an important role.

Through communication activities and practices, individuals and groups can imagine, create, and enact different relationship arrangements and expectations. It is also through such communicative actions that individuals and groups can develop ways to honor, embrace, and celebrate human sexual diversity that is based on the recognition of difference rather than the imposition of a heterosexual contract and the concomitant devaluation of individuals and groups who deviate from it. These "life experiments" and relational networks can be quite diverse as they are created and transformed by the individuals themselves. They can consist of friends, lovers and ex-lovers, same-sex and different-sex mixing in dyads or groups, who develop their rules and expectations based on respect and consent. Further, these individuals are engaged in exploration of pleasure that may or may not be genitally focused, and connected with a deep sense of care, affection, and community.

Communication consists of symbols, which are representations of ideas, values, thoughts, emotions, events, and people. Such representations are generally arbitrary but culturally and historically specific. For example, in the United States, the term **"queer"** was used in the context of insult, contempt, derision, and verbal abuse several decades ago. Current use of the term by lesbians and gay men has come to signify empowerment and challenge to normalized sexualities. Through the use of symbols, individuals can assign meanings to situations and events. The symbols themselves do not contain inherent meaning. Because individuals assign meanings to symbols, meanings are in people. Although the process of assigning meaning might be theoretically unlimited, there are cultural codes, or systems of meaning production, that are shared by individuals in a community, society, or culture. These dominant cultural codes are heteronormative. However, these dominant systems of meaning can be resisted or "queered." For example, teachers can talk about how many lesbians and gay men are currently using labels such as "wife" and "husband," respectively, to refer to their partners, and how this labeling process resists and resignifies heteronormative meanings associated with such terms.

Meanings are both unique (individually held) and shared (common understanding). They also have denotative and connotative dimensions. Returning to the term "queer," it might be slang for homosexual (denotation), a term of contempt, empowerment, difference, or challenge to the sexual status quo (connotation) depending on the individual's personal experience and history, relationship to the name-caller, and the broader cultural context where such individual was raised. This symbolic process is always ongoing, ever changing, and never-ending.

Communication consists of verbal (e.g., words) and nonverbal (e.g., gestures, tone, images) components. Although generally used together, they can also occur separately. Such verbal and nonverbal components can be used intentionally or unintentionally. Intentionally one may choose words and gestures to encourage, motivate, undermine, or punish others, such as the word "**sissy**." It can be used in the context of presumable encouragement and motivation ("Don't be a sissy!") or punishment and ridicule ("You are such a sissy!"). However, by telling another person not to be a sissy, one is intentionally telling the other that a sissy is undesirable, repulsive, loathsome, and shameful. If the listener is a queer youth (or LGBTQ young person), one might be unintentionally harassing and tormenting such person. Living in a heteronormative society, these communication messages are persistent and harmful, as one can easily imagine the lasting effects of the being called a "sissy" for gay, bisexual, transgendered, and questioning youth and young adults.

The heterosexual contract (Wittig 1992) is continually produced and reproduced in our everyday communication practices—ranging from how we talk about relationships and assumptions that we make about others to how we formulate laws and policies and represent people in the media. In this sense, communication creates and perpetuates the sexual status quo. Because communication constructs social realities, it is important to remember that envisioning and constructing different social realities is also accomplished through communication.

Communication constructs new social realities. Through communication we can contest heteronormativity by identifying the pain and suffering it causes, highlighting the social injustices against nonheteronormative individuals, demystifying the patriarchal nature of heterosexuality, and unpacking heterosexuality as an institution, identity, practice, and experience. Through communication we can repair and transform these oppressive realities by envisioning new forms of social organization and human expression. **Queer theory**, for example, has been particularly helpful in this endeavor. It has been used both in the academy and in activism to deconstruct current sexual hierarchies, to identify the psychological, physical, and material costs of heteronormativity for individuals both inside and outside heteronormative regimes, and to offer new possibilities for self-actualization, relationship formation, and community building. In other words, a "queer world" is both an imaginable and possible new social reality (Yep, Lovaas, and Elia 2003).

Educators committed to equality and social justice can intervene in a number of ways. With the understanding that language and communication are saturated with heteronormative ideology, educators can participate in the reparation and transformation of social reality through teaching and in the **curriculum**. For example, educators can both model and encourage others—students, staff, other teachers, parents—to recognize and interrogate presumptions of heterosexuality in our everyday talk and popular discourse, and understand and use noninjurious language in their daily interactions. Educators can also increase awareness of representations of LGBTQ people in textbooks, media images, and **popular culture** by posing some important questions. For example, if LGBTQ representations are present, how are these individuals characterized? What features are emphasized? What views are implied? What characterizations are invisible or absent? What are their consequences for LGBTQ and non-LGBTQ people? Through this examination, educators can unpack dominant ideologies in texts and images and improve understanding of the effects of such ideologies on all individuals across the spectrum of sexualities. Educators can also increase the possible range of representations and meanings and offer validation and hope to those individuals and groups whose social realities have been fundamentally erased, ignored, marginalized, or damaged by current communication systems.

Bibliography

Baker, Jean M. 2002. *How Homophobia Hurts Children: Nurturing Diversity at Home, at School, and in the Community*. Binghamton, NY: Harrington Park Press.

Chesebro, James W., ed. 1981. *Gayspeak: Gay Male and Lesbian Communication*. New York: Pilgrim Press.

Cramer, Elizabeth P., ed. 2002. *Addressing Homophobia and Heterosexism on College Campuses*. Binghamton, NY: Harrington Park Press.

Gross, Larry. 2001. *Up from Invisibility: Lesbians, Gay Men, and the Media in America*. New York: Columbia University Press.

Henderson, Lisa. 2000. "Queer Communication Studies." Pp. 465–484 in *Communication Yearbook*. Vol. 24. Edited by William B. Gudykunst. Thousand Oaks, CA: Sage.

Ringer, R. Jeffrey, ed. 1994. *Queer Words, Queer Images: Communication and the Construction of Homosexuality*. New York: New York University Press.

Unks, Gerald, ed. 1995. *The Gay Teen: Educational Practice and Theory for Lesbian, Gay, and Bisexual Adolescents*. New York: Routledge.

Wittig, Monique. 1992. *The Straight Mind and Other Essays*. Boston: Beacon Press.

Yep, Gust A., Karen E. Lovaas, and John P. Elia, eds. 2003. *Queer Theory and Communication: From Disciplining Queers to Queering the Discipline(s)*. Binghamton, NY: Harrington Park Press.

Web Site

National Communication Association. May 2005. Lisa Millhous. Accessed May 28, 2005. http://www.natcom.org/nca/Template2.asp. The National Communication Association (NCA) is the largest United States-based professional organization promoting the study, criticism, research, teaching, and application of the principles of communication. NCA has a number of units and divisions, including the Gay, Lesbian, Bisexual and Transgender Communication Studies Division and the Gay and Lesbian Caucus http://communication.wcupa.edu/glbt.

Community and Technical Colleges

Kristen A. Renn

Community and technical colleges, sometimes called junior colleges, are those post-secondary institutions that offer associate's degrees, nondegree programs, and adult education. Community and technical colleges typically serve a local or regional audience, provide few or no on-campus residential arrangements, and attract a student body that is predominantly female, as well as chronologically older, more racially and ethnically diverse, and more likely to be part-time than those at four-year institutions. LGBT **school climate** surveys conducted at community and technical colleges have not received as much publicity as those at four-year institutions, though there are examples available (National Consortium 2003). Campus climates vary widely as welcoming environments for LGBT students and faculty according to region, setting (urban, suburban, rural), and institutional mission (broad, general education curriculum or single academic focus, such as automotive technology,

See also College Age Students; College Campus Organizing; Coming Out, Teachers; Coming Out, Youth.

200

medical technology, or cosmetology). Two-year institutions are less likely than four-year institutions to include sexual orientation in their nondiscrimination clauses, and nearly all research on LGBT issues in higher education has been conducted at four-year institutions. In the United States, of the 1,171 community colleges operating in 2002, the majority (992) were state-supported public institutions, with independent institutions and tribal colleges accounting for the remainder (NCES 2003). The community college is unique to the United States. However, technical colleges, which do not serve the transfer function of U.S. community colleges, exist in most other nations but are considered part of larger, typically centralized postsecondary systems governed by ministry of education. In fall 2000, community colleges enrolled over six million students, nearly 40 percent of all U.S. undergraduates.

Students at community and technical colleges may pursue a terminal associate's degree, seek transfer to a four-year institution, obtain a certificate in a vocational area, or engage in a variety of continuing education courses in arts, science, technical, or other areas. There are no reliable data on the number of LGBT community and technical college students, the exact number of active LGBT student organizations, or unique challenges faced by these students. Like their peers at four-year institutions, community college students have organized formal and informal student organizations to meet their social, support, and political interests as well as to provide structures for educational programs and political organizing. At some institutions, the groups take the form of an LGBT student organization, while the student groups at others actively include **allies** and other non-LGBT students in the form of a **gay–straight alliance** or a more general multicultural collective. It is estimated that about one in four community colleges has some sort of LGBT student organization.

Leaders of LGBT student organizations at community colleges face some issues that their peers at four-year institutions may not. The more transient nature of community college student populations creates a challenge for leadership development within student organizations, and the funding structure for student organizations is often not as well developed and consistent as it is at four-year institutions. Community colleges may lack administrative staff support for student organizations or offer limited services. The nonresidential and more part-time student nature of the student body results in less participation in **cocurricular activities**. Community college students are more likely than students at four-year institutions to live at home with parents, which may lead to fewer students willing to take on leadership responsibilities or to come out publicly.

Campus climate surveys at two-year institutions reveal rates of **harassment** and violence similar to those at other educational institutions in their area and LGBT community college students are believed to be at least as subject to antigay harassment and violence as are students at other institutions. A multicampus study of antigay violence at two-year colleges found that more than one in three community college students had engaged in hate speech or committed a **hate crime** against individuals perceived to be gay or lesbian (Franklin 1998).

Faculty at two-year institutions are more likely than those at four-year institutions to be female, to be part-time instructors, to hold a master's degree instead of a Ph.D., and to work without the constraints and benefits of a tenure system (Cohen and Brawer 1996). Like LGBT students, very little is known about LGBT employees of community and technical colleges. A very small number of community colleges have faculty and staff LGBT organizations, and about 15 percent of community colleges offer benefits to the same-sex domestic partners of employees under similar conditions to those offered to married employees (Human Rights Campaign Foundation 2003). However, since community colleges employ many part-time faculty members, even these benefits are not available to all employees.

An increasing number of community colleges offer coursework in **LGBT studies**. The City College of San Francisco (CCSF) has been a pioneer in this area, offering an Associate of Arts degree in Lesbian, Gay, and Bisexual Studies. At other institutions such as Santa Monica College and South Seattle Community College, there are courses, or concentrations within majors. Because anyone with a high school degree can be admitted for study, because one need not be enrolled in a degree program to take in a course, and because of the relatively low tuition, LGBT studies courses at 2-year institutions are more accessible to the public than those at four-year institutions.

Bibliography

Arnold, Carolyn L. 1995. *Chabot College Campus Climate Survey Results: Fall 1994*. Hayward, CA: Office of Institutional Research, Chabot College. ERIC Document: ED 402 982.

Cohen, Arthur M., and Florence B. Brawer. 1996. *The American Community College*. San Francisco: Jossey-Bass.

Franklin, Karen. 1998. *Psychosocial Motivations of Hate Crimes Perpetrators: Implications for Educational Intervention*. Paper presented at the 106th Annual Convention of the American Psychological Association at San Francisco, CA, August 16. ERIC Document ED 423 939.

Human Rights Campaign Foundation. 2003. *Domestic Partner Benefits*. Accessed December 29, 2003. http://www.hrc.org/Template.cfm?Section=The_Issues& Template=/TaggedPage/TaggedPageDisplay.cfm&TPLID=26&ContentID=13399.

Leck, Glorianne M. 1998. "An Oasis: The LGBT Student Group on a Commuter Campus." Pp. 373–382 in *Working with Lesbian, Gay, Bisexual and Transgendered College Students: A Guide for Faculty, Staff, and Administrators*. Edited by Ronni Sanlo. Westport, CT: Greenwood.

Leider, Steven. 1999. *Sexual Minorities on Community College Campuses*. Unpublished paper. Los Angeles: UCLA. ERIC Document: ED 427 796. Accessed June 12, 2005. http://www.ericdigests.org/2001-3/sexual.htm.

National Center for Education Statistics. 2003. *Digest of Education Statistics, 2002*. Washington, DC: Department of Education.

National Consortium of Directors of LGBT Campus Resources in Higher Education. 2002. *Bibliography: "Campus Climate" Reports*. Accessed June 26, 2005. http://www. lgbtcampus.org/resources/campus_climate.html.

Ottenritter, Nana. 1998. "The Courage to Care: Addressing Sexual Minority Issues Campus." *Removing Vestiges* 1 (April): 13–20. Accessed June 26, 2005. http:// www.aacc.nche.edu/Content/NavigationMenu/ResourceCenter/Services/ Access_ and_Equality/Publications2/vestiges.htm.

Web Sites

Gay Straight Alliance of Mott Community College. September 2005. Accessed May 28, 2005. http://www.mcc.edu/clubs/gsa/gsa_index.shtml. The home page of the Mott Community College (Flint, Michigan) Gay Straight Alliance, includes examples of campus–community resource sharing.

Prince-Hughes, Tara, Kathy Seibert, and Bree Herndon. 2003. *The Gay-Straight Alliance at Whatcom Community College: A Student-Faculty Collaboration*. Accessed May 28,

2005. http://www.evergreen.edu/washcenter/Fall2003Newsletter/Pg22-23.pdf. An article describing a successful community college student–faculty partnership in creating a gay–straight alliance.

Younger, John G. 2003. *University LGBT/Queer Programs.*February 2005. Accessed May 28, 2005. http://www.people.ku.edu/~jyounger/lgbtqprogs.html. Information about postsecondary institutions, including women's colleges, that offer LGBT/Queer programs, courses, and study abroad programs.

Community LGBT Youth Groups

Steven E. James, Mary M. Clare and *James T. Sears*

LGBT youth face a wide range of intrapersonal, familial, and social challenges that are increasingly addressed by community support groups. About 400 of these institutional resources are available to **queer** youth throughout the United States (Cohen 2005). The variety of these groups reflects the diversity of the surrounding neighborhoods and the needs of the youth they serve. Some groups focus on supporting sexual minority youth who face homelessness, some focus on **substance abuse** treatment, some support youth engaged in **sex work**, and some simply help youth to integrate into typical community activities. Many of these groups meet face-to-face, but increasingly virtual groups offer **rural youth** and those unwilling or unable to meet in person opportunities for support. Successful LGBT community youth groups respond to the needs and challenges of such youth with an acceptance of the members' strengths and an understanding of how to bring the community's resources to their assistance.

LGBT youth groups are not new phenomena. **Gay youth activism** in the mid- to late-1960s resulted in grassroots youth groups forming in a few cities like San Francisco (Vanguard Youth Group) as well as some on college campuses, notably Student Homophile League at Columbia University. By the early 1970s, these youth-led, independent groups had expanded into more communities, from Young Peoples Group in Miami to Chicago's Alternatives for Teenage Gays, as well as to colleges and schools, including a gay–straight club initiated by George Washington High School in New York City (Cohen 2005). In some places, they initiated the first pride parades and were generally a focal point for political activism. The growing visibility of these early groups sped up the **coming out** process as more LGBT youth disclosed their sexual identities to family, peers, and educators at a younger age.

The emergence of these groups also altered the nature of the gay rights movement by putting a new face on "gay America," that of healthy young people fighting oppression and attracting **allies**, like the founders of Parents, Families, and Friends of Lesbians and Gays (PFLAG). Jeanne and Jules Manford walked with their activist son, Morty, in the 1972 Pride Day Parade and formed their organization the following year. Near the end of this decade, community-based LGBT youth

See also Activism, Activism, LGBT Teachers; LGBT Youth; Agency; Canada, LGBT Youth in; College Campus Organizing; Legal Issues, Students; Secondary Schools, LGBT; Youth Culture; Youth, Homeless.

groups were being formed by professionals in education, **counseling**, and **social work**. Social service type programs such as the Horizons youth group in Chicago and the Hetrick-Martin Institute in New York were established *for* queer youth whose needs were not being met within the school system.

The greater visibility of the gay rights movement and the emergence of a more visible generation of queer youth—coupled with the reluctance of schools to address this minority group—have resulted in a growing number of community-based youth groups. These, too, have often served as catalysts for the development of school-based counseling programs, such as **Project 10**, and **gay–straight alliances**, which emerged in the 1990s.

In every community there is a need for community-based LGBT youth support groups. In practical terms, this support extends not only to the youth most directly affected by acculturated **homophobia**, but it also extends to the broader community in the form of education about queer people. In some instances, advocates from LGBT youth organizations have shifted the awareness of a school principal or guidance counselors, leading to their supporting the initiation of school-based programs like gay–straight alliances. In other cases, years of presence, education, and several layers of community involvement have been required to get even the most basic support services started within a school.

In the wake of the landmark civil case *Nabozny v. Podlesny* (http://www.lambdalegal.org/cgi-bin/iowa/cases/record?record=54), there have been growing numbers of queer high school students (and their parents) who are suing school boards when their **school safety** is not protected. The threat of potential litigation coupled with the growing number of successful law suits have motivated school boards and **administrators** to evidence greater concern with issues such as **bullying** and **harassment** of LGBT students, even if they are more reluctant to initiate student services or curriculum reform.

Some communities and states have launched multiyear education initiatives to address the serious concerns of harassment and violence toward LGBT youth. A notable example of such effort is the curriculum developed by the Safe Schools Coalition (http://www.safeschoolscoalition.org). This organization emerged from a 1988 recommendation by the Seattle Commission on Children and Youth for an Advisory Committee on Gay/Lesbian Youth and Schools. Aimed at understanding, reducing, and preventing antigay harassment and violence, it has produced a "Safe Schools Resource Guide," a five-year qualitative study, "Safe Schools Anti-Violence Documentation Project," as well as providing workshops educators and community groups and advocating for queer youth.

In 1992, the Commission on Gay and Lesbian Youth was appointed by the governor of Massachusetts to address the problems and needs of LGBT youth. The major recommendations from its, "Making Schools Safe for Gay and Lesbian Youth," were adopted by the Massachusetts Board of Education the next year. This resulted in a state-wide program offering free training sessions for students, teachers, and parents and resources to schools interested in raising awareness of LGBT students' issues and reducing harassment.

Once the issues of queer youth have been publicly raised, communities and schools experience their own coming out process. School and community leaders emerge as supportive or not. Political turmoil and community debate often ensue, though not always. There have been schools that have established gay–straight alliances without clamor or dissent. There are communities that have broad support for LGBT youth groups that meet in churches or other civic venues. But often a conflict emerges, as in the highly publicized controversy in Salt Lake City where the school board ceased all extracurricular student organizations rather than allow a gay–straight alliance, in 1996. Thus, it is important to understand the dynamics involved, to better appreciate what works, and why in one community a project fails only to succeed elsewhere (Macgillivray 2003).

Old political and interpersonal wounds can be reopened by the introduction of the needs of queer youth and their families. Underlying political dynamics are often expressed through these issues. Communities may struggle with religious or moral or racial or economic conflicts that may have been long suppressed. Funding issues also are raised whenever new projects and services are debated, sometimes legitimately and sometimes as red herrings. Political and religious leaders may fear how such debates will impact their standing in the communities. And some closeted educators, politicians, and religious leaders may also worry about being outed.

School safety issues are compelling to community leaders. Although national statistics on **suicide, substance abuse**, and **academic performance** of queer youth can be used to demonstrate the costs of nonsupport, examples from local LGBT youth's experiences may be more effective in getting local law enforcement and elected officials to act for the safety of their citizens. Certainly, many communities were galvanized around the difficulties faced by LGBT youth following the murder of **Mathew Shepard** in Wyoming. But, in every community there are tragedies that befall its young queer citizens.

Communities are beginning to address these issues using a variety of strategies. Existing organizations such as liberal churches, crisis centers, theater groups, and community service agencies have created supportive programming for queer youth and their allies. In many communities, for instance, Unitarian Universalists and Metropolitan Community Churches host gay and bisexual **spirituality** groups, which are inclusive of LGBT youth. Other LGBT youth groups are sponsored by a community service agency, such as Oregon's Vanguard Youth Services, which supports the Sexual Minority Youth Recreation Center (SMYRC, http://www.smyrc.org/). Among the activities at SMYRC is a Bikes Program where volunteer mechanics work with queer youth to repair donated bicycles, illustrating how LGBT adults and allies can contribute their expertise in nontraditional and non-school settings. This Portland-based group also offers a trans-youth group, art therapy, counseling and case management, Bridge 13 (a community speakers bureau), and HIV testing.

Most community LGBT youth groups, however, are formed and operated by LGBT adults and their allies, who then seek public and corporate funding. Many, like the Bay Area Sexual Minority Youth Network in San Francisco and the Gay and Lesbian Community Service Center–Youth Outreach, located in Los Angeles, serve the wide spectrum of queer youth as they attempt to address their varied needs. Others, however, are more focused.

In Boston, the Justice Resource Institute (JRI) had already organized an outreach program to homeless youth, but its leaders soon recognized that there was a significant number of New England kids who were LGBT or questioning. JRI created the Boston Gay and Lesbian Adolescent Social Services (http://www.bostonglass.org/), which initially offered free mental health services in a walk-in clinic, and had evolved into a drop-in center that offered job training and daily social support.

The Lambda Center (http://www.thelambdacenter.com.) of Washington, D.C., sprang from a shared concern by professionals at the Psychiatric Institute of Washington and the Whitman–Walker Clinic of the greater risk for substance abuse among queer youth coupled to increases of drug-related overdoses and deaths, as well as an increase in HIV infections among young men who have sex with men. Lambda Center is an example of the impact that health service agencies can have when they collaboratively address a minority need. Such collaborations reduce costs to participating agencies, as they can avoid duplicating some functions and services, and increase their net impact on the target population in their community.

For many homeless LGBT youth, survival sex is a way for them to support themselves. Although the needs of such youth are increasingly addressed by homeless outreach programs that exist across North America (from Boston to Vancouver), and by substance abuse treatment agencies, there are less conventional means of community support for queer youth. In Manhattan, there are "houses" of homeless LGBT youth and adults, mostly drug-addicted and many engaged in sex work. They emotionally support one another while competing with other houses at fashion, dance, and voguing contests. Vividly portrayed in the film documentary *Paris Is Burning* (USA 1990), the support and guidance queer youth get from peers and the "house mothers" are often the best they've received since coming out.

There, too, are community youth groups specifically for queer youth of color. For instance, BQY: The Black Queer Youth Initiative (http://www.soytoronto.org/current.html.) is a project of Supporting Our Youth, itself founded in 1997 by the Toronto Coalition for Lesbian, Gay and Bisexual Youth. BQY provides safe and social space for queer youth under age twenty-nine. Similarly, the Joseph Beam Youth Collaborative is a nonprofit organization, launched in the fall of 2003, providing antiracist safe havens for LGBT and allied youth of color through programs and services offered directly and through collaborations with schools and other community-based organizations.

Such organizations may need additional sources of support, since, ironically, they may be challenged by **racism** in the LGBT community and homophobia in their community of color. In some cases, these organizations benefit from the support of other allies, individuals and agencies, who serve both communities of color and LGBT populations, but not traditionally where they overlap.

The progress made in valuing diversity in schools is an important window of opportunity for many communities interested in beginning to offer some support to queer youth, their families, and other LGBT members. Diversity Day's celebrations of various local constituencies may already exist and can incorporate queer themes and examples. Again, those who advocate visible queer youth participation in these activities may confront controversy, as evident in the struggle over St. Patrick's Day celebrations in New York City. Gay community events also afford opportunities to involve LGBT youth, ranging from **National Coming Out Day** to Gay Pride.

For youth living in rural areas or those who cannot meet in person, opportunities for support have increased with the advent of the **Internet**. Virtual groups and online communities have emerged offering support and contact for LGBT youth who are isolated or who isolate themselves. While some of these virtual communities support spin-off from existing organizations, such as Children Of Lesbians And Gays Everywhere (http://www.colage.org/), many are created by individuals who access those Internet Service Providers giving their customers the capability to create chat rooms, bulletin boards, Web pages, **queer zines**, and blogs. As might be expected, these creations range widely in their sophistication, helpfulness, and stability. Nonetheless, they are emerging as a new alternative, one that may increasingly challenge more traditional support groups in their outreach to LGBT youth who by choice or necessity remain hidden. Similarly, LGBT youth are exploring increasing access to other media, including radio. "Homofrecuencia," for example, is a Chicago-based radio program broadcasting locally and internationally in Spanish for and by queer Latino and Latina youth via the web (http://www.wrte.org/homofrecuencia.)

Bibliography

Cohen, Stephen. 2005. "Liberationists, Clients, Activists: Queer Youth Organizing, 1966–2003." *Journal of Gay and Lesbian Issues in Education* 2, no. 3.

Hunter, Joyce. 1990. "Violence against Lesbian and Gay Male Youths." *Journal of Interpersonal Violence* 5: 295–300.

MacGillivray, Ian. 2003. *Sexual Orientation and School Policy: A Practical Guide for Teachers, Administrators and Community Activists.* Lanham, MD: Rowman and Littlefield.

Web Sites

Sexual Minority Youth Assistance League. 2004. Accessed December 18, 2004. http://www.smyal.org/main.htm D.C.-based group that provides a variety of activities to help youth who are questioning their sexual orientation and to help foster self-esteem among youth LGBT youth.

U.S. Local GLBT Youth & Teen Organizations. October 2004. Accessed December 2, 2004. http://www.dv-8.com/resources/us/local/youth.htm/. Extensive list of community-based queer youth groups with contact information.

Compulsory Heterosexuality

Glorianne M. Leck

It is characteristic of patriarchal societies that they promote and engage in rituals that make heterosexuality seem to be the only appropriate sexual behavior (Rich 1980). This dominant social view disregards individual preferences for kinds of expressions of affection, types of erotic stimulation, gender compatibility, and lifestyle preferences. The patriarchal society harbors a belief that each and every male is sexually attracted to females and that each and every female is naturally attracted to males. Because of the abundance of heterosexual images same-sex attractions and **bisexuality** are made to appear "abnormal" or "unnatural." Cultural celebrations such as weddings, dances, puberty rituals, dowries, arranged marriages, and engagements reward and promote heterosexual relationships. The organizing of festivals and parties around events that celebrate heterosexuality and reproduction make it so dominant that heterosexuality appears to be the only "natural" human sexual response. Same-sex couples attending a school **prom**, a teacher's revelation that a famous poem was written for the poet's same-sex partner, or a **sexuality education** discussion on using "dental dams" for protection when lesbians have oral sex remain a source for great controversy in many schools. The denial of same-sex

See also Feminism; Heterosexism; Sexism; Stereotypes.

imagery and the prohibitions against same-sex expressions of affection continue to create a hostile and unaffirming **school climate** for students, faculty, and staff who are lesbian, gay and/or bisexual. **Homophobia** is the direct result of this emphasis on heterosexuality and the social efforts to promote and enforce it (Pharr 1988).

In many elementary, middle, and secondary schools, the illustrations in textbooks and in classic **literature** assume that families are all made up of a heterosexual couple and their biological offspring. When viewing illustrations of males and females in European Caucasian Christian-based cultures, males often are portrayed as taller, stronger, darker, braver, and dominant over females. Males are represented as rescuing females, conquering females, marrying females, and fathering children who then bear their last name. Men who elect not to follow those male prescriptions are targeted as traitors to their gender.

Females have traditionally been portrayed so they will appear to be weaker, younger, more fearful, and more light complexioned. This model changes somewhat with cultural, racial, and religious differences. In **rural** settings or in societies where physically strong women are a necessary source of labor on a family farm, for example, we will see some different images of women's bodies and thus of men's choices of their marital partners. It is well worth picking up many books and looking at the illustrations and stories in order to learn how cultural groups construct those differences, but more importantly to see the similarities in the underlying assumptions across patriarchal cultures.

Patriarchy is a social system that holds that whatever men do should be more highly valued than whatever women do (Gray 1982). Patriarchy places men's activities at the center of public life and rewards masculine behaviors that have been designed to contrast with feminine behaviors. This arrangement promotes heterosexuality and social reproduction.

Schools are institutions of the patriarchal society, and it is in schools that many of the values of compulsory heterosexuality are taught and enforced in the **curriculum** as well as through teaching and **educational policies**. In elementary school, animals are usually described in a way that displays gender characteristics of masculinity and femininity. Females with long eyelashes and the nonverbal gesture of looking up in admiration at the male figure are key features assigned to many of the female characters in traditional children's books. Gay and lesbian families are rarely portrayed or mentioned, so ultimately the child's picture is that everything in life is about heterosexual courtship and reproduction. It is not uncommon to hear adults asking first and second grade children about their "opposite sex" girlfriends and boyfriends.

References to domestic animals and pets reinforce compulsory heterosexuality. Dogs are generally referred to as "he," associated as pets for men, and are often described as "man's best friend." Cats are generally referred to as "she." This pattern seems to be based on both the size of dogs and cats, as they are seen in relation to each other, and on their portrayal as having features that characterize masculine aggression and feminine cunning.

Gender is associated with masculinity and femininity and, as such, includes **stereotype** features designed to represent opposites, suggesting that each person is a half of a human whole. Traditional men can often be heard referring to their female spouses as their "better half." Wedding rings have been described as the circle of "completion" and the bond that holds them together. And, we frequently speak of the "other sex."

Children's books converted to **film** have had a particularly strong influence in reinforcing heterosexuality through old cultural stories and traditions. *Cinderella*, featuring her charming prince and her ugly step sisters, is one example. Here, Cinderella is rescued from the company of her family of nasty, gossipy women and chosen to serve as the wife of the prince. This is a very strong theme in Western culture. Women are systematically taught to dislike other women and themselves. It seems that all that can rescue her is the love of a man and her appearance as an appropriately diminutive body. Review Disney's *Littlest Mermaid* to notice what it is she has to give up to be married to the man. *Snow White* needs only to be kissed by a prince in order to wake from her long sleep, which an evil woman inflicted upon her.

In middle and secondary schools male football players serve as competitive gladiators representing the school. Men and women stand or sit on the side and cheer as the more physically competitive masculine persons perform acts of strength in order to defeat the men from other schools or villages. Many athletic and social events from bullfighting to movie acting reflect this courtship ritual in which men compete for the favors of the lady on the sidelines or in the viewing box. The emphasis on differences between men and women doesn't stop or start with the game itself. There are the support programs such as pep rallies, bake sales, separate men's and women's choruses, cheerleading, and press coverage. In many countries, laws and family traditions actually forbid men and women to participate together in certain **sports** (*Bend It Like Beckham*, UK/Germany 2002).

Title IX, on the other hand, was a federal provision in the United States enacted in 1972, meant to balance the number of opportunities offered to women and men in sporting events as well as in school **cocurricular** and recreational activities. In 2003, Title IX provisions were reviewed and left in place.

Physically combative sports continue to be promoted above recreational opportunities. Outside of schools, professional sports are rigidly segregated by gender. Even when a woman appears in a match against men in tennis or golf, which are not considered highly combative, the event is depicted as entertainment and not legitimate sport. All of these patriarchal rituals, rules, and exercises promote the illusion that men are dominant over women and that masculine activities and physiological manifestations are to be more valued than feminine characteristics and abilities. This perpetuates the notion of and the perceived advantage of heterosexuality as it would be based in a woman's need for male protection of any children she would bear. It also promotes the notion of sexual conquest by the strongest over the more nurturing or verbal contestant. A sexuality based on reproduction and the rearing of children is key to the culture of compulsory heterosexuality.

In contemporary society, there are some indications of greater hope for sexual freedom from patriarchal ritual. **Gays, lesbians, transgender, transsexual, bisexual youth,** their families, friends, and **allies** are challenging those long held patriarchal sex and gender stereotypes and the patriarchal social rules they have fostered. Women in cultures with economic surplus are now more likely to be able to earn their living and support themselves and their children. A man can live with and love another man and, if they prefer in some regions, adopt or father children that they will raise. And, in a few schools, same gender couples have attended proms and other school-sponsored events.

These relationships, however, are still defined in terms of child rearing and pairing off with a partner in a lifetime bond. What remains unacknowledged is the possibilities of two men or two women or numbers of men and women living and loving happily outside of some social commitment to either a religious community life or to a lifelong bond committed to the raising of children. Compulsory heterosexuality is not fundamentally altered if only some "couples" of the same-sex gain approval and sanction by the same or similar means of being able to say: "We too can have children, raise them and can appear to be normal like heterosexuals."

Plato, the ancient Greek philosopher, after exploring the skills and abilities of men and women indicated that he found that gender was a difference that makes no difference. When gender, unlike something such as eye color, is tied to a hierarchy of social values then the differences are deemed to be of social significance. It is in that context that judgments are derived for and against same-gender sexual relations.

Bibliography

Doyle, Joan. 2002. "Who's Safe in School?: Contradictions and Inconsistencies in Federal Educational Policy." *Progressive Perspectives: Monograph series* 4, no. 1. http://www.uvm.edu/~dewey/monographs/mono.htm. Last Accessed March 3, 2004.

Gray, Elizabeth Dodson. 1982. *Patriarchy as a Conceptual Trap.*Wellsley, MA: Roundtable Press.

Letts, William J., IV, and James T. Sears, eds. 1999. *Queering Elementary Education: Advancing the Dialogue about Sexualities and Schooling.* Lanham, MD: Rowman and Littlefield.

Pharr, Suzanne. 1988. *Homophobia: A Weapon of Sexism.* Little Rock, AK: Chardon Press.

Rich, Adrienne. 1980. "Compulsory Heterosexuality and Lesbian Existence." *Signs: Journal of Women in Culture and Society* 5, no. 4: 631–660.

Counseling

Kathleen J. Bieschke

Affirmative counseling and psychotherapy celebrate and advocate for the authenticity and integrity of LGB persons and their relationships. Competencies for counseling lesbian, gay, bisexual, and transgender clients are articulated by the Association of Gay, Lesbian, and Bisexual Issues in Counseling (AGLBIC) and guidelines for psychotherapy with lesbian, gay, and bisexual clients have been issued by the American Psychological Association (APA). While LGB clients have a preference for working with LGB therapists, heterosexual therapists can be effective if they attend to the influence their attitudes and those of society have on their clients. Therapists must also be aware of and understand the unique ways that LGB clients view relationships and create families as well as be mindful of the unique ways in which diversity issues (e.g., **race, ethnicity, disabilities**, age) operate in this population. Finally, they must stay informed about this population through professional development and community awareness. In particular, counselors need to be aware of the unique concerns and risks LGBT youth face as well the difficulties they often encounter

See also College Campus Resource Centers; Educational Policy; Prejudice; Professionalism; Reparative Therapy; Youth, At Risk.

when seeking counseling services. Working with transgender clients also includes attending to specific issues such as decisions regarding transitioning.

Prior to the early 1970s, treatment of LGB clients was predicated on the assumption that same-sex attraction represented a form of pathology. Thus, the goal of such therapy was to "convert" the client to a heterosexual identity (hence the term "conversion therapy" was applied to such treatment). All major mental health organizations in the United States and many other countries—most recently **China**—have recognized that identifying as lesbian, gay, or bisexual is not a form of mental illness. Indeed, in 1997 the APA reiterated its opposition to the portrayal of LGB youth and adults as mentally ill due to **sexual orientation** and called for the dissemination of accurate information about sexual orientation, **mental health**, and appropriate interventions.

Recent studies of counselor attitudes suggest that mental health providers do not perceive same-sex attraction as psychopathology, that they exhibit lower levels of **homophobia** than the general public, and that that they are supportive of LGB clients; however, there is also some evidence that therapists seem vulnerable to acting in accordance with **stereotypes** held by the general public (Bieschke et al. 2000). Thus, as articulated by both APA and AGLBIC, **counselor education** programs play an important role in preparing future clinicians to work effectively with an LGB client population. Elements of LGB-affirmative training programs include raising trainee awareness of LGB issues and increasing understanding of counselor biases and stereotypes, expanding trainee knowledge about the LGB population, and providing trainees with opportunities to work with LGB clients.

One might expect that clients might be reluctant to seek mental health services given the continued controversy regarding conversion therapy and the empirical evidence that the heterosexual biases held by therapists may be evident in their work with clients. To the contrary, lesbian and gay clients use mental health services at a relatively high rate. In general, lesbian and gay clients report feeling satisfied with the mental health services they receive (little is known about bisexual clients' use of and satisfaction with therapy). Research indicates that LGB individuals have slight preference for therapists who are of the same-sex and sexual orientation. Further, female therapists, regardless of sexual orientation, are perceived as more helpful than heterosexual male therapists, particularly for lesbian clients. Empirical research indicates that LGB clients' views of helpfulness were dependent on therapists' practices in regard to LGB issues; best practices have been standardized through the articulation of competencies and guidelines for working with LGB clients issued by the APA and the AGLBIC (Bieschke et al., 2000).

Lesbian, gay, and bisexual clients seeking counseling might consider prescreening therapists. That is, potential clients should consider seeking recommendations of therapists from members of the LGB community or asking therapists about his or her experience and training in LGB issues. Those who have engaged in prescreening activities rated their therapists as significantly more helpful than those who did not (Liddle 1997). Should prescreening prove not to be an option, clients may be able to infer whether their counselor is affirmative based on behaviors the counselor engages in with all clients. Affirmative therapists are aware that clients' decisions about whether to be forthcoming about **sexual identity** issues may be dependent on such behaviors. Affirmative in-session behaviors include (but are not limited to) displaying affirmative symbols, using language inclusive of same-sex relationships (e.g., using the term "partner" rather than "husband" or "wife"), and not making the assumption that all clients are heterosexual.

Lesbian, gay, and **bisexual youth** may find it especially challenging to identify affirmative counselors. Though affirmative counselors may not be listed as such in phone books as such, counselors can be asked directly about their approach to working with sexual minority youth in an exploratory phone call. Accessing a Web site such as GLB Central (http://www.glbcentral.com) is another way youth can find counselors who are affirmative. Contacting a Parents, Families, and Friends of Lesbians and Gays chapter (http://www.pflag.org/chapters/find.html) will likely provide support as well as access to affirmative community resources for youth. Other resources include the local gay switchboard; in **urban** areas, the LGB community center often has programs for youth.

Counselors providing services to youth who identify as LGB must strive to understand that the special problems and risks for LGB youth as the processes of adolescence and "**coming out**" as LGB are often intertwined. First, it is important to distinguish between sexual identity and sexual behavior because the two are not interchangeable. Youth who are exploring a LGB sexual identity will often experience and internalize some degree of conflict and shame regarding their sexual orientation. Further, LGB youth will attempt to achieve self-understanding regarding their sexual orientation in either total isolation or with a few others who are likely also to be struggling with similar issues. Persistent stressors identified by LGB youth include coming out to others and having their sexual orientation discovered and ridiculed. LGB youth must also struggle with bias-motivated attacks, particularly in the high school setting. Such social isolation results in fewer resources to deal with such stress. For sexual minority youth who attempt to act on their feelings, there are few opportunities for healthy **dating** experiences. LGB adolescents may be left feeling that satisfying needs for emotional and sexual intimacy are not attainable. Thus, the normative developmental tasks of LGB adolescents frequently may be complicated or compromised by concerns about sexual identity which may manifest in counseling as suicidal ideation/behavior, family dysfunction, STD/HIV infection, academic failure, homelessness, and **substance abuse**.

Given the nature of the complex issues often faced by LGB youth, it perhaps seems obvious that counseling has the potential to be a useful and productive activity. Yet, youth may face significant obstacles in their attempts to obtain counseling. School counselors and teachers may be forbidden by school districts to discuss issues of sexual identity with students. Counselors may feel obligated or be required to inform parents about the nature of counseling discussions, which may result in prematurely forcing clients to share their thoughts about their sexual identity. Even parents who are supportive may be stymied by their inability to identify an affirmative counselor given their lack of knowledge of either the mental health or LGB community.

Despite these challenges, a number of options exist for school personnel, counselors, parents, and youth themselves. While school personnel may be limited in their ability to directly address issues of sexual identity, such individuals as professionals can and must intervene when LGB students are being harassed and victimized since these students are often unable or afraid to act as advocates. And although school counselors may not be able to discuss sexual identity specifically with youth or their parents, a referral to an affirmative counselor can be made on the basis of symptoms manifested by the youth. Counselors and parents should be careful to distinguish between sexual identity and **gender identity** issues. Youth struggling with issues in regard to their gender identity should be referred to counselors who are knowledgeable about and affirming of the transgender population.

Lesbian, gay, and bisexual **college students** face many of the same issues as their K-12 counterparts, including experiencing victimization, making decisions regarding disclosure of their sexual orientation to significant others, and identifying supportive and affirmative resources. Further, given the complexities associated with sexual **identity development**, college students may find it difficult to engage in other typical developmental tasks such as career exploration and decision-making. Yet, LGB college students may be better positioned to seek out affirmative resources given their legal status as adults, their increased independence, and the availability of such services on many campuses. Many universities staff offices devoted to LGB students. Often there are both undergraduate and graduate student associations devoted to LGB issues. In addition, most college campuses have a university counseling center that provides both individual and group counseling intended to be affirming of the LGB population.

Although working with youth presents special challenges, identity formation and stigma management are ongoing developmental tasks that span the lives of LGB persons. Further, due to the coming out process, LGB individuals may experience a lag between their chronological ages and the developmental stages delineated by current theories. This can complicate life tasks such as **career development**, partnership formation, and decisions about childbearing and rearing. With all LGB clients, attending to the sociocultural–political and historical context of a client's development is essential as rapidly changing societal views of LGB individuals will affect clients' perceptions. LGB clients must also cope with the lack of protection of their civil rights regarding end-of-life decisions (e.g., living wills, power-of-attorney), partner benefits, and affirmative living accommodations for elderly LGB clients. Therapists working with such clients may be increasingly called upon to serve in an advocacy role.

Regardless of age, LGB clients presenting with multiple salient identities (e.g., racial, religious, gender) raise a range of therapeutic issues, particularly if more than one of these identities represent marginalized groups. It is important to approach such clients from a multicultural perspective by assessing and understanding the totality of the client's experience rather than focusing on one identity in isolation. Therapists and clients may want to explore multiple identities, societal and family message, group memberships, oppression, and power. Although clients may want to come out and affirm their sexual identity, some may not be prepared to leave their cultural environment. Such clients may be unprepared to enter the LGB community or perhaps doing so may lead to disenfranchisement from a salient cultural community.

Bibliography

American Psychological Association. 2000. "Guidelines for Psychotherapy with Lesbian, Gay, and Bisexual Clients." *American Psychologist* 55: 1440–1451.

Bieschke, Kathleen J., Mary McClanahan, Erinn Tozer, Jennifer L. Grzegorek, and Jeeseon Park. 2000. "Lesbian, Gay, and Bisexual Vocational Psychology: Reviewing Foundations and Planning Construction." Pp. 309–336 in *Handbook of Counseling and Therapy with Lesbian, Gay, and Bisexual Clients.* Edited by Ruperto M. Perez, Kurt A. DeBord, and Kathleen J. Bieschke. Washington, DC: American Psychological Association.

Liddle, Becky J. 1996. "Therapist Sexual Orientation, Gender, and Counseling Practices as they Relate to Ratings of Helpfulness by Gay and Lesbian Clients." *Journal of Counseling Psychology* 43: 394–401.

———. 1997. "Gay and Lesbian Clients' Selection of Therapists and Utilization of Therapy." *Psychotherapy* 34: 11–18.

Perez, Ruperto M., Kurt A. DeBord, and Kathleen J. Bieschke, eds. 2000. *Handbook of Counseling and Therapy with Lesbian, Gay, and Bisexual Clients*. Washington, DC: American Psychological Association.

Web Sites

Association for Gay, Lesbian, and Bisexual Issues in Counseling (AGLBIC). Spring 2004. Accessed December 1, 2004. http://www.aglbic.org/. Resources for counselors and clients are provided here, including a therapist directory, description of books specific to counseling with LGB individuals, and the counselor competencies AGLBIC recommends counselors strive to adhere to when working LGBT individuals.

GLBT Central. October 9, 2003. Accessed December 1, 2004. http://www.glbtcentral.com/counselors.html. List of counselors and agencies that provide services to gay, lesbian, bisexual, and transgendered individuals. Contact information for each listing.

Society for the Psychological Study of Lesbian, Gay, and Bisexual Issues. November 2004. Accessed December 1, 2004. http://www.apa.org/divisions/div44/. Provides information relevant to psychologists and the general public about research, education, and service activities of the Society relative to LGB issues. Links to the American Psychological Association's Guidelines for Psychotherapy with Lesbian, Gay, and Bisexual Clients as well as other online resources LGB individuals.

Counselor Education

Jodi A. Boita

Counselor education broadly describes the training of individuals who will provide **counseling**, therapy, or psychotherapy. Formal training typically occurs at the graduate level of education within master's and doctoral degree programs. More narrowly, counselor education is one such program that trains individuals to work in various settings, some of which include schools, community centers, and private counseling facilities. Counseling psychology programs share common ground in training agenda, preparing trainees for professional work in psychotherapy, teaching, and **research**, but serve distinct purposes. These training programs have the potential to serve as conduits for social justice for the LGBT community as a whole and support for queer youth, in particular. Professional standards and ethical codes of conduct by the professional organizations that govern professional counseling, notably the American Counseling Association (ACA) and the American Psychological Association (APA), clearly articulate that counselor training programs must promote lesbian, gay, and bisexual (LGB) affirmative behavior. Additionally, accrediting organizations, such as the Council for Accreditation of Counseling and Related Educational Programs (CACREP) and APA, mandate that accredited training programs include exposure to **sexual orientation** issues. These professional standards

See also Allies; Homophobia; Multicultural Education; Professional Educational Associations; Professionalism.

and ethical guidelines, as well as the bulk of empirical and theoretical literature, fail to include information about **transgender** individuals. Currently, accreditation regulations do not detail how competency training ought to be accomplished, and counselor education programs do not uniformly attend to such training. Researchers and scholars have only begun to address this issue by analyzing the competency of counselor education and counseling psychology program graduates as well as the efficacy of specific training components. While the field of counseling is broadly supportive of LGBT youth, both covert and overt heterosexist and homophobic actions continue to be displayed in professional and training venues. The Association for Gay, Lesbian and Bisexual Issues (AGLBIC) was developed as a division of ACA to address these problems, to promote social equality for LGBT individuals, and to advocate LGBT inclusive counselor education curricula. Specifically attending to LGBT adolescents, AGLBIC counselor competencies call for familiarity with experiences that challenge normative adolescent development and that acknowledge critical challenges facing LGBT adolescents such as identity confusion, suicidal ideation, and HIV/STD infection.

In the United States, ethical codes and standards of practice document the responsibilities of professional behavior required of members of counseling professions. The ACA, APA, and National Board for Certified Counselors (NBCC) mandate similar directives for respect for diversity within codes of ethics published by each organization that serve as benchmarks for the counseling professions. They warn against **discrimination** based on sexual orientation, and call for awareness of **stereotypes** and their impact on LGBT individuals. Recently, articulation of psychotherapeutic guidelines (APA 2000) for work with LGB clients recommended knowledge of personally held beliefs and values, societal treatment, family issues, and community resources related to LGB individuals. For example, counselors should be aware of the development of common issues for LGB youth, such as social and emotional isolation, rejection by family members, and suicidality. Exploration of one's personally held beliefs regarding sexual orientation may illuminate biases likely to influence the therapeutic relationship and significant issues that one may have unintentionally overlooked.

While there are no standards of training for counselors in most other countries, the Canadian Counseling Association (CCA), guided, in part, by Council on Accreditation of Counsellor Education Programs (CACREP) standards, developed core competency standards for accrediting counseling programs and certifying professional counselors, including sexual orientation, which is listed within factors that fall in a range of social and cultural diversity issues. CACREP standards further detail the need for programs to disperse information about societal trends, provide experiential activities for enlightenment of personal attitudes and beliefs, teach practical skills, reveal contributions to social justice efforts, and teach counseling theories and competencies related to multicultural issues and diverse populations. Standards demand elimination of heterosexist assumptions, such as the automatic guided expectation that an individual is heterosexual until presented with evidence to suggest otherwise, that **curriculum** development in the past and support the current existence of cultural intolerance.

As in many other countries, in **Canada** there is currently no legal standard preventing individuals from practicing without meeting such requirements for certification as a Canadian Certified Counsellor. In the **United Kingdom**, the British Association for Counseling and Psychotherapy (BAC) offers accreditation for training courses based on accrual of a set number of theory and skills training hours, although it is also not necessary for an individual to complete such programs in order to practice as a counselor. These guidelines do not specifically address issues regarding LGBT youth.

The challenge for counselor educators is to add to existing programs in a reasonable way. Some researchers argue for the curriculum inclusion of coursework specific to training in LGBT issues (Pearson 2003; Phillips 2000). Others suggest that the components of general diversity training can be applied (Israel and Selvidge 2003). Currently, a limited number of training programs offer courses exclusively to address learning about sexual orientation, sexual and **gender identity** development, and LGBT issues, while even fewer programs offer training focused specifically on counseling LGBT youth. In the majority of training programs that include specific exposure to LGBT issues, such training is a segment within a general multicultural issues course. Other programs fail to incorporate formal attention to sexual and gender orientation within any course, although trainees may choose to seek training experiences in the provision of counseling for clients who identify as LGBT within practicum or internship experiences. In such instances, formal supervision serves as the training resource for students. Few, if any, programs require the completion of practica or internships regarding LGBT issues; however, those devoted solely to child and adolescent populations are available. But, the likelihood of gaining counseling experience with LGBT youth at those training sites is variable.

Graduate students' low self-perceived competency with regard to treatment of LGB clients supports the need to incorporate specific training within program curricula. Further, research highlights the existence heterosexist and homophobic attitudes and behaviors in educational arenas as well as in therapy (Phillips 2000). These can be as overt as hate comments and as covert as automatically asking about one's husband or wife instead of using the term "partner."

Nevertheless, current training programs do not adequately prepare graduates to deal with LGBT issues or work with LGBT youth and accreditation guidelines do not require specific coursework or experiential training components targeting work with LGBT individuals (Phillips and Fischer 1998). Professional ethical guidelines do call for competency in such areas.

Another challenge facing counselor education is the limited empirical evidence to dictate the best manner of training individuals to act affirmatively. Researchers have made suggestions based on what is known about counselor training in general, multicultural issues, and LGBT specific information. At a very basic level, Israel and Hackett (2004) found that counselor trainees who received information about LGB issues were more knowledgeable about working with LGB clients than their counterparts who did not receive the information. In the same study, trainees who were exposed to a short attitude exploration exercise regarding LGB issues showed an *increase* in negativity about LGB subject matter following the attitude training. These researchers concluded that the limited time spent on attitude exploration made participants uncomfortable due to uncovering and challenging embedded heterosexist assumptions. Although this may be the first step in acknowledging and changing true attitudes of counselor trainees, Israel and Hackett suggested that a longer more substantial training program would be necessary to bring about positive change in counselor trainees' attitudes toward LGB issues.

Qualitative research targeting the process of developing LGB affirmative attitudes in counselor training shows the need for self-reflection surrounding personal beliefs about one's **sexual identity**/orientation development and attitudes about LGB individuals (Dillon et al. 2004). Such self-reflection helped the counselor trainees to change heterosexist assumptions and behaviors. It would be a heterosexist behavior, for instance, to assume that a male adolescent client who shows anxiety about **dating** is anxious over being rejected by females. Exposing and challenging one's belief that all individuals are heterosexual until proven otherwise would allow the counselor to behave affirmatively regardless of knowledge of the client's sexual orientation. The possibility that this client is interested in dating males would be integrated into the counselor's initial conceptualization.

The general components of multicultural training, which are knowledge, attitudes, and skills, can be applied to counselor training for work with LGB clients (Israel and Selvidge 2003). Informational training imparts knowledge that can help individuals to identify **heterosexism** and serve to challenge heterosexist manners of interacting and thinking. Training can be infused in the current curriculum of counselor education programs. Specific training seminars focused on the unique and shared experiences of LGBT youth will add to students' general knowledge of multicultural issues currently incorporated into counseling programs. Experiential instruction in sexual **identity development**, effects of stereotyping, and counseling interventions have been endorsed by graduate level counseling students as beneficial to their knowledge about sexual orientation issues and interest in working with LGB clients (Pearson 2003).

Although published research attending to LGBT issues has increased, there is still much to be done regarding the training of counselors to work with LGBT youth. Calling for improved research training environments, Bieschke et al. (1998) have made specific proposals to create an LGB affirmative atmosphere that would increase the programmatic research regarding LGBT issues in counselor education programs. In addition to faculty support for LGBT related research, creating graduate assistantship opportunities, promoting membership in LGBT and ally groups, and advertising the affirmative stance of its training programs can enhance an LGBT affirmative environment.

Bibliography

American Counseling Association. 1995. *Code of Ethics and Standards of Practice.* Alexandria, VA: Author.

American Psychological Association. 2000. "Guidelines for Psychotherapy with Lesbian, Gay, and Bisexual Clients." *American Psychologist* 55:1440–1451.

Bieschke, Kathleen J., Amy B. Eberz, Christine C. Bard, and James M. Croteau. 1998. "Using Social Cognitive Career Theory to Create Affirmative Lesbian, Gay, and Bisexual Research Training Environments." *The Counseling Psychologist* 26: 735–753.

Council for Accreditation of Counseling and Related Educational Programs. 2001. *The 2001 Standards.* Alexandria, VA: Author.

Dillon, Frank. R., Roger L. Worthington, Holly Bielstein Savoy, S. Craig Rooney, Ann Becker-Schutte, and Rachael M. Guerra. 2004. "On Becoming Allies: A Qualitative Study of Lesbian, Gay, and Bisexual Affirmative Counselor Training." *Counselor Education & Supervision* 43: 162–178.

Israel, Tania, and Gail Hackett. 2004. "Counselor Education on Lesbian, Gay, and Bisexual Issues: Comparing Information and Attitude Exploration." *Counselor Education and Supervision* 43: 179–191.

Israel, Tania, and Mary D. Selvidge. 2003. "Contributions of Multicultural Counseling to Counselor Competence with Lesbian, Gay, and Bisexual Clients." *Journal of Multicultural Counseling and Development* 31: 84–98.

Pearson, Quinn. M. 2003. "Breaking the Silence in the Counselor Education Classroom: A Training Seminar on Counseling Sexual Minority Clients." *Journal of Counseling and Development* 81:292–300.

Phillips, Julia C. 2000. "Training Issues and Considerations." Pp. 337–358 in *Handbook of Counseling and Psychotherapy with Lesbian, Gay and Bisexual Clients*. Edited by Ruperto M. Perez, Kurt A. DeBord, and Kathleen J. Bieschke. Washington, DC: American Psychological Association.

Phillips, Julia C., and Amy R. Fischer. 1998. "Graduate Students' Training Experiences with Lesbian, Gay, and Bisexual Issues." *The Counseling Psychologist* 26: 712–734.

Web Sites

American Counseling Association (ACA). 2004. Accessed December 3, 2004. http://www.counseling.org. Resources on public policy, publications, and career information.

American Psychological Association (APA). December 2004. Accessed December 3, 2004. Professional resources for psychologist, ethical guidelines for psychologists, and accreditation standards for counseling psychology training programs are outlined within this Web site.

Association for Gay, Lesbian, and Bisexual Issues in Counseling (AGLBIC). Spring 2004. Accessed December 3, 2004. http://www.aglbic.org/. Recommended resources for counselor training with regard to affirmative counseling with LGBT individuals are offered here.

British Association for Counselling and Psychotherapy (BAC). 2004. Accessed December 3, 2004. http://www.bacp.co.uk/. Suggested professional guidelines and resources for counselors in the United Kingdom are offered.

National Board of Certified Counselors Code of Ethics (NBCC). Accessed May 30, 2005. http://www.nbcc.org/pdfs/ethics/NBCC-CodeofEthics.pdf. The code of ethics mandated for counselor certification are outlined here.

2001 Standards. 2004. Council for Accreditation of Counseling and Related Educational Programs (CACREP). Accessed December 4, 2004. http://www.cacrep.org/2001 Standards.html. CACREP Accreditation Standards (2001) for counselor training programs are offered within this Web site.

Critical Social Theory

André P. Grace

As it relates to education, critical social theory provides a framework for discussing democratic forms of education, teacher and student freedom, social justice issues, and ethical educational practices. Moreover, critical social theory provides an encompassing lens to investigate how education legitimates particular ways of being and acting as a function of its role as a social and political enterprise caught up in

See also Agency; Canada, LGBT Youth in; Curriculum, Higher Education; Philosophy, Teaching of; Professional Educational Organizations; Queer Pedagogy; Sexual Identity; Secondary Schools, LGBT; Social Class; White Antiracism.

the larger contexts that shape society (McLaren 2003). As a theory of resistance, critical social theory can also help us analyze how education can also play a key role in political and cultural action for social transformation (Allman 1999). In this light, in relation to **lesbian, gay, bisexual,** trans [**transgender** and **transsexual**], and **queer** (LGBTQ) issues, all students ought to build knowledge and understanding regarding why and how LGBTQ students have been historically marginalized. From an educational perspective, such analysis begins by investigating what schooling is and what schooling means in relation to the social, cultural, historical, political, and economic contexts that shape it. Furthermore, it involves investigating what democratic forms of education might look like, and what constitutes ethical and just educational practices. Critical social theory and critical pedagogy, as its educational expression, have value here. They provide a theory–practice framework to help us interrogate and transform schools as social and cultural sites that have historically tolerated **heterosexism** and **homophobia,** thus normalizing the exclusion of those not heterosexual or biologically male or female.

Building such knowledge and understanding has been the central mission of critical studies (McLaren 2003; Peters, Lankshear, and Olssen 2003). As a way of analyzing how education functions, critical studies examine how schools, as central social and cultural institutions, are expected to maintain the status quo with its established hierarchies, values, and ways of doing things. In other words, critical studies analyze how schooling, which is shaped by power and interests, "always represents an introduction to, preparation for, and legitimation of particular forms of social life" (McLaren 2003, 186–187). From this perspective, schooling is about fitting in, being accepted, and being acceptable in the face of power and interest groups. Critical studies explore the limitations of this conditioning. They examine what happens when alternative kinds of knowledge, beliefs, and social forms collide with dominant kinds that have power, support, and value within the status quo. It is in this exploration that critical studies find purpose and a call to action: "to empower the powerless and transform existing social inequalities and injustices" (McLaren 2003, 186).

Critical theory emerged in Germany, in 1923, with the founding of the Frankfurt School (Institute for Social Research at Frankfurt am Main). During the twentieth century it became known as a way to analyze *the social* as a construction shaped and impacted by contexts, beliefs, and the power maintained within dominant groups. Critical theory continues to critique *the dominant social* characterized by categories like whiteness, maleness, heterosexuality, and wealth. This social theory has linked scientific progress to such domination, interrogating the systems and structures that affirm science as a powerful agent of order, progress, and predictability supporting the status quo. While some feminists and postmodern theorists have rightly critiqued critical theory for its inadequate attention to relationships of power like **race** and gender, new versions of critical theory have emerged to take race (critical race theory) and gender (critical **feminism**) into account. Critical theory remains important in education to help us think about the challenges, risks, and possibilities of reframing schooling as an inclusive project that makes space for students across the spectrum of differences like race, sexuality, and gender that characterize them.

Critical pedagogy is the application of critical theory to schooling. As a discourse, critical pedagogy is a group of concepts that can help us understand the relationship between power and knowledge. Thus, critical pedagogy can help students understand how knowledge is socially constructed and how schooling is a political venture. It does this by encouraging teachers and students to examine knowledge "both for the way it misrepresents or marginalizes particular views of the world and for the way it provides a deeper understanding of how the student's world is actually constructed" (McLaren 2003, 186). This situates critical pedagogy as a conceptual framework for inquiry and a guide for questioning and acting in schools and other social and cultural sites. Moreover, it situates critical pedagogy at the point where theory and practice meet: "Theory emerge[s] soaked in well-carried-out practice" (Freire 1998, 21). What this means is that theory and practice ally in particular ways to inform communicative learning and the possibility of social change.

In contemporary times, critical theory can help us understand change, oppression, and disenfranchisement in terms of new social relationships of domination, control, and racial and ethnic profiling associated with globalization and terrorism. It can also help us understand the twists and turns **homophobia** can take in response to the fears and misunderstandings some heterosexuals have to the increased visibility of LGBTQ persons. For example, it can help us understand the challenges, risks, and intricacies of forming **gay–straight alliances** (GSAs). Moreover, it can help us determine the degree to which GSAs are inclusive, transgressive sites that reflect human diversity and engage in resistance to revitalize schools as sites of cultural democracy.

Working in the intersection of critical theory and **queer theory**, one can find similarities and tensions in comparing these competing theories. The tensions arise because certain feminist and cultural discourses that variously contest critical theory have influenced the development of queer theory's discourse. The similarities are found in the common concerns of critical theory and queer theory with domination, oppression, resistance, and social change. Queer theory engages how the realities of societal ignorance, fear, hate, and violence harmfully impact the outsider or outlawed sex-and-gendered subject (what has been historically usual). At the same time, queer theory focuses on fighting heterosexism and homophobia so LGBTQ citizens can be respected and accommodated (what is sometimes achieved through social, cultural, and political resistance). Thus, both critical theory and queer theory are concerned with building cultural democracy and ensuring ethical public practices (framed in education around being there for every student).

"Agape," an education-and-culture action group located in the Faculty of Education, University of Alberta, provides an example demonstrating how both critical and queer theory can impact resistance in education and the move toward more inclusive, ethical, and just practices (Grace and Wells 2004). Agape engages in deliberations, social action, and cultural work—all of which have political intent—to provide a space for undergraduate and graduate students, faculty, and staff to take up issues of sex, sexuality, and gender differences in relation to access and accommodation in educational and other social and cultural contexts. In addition, the group invites participation from teachers working in K-12 schools as well as junior and senior high-school students and interested community members. Agape participants assess changes, progress, and possibilities regarding inclusivity for LGBTQ students and teachers in Canadian education. In this work, they address issues necessary to mobilize queer work for social action in vital and vigorous ways that attend to ethics, politics, justice, agency, and results (Ristock and Taylor 1998). Group facilitators, working with participants, have eclectic backgrounds. Some have worked on antiracist community projects, others have worked with queer street kids for whom **drug use** and **prostitution** are parts of everyday living, and still others have worked with youth in **community LGBT support groups**. There is a focus on resistance, change, and youth **resilience**. For example, as a result of a recent Agape initiative that involved community education, group mobilization, and using the media to get the word out, Edmonton's public-school district is encouraging and supporting school principals to enable queer and allied students and teacher sponsors to set up GSA clubs in the district's schools.

The Alberta Teachers' Association's *Sexual Orientation and Gender Identity Educational Resources Online* demonstrates how critical pedagogy can be used in workshops with teachers to educate them about the positionalities and needs of LGBTQ persons in schools and communities. Through a series of three workshops, developed by educator Kristopher Wells, teachers are invited to engage in critical learning and dialogue to build awareness of students' safety, health, and inclusive educational issues related to **sexual orientation** and **gender identity**. Teachers grapple with stereotypes, profiling, and binary thinking (male–female and heterosexual–homosexual) as they build understanding of their professional, ethical, and legal responsibilities in relation to the equitable and fair treatment of LGBTQ students. In the spirit of Paulo Freire's (1998) mutuality of theory and practice, they explore specific strategies and resources that can enable them to transform classrooms, schools, and communities into safe, caring, and inclusive social and cultural sites.

Bibliography

Allman, Paula. 1999. *Revolutionary Social Transformation: Democratic Hopes, Political Possibilities and Critical Education.* Westport, CN: Bergin and Garvey.

Freire, Paulo. 1998. *Teachers as Cultural Workers: Letters to Those Who Dare Teach.* Translated by Donaldo Macedo, Dale Koike, and Alexandre Oliveira. Boulder, CO: Westview Press.

Grace, André P., and Kristopher Wells. 2004. Engaging Sex-and-Gender Differences: Educational and Cultural Change Initiatives in Alberta. Pp. 289–307 in *I Could Not Speak My Heart: Education and Social Justice for Gay and Lesbian Youth.* Edited by James McNinch and Mary Cronin. Regina, SK: University of Regina, Canadian Plains Research Centre.

McLaren, Peter. 2003. *Life in Schools: An Introduction to Critical Pedagogy in the Foundations of Education.* 4th ed. Boston: Allyn and Bacon.

Peters, Michael, Colin Lankshear, and Mark Olssen, eds. 2003. *Critical Theory and the Human Condition: Founders and Praxis.* New York: Peter Lang.

Ristock, Janice L., and Catherine G. Taylor, eds. 1998. *Inside the Academy and Out: Lesbian/Gay/Queer Studies and Social Action.* Toronto: University of Toronto Press.

Web Sites

AERCQUEERSPACE. June 4, 2003. Robert J. Hill. Accessed December 16, 2004. http://www.arches.uga.edu/~bobhill/AERCQUEERSPACE/refs.htm. Includes an extensive bibliography of LGBTQ books, journal articles, and videos. As well, it provides an annotated list of links to other Web sites intersecting LGBTQ and critical perspectives.

Building Safe, Caring and Inclusive Schools for Lesbian, Gay, Bisexual and Transgendered (LGBT) Students—Workshop Series. May 2005. Kristopher Wells. Accessed May 26, 2005. http://www.teachers.ab.ca/Issues+In+Education/Diversity+and+Human+Rights/Sexual+Orientation/Index.htm. Sponsored by the Alberta Teachers' Association, this site describes three workshops for teachers that are intended to engender critical dialogue around contexts, relationships, and dispositions impacting school and community responses to LGBTQ teachers and students and their collective needs.

Introductory Guide to Critical Theory. November 28, 2003. Dino Felluga. Accessed December 16, 2004. http://www.purdue.edu/guidetotheory/introduction. Provides a resource for both undergraduate and graduate students who are beginning to learn critical theory, includes guides to terms. It also includes sample applications, annotated links to existing Web sites, and more-in-depth modules on specific authors.

Cross-Dressing

Brett Genny Beemyn

Cross-dressers, commonly defined as individuals who wear clothing and take on an appearance and behavior considered by a given culture to be appropriate for another gender but not one's own, have often been misunderstood and maligned, especially in societies with strict, dichotomous **gender roles**. As a result, many cross-dressers choose to hide this part of themselves, sometimes internalizing a sense of shame and guilt. The individuals who were tormented by their cross-dressing were more likely than others to seek the assistance of doctors, leading many medical authorities in the nineteenth and twentieth centuries to view cross-dressing as a mental illness. Not until the 1960s, when generally well-adjusted cross-dressers formed support groups and became more visible to researchers, did the practice start to become less stigmatized and more accepted. Many psychiatrists, though, still consider cross-dressing pathological. Frequently, teenagers and preteens today discovered to cross-dress are required to undergo therapy and are sometimes institutionalized. Nevertheless, cross-dressing youth are finding support, often through creating their own resources.

Every generation of queer youth has appropriated cross-dressing in some form. Interest in "gender bending" and cross-dressing among youth is widespread, as evident in the institutionalization of "Miss Teen" pageants. Synthia Sanchez (Miss Teen Iowa Unltd., 2004) with Savannah (on the far left) and Antoine (in the center). Courtesy of Gay Youth Unlimited, www.youth-unlimited.org

Accounts of women and men who cross-dress have appeared in newspapers, legal records, and medical journals in Europe and the United States for centuries. For example, white explorers and missionaries in the seventeenth and eighteenth centuries found that many Native American tribal cultures recognized **multiple genders**, including "women–men" and "men–women" who took on cross-gender roles, often involving cross-dressing. In the nineteenth century, European and United States' sexologists discussed cases of individuals who cross-dressed, typically categorizing them as "homosexuals" or as having a "contrary sexual feeling."

See also Adolescent Sexualities; Native and Indigenous LGBT Youth; Passing; Psychoanalysis and Feminism; Sissy Boy; Tomboy.

Like sex researchers, many contemporary historians have contended that men and especially women who cross-dressed in the past did so as a cover to pursue same-sex relationships or, in the case of women, to take advantage of male privilege, such as being able to escape narrow gender roles or enter traditionally male occupations. These women are said to have "posed" or "passed" as men and to have been in a lesbian relationship if they lived with another woman. Generally, there is no consideration given to the possibility that they identified as men or felt more comfortable dressed in traditionally male clothing.

In order to distinguish gender expression from sexual behavior, German physician **Magnus Hirschfeld** coined the term "transvestism" (Latin for "cross-dressing"), in 1910. Hirschfeld, a cross-dresser himself, argued that transvestites were not fetishists, but were overcome with a "feeling of peace, security and exaltation, happiness and well-being . . . when in the clothing of the other sex" (Hirschfeld 1910, 125). Challenging the claim by other sexologists that cross-dressers were homosexuals and almost entirely men, Hirschfeld demonstrated that transvestites could be male or female and of any **sexual orientation**. In fact, most of the individuals he studied were heterosexual.

After Hirschfeld, most of the work published on cross-dressing through the 1960s was by psychiatrists. Based on the distressed patients in their care, they considered cross-dressing to be a perversion treatable through psychotherapy. Ignoring Hirschfeld's groundbreaking research, these psychiatrists argued that transvestism was a male phenomenon often associated with fetishism. Psychoanalytic literature tended to explain cross-dressing as either a form of homosexuality or an escape from homosexuality resulting from "castration anxiety."

Prior to the 1960s, there was little organizing among cross-dressers; many doctors even urged the cross-dressers who came to them to hide their transvestism and avoid contact with other cross-dressers. A new era began in 1960, when Virginia Prince started publishing *Transvestia* magazine and helped found the first national organization for cross-dressers in the United States. Known today as Tri-Ess (the Society for the Second Self), the group has more than thirty chapters

Even though drag kings and drag queens had presented the most visible image of cross-dressing since the early twentieth century, Prince refused to acknowledge lesbian and gay male cross-dressers and excluded them from the society. Many other cross-dressing clubs followed suit. As a result, the cross-dressing movement consisted primarily of married, heterosexual men, and drag kings and drag queens aligned themselves with the emerging homosexual movement.

As the number of clubs grew in the 1970s and 1980s, researchers were able to conduct surveys of cross-dressers who were not patients and thus were more comfortable with their cross-dressing. The fact that most club members were white, middle-class, heterosexual men meant that the resulting samples were still not representative of cross-dressers. Nevertheless, these studies provided the first scientific look at the experiences of a significant segment of cross-dressers.

Research on cross-dressers finds that rarely does this behavior begin in adulthood. Most began cross-dressing clandestinely before puberty, with some starting as early as preschool. Contrary to the popular belief that cross-dressing was first initiated or encouraged by a parent, the studies show that this was usually the decision of the young person, often without the knowledge of anyone else (Docter 1988). As these individuals grew older and had greater autonomy, they were able to cross-dress more completely and more frequently.

Although research studies involving members of cross-dressing clubs have helped change the medical community's image of transvestites, many psychiatrists continue to view cross-dressing as a mental illness amenable to treatment. Since 1987, the American Psychiatric Association's *Diagnostic and Statistical Manual* (*DSM*), the profession's guide to mental disorders, has included the diagnosis "Transvestic Fetishism," which it defines as a heterosexual male who has "recurrent intense sexual urges and sexually arousing fantasies involving cross-dressing" and "has acted on these urges or is markedly distressed by them" (American Psychiatric Association 1987, sec. 302.3). The most recent edition of the *DSM* (1994) acknowledges that some transvestites are attracted to others of the same sex and that the fetishistic aspect may diminish over time, but the clinical definition of transvestism remains a heterosexual male who compulsively dresses in women's clothing because of the erotic pleasure he derives from doing so. Because "transvestite" connotes a perversion and excludes female, gay, and bisexual male cross-dressers, as well as heterosexual men who cross-dress for nonsexual reasons, this term is rejected today by many transpeople in favor of "cross-dresser."

In addition to stigmatizing adult cross-dressers, the *DSM* pathologizes gender nonconforming children and teenagers. A prepubescent girl who insists on "wearing only stereotypical masculine clothing" or a boy who has a "preference for cross-dressing or simulating female attire" can be diagnosed with a **Gender Identity Disorder** (GID) and be forced into psychotherapy or committed to a psychiatric hospital (American Psychiatric Association 1994, sec. 302.6). While no figures exist for the number of children and young adults who have been institutionalized for GID, the former patients who have been willing to discuss their experiences demonstrate the ease with which this diagnosis has been applied.

Faced with a traditionally hostile psychiatric community and often parents and other relatives who do not or would not understand, many cross-dressing youths have turned to each other for support. The **Internet**—especially chat rooms, instant messaging, and blogs—has made it possible for many preteen and teenage cross-dressers to share information and discuss their experiences. They can also do so without having to come out publicly, enabling them to explore their gender identities as they see fit.

In the last fifteen years, close to 2,000 **gay–straight alliances** (GSAs) have been formed to support each other and to educate teachers, administrators, and other students about LGBT issues. But because many GSAs do not specifically address the needs of **transgender youth** or focus on **gender identity** issues, some schools and transgender organizations are beginning to form after-school trans youth groups. As a result, young cross-dressers today are often less isolated and more self-assured than previous generations of cross-dressers.

Bibliography

American Psychiatric Association. 1987. *Diagnostic and Statistical Manual of Mental Disorders*. 3rd ed. Washington, DC: American Psychiatric Association.

———. 1994. *Diagnostic and Statistical Manual of Mental Disorders*. 4th ed. Washington, DC: American Psychiatric Association.

Bullough, Bonnie, Vern L. Bullough, and James Elias, eds. 1997. *Gender Blending*. Amherst, NY: Prometheus Books.

Bullough, Vern L., and Bonnie Bullough. 1993. *Cross Dressing, Sex, and Gender*. Philadelphia: University of Pennsylvania Press.

a

Cromwell, Jason. 1999. *Transmen and FTMs: Identities, Bodies, Genders, and Sexualities.* Urbana: University of Illinois Press.

Docter, Richard F. 1988. *Transvestites and Transsexuals: Toward a Theory of Cross-Gender Behavior.* New York: Plenum Press.

Hirschfeld, Magnus. 1991 [1910]. *Transvestites: The Erotic Drive to Cross Dress.* Translated by Michael A. Lombardi-Nash. Buffalo, NY: Prometheus Books.

Web Sites

Trans Proud. 2004. The National Coalition for GLBT Youth. Accessed December 20, 2004. http://www.transproud.com Answers questions about transgenderism, trans coming out stories, message boards, resources for parents whose children have come out as transgender, and other valuable information.

Tri-Ess, The Society for the Second Self. November 2004. Accessed December 20, 2004. http://www.tri-ess.org Web site includes information about the group's chapters and events and resources specifically for the partners and children of cross-dressers.

Crush

John C. Spurlock

A crush is an intense, emotion-filled interest in another individual. Although today it generally refers to a heterosexual interest, until at least the 1940s a crush meant an interest in someone of the same sex. The term "crush" refers both to the emotional script, which includes affection and near-obsessive interest in someone who is not a parent ("I have a crush on Jennifer"); and also to the object of interest ("Jennifer is my crush"). Although crushes first appear for most people in early **adolescence**, they can continue as part of an individual's emotional repertoire throughout life. In early adolescence the crush may be someone who is an older peer or an adult and almost always someone of the same sex; these have traditionally been called "hero worship." In contemporary American adolescent culture, crushes typically are short-lived. They may be the initial phase of a longer-term relationship, but the object of the crush frequently will remain unaware that a crush exists. Today same-sex crushes are possible for **gay, lesbian, bisexual**, and **transgender youth** and may also be part of the sexual experimentation typical of youth.

Intense same-sex friendships are quite common among adolescents. Although these friendships are likely to contain some homoerotic feelings, such feelings will more likely find expression in single-sex environments where young people have time away from adult supervision. During the nineteenth and much of the twentieth century, the English "public schools," private boarding schools for middle-class boys, offered an ideal setting for strong friendships and sexual experiments among the boys and young men who lived together for months of each year. Similar settings for male bonding appeared in American boarding schools and military academies.

See also Adolescent Sexualities; Childhood; Desire; Japan, Lesbian and Bisexual Youth in; Single-Sex Schools; Social Class; Women's Colleges.

The crush is distinctive in being mainly an experience among girls and young women. It began at least as early as the late nineteenth century at women's colleges. Middle-class women in that century commonly formed strong, emotionally intense relations with other women as they grew up in a network of family and friends. As college education became available to a wider portion of middle-class women late in the century, young women already had a context for emotional closeness to other women. College life, however, brought together young women who were not part of one another's network of family and kin. At college these women had ample opportunity to discover interesting and attractive peers. The passionate attachments that grew out of this setting were known as "smashing," and they became so prevalent that faculty and administrators considered them a threat to the peace of the colleges.

Crushes appeared more frequently as social changes during the late nineteenth and early twentieth centuries gave more opportunities for children and adolescents to spend long periods of time together in single-sex settings. For middle-class boys and girls, summer camps became a common experience. A wave of hero worship of camp counselors, and crushes among the campers, could completely disrupt the camp activities. A more important setting, particularly for girls, was the public high school. The proportion of teenagers in high school grew rapidly in this period. Because boys continued to leave school for work in their teenaged years, girls greatly outnumbered boys in high school until the 1920s.

By the early twentieth century, crushes were well-known to both the young girls and boys who had them, and to the adult authorities who taught, administered, and studied youth. The individual with the crush would realize that she had a powerful interest in and affection for another individual. At first this interest would be a secret, providing opportunity for the individual to observe and long for the object of the crush. The crush might remain secret, but during the life of the crush the person who experienced it might feel compelled to share her feelings with parents or peers, or even with the object of the crush. The feelings of the crush alternated between glowing happiness when it seemed that the object recognized and reciprocated the crush feelings, and despair when the object of affection seemed to reject the crush. As children grew older, hero worship generally gave way to crushes on peers. Crushes on peers were more likely to lead to reciprocal feelings of affection, and during the early twentieth century girls who had special relationships often referred to one another as their crushes (other terms such as "grand passion" were also common). A survey of college women in the late 1920s found that half of the sample had experienced some form of affectionate or sexual involvement with another woman, with a large portion fitting into the style of the crush. High school girls took the existence of crushes for granted.

By the 1950s "crush" had acquired an almost exclusively heterosexual meaning. Although heterosexual **dating** had become widely accepted in American high schools by the 1920s, girls could have crushes on other girls while they dated boys. As the proportion of boys and girls in high school became more equal, more possibilities developed for relationships between the sexes. Heterosexual dating was a central feature of high school social life, and success at dating became an important measure of status. High school extracurricular events included a variety of heterosexual rituals such as school dances and the senior **prom**. Probably the most important indication of the shift from the same-sex crush was the appearance during the 1930s of heterosexual "steady" relationships. Although steadies might change partners after only a short period of time, the steady had many of the same features as the crush. It was relatively long-term and emotionally significant.

Bibliography

Faderman, Lillian. 1981. *Surpassing the Love of Men: Romantic Friendship and Love between Women from the Renaissance to the Present.* New York: Morrow.

Rupp, Leila. 1999. *A Desired Past: A Short History of Same-Sex Love in America.* Chicago: University of Chicago.

Spurlock, John C. 2002. "From Reassurance to Irrelevance: Adolescent Psychology and Homosexuality in America." *History of Psychology* 5: 38–51.

Curriculum, Antibias

Nina Asher

Antibias curricula focus on promoting social justice, enabling teachers, students, and parents to address **prejudice** based on race, class, culture, gender, sexuality, religion, and ability. These curricula can focus on creating a critical awareness regarding **heterosexism** and **homophobia** as forms of oppression and representing different sexual identities as integral aspects of human life. Overall, **multicultural education** has, to date, focused mainly on addressing marginalization based on race and culture, with limited attention to issues of gender, sexuality, and **social class**. However, as critical theorists and antibias educators recognize, these oppressions are interconnected. Thus, antibias curricula, which focus on sexuality, would enable students, teachers, and parents to develop a critical consciousness, engage a multiplicity of perspectives, and broaden the ways they relate to different "others."

Antibias educators, multiculturalists, and critical theorists offer a number of strategies for addressing homophobia and heterosexism in elementary, middle, and secondary school settings. Lesbian, gay, bisexual, and transgender/transsexual (LGBT) peoples, their stories, and their literature can be made visible in the school context such as on bulletin boards and in libraries. In the earlier grades, teachers can draw on **early childhood literature** (e.g., *Heather Has Two Mommies* or *Asha's Two Mums*) which features and validates LGBT youth and families. In higher grades, teachers may use individual case studies and specific examples of antibias curriculum (Bigelow et al. 2001) to lead a discussion of issues pertaining to sexuality and homophobia.

Antibias curricula at all levels of K-12 schooling can draw on (auto)biographies and narratives of LGBT youth and families. Teachers may bring in guest speakers from LGBT families and community organizations such as **Gay, Lesbian, Straight Education Network** or Parents and Friends of Lesbians and Gays. At all levels, teachers can use critical, reflective questioning (e.g., "What do we think when we hear the word 'gay?' Why?" "Where do we get the information/ideas we get?") to foster a dialogue and deconstruct stereotypes. Representing diversity of race, class,

See also Families, LGBT; Heteronormativity; Literature, College; Literature, Middle School; Literature, Secondary School; Queer Pedagogy; Race and Racism; White Antiracism.

culture, ability, religion, and language *within* the LGBT population is also important. The video, *It's Elementary* (USA 1997) also offers examples of curricular innovations, undertaken by particular schools, such as inviting guest presenters from LGBT community organizations, organizing a photo exhibit representing gay and lesbian families, and celebrating Pride Day. In one scene, a young gay presenter informs his eighth grade audience that he is part Puerto Rican and part Mexican and that he comes from a very religious background, since his father is a clergyman.

Effective antibias curricula addressing sexuality are not focused on sex (a homophobic assumption) but rather on understanding the experiences and struggles of LGBT individuals in terms of negotiating **sexual identity** and community. For instance, discussions on the topic of family can focus on the acceptance of young children who have gay or lesbian parents. Or, in the case of older students, readings/discussions related to issues of identity can engage the **discrimination** and isolation **lesbian** and **gay youth** encounter in schools. Through such a **curriculum**, it also becomes possible to rethink such oft-raised issues as the gender of the teacher (for instance, the homophobic association of male elementary school teachers with pedophilia or the high school female **physical education** teacher as a lesbian) and whether or not it is appropriate to address LGBT issues at the elementary school level (for instance, the battle over implementing the **Children of the Rainbow curriculum** in New York City).

Another important consideration in an antibias curriculum is adapting it to particular cultural contexts. For instance, students in many **urban** schools are likely to have greater exposure (whether the information is accurate or not) to the presence of LGBT issues and persons than are kids in a **rural** areas where homophobia may be compounded by **religious fundamentalism** and few **community LGBT support groups** and resources. Similarly, gay and lesbian identities and gender representations in, say, cultures in **Africa** or **Asia** may be very different from those commonly encountered in North America. For instance, the documentary *Woubi Cheri* (France 1998), based in the city of Abidjan in the Ivory Coast, highlights nuanced constructions of male homosexual relationships. In this context, a "woubi" is a man who chooses to play the **gender role** of the "wife" in a relationship with a "yossi," a **bisexual**—perhaps married—man, who accepts the role of the woubi's husband.

All schools, however, need to integrate curricular materials, ranging from posters, to biographies of famous people, to first-person narratives of **queer** students/parents/families, to statistical data and **educational policies** regarding **harassment** against queer students. Such curricula can be used to engender dialogue so that young people learn about the particular struggles queer students encounter, identify strategies for combating homophobia in their particular schools and communities, and, in the process, become **allies**.

By interrogating identities, cultures, and even families as dynamic, evolving constructs rather than fixed entities, antibias curricula serve as a form of social justice intervention, requiring teachers and students to rethink issues of sexuality, race, culture, and gender. By engaging children in a critical interrogation of popular stories such as *The Ugly Duckling*, for instance, teachers can open up discussions related to issues of isolation, identity, and self-worth and relate the same to the larger issue of validating differences. With older students, teachers can interrogate **stereotypes** by beginning with those that they, as teenagers, might encounter and then broadening the discussion to focus on race, gender, class, and so on. Thus, curricula which deconstruct heterosexism and homophobia and foster an awareness and acceptance of different sexual identifications also contribute to the broader mandate of multicultural education and the effort to realize the vision of a democratic society.

Bibliography

Bigelow, Bill, Linda Christensen, Stan Karp, Barbara Miner, and Bob Peterson, eds. 1994. *Rethinking our Classrooms: Teaching for Equity and Justice*. Milwaukee: Rethinking Schools.

Bigelow, Bill, Brenda Harvey, Stan Karp, and Larry Miller, eds. 2001. *Rethinking our Classrooms: Teaching for Equity and Justice, Volume 2*. Milwaukee: Rethinking Schools.

Derman-Sparks, Louise, and the Anti Bias Task Force. 1989. *The Anti-Bias Curriculum*. National Association for the Education of Young Children. Washington DC: Author.

Kissen, Rita M., ed. 2002. *Getting Ready for Benjamin: Preparing Teachers for Sexual Diversity in the Classroom*. Lanham, MD: Rowman and Littlefield.

Letts, William J., IV, and James T. Sears, eds. 1999. *Queering Elementary Education: Advancing the Dialogue about Sexualities and Schooling*. Lanham, MD: Rowman and Littlefield.

Sears, James T., and Walter L. Williams, eds. 1997. *Overcoming Heterosexism and Homophobia: Strategies that Work*. New York: Columbia University Press.

Theory and Research in Social Education. 2002. 30, no. 2. Special Issue: Social Education and Sexual Identity.

Web Sites

Gay Lesbian and Straight Education Network (GLSEN). May 2005. Accessed May 30, 2005. http://www.glsen.org/templates/index.html News pertaining to LGBT issues in relation to school, links discussing current issues, and educational resources to address the same (e.g., same-sex marriage) in the classroom. Links to locate local GLSEN chapters and to obtain state-by-state listings of Gay–Straight Alliances are also available.

GLEE Project Gay Lesbian Bisexual Transgender (GLBT) Educational Equity. February 25, 2003. Accessed May 30, 2005. http://glee.oulu.fi. Participants learn to use an Internet-based support network (GLEENET), which also serves as a resource center for on-going communication between participant schools from different countries to share ideas and collectively develop materials for their own local actions.

Parents, Families and Friends of Lesbians and Gays (PFLAG). May 2005. Accessed May 30, 2005. http://www.pflag.org. Facts, publications/resources, and strategies for addressing issues such as hate crimes, parenting and families, and civil rights. Links pertaining to "communities of color" and "moving towards a multicultural PFLAG" speak to the intersections of race–class–gender–culture.

Rethinking Schools Online. Spring 2005. Accessed May 30, 2005. http://www.rethinkingschools.org/index.shtml. Current and past issues of *Rethinking Schools* focused on promoting social justice and curriculum strategies for addressing issues of race, class, gender, culture, and language in a global context. Includes an extensive listing of additional web resources for educators.

Southern Poverty Law Center (SPLC). May 2005. Accessed May 30, 2005. http://www.splcenter.org. The link for "Teaching Tolerance" is of key interest on the SPLC homepage. Resources and specific strategies for teachers, parents, and students (with separate links for teens and kids) to combat hate and prejudice as well as discussions of current issues (such as discrimination against gays by the Boy Scouts of America) are available.

Curriculum, Early Childhood

Kerry H. Robinson

Addressing **homophobia** and **heterosexism** in early childhood curricula and including sexual diversity in the **curriculum** are critical given that much of the **prejudice** held and **harassment** directed by youth toward sexual difference is constituted in their early years. Since the late 1980s, there has been a significant increase in awareness of the importance of early childhood education positively reflecting and empowering the diverse identities of children and their families. Today, this is a central feature of early childhood education philosophies and practices. One of the most influential and pioneering publications in this field has been *The Anti-Bias Curriculum* (Derman-Sparks 1989), which provided a framework for dealing with diverse families, including gay- and lesbian-headed families. Recently, there has been an increased focus in the literature on addressing gay and lesbian issues in early childhood education, but LGBTQ equity issues are largely considered to be irrelevant to young children's lives and, in some cases, detrimental to their education.

Several factors contribute to the perceived irrelevance and inappropriateness of LGBTQ issues in early childhood curricula, often resulting in their exclusion. Young children are generally perceived to be asexual and "too young" to understand or deal with sexuality. This perception is primarily linked to traditional understandings of **childhood** that are based on theories of child development, such as those devised by the Swiss psychologist Jean Piaget. In Piagetian theory, children progress through a set of biologically predetermined, fixed, developmental stages that correlate with chronological age. Along this perceived lineal progression to adulthood, they are considered to gradually become more cognitively developed, reaching the ability to engage in abstract and hypothetical thinking in adulthood. Children are constructed as "naturally" dependent, immature, and the powerless "Other" in relation to the independent, mature, and powerful adult. Thus, addressing sexuality issues is generally upheld to be developmentally inappropriate for children.

Sexuality, like childhood, has been traditionally understood as fixed, biologically determined, and linked to human biological development. The boundary between adulthood and childhood is considered to be physiological sexual maturity, which begins at puberty. Prior to puberty, children's sexuality is perceived to be immature or nonexistent.

Scholars (Butler 1990; Gittins 1998) have begun to critique these understandings of childhood and sexuality, arguing that both are socially constructed. Educators, such as Robinson (2002, 418), have begun to challenge the assumption that adults must define "what children should/should not be, or should/should not know." Robinson (2002) and others (Cahill and Theilheimer 1999) highlight the contradiction that children are "too young" to deal with sexuality issues although heterosexual **desire** is part of everyday early childhood settings. Mock heterosexual weddings, for example, along with young children's participation in kissing games and girlfriends/boyfriends normalises the construction of heterosexual desire and gendered performances in young children's lives.

See also Children of the Rainbow Curriculum; Curriculum Primary; Families, LGBT; Gender Roles; Identity Development; Literature, Early Childhood; Parents, LGBT; Sexism; Sexuality Education.

Heteronormativity and **compulsory heterosexuality** also contribute to the difficulty of integrating LGBTQ issues in the early childhood curriculum. Unless lesbian or gay parents are known to early childhood educators in their children's settings there is an assumption that children's parents are heterosexual. Most often early childhood educators have contact with one parent, usually the mother; the absent parent is often assumed to be a working male. Hence, many gay and lesbian parents are invisible or engage in **passing**, out of fear and/or concern for themselves or their children. Compulsory heterosexuality is institutionalized in everyday school practices. For example, administrative forms frequently assume language anticipating a partner of the other gender, and children's books routinely feature stories of families headed by a mother and father. Even in early childhood settings that are more inclusive, LGBTQ issues are often only seen as relevant to educators and children if there are same-sex or transsexual parents participating in the program.

Homophobia also manifests itself in a variety of ways and may be experienced by educators, children, parents, and nonteaching staff. Some adults might believe in destructive myths that link pedophilia with lesbians and gay men who work in the school, or to lesbian and gay parents whose children are in attendance. Children, too, can be teased by other children for having parents who do not fit the two-gender model. LGBTQ issues are often excluded from early childhood education curriculum for fear of negative responses of parents or the community.

Despite the existence of these and other barriers to incorporating LGBTQ content and redressing homophobia and heterosexism in the early childhood curriculum, educators throughout the Western world are taking up these issues with children, as a crucial part of their planning, programming, and policy development. In some early childhood settings, dealing with these issues are legitimated through curriculum planning. For example, particular LGBTQ events throughout the year, such as **National Coming Out Day** in the United States or the Sydney Gay and Lesbian Mardi Gras in Australia, provide valuable opportunities for educators to work with children around difference, LGBTQ content, homophobia, and **heterosexism**. In terms of programming, LGBTQ content is incorporated into broader discussions of family diversity through the utilization of reading books that have positive lesbian and gay characters and themes. The introduction of LGBTQ issues also occurs through discussions around the meanings of different symbols, such as using yellow triangles to identify Jewish people and **pink triangles** to identify gays and lesbians

My House. Courtesy of Vicki Harding. Illustrated and © by Chris Bray-Cotton

during the Holocaust, or developing a portfolio of positive alternative family images. Such strategies are supported by **educational policies** inclusive of LGBTQ people, which specifically incorporate LGBTQ terminology rather than less specific terms such as family diversity or lifestyle choices.

Nevertheless, there is still inadequate recognition of this area in official early childhood education accreditation guidelines and policies. Most frequently, these documents allude to recognizing the cultural diversity that exists in children's families. Here there is some scope for interested parties to include a focus on nonheterosexist education, although it is not actually specified in the documents. In some states in Australia, for example, the generic term "lifestyle choice" is used to include sexual orientation in official early childhood curriculum frameworks. However, some debate has arisen about the problematic usage of this term and its failure to reflect appropriate understandings and the complexities of constructions of identities. That is, the term "lifestyle choice" once again renders LGBTQ identities as invisible, silencing the differential power relations that surround nonheterosexual and heterosexual relationships. Ironically, the latter are not considered a "lifestyle choice."

So what are some principles or key aspects for a nonheterosexist, LGBTQ inclusive early childhood curriculum? First, there should be a recognition of the widespread prevalence of heteronormativity in the every day lives of children (in and outside early childhood education contexts) and of the active role that children play in its constitution and policing. This recognition would include an understanding of the notion of compulsory heterosexuality and the way that it operates to make LGBTQ people invisible, such as the assumed absence of gay and lesbian parents in early childhood settings or, more broadly, in the lives of children. Proactive early childhood eductors can challenge and deconstruct children's everyday heteronormative assumptions such as only men and women can love one another, get "married," or have children. These discussions primarily aim to disrupt normalizing gender/sexuality binaries (e.g., male/female; heterosexual/homosexual) that underpin heteronormativity.

Secondly, there would be a focus on the development of children's critical thinking around heteronormativity and the social, political, and economic factors that underpin inequities faced by LGBTQ people. This would include an awareness of the diversity that exists in LGBTQ people's lives, as well as the pleasure and success that can be experienced within nonheterosexual relationships. Discussing "out" sporting, music, or media celebrities that may be known to young children, or encouraging educators and parents who are in committed relationships to share their experiences are two examples. Such discussions also include a focus on developing children's critical thinking in relation to the social and political factors contributing to exclusion, harassment, and bullying based on homophobia and heterosexism.

Third, an inclusive early childhood curriculum would incorporate a nonheterosexist perspective through using the increasing number of multimedia resources available (e.g., *It's Elementary*). This could also include utilizing relevant local community symbols and celebrations such as the **Rainbow Flag**, Pride Week and the Sydney Gay and Lesbian Mardi Gras to foster a positive, critical awareness of difference and to celebrate diversity.

Finally, such a curriculum works in conjunction with a whole setting approach to antiheterosexism from organizational frameworks and policies (e.g., antiharassment/antibullying) to practices (e.g., reviewing enrollment forms for assumptions of heterosexuality) and pedagogy. This not only includes integrating LGBTQ perspectives in curriculum programming, planning, and policy, but developing a comprehensive educational program for teachers, nonteaching staff, families, and the broader community. Workshops can be offered to educators and other staff members around homophobia and heterosexism, which may include deconstructing the intersections of the discourses of childhood and sexuality. Parents and friends could be invited to a screening and discussion of *It's Elementary: Talking about Gay Issues in Schools* (USA 1997) and relevant articles for inclusion in the school's newsletter.

Bibliography

Baker, Jean M. 2002. *How Homophobia Hurts Children*. Binghamton, NY: Harrington Park Press.

Butler, Judith. 1990. *Gender Trouble*. New York: Routledge.

Cahill, Betsy and Rachel Theilheimer. 1999. "Stonewall in the Housekeeping Area: Gay and Lesbian Issues in the Early Childhood Classroom." Pp.39–48 in *Queering Elementary Education*. Edited by William J. Letts IV and James T. Sears. Lanham, MD: Rowman and Littlefield Publishers.

Casper, Virginia, Harriet K. Cuffaro, Steven Schultz, Jonathan Silin, and Elaine Wickens. 1998. "Towards a Most Thorough Understanding of the World: Sexual Orientation and Early Childhood Education." Pp. 72–97 in *Gender in Early Childhood*. Edited by Nicola Yelland. London: Routledge.

Derman-Sparks, Louise, and the Anti Bias Task Force. 1989. *The Anti-Bias Curriculum*. National Association for the Education of Young Children. Washington DC: Author.

Gittins, Diana. 1998. *The Child in Question*. London: Macmillan.

Kissen, Rita, ed. 2002. *Getting Ready for Benjamin: Preparing Teachers for Sexual Diversity in the Classroom*. Lanham, MD: Rowman and Littlefield.

Robinson, Kerry H. 2002. "Making the Invisible Visible: Gay and Lesbian Issues in Early Childhood Education." *Contemporary Issues in Early Childhood* 3, no.3: 415–434.

Web Sites

Early Childhood Care and Education Resources. January 2005. Peggy Riehl. Accessed May 30, 2005. http://home.sprintmail.com/~peggyriehl/ Links to a range of resources around early childhood education, and includes a very useful link to resources for dealing with LGBT issues in early childhood contexts.

GLSEN Resource Centre, Curricula. Gay Lesbian and Straight Education Network. May 2005. Accessed May 30, 2005. http://www.glsen.org/cgi-bin/iowa/home.html. Provides numerous curricula resources that deal with a range of issues on discrimination based on sexual orientation and gender identity that are relevant to early childhood education.

Resources and Networking for Gender Equity in Early childhood (RANGE). March 2005. Accessed May 30, 2005. http://www.edfac.unimelb.edu.au/LED/RANGE/links.htm. An informal network of early childhood professionals in Australia who are committed to gender equity in early childhood. Gives valuable links to resources for educators in the area of LGBT issues, including those developed in Australia.

Curriculum, Higher Education

Jeremy P. Hayes, Todd K. Herriott, and Penny J. Rice

The experiences of students in higher education encompasses not only the curriculum taught within the classroom but also extracurricular experiences such as student organizations, **residence life**, **fraternities** and **sororities**, athletic participation, and daily campus activities. For lesbian, gay, bisexual, and transgender (LGBT) **college age students**, the degree to which they feel included or safe in these activities varies from campus to campus and from activity to activity. While the presence of

See also Curriculum, Antibias; Cocurricular Activities; College Age Students; College Campus Programming; Coming Out, Youth; Dance, Teaching of; Educational Policies; Geography, Teaching of; Men's Studies; Political Science, Teaching of; Science, Teaching of.

233

LGBT persons on college campuses both in the United States and internationally is not a new phenomenon, the presence of students who openly identify as LGBT is more recent. As their visibility has increased, so, too, has the visibility of LGBT-related issues. Campuses, as microcosms of the larger society, have met this increased visibility of LGBT people and issues with mixed reactions. On many campuses, **homophobia** and **heterosexism** have become more evident, contributing to a hostile or unsafe campus environment. In the classroom, LGBT-related issues and portrayals of LGBT people are often based solely on **stereotypes** or they are left out entirely even though there are many colleges which include LGBT courses and support LGBT student organizations.

The earliest official student organizations for gay and lesbian individuals emerged in the 1970s. From their beginnings, these organizations have served as a primary location for LGBT people to interact socially as well as politically. These organizations have often been the source of LGBT-related campus **activism**. Throughout modern history, college campuses and college students have played a role in many social movements around the world. The LGBT movement is no exception. These early pioneers in LGBT activism did much to improve the **school climate** simply by being open about their sexual orientations and gender identities. For many, the presence of openly identified LGBT individuals helped to alleviate fears of being the only one. The continued LGBT-related activism of the 1980s and the outbreak of **AIDS** brought LGBT health issues into mainstream media and contributed to a further increase in the visibility of LGBT students and issues on campuses.

LGBT youth and issues have also begun to be more explicitly included in non-LGBT-specific student organizations and activities. Other diversity-related or social justice-oriented organizations have intentionally taken on LGBT-related issues. LGBT students have visibly and invisibly taken on leadership roles in non-LGBT-specific organizations and have served as the LGBT voice within those organizations. Student government bodies have created positions specifically designed to address LGBT-related issues as part of initiatives related to diversity and multiculturalism. On some campuses, LGBT students can choose not only from a number of LGBT-related organizations, but also from a host of other groups in which they can openly identify.

An additional arena in which LGBT students have become more visible is within university housing or residence life. For many LGBT students, these close living quarters and shared bathroom spaces have been some of the most daunting places in which to come out. Residence halls are often areas of increased hostility toward LGBT people (Evans and Briodo 1999). Heterosexist attitudes pervade the majority of campus life but tend to be particularly intense within living areas where there is a greater opportunity for violence and hostility. The proximity to non-LGBT people in what can easily be seen as intimate spaces has been the cause of a great deal of fear for LGBT students.

As LGBT students have continued to become more visible throughout campus life, their presence is being seen more and more in areas previously considered out of bounds, including athletics and the Greek system of fraternities and sororities. Historically these areas have been areas in which it is particularly difficult for LGBT people to be open because of the strong gender norms and assumptions. The increase of visible LGBT Greek community members has forced the larger Greek campus communities to reevaluate previously held beliefs and stereotypes. This increase has not been met without resistance. Nevertheless, more LGBT Greek community members have begun to openly identify as LGBT and challenge a Greek community system that historically not only denied them access, but also acted openly hostile to LGBT people outside of the Greek community. Similarly, there has been an increase in openly LGBT identified athletes in colleges and universities. **Sports,** a bastion of hypermasculinity and heterosexuality, has also been faced with the challenge of reconciling its ingrained homophobia and **gender role** constraints with the reality of their proven, star athletes coming out and openly identifying as LGBT.

In general the inclusion of LGBT-related issues in the academic courses has been limited. However, the last thirty years have seen an expansion of the curriculum and an increase in visibility of LGBT experiences. The advent and rise of **women's studies** programs on campuses—primarily in the United States—brought with it the inclusion and open discussion of lesbian experiences as part of the larger **women's movement.** This was then followed by larger discussions of men and masculinities and issues of **gender identity.** These discussions gave birth to **LGBT studies** or **queer studies.** Following patterns similar to various ethnic studies programs, LGBT studies programs offered for many their first glimpse into the lives and experiences of LGBT identified individuals in a classroom context. Just as the scholarship increased and expanded, so did the call for a more inclusive curriculum.

While much more typical within humanities fields, information regarding LGBT people, experiences, and history has begun to work its way into the previously heterosexually dominated classroom discussions. As was the situation with women's studies, it has become clear that there is a need not only for specialized curriculum focused on LGBT issues, but also for cross-disciplinary inclusion of LGBT themes. This impact of LGBT studies has meant that there has been an increased demand for resources and information regarding LGBT issues from a wide range of disciplines, including **psychology, theater; biology, art, history,** religion, **music, literature,** economics, **philosophy,** and even business and marketing. Many students today find themselves face-to-face with queer-related content or even an LGBT-identified instructor. Within the field of education, particularly teacher preparation programs, there have been initiatives toward gender-free and **multicultural education.** These initiatives, while not exclusively LGBT-focused or even LGBT-positive, have challenged the current hegemonic power of white, male, heterosexuality in the academy.

As campuses face an increasingly diverse student population, the curriculum has diversified. Professors of art history or literature are less likely to avoid discussions of artists' and writers' **sexual orientation** or same-sex behaviors, especially when looking at motivations, experiences, and personal expressions of self in their work. For example, Willa Cather's *O Pioneers* can be better understood when given in the context that she was not only a woman on the frontier but a woman-identified woman. Likewise, the subtle sensuousness of Caravaggio's male figures, depicted in his *Narcissus* or *St. John the Baptist (Youth with Ram),* becomes more telling when the viewer understands the same-sex attraction of the painter. Women's studies programs have continued to become more inclusive of different sexual orientations and gender identities as part of their criticism of the dominant heterosexual paradigm. Since the delisting of homosexuality as a disorder in the ***Diagnostic & Statistical Manual of Mental Disorders*** and by the American Psychological Association, psychology and counseling curricula have become more inclusive, and even general history courses are more likely to cover LGBT events such as the Nazi's persecution of gays and lesbians during World War II or the **Stonewall**

Riots of 1969. The inclusion of such content and courses is, in part, the result of a new generation of faculty with expertise in this area and an academic infrastructure that support LGBT **research** and scholarship.

Still, proponents of LGBT-inclusive curricula argue that by not including LGBT information, academia perpetuates a conspiracy of silence and an egregious neglect of the developmental needs of LGBT students and their **allies**. The relative absence of discussions of LGBT people and experiences within the curriculum creates disequilibrium for LGBT students and negatively impacts their growth and **identity development** when they do not see their identities and experiences reflected as do non-LGBT students. Opponents of wider inclusion of LGBT themes question the propriety of such information, the level to which inclusion would be germane to the topic, or the application of twenty-first century identity constructs to historic figures and cultural contexts.

The past twenty years also have seen the development of campus LGBT centers across the United States and in Canada. These **college campus resource centers** are frequently staffed by student affairs professionals charged with the mission of providing support to LGBT people on campus as well as educating the general campus community about LGBT-related issues. This increase in LGBT-related services and staff positions has prompted higher education programs to include LGBT student identity development theory and other training in supporting and working with LGBT students, as part of their student affairs curriculum. On campuses with and without specific LGBT centers, **Safe Zone programs** have developed to help LGBT students visually identify LGBT-supportive faculty and staff. Campus policies have continued to become more inclusive by adding sexual orientation and **gender identity** to **antidiscrimination** and nonharassment policies; extending employment benefits to same-sex domestic partners is becoming standard practice across the United States.

Bibliography

Cramer, Elizabeth P., ed. 2002. *Addressing Homophobia and Heterosexism on College Campuses*. Binghamton, NY: Haworth Press.

Evans, Nancy J., and Ellen M. Briodo. 1999. "Coming Out in College Residence Halls: Negotiation, Meaning Making, Challenges, Supports" *Journal of College Student Development* 40, no. 6: 658–667.

Evans, Nancy J., and Vernon A. Wall, eds. 1991. *Beyond Tolerance: Gays, Lesbians and Bisexuals on Campus*. Lanham, MD: University Press of America.

Howard, Kim, and Annie Stevens, eds. 2000. *Out & About Campus: Personal Accounts by Lesbian, Gay, Bisexual, & Transgendered College Students*. Los Angeles: Alyson Books.

Sanlo, Ronni L., ed. 1998. *Working With Lesbian, Gay, Bisexual, and Transgender College Students: A Handbook for Faculty and Administrators*. Westport, CT: Greenwood Press.

Wall, Vernon A., and Nancy J. Evans, eds. 1999. *Toward Acceptance: Sexual Orientation Issues on Campus*. Lanham, MD: University Press of America.

Web Site

Finding an LGBT-Friendly Campus. April 2004. Gay Lesbian Straight Education Network. Accessed May 30, 2005. http://www.glsen.org/cgi-bin/iowa/all/library/record/1652.html GLSEN has recently begun addressing issues within higher education as well, including information about queer friendly campuses and scholarships for LGBT students.

Curriculum, Primary

Emma Renold

The ways in which lesbian, gay, bisexual, transgender, and questioning (LGBTQ) issues are perceived as both irrelevant and inappropriate to an early childhood curriculum persist well into the primary years and the primary curriculum. Preteen **childhood** continues to be represented as a time of presumed sexual innocence. Often, the only option available when discussing children and sexuality is within the context of **sexual abuse** and exploitation. There continues to be widespread belief that children should not know anything about sexuality. Sexuality is continually reinscribed as the property of the adult, where adult power erases any notion of children as active social agents in thinking, feeling, and doing sexuality. By and large, children are assumed to be either immune to, or passive recipients of sexual representations within the entertainment and media industry. Primary school-aged children (ages five through eleven), however, show considerable knowledge about a range of sexual issues (Buckingham and Bragg 2003). Some scholars have suggested that educators and policy makers should not debate whether children are sexual beings, but critically think about the ways in which adults respond to, treat, regulate, punish, and ultimately create children's sexualities, much of which is highly hetero-gendered and age-specific.

When it comes to sexuality, the primary school curriculum generally operates to protect, promote, and nurture children's sexual innocence. The idea that sexuality is something peculiar to adults and adulthood or even "older" teenage childhood has been challenged by scholars as both short-sighted and dangerous. How children are taught and how they learn about sexuality is either delayed (until they are older) or limited to **sexuality education** programs, which focus only upon heteronormative biological and reproductive issues and thus silence teaching and learning about LGBTQ sexualities as well as homophobic and heterosexist abuse and **discrimination**. Heterosexuality has only recently been explicitly addressed by **research** as a pervasive and normalizing presence within the primary school. The ways in which **heteronormativity** is embedded within official **educational policies** and practices of the taught curriculum and children's informal and tacit sexual learning within the hidden curriculum is a key feature of this literature (Epstein, O'Flynn, and Telford 2003; Renold 2005). Overcoming **heterosexism** and **homophobia** will involve some radical disruptions of what society thinks children should or shouldn't "know," "be," or "do" sexually.

Feminists have long shown how romanticized notions of the sexually innocent child profoundly endanger children (Kitzinger 1997). Social scientists drawing on **queer theory** have reiterated the danger of sexual innocence by drawing attention to the gendering of sexual innocence. Although children's sexuality or sexual knowledge has been the focus of primary school research, much of the discussion has revolved around girls' emerging heterosexualities, as indicated by their changing pubertal bodies and their induction in and graduation to a heterosexualised

See Also Agency; Curriculum, Antibias; Biology, Teaching of; Compulsory Heterosexuality; Curriculum, Early Childhood; Feminism; Gender Roles; Identity Development; Literature, Early Childhood.

adolescence (Thorne 1993). Boys, however, are also inscribed within discourses of heterosexuality as they "do" and "become" boys. They must prove they are "real boys" by engaging in "masculine" behavior (e.g., fighting) or traditional sporting activities (e.g., soccer) and by avoiding traditionally "feminine" behaviors or activities (e.g., crying or playing with Barbie dolls). Failure to conform to dominant gender traits can result in gendered (e.g., **"sissy boy"** "girl" **"tomboy"**) and homophobic (**"queer,"** "poof") name-calling.

Writing over twenty years ago, Raphaela Best's educational ethnography of boys and girls in their first four years of schooling was one of the first published accounts of the primary school as key social and cultural site for the production of children's sexual learning and **sexual identity** work. Describing children's sexual learning as the "third hidden curriculum" (the former two being the official academic and hidden gender curriculum), Best (1983) recognized the school arena as a central erotic and sexual playground for children. Only recently has research focused upon the heteronormativity of children's sexual learning, most notably in studies of preteenage gender relations.

From clothes and sports to friendship and play, research is starting to explore the (hetero)sexualization of school-based gender identities and peer group cultures within Best's third hidden curriculum (Epstein 1997). Sexual learning takes place within:

- Children's imagined heteronormative futures (through writing, reading, and story-telling)
- Traditional games, rhymes, and **popular culture** (e.g., kiss-chase)
- Heterogendered/heterosexualized "curriculum of the body" (e.g., from popular fashion and cosmetics, to **body image** and body language)
- Children's (hetero)dating cultures: "going out," **"dating."** "two-timing," and "dumping"
- Heterosexual/heterosexist **harassment** and gender-based **bullying** (e.g., sexually abusive language, e.g., homophobic name-calling).

Debunking the myth that heterosexual relations symbolize entry into **"adolescence,"** studies into children's romantic cultures highlight the pressures of compulsory heterosexuality through an increasingly prevalent boyfriend/girlfriend culture. Research has shown how children's friendships are often organized and mediated around children's dating cultures and how everyday interactions between boys and girls are heterosexualized (Davies 1993). Other researchers have explored how sexual and romantic teasing creates and maintains social, gendered, and sexual hierarchies and how children's sexual cultures cannot be separated from other social and cultural differences such as race, ethnicity, religion, and disability.

Researchers are also attending to the ways in which primary school-aged children are subjected, or subject others, to physical and verbal forms of homophobic/ antigay and heterosexist bullying and harassment. Such behaviors are often the means by which many children define themselves as "normal" (heternormative) boys and girls. Some research suggests that although all children experience some form of gendered and sexualized teasing, it is often those girls and boys who subvert and resist (hetero)normative gender identities who routinely receive homophobic and antigay abuse (Renold 2002). Children may well express prejudice and fear, and these must be supportively dealt with (Ray and Jolly 2002); lessons tackling gendered/sexual bullying will need careful thought and planning.

The forces of heteronormativity regulating peer group relations also underpin official "sex and relationship" education guidance and the formal curriculum in primary schools. Teachers are complicit in reinforcing children's heteronormative values and imagined futures (Epstein 1997). Such (hetero)familial discourses (e.g., marriage and babies) are explicitly prescribed within much of sex education. For example, the United Kingdom's Sex and Relationship Education guidance states that "children should be taught about the nature of marriage and its importance for family life and for bringing up children" (DfEE 2000, 11: para 1.21). Throughout the teacher guidelines there are numerous references promoting "heterosexuality" despite the DfEE's specific claim that the guidance "is not about the promotion of **sexual orientation.**" Gay, lesbian, bisexual, transgender, or questioning identities are either invisible or only raised in relation to (homophobic) "bullying" or "harassment."

Observing a primary school sex education lesson for ten-year-olds, Epstein, O'Flynn, and Telford (2003) illustrate just how disenabling and disempowering working within the constraints of a (hetero)normative and narrow pedagogic practice can be for both teachers and pupils. For instance, the lesson Epstein observed added little to children's existing knowledge and provided no opportunity for any kind of real learning to take place, particularly in relation to responding to children's concerns, knowledge, and experiences. Lesbian and gay sexualities raised by the children, within the context of "rude" words or as terms of abuse, went unchallenged. Children's attempts to draw upon their relationship cultures or accounts of "bad" or "dangerous" sexual encounters (e.g., **sexual harassment**) were quickly dismissed.

In contrast, teachers specifically need to:

- Recognize the prevalence of heteronormativity in the everyday lives of children and the active role they play in its policing.
- Encourage children's critical thinking around heteronormativity.
- Develop an inclusive curriculum incorporating a nonheterosexist perspective.
- Construct a whole-school approach to antiheterosexism from organizational frameworks and policies and practices such as antibullying and equal opportunity policies (Claire 1993).

Many educators committed to a fully inclusive sexuality education stress the importance of using pupils' experiences as starting points for the development of programs and policies. First, however, educational practitioners need to reflect on their experiences and disrupt their normalised assumptions about what constitutes "age-appropriate," "gender-appropriate," and "sexually-appropriate" knowledge and behavior. An examination of how these assumptions are reinforced in their practice, embedded in the official and informal school curriculum and policy should follow.

Developing children's critical thinking can be achieved using a variety of pedagogic child-friendly strategies (Ray and Jolly 1998). These could include:

- Drama, games, and role-play to explore themes critiquing heteronormative accounts of "what is a family" or "being a boy"/ "being a girl."

- Pictures, **cartoons**, advertisements, and magazines to trigger discussions on a range of topics such as gender/sexual **stereotyping**, bullying, relationships, appearance, and dating.

- Anonymous question boxes that encourage children to place anonymous questions they want answered or debated about gender, sexuality, and LGBTQ issues.

- Circle time where small groups of children seated in a circle undertake weekly planned activities (e.g., on diversity, difference, and discrimination). Stories, poems, songs, media events, like Gay Pride Week, can all be used as "starting points" to discuss LGBTQ issues. Circle time encourages children to consider the views of others and helps them express their own.

- Using fiction and poetry to explore LGBTQ issues (e.g., relationships, families, etc.) and challenge heterosexist storylines. Useful texts include: *Asha's Mums* (Elwin and Paulse 1990), *Everybody's Different* (Langoulant 1990), *Daddy's Wedding* (Willhoite 1996), *Oliver Button is a Sissy* (de Paola 1990), *Gloria Goes to Gay Pride* (Newman 1992).

Bibliography

Best, Raphaela. 1983. *We've All Got Scars: What Girls and Boys Learn in Elementary School*. Bloomington: Indiana University Press.

Buckingham, David, and Sara Bragg. 2003. *Young People, Sex and the Media: The Facts of Life?* Basingstoke: Palgrave.

Claire, Hilary, Janet Maybin, and Joan Swann, eds. 1993. *Equality Matters: Case Studies from the Primary School*. London: Multilingual Matters

Davies, Bronwyn. 1993. *Shards of Glass: Children Reading and Writing Beyond Gendered Identities*. New Jersey: Hampton Press.

Department of Education and Employment (DfEE). 2000. *Guidance of Sex and Relationship Education*. London: Author.

Epstein, Debbie. 1997. "Cultures of Schooling/Cultures of Sexuality." *International Journal of Inclusive Education* 1, no. 1: 37–53.

Epstein, Debbie, Sara O'Flynn, and David Telford. 2003. *Silenced Sexualities in Schools and Universities*. Stoke on Trent: Trentham Books.

Kitzinger, Jenny. 1997. "Who Are You Kidding? Children, Power and the Struggle Against Sexual Abuse." Pp. 165–190 in *Constructing and Reconstructing Childhood: Contemporary Issues in the Sociological Study of Childhood*. Edited by Alison James and Alan Prout. 2nd ed. London: Falmer Press.

Ray, Caroline, and Janine Jolly. 2002. *Sex and Relationships Education for Primary Age Children: Sex Education Forum Factsheet 28*. National Children's Bureau Publications: London.

Renold, Emma. 2002. "'Presumed Innocence': (Hetero)sexual, Homophobic and Heterosexist Harassment amongst Children in the Primary School" *Childhood* 9, no. 4: 415–433.

———. 2005. *Girls, Boys and Junior Sexualities: Exploring Gender and Sexual Relations in the Primary School*. London: RoutledgeFalmer.

Thorne, Barrie. 1993. *Gender Play: Boys and Girls in School*, Buckingham: Open University Press.

Walkerdine, Valerie. 1999. "Violent Boys and Precocious Girls: Regulating Childhood at the End of the Millennium." *Contemporary Issues in Early Childhood* 1, no.1: 3–23.

Web Sites

Educational Action Challenging Homophobia (EACH). Accessed November 16, 2004. http://www.eachaction.org.uk. Challenges homophobia through education and schools specifically. EACH Web site provides useful links to resources for educators, offers a confidential helpline and delivers training to schools on a range of issues concerning sexual orientation and homophobia (including schools and youth groups).

Schools Out! Sue Sanders, Paul Patrick and AnneMarie Talbot. October 2004. Accessed November 16, 2004. http://www.schools-out.org.uk/ A range of formal and informal support networks and campaigns for all lesbians, gay men, bisexuals and transpersons in education. Offers downloadable curricula materials on LGBTQ issues (including primary years).

Sex Education Forum. 2003. Accessed November 17, 2004. http://www.ncb.org.uk/sef UK-based NGO that aims to ensure that *all* children and young people receive their entitlement to good quality sex and relationship education in a variety of settings. Web site offers free and downloadable publications and fact sheets for educators on a range of sexuality issues.

Curriculum, Secondary

Arthur Lipkin

Gay-inclusive curricula include readings, guided discussions, guest presentations, media representations, and student research typically serving students in middle through high school. Same-gender sexuality in individual, cultural, and political contexts across disciplines, particularly the arts and human sciences, are seldom found in existing school curricula. Inclusive curricula can increase understanding of diversity, lessen antigay bigotry, and foster the healthy development of all youth by helping students:

- understand the nature of **sexual identity** and same-gender attraction, and how they have been expressed in various times and cultures;
- understand the significance of past and current **research** and theories about the "causes" of homosexuality;
- analyze how the homosexuality or **bisexuality** of an historical figure, author, artist influenced or might have influenced his or her life and work;
- know something about the history of the gay/lesbian community in Western societies and current issues in LGBT life;
- appreciate the diversity and different experiences of sexual minorities within a country and around the world.

See also Adolescence; Curriculum, Antibias; Films, Youth and Educators in; Literature, Secondary School; LGBT Studies; Multicultural Education; School Safety and Safe School Zones.

More than a description of particular kinds of people, an inclusive secondary curriculum explains how same-gender attraction became a part of human identity historically, how sexual identity labels were invented, and how such labeling influences our contemporary understanding of the past and present. Moreover, it connects sexuality to a variety of other equity issues regarding **race**, gender, **social class**, and other categories.

In **Europe** and North America such school curricula are rare. Spontaneous comments or brief discussions of homosexuality arise occasionally and special events like a diversity day panel may appear. Curriculum units have been made available in only a few public school systems in the United States like San Francisco and Cambridge, Massachusetts. **GLBT Educational Equity** (GLEE), established in 1999, has encouraged curriculum development and distribution in Europe. However, there is no evidence that comprehensive gay-inclusive curricula are being employed consistently anywhere.

The absence of a gay curriculum, however, does not maintain schools as "sexuality-free" or neutral spaces. Classrooms and lessons are already sexualized. Moreover, many students, at least from preadolescence, are active players in the cultural dramas of sex and gender. Having a **crush**, **dating**, going steady, breaking up, and the prescriptions/proscriptions of masculinity and femininity preoccupy many young people. Curricula reinforce a heterosexual norm in arguably every subject area. Examples of this **heteronormativity** include glorifying the heterosexual affair in Hemingway's *A Farewell to Arms*, while ignoring the homosocial/homoerotic themes in Melville's *Moby Dick*, or highlighting Anthony's relationship with Cleopatra, but not Alexander's with Hepahaestion. At the same time, there is a hidden curriculum of heterosexist notions and homophobic behaviors. Tchaikovsky's homosexuality is either unrecognized or thought irrelevant to his musical genius, and teachers commonly "don't hear" antigay slurs in the classroom.

LGBT students are major beneficiaries of inclusive curricula. But studying the range of human sexual feeling and gender expression is also beneficial to straight-identified students who find themselves pressured into narrow, inflexible sexuality and **gender roles**. Moreover, presenting sexual diversity without embarrassment or condemnation evidences a teacher's acceptance of sexuality and facilitates better **communication** with all students. When students volunteer that they or people dear to them are not heterosexual, the class has an opportunity for immediacy. People learn first how to be considerate of those around them for whom they have a predisposition to care and with whom they share a community.

An effective and sexually inclusive curriculum is open, nuanced, and based on good scholarship. Merely challenging homophobic **harassment** can be the germ of a curriculum when it leads to a disruption of the hidden heterosexist curriculum. Other beginning strategies might include:

- putting up a "Safe-Zone for LGBT People" sticker;
- putting up a poster of LGBT youth of all backgrounds;
- putting up a poster of famous LGBT people of all backgrounds;
- addressing some **stereotypes** and misconceptions;
- inviting guest speakers from the LGBT community;
- celebrating **National Coming Out Day**, Gay Pride Day, the **National Day of Silence**

Incorporating LGBT content into existing or new courses is not easy, even beyond religious, cultural, and political considerations. It takes time to build the trust required for self-exposure and honest dialogue, without defensiveness or disapproval.

Homosexuality might be discussed in health classes (Telljohan and Price 1995). Yet national and regional differences abound. Homosexual inclusion in British secondary school sex education, for example, has been hampered by political interference, whereas mention of gays in Dutch sex education curricula is determined by educators and is nonjudgmental, albeit brief (Lewis and Knijn 2003). Homosexuality is frequently raised in connection with **HIV education**. Even so, prevention typically is taught with a heterosexual slant. And when homosexuality is broached only in this context, students can conclude that it is mainly about pathology and the physical and not about pleasure, **spirituality**, and power, like other sexual relationships. Secondary family life curriculum could be expanded to include **families** who are LGBT alternative families along with issues such as spousal relationships, **adoption**, child rearing, and **children of LGBT parents**.

The needs of disabled adolescents are often ignored in health curricula. Although they are as sexually experienced, severely disabled boys and girls have less other-sex attraction and are less sure about their **sexual orientation;** those with mild **disabilities** are *more* likely to experience same-sex attraction than are the nondisabled (Cheng and Udry 2002). Courses are good venues for LGBT inclusion. Topics might include: same-gender sexuality and **multiple genders** from North and **South America** to **Asia** and **Africa**; the emergence of gay and lesbian geographic communities; the **Stonewall** riots, homosexuality as a mental illness; the role and image of women and **transgender** people in the movement; the effect of HIV/**AIDS** on the community; gays in the military; marriage rights; and how the gay movement compares to other struggles. LGBT history offers universal insights into stigma, identity, subcultures, and survival. Often, current events can be a springboard. For instance, in 2004, public debate about same-sex marriage prompted the Gay, **Lesbian, and Straight Education Network** to develop a curriculum guide for discussing the topic in high schools.

Support Services for Sexual Minority Youth of the San Francisco School Health Department has prepared units for United States and world history classes on **homophobia** and **heterosexism**, civil rights and lesbian and gay organizing in the 1960s and 1970s as well as lesbians, gays, and bisexuals in the Harlem Renaissance and the Holocaust. There are no resources, however, to monitor the extent of their use and impact in the city's twenty-two high schools.

More typical are the efforts of a few individuals in a handful of schools. For instance, a heterosexual sociology teacher at Glastonbury Connecticut High School uses newspaper clippings and taped television shows for a two-week unit on gays and lesbians, which concludes with LGBT speakers.

Homosexuality in autobiography and literature can be explicit or implied. Asking whether particular authors experienced same-gender attractions, what these feelings may have signified to them, and how both are reflected in their work can bring a new perspective to writers like Henry Thoreau, Willa Cather, Langston Hughes, Federico Garcia-Lorca, and Somerset Maugham. Writing classes can include gay-related exercises such as opinion pieces about gay rights, research on historical figures, fiction with LGBT characters, and first-person exercises in a **queer** voice. Writing is vital self-expression for some sexual minority youth. As an incentive to authenticity, instructors might divide classes into small private writing groups and students might mark some of their writing "teacher's eyes only."

Tenth grade American literature classes at Lyman Hall High School in Wallingford, Connecticut read *The Laramie Project*, a play based on the homophobic murder of **Matthew Shepard**. Each teacher is free to devise a two to three week curriculum around the text. One asks students to research state and national **hate crimes** laws as well as specific hate incidents involving other prejudices and to keep a journal while reading the play. They also perform scenes and view a taped production. A few participated in a panel discussion after a live performance. Some interviewed **administrators** about the numbers of minorities at their school and how minority issues are addressed in the curriculum.

A **gay–straight alliance** at another Connecticut high school received a $1,000 grant from a television station to develop fifteen sociology units, ranging from gay parenting to antihomophobia school reform. Teachers choose the lessons, but the donors require proof of the curriculum's use.

Film-related activities can teach critical viewing skills and content. *Ma Vie en Rose* (1997) from Belgium and *Blue Gate Crossing* (2002) from Taiwan can enhance students' appreciation of the international scope of homosexualities. Likewise, gay content in English as a Second Language (**ESL**) materials creates opportunities to broach sexual diversity with students from other cultures (Nelson 1995).

Students can also explore sexual identity issues in the graphic and performing **arts**. Much painting, sculpture, **theater**, photography, **music**, and **dance** is related to sexual imagination, relationships, and **desire**—from Michelangelo to Kahlo, Schubert to Strayhorn, and Diaghileff to Ailey. Photo essayist Duane Michaels' *Salute, Walt Whitman* (1996), for example, literally illustrates the influence of the poet on the gay artist.

Biography is also usually part of general **science** courses. Leonardo DaVinci, Francis Bacon, Florence Nightingale, John Maynard Keynes, and Margaret Mead were gay or bisexual and there are resources, ranging from the *Encyclopedia on Homosexuality* to full-length books that detail the lives of these and other scientists. Homosexuality can be more thoroughly studied in **biology**, biochemistry, and psychobiology. Biological theories of the etiology of same-sex desire have been offered in language accessible to high school readers (e.g., Bailey 1995). Even word problems can be structured to remind students not to assume a heterosexual context, e.g., "Linda and Maryann are measuring their bedroom for carpet. . . ."

Physical education and **sports** curricula can address the homophobic insults that typically encourage solidarity and performance among males. It can deal with girls' being lesbian-baited for their skill and dedication to sport. Moreover, physical education can include cooperative games and dance that deemphasize conventional gender roles.

Willing teachers might begin modestly and build support among hesitant colleagues through peer persuasion, model teaching, and sharing of lesson plans. They can also devise strategies to respond to student or parent discomfort and opposition. It may help to know that in the United States over 80 percent of teens consider human sexuality and relationships equal or more important than other school subjects; three-fourths of parents support instruction on sexual orientation in comprehensive health education for grades nine and ten and 85 percent for grades eleven and twelve (SIECUS 1999).

Bibliography

Allan, Christina. 1999. "Poets of Comrades: Addressing Sexual Orientation in the English Classroom." *English Journal* 88, no. 6: 97–101.

Bailey, J. Michael. 1995. "Biological Perspectives on Sexual Orientation." Pp. 119–135 in *Lesbian, Gay and Bisexual Identities Over the Lifespan: Psychological Perspectives*. Edited by Anthony R. D'Augelli and Charlotte J. Patterson. New York: Oxford University Press.

Cheng, Mariah Mantsun, and J. Richard Udry. 2002. "Sexual Behaviors of Physically Disabled Adolescents in the United States." *Journal of Adolescent Health* 31, no. 1: 48–58.

Lampela, Laura. 2001. "Lesbian and Gay Artists in the Curriculum: A Survey of Art Teachers' Knowledge and Attitudes." *Studies in Art Education* 42, no. 2: 146–162.

Lewis, Jane, and Trudie Knijn. 2003. "Sex Education Materials in the Netherlands and in England and Wales: A Comparison of Content, Use and Teaching Practice." *Oxford Review of Education* 29, no. 1: 113–150.

Michaels, Duane. 1996. *Salute, Walt Whitman*. Santa Fe: Twin Palms Publishers.

Nelson, Cynthia. 1995. "Heterosexism and ESL: Examining Our Attitudes." *TESOL Quarterly* 27, no. 2: 143–150.

SIECUS and Advocates for Youth. 1999. *SIECUS/Advocates for Youth Survey of Americans' Views on Sexuality Education*. Washington, DC: Sexuality Information and Education Council of the United States and Advocates for Youth, 1999.

"Social Education and Sexual Identity." 2002. Special Section of *Theory and Research in Social Education* 30, no. 2: 178–319.

Telljohan, Susan K., and James H. Price. 1995. "Teaching About Sexual Orientation by Secondary Health Teachers." *Journal of School Health* 65, 1: 20.

Walling, Donovan R. 2003. "Gay- and Lesbian-Themed Novels for Classroom Reading," *Journal of Gay and Lesbian Issues in Education*, 1, no. 2: 97–108.

Web Sites

The Rainbow Special Interest Group of the National Association of Foreign Student Advisers. Accessed December 1, 2004. http://www.indiana.edu/~overseas/lesbigay/advise/esl.html. Suggestions for LGBT curricular integration on its Web site.

The Sexuality Information and Education Council of the U.S. December 2004. Accessed December 1, 2004. http://www.siecus.org. Promotes inclusive sex-education curricula for grades K-12.

D

Dance, Teaching of

Michael Gard

The teaching of dance, as with most areas of formal education, is shaped by the ongoing struggles over sexualities and "appropriate" ways for bodies to move. Dance can be a site of resistance for **queer** youth who do not fit into mainstream physical cultures, which are often dominated by the openly heterosexist and homophobic worlds of sport. By failing to conform, queer youth expose a contradiction at the heart of the idea of teaching people to dance. That is, where *dance* invites us to imagine a space in which bodies are freed from the movement conventions and constraints of everyday life, the act of *teaching* always threatens to bring bodies back under the control of wider social forces. Understanding this contradiction should remind dance teachers and educators that choices about **curriculum** and pedagogy always mean that certain ways of moving are ruled in while others are ruled out. Even more importantly, it is a reminder that movement, including the ways young people like to move and the degree to which they feel safe to move in particular ways and in particular contexts, is not the same for all people. Movement, after all, is one of the ways we announce to the world who we are.

The different ways bodies look, they ways we experience our bodies and the ways other people interpret the meaning of bodies all shape and are shaped by culture (Turner 1996). For example, substantial anthropological and sociological literatures show how apparently "natural" bodily acts such as walking, eating, and having sex vary across and within different cultures (Blacking 1977). How cultures dance has also been studied extensively; it is clear that the norms which govern general social behavior within cultural groupings are also reflected in their dance movement. The process of "teaching" young bodies (either implicitly or explicitly) in activities such as dance, then, is one of the ways in which social norms are reinforced.

Perhaps the most obvious Western example of this has been the notoriously ambivalent relationship between school **physical education** and dance. Although dance is an official component of many school physical education curricula, it has often been erased from classroom practice or taught reluctantly. In attempting to explain this phenomenon, a number of scholars have argued that physical education has generally embodied masculinist and heterosexist norms and simply perpetuated two centuries of heterosexual, white, Western anxiety about males who dance (Gard 2001; Gard 2002). Prominent among these norms are physical education's preoccupation with male-dominated competitive **sports** (and their never-too-far away homophobic traditions and practices) and its apparent aversion to movement and bodies which do not conform to its ideal of aggressive and competitive athleticism. Dance movement in general, and creative dance in particular, is often thought of as "gay" by male students, and it is this negative reaction which appears to marginalize dance within physical education (Keyworth 2001). However, we should not forget that physical education teachers often display many of these anxieties. Each year, the ranks of new physical education teachers are bolstered by youth embodying an archetypal straight, Western, sports-focused athleticism. Scholarly and anecdotal

See also Feminism; Heteronormativity; Heterosexism; Homophobia; Japan, Gay and Transgender Youth in; Queer and Queer Theory; Sexism; Sissy Boy.

evidence show that physical education has not always been a safe cultural space for queer students and teachers (Clarke 2004). Whether or not queer teachers should or are able to name their sexual identities within the school community—and for what reason—become questions which politicize the practice of teaching in ways which straight educators rarely, if ever, face.

In this context, it is interesting that some dance educators have wondered about the absence of dance within physical education as well as the comparatively small number of boys who voluntarily enroll in dance classes in or outside of school. Some have suggested that in order to attract boys, dance education experiences should be structured so that they more closely resemble sport (Crawford 1994). Here the logic appears to be that if dance can somehow be tethered to the (implicitly heterosexual) "respectability" of sports, more boys will want to dance. Incorporating sporting movements into the movement experiences that dance educators offer, these advocates try to convince boys that dance will improve their performance in sports such as football. However, if we acknowledge that the movement cultures of Western societies already privilege boys and girls who enjoy and are good at sports, then advocating for more "boy friendly" dance education experiences seems a questionable pedagogical move. Pedagogical spaces which value queer identities and allow bodies to move in unconventional ways are already scarce.

None of this is to suggest that queer youth are by definition disinterested in sport or drawn automatically to other forms of movement such as dance. At the very least, it is important to acknowledge that dance and sport have related very differently to the movement aspirations of young **gay** males and **lesbian youth**. For example, a number of feminist dance scholars have considered the historical connections between the image of the ballerina and idealised, heterosexist Western conceptions of femininity. Indeed, despite the influence of feminism and ballet's archaic traditions and high-brow trappings, ballet classes remain an extremely popular and thoroughly "normal" activity for girls, which is still not true for boys. Even though it is always dangerous to generalize or speculate about the "true" sexual identities of young women who take ballet classes and aspire to become ballerinas or professional dancers, formal dance teaching remains a space for very particular female body shapes and identities (Aalten 1997). The practice of ballet teaching, for example, is premised upon the image of thin and compliant female students; big girls, who constantly want to know why they are being asked to move in a particular way, are unlikely to be welcome.

Formal dance teaching for boys and young men presents a somewhat different picture. It is certainly true that ballet and other forms of professional dance have lost some of their stigma as "deviant" career choices. The recent popularity of mainstream movies such as *Billy Elliot* (UK 2000) and *Bootmen* (Australia 2000), which openly celebrate boys' decision to dance, suggests this stigma may continue to wane. However, the images of dancing boys crafted in these films are anything but queer, emphasizing a very straight male athleticism, no doubt with the intention of communicating the message that not all male dancers are gay. And yet it is undeniable that queer youth remain significantly overrepresented in dance training institutions. Published **research** into their experiences within dance training institutions is extremely limited, but evidence suggests that these experiences are variable (Gard 2004a; Wulff 1998). For example, some dancers have described the dance training milieu as one in which a kind of gay sexual awakening is possible, particularly if they have come from social contexts where being gay was unusual or unacceptable. In contrast, other dancers feel that, despite the presence of queer boys and young men, dance training institutions sometimes maintain a conspicuous silence about their presence, particularly if the institution is connected to a dance company which relies on corporate or government support.

On another level, it is worth pointing out that although dance training institutions appear to be comparatively welcoming to queer youth, it is equally true that much of the pedagogy and content of dance training, particularly in ballet, make sharp distinctions between the physical skills and body shapes required of male and female dancers. Although there are contemporary choreographers and dance companies that have explicitly made conventional masculinities and femininities problematic through their choreographic work (for example Pina Bausch, Michael Clarke, and Lloyd Newson's *DV8 Physical Theatre*), becoming a ballet dancer still requires male and female students to practice and perform highly dichotomized **gender roles**. Matthew Bourne's *Swan Lake* and David Bintley's *Edward II* are two rare examples of ballets which depict nonheterosexual relationships. There are also a small number of ballet companies which have used male dancers to perform the roles and movements of ballerinas, most notably the comedic *Les Ballets Trockadero de Monte Carlo*. In contrast, a number of high-profile straight-identifying male ballet dancers have been at pains to liken themselves to elite sportsman and to close what they see as an unnecessary divide between dance and sport. Not everyone would see this as a helpful comparison, particularly those who want to emphasize and celebrate dance's uniqueness. Some gay male dancers have recalled that a significant dimension of their original attraction to ballet as young boys was precisely its difference from traditional sports (Gard 2004a; Kavanagh 1996).

Dancers and dance educators have rarely claimed their queer history. However, a solid case could be made for the dominant role played by gay men and lesbians in establishing dance as a serious Western art form during the twentieth century. These include: Russian impresario Sergei Diaghilev whose company, *Les Ballets Russes*, first toured Western Europe in 1909 and captured a new middle-class audience for ballet; Frederick Ashton, the founding and long-time choreographer for England's Royal Ballet; Robert Helpmann, Australia's first international ballet star; and Loie Fuller and Isadora Duncan, both immensely important pioneers in what would later became known as modern dance.

A limited amount of research into the gender and sexual politics of dance teaching in non-Western countries has been published in English. Nonetheless, this research shows that similar concerns about the "right" ways for boys and girls to move are often at stake. For example, Hayashi (1998) argues that, prior to the 1870s, traditional Japanese dances were performed only by men and were not taught in schools. Later, authorities began to import a more European style physical education system which stipulated martial arts and sports for boys and gymnastics and folk dance for girls. Hayashi claims that authorities were clear about their belief that this would produce war-ready men and a beautiful, male-serving female population. Since that time the **prejudice** against males dancing has been very strong and it was not until as late as 1994 that dance became coeducational in Japanese high schools. Perhaps not surprisingly, this has been a shift which older and more senior male physical education teachers have resisted. In a similar vein, Van Zile (1998) charts the development of the South Korean sword dance, the *Chinju kommu*. Once again, whether or not the dance should be taught to and performed by males or females and the exact movements which are considered gender appropriate are evolving and historically contingent matters.

Explicitly antiheterosexist and antihomophobic approaches to dance teaching are rare, particularly in formal dance training institutions, although the ideas of **critical social theory** have begun to be taken up by some school and university teachers and researchers (Shapiro 1998). For instance, some feminist dance educators emphasize the need for students to study, understand, and critique the historical traditions, which have shaped the ideas and practices of institutional artistic dance. However, given that critical pedagogy has been widely criticized for its ponderous reliance on rational critique, a more playful and spontaneous approach to teaching dance movement may be a useful alternative. Gard (2004b), for instance, has employed the concepts of parody, exaggeration, and juxtaposition such that students are asked to observe and, through movement, "comment" on the way cultures discipline and normalize bodies. Students are asked to create scenarios in which "normal" movement for a boy or a girl is juxtaposed with "abnormal" movement or movement which parodies "normal" movement. In this approach, the arbitrary codes which shape our embodied lives are the focus of teaching, rather than some standard of technical movement proficiency. This approach draws from the performance work of the dancer Joe Goode, particularly his *29 Effeminate Gestures*, in which he both celebrates and analyzes the subtle ways in which "effeminacy" is read from male bodies (Gere 2001).

Bibliography

Aalten, Anna. 1997. "Performing the Body, Creating Culture." Pp. 41–58 in *Embodied Practices: Feminist Perspectives on the Body*. Edited by Kathy Davis. London: Sage.

Blacking, John, ed. 1977. *The Anthropology of the Body*. New York: Academic Press.

Clarke, Gill. 2004. "Threatening Space: (Physical) Education and Homophobic Body Work." Pp. 191–203 in *Body Knowledge and Control: Studies in the Sociology of Physical Education and Health*. Edited by John Evans, Brian Davies and Jan Wright. London: Routledge.

Crawford, John R. 1994. "Encouraging Male Participation in Dance." *Journal of Physical Education, Recreation and Dance 65*, no. 2: 40–43.

Gard, Michael. 2001. "Dancing Around the "Problem" of Boys and Dance." *Discourse: Studies in the Cultural Politics of Education* 22: 213–225.

———. 2002. "What Do We Do in Physical Education?" Pp. 43–58 in *Getting Ready for Benjamin: Preparing Teachers for Sexual Diversity in the Classroom*. Edited by Rita M. Kissen. Lanham, MD: Rowman and Littlefield.

———. 2004a. *Men Who Dance: Aesthetics, Athletics and the Art of Masculinity*. New York: Peter Lang.

———. 2004b. "Movement, Art and Culture: Problem-Solving and Critical Inquiry in Dance." Pp. 93–104 in *Critical Inquiry and Problem-Solving in Physical Education*. Edited by Jan Wright, Doune Macdonald and Lissette Burrows. London: Routledge.

Gere, David. 2001. "29 Effeminate Gestures: Choreographer Goode and the Heroism of Effeminacy." Pp. 349–381 in *Dancing Desires: Choreographing Sexualities On and Off the Stage*. Edited by Jane C. Desmond. Madison: University of Wisconsin Press.

Hayashi, Michie. 1998. "Dance Education and Gender in Japan." *Choreography and Dance 5*, no. 1: 87–102.

Kavanagh, Julie. 1996. *Secret Muses: The Life of Frederick Ashton*. London: Faber and Faber.

Keyworth, Saul A. 2001. "Critical Autobiography: 'Straightening' Out Dance Education." *Research in Dance Education* 2, no. 2: 117–137.

Shapiro, Sherry B., ed. 1998. *Dance, Power and Difference: Critical and Feminist Perspectives on Dance Education.* Champaign, IL: Human Kinetics.

Turner, Bryan S. 1996. *The Body and Society: Explorations in Social Theory.* 2nd Edition. Thousand Oaks, CA: Sage.

Van Zile, Judy. 1998. "For Men or Women? The Case of *Chinju kommu*, A Sword Dance from South Korea." *Choreography and Dance 5*, no. 1: 53–70.

Wulff, Helena. 1998. *Ballet across Borders: Career and Culture in the World of Dancers.* Oxford: Berg.

Web Sites

DV8 Physical Theatre. 2004. Accessed October 8, 2004. http://www.dv8.co.uk/dv8.html. Home page for this groundbreaking and often controversial English contemporary dance company, which includes current productions, archives, and a bibliography.

Les Ballets Trockadero de Monte Carlo. 2004. Accessed October 8, 2004. http://www.trockadero.org. Home of this all male troupe, showing that tutus and pointe shoes also look great on men.

San Francisco Queer Dance Camp Exchange. March 2004. Accessed October 8, 2004. http://www.SFQueerDanceCampExchange.com. Home page of one of the many specialist dance teaching exchanges for queer people of all ages.

Dating

John C. Spurlock

A form of socializing in which two people agree to do some brief activity together, dating has become pervasive in American culture as a form of socializing and courtship. But it can have a variety of meanings and functions depending on the goals of the individuals involved. Because of its origins as a form of heterosexual socializing, dating presents special challenges for **lesbian, gay, bisexual,** and **transgender youth** (LGBT). The ritualized form that evolved in the United States required that a young man ask a young woman to attend a public or school-sponsored amusement with him, with the understanding that the male would bear all of the expenses of the excursion. This removed the couple from parental oversight and often from all adult supervision, and so greatly increased the possibilities for social exchange and sexual intimacy. This heterosexual ritual generally required acceptance of gender-specific behavior. Because gendered behaviors often do not apply, or apply in different ways, to sexual minority youth, dating has required development of new, sometimes extemporaneous rules.

Although dating appears to have begun in the late nineteenth century among working class heterosexual youth, by the 1930s it had spread to all **social class**es and to most regions of the United States. The wide acceptance of dating as heterosexual socializing and sex play has made heterosexual couples, even at relatively early ages, an expected norm for adolescents. Girls in the 1920s began dating on average at age sixteen; today they begin three years earlier (Thornton 1990). In the course of the twentieth century, North American youth and their parents have

See also Adolescent Sexualities; College Age Students; Compulsory Heterosexuality; Heteronormativity; Identity Development; Mental Health; Passing.

generally accepted that young people will control most of the terms of who they so-cialize with and ultimately with whom they become intimate.

From its beginning, dating has been based on widely accepted **gender roles**. Both working and middle-class male youth paid the costs of the date, expecting that they should have a good time with the women they escorted. By the 1920s, middle-class males generally expected some sex play on dates. This set the stage for the wide acceptance of petting. Girls and young women had to negotiate for them-selves the balance between rejecting requests for sexual intimacy, and so possibly losing the chance for more dates, or assenting and so losing their sense of re-spectability. For heterosexual couples, this conflict at the heart of the dating system continues, in some forms, to the present. As late as the 1980s, a study showed that one of the most frequent problems associated with dating for university women is pressure for sex play (Rice 1996).

For LGBT youth, dating serves the same purposes as for heterosexuals, but the context is far different. In its origin a ritual of heterosexual socializing, dating grew in prominence during the same decades that formerly widespread forms of same-sex relationships such as the **"crush"** declined in importance. Especially in early **adolescence**, dates often take place in groups. This gives young people some sup-port in what might be a difficult social situation, but it also provides a means for peers to monitor the sexuality of other peers, and so increases the likelihood that individuals will pair off into heterosexual couples. High schools have institutional-ized a variety of social rituals that affirm heterosexual socializing. School dances, newspaper columns, and **proms** all support the dating system and all tend to mar-ginalize homosexual experience. Adolescents can safely lay claim to a LGBT identi-ties only in schools or communities where peers, teachers, and other important adults have accepted sexual minority experience as a fact of life. Since the 1990s, a few **urban** areas have become accepting enough that same-sex dating and even prom dates do not raise concerns.

Most sexual minority youth, however, are confronted with expectations of pairing off with partners of the other gender. They may deal with this in a variety of ways. Some youth will simply delay dating and sex play. Others, who manage to find similarly marginalized friends, may "pass" as heterosexuals who have same-sex "best friends." Some sexual minority youth delay dating with the people they are really attracted to until late in adolescence or even into early adulthood. Conse-quently, they have less practice at socializing and can enter the adult dating scene feeling unprepared for it.

No matter when they begin dating, LGBT individuals face special problems. The practice of dating grew from heterosexual gender norms with males generally taking the active role. Young people who have not embraced mainstream gender roles cannot rely on these norms as guides for dating. While the issue may be greater for younger people who are still working out their **sexual identity**, the shades of differences among lesbians and gay males make negotiating dating roles extremely difficult. Adding bisexual and transgender sexualities to the mix in-creases the complexity of even a simple date. Consequently, dating rules must be worked out by the couple, and this generally takes place without explicit discus-sion. If one member of the couple is consistently more assertive, this may take the place of gender roles.

Dating can serve many purposes. It will usually have the most importance early in a relationship when two people are still developing their acquaintance. Even at the college level, both women and men report that one of the major problems with dating is "**communication**." When both people run out of ready topics for conversation, feelings of discomfort can quickly follow, and this seems to be equally true for homosexual and heterosexual couples. Adolescents also typically use dates for sexual experimentation; sex play remains one of the most important goals of dating for people of all ages. Progressively more intimate sex play becomes more typical with increases in age, acquaintance, and frequency of dating. Gendered differences play important roles in dating for couples of all **sexual orientation**s. Males still press for sex sooner than females. Gay male couples have often been characterized as more interested in sex; lesbian couples often seek commitment early in a social relationship. Since the 1990s, however, many observers have seen a lessening of this gendered divide, with more gay men seeking longer-term relationships and many lesbian women enjoying sexuality.

In the United States, dating has also become the principal form of courtship as a result of two trends. School attendance expanded for both boys and girls throughout the early twentieth century while at the same time the marriage age declined. By the 1930s, high school graduation and marriage came close to coinciding for girls. Dating by then had become widespread on college campuses and among working young adults, so it served to broaden and deepen the acquaintance of youth and young adults considering marriage. As early as the 1920s, advice literature urged young people to become acquainted with many other young people, dating with a variety of people in order to find the right person for a lifetime commitment. Today this viewpoint is popularly accepted in North American culture. Even though traditional marriage remains unavailable to most sexual minorities in the United States, dating has become important in courtship for individuals seeking a long-term partner of the same gender. The Netherlands, which since 2001 has legally sanctioned marriage for gay couples, has a longstanding practice of social acceptance for sexual minorities. Especially in Amsterdam, sexual minority couples socialize easily in public, making the dating process less difficult for LGBT youth.

Dating probably reached its peak as a fundamental practice of adolescent heterosexual conviviality during the 1950s. Frequent dating in the two decades following World War II was directly linked to status for high school youth. Girls who dated most frequently in the 1950s were most likely to marry early during a decade that witnessed the highest level of adolescent **pregnancy** and marriage in that century. Both dating and going steady had elaborate rituals such as pinning and the prom that readily allowed heterosexual adolescents to learn the roles of romantic love, engagement, and even marriage. During the 1960s, however, young people in colleges and ultimately in high schools began to question and even disregard the norms of the dating and steady system. Although the forms and many of the rituals of earlier periods remain, traditional dating has become less central to the social life of contemporary youth.

Sexual minority youth often enjoy a broader range of opportunities for socializing with one another. Many cities have **community LGBT support groups** that often include programs for adolescents. Sexual minority organizations have sponsored events that provide alternatives to the traditional high school prom, online services to help match young people with similar sexual orientations, and **Internet** chat rooms provide opportunities to meet and socialize with others. Magazines, such as *X/Y*, targeted at specific sexual minority youth include columns dealing with issues surrounding pairing off, whether for dates or for longer relationships. The media, too, have provided some models of gay dating and homosexual couples in television shows like *Queer as Folk* and *My So Called Life* as well as **films** such as *Get Real* (UK 1998) or *Lan Yu* (Hong Kong 2001).

Bibliography

Bailey, Beth. 1988. *From Front Porch to Back Seat: Courtship in Twentieth-Century America*. Baltimore: Johns Hopkins University Press.

Raymond, Diane.1994. "Homophobia, Identity, and the Meanings of Desire: Reflections on the Cultural Construction of Gay and Lesbian Adolescent Sexuality." Pp. 115–150 in *Sexual Cultures and the Construction of Adolescent Identities*. Edited by Janice M. Irvine. Philadelphia: Temple University Press.

Rice, F. Philip. 1996. *The Adolescent: Development, Relationships, and Culture*. 8th ed. Boston: Allyn and Bacon.

Tessin, Tina. 1989. *Gay Relationships*. New York: Putnam.

Thornton, Arland. 1990. "The Courtship Process and Adolescent Sexuality." *Journal of Family Issues* 11: 239–273.

Web Site

The Lesbian, Gay, Bisexual & Transgender Community Center. December 2004. Accessed December 18, 2004. http://www.gaycenter.org/. This New York City center sponsors programs to assist sexual minority youth and adults meet and sustain relationships.

Day of Silence or Silencing

Tania Ferfolja

The Day of Silence, first implemented at the University of Virginia in 1996, is an effective and important form of student-led **activism** that protests against and draws attention to the LGBTQ **discrimination** and **prejudice** that occurs in educational institutions which silence sexual minorities. Participation in this mass action involves remaining silent on an organized date every year. The Day of Silence has expanded to other industrialized countries, including **Canada, New Zealand**, and **Australia**. Because of its inclusion of broader educational initiatives and its burgeoning international profile and popularity, the name was changed from the National Day of Silence to the Day of Silence Project in 1998.

The idea for a silent protest organized and implemented by youth originally stemmed from Maria Pulzetti, a University of Virginia student who, at eighteen, wrote a paper on activism and grassroots protest. This resulted in the first campus protest where over 150 students participated. Participants remained silent for a day while explaining their action through other means, such as information cards that pointed out their personal support for **lesbian, gay, bisexual, transgender**, and questioning (LGBTQ) individuals and questioned how others would address discrimination. The event received media coverage, and its success inspired Pulzetti

See also College Campus Organizing; Heteronormativity; Identity Politics; National Coming Out Day; School Safety and Safe School Zones.

(along with nineteen year-old Jessie Gilliam) to expand the concept nationally. Over one hundred schools, colleges, and universities across the United States participated; some educational institutions in Australia implemented a similar protest. To sustain the rapid expansion of the project required regional coordinators whose local understandings could better work with schools.

The Day of Silence promotes a safer environment for LGBTQ students, teachers, and their **allies**. Partly because of its direct integration with student life, it enables activists to communicate and intermingle with a diverse audience. Other educational events, such as reflection periods, were added to the initial action of silence to further develop positive understandings of these issues. The event has burgeoned to include more than 2,000 educational institutions on three continents. The initiative received sponsorship from the Advocates for Youth and later, officially, by the **Gay, Lesbian and Straight Education Network** (GLSEN). The latter organization further established the protest through the institution of a student leadership team and, in partnership with the United States Student Association, provided support for both schools and tertiary educational institutions.

The Day of Silence is an important student-led event that seeks to give voice to, and make visible, the silences often imposed on LGBTQ individuals in heteronormative schools, colleges, and universities. Despite the rhetoric that educational institutions, particularly schools, are sexless organizations where pedagogies, policies, and practices are objective, these institutions are saturated with heterosexual ideologies that are overtly and covertly perpetuated and promoted (Epstein and Johnson 1998). In actuality, schools are highly sexualized sites where representations of heterosexuality are normalized and celebrated, reinforcing the status quo. This myth of the sexless institution is problematic for LGBTQ students and **teachers** who, by definition, are frequently reduced to their sexual identities. The Day of Silence highlights this culture of silencing within educational institutions where pedagogical policies, practices, and curricula marginalize and police sexual "difference."

In most countries, the inclusion of **sexual orientation** components actually written into the **curriculum** is limited, and teachers have few skills to address these issues. Positive education through nonviolent political action such as the Day of Silence aims to redress these omissions and prejudices. Through mass action, this event illustrates the often hidden support for LGBTQ individuals by many in the broader community while empowering organizers and participants.

Institutional and interpersonal silences often, but not always, result in the self-silencing or "**passing**" of LGBTQ individuals. However, negotiating safe spaces in educational institutions is a complex and contradictory skill that, in many instances, simultaneously challenges marginalization while also demonstrating the **agency** and power of the individual. Though silent, LGBTQ individuals disrupt the heterosexual status quo through their **sexual identity**. The Day of Silence makes visible this plight of LGBTQ individuals by turning this imposed silence into a political and educational tool. Rather than silence being imposed on minority individuals, this event enables individuals who support LGBTQ people to reclaim this silence through a nonviolent, yet highly visible political protest.

Bibliography

Epstein, Debbie, and Richard Johnson. 1998. *Schooling Sexualities*. Buckingham: Open University Press.

Web Site

Day of Silence Project—GLSEN and USSA. GLSEN (Gay, Lesbian and Straight Education Network) and the USSA (United States Students Association). April 2005. Accessed May 30, 2005. http://www.dayofsilence.org. Provides information about this day of student-led activism, including information about its history, how to get involved, and making contact.

Deaf LGBT Youth

Lynda Rae Myers

Deaf **lesbian, gay, bisexual,** and **transgender youth** (LGBT) represent a diverse population with differing communication, social, and educational needs. **Communication** with, and access to, the larger hearing society is a struggle for members of the deaf community. The specific communication and social support needs of deaf youths differ based on auditory capabilities, preferred communication models (American Sign Language, cued speech, contact signs, oral), educational background (institutional/mainstreamed), cultural identification, and the coping skills developed to negotiate with the larger hearing majority. The communication difficulties inherent in interactions between deaf people and the larger society also limit deaf youths' access to the resources of the hearing LGBT community. There are an estimated 2.8 million deaf and hard of hearing LGBT people in the United States. There are also numerous deaf LGBT organizations across the globe. In spite of such large numbers, few role models and community resources are available for deaf LGBT youth in either the LGBT or Deaf communities. The deaf population is diverse, including born deaf or hard-of-hearing, late deafened, deaf blind, and physically disabled individuals from all ethnic and cultural groups. Deaf people in the United States can be born into hearing or deaf families; they can be native users of American Sign Language or use English, written or spoken, as a first language. As well, deaf youth may or may not identify themselves as members of a cultural minority.

Deaf LGBT youth are members of a dual (or multiple) minority group. The larger LGBT community often overlooks minority and deaf youth. In the United States, groups such as **Gay, Lesbian, and Straight Education Network** (GLSEN) may occasionally provide interpreters (of varying skills) for their local educator workshops, but mainstream LGBT youth organizations usually do not extensively outreach into the deaf community due to a lack of knowledge, limited resources, and funding considerations. For example, accommodations (TTY communication devices for phones, ASL/cued speech/real time captioning, and interpreters) that help provide access for deaf people are often expensive ongoing expenses. Cultural naïveté makes it difficult for traditional LGBT program organizers to locate, identify, and provide the necessary accommodations to adequately serve a diverse deaf population. The deaf community itself is not always aware of its needs. Deaf institutes

See also Community LGBT Support Groups; Disabilities, Physical; Discrimination; Mentoring; Parents, Responses to Homosexuality; School Safety and Safe School Zones; Youth, At Risk.

have only a few LGBT youth chapters. The result is that these youth are left underserved, isolated, and in need of specialized outreach efforts.

It is important for mainstream LGBT educational programs that outreach to deaf LGBT youth to understand the differing needs of deaf and hard of hearing youth:

- Prelingual deaf individuals were identified as deaf prior to developing an auditory language and usually are educated by use of American Sign Language (ASL), auditory/oral training, or some kind of manual/contact sign system. They may or may not have the capacity of speech or speech reading. Educational services are usually specialized/segregated—offered in self-contained classrooms in regular educational settings or in separate institutions that use ASL or other unique communication systems for instruction.

- Hard-of-hearing individuals may be educated in regular public schools or in special educational programs and tend to have the ability to speak and may speech read.

- Late-deafened individuals have experienced their hearing loss after learning language and usually can converse via spoken language and writing, though they may or may not be able to speech read or use signed communication.

Deaf gay youth often are hidden and isolated in the deaf community, relying on private codes to disclose their identities to each other. For example, green and yellow is a code for G A Y (G green A and Y yellow, used in a sentence such as: "He plays with green and yellow golf balls."). The fear of disclosure and the dread of rejection by their peers experienced by LGBT youth are especially high in the close deaf community where personal information travels quickly. Deaf people cannot easily change social groups since the community is very small and communication with outsiders is limited to those who can sign or are willing to make adaptations. Actually, due to their close social ties and increasing awareness in the deaf community, deaf peers are somewhat less likely to ostracize LGBT members of their community.

There are some concerns that are unique to deaf LGBT youth. Since many deaf youth are educated in residential settings with close quarters, shared showers, and a lack of privacy, unanticipated disclosure of sexuality is a greater possibility. Deaf peers, being sensitive to nonverbal information, may notice a teen's sexual curiosity before his or her own awareness, or a hand-holding couple may be "caught" in the dorms. Deaf youths may be "outed" before they have the self-awareness and self-confidence to negotiate homophobic responses from their peers. LGBT awareness training is still rather new in deaf education. Some schools do not allow teachers to disclose their own **sexual identities**. However, a few progressive schools in California and Washington, D.C., have allowed youth support groups and posted safe zone stickers on doors of staff willing to be supportive to youth.

Concerns regarding **coming out** may be focused more on family and contacts in the larger nondeaf community. The majority of deaf youth have hearing parents. If parents do not sign well or they do not understand their child's speech, then daily communication can be strained. Parent–child interactions may be frustrating or otherwise unrewarding, making discussion of sensitive issues more difficult. If the parents and child have difficulty negotiating borrowing the car, how comfortable will they be discussing homosexuality, assuming that the parents even know the sign for it? The challenges faced by "coming out" to parents and other family members loom even larger for deaf LGBT youth.

Deaf youth are thought to have less factual information about sexual mores and practices then their hearing peers. A hearing parent and a deaf child may not have a shared language in which to discuss sexuality. Further, educational materials such as safer sex/**HIV education**, traditional media (radio/newspapers) or community workshops on STDs, or gay-related information provided by mainstream LGBT outreach programs often do not address the reading levels, which are well below the national average, and the visual needs of deaf youth.

Being a member of both a low incidence population and a small sexual minority group reduces the likelihood of chance meetings with other deaf LGBT adults. Deaf youth have a desperate need for deaf role models who share their language and worldview Deaf youth need access to reflections of themselves, as well as guidance regarding HIV/**AIDS**, deaf LGBT social norms, coming out processes, deaf-friendly resources, stigma management, and leadership skills. Deaf youth who are most comfortable using ASL may need direct face-to-face contact with deaf role models in order to access social supports because e-mail and other media may not meet their communication needs. There is a need for such programming, specifically targeted to the deaf community's unique needs, provided by deaf people within the deaf community, for its deaf youth. If mainstream LGBT groups wish to outreach to deaf youth, they need to partner with the deaf community. Providing access via advertising in the deaf media, using assistive technology such as teletype devices for phones, audio loops, e-mail addresses, Web sites, and providing ASL/cue interpreters are critical to meet this need. Networking with deaf service agencies and community groups to exchange information and share the costs of theses resources also increases the level of support available to deaf LGBT youth.

Services targeted to the deaf community are still rather recent interventions, and resources to provide services for deaf youth remain limited and underfunded. The Deaf Gay and Lesbian Center, formed in 1992 under the Deaf Counseling Advocacy and Referral Agency of Los Angeles, provides services to adults. The deaf community also has several community **LGBT support groups** that serve its adult population, including the Rainbow Association of the Deaf (founded in 1977) and the Deaf Lesbian Festival (established in 1998). Various international communities have strong LGBT organizations but little is known about their services to youth. The Rainbow Association of the Deaf has many local chapters, some of which hold youth group activities. The National Technical Institute for the Deaf sponsored the first campus-wide, week-long, Deaf Gay and Lesbian Conference in January 1993. There was also an attempt to provide more support for Deaf LGBT youth by holding the Rainbow Deaf Youth Conference (RDYC), in Washington, D.C., in 1999. A survey conducted at that time found that the needs of these youth, ages fourteen to twenty-one, were social and cultural events, field trips, support/discussion groups and workshops (held in American Sign Language).

More **research** to identify the specific needs of deaf youths as dual (and triple) minority group members is necessary. What are the cultural barriers to accessing traditional services, funding sources, and supports for LGBT youth? How can deaf grassroots organizations become sensitized to the needs of its LGBT youth? What antibias techniques can be adapted to meet the needs of the deaf educational systems?

Bibliography

Gutman, Virgina. 1999. *Therapy Issues with Deaf Lesbians, Gay Men and Bisexual Men and Women.* Pp. 97–120. In *Psychotherapy with Deaf Clients from Diverse Groups.* Edited by Irene Leigh. Washington DC: Gallaudet University Press.

Langholtz, Daniel, and Marie Rendon. 1991–1992. "The Deaf Gay/Lesbian Client: Some Perspectives." *Journal of the American Deafness and Rehabilitation Association* 25, Spring 91–92: 31–34.

Lucak, Raymond. 1993. *Eyes of Desire: A Deaf Gay and Lesbian Reader.* Boston: Alyson.

Phaneuf, Jean. 1987. "Considerations on Deafness and Homosexuality." *American Annals the Deaf* 132: 52–55.

Zakarewsky, George. 1979. "Patterns of Support among Gay and Lesbian Deaf Persons." *Sexuality and Disability* 2, no. 3: 178–191.

Web Sites

The Deaf Gay and Lesbian Center. May 2005. The Deaf Counseling and Advocacy/Referral Agency. Accessed May 30, 2005. http://www.dcara.org/dglc. Information and referral for deaf youth on a site that includes photo galleries and links for parents.

Deaf Queer Resources Center. February 2005. D. Renteria. Accessed May 21, 2005. http://www.deafqueer.org. International gatherings listed along with chat, coming out stories, and support.

Deaf Youth Rainbow. May 2000. http://www.deafqueer.net/cmra/dyr. Accessed May 21, 2005. Sponsored by the Capitol Metropolitan Rainbow Alliance, this site provides discussion forum, links, and a history of the group.

National Association of the Deaf. May 2005. Accessed May 21, 2005. http://www.nad.org/. Accessed December 6, 2004. Human rights organization for the deaf.

The Rainbow Society of the Deaf. December 2004. Accessed May 21, 2005. http://www. Rad.org. The Web site for the oldest deaf GBLT organization in the United States includes membership information, events, and many national and international links.

Youth Resource. 2004. Accessed May 21, 2005. http://www.youthresource.com/community/deaf. Mainstream youth resource—deaf youth conference pages RDYC.

Desire

jan jagodzinski

Desire is colloquially understood as consciously wanting something, but the more interesting and difficult question is that of *unconscious* desire. Such unconscious desire is not so immediately apparent and may never be known to the subject. **Jacque Lacan**'s (1998) dictum was that human desire finds its meaning *in the desire of the Other*. For **lesbian, gay, bisexual**, and **transgender youth** (LGBT), unconscious same-sex desire is far more troubling than heterosexual unconscious desire

See also Mentoring; Psychoanalysis and Education; Psychoanalysis and Feminism; Queer Studies; Queer and Queer Theory; Sexual Identity; Transsexuality.

because of the obvious suppression of this erotic discourse in school contexts and the symbolic order of society as such. Same-sex *conscious* desire between teachers and students is often disavowed, as it usually is with heterosexual relations, confined to *fantasy formations only* at the level of the "imaginary" psychic register. Love (and hate) for the teacher is a *normative* part of transference and countertransference if learning (or resistance) is to take place.

Unconscious desire and fantasy are intimately linked. Lacan had a special term for this unknown aspect of fantasy that harbors unconscious desire—*objet a* which belongs to the "Real" psychic register. This is not an "object," but what the lure or structure of the fantasy promises—the "a." Desire can take the form of either narcissistic desire to or anaclitic desire to *have*. For LGBT same-sex desire, the student may narcissistically desire the teacher by *actively* becoming like him or her; or narcissistically desire the teacher *passively* by being the object of admiration, idealization, or recognition. Anaclitic desire is also possible. The student can actively desire to possess the teacher or passively desire to be possessed by the teacher. The same possibilities structure teacher conscious desires as well. The imaginary fantasy of a sexual relationship provides the sense that the subject's ego is whole and intact, confirmed by a social authority figure, especially crucial for LGBT youth who have no support systems. This imaginary relationship fills the *lack* in the subject. Unconscious desire in the Real has a metonymic structure. This means that there is never *one* final fantasy object (relationship) that will satisfy desire completely. A continual procession of fantasies is necessary as we change as human beings who are in the process of becoming.

When can it be said that desire is "free" of this Other? That our unconscious desired objects change? Only when a conflict arises within the self's coherent ego structure, and the fantasy collapses. The subject suffers a "subjective destitution." Such moments reveal the "true" Real self (*Je*) of unconscious desire rather than the imaginary *moi* of fantasy. The paradox of desire is that once the fantasy frame collapses, the drives (*Triebe*) of the body takes over. There is a certain self-destructive excessive element at work here that is referred to as the "death drive." A point is reached where pleasure turns to pain, and the act of transgression against the lawful limits manifests itself as painful–pleasure which Lacan called *jouissance*. This raises an ethics of the Real as to the responsibility teachers have for their *unconscious* desires. The superego is a conflicted paradoxical internalized voice. On the one hand there is a societal pressure to obey the laws; on the other there is pressure to transgress them as well. Conflict and guilt *can* emerge when a teacher–student relationship collapses into sexual relationship. Gallop's (1997) defense for this possibility within an educational context sets up the terms of the debate. Others argue that the student has misrecognized his or her unconscious desire in the way the teacher "gets off" (jouissance), and has directed it at the teacher's *body* as the *objet a*.

This background to the question of unconscious desire in the Real raises significant and difficult questions for LGBT. What is **queer** desire? How is it to be theorized? This has been a highly contested theoretical zone of postmodernism where accusations of essentialism and the difficulties of specificity of LGBT have been impossible to define. The lesbian theorist Teresa de Lauretis (1994) has attempted to "re-theorize" Lacan's heterosexual privileging, in the 1950s, of the "phallus" as being *descriptive* of the paternal law. The use of this term "phallus" is perhaps the most controversial aspect of Lacanian psychoanalysis. It refers to a transcendental signifier of desire—to the lack or missing piece that we unconsciously desire. It is a transcendental because there is no *one particular object* that could represent it. This is precisely the way de Lauretis theorizes the "lesbian phallus," as a fetishistic object that could be any body part (breasts, clitoris, hips, and so on) that fulfills lesbian desire for the loss of the mother's body. For gay theorist Tim Dean (2000), however, Lacan was already a "queer theorist" whose notion of perverse unconscious desire in the Real already could accommodate a multiple range of possibilities of sexual differences. Heterosexual sexual desire becomes simply one of the many possible unconscious ways of fantasying being whole, receiving a privileged position *only* at the socio–political level (symbolic order). Controversially, Dean argues that perversion or queerness is "an internal division akin to that of the unconscious, rather than being substantive or an external oppositional force" (Dean 2000, 245–246). As soon as a "body" is attached to perversion in terms of a queer identity, *it loses its subversive effects*. Champagne also argues along the same lines as Dean. Queer, for her, "refers not to the fact of gay or lesbian, transgendered or bisexual identity, but to the *political and epistemic* meaning of homosexuality. . . . The queer turn away from identity politics can be traced to Lacan who saw identifications as one of the three sources of human aggression (along with cultural prohibitions and forced sacrifices)" (Champagne 1998, 292, original emphasis). The danger, as these queer theorists see it, lies in the ideological constructions confining each of LGBT into ideological categories. In Lacanian terms, the claim that "The" Lesbian, "The" Gay, "The" Bisexual, "The" Transsexual exist. Lacan purposely placed a "bar" through Woman to indicate the impossibility of such a subject position to maintain it as an open category. With transsexual identity, unconscious desire is a particularly difficult concern. Modern technological science grants sex-change operations without questioning unconscious desire. In some cases the sex change is achieved to reach the fantasy of becoming "The" Woman, believing that the difficult question of sexual difference will be solved (Millot 1990).

Lacan took seriously **Sigmund Freud**'s radical statements. "[I]n human beings pure masculinity and femininity is not to be found either in a psychological or biological sense" (Freud SE 7, 220), and "[P]ure masculinity and femininity remain theoretical constructs of uncertain content" (Freud SE XIX, 258). These are passages Dean and Champagne can identify with as well. This also means that heterosexuality, itself, is not a distinct pure category, but fluid as testified by bisexual and gay men in some cultures who do not identify themselves as such because they take the dominant position.

What is unnerving and radical about Lacan's (1998) "formulae of sexuation" is his understanding of sexuality in purely logical terms. Masculine and feminine as orientations toward sex (not gender) are but *two failed accounts of language to articulate unconscious desire*. Language can never provide an adequate answer as to one's **sexual orientation**, only unconscious desire can, which is "beyond" language and caught by an unknown element in the imagination. Masculine and feminine pairings in the LGBT community, as well as in the heterosexual community do not escape the impossible gap between them. Identity is at the level of unconscious desire and not body. This means there are many biological females that have masculine structure and vice versa. As odd and inconceivable as it may sound, lesbian desire may be "trapped" in a male biological body at the level of the unconscious. Cross identification of sexes in the hetero community has also starkly emerged in online cyber communities and in video games.

Since LGBT educational politics have centered themselves on **identity politics**, Lacanian views of unconscious desire have proven to be either "too" theoretical or abstract when applied to the everyday life of the classroom where the stress has been on body politics. Identity politics has been divisive among the LGBT community, with "queer" emerging as a signifier that attempts to unify the factional differences among competing groups and ideologies. Thus far unconscious desire as applied to queer education has not received much attention except in the larger more controversial context of Platonic pederasty (Bredbeck 1995).

Bibliography

Bredbeck, Gregory W. 1995. "Analyzing the Classroom: On the Impossibility of a Queer Pedagogy." Pp. 89–109 in *Professions of Desire: Lesbian and Gay Studies in Literature.* Edited by George E. Haggerty and Bonnie Zimmerman. New York: Modern Language Association of America.

Champagne, Rosaria. 1998. "Queering the Unconscious." *The South Atlantic Quarterly* 97, no. 2: 281–296.

Dean, Tim. 2000. *Beyond Sexuality*. Chicago: University of Chicago Press.

De Lauretis, Teresa. 1994. *The Practice of Love: Lesbian Sexuality and Perverse Desire.* Bloomington: Indiana University Press.

Freud, Sigmund. 1953–1974. *The Standard Edition of the Complete Psychological Works of Sigmund Freud.* Edited and translated by James Strachey London: Hogarth.

Gallop, Jane. 1997. *Feminist Accused of Sexual Harassment.* Durham, NC: Duke University Press.

Lacan, Jacques. 1998. *On Feminine Sexuality, the Limits of Love and Knowledge, 1972–1973. The Seminar of Jacques Lacan XX, Encore.* Translated with notes by Bruce Fink. Edited by Jacques-Alain Miller. New York: Norton.

Millot, Catherine. 1990. *Horsexe: Essay on Transsexuality.* Translated by Kenneth Hylton. New York: Automedia.

Diagnostic and Statistical Manual of Mental Disorders (DSM)

Shawn M. Coyne

The *Diagnostic and Statistical Manual of Mental Disorders* (DSM), a bible of diagnostic categories and criteria for professionals in the field of American psychology, has undergone an evolution in terms of how it defines homosexuality. Early versions classified homosexuality as pathology and a mental disorder. By the time the third version was published, in 1973, homosexuality had been removed, but an additional category, Ego-Dystonic Homosexuality, was included. This diagnosis referred to those who identified themselves as homosexuals, but experienced distress over the **sexual identity** and wished to be otherwise. The current version of the DSM does not include **sexual orientation** as a mental disorder, however "persistent and marked distress about sexual orientation" (American Psychiatric Association

See also Behavior Disorders and LGBT Youth; Disabilities, Intellectual; Identity Politics; Professionalism; Reparative Therapy.

2000, 582) is still listed as a possible example of a Sexual Disorder Not Otherwise Specified. All changes to the DSM have occurred with controversy, conflict, and political influence. But despite these struggles, the changes have had a strong impact on the field of psychology and beyond. This impact includes effects for both educators and youth.

The first edition of DSM, dating back to 1952, defined homosexual attraction, behavior, or identity as a mental disorder. At the time, the diagnosis led clinicians to conclude that conversion therapy was the best course. Conversion therapy took many forms including behavioral intervention, electric shock therapy, medication, and surgery, such as sterilization, breast amputation, castration, clitoridectomy, and brain surgery. In 1973, homosexuality, as a category of dysfunction, was removed from DSM. Earlier research by UCLA psychologist Evelyn Hooker had shown no difference between homosexuals and heterosexuals in term of **mental health**, so there was little empirical argument to continue to view one orientation as pathology. However, in the fifteen years between her research and the change in the DSM, significant social changes had occurred. At the 1972 meeting of the Association for Advancement of Behavioral Therapy, gay activists protested the conference due to one speaker having a history of using aversion therapy for conversion. In turn, they were invited to present to the APA Nomenclature Committee, the group responsible for any revisions to the DSM. Under the political leadership of gay activist Frank Kameny, and supported quietly by several homosexual psychiatrists, they argued that inclusion of homosexuality as a disorder was a moral value and political judgment rather than a psychologically-based one. This proposition was not a novel one, since some early homophile activists had long challenged the "sickness doctrine."

The committee preparing the revision to the DSM rewrote the draft, eliminating homosexuality as a disorder and adding Sexual Orientation Disturbance for those people who have a homosexual orientation but are disturbed by it or want it changed. This change, however, did not sit well with all APA members attending the annual conference in May 1973. Opponents called for a referendum vote of the entire membership to approve the change. The decision, however, was finalized by the APA Board in December 1973; it was upheld by a referendum of 10,000 votes four months later by a ratio of nearly 3 to 2.

Years later the issue of the categorization of homosexuality within DSM would surface again. As DSM-III was being written, the same individual who chaired the Task Force on Nomenclature and Statistics in 1973, Robert L. Spitzer, was again chairperson. Spitzer now directed his task group towards a different kind of revision. Recognizing that there were still homosexuals who experience distress, he focused on how the Association defined mental disorder. Spitzer saw disorder as subjective distress or general impairment of social effectiveness. He recognized, however, that the APA was not in a position to determine whether lack of heterosexual functioning represented impaired social effectiveness. He then focused on the condition causing inherent disadvantage as an additional criterion. Defining disorders this way, he argued that some cases of homosexuality should be categorized as mental disorders. To separate these cases from the cases that did not qualify, he developed the category of Ego-Dystonic Homosexuality. There were two criteria for this disorder. First, an individual must complain that heterosexual arousal is persistently absent or weak and that this significantly interferes with initiating or maintaining wanted heterosexual relationships. Second, the individual needs to report a sustained pattern of homosexual arousal that is unwanted and a persistent source of distress (American Psychiatric Association 1980, 282).

By 1988, Ego Dystonic Homosexuality was dropped from the next revision of DSM. The current version, DSM-IV-TR, has no discussion of homosexuality as a specific mental disorder nor of Ego-Dystonic Homosexuality. Nonetheless, there are those who still argue that the DSM has still not gone far enough because a clinician could still diagnose a gay or lesbian individual with Sexual Disorder Not Otherwise Specified.

Important to understand in this history of changes are the arguments and ideologies that were considered in the process. When homosexuality was first removed, those who opposed the modification claimed—most notably the outspoken psychiatrists Edmund Bergler, Irving Bieber, and Charles Socarides—that it was deviance worthy of a disorder status and that there were plenty of cases of successful conversion to support their argument. However, researchers found significant flaws in nearly every cited example. Those who argued for the first removal of the diagnosis argued that homosexuality is merely another form of sexual expression and that its existence as a mental disorder was only in response to current cultural values. When Spitzer moved to develop a case for Ego-Dystonic Homosexuality, many saw his efforts as a step backwards and an action against the spirit of the 1973 decision. They argued that the disorder lay in **homophobia** and a nonaccepting society. Some argued with Spitzer that his additional category would only be acceptable if a parallel Ego-Dystonic Heterosexuality was created. Spitzer did not support this idea. What these arguments demonstrate, however, is significant. This request for and denial of a category for Ego-Dystonic Heterosexuality demonstrates that the DSM committees continued to work from a **heteronormative** perspective.

Critics of the DSM and of the categorization of any disorder support the changes regarding sexual orientation, but feel the committee made the changes for the wrong reasons. Their argument is that the **psychology** field holds significant power to define normalcy. More than anything else, these critics assert that the field needs to recognize its power and respond appropriately. Difference is not enough of a criterion to define disorder.

Whether one thinks the changes in the DSM have come far enough or whether these changes should be merely a beginning, they have had broad impact. After the removal of homosexuality from the DSM in 1973, the American Psychological Association came out with a resolution and two policies on sexual orientation. These statements recognized it not to be a disorder, urged the removal of its stigma, pledged to teach and approach client's needs appropriately, took a stand against LGBT **discrimination**, urged equal civil rights for the LGBT community, and did not recognize conversion therapies. These statements began an ethical framework for working with LGBT clients that shifted the focus to treating the socially induced problems of these people. Additionally, the International Statistical Classification of Diseases (ICD), being influenced by the DSM, removed its classification of homosexuality as a mental disorder in 1992 for its tenth version. The American Psychological Association pushed for this when, in 1987, it publicly urged its members not to use the ICD classification found in the ninth version. However, the ICD-10 still maintains a catch-all category for "disturbances of sexual preference, unspecified."

Having homosexuality removed as a category of pathology has helped to pave the way for acceptance of LGBT issues and persons in schools. Educators with diverse sexualities are no longer denied certification or fired solely on the basis of their sexual orientation. Further, the removal of homosexuality from the DSM has facilitated the development and growth of **gay–straight alliance** and organizations like **GLSEN** and **Project 10**, along with gaining support from major **professional educational associations** and school counselor groups. Teacher and **counselor education programs** now promote LGBT affirmative practices while accreditation standards routinely include sexual diversity issues.

The DSM changes provide support to the argument that conversion therapy is inappropriate for anyone, especially adolescents. When homosexuality is not defined as a disorder, the only remaining reason for conversion therapy would be out of a judgment that a person *should not* be something. Therapists do not hold a moral high ground over the public to make that decision. This was made very clear in the American Psychological Association's resolution and two policies on orientation. Further, the primary goals of adolescent development are **identity development** and independence, which should be the focus of psychological services.

Bibliography

American Psychiatric Association. 1980. *Diagnostic and Statistical Manual of Mental Disorders*. 3rd ed. Washington, DC: Author.

American Psychiatric Association. 2000. *Diagnostic and Statistical Manual of Mental Disorders*. 4th ed. Washington, DC: Author.

Bayer, Ronald. 1987. *Homosexuality and American Psychiatry: The Politics of Diagnosis*. 2nd ed. Princeton, NJ: Princeton University Press.

Clendinen, Dudley, and Adam Nagourney. 1999. *Out for Good: The Struggle to Build a Gay Rights Movement in America*. New York: Simon and Schuster.

Greenberg, Gary. 1997. "Right Answers, Wrong Reasons: Revisiting the Deletion of Homosexuality from the DSM." *Review of General Psychology* 1: 256–270.

Miller, Neil. 1995. *Out of the Past: Gay and Lesbian History from 1869 to the Present*. New York: Vintage.

Spitzer, Robert L. 1981. "The Diagnostic Status of Homosexuality in DSM-III: A Reformulation of the Issues." *American Journal of Psychiatry* 138: 210–215.

Web Sites

APA Lesbian, Gay, Bisexual Concerns Office. 2004. Accessed December 5, 2004. American Psychological Association. http://www.apa.org/pi/lgbc/office/homepage.html. Provides answers to commonly asked questions, statements about the office's mission, and additional links to other services.

Evelyn Hooker: In Memoriam. 2004. Gregory M. Herek. Accessed December 4, 2004. http://psychology.ucdavis.edu/rainbow/html/hooker.html. This Web site provides historical background information regarding Evelyn Hooker and her groundbreaking study of homosexuality. The Web site also provides insight into how her study and other features of the culture impacted the DSM.

Fact Sheet: Gay, Lesbian, and Bisexual Issues. 2000. American Psychiatric Association. Accessed December 4, 2004. http://www.psych.org/public_info/gaylesbianbisexualissues22701.pdf.

Fact Sheet: Homosexual and Bisexual Issues. February 2000. American Psychiatric Association. Accessed December 4, 2004. http://www.psych.org/news_stand/homosexual12.pdf. The American Psychiatric Association publishes the DSM and provides psychology-related information to the public. These Web sites discuss the evolution of their classification and the nature of sexual orientation.

Disabilities, Intellectual

S. Anthony Thompson

Intellectual disability is subaverage intellectual functioning and limited adaptive behaviors, such as communication, social, self-care, and community use. For various reasons, **lesbian**, **gay**, **bisexual** and questioning youth with intellectual disabilities have only recently been acknowledged as a distinct group and identity. There are many false and conflicting myths surrounding the sexualities of youth with intellectual disabilities. These youth are variously seen as nonsexual and/or oversexed, forever childlike, or exclusively heterosexual. These myths serve to control sexualities of youth with intellectual disabilities. For example, historically, many such youth have been involuntarily sterilized through surgery and/or drugs. These efforts at containment are particularly salient within the context of same-gender sexualities. Therefore, it is difficult to talk about LGBQ issues as cultural identities for youth with intellectual disabilities without talking about sexual behaviors and efforts to suppress homosexualities.

In attempting to construct a positive LGBQ identity, youth with intellectual disabilities (such as mental retardation, fetal alcohol syndrome, autism spectrum disorder) must navigate the everyday manifestation of disabling myths at school, in the community, and at home. Therefore, it is important to appreciate the attitudes of teachers, school **administrators**, community caregivers, and parents because educational programming occurs in these environments and has a large impact on the kinds of identities possible for LGBQ youth.

Ellen Brantlinger (1992) reported that teachers perceived their values about sexuality to be significantly different from those of their students with intellectual disabilities. She also found that "although teachers believed students would benefit from comprehensive and realistic [**sexual education**] training, they feared adverse reactions from students, parents, and administrators" (32). Differential expectations were also found in that teachers and school administrators rated expressions of heterosexuality as 80 percent appropriate for students with moderate intellectual disabilities; homosexuality, as 19 percent appropriate. For students with severe intellectual disabilities, heterosexuality was assessed as 46 percent appropriate; homosexuality, as 17 percent (Wolfe 1997).

Within residential settings, caregivers' attitudes are similarly homophobic (Scotti 1996). Although they tolerate masturbation fairly comfortably; less tolerated is heterosexual petting and kissing followed by heterosexual oral sex, heterosexual intercourse, and finally, least tolerated is any homosexual behavior. Another finding among Scotti's **research** was that some caregivers conflate **AIDS** with homosexual activity.

Hingsburger (1993) traces the evolution of such attitudes to the past when institutional-living was practically the only residential option for those with intellectual disabilities. Historically, same-sex behaviors were tolerated in private, although publicly renounced by caregivers. Paradoxically, in public, caregivers

See also Adolescent Sexualities; Community LGBT Youth Groups; Discrimination; Educational Policy; *Lawrence v. Texas*; Mental Disorders; Parents, Responses to Homosexuality; Prejudice; Special Education, LGBT Youth in.

tended to approve of heterosexual activities, and privately restricted them. Recently, these sexual attitudes have changed; heterosexual expressions are privately and publicly sanctioned, although any display of homosexuality remains verboten. Caregivers, including parents, often feel directly responsible for the consequences of sexual behaviors of youth with intellectual disabilities, and given the conflation of AIDS with same-sex behavior as well as the generally negative attitudes about homosexuality, such attitudes are as understandable as they are unacceptable.

Parental sexual attitudes vary with respect to the **sexual orientation** of their offspring. Parents are often more progressive and informed than teachers and caregivers give them credit; however, often homosexuality is not viewed favorably.

There is some evidence that youth with intellectual disabilities have adopted some of these negative beliefs about sexualities, particularly same-sex behavior, although researchers in the field of intellectual disability often include youth and adults in the same sample. Brantlinger (1992) found several adolescents with disabilities that thought that sex was a dirty and nasty business, and many disapproved of homosexuality. Lunsky and Konstanareas (1998) interviewed people with mental retardation and those with autism (ranging in age from sixteen to forty-six) around topics of sexuality. Their results were consistent with other researchers; same-sex expressions were least favored compared to various heterosexual expressions. McCabe and Cummins (1996, 19) found that, in their sample of people with mild intellectual disabilities who ranged from sixteen to forty years of age, "people with intellectual disabilities were more likely to have negative feelings in relation to a range of sexual experiences including . . . homosexuality." And, in an ethnography of Opportunity House, a Florida community residence for people and youth with intellectual disabilities, residents lacked awareness of the diverse choices around sexuality and sexual behaviors, and mocked possibilities of mutually consenting same-sex behavior (Angrosino 1998).

The cumulative result of these attitudes, rooted in myths, is that often LGBQ youth with intellectual disabilities are left vulnerable. The rates of **sexual abuse** of youth with intellectual disabilities (of any sexual orientation) are alarmingly high; one study found that for girls with developmental disabilities the rate was 1.5 times higher than, and for boys with disabilities, the rate was about twice that of the general population (McCreary Centre 1993). Some advocates suggest that youth with intellectual disabilities attempting to fashion an LGBQ **sexual identity**—or perceived as LGBQ—may be vulnerable to other kinds of violence from caregivers. Staff **homophobia** is cited as a condition leading to abuse for youth with intellectual disabilities in the 1997 postings on the International Coalition on Abuse and Disability listserv.

There are also **legal issues** for youth with intellectual disabilities who engage in same-sex behaviors. In the United States, Matthew Limon, who some refer to as the other Matthew, received a seventeen-year prison sentence because two weeks after he turned eighteen he performed oral sex on another male teenager at a Kansas residential school for youth with intellectual disabilities. The other youth asked Matthew to stop and by all reports he did. The American Civil Liberties Union appealed on the basis that heterosexual behaviors under the same circumstances would have resulted in a far more lenient sentence. In August 2004, the *American National Association of Social Workers* called for the Kansas Supreme Court to reverse the conviction, although to date Mathew remains in prison.

Consequently, there is a movement of late to educate youth with intellectual disabilities in the areas of healthy sexuality, sexual abuse prevention, and STD prevention (including AIDS). Until recently, many in special education circles believed another myth; namely, teaching and talking about sexuality leads to sexual behavior among youth with intellectual disabilities. Of course, youth are sexual, and sexuality is a normal part of the human condition. However, without proper teaching and guidance youth with intellectual disabilities may engage in unsafe sexual behaviors. LGBQ youth with intellectual disabilities require individualized approaches to support their sexualities. Some community agencies strike a Sexuality Review Committee (SRC), composed of professionals, paraprofessionals, parents, and others for such a purpose. An SRC considers particular cases with respect to relationships and sexuality; members may survey existing information within the agency, determine whether more expertise or information is required, consider the benefits and risks of those involved—all to better support youth with intellectual disabilities.

For LGBQ youth with intellectual disabilities, sex education curricula need to be visual, clear, simple, and written in plain language. Within the mainstream of sex education, these youth are disenfranchised since they cannot typically understand the abstract language often used. However, materials for youth with intellectual disabilities frequently lack specificity and clarity when representing same-sex activities. An exception is the *The Sexuality Series* (1997) produced by the Young Adult Institute. In the series, pictures and accompanying videos of same-sex relationships, sexual activities, and safer sex practices (both male and female) are presented as the basis for educational discussion.

Of course, in order to educate LGBQ youth, educators and caregivers must become informed about sexual diversities. To this end, in North America and **Europe**, programs promoting healthy sexuality (including homosexualities) for youth with intellectual disabilities have been created. These programs usually provide in-service training for professionals as well as para-professionals and—often to a lesser extent—direct support and teaching for LGBQ youth. There are some LGTBQ youth agencies and community centers that provide support services to youth with intellectual disabilities, although usually on an as-needed basis. One example is Vancouver's The Centre, a community resource providing support, health and social services, and public education for the well-being of lesbians, gay men, transgender, and bisexual people and their allies. It makes explicit its support of youth with disabilities, among other groups it supports, by naming "disability" in its mission statement.

Additionally, there is a need for community living agencies to adopt progressive policies that embrace LGBQ expressions for youth with intellectual disabilities. The government of Nova Scotia has taken positive steps in this regard, producing a policy guide for all provincial residential service providers (Regional Residential Services 1998). There is recognition that some persons with intellectual disabilities may require assistance in exploring their sexual orientation and that staff must contact the SRC to determine how to best offer support.

The visibility of LGBQ youth with intellectual disabilities within the larger queer communities is limited; despite evidence indicating their vulnerability—even within queer communities (Withers et al. 2001). Often, youth lack skills to negotiate safer sex since frequently they are not taught healthy sexuality practices within disability-related services. Further, to be labeled with an intellectual disability is to be stigmatized and ostracized within queer communities (as in the larger society) so these youth will frequently act in ways to hide their disability—often through unquestioning acquiescence to able-bodied persons.

Currently, there are a few support groups exclusively for LGBQ persons, including youth, with intellectual disabilities across North America and Europe. The Rainbow Support Group meets monthly and provides a safe space in which members can explore homosexualities from their perspectives (Allen 2003). Ron, a twenty-four-year-old man diagnosed with an intellectual disability as well as Attention Deficit Hyperactivity Disorder (ADHD), began attending the Rainbow Support Group a few years ago, encouraged by several staff members from his residential agency. Charming and charismatic, Ron helped other participants see themselves differently—as legitimate members of queer communities—after only his first meeting. Pam, also age twenty-four and a member of the Rainbow Support Group, was always clear in her intention to meet a partner (although the group is not a dating service). She met Dana, another woman with an intellectual disability, through the group and they are currently living together with the support of Dana's nearby family and their mutual staff support teams.

Such groups are critical—not only for LGBQ youth to obtain more appropriate information on safer sex, to translate gay jargon, and to have an open forum to discuss issues usually ignored—but just as important, to help facilitate LGBQ as cultural identification (Thompson 2003).

Bibliography

Allen, John. 2003. *Gay, Lesbian, Bisexual and Transgender People with Developmental Disabilities and Mental Retardation.* Binghamton, NY: Harrington Park Press.

Angrosino, Michael V. 1998. *Opportunity House: Ethnographic Stories of Mental Retardation.* London: Alta Mira Press.

Brantlinger, Ellen. 1992. "Sexuality Education in the Secondary Special Education Curriculum: Teachers' Perceptions and Concerns." *Teacher Education and Special Education* 15, no. 1: 32–40.

Hingsburger, David. 1993. "Staff Attitudes, Homosexuality and Developmental Disability: A Minority within a Minority." *The Canadian Journal of Human Sexuality* 2, no. 1: 19–22.

Lunsky, Yona, and Mary Konstantareas. 1998. "The Attitudes of Individuals with Autism and Mental Retardation towards Sexuality." *Education and Training in Mental Retardation and Developmental Disabilities* 33, no. 1: 24–33.

McCabe, Marita, and Robert Cummins. 1996. "The Sexual Knowledge, Experience, Feelings and Needs of People with Mild Intellectual Disability." *Education and Training in Mental Retardation and Developmental Disabilities* 31, no. 1: 13–21.

The McCreary Centre Society. 1993. *Sexual Abuse and Young People with Disabilities Project: Results and Recommendations.* Vancouver, BC: Author.

Regional Residential Services Society and the Nova Scotia Department of Health. 1998. *Relationships and Sexuality: A Guide for Individuals with Intellectual Disabilities and Their Residential Service Providers.* Halifax, Nova Scotia: Author.

Samowitz, Perry. 1997. *Relationship Series #3: The Sexuality Series.* New York: Young Adult Institute, National Institute for People with Disabilities.

Scotti, Joeseph, Kimberley Ujcich, Douglas Nangle, Karen Weigle, James Ellis, Karen Kirk, Glenda Vittimberga, Angela Giacoletti, and Rebecca Carr-Nangle. 1996. "Evaluation of an HIV/AIDS Education Program for Family-Based Foster-Care Providers." *Mental Retardation* 34, no. 7: 75–82.

Thompson, S. Anthony. 2003. "Subversive Political Praxis: Supporting Choice, Power and Control for People with Developmental Disabilities." *Disability & Society* 18, no. 6: 719–735.

Withers, Paul, Ian Ensum, Daniel Howarth, Patrick Krall, Damian Thomas, Donald Weekes, Charles Winter, Andrew Mulholland, Tim Dindjer, and John Hall. 2001. "A Psychoeducational Group for Men with Intellectual Disabilities who Have Sex with Men." *Journal of Applied Research in Intellectual Disabilities* 14, no. 4: 327–339.

Wolfe, Pamela. 1997. "The Influence of Personal Values on Issues of Sexuality and Disability." *Sexuality and Disability* 15, no. 2: 69–89.

Web Sites

The Association for Persons with Severe Handicaps (TASH). October 2004. Accessed May 26, 2005. http://www.tash.org. Offers various resources useful for LGBQ persons with intellectual disabilities and their supporters.

International Coalition on Abuse and Disability. 2003. Dick Sobsey. Accessed May 26, 2005. http://www.ualberta.ca/~jpdasddc/abuse/. Includes an international listserv with contributions from people with various disabilities and their allies.

Disabilities, Physical

Maria Pallotta-Chiarolli

Physical disabilities include speech impediments, sensory impairments such as various degrees and forms of visual and hearing impediments; and mobility impairments such as those which require the use of a wheelchair, scooter, or walking aids. Same-sex attracted young people with such disabilities generally experience exclusion and **harassment** in relation to their sexuality as well as in relation to their disability. **Lesbian** and **bisexual** female youth with physical disabilities find themselves also experiencing gender-based harassment. Similarly, heterosexual-identifying young people with physical disabilities often experience **homophobia** if the movement and appearance of their bodies transgress dominant constructions of masculinity and femininity. They also often express overt homophobia and hyperheterosexuality as a means of compensating for their disability. There has been an absence of educational research on how homophobia and **heteronormativity** impact on same-sex attracted young people with physical disabilities.

The limited **research** that has been conducted shows that the disability/heterosexuality interface is a significant issue in schools for young people with physical disabilities. For example, Shakespeare (1996) reports how a young man with neuromuscular impairment received homophobic harassment from peers at school due to his arched back and thrust-forward chest because his appearance suggested he had "a womanly bust." Thus, boys with physical disabilities often find that their disability becomes a signifier of marginal heterosexual masculinity. In other words, by not possessing a body that "looks like a normal man's body" or "moves like a normal man's body," this "abnormality" is equated with not being a "normal" heterosexual boy. Any movement or stance that is defined as feminine or less than

See also Community LGBT Youth Groups; Gender Roles; Physical Education, Teaching of; Special Education, LGBT Youth in; Coming Out, Youth.

masculine is seen as indicative of asexuality or homosexuality. For example, to be a boy in a wheelchair is to be "impotent, unable to be a (hetero)sexual being, and therefore not a 'complete' man" (Morris 1991, 96).

In order to achieve a measure of normalization, young people often use various strategies of compensation for their disability. One of the strategies is to perform or fashion a hyper-heterosexual masculinity and femininity (Shakespeare 1999; Martino and Pallotta-Chiarolli 2003). For example, Kieran is an adolescent boy with a speech impediment, which often led to homophobic harassment by other boys at school. The homophobia ceased only when he had a girlfriend because he had gained some hetero-masculinist status among his male peers: "I'm not worried anymore. Being in a relationship with a girl, it makes you feel like you're worth something." Likewise, Marc, another Australian youth, uses various walking aids and occasionally a wheelchair due to bone weakness. He became a member of a rock band and worked very hard to achieve popularity with girls:

> I've had that [homophobic harassment from able-bodied boys], but now who's laughing? They say, "If you have sex, will you break?" Because I break bones easy, they go, "Does your dick break in half?" And then . . . the chicks started in Year 9 . . . I got seven chicks after me . . . As soon as I did start going out with girls it didn't matter if they [boys] were paying me out because I was having the last laugh because I actually was with a girl.

Young people with disabilities may also homophobically harass able-bodied and disabled students as a way of positioning others below themselves on the social ladder (Morris 1991; Martino and Pallotta-Chiarolli 2003).

Schools are sites for the stigmatization of disabilities and the harassment of same-sex attracted young people with disabilities (Martino and Pallotta-Chiarolli 2003). To the extent that antiharassment and anti**bullying** policies and programs exist within schools, they do not equitably address sexual diversity, cultural diversity, and physical diversity. If they are addressed, they are constructed as separate rather than inter-weaving categories (Shakespeare 1996; Vernon 1999). Thus, these policies and programs need to acknowledge and cater to students who are receiving multiple forms of harassment. This can be done by specifying the various forms of harassment in any policy and program for all students and staff, and explaining how they can be experienced in interwoven and multiple ways. School **curriculum**, particularly in health education and personal development, can be used to raise awareness of various forms of physical disabilities and their impact on bodily functions and performances. A young man, Tony, who is in a wheelchair with muscular dystrophy, recalls the interwoven forms of homophobic, racist, and ableist harassment he received at school:

> I had my chair rammed into. . . . They called me Squealer because of my funny high voice. . . . They called me fag. . . . They picked on me because I was Greek. I was scared of some of those guys. . . . There was no one else there with disabilities as obvious as me and I remember being really traumatized and crying myself asleep at night not wanting to go to school.

Physically disabled LGBT youth also face challenges with respect to sexual behavior. School **sexuality education** programs seldom address homosexuality or disability, so for young people with disabilities who have limited access to information and resources, the articulation of their sexuality with their disability may be especially problematic (Sipski and Alexander 1997; Martino and Pallotta-Chiarolli 2003). Schools are important sites for dispelling predominant myths regarding people with disabilities. Namely, that they are asexual, all heterosexual, or physically unable to be sexual. Not only do LGBT young people with disabilities require education about puberty, sexual function, sexual **desire**, and sexual safety like able-bodied hetero-sexual youth, there are added dimensions that schools need to address. These include handling homophobia, developing a positive **body image**, knowing their sexuality is valid and that they can form relationships, and understanding the specificities of their particular physical needs in order to enjoy sexual activity. Indeed, such education is important for all students to understand and engage with the multiple facets of sexu-alities and bodies. Schools can also enlist counselors and **social work**ers who can undertake private sessions with LGBT young people with disabilities. These profes-sionals can connect them with LGBT-friendly disability services and disability-friendly queer services and venues in the community as well as assume a significant role in mediating with parents as the young person "comes out."

Insufficient attention has been given to LGBT youth with physical disabilities within the predominantly able-bodied queer communities, which are also sites of **discrimination** (Shakespeare, Gillespie-Sells, and Davies 1997, Tony 2005). Thus, these disabled youth may also experience alienation, not only at school, but in the wider heteronormative able-bodied society and in the queer community. Mainstream LGBT organisations, including queer youth organizations, do not usually undertake much research or activism to affirm and encourage participation of queer youth with disabilities. This is often due to a lack of awareness of the issues and limited funding or other resources. Thus, LGBT people with disabilities will often endeavor to form their networks and subgroups under the umbrella of LGBT communities. For exam-ple, the Safe Schools Coalition Web site (http://www.safeschoolscoalition.org/RG-glbt_youth_with_disabilities.html.) provides a comprehensive list of LGBT peo-ple with disabilities' Web sites, organizations, and listservs, through which young people with various physical disabilities can access and construct community.

The multiple exclusions and **prejudices** result in isolation and impeded **mental health** for many young people (Morris 1991; Taleporos and McCabe 2002; Vernon 1999). For example, many LGBT young people with disabilities are completely re-liant upon parents and caregivers to transport them to social events. If they have not come out to their families and caregivers, it is highly unlikely they will be able to attend LGBT community events (Tony 2005). Thus, this lack of independence can lead to depression, isolation, and loneliness. On the other hand, those young people who are able to participate in LGBT community may find venues to be pro-hibitive of safe, sociable, and accessible mobility. Able-bodied queer youth, too, may not wish to engage socially and sexually with those who are disabled. Simi-larly, within mainstream social networks for young people with disabilities, LGBT young people may not feel that their sexuality will be accepted, or they may be the only participant who identifies as same-sex attracted.

Bibliography

Martino, Wayne, and Maria Pallotta-Chiarolli. 2003. "'You're Not a Real Boy if You're Disabled': Boys Negotiating Physical Disability and Masculinity in Schools." Pp. 159–180 in *So What's a Boy? Addressing Issues of Masculinity in Education.*

Edited by Wayne Martino and Maria Pallotta-Chiarolli Buckingham, UK: Open University Press.

Morris, Jan. 1991. *Pride against Prejudice: Transforming Attitudes to Disability*. London: Women's Press.

Shakespeare, Tom. 1996. "Power and Prejudice: Issues of Gender, Sexuality and Disability" Pp. 191–214 in *Disability and Society: Emerging Issues and Insights*. Edited by Len Barton. London: Longman.

———. 1999. "The Sexual Politics of Disabled Masculinity." *Sexuality and Disability* 17, no. 1: 53–64.

Shakespeare, Tom, Kath Gillespie-Sells, Dominic Davies, eds. 1997. *The Sexual Politics of Disability: Untold Desires*. London: Cassell.

Sipski, Marca. L., and Craig Alexander, eds. 1997. *Sexual Function in People with Disability and Chronic Illness: A Health Professional's Guide*. Frederick, MD: Aspen.

Taleporos, George, and Marita P. McCabe. 2002. "The Impact of Sexual Esteem, Body Esteem, and Sexual Satisfaction on Psychological Well-Being in People with Physical Disability." *Sexuality and Disability* 20, no. 3: 177–183.

Tony. 2005. "Coming Out and Being Disabled: Risky Business." Pp. 202–203 in *When Our Children Come Out*. Edited by Maria Pallotta-Chiarolli. Sydney: Finch Publishing.

Vernon, A. 1999. "The Dialectics of Multiple Identities and the Disabled People's Movement." *Disability and Society* 14, no. 3: 385–398.

Web Site

Susan's Sex Support Site. March 2004. http://sexsupport.org/GLBTlinks.html. Accessed May 25, 2005. Includes a range of academic readings, community listings, and other resources regarding LGBT youth and disabilities.

Discrimination

Laura J. Gambone

Discrimination is the unequal and often unkind treatment of a member of a minority group based on group membership. Discrimination has two subcategories, interpersonal discrimination and institutional discrimination, which work together to create and maintain the oppressed status of a social group. Interpersonal discrimination consists of avoiding, distancing, excluding, or physically violating a minority group member due to his/her group status (Lott & Maluso 1995; Rey & Gibson 1997). Institutional discrimination is the exclusion or unequal treatment of members of a minority group by social institutions. **Lesbian, gay, bisexual**, and **transgender** youth experience interpersonal discrimination in the forms of family and peer rejection, slurs, **harassment**, threats, the absence of positive role models, mistreatment by medical and mental health workers, and the absence of supportive adults or **allies** at school, at home, and in the community. Common examples of institutional discrimination against LGBT youth include exclusion of relevant

See also Coming Out, Youth; Disabilities, Intellectual; Disabilities, Physical; Educational Policies; Heterosexism; Legal Issues, Students; Prejudice; Religion and Psychological Development; Sexism; Youth, At Risk.

knowledge or information from school **curriculum**, lack of relevant school programs and **community support groups**, and exclusion from **cocurricular activities** and events such as **proms**. Interpersonal and institutional discrimination does not end with adulthood; rather, it continues into the work force, housing, legal relationship options, child custody and **adoption**, and overall civil rights protection.

LGBT youth face multiple forms of interpersonal discrimination. Slang like "dyke," "fag," and their equivalents are commonplace and communicate to LGBT youth that their **sexual identity** is unacceptable and that **bullying** by others is acceptable. Rejection, verbal and physical harassment, threats, or even **sexual assault and abuse** at the hands of teachers, fellow students, and/or family members is among the interpersonal discriminatory experiences of many LGBT youth. Some teachers and **administrators** participate in discrimination by using negative slang themselves, framing homosexuality in a negative light, failing to intervene in the mistreatment of LGBT students, or ignoring LGBT issues in the school.

Facing discrimination or a hostile **school climate**, adolescents may turn to school counselors or social workers, mental health or medical professionals, or religious groups for support. These professionals, however, are often untrained on handling of LGBT clients or issues and may be heterosexist or homophobic themselves. Further, a number of religious institutions, particularly in **Jewish, Christian,** and **Muslim** traditions, teach that homosexuality is sinful and/or changeable, rendering such places unlikely sources of support. Positive LGBT adult role models in schools and in communities can be valuable sources of information and support for LGBT youth, however, decades of discrimination against homosexuals can result in a hesitancy to develop these **mentoring** relationships due to perpetuation of myths such as "recruitment."

LGBT individuals of color may face additional discrimination due to their multiple minority statuses. Especially for **Asian American** and **Latino/a** queer youth, family duty and traditional **gender roles** within the family are often considered primary cultural responsibilities, and negative familial reactions are likely to result from their perceived rejection. Religious-based discrimination, particularly **religious fundamentalism**, and familial rejection may be especially harmful—although religion and family can serve extremely important roles as sources of **resiliency** for some youth. Homosexuality may also be seen as a "white disease" in many communities of color, while **racism** exists in many LGBT communities. Thus queer youth of color may feel a need to choose between forms of discrimination, since it can be difficult to belong to both communities.

Legally, institutional discrimination and institutional protections available against it vary greatly from country to country. In some places, such as northern **Europe**, parts of Central and **South America**, and most of **Canada**, as well as **New Zealand, South Africa,** and **Australia**, sexual orientation is a protected category in discrimination legislation. These protections generally encompass, or coexist with legislation that encompasses, treatment at school and on the job. One example of this type of law is the Republic of South Africa, which, in 1996, became the first country to offer specific **sexual orientation** protection in its constitution. At the other extreme, a number of Muslim countries in Northern Africa and the Middle East uphold Sharia law (religious courts in which strict interpretations of Islam hold sway), which forbids the practice of homosexuality. Same-sex partners, for example in Egypt, caught in any form of intimacy are subject to corporal punishment, lengthy imprisonment, or even death. LGBT individuals have little protection from institutional discrimination in these places. In some other locales, particularly in parts of **Asia**, homosexuality and **transsexuality** have been made invisible to the extent that no mention of their legal status exists in the law. Nevertheless, institutional discrimination can still exist in education, group membership, housing, employment, military, marriage, adoption, and child custody.

In the United States, although sexual orientation is not a protected category in federal discrimination legislation, federal protection against discrimination exists in publicly funded schools via Title IX, a federal statute designed to require equal treatment of the sexes in schools. This statute specifically includes gay and lesbian students in its protection against sexual harassment, and school districts and/or administrators can be held legally responsible for failing to protect LGBT students from harassment. Title IX also guarantees LGBT students equal rights to organize groups and clubs using school property and funds. The statute is not always adhered to, but the number of school-based organizations such as **gay–straight alliances** is increasing rapidly. Regarding group membership outside of school, however, the Supreme Court ruled, in June of 2000, that the **Boy Scouts of America** have the right to ban homosexual individuals from leadership positions. Although the Court did not specifically state that sexual minority boys can also be excluded from the group, it is implied.

Institutional discrimination against LGBT individuals in schools involves the frequent omission of discussions or teachings related to homosexuality and LGBT historical figures from the curriculum, even when these topics are relevant. In some places, particularly in parts of **Africa**, the Middle East, and parts of North America, it is policy-mandated that homosexuality not be presented in a positive light or that it be excluded entirely. Other ways in which schools and other institutions more subtly discriminate via the invisibility of LGBT individuals include devising forms for heterosexual couples and only displaying representations of heterosexual families.

Interpersonal and institutional discrimination work together. One example is the failure of **teachers** and administrators to intervene in discrimination against LGBT youth. Scholars suggest that this hesitancy is due to the fear of being thought to be gay or lesbian oneself and the actuality that outing, whether accurate or inaccurate, could legally result in job loss in some places and corporal punishment or death in others.

The **workplace** is one example where institutional discrimination follows LGBT youth into adulthood. In the United States, only federal civilian employees are protected from job and housing discrimination via federal law and, as of 2004, just fourteen states and the District of Columbia offered such protections. However, in the private sector, major corporations, from Wal-Mart to IBM, have adopted **antidiscrimination policies** for their LGBT employees. Legal protection from sexuality-based employment discrimination is found in most of Europe and Canada as well as in Australia, **Israel**, and South Africa.

For many youth, the military is an important option in lieu of education or the workplace. However, LGBT youth are unable to join the military in many countries, including **Japan**, Greece, Hungary, Turkey, and **Brazil** among many others. In the United States, though LGB military participation is not banned outright, the "Don't ask, don't tell" policy allows LGB individuals to join the military only if they are willing and able to keep their sexuality hidden. Transsexual individuals are medically disqualified from joining. Exceptions to these policies are found in much of Europe, Israel, Australia, New Zealand, South Africa, Lithuania, Canada, the Czech Republic, and several other countries.

Institutional discrimination may be a problem for youth once again when it comes to sexual expression. In many countries, particularly in countries where government is heavily influenced by conservative Islamic or Judeo-Christian beliefs, such as most of Africa and the Middle East as well as parts of the Americas, same gender sexual intimacy remains criminalized. Further, even in countries where homosexuality has been decriminalized, the legal age of homosexual consent generally is much older than for heterosexuals, unfairly limiting the legally available means of sexual expression. Similarly, restrictions on youth access to sexually-explicit materials, from the **Internet** to magazines, are also common in most countries. Censorship in the United States has been extended to schools where blocking software restricts information relevant to LGBT youth.

Institutional discrimination may again become an obstacle as LGBT youth choose a life partner or wish to have children. Currently full marriage rights are available to same-sex couples only in the Netherlands, Belgium, most of Canada, and to citizens of the state of Massachusetts. "Registered Partnerships" and other legal statuses in which most, but not all, rights associated with marriage are obtained exist in Australia, much of Europe, Vermont, Connecticut, California, Hawaii, Maine, New Jersey, and the District of Columbia. In the United States, the federal government opposed the legalization of same-sex marriage in 1996 via a statute called the "Defense of Marriage Act," which defines marriage as "a union between a man and a woman." Forty American states have laws or amendments banning gay marriage.

Two of the several hundred legal rights associated with marriage are the rights to adopt a spouse's children and to maintain custody of one's own children in the case of divorce. These are particularly significant for **children of LGBT parents**. Legal adoption of a partner's children is specifically permitted by law only in Scandinavian countries. Elsewhere, children of LGBT individuals risk being uprooted from their homes and their remaining parent in the event of the death, divorce, or abandonment by their biological parent. In many countries, parental sexual orientation plays an important role in determining which parent is deemed most fit. This also contains the danger of unnecessarily disrupting the lives of youth whose parent(s) identify as LGBT. General adoption, too, is limited for LGBT individuals in most countries.

Bibliography

Baker, Jean M. 2002. *How Homophobia Hurts Children: Nurturing Diversity at Home, at School, and in the Community*. Binghamton, NY: Harrington Park Press.

Harper, Gary W., and Margaret Schneider. 2003. "Oppression and Discrimination among Lesbian, Gay, Bisexual, and Transgendered People and Communities: A Challenge for Community Psychology." *American Journal of Community Psychology* 31: 243–252.

Lott, Bernice, and Diane Maluso, eds. 1995. *The Social Psychology of Interpersonal Discrimination*. New York: Guilford Press.

Rey, Amy M., and Pamela Reed Gibson. 1997. "Beyond High School: Heterosexuals' Self-Reported Anti-Gay/Lesbian Behaviors and Attitudes." Pp. 65–84 in *School Experiences of Gay and Lesbian Youth: The Invisible Minority*. Edited by Mary B. Harris. Binghamton, NY: Haworth Press.

Web Sites

Human Rights Campaign Homepage. December 2004. Accessed December 3, 2004. http://www.hrc.org. Information on current LGBT issues, laws, political campaigns, and related news.

The International Gay and Lesbian Human Rights Commission Homepage. December 2004. Accessed December 3, 2004. http://www.iglhrc.org/site/iglhrc/. Frequently updated information regarding the LGBT news, rights, and campaigns worldwide.

The International Lesbian and Gay Organization Homepage. December 2004. Nigel Warner. Accessed December 3, 2004. http://www.ilga.org. World news related to LGBT issues and information on laws impacting LGBT rights worldwide.

Domestic and Relationship Violence

Peggy Lorah

Domestic violence describes a pattern of coercive and/or abusive behavior used by a current or former intimate partner or a family member for the purpose of gaining or maintaining power and control. Domestic and relationship violence are problems that face many **lesbian, gay, bisexual**, and **transgender** (LGBT) individuals, particularly high school and college students. The abuse can be verbal, economic, emotional, psychological, physical, or sexual in nature, and it is typically committed by a **dating** partner or a life partner, although parents and siblings can also be abusive under this definition. A review of **research** studies shows that the prevalence of same-sex relationship violence ranges from 17 percent to 46 percent of those surveyed, about the same as for the heterosexual population (Elliott 1996).

Verbal abuse includes behaviors such as criticizing, name-calling, yelling, and threats of emotional or physical harm. Examples of economic abuse are keeping money from the victim, keeping the victim from getting a job or constantly appearing at the job site, and interfering with schooling. Emotional abuse includes the use of isolation or blackmail. Questioning the victim's sanity or saying that the victim is "messed up" are examples of psychological abuse. Behaviors such as slapping, hitting, punching, pushing, kicking, and throwing objects evidence physical abuse. **Sexual abuse** includes forcing unwanted sexual activities, inflicting pain during sex, and threatening transmission of HIV or sexually transmitted infections. Abuse is not the victim's fault. No one deserves to be treated badly. Victims cannot prevent abuse, and they cannot control someone else's violent behavior. Only the abusive partner can do that.

LGBT individuals who are victims of domestic violence have to deal with these behaviors, but there are also additional issues that are specific to them. These include threats to "out" them or actually outing them, alleging that no one will believe them or help them because of their **sexual orientation** or **gender identity**, telling them that abuse does not happen in LGBT relationships, saying that the abuse is mutual, and portraying themselves as the victim in the relationship.

See also Coming Out, Youth; Community LGBT Youth Groups; Parents, Responses to Homosexuality; Sexual Abuse and Assault; Youth, At Risk.

Relationship/domestic violence occurs in at least 25 percent of heterosexual relationships, and even though the LGBT population is largely silent about this problem, it is believed that the rate of domestic violence is at least as high for them. For young adults, in general, studies have shown that between one-third and one-half of high school students report having been in violent dating relationships, while between 65 and 70 percent report a history of dating violence (Wingspan 1998). Those who provide services for gay and lesbian youth estimate that their percentages of violence are even higher, because **homophobia** is added to the risk factors that exist for heterosexual victims (Wingspan 1998). It feels even less safe for an LGBT victim to share with anyone, either because the perpetrator of violence has said that no one will believe the victim or that the victim deserved the violence because of sexual orientation/gender identity, or because victims, themselves, believe they deserve the violence. There also is less information available about transgender relationship violence. The few studies that have been done indicate that abuse incidences are even more common for youth in this population (Wingspan 1998). As is the case with heterosexual relationship violence, relationship violence in the LGBT community occurs across the spectrum of gender, **race**, **ethnicity**, and **social class**.

Victims of LGBT relationship violence may be reluctant to report the violence to anyone, believing that there is no help for them. They may also fear the threats their abusive partner has made or fear violent retaliation. Victims may love their abusive partners and may believe that they can change. They may also fear homophobic responses from law enforcement or medical facilities or even from hotline and shelter personnel. Law enforcement officers and medical providers may not be trained to deal with LGBT relationship violence in affirming ways, and shelter and advocacy services may not be responsive to the particular needs of LGBT victims. Additionally, in most, if not all, regions of the United States, LGBT individuals may not have the same access to protection orders and other civil remedies as heterosexual individuals do. Both the perception and the reality of these barriers can keep victims from sharing their circumstances with anyone.

LGBT youth are also at risk of violence committed by parents or guardians. Domestic violence can occur particularly when a child has "come out" within the family. This is particularly the case with fathers and GBT sons, and the violence often has to do with expectations of manhood. For example, a father may feel that he can beat his GBT son into being a "real man," which is to say a heterosexual man.

Safety planning is the most important consideration for victims of relationship violence. Although safety plans may vary with situations, a key element is sharing one's circumstances with someone else. LGBT victims are often reluctant to talk to anyone, including friends and family members. They fear that no one will believe them and they may believe that telling someone is betraying their partner. Within LGBT communities, there has been silence about relationship violence; many individuals believe that abuse happens only in heterosexual relationships. LGBT victims of abuse are often reluctant to talk with anyone outside of their communities, fearing that they are betraying not only their partner, but also the entire LGBT population. Many victims find it helpful to talk with an advocate affiliated with a domestic violence program. This can be done anonymously by phone.

If the victim lives with family members or on a campus and is in a dating violence situation, it is again important to identify a safe person to talk to. In high school settings, that person could be a trusted teacher, a guidance counselor, a **gay–straight alliance** advisor, or a member of a student assistance program who is known to be LGBT-friendly. Even if such individuals do not have experience dealing with relationship violence, they will be able to connect the victim with community resources. Since school districts have **educational policies** about confidentiality when any type of interpersonal violence is reported, victims should always ask what school personnel are required to report before they share information. If it does not feel safe to talk to someone at school about a situation, victims can always call their local domestic violence program (found in the blue pages of the phone book under "Abuse") or the National Domestic Violence Hotline (800–799-SAFE). Calls to such hotlines can be anonymous, but even if the victim identifies herself or himself, individuals who work for domestic violence programs are protected by confidentiality regulations in a different way than school personnel. Hotline workers have taken special training that exempts them from having to report to anyone. An exception to this might be when the victim is in danger because a parent or guardian is violent, and then state mandated reporting guidelines could take precedence.

In college or university settings, victims can talk with student affairs staff members, most of whom have LGBT diversity training. There are several units within student affairs that are likely to provide the best assistance. Many campuses also have women's centers that are LGBT-affirming and that deal with relationship violence for women and men students. College **counseling** centers often have designated therapists who are both LGBT-affirming and trained to deal with relationship violence issues. Campus health care providers are also likely to employ staff trained to provide information and support. Some have either **college campus resource centers** or multicultural centers with LGBT offices, which typically employ individuals who can deal with relationship violence, either themselves or by referral. Many schools across the country have received Department of Justice Violence Against Women on Campus grants, and any school that administers one of these grants should have programs in place to deal with LGBT relationship violence.

Bibliography

Elliott, Pam. 1996. "Shattering Illusions: Same-Sex Domestic Violence." *Journal of Gay and Lesbian Social Services* 4: 1–8.

National Coalition of Anti-Violence Programs. 2003. *National Report on Lesbian, Gay, Bisexual and Transgender Domestic Violence.* 7th ed. New York: Author.

Renzetti, Claire M. 1997. "Violence and Abuse in Same-Sex Couples." Pp. 70–89 in *Violence Between Intimate Partners: Patterns, Causes, and Effects.* Edited by Albert P. Cardarelli. Boston: Allyn and Bacon.

Wallace, Harvey. 1999. *Family Violence: Legal, Medical, and Social Perspectives.* 2nd ed. Boston: Allyn and Bacon.

Wingspan Domestic Violence Project. 1998. *Abuse and Violence in Same-Gender Relationships: A Resource for the Lesbian, Gay, Bisexual and Transgender Communities.* Tucson, AZ: Author.

Web Sites

Community United Against Violence Domestic Violence Program. 2003. Accessed December 7, 2004. http://www.xq.com/cuav/domviol.htm. Provides good general information and links to other sites.

Gay Men's Domestic Violence Project. 2004. Accessed December 7, 2004. http://www. gmdvp.org. Information and resources about domestic/relationship violence, myths, and facts about same-sex violence, and an excellent reading list, as well as links to other sites.

Love Doesn't Have to Hurt. 2003. Accessed December 7, 2004. http://www.apa.org/pi/ pii/teen/. Offers good information for teens and young adults. Although it focuses mostly on heterosexual relationships, it addresses gay and lesbian situations.

Texas Council on Family Violence. National Domestic Violence Hotline. 2004. Accessed December 7, 2004. http://www.ndvh.org. This has an excellent section on teen and young adult dating violence that addresses LGBT concerns.

Drug Use

Pamela K. Autrey

Drug use, including both legal and illegal substances, refers to aesthetic use of mind-altering substances to create alternate realities or to ameliorate stress. Drug use refers to its occasional and social usage while drug abuse intersects with multiple factors, including genetic/biochemical, psychological, and social/environmental factors, in its emergence as a behavior pattern and/or addiction. Although **lesbian, gay, bisexual, transgender,** and questioning (LGBTQ) youth have similar reasons to use drugs as their heterosexual counterparts, the additional stress of dealing with issues such as **sexual identity** and **coming out**, compounded by **homophobia**, increases the likelihood of drug use or abuse. Although there is a downward trend in drug use and abuse among youth, this is not supported for LGBTQ youth and heterosexual girls.

Homosexuality does not cause drug use and/or abuse. By and large, LGBTQ students are stigmatized in schools, which often have negative psychosocial impact on these youth. From routine **harassment** and bullying to heteronormative activities like **proms** and a **curriculum** that seldom includes LGBTQ topics, to the lack of knowledge or support among teachers, counselors, and **administrators**, schools are the principal site of social/environmental factors that contribute to stress. Although all adolescents must integrate the biological, cognitive, psychological, and social changes of the transition to adulthood, heterosexual students have resources that LGBTQ youth do not have, including institutionalized **dating** rituals (school dances, open dating, **cocurricular activities**), the blessings of society, schools, churches, and families, appropriate role models, and access to accurate information about heterosexuality. Instead, the LGBTQ student has to negotiate a stigmatized identity, generally without these supports.

See also Adolescent Sexualities; AIDS; Identity Development; Gender Roles; Latinos and Latinas; Mental Health; Passing; School Climate, K-12; Mentoring; Youth, At Risk; Youth, Homeless.

Early **adolescence** is when LGBTQ youth begin to struggle with their **sexual orientation**—one they have been socialized to believe is shameful and perverted. Internalized homophobia, experienced as self-loathing and low self-esteem, is experienced by many LGTQ youth. Struggling not only with a stigmatized identity but with a crucial need for community belongingness, these youth may adopt dysfunctional coping mechanisms, including drug use. And many behavior patterns are set during adolescence and continue into adulthood.

The Youth Risk Behavior Surveillance System (YRBSS) of the United States Centers for Disease Control monitors sex categories of priority health-risk behaviors among youth and young adults; one of these categories is substance use. **The Youth Risk Behavior Surveys** are administered in public secondary schools every two years. Most states do not differentiate on the basis of sexual orientation. Nationwide, based on 13,601 completed questionnaires in 150 schools, 42.4 percent of ninth-through twelfth-grade students used marijuana, 9.8 percent of students used methamphetamines, and 9.4 percent of students used a form of cocaine (e.g., powder, crack, or freebase) during their lifetimes (Grunbaum et al. 2001). In this 2001 survey, 28.5 percent of students had been offered, sold, or given an illegal drug on school property during the twelve months prior to the survey. Whites and Hispanics were substantially higher users of illegal drugs than **African Americans** in the most recent YRBSS survey. **Asian Americans** have the lowest rate of illicit drug use although there are variations among Asian subgroups, the highest being 5.1 percent of Koreans. Females and males of the same race used drugs at about the same rate.

A few states do include questions(s) in their YRBSs that address sexual identity. One study (Faulkner and Cranston 1998) analyzed data from the 1993 Massachusetts Youth Risk Behavior Survey for the prevalence of high risk behaviors among sexually-experienced LGB youth compared to that of sexually-experienced heterosexual youth. Because of the small subgroup sizes, homosexually and bisexually experienced students were grouped together and comprised 6.4% of sexually-experienced youth. Compared to heterosexual youth, this group was almost four times more likely to have used marijuana forty or more times in the thirty days before the survey and were six times more likely to have used cocaine recently—nineteen times more likely to have used it ten or more times in the preceding month. Same-sex students were five times more likely to have used other illegal drugs twenty or more times in their lives and to have injected illegal drugs seven times more often. Another recent study found bisexual youths to be at highest risk among LGBTQ students and questions whether the high percentages of risk found in representative studies for **substance abuse** is driven by bisexual youths, "who in fact have made up the largest portions of LGB youths in these studies" (Russell, Driscoll, and Truong 2002, 2013).

Similarly, higher rates of drug use among lesbians and gay youth have been found in other countries. A summary of a study of 2,987 Norwegian LGB youth (Hegna 2001) produced by Norwegian Social Research (NOVA) reported that twice as many LGB adolescent youth had used illegal narcotic substances in the year preceding the survey. A 21-year longitudinal study of 1,265 children born in Christchurch, **New Zealand** (Fergusson, Horwood, and Beautrais 1999) found 61 percent of LGB youth reported substance abuse at age 21 compared to 44 percent of heterosexual youth.

LGBTQ youth experience isolation—social, emotional, and cognitive—and many LGBTQ youth live with multiple identities negotiated within the politics of different social situations, which create further isolation. For those who decide to, "coming out" is fraught with stressful possibilities whereas for those who do not come out or who try to "pass" as heterosexual, there is the constant threat of discovery. When one is forced to "live a lie" in order to survive, when the gap between the norms and what is necessary to live one's everyday life grows too wide, stopgap measures emerge; one of these is drug use.

Drugs have different effects and those popular in the youth market can be separated into three broad categories: those which ease negative feelings via a tranquilizing effect, such as Xanax, Valium, and marijuana; "club" or "party" drugs, including Ecstasy, methamphetamines, and LSD, stimulants that noticeable alter personality and behaviors; and steroids which enhance body image. The part drugs play in cultural production for LGBTQ youth is partially due to the coproduction of **youth culture** with heterosexual youth, of which drug use is already a dividing line between users and nonusers. The here-and-now emphasis of youth experiences makes identity ever-changing and must be considered as a factor in how they use social and cultural practices to shape their worlds. For both LGBTQ youth and heterosexual youth, drug use is contextual. A recent study found that adolescent girls are more likely to be offered illicit drugs in private places such as a friend's home whereas boys are more likely to receive such offers in public situations such as parks (Albert, Brown, and Flanigan 2003). Teenage girls are also more likely than boys to report that cocaine, LSD, and heroin are fairly or very easy to obtain. The study faults the availability of private homes where both parents work as one of the dimensions of teenagers' drug use and, for girls, the presence of boys two or more years older. They also cite evidence that substance use before the age of fifteen is a predictor of adult substance abuse.

Community is vital to healthy development for adolescent youth. For some, small friendship groups organize around drug use. Raves (also called "trances") and gay clubs provide opportunities for hyper-release of stress and self-expression in the context of a community based on drug use. Club drugs taken in the context of a gay bar or rave provide a pseudo-reality enhanced by their psychotropic effects in which the one reality of their lives problematic in other social situations can be expressed.

Club drugs include "poppers' (amyl nitrate), methamphetamine (speed, meth, ice, crystal, and crank), Viagra, Ecstasy (MDMA, Adam, and XTC), hallucinogens (LSD, cocaine), and depressants (Special K, Disco biscuits, Sopers, Quads). The effects of these kinds of drugs enhance the effects of music, lights, dance, sex, and alcohol, while weakening inhibitions. Designer drugs refer to drug cocktails. Drugs like Ecstasy, crystal Meth, and LSD produce long-term effects, making the body pulsate with hyper-energy for hours. Other drugs are used as the night progresses to refresh and/or intensify the high, including cocaine and amyl nitrate. Drugs like Viagra, marijuana, and depressants moderate the undesirable side effects of these club drugs, while making long-lasting sex binges possible.

These drug-saturated contexts provide community for queer youth to congregate without fear of judgment, stigmatization, or violence. The pairing of drug use and sex may persist into adulthood; loss of inhibitions often leads to unprotected sex—a particular concern given the possibilities of HIV infection and other sexually-transmitted diseases (STDs). Methamphetamine users report more unsafe receptive anal intercourse, greater condom breakage, and more unprotected sex with HIV-positive partners (Midwest AIDS Prevention Project 2001).

For other LGBTQ students who are trying to "pass" as heterosexual, hyper-surveillance of their behaviors and fears of inappropriate reactions in sexually-charged spaces may make drug use risky for them. Those young gay men for whom masculinity is important may also not want to lose control and engage in gender inappropriate or effeminate behaviors.

Girls and young women use drugs for different reasons than boys and young men and get addicted faster with greater consequences. Increased rates of depression or anxiety and eating disorders are two culprits, but a recent study also found that national antidrug campaigns do not address adolescent female causes of substance use and abuse (CASA 2003). The hormonal differences between girls and boys may be the cause of a gender difference in susceptibility to the toxic effects of some drugs such as Ecstasy. When women use this drug, they lose significantly more brain cells (Albert, Brown, and Flanigan 2003). **Research** has not examined the relevance of drug use and abuse among young lesbians.

Bibliography

Albert, Bill, Sarah Brown, and Christine M. Flanigan, eds. 2003. *14 and Younger: The Sexual Behavior of Young Adolescents* (Summary). Washington, D.C.: National Campaign to Prevent Teen Pregnancy. Accessed August 9, 2004. http://www.teenpregnancy.org. (Type "14 and younger" into search engine.)

CASA—The National Center on Addiction and Substance Abuse at Columbia University. 2003, February. *The Formative Years: Pathways to Substance Abuse among Girls and Young Women Ages 8–22.* Accessed August 9, 2004. http:www.casacolumbia.org. (Type The Formative Years into search engine.)

Faulkner, Anne H., and Kevin Cranston. 1998. "Correlates of Same-Sex Sexual Behavior in a Random Sample of Massachusetts High School Students." *American Journal of Public Health* 88, no. 2: 262–266.

Fergusson, David M., L., John Horwood, and Annette L. Beautrais. 1999. "Is Sexual Orientation Related to Mental Health Problems and Suicidality in Young People?" *Archives of General Psychiatry* 56: 876–891.

Grunbaum, Jo Anne, Laura Kann, Steven A. Kinchen, Barbara Williams, James G. Ross, Richard Lowry, and Lloyd Kolbe. 2001. "Youth Risk Behavior Surveillance—United States, 2001." *Morbidity and Mortality Weekly Report.* Accessed August 9, 2004. http://www.cdcgiv/mmwr.

Hegna, Kristinn. 2001. "Norway's GLB Suicide Problems: A Summary of the Hegna et al. (1999) Study of 2987 Norwegian GLB Individuals." Accessed August 8, 2004. http://www.fsw.ucalgary.ca/ramsay/homosexuality.

Kus, Robert J., ed. 1995. *Addiction and Recovery in Gay and Lesbian Persons.* Binghamton, NY: Haworth Press.

Massachusetts Department of Education. 2001. *1999 Massachusetts Youth Risk Behavior Survey.* Accessed August 9. 2004. http://www.doe.mass.edu/yrbs99.

Philleo, Joanne, Frances Larry Brisbane, and Leonard G. Epstein, eds. 1995. *Cultural Competence in Substance Abuse Prevention.* Washington, D.C.: National Association of Social Workers Press.

Russell, Stephen T., Anne K. Driscoll, and Nhan Truong. 2002. "Adolescent Same–Sex Romantic Attractions and Relationships: Implications for Substance Use and Abuse." *American Journal of Public Health* 92, no. 2: 198–202.

U.S. Department of Health and Human Services: Substance Abuse and Mental Health Services Administration. 2002, September 4. *Results from the 2001 National Household Survey on Drug Abuse: Volume I. Summary of National Findings.* (Office of

Applied Studies, NHSDA Series H-17 ed.) (BKD461, SMA 02–3758) Washington, DC: U.S. Government Printing Office.

Wichstrøm, Hans Wiggo, and Kristinn Hegna. 2003. "Sexual Orientation and Suicide Attempt: A Longitudinal Study of the General Norwegian Adolescent Population." *Journal of Abnormal Psychology* 112, nos. 4/5: 144–151.

Web Sites

Center for Disease Control. [updated daily]. Jo Anne Grunbaum, Laura Kann, Steven A. Kinchen, Barbara Williamas, James G. Ross, Richard Lowry, and Lloyd Kolbe. "Youth Risk Behavior Survellance—United States, 2003." Accessed December 7, 2004. http://www.cdc.gov/HealthyYouth/YRBS. Study including data on drug use.

Midwest AIDS Prevention Project: Fact Sheet about Gay/Lesbian Substance Abuse. January 2004. ADAPT: Alcohol & Drug Abuse Prevention Training. Accessed December 7, 2004. http://www.aidsprevention.org/ADAPT/facts.htm. Basic data on substance abuse provided by ADAPT, a project designed to reduce substance abuse among LGBT youth by increasing LGBT population's knowledge about the link between alcohol and other drug use with AIDS, sexually transmitted diseases, family violence, drunk driving fatalities and injuries, and exposure to date rape and other crime, and increase LGBT people's ability to receive substance abuse services that are sensitive to their specific needs.

Sexuality Information and Education Council of the United States—SIECUS. December 2004. Accessed December 7, 2004. http://www.siecus.org. Includes links for policy makers and advocates regarding LGBTQ youth, a school health education clearinghouse, media, and international studies. There is also an international bibliography.

SoberDykes: Women in Recovery for Substance Abuse. 2004. Accessed December 7, 2004. http://www.soberdykes.org. Supports all women, including adolescents, who wrestle with alcohol and drug use and includes those who are not sure they have substance abuse problems.

Eating Disorders and Body Image

Katherine van Wormer

The category of eating disorders includes two disorders listed in the body of the *Diagnostic and Statistical Manual* (DSM) (APA 2000)—anorexia nervosa and bulimia nervosa. Also included is binge eating disorder, whose definition and criteria appear in the DSM appendix. All three varieties of disordered eating have special relevance for youth and for male **gay youth**. Negative body image, as influenced by images and norms in their dominant gay subcultures, is associated with the development of eating disorders (Williamson 1999). Anorexia is the eating disorder most often associated with gay males and heterosexual females. Although anorexia is rare among lesbians, obesity may be disproportionately represented. To understand and work with gays and **lesbian youth** with eating disorders it is first necessary to know something about the dynamics and causes of eating disorders generally, as well as how these are alike and different by gender and **sexual orientation**.

Studies indicate that a complex combination of biological, psychological, and cultural factors is responsible for the onset of eating disorders. In anorexia nervosa, biological and psychological factors are inextricably intertwined. Anorexia is characterized by a refusal to maintain a minimally normal body weight, even to the extent of self-starvation. One of the most perplexing aspects of anorexia is that its victims continue to think they are "fat," even when their ribs and bones are showing. Bulimia, in contrast, is characterized by repeated episodes of binge eating followed by vomiting, abusing laxatives or diuretics, taking enemas, or exercising obsessively in order to get rid of the food or burn the calories (National Institute of Mental Health [NIMH] 2004). Some anorexics binge and purge as well to maintain their low weight. Family, friends, and physicians have difficulty detecting bulimia in someone they know because that person's body weight may be normal. Dentists may detect tell-tale teeth enamel damage due to frequent vomiting.

The *DSM-IV-TR* (APA 2000) includes in its diagnostic criteria for anorexia: that weight loss be less than 85 percent of normal body weight; intense fear of weight gain; and amenorrhea in young women (the absence of at least three consecutive menstrual cycles). Many of the physical signs and symptoms are attributable to starvation—cold intolerance, lethargy, constipation, and the appearance of lanugo or fine body hair. Mortality from anorexia is over 10 percent; death most commonly results from starvation, **suicide**, or electrolyte imbalance.

Genetic factors undoubtedly play a role. Children from families with problems of addiction and depression are disproportionately at greater risk of developing an eating disorder than are other children. Phobias about becoming overweight and strange eating compulsions or rituals are closely related to obsessive-compulsive disorder (OCD) (van Wormer and Davis 2003). Scientists, according to NIMH (2004) have found biochemical similarities between people with eating disorders and OCD. The similarities relate to abnormal serotonin levels. A genetic trait is

See also Gender Identity; Harassment; Mental Health; Race and Racism; Substance Abuse; Youth, At Risk.

likely a key factor in the development of eating disorders, according to psychiatric research at the University of Iowa (Segall 2001). Interestingly, OCD, like anorexia, often begins in adolescence (Schwartz 1996).

These eating disorders occur primarily in cultures or subcultures that value thinness and present media images of Barbie Doll-shaped bodies, attesting to their cultural aspect. The usual explanation is that mothers, concerned about their weight, transmit the cultural prescription to their daughters. However, the journal *Pediatrics* reported that constantly dieting girls attributed it to their fathers' opinion (Davison and Birch 2001). Gay youth and homosexual men are also at risk, owing to stress on the Adonis-like body image within the gay community.

Unlike anorexics, bulimics may have a history of weight gain or come from a family in which overweight is a problem. Personality-wise, bulimics usually are extroverted, have voracious appetites, and experience episodes of binge (van Wormer and Davis 2003). A key characteristic of bulimia is its common association with alcohol and other drug misuse; estimates of their co-occurrence ranges from 30 to 70 percent, according to a recent report in the *Journal of the American Medical Association* (Vastag 2001).

As with anorexia, bulimia typically begins in **adolescence**. More than 90 percent of cases of these two eating disorders occurs in females. The lifetime prevalence of anorexia among girls and women is .5 percent and approximately 1 to 3 percent for bulimia (APA 2000). A surprise finding is that when bulimia does exist in men, its medical consequences are severe, and its occurrence is related to low levels of the male hormone testosterone ("Anorexia, Bulimia Found More Dangerous in Men" 2000).

People with eating disorders share certain personality traits: low self-esteem, clinical depression (which often runs in their families), and an inability to handle stress (NIMH 2004). Low self-esteem related to body image is a research theme especially pertinent to adolescents. It is also the theme that most closely relates to the cultural component of the biological–psychological–cultural model of eating disorders.

The cultural component is perhaps the most widely studied aspect of the etiology of these illnesses. Whether the samples were of **college-age students** or more mature subjects, the results have been consistent and are highly relevant to gay and lesbian youth. Lydens (1999) measured levels of body dissatisfaction in non-student populations consisting of an equally divided sample of 160 lesbians, gay men, heterosexual women, and heterosexual men. Heterosexual men and gay men tended to objectify their bodies and experience "body shame." Lydens' findings parallel those drawn from samples of younger persons. In all such studies gay males had significantly lower levels of body satisfaction and self-esteem than their heterosexual peers.

Gay males consistently have been found to have a higher gender propensity for eating disorders than do heterosexual men, whereas among lesbians, anorexia is rare. The explanation offered by Siever (1994) is that lesbians like heterosexual men are less invested in societal norms of attractiveness than are heterosexual women or gay men. In his sample of 250 college students, which included about an even number of heterosexuals and homosexuals, Siever found that young men place priority on physical attractiveness in evaluating potential partners, whereas young women place a higher value on factors such as personality, status, power, and income. Therefore, one could conclude that youth seeking male attention internalize these standards and that this leads, in extreme cases, to eating disorders. The cultural imperative equating thinness with desirability and the stress on appearance in girls and women appear to impact on females' formation of body image. Media images of Barbie Doll-type figures reinforce unrealistic cultural norms for girls. The emerging research on body image within the gay and lesbian population, however, is more complex.

The body image to which most gay males aspire is a thin but muscular build. Strong, Singh, and Randall (2000) differentiate between a "high feminine" or gender nonconforming subtype of gay males who manifest greater body dissatisfaction and a "less feminine" subtype who take more pride in their physical appearance but whose risk may be in the opposite direction—obsessive body building efforts. These researchers report that eating disorders in males also are associated with **childhood** gender nonconformity. The key variable here is the relentless teasing and ridicule to which gender nonconforming males are subjected in school. Often called "**sissy**" and "**queer**," such males (many of whom are not gay) are apt to internalize this rejection at great psychological cost. Beren (1997) has related internalized **homophobia** in young males to disordered eating patterns.

Schoolgirls who are gender nonconforming also are exposed to their share of teasing (van Wormer, Wells, and Boes 2000). However, girls who are considered **tomboys** are often good at **sports** and, unlike feminine boys, are apt to achieve recognition in this arena. Regarding body image, lesbians are shown in empirical investigations to exhibit lower levels of cultural norms for slimness and higher levels of body esteem (Share and Mintz 2002). Anorexia is rare among lesbians (Andersen 1999). This is not to say that lesbians do not have worries concerning their weight levels, however. Although the **research** is mixed on this point, there is some evidence that binge eating may be a problem for lesbians of all ages. Heffernan (1996), who assessed eating disorder problems in 200 lesbians, found that binge eating related to low self-esteem was more frequent in lesbian than in heterosexual women, but that bulimia was equally common.

Although **African American** women are less subject to anorexia and more subject to overeating than the general population, there is some evidence that as they move into the predominantly white lesbian community their body image may undergo a change. Auerbach and Bradley (1998) found that several women of color in their lesbian sample had developed serious body image problems in the context of racial assimilation. Further research on lesbians of color is clearly needed.

There is a paucity of information in the literature on eating disorder problems in **transgender** and **bisexual** populations. One rare exception is the collection of personal essays and narratives on body image in LBGT communities (Atkins 1998). Selections concerning bisexuals and male-to-female **transsexuals** show that Western culture's narrowly defined ideal of female beauty can lead to unhealthy attitudes and behaviors. Further research is needed as well to clarify the form that eating disorders take in lesbians and the incidence of such disorders among lesbians and gay adolescents of color.

Bibliography

American Psychiatric Association. 2000. *Diagnostic and Statistical Manual of Mental Disorders*, 4th ed. Washington DC: Author.

Andersen, Arnold E. 1999. "Gender-Related Aspects of Eating Disorders: A Guide to Practice." *Journal of Gender-Specific Medicine* 2, no.1: 47–54.

"Anorexia, Bulimia, Found More Dangerous in Men," 2000, June 7. *Chicago Tribune,* evening update, p.7.

Atkins, Dawn, ed. 1998. *Looking Queer: Body Image and Identity in Lesbian, Bisexual, Gay, and Transgender Communities.* Binghamton, NY: Harrington Park Press.

Auerbach, Sara, and Rebekah Bradley. 1998. "Resistance and Reinscription: Sexual Identity and Body Image among Lesbian and Bisexual Women." Pp. 27–36 in *Looking Queer: Body Image and Identity in Lesbian, Bisexual, Gay and Transgender Communities.* Edited by Dawn Atkins. Binghamton, NY: Harrington Park Press.

Beren, Susan E. 1997. "Stigmatization and Shame as Determinants of Subclinical Eating Disorder Pathology." *Dissertation Abstracts* 58, no. 4B: 2109.

Davison, Kirsten K., and Leann L. Birch. 2003. "Weight Status, Parent Reaction, and Self Concept in Five Year Old Girls. *Pediatrics* 107, no. 1: 46–53.

Heffernan, Karen. 1996. "Eating Disorders and Weight Concern among Lesbians." *International Journal of Eating Disorders* 19, no. 2: 127–138.

Lydens, Greta C. 1999. "Body Image and Attitudes toward Eating: The Influence of Objectified Body Consciousness and Variations by Gender and Sexual Orientation." *Dissertation Abstracts* 60, no. 4B: 1861.

National Institute of Mental Health (NIMH). 2004. Eating Disorders. Accessed September 3, 2004. http://www.nimh.nih.gov/publicat/eatdis.htm.

Schwartz, Jeffrey M. 1996. *Brain Lock: Free Yourself from Obsessive-Compulsive Behaviors.* New York: Regan.

Segall, Rebecca. 2001, March/April. "Never Too Skinny." *Psychology Today* 34: 22.

Share, Tamara, and Laura B. Mintz. 2002. "Differences between Lesbians and Heterosexual Women in Disordered Eating and Related Attitudes." *Journal of Homosexuality* 42, no. 4: 89–106.

Siever, Michael D. 1994. "Sexual Orientation and Gender as Factors in Socioculturally Acquired Vulnerability to Body Dissatisfaction and Eating Disorders." *Journal of Consulting and Clinical Psychology* 62, no.2: 252–260.

Strong, Scott M., Devendra Singh, and Patrick K. Randall. 2000. "Childhood Gender Nonconformity and Body Dissatisfaction in Gay and Heterosexual Men." *Sex Roles: A Journal of Research* 43, nos. 7–8: 427–439.

van Wormer, Katherine, Joel Wells, and Mary Boes. 2000. *Social Work with Lesbians, Gays, and Bisexuals: A Strengths Perspective.* Boston: Allyn and Bacon.

———, and Diane R. Davis. 2003. *Addiction Treatment: A Strengths Perspective.* Boston: Allyn and Bacon.

Vastag, Brian. 2001. "What's the Connection? No Easy Answers for People with Eating Disorders and Drug Abuse." *Journal of the American Medical Association* 285, no. 8: 1006–1008.

Williamson, Iain. 1999. "Why are Gay Men a High Risk Group for Eating Disturbance?" *European Eating Disorders Review* 7, no. 1: 1–4.

Web Sites

Faculty of Social Work at the University of Calgary 2004. Accessed May 31, 2005. http://www.fsw.ucalgary.ca/ramsay/gay-lesbian-bisexual. Professor Ramsay's Web site has numerous links to issues, including studies on male eating disorders.

National Institute of Mental Health. May 2004. Accessed May 31, 2005. http://www.nimh.nih.gov/publicat/eatingdisorders.cfm. Promotes results of recent research on the etiology and treatment strategies for persons with eating disorders.

Educational Policies

Catherine A. Lugg

Educational policies cover every aspect of a given school's operations. *Formal* educational policies include laws, budgetary regulations, executive orders, state department guidelines, federal education mandates, judicial decisions, consent decrees, and local school board regulations. Formal policies are found in documents, budget reports, minutes, case law, consent decrees, published guidelines, memoranda and the like. *Informal* educational policies are more related to professional socialization of the staff, student peer culture, and the larger school culture. Informal policies are the unwritten rules that everyone (or almost everyone) within a given school environment follows or is expected to follow. In every day language, informal policy "is how things really get done around here." Historically, formal educational policies have generally either ignored **lesbian, gay, bisexual**, and **transgender** (LGBT) youth and personnel or targeted them as a problem that needed to be repressed or eliminated. The early school policies that were specifically directed at LGBT people were punitive—any possible LGBT influence was to be erased.

At the height of the Cold War, LGBT status was repeatedly and erroneously equated with communism. Hence, LGBT school workers were seen as a dire threat both to the well-being of public school children and the nation. Operating under this rubric, the Florida state legislature established the "**Johns Committee**," which instituted a massive six-year witch-hunt searching for suspected homosexual subversives throughout its educational system. University professors, college students, and public school teachers were questioned—without legal counsel—regarding their possible homosexuality and threatened with public exposure. College students were expelled or quietly transferred, and professors and teachers were fired or resigned. Roughly seventy-one teachers lost their professional licenses for "moral misconduct" (Sears 1997). More contemporary examples of LGBT "erasure policies" include state bans on mentioning homosexuality in **sexuality education** curricula, except for explicitly equating it with possible health risks and immorality (Lugg 2003). In South Carolina, for example, "alternative sexual lifestyles" are banned from health education classes, except in the context of discussing sexually transmitted diseases. Arizona bars any material that would promote "a homosexual life-style" or portrays "homosexuality as a positive alternative life-style."

With the rise of the modern-day gay rights movement during the early 1970s, some states and local public school districts passed policies designed to protect LGBT people from **harassment** and abuse. A few have gone further and embraced LGBT people under a broader multicultural/antiracism educational rubric. Nevertheless, while the formal policy environment for LGBT youth appears to be less overtly hostile than during the Cold War, many LGBT individuals—both adults and students—still find that the public school environment is detrimental to their well-being. In the vast majority of American states, there are few formal policies to

See also Africa, LGBT Youth and Issues in; Antidiscrimination Policy; Asia, LGBT Youth and Issues in; Europe, LGBT Youth and Issues in; Legal Issues, Students; Licensure; Parents, LGBT; School Climate, K-12; School Safety and Safe School Zones; South America, LGBT Youth and Issues in; Workplace Issues.

combat fiercely homophobic *informal* school policies. Such informal policies include: teachers and **administrators** turning a blind eye to the **bullying** and harassment of LGBT students, ignoring or demeaning LGBT parents, educational leaders quietly insisting that LGBT school workers remain "closeted," school personnel blaming LGBT students for their harassment, students using **"queer"** or some other homophobic taunt as the universal insult. While most public schools have formal policies banning bullying and harassment, comparatively few have formal policies that specifically address the welfare of LGBT students and school personnel.

Consequently, a recent report found that: 84 percent of LGBT students were verbally harassed because of their orientation, 91 percent heard homophobic remarks either frequently or often, nearly one-half of LGBT students of color reported being harassed because of their **sexual orientation** *and* **race,** and eight out of ten LGBT students reported that faculty and staff failed to intervene when in the presence of homophobic remarks (Kosciw and Cullen 2003). Furthermore, almost 58 percent of LGBT students reported having property stolen or vandalized, which was one-fifth higher than their straight peers. Transgender students were at the greatest risk of physical harassment, nearly a third more likely than their LGB peers (Kosciw and Cullen 2003).

Even in those U.S. locations that have specific formal policies addressing LGBT people in public education, these formal policies can be subjected to conflicting policy directives, particularly in the area of funding. For example, beginning in the early 1990s, Massachusetts had a fairly innovative and well-respected program that targeted the needs of LGBT students in public schools. Nevertheless, during an economic downturn, the program fell victim to state budgetary pressure in the summer of 2002 and was eliminated.

One of the most important formal policies currently available for LGBT students in public schools actually arose from what can be called "policy subversion." In 1984, then President Ronald Reagan signed into law the "Equal Access Act" (EAA). This federal act permits student-initiated noncurricular clubs to meet during noninstructional time, if a given public secondary school maintains a "limited public forum." In addition, a public school that permits other noncurricular organizations to meet on school grounds outside of instructional time cannot discriminate against religiously-oriented student groups. The original legislative intent behind EAA was *specifically* religious. EAA was passed on the heels of a thrice-defeated proposed amendment to the U.S. Constitution that would have permitted state-sanctioned prayers in public schools. However, in the midst of the legislative process, the original wording was modified to include secular noncurriculum groups.

EAA's constitutionality was later upheld in the 1990 decision of *Board of Education v. Mergens*. At the time, religious conservatives hailed the Supreme Court's 8 to 1 decision. However, the *Mergens* decision also opened the window for **gay–straight alliances** (GSAs), which are student-initiated clubs for both straight and gay secondary students. By the mid-1990s, GSAs had formed at public schools across the country. In some cases, public school officials permitted the groups to meet on school property. However, the Salt Lake City school board chose to ban all noncurricular groups rather than permit the GSA, which was their only other option under the constraints of *Mergens* and EAA. The school board and student group entered into a litigation battle, finally settling in 2001, after the student group had evolved into a curricular-related group called PRISM (People Respecting Important Social Groups).

There is some evidence that GSAs have a positive influence in ameliorating some of the more corrosive elements of the informal policies that harm LGBT students. The GLSEN survey found that students who attended public schools with GSAs felt slightly safer than those who did not. However, the percentage difference was roughly seven points (68 to 61 percent).

With the U.S. Supreme Court's invalidation of all consensual sodomy laws in *Lawrence v. Texas*, school boards have lost their last legal justification for banning GSAs (the possibility that they might "promote illegal behavior"). It is still too early to predict the impact from the *Lawrence* decision, but it has the potential to be as important for LGBT people and public education as *Brown v. Board* has been for **African Americans**. Given the Supreme Court's rare expansive language in *Lawrence*, legal and policy restrictions on LGBT people should not withstand judicial examination. Potentially, LGBT students could have the same rights as their heterosexual peers, and LGBT school workers would enjoy the same employee rights and benefits (including spousal insurance coverage), and LGBT parents would be accorded the same respect and responsibilities as nonqueer parents.

The **United Kingdom, Australia, New Zealand**, and **Canada** also have been addressing LGBT students and personnel in both formal and informal policies since the 1980s. As such, they have been generally ahead of the United States in developing formal policy mechanisms. In each instance, policies specifically covering LGBT people in schools have been the logical outgrowth of increasingly expansive policies addressing gender equity in schools. Nevertheless, like those in the United States, formal policies elsewhere can run into a fair amount of resistance when these policies conflict with a given school's informal policies.

In the United Kingdom, many of these policies arose in the midst of a hostile policy environment thanks to the 1986 law, **Section 28**. Although some educators believe that Section 28 banned the teaching about LGBT issues in schools, the law actually banned "the promotion of homosexuality" by local school authorities. Since local authorities were not directly responsible for sexuality education, the law did not limit the scope of this **curriculum**. Nevertheless, it did contribute to a homophobic climate, which in turn intimidated less intrepid and policy-subversive educators Section 28 was finally repealed in 2003.

Bibliography

Cooper, Bruce S., Lance D. Fusarelli, and E. Vance Randall. 2004. *Better Policies, Better Schools*. Boston, MA: Pearson.

Harbeck, Karen M. 1997. *Gay and Lesbian Educators: Personal Freedoms, Public Constraints*. Malden, MA: Amethyst Press.

Gaskell, Jane, and Sandra Taylor. 2003. "The Women's Movement in Canadian and Australian Education: From Liberation and Sexism to Boys and Social Justice." *Gender & Education* 15, no. 2: 151–168.

Grattan, R. M. 1999. "It's Not Just for Religion Anymore: Expanding the Protections of the Equal Access Act to Gay, Lesbian, and Bisexual High School Students." *George Washington Law Review* 67: 577–599.

Kosciw, Joseph, and M. K. Cullen. 2003. *The GLSEN 2001 National School Climate Survey: The School-Related Experiences of Our Nation's Lesbian, Gay, Bisexual, and Transgender Youth*. New York: Gay, Lesbian, and Straight Education Network.

Lindblom, Charles E., and Edward J. Woodhouse. 1993. *The Policy-Making Process*. 3rd ed. Englewood Cliffs, NJ: Prentice Hall.

Lugg, Catherine A. 2003. "Sissies, Faggots, Lezzies and Dykes: Gender, Sexual Orientation, and a New Politics of Education?" *Educational Administration Quarterly* 39, no. 1: 95–134.

Narin, Karen, and Anne B. Smith. 2003. "Taking Students Seriously: Their Rights to be Safe at School." *Gender & Education* 15, no. 2: 133–149.

Russ, IV, John A. 1997. "Creating a Safe Space for Gay Youth: How the Supreme Court's Religious Access Cases Can Help Young People Organize at Public Schools." *Virginia Journal of Social Policy & the Law* 4: 545–577.

Sears, James T. 1997. *Lonely Hunters: An Oral History of Lesbian and Gay Southern Life, 1948–1968*. New York: HarperCollins/Westview.

Web Site

National Gay and Lesbian Task Force Policy Institute. October 2004. Accessed December 3, 2004. http://www.thetaskforce.org/ourprojects/pi/index.cfm. Founded in 1995, this project of NGLTF produces policy reports on a range of topics, including education, which are available for download.

Egypt, LGBT Youth and Issues in

Didi Khayatt

When fifty-two young men were arrested in Egypt in May 2001 for "practicing debauchery with men," European and North American news media reported the incident as the arrests of fifty-two *homosexuals*. Reporters assumed that the meaning of "homosexual" was universal and few noticed that the charge against these men was not "homosexuality" but "debauchery." The former term could not be used because there is no equivalent word in Arabic that describes two men engaged in sexual activity as having a "homosexual identity," hence *being homosexual*. Of course, Egyptian men engage in same-sex practices, as do women, but *being* "gay" or "lesbian" or "bisexual" (terminology that grew out of late nineteenth-century Europe) is restricted to men and women who have access to English and, hence, are of upper or middle **social class**, and literate. For those men who engage in same-sex practices (little is known about women other than that same-sex practices exist as well), Egypt is currently a dangerous place (http://www.sodomylaws.org/world/egypt/egnews164.htm), a place where men are systematically entrapped by the police, where, according to the Al Fatiha Foundation (an organization serving LGBT Muslims), human rights of such men are regularly disregarded, and where no public education regarding sex between men exists. By implication, there is equal danger for youth who may want to engage in same-sex activities, although the culture is slightly more lenient in their case. They are expected to marry eventually, and, since they have no access to women because of their age, such activity may be seen as a temporary alternative.

See also Colonialism and Homosexuality; Gender Roles; Identity Politics; Muslim Moral Instruction on Homosexuality; Queer and Queer Theory; Race and Racism; Religious Fundamentalism; Sexual Identity; Transsexuality.

There exists a vast literature that expounds on the sexual virtues of the males of Egypt and what is now called the Middle East. From writers such as André Gide and Albert Camus, to the travelogues of Renaissance Europe, to Lawrence of Arabia, to modern sex holidays, this discourse describes and expresses Western Europe's attraction to a concept of "the East" that it created almost in opposition to itself. Edward Said (1979, 1) refers to this phenomenon as "orientalism," a place in the European imagination, almost a European invention that, since antiquity, has held the promise "of romance, exotic beings, haunting memories and landscapes, remarkable experiences." Set in opposition to the "Occident," the Orient, Said argues, is experienced through a set of restricted and typical encapsulations: the journey, the history, the fable, the stereotype, the polemical confrontation. These provide the lenses "through which the Orient is experienced, and they shape the language, perception, and form of the encounter between East and West" (58).

Within the Orient, Egypt, specifically, was a land of mystery. Its history was immense, its peoples exotic, and its cultures and languages confounding. Of the many attractions that Egypt held for the European traveler, none was as seductive as the image of the Orient as a place of sexual license, where gender segregation was perceived to lead to sexual perversions and where it was assumed that every sexual proclivity could be satisfied.

For a British traveler, for instance Edward William Lane, author of *An Account of the Manners and Customs of the Modern Egyptians* (1836), Egypt was a place that offended British propriety on every level, from what constituted a "family" to notions of hygiene. It embraced a sexuality that was permissive, and seen to be excessive in its "freedom of intercourse," as Lane put it. (Said 1979, 167). This salacious image of Egypt is an example of what Anne McClintock (1995, 22) calls *porno-tropics*, a notion that describes the exotic in the European imagination: "a fantastic magic lantern of the mind onto which Europe projected its forbidden sexual desires and fears." These desires and fears included same-sex practices that were mostly outlawed in Western Europe during the Victorian era, but that were seen as prevalent, if not condoned, in a sexually segregated Egypt. French and British travelers described, with lewd detail, such "perversions" shamelessly practiced by men and women. Knowledge of the Turkish baths, the harems, the eunuchs, the Circassian slaves, the sheer wealth and opulence of the Ottoman Empire lent some veracity to the many chronicles of the time. Gerard de Nerval, for instance, a Frenchman traveling in the early nineteenth century, describes watching beautifully made-up dancers and practically falling in love with one of them, only to discover they were men. These men, he informs us, were known locally as *khawal*—a pejorative word that exists today in Egyptian colloquial Arabic that refers to effeminate men, or men who engage in same-sex practices.

Numerous scholarly articles record same-sex practices among the Ancient Egyptians. For instance, R. B. Parkinson (1995, 81) reviews the literature on "homosexual" **desire** during the Ancient Egyptian Middle Kingdom, stating: "Textual evidence shows that Egypt did not witness a sense of categorization by sexuality, but that sexual acts between men were acknowledged to occur." Parkinson remarks that "it seems that Egyptian texts provide no terms for 'sexualities;' most of the relevant extant vocabulary is derived from descriptions of penetrative sexual activity rather than expressions of desire" (61). Lise Manniche (1992, 11), in another article about Ancient Egyptian sexual life, argues that same-sex practices were used as an act of aggressive power over enemies of Egyptians, that "homosexual" activities for pleasure "are much less well-tested, almost the only example being the adventure of King Neferkare with his general." Parkinson (1995, 81) agrees that "sexual acts between men seem to be predominantly expressions of power, and the relationships are uneroticised." Little is known about female same-sex practices in Ancient Egypt, and what is mentioned seems to be a copy of a male form of negative confessions in the Book of the Dead. Montserrat (1996, 166) attributes this to women's lack of access to writing. Some scholars have looked to the famous Queen Hatchepsut of the Middle Kingdom as an instance of cross-dressing. However, Hatchepsut likely cross-dressed for necessity and power, to appear in the traditional image of the Pharaoh, and not for erotic pleasure. Later in history, during the Greco-Roman period in Egypt, many more instances appear in various papyruses. Same-sex practices between men are mentioned in the Bible, with special reference to such behavior existing in Egypt.

Egypt became Christian in 50 CE during the time of the Eastern Roman Empire, and Greco-Roman influences on its habits and customs are well documented. By the seventh century, Egypt has fallen under Islamic rule, and cultural mores changed accordingly. During this era, same-sex activities were more prevalent, despite religious and civil prohibitions (Montserrat 1996). The poetry, fables, and stories that were developed during the time that the various Islamic dynasties ruled Egypt fill many tomes (A Thousand and One Nights; Wright and Rowson, 1997).

In a controversial book, Arno Schmitt and Jehoeda Sofer (1990, 8) argued that: "In Classical Arabic there was no word meaning homosexuality; the translations given in modern dictionaries are either recently coined literal translations of 'homosexuality' or simply wrong." However, other scholars such as As'ad AbuKhalil (1993) have dismissed their work as largely anecdotal, and have presented the various conceptualizations that emerged from the Arab/Islamic Civilization with respect to the concept of "homosexuality."

In modern Egypt, same-sex practices are present and some would say are prevalent particularly because of a sexually segregated society. However, as previously mentioned, homosexuality as an identity exists only among Egyptians who have access to Western information technologies or that have a European education, a vestige of Egypt's colonial past. Youth (of both genders) who belong to a social class that has access to Western books and to the **Internet** may also have access to notions of gay and lesbian identities. These youth would still have to hide their sexual activities from their parents because of the stringent rules of local gender conformity to which their parents may adhere. Little is known of their everyday lives, but some queer youth emigrate to the West. There is little information about transsexuals in Egypt. As a result of **research** completed in Egypt between 1993 and 1999, one informant reported that several male-to-female sex changes occur each month in state hospitals. There can be no confirmation of such a statement.

Bibliography

AbuKhalil, As'ad. 1993. "A Note on the Study of Homosexuality in the Arab/Islamic Civilization." *The Arab Studies Journal* 1/2, Fall: 32–34, 48.
———. 1997. "Gender Boundaries and Sexual Categories in the Arab World." *Feminist Issues*, 15, nos. 1–2: 91–104.

Dunn, Bruce. 1998. "Power and Sexuality in the Middle East." *Middle East Report* 206, Spring: 8–38.

Manniche, Lise. 1992. "Some Aspects of Ancient Egyptian Sexual Life." Pp. 11–23 in *Homosexuality in the Ancient World*. Edited by Wayne R. Dynes and Stephen Donaldson. New York and London: Garland.

McClintock, Ann. 1995. *Imperial Leather: Race, Gender and Sexuality in the Colonial Contest*. New York and London: Routledge.

Montserrat, Dominic. 1996. *Sex and Society in Græco-Roman Egypt*. London and New York: Kegan Paul.

Murray, Stephen O., and Will Roscoe, eds. *Islamic Homosexualities: Culture, History, and Literature*. New York and London: New York University Press.

Parkinson, R. B. 1995. "'Homosexual' Desire and Middle Kingdom Literature." *The Journal of Egyptian Archeology* 81: 57–76.

Said, Edward W. 1979. *Orientalism*. New York: Vintage.

Schmitt, Arno, and Jehoeda Sofer, eds. 1990. *Sexuality and Eroticism among Males in Moslem Societies*. Binghamton, NY: Harrington Park Press.

Wright, J. W., Jr., and Everett K. Rowson, eds. 1997. *Homoeroticism in Classical Arabic Literature*. New York: Columbia University Press.

Web Sites

Al Fatiha Foundation. February 2004. Accessed December 4, 2004. http://www.al-fatiha.net/ A United States-based nonprofit foundation serving LGBT Muslims.

Behind the Mask: A Web site on Gay and Lesbian Affairs in Africa. Accessed February 23, 2004. http://www.mask.org.za/sections/AfricaPerCountry/abcnew/egypt/journey.

Sodomy Laws. September 2003. Accessed May 31, 2005. http://www.sodomylaws.org/world/egypt/egnews164.htm.

Third Gender in Ancient Egypt. 1999. Accessed May 31, 2005. http://www.well.com/user/aquarius/egypt.htm. Details gender complexity in ancient Egypt with examples from pottery and links to other sites.

The Tomb of Niankhkhum and Khnumhotep. Accessed May 31, 2005. http://www.egyptology.com/niankhkhnum_khnumhotep.

ESL, Teaching of

Cynthia D. Nelson

Over the past few decades, massive migration and displacement on a global scale, combined with the rise of English as an international language, have led to the worldwide proliferation of educational programs in which immigrants, refugees, and international students learn English as a Second (or Foreign) Language (ESL/EFL). Although learning English involves talking, reading, and writing in English about contemporary issues, it was not until the early 1990s that teaching publications and conference presentations began to explore ways of acknowledging and incorporating a range of sexual identities in ESL/EFL curricula and teaching practices. To date the main emphases have been introducing lesbian, gay,

See also Antibias Curriculum; Language Arts, Teaching of; Licensure; Queer Pedagogy.

bisexual, and (to a lesser extent) transgender (LGBT) topics into curricula along with creating supportive environments for openly LGBT students and teachers. A case has also been made for moving beyond a focus on mere inclusion, in which "minority" sexual identities are acknowledged and affirmed, in favor of a focus on inquiry, in which all sexual identities are critically examined and "unpacked." Despite this groundswell of work, within the international field of ESL/EFL the topic of sexual identity remains contentious.

For some, the concern is not how but whether to discuss **sexual identity** in the classroom. A survey of lesbian, gay, and bisexual teachers of ESL in the United States found that mostly heterosexual ESL teachers attending workshops on including gay and lesbian literature in ESL classes typically express four types of concerns: fear of criticism from **administrators**, parents or students if such themes are included in their teaching; lack of confidence in their capability and sensitivity regarding these matters; a dearth of appropriate materials and training; and failure to see the relevance of **queer** issues to their students (Snelbecker 1994). These concerns are not unique to U.S. teachers. A teacher educator in **Australia**, for example, noted that some teachers have expressed reluctance to address this topic because they worry about offending learners, citing learners' cultural backgrounds as the reason for their concern (O'Loughlin 2001).

A handful of commercially produced ESL textbooks include gay or lesbian characters or issues. One includes a reading about a boy whose two fathers are gay (Clarke, Dobson and Silberstein 1996), and another includes a grammar exercise featuring two gay men who live together (Thewlis 1997). In the latter, students are asked to identify the "coordinating conjunctions" (such as "and" or "but") in a reading that includes this sentence: "Matt liked staying out late every Friday night, but Jeff always wanted to get up early on Saturday mornings to clean the house and to finish chores so they could spend the afternoon relaxing or playing with their new puppy in the park" (186). A third textbook prompts students to offer advice to a **gay youth** who writes: "Most of my classmates have started dating girls. But not me. I have no interest in dating girls. I fantasize about boys. I guess I'm gay. Will I spend all my life in mistery and frustration?" (85). Yet, such examples remain rare, and even these are restricted to depictions of gay males.

Given the dearth of LGBT themes within ESL/EFL curricula and textbooks (and **research**), some teachers are describing their efforts to develop gay-themed activities and teaching materials. One English teacher in **Japan** makes a point of integrating discussions of sexual identity into discussions of human rights (Summerhawk 1998). When students are talking about types of social **discrimination** evident in their country (in this case, Japan), she prompts them to bring up discrimination against "homos" and to discuss this form of discrimination in terms of housing, employment, marriage, and so on. Other activities that have proven popular with students include discussing books and films with gay or lesbian characters, discussing newspaper articles on gay actors, and inviting lesbian, bisexual, or gay speakers to talk about their experiences (Summerhawk 1998).

The fact that LGBT subject matter may generate controversy is precisely why it may be worth talking about in language classes, as noted in a three-way dialogue between teachers in Australia, Japan and the United States. One of the teachers (Nelson) contests the notion that teachers should "protect" students from challenge, complexity or discomfort: "Do teachers need to decide for students what is culturally appropriate with regard to gay or lesbian themes? Or examine with students the intercultural complexities of negotiating these themes?"(Ó'Móchain, Mitchell, and Nelson 2003, 134).

In the same dialogue, an EFL teacher (Ó'Móchain) in Japan offers an example from his classroom of what a questioning approach might look like that makes sexual identities a productive subject of discussion:

> [A]student recounted an incident in which he experienced an irate reaction from a customer at a health club. The student had a summer job as a receptionist at the club. The customer called by telephone and expressed amazement that his call was taken by a male receptionist. "You should be a woman, not a man!" he repeated loudly. I [then] . . . put some questions to the class: "What makes one job masculine and another feminine? Does this change depending on time or place? Why do some people feel uncomfortable when something like this happens?" The students seemed a little surprised by these questions, but they generated a valuable discussion that broadened out around questions of sexual identity and how some behavior draws the label *gay* or *straight* in some places and not in others. The discussion was relatively brief (15 minutes), [and] unplanned . . . [but] most of the students seemed truly engaged. (Ó'Móchain, Mitchell and Nelson 2003, 126)

Discussions of LGBT subject matter tend to engage students' interest, which in turn facilitates the learning process.

There is generally a lack of research exploring the perspectives of ESL students or teachers who openly identify as LGBT. One study notes the alienation experienced by a **transgender** ESL student in Australia, whose ESL textbooks failed to represent a plurality of sexual and **gender identities** (Jewell 1998). In another study, a gay man from **Mexico** studying English in the United States recounted his excitement at having a lesbian teacher with whom he could speak openly about his life (Nelson 2004). Creating spaces in which LBGT students feel they can speak freely may be especially important in language classes. If students feel they must constantly monitor and censor what they say in class while attempting to use the new language, learning opportunities may be impeded rather than enhanced.

Somewhat more prevalent are published accounts of LGBT teachers' **coming out** dilemmas and experiences. While some LBGT teachers are reluctant to come out because they think it might disrupt their rapport with students, one study suggests that when teachers do, the experience is rarely negative (Snelbecker 1994). ESL teachers report that coming out in the classroom or to the school community can be a positive experience because it can be a way of supporting LGBT students, educating straight students, or prompting critical thinking (Saint Pierre 1994; Snelbecker 1994). One study of teachers' coming out conundrums highlights the potential for misunderstandings in ESL classes, where interactions are intercultural and multilingual (Nelson 2004). This study found that a gay-identified teacher decided to present himself as straight to his students, but some students strongly suspected that he was gay; conversely, a lesbian-identified teacher decided to come out in class, but afterwards at least one student did not understand what this teacher had been saying.

In some regions there may be limited opportunities for teachers to come out in the classroom. Even having the opportunity to pursue a Master of Arts in Teaching ESL degree can be dependent upon being perceived as heterosexual. Despite the critical need for ESL teachers, some LGBT people are prevented from enrolling in teacher education programs due to anticipated problems in student teaching at cooperating schools (Ó'Móchain, Mitchell, and Nelson 2003).

In encouraging ESL teachers and teacher educators to integrate LGBT themes and perspectives into their **curriculum**, one researcher distinguishes "pedagogies of inclusion" from "pedagogies of inquiry," making a case for the latter (Nelson 1999). This means that instead of aiming merely to include and affirm "minority" sexual identities, ESL teachers would encourage students to investigate and question the ways in which all sexual identities are represented and negotiated in everyday linguistic and cultural practices. To this end, Nelson (1999, 378) proposes that ESL students discuss questions such as the following:

- In this country, what do people do or say (or not do or say) if they want to be seen as gay [lesbian] [straight]?
- How is this different in another country? How is it similar?
- Why do people sometimes want to be seen as straight [bisexual] [lesbian]? Why do they sometimes not want to?
- Why do people sometimes want to be able to identify others as straight [gay] [bisexual]? When is it important to know this about someone? When is it not important at all?
- Is it easy to identify someone as gay [straight] [lesbian]? Why or why not? Does it make a difference if the person is old or young, a man or a woman, someone you know or someone you only observe? What other things can make it easier or more difficult? [. . .]
- In this country [in this city] [on this campus], which sexual identities are seem natural or acceptable? Which do not? How can you tell?
- After people move to this country, do they change how they think about sexual identities? If so, how? If not, why not?

Such questions draw on queer theorizations of sexual identities as "acts" not facts, and they demonstrate how queer theory may be of practical use in increasingly globalized classrooms. New empirical research on "queer inquiry in language education," which is the theme for a 2006 special issue of the *Journal of Language, Identity, and Education* (vol 5, no. 1), shows how language teachers and researchers in Australia, Brazil, Canada and Japan are putting queer theory into practice in education contexts.

Bibliography

Clarke, Mark A., Barbara K. Dobson, and Sandra Silberstein. 1996. *Choice Readings*. Ann Arbor: Michigan University Press.

Jewell, Jason B. W. 1998. "A Transgendered ESL Learner in Relation to Her Class Textbooks, Heterosexist Hegemony and Change." *Melbourne Papers in Applied Linguistics* 10: 1–21.

Nelson, Cynthia D. 1999. "Sexual Identities in ESL: Queer Theory and Classroom Inquiry." *TESOL Quarterly* 33, no. 3: 371–391.

———. 2004. "A Queer Chaos of Meanings: Coming Out Conundrums in Globalised Classrooms." *Journal of Gay and Lesbian Issues in Education* 2, no. 1: 27–46.

———. (Forthcoming). *Out to Educate? Sexual Identities in Language Education*. Mahwah, NJ: Lawrence Erlbaum.

O'Loughlin, Kieran. 2001. "(En)gendering the TESOL Classroom." *Prospect: An Australian Journal of TESOL* 16, no. 2: 33–44.

Ó'Móchain, Roibeárd, Maren Mitchell, and Cynthia D. Nelson. 2003. "Dialogues Around 'Heterosexism in ESL: Examining Our Attitudes' and 'Sexual Identities in ESL: Queer Theory and Classroom Inquiry,' by Cynthia Nelson (1993, 1999)." Pp. 123–140 in *The TESOL Quarterly Dialogues: Rethinking Issues of Language, Culture, and Power*. Edited by Judy Sharkey and Karen E. Johnson. Alexandria, VA: TESOL.

Saint Pierre, Raymond. 1994. "On Being Out in the Classroom: Dilemma or Duty?" Pp. 164–172 in *One Teacher in Ten: Gay and Lesbian Educators Tell Their Stories*. Edited by Kevin Jennings. Boston: Alyson.

Snelbecker, Karen A. 1994. *Speaking Out: A Survey of Lesbian, Gay and Bisexual Teachers of ESOL in the US*. Unpublished Master's thesis. Brattleboro, VT: School for International Training. ERIC Document ED 375 680.

Summerhawk, Barbara. 1998. "From Closet to Classroom: Gay Issues in ESL/EFL." *The Language Teacher (Japan Association for Language Teaching)* 22, no. 5: 21–23.

Thewlis, Stephen H. 1997. *Grammar Dimensions: Book Three*. 2nd ed. Pacific Grove, CA: Heinle and Heinle.

Voller, Peter, and Steven Widdows. 1989. *Chatterbox: A Conversation Text of Fluency Activities for Intermediate Students*. Pacific Grove, CA: Heinle and Heinle.

Web Sites

NAFSA: Association of International Educators, Rainbow Special Interest Group. 2000. Indiana University Office of Overseas Study. Accessed May 30, 2005. http://www.indiana.edu/~overseas/lesbigay/. Counsels international students and study abroad students who are gay, lesbian, bisexual or transgender; to support LGBT professionals in international education; and to combat homophobia, heterosexism and transphobia within NAFSA.

TESOL: LGBTF Caucus. 2005. Accessed May 30, 2005. http://www2.tesol.org/communities/lgbtf/. Aims to create fair, safe, and accepting environments for students and colleagues of all sexual orientations.

Ethnic Identity

Maria Pallotta-Chiarolli

Ethnic identity is a person's sense of belonging to a particular ethnic group, within the context of a larger dominant culture such as in the United States. This identity involves participating in and negotiating that group's cultural, religious, and other traditions, beliefs, and values. Being a same-sex attracted young person raised within an ethnic group requires the negotiation and interweaving of varying and multiple regulations, expectations, and social codes in relation to gender, sexuality, and ethnicity. These regulations, expectations, and codes are coming from the young person's ethnic families and communities, predominantly white LGBT communities, and predominantly white homophobic schools within a wider predominantly white homophobic society. **Lesbian, gay, bisexual**, and **transgender** youth from diverse

See also Curriculum, Antibias; Europe, LGBT Youth and Issues in; Parents, Responses to Homosexuality; Mental Health; Multicultural Education; Racial Identity; Religion and Psychological Development; Religious Fundamentalism; Social Class; South America, LGBT Youth and Issues in; Youth, At Risk.

ethnic backgrounds call for various policies, practices, and other strategies to be implemented in education systems, gay community and ethnic community media and health services, and in the wider society's media and health services.

Savin-Williams (1998) presents three main developmental tasks of same-sex attracted young people from diverse ethnic backgrounds that are not necessarily experienced by same-sex attracted young people from dominant Anglo-white backgrounds. First, the young person needs to cultivate both a **sexual identity** and an ethnic identity. Second, the young person must resolve any conflicts that may arise in claiming allegiance to an ethnic reference group and to a gay community; and third, the young person needs to negotiate any stigmas and **discrimination** encountered because of the interconnections of **homophobia, racism,** and **sexism.**

> Many same-sex attracted young people from diverse ethnic backgrounds want to belong to and feel they have a place in their families and ethnic communities. Their ethnic community and family can nurture a cultural identification, offer a deep sense of ethnic heritage and values, and provide a sense of self within the context of a family that shares a youth's struggles and oppressions such as racism and classism (Greene 1997; Pallotta-Chiarolli 1998).

Two factors appear to be significant in leading to changing attitudes toward homosexuality within ethnic families. First, the growing visibility and diversity of LGBT lives both within their country of residence and in their homelands are chipping away at the rigid **stereotypes** preserved in migrant communities (Drucker 2000). Second, the longer the family is in its new country, the more it ceases to be bound by traditional religious and cultural values in relation to gender and sexuality, or it appears to become increasingly similar to **urban,** educated, middle class understandings of sexual diversity in their countries of origin (Greene 1997).

Research also shows that many ethnic families and communities adopt a "don't ask, don't tell" strategy. Denial and silence are forms of internal community control and group cohesion, the construction of a united front, against the real and/or imagined pressures from the wider Anglo society. A young person's **coming out** is often equated with assimilating the Anglo-white culture's norms and losing one's cultural self, of losing the remnants of the "home" that was left behind in the migration process. Notions of collectivism rather than individuality are dominant as members of a family and community rely on each other in negotiating external alien official and unofficial socio-economic and political structures and realities (Pallotta-Chiarolli 1998; Ratti 1993). Belonging to an ethnic family means that traditional constructions of gender are interconnected with sexual behavior, identity, and expression. For example, in South American and Mediterranean ethnic groups, sons are inheritors, expected to provide life-long support to the family, to marry, and to carry on the family name. Women are also expected to get married and have children as their performance of a heterosexual femininity is a key marker of the family's success and honor within the community (Jackson and Sullivan 1999; Pallotta-Chiarolli 1998). Likewise, for these cultures, some of the social stigma against LGBT people is based on anxiety about their existence outside the family structure and its support mechanisms. Aging migrants are often concerned with sustaining intergenerationally supportive families. Yet, the very silences and discriminations against LGBT family members, often bolstered by a rigid adherence to religious dogma, are what actually drive them away from their parents and extended family, and prevent them from making choices about having children and thus providing grandparents with grandchildren (Greene 1997; Pallotta-Chiarolli 1998).

Some ethnic families, such as those from diverse countries in **Asia** and **Africa**, see homosexuality as a manifestation of secularization imposed by a decadent, urbanized Western white culture (Ratti 1993). As Teddy Consolacion writes,

> Most people think it was great that I was a lesbian with the opportunity to grow up in San Francisco where the general attitude towards lesbians and gays is fairly positive. I remind those people that I did not grow up in the queer-positive milieu everyone thinks of at the mention of my home city. I grew up in a Catholic, Filipino home . . . [my Mum] became very embittered to the American culture that had corrupted my morals and influenced me into becoming a lesbian (Kumashiro 2001, 84).

Oral history and other community projects are needed to explore sexual diversity in non-Western countries of origin as part of migration experiences.

Linked to ethnicity and family expectations is religion, both within the ethnic community and framed by the wider society's often homophobic religious institutions. For example, the breaking of religious regulations for LGBT young people from diverse Islamic backgrounds generally leads to guilt, intimidation, and excommunication from the family and community. In non-Islamic countries where these LGBT youth may reside, this is often framed by mainstream **Christian** condemnation that perpetuates and reinforces the fundamentalist non-Christian views of some ethno-religious community gatekeepers (Jackson and Sullivan 1999; Ratti 1993). Arik, a **Muslim** gay youth explains, "Muslims and Christians think they're so different, but when it comes to gay kids, we're scum to both religions. They gang up on us, and it's harder when you got both religions out to get you. . . . I still want to be part of my Muslim community and part of the Christian gay community."

Same-sex attracted young people from diverse ethnic backgrounds identify seven significant factors in the successful negotiation of their various identities and communities. First, strong support networks and friendships with other same-sex attracted people of same and/or similar cultural and religious backgrounds are considered of great significance (Jackson and Sullivan 1999). Likewise, access to and participation in both the LGBT and ethnic communities (while transcending both to live with a code of their own) is important (Emslie 2005; Pallotta-Chiarolli 1998). Third, young people want control over how, when, and if to "come out" to their ethnic families, as well as receiving acceptance and support for those decisions from their LGBT friends, ethnic and school friends (Greene 1997). Fourth, media coverage of same-sex attracted individuals and role models from diverse ethnic backgrounds, and historical facts about sexual diversity within their "home" cultures needs to be made available in both ethnic community and mainstream papers, ethnic and mainstream television, film, and music (Drucker 2000; Savin-Williams 1998; Sears and Williams 1997). **Films** such as *The Crying Game* (UK 1992), *My Beautiful Laundrette* (UK 1985), *Fire* (India 1996), *Bend It Like Beckham* (UK/Germany 2002), *Mambo Italiano* (Canada 2003), and *Hsi Yen* (*The Wedding*

Banquet) (Hong Kong 1993) deal with cross-cultural LGBT issues and same-sex at-tracted young people within ethnic communities.

Similarly, schools and other educational systems can address racism, sexism, and homophobia equally, consistently, and in interconnected ways. For example, the school **curriculum** can incorporate texts, lessons, research assignments, and commu-nity involvement projects that address and explore historical cross-cultural sexuali-ties, as well as ethnic LGBT realities and issues within mainstream Western societies. Student welfare policies such as antiharassment and equal opportunity policies can specify and provide strategies to address the intersection of racist, sexist, and homo-phobic harassment that young lesbians and bisexual girls from diverse cultural back-grounds may experience in schools (Kumashiro 2001; Sears and Williams 1997).

Finally, **queer** youth from diverse ethnic backgrounds want **community LGBT youth groups**, organizations and services, gay venues, papers, and other media av-enues to promote and implement policies and practices that cater for their diverse ethnic backgrounds (Pallotta-Chiarolli 1998). This can include ethno-specific sup-port services and social groups within mainstream LGBT communities as well as multicultural content and events within mainstream LGBT film, food, and other cultural festivals.

Bibliography

Drucker, Peter, ed. 2000. *Different Rainbows*. London: Gay Men's Press.
Emslie, Mic. 2005. "Working with GLBT Young People and Their Ethnic Communities." Pp. 212–215 in *When Our Children Come Out*. Edited by Maria Pallotta-Chiarolli. Sydney: Finch Publishing.
Greene, Beverly, ed. 1997. *Ethnic and Cultural Diversity among Lesbians and Gay Men*. Thousand Oaks, CA: Sage.
Jackson, Peter, and Gerard Sullivan, eds. 1999. *Multicultural Queer: Australian Narratives*. Binghamton, NY: Haworth Press.
Kumashiro, Kevin, ed. 2001. *Troubling Intersections of Race and Sexuality: Queer Students of Color and Anti-Oppressive Education*. Lanham, MD: Rowman and Littlefield
Pallotta-Chiarolli, Maria. 1998. *Cultural Diversity and Men Who Have Sex with Men*. Commonwealth Department of Health and Family Services and the National Centre in HIV Social Research, University of New South Wales, Australia.
Ratti, Rakesh, ed. 1993. *A Lotus of Another Color: An Unfolding of the South Asian Gay and Lesbian Experience*. Boston: Alyson.
Savin-Williams, Ritch C. 1998 *". . . And Then I Became Gay:" Young Men's Stories*. New York: Routledge.
Sears, James T., and Walter L. Williams, eds. 1997. *Overcoming Heterosexism and Homophobia: Strategies That Work*. New York: Columbia University Press.

Web Sites

Magenta Foundation. Gay and Lesbian Resources. 1999. http://www.magenta.nl/crosspoint/gay.html. Accessed December 5, 2004. This site is a collection of LGBT resources and support/social groups throughout the world including Asia, the Pacific, North and South America, Europe, Russia, Africa, and the Middle East.
Tremblay, Pierre. A GLBTQ Education Internet Resources. September, 1998. http://www.youth-suicide.com/gay-bisexual/links5.htm. Accessed December 5, 2004. This is a collection of LGBT resources that address race and ethnic minority issues in North America, Europe, Australia and New Zealand.

Europe, LGBT Youth and Issues in

Loykie Loïc Lomine

That Europe has long ignored its **lesbian, gay, bisexual**, and **transgender youth** (LGBT) appears paradoxical on the continent that proudly boasts the Enlightenment and the concept of human rights. Despite important regional and national disparities due to economic, socio-cultural, and religious differences, Europe, as a whole, is the theater of numerous tensions and debates pertaining to LGBT issues. Although most topics under discussion (such as **adoption** rights and legal protection against **discrimination** at the **workplace**) may not be primarily relevant for LGBT youth, they have nonetheless brought the needs and experiences of LGBT people into the public sphere. The younger generations have started to benefit from more visibility and more protection against **homophobia**. The main political strength in favour of LGBT European youth is the combination of two key factors: the existence of active, local LGBT youth grass-roots support movements; and, the development of European legal frameworks.

In 2000, the Council of Europe published a report entitled *The Situation of Lesbians and Gays in Council of Europe Member States*. Out of the seventy-four points developed in the document, only two short paragraphs specifically deal with the situation of LGBT youth, confirming the view that the experience of young people and their specific needs are usually forgotten. These two paragraphs provide a very bleak overview: "The problems faced by young lesbians and gays are particularly acute. Research carried out in many countries confirms that negative images of homosexuality, rejection by family, peer group hostility, isolation, and lack of information and support can combine to create the most intense pressures. Moreover homophobic violence and bullying are a common experience for many young lesbians and gays" (Tabajdi 2000, paragraphs 59 and 60).

As a whole, Europe appears to be a rather homophobic continent, but generalizing over Europe is difficult since situations vary from country to country. An emerging pattern is the difference between Western Europe and Eastern Europe. Western European countries, more developed economically and with more liberal political traditions, have started to adopt more inclusive policies as their governments increasingly legislate about discrimination on the basis of **sexual orientation** and the prevention of homophobia. Although not directed toward young people, these Laws and Acts (such as the 2003 *Employment Equality Sexual Orientation Regulations*, in the United Kingdom, and the 1999 *Pacte Civil de Solidarité*, enabling gay couples to register their partnerships in France) constitute official statements that send positive messages to young people. The situation is far from ideal for LGBT youth, however. In one survey within the United Kingdom, 48 percent of LGBT youth under the age of eighteen reported violent attacks, and 50 percent of these attacks took place in schools and were carried out by fellow students (Mason and Palmer 1996).

See also Bulgaria, LGBT Youth in; College Campus Organizing; Coming Out, Youth; Community LGBT Youth Groups; Drug Use; Educational Policies; France, LGBT Youth in; GLBT Educational Equity (GLEE); Ireland, LGBT Youth and Issues in; Jewish Moral Instruction on Homosexuality; Muslim Moral Instruction on Homosexuality; Scouting; Substance Abuse and Use; United Kingdom, LGBT Youth and Issues in; Youth, At Risk.

In contrast, Eastern European countries often ignore, if not violate, the human rights of LGBT youth in the process of their political and economic transition: "LGBT youth is not protected from different forms of hate speech, many times also reflected in the media. . . . Being open about one's sexual orientation will cause intolerance. . . . Young lesbians and gays are also often victims of police **harassment** and/or gay-bashing in public places" (Vanhemelryck 2002, 6). Despite these problems and the absence of a supportive legal framework, active LGBT youth movements exist in Eastern Europe. For example the Serbian LGBT organisation Queeria, founded in 2000, is active through media campaigns, exhibitions, and partnerships. The International Gay and Lesbian Youth Organisation (IGLYO) now has a permanent office in Slovenia's capital of Ljubljana, a location most symbolic as a bridge between Western and Eastern Europe.

Across Europe, a distinction has to be made between **urban** and **rural** areas. The concentration of population and the presence of alternative subcultures in urban areas, give LGBT youth more opportunities for existence and protection. Two dynamic factors—a pull factor, the visibility of LGBT adults in urban areas, and as a push factor, the traditional conservative homophobia of the rural world— work in combination and explain the "queer rural exodus" of many LGBT youth.

Religion is another factor that, within Europe, contributes to creating a hostile environment for queer youth. Catholicism is dominant in the countries of southwest Europe (e.g., Spain and Italy) and in Central Europe (e.g., Austria and Poland). Its explicit homophobia represents a major socio-cultural obstacle for LGBT youth's expression and visibility. The official line from the Vatican, as expressed in the 1992 Catechism of the **Catholic** Church (paragraphs 2357–2359), is one of strict condemnation, which makes life particularly difficult for LGBT youth. Living in Catholic environments, they cannot safely discuss issues of sexuality or come out. The more Catholic one's family background, the more difficult it will be. The **Christian** Orthodox Churches, in the eastern parts of Europe, have traditionally held similar views. For example, in August 2000, the Russian Orthodox Church adopted a strictly conservative social policy platform that contained harsh criticisms of homosexuality. In the Protestant regions of northwest Europe (such as the United Kingdom and Scandinavia), the situation is difficult but improving. Numerous denominations and **religious fundamentalist** groups (such as the evangelical wing of the Church of England) are openly homophobic, yet one can witness recent condemnation of homophobia within some Protestant churches. In December 2003, the Right Rev. Professor Iain Torrance, leader of the Church of Scotland, called upon the Christian congregations everywhere to shed their homophobia. Other religions present in Europe (such as Islam, Hinduism, and Judaism) have been opposed to nonheterosexual forms of sexuality. Young Europeans growing up in religious or semireligious environments (parents, family, school, youth groups) are, therefore, quite likely to remain silent, to suppress or repress their **desires**, and to leave home before they come out.

With a few exceptions such as the Netherlands (Dankmeijer 1995), in most countries, the educational system does not provide any information on nonheterosexual sexualities and alternative lifestyles, reflecting heterosexual **prejudice** and **heteronormativity**. Dutch gay and lesbian organizations promote healthier development by giving gay and lesbian education sessions in schools. The schools invite gays and lesbians to tell something about their lives and to answer questions, and the Dutch government supports integration of education about homosexuality in the **curriculum**.

For LGBT youth in Europe, the current picture is bleak until they reach their late teens and early twenties, when opportunities multiply. For example, most universities accept LGBT **activism** as part of their student structures with LGBT student societies, clubs, and associations officially endorsed by the institution, falling under "special interest" or "lifestyle" categories. Additionally, some universities are openly LGBT-friendly, such as the University of Utrecht which has a **LGBT studies** program, or the University of Essex where scholars such as sociology professor Ken Plummer have traditionally attracted high numbers of Ph.D. students from all over Europe, keen to conduct **research** in LGBT areas. These institutions appear as academic landmarks of tolerance, but the downside is an "ivory tower" **school climate** where LGBT students may be too remotely detached from the rest of the world.

Heteronomativity and homophobia are pervasive throughout European society, including the media, especially in television programs where programmers and producers often indulge in easy clichés of effeminate men and masculine women. Representations often conform to mainstream norms and **stereotypes** with limited attention to the psychological and emotional effects on young LGBT viewers and on society as a whole. Positive representations of happy gay youth, such as in Cesc Gay's Spanish **film** *Nico and Dani—Krámpack* (2000) and Hettie Macdonald's *Beautiful Thing* (UK 1996), are very important in terms of representation, but they are few in number and do not show how difficult coming out in Europe can be, especially when one does not have LGBT-friendly people around.

Given this less than hospitable climate for LGBT youth, there is a "self-hate that leads an alarmingly high percentage of gay and lesbian youth to inflict violence upon themselves through suicide attempts, drug and alcohol abuse, or other high-risk behaviors. Studies in several countries show that young lesbians and gays are between two and three times more likely to attempt suicide than their heterosexual counterparts" (Tabajdi 2000, Paragraph 60). Research in Italy (Bertozzo 1998) and France (Firdion 2001) has showed that **suicide** rates are much higher among LGBT youth. Bertozzo, for instance, found that 40 percent of young LGBT Italians surveyed had contemplated suicide, and 13 percent had attempted it. The relatively little research on LGBT youth in Europe also underscores the inhospitable climate.

In the absence of any systematic research, organizations such as the IGLYO and, to a lesser extent, the European branch of the International Lesbian and Gay Association, provide information based on their networking, educating, and campaigning throughout Europe. National case studies (not always widely publicized abroad and translated) are useful, too, as well as the few other texts which include LGBT youth issues, even though it may not necessarily be their primary objective. Graupner's (1997) legal analysis, comparing the provisions of the criminal law in all European jurisdictions, occasionally tackles issues of sexual self-determination of "minors."

The Treaty of Amsterdam, which revised the Treaties on which the European Union (EU) is founded, came into force in May 1999, marking a significant milestone for European lesbians and gay men. It includes Clause 13, which covers discrimination on the basis of sexual orientation. Lacking substantive legal power, it symbolically shows that the EU will not tolerate discrimination (including anti-LGBT) in its twenty-five member states. Toward that end, in 2000, the European Council passed Recommendation 1474, urging member states to "take positive measures to combat homophobic attitudes, particularly in schools" (point 11 iii e). An international hearing on the discrimination of gay and lesbian youth in the EU accession countries, held in Ljubljana in 2002, demanded that no EU candidate country should be allowed to join the EU unless legislation discriminating against lesbians and gays was repealed before accession. This was only partly successful. Ten countries have joined the EU since then, including ultra-Catholic Poland where gay rights are hardly even acknowledged. Governments may pay lip service and promise to fight against discrimination, but it will be years before LGBT youngsters start benefiting from more liberal attitudes. Likewise, private groups (especially religious and quasi-religious ones such as the Scouts) might claim that they welcome all youngsters, irrespective of their sexual orientation, but seldom is there a genuine cultural shift towards socio-cultural inclusion. Ostracism, harassment, and bullying against LGBT youth will not cease because of supranational EU policies. Likewise, LGBT teachers might get some legal protection against discriminatory dismissal, but most will usually keep silent, except in the most tolerant countries such as the Netherlands.

Across Europe, several organizations, such as London-based "Press for Change" and Paris-Based "Association du Syndrome de Benjamin," campaign for respect and equality for all transpeople. Some of these charities, such as the United Kingdom parents support group "Mermaids," focus on youth's experience. Their multidimensional work gives voice to transgender children and their families while keeping archives of related articles and stories, lobbying politicians, raising awareness among social workers and medical providers, as well as offering a public platform to discuss issues of **gender identity** and gender ethics.

Bibliography

Bertozzo, Graziella. 1998, October. "Da Internet le Voci di Quella Ragazza, di Quel Ragazzo" (From the Internet the Voices of that Girl, that Boy). Firenze: *Finisterrae* no. 1: 10–11.

Dankmeijer, Peter. 1995. *Gay and Lesbian Education in Dutch Schools.* http://www.tolerantescholen.net/educonte.htm. Accessed December 4, 2004.

Firdion, Jean-Marie. 2001. Le risque de Suicide Chez les Jeunes à Orientation Sexuelle non Conventionnelle (Lesbiennes, Bisexuels, Gais). Rapport du Groupe de Travail pour Homosexualités et Socialisme. (Suicide Risk amongst LGBT Youth: Report from Working Group on Homosexuality and Socialism). Paris: Montblanc H & O.

Graupner, Helmut. 1997. *Sexualität. Jugendschutz & Menschenrechte: Über das Recht von Kindern und Jugendlichen auf Sexuelle Selbstbestimmung.* (Sexuality – Youth and Human Rights: About Youngster's Right to Choose their Sexuality). Wien: Peter Lang.

Mason, Angela, and Palmer, Anya. 1996. *Queer Bashing: A National Survey of Hate Crimes against Lesbians and Gay Men.* London: Stonewall.

Tabajdi, Csaba. 2000, June. *Situation of Lesbians and Gays in Council of Europe Member States.* Report of the Committee on Legal Affairs and Human Rights. Parliamentary Assembly, Doc. 8755—Followed by Recommendation 1474. http://assembly.coe.int/Main.asp?link5http://assembly.coe.int/Documents/WorkingDocs/Doc00/EDOC8755.htm. Accessed December 4, 2004.

Vanhemelryck, Kris. 2002. *ILGA-Europe Newsletter* 2, no. 1: 6–7.

Web Sites

Catechism of the Catholic Church. November 2003. Accessed May 31, 2005. http://www.vatican.va/archive/ccc/index.htm 1992 official version, full text available in several languages, including English. Homosexuality is discussed within part three, section two, chapter two, article 6, subsection 2 (entitled "The Vocation to Chastity").

IGLYO. 2003. Accessed December 3, 2004 http://www.iglyo.net/ Based in Ljubljana (Slovenia), this European organization's Web site (even if its name seems to have a global dimension) is promising in terms of resources and actions, although many pages are still under construction.

ILGA Europe. December 2004. Accessed December 3, 2004. http://www.ilga-europe.org. The European Region of the International Lesbian and Gay Association's free quarterly newsletter often include youth-related papers and briefings.

Pink Quest. 2003. Accessed October 8, 2004. http://www.pinkquest.nl/ From the Netherlands, this Dutch-only site has news facts and a help desk, among other features.

Queeria: Where Queers Feel at Home. 2004. Accessed October 8, 2004. http://www.queeria. org.yu. Serbian queer youth Web site, available in English, which includes sections on activism, the arts, and theory.

Queer Youth Alliance. 2004. Accessed October 8, 2004. http://www.queeryouth.org.uk The UK Alliance of LGBT People hosts this site with message boards, underground magazines, advice and support, and current projects.

F

Families, LGBT

Connie R. Matthews and *Peggy Lorah*

Despite its limited definition in the culture at large, family can have many meanings for the lesbian, gay, bisexual, and transgender (LGBT) community, and young people must learn to negotiate their way with family on many fronts. **Lesbian, gay, bisexual,** and **transgender youth** exist in families in a variety of ways: families they are born into (family of origin), often through heterosexual marriage and sometimes from permanent relationships with individuals of the same gender; kinship networks of close friends (family of choice); and the LGBT community as a whole. LGBT individuals may exist in families as children or as parents of children or without children. Creating and maintaining family can often be a struggle for LGBT individuals due to cultural prescriptions about the nature of family. These struggles can be legal, financial, psychological, and physical. At the same time, struggle can lead to creativity; the LGBT community has found ways to help its members experience the bonds and support of family on many levels. LGBT youth who are ethnic minorities experience additional stresses, but also additional resources in negotiating the realm of family.

An Extended LGBT Family. © Gigi Kaeser from the book and the touring photo-text exhibit LOVE MAKES A FAMILY: Portraits of Lesbian, Gay, Bisexual, and Transgender People and Their Families. For information, visit www.familydiv.org or email info@familydiv.org.

See also Children of the Rainbow Curriculum; Children of LGBT Parents; Community LGBT Youth Groups; Curriculum, Early Childhood; Curriculum, Primary; Educational Policies; Ethnic Identity; Literature, Early Childhood; Parents, LGBT; Parents, Responses to Homosexuality; Passing; Race and Racism; Transsexuality.

The first family that LGBT youth experience is the family of origin. At whatever age an individual comes out as LGBT, the issue of what and when to tell this family must be addressed. For LGBT adolescents, this is further complicated by financial and emotional dependence on their family. Even when the end result is positive, this process is almost always disruptive. Families go through an adjustment to incorporating an LGBT member, just as individuals go through an adjustment process in coming out (Matthews and Lease 2000). It is important for anyone working with youth or families to understand this longer-term process to avoid getting trapped in short-term reactions.

For LGBT youth from ethnic minority communities, the process of **coming out** to family can be even more complicated. Because societal oppression strengthens the bonds many minority youth have with their families of origin and their extended families, young people will often choose not to discuss **sexual orientation** or **gender identity** with their families. Furthermore, the family, and perhaps the religious institution, are often the only refuges ethnic minority youth have from the racism of the dominant culture. Many are not willing to risk their strong connections for the sake of identifying as a sexual minority. Many LGTB minority youth choose not to act on, or even to acknowledge, their orientation or identity. All of this may be exacerbated by norms in some cultures against any open discussion of sexuality, regardless of orientation. Thus, coming out to parents can mean violating multiple cultural norms. This can be compounded by cultural values that discourage individuals from violating cultural expectations and bringing shame to the family.

Paradoxically, the commitment to family that is prevalent in many ethnic minority cultures can serve as an avenue for acceptance, or at least tolerance, of minority sexual identities. Parents find ways to accept and support their children rather than risk severing family ties. Furthermore, such estrangement itself might bring shame or disgrace to the family. Sometimes this involves simply not talking about it. Partners of LGBT children may even be incorporated into family functions, identified simply as "friends." Although this facilitates relationships within the family of origin, it can create strains within the LGBT community for ethnic minority youth. Political elements of the community may place great importance on being "out" and disparage those individuals who are unwilling to do this.

Cultural assumptions and prescriptions of heterosexuality lead many LGBT individuals into heterosexual marriages, sometimes without a prior awareness of their sexual orientation or gender identity. Approximately one-third of lesbian and bisexual women and one-fifth of gay and bisexual men in same-sex relationships were once in heterosexual marriages (Cahill, Mitra, and Tobias 2002). This adds a further layer to the coming out process as more people are affected by it. Further, legal complications may make it difficult for LGBT individuals to leave these marriages and/or retain custody or even visitation with children from the marriage. These families may or may not remain in tact once the LGBT individual identifies.

For transgender individuals, there are special considerations, particularly if the need to dress or to live as a different gender or to have gender reassignment surgery is a concern. Some marriages are severed immediately upon a coming out discussion or dissolve as soon as any outward signs of transgender status are evident. Sometimes marital partners are so totally estranged that loving parents are no longer permitted contact with their children. This is not always the case. Because gender identity is not about sexual orientation, these individuals may deeply love their spouses and may wish to remain married and full partners in parenthood.

Many transgender persons work this out with their spouses and continue living with their families and raising their children (Boylan 2003).

The question of whether or not same-sex couples should be able to marry legally or to enjoy the benefits and protections of marriage has become a politically charged one in the United States. Massachusetts is the only state to grant marriage licenses to same-sex couples, and only Vermont recognizes civil unions for gay men and lesbians; a few more offer domestic partner benefits. At the federal level, the 1996 Defense of Marriage Act limited the definition of marriage to heterosexual couples and relieved states of recognizing civil unions conducted elsewhere. However, this may be complicated by constitutional rulings in state courts (as in the case of Massachusetts) as well as by the more recent *Lawrence v. Texas* decision. A number of other countries have progressed further. The Netherlands, Germany, Denmark, Iceland, Sweden, Portugal, and Greenland all offer national recognition of nonheterosexual partners. Several Canadian provinces also recognize partnerships, as do a number of other countries in more limited degrees. Legal recognition is important, not only for the benefits and protections offered within the relationship, but also should the partnership dissolve (Cahill, Mitra, and Tobias 2002). This has particular ramifications for children who often have biological or legal ties to only one adult in the family, leaving the other partner and the children without recourse for maintaining connection.

With or without legal recognition, LGBT individuals create families in a variety of ways. Couples may live together or apart. Such partnerships can include children from previous marriages, through **adoption**, or from insemination or surrogate parenting. It can also include communal arrangements and shared parenting. Such arrangements may involve former heterosexual and/or LGBT partners.

Children in LGBT families sometimes must adjust to new relationships with their parents. These same children may also face **harassment** or **discrimination** due to their parents' sexual orientation. Educators must be prepared to offer support and assistance to these young people and their families. This is an area in which Parents, Families, and Friends of Lesbians and Gays (PFLAG) can be a useful resource.

The LGBT community itself often serves as family for its members. Friendship networks within the community also act as kinship networks, taking on roles common within families. This may involve celebrating holidays, offering emotional support, sharing financial and other resources. In addition, the LGBT community serves as a socializing mechanism, helping individuals to develop healthy gay, lesbian, bisexual, or transgender identities in the face of **prejudice**, discrimination, or even hostility in the larger culture. Dahlheimer and Feigal (1994, 66–67) address five ways in which the LGBT community functions as family that seem particularly applicable to youth. They suggest that family serves to "directly protect its children from harm or danger . . . teach its children how to socialize appropriately in the culture . . . promote self-esteem and a sense of value and worth in its children . . . help its children develop a sense of identity . . . [and] teach survival skills to cope in the larger world."

These functions seem especially important for young people coming out. Unlike many other minority cultures in which parents share the cultural attributes and any social ramifications with their children, the vast majority of LGBT youth are raised by parents who do not share their minority status. When parents do share this, for instance in ethnic minority families, they are able to provide a buffer from the racism or other discrimination their children face in the dominant culture. They are also able to help their children to feel valued as the people they are, which is necessary if they are to develop a healthy and positive sense of identity. Often, parents of LGBT youth share, at least initially, many of the biases of the dominant culture, thus making the family a place of additional turmoil rather than refuge, at least temporarily. Even when parents of LGBT youth are supportive, they lack the familiarity with the culture to really assist their children in becoming acculturated.

The LGBT community generally provides some of these family functions for LGBT youth through community youth groups and other support groups. Many metropolitan areas, as well as most large universities, have visible and somewhat accessible organizations and services for LGBT youth. Here they can find the companionship of others like themselves as well as adults who can help mentor them in developmental tasks. This is often not the case in smaller cities or more rural areas, and more effort is usually needed to help youth connect with more informal communities. The **Internet** is an important resource as are local educators who make the effort to locate such communities, to encourage them to reach out to young people, and then to help young people connect with them.

Bibliography

Boylan, Jennifer. 2003. *She's Not There: A Life in Two Genders*. New York: Broadway Books.

Cahill, Sean, Ellen Mitra, and Sarah Tobias. 2002. *Family Policy: Issues Affecting Gay, Lesbian, Bisexual, and Transgender Families*. New York: National Gay and Lesbian Task Force Policy Institute.

Dahlheimer, Darryl, and Jennifer Feigal. 1994. "Community as Family: The Multiple-Family Contexts of Lesbian and Gay Clients." Pp. 63–74 in *Transitioning from Individual to Family Counseling*. Edited by Charles H. Huber. Alexandria, VA: American Counseling Association.

Greene, Beverly. 1998. "Family, Ethnic Identity, and Sexual Orientation: African-American Lesbians and Gay Men." Pp. 40–52 in *Lesbian, Gay, and Bisexual Identities in Families: Psychological Perspectives*. Edited by Charlotte J. Patterson and Anthony R. D'Augelli. New York: Oxford University Press.

Liu, Peter, and Connie S. Chan. 1996. "Lesbian, Gay, and Bisexual Asian Americans and Their Families." Pp. 137–152 in *Lesbians and Gays in Couples and Families: A Handbook for Therapists*. Edited by Joan Laird and Robert-Jay Green. San Francisco, CA: Jossey-Bass Publishers.

Matthews, Connie R., and Suzanne H. Lease. 2000. "Focus on Lesbian, Gay, and Bisexual Families." Pp. 249–273 in *Handbook of Counseling and Psychotherapy with Lesbian, Gay and Bisexual Clients*. Edited by Ruperto M. Perez, Kurt A. DeBord, and Kathleen J. Bieschke. Washington, DC: American Psychological Association.

Weston, Kath. 1994. "Building Gay Families." Pp. 525–533 in *The Psychosocial Interior of the Family*. 4th Ed. Edited by Gerald. Handel and Gail. G. Whitchurch. New York: Aldine deGruyter.

Web Sites

National Gay and Lesbian Task Force. May 2005. Accessed May 31, 2005. http://www.thetaskforce.org/. The Policy Institute offers publications and information about the status of major policy issues, including gay marriage and gay family issues.

Parents, Families, and Friends of Lesbians and Gays (PFLAG). May 2005. Accessed May 31, 2005. http://www.pflag.org/. Provides educational resources, information about support groups throughout the country, advocacy updates, and news about current issues.

Feminism

Mahoney Archer

Feminism is a movement of thinking and action that seeks to address oppression, principally that of women. From the eighteenth century, women have sought to challenge the notion of "masculine truth" whereby men and masculine social constructions are inherently superior, and women and the feminine are inferior. The mission of feminism is to displace traditional social systems that determine privilege to some and not to others. Feminism is a response to patriarchy, wherein knowledge and power have been arbitrarily gendered as masculine and universal. Feminism seeks to address patriarchy's conceptual foundation that suggests human traits are intrinsically male or female. Education and educational institutions are keys in this socialization process—and they are the means by which patriarchy can be discussed and disrupted. Feminism is involved in school-related issues with many implications for lesbian teachers, **curriculum**, and queer youth.

The ownership of knowledge and power has historically enabled men to "own" society. Among the first efforts to respond to the systematic exclusion of women/the feminine was the writing of Mary Wollstonecraft during the late 1700s. Wollstonecraft is identified as one of the first *egalitarian feminists*. She sought equal opportunity and advantage for both sexes/genders, arguing that gender differences were the result of socialization and education rather than **biology** (Cole 1993). Society, Wollstonecraft asserted, taught males and females differently so that males would be powerful and females would not. Simone de Beauvoir is another luminary egalitarian feminist. De Beauvoir's contribution to feminism is located predominantly in her critical work *The Second Sex* (1949). In this, she illustrates that through social (masculine) tradition and education women's dignity and independence are diminished.

Egalitarian feminist approaches assert that women are as capable as men, to operate within a male-determined social structure. The 1960s and 1970s saw numerous influential works by authors such as Germaine Greer (*The Female Eunuch*), Betty Friedan (*The Feminine Mystique*), Kate Millett (*Sexual Politics*), and Shulamith Firestone (*The Dialectic of Sex*). Juliet Mitchell and Nancy Chodorow also made significant contributions through their discussion of **psychoanalysis**. Both reappropriated Freudian psychoanalysis, using psychoanalysis to explain the means by which patriarchy is replicated generationally. Broadly considered egalitarian feminists, these authors are some of the leaders of second-wave feminism.

Over time, numerous egalitarian feminists became frustrated in efforts toward gender equity within a gender-biased system. *Radical feminism* seeks to illustrate male control in all spheres of women's lives. The slogan, "personal is political" emerged, meaning that all personal experiences of women are points for political **activism**. Thus, reproduction, marriage, **compulsory heterosexuality,** and motherhood are at the forefront as possible sites where change can be positively effected. Here the body is analyzed as a site of women's oppression through discussions of sexuality and a continually growing body of knowledge regarding women's health.

See also Graffiti; Heteronormativity; Lesbian Youth; Men's Studies; Mentoring; Sexual Health, Lesbian and Bisexual Women; Sexism; Sports, Lesbians in; Stereotypes; Teachers, LGBT and History; Women's Movement; Women's Studies; Workplace Issues.

Ensuring women's autonomy, a woman's control over her body was regarded as key to her liberation.

Lesbian feminism grew from this, addressing heterosexual privilege, **gender role** stereotyping, and gender inequity. Lesbian feminists focused on discovering that lesbians exist in a dynamic that is not dependent upon men. During this era, the concept and practice of "elective lesbianism," emerged as heterosexual feminists who "slept with the enemy" were challenged. And, radical feminist philosophers—Luce Irigaray, Michele Le Doeuff, Mary Daly, Elizabeth Grosz and Genevieve Lloyd—pinpointed the origins of such Western binaries with their associated valuations (e.g., masculine=good, feminine=bad) rooted in patriarchy. Their charge was to illustrate positive constructions of the feminine, creating a space and a voice for women.

These feminisms have applications for schools, learning, teachers, and students. For example, contemporary feminists underscore how women teachers have been historically cast as "nurturers," with schools as the extension of the home and their "natural" maternal role (Khayatt 1992). Women predominate as elementary teachers and, when teaching in secondary schools, preponderantly teach **literature** and the arts; men have assumed administrative (and higher paid) positions and predominate in the "hard" sciences. Schools socialize the next generation into this gendered hierarchy. Families and religions are also regarded in this way.

In the 1970s, philosopher Louis Althusser theorized that these institutional sites (educational, familial, political, religious, **communication**, and cultural) are based on ideas and values that create the conditions necessary for the dominant patriarchal discourse to exist, allowing the gender, **social class**, racial, and sexual status quo to be maintained (Khayatt 1990). These "institutional state apparatuses," as Althusser calls them, promote the heterosexual model of sexuality in which the masculine is reasonable, strong, capable, and active while the feminine is hysterical, unreliable, and passive.

Schools have not only exercised a powerful social control over women and girls, but privileges and transmits certain types of "knowledge," presented as "truth." Curricula, processes, and instruments of the schooling system have done more than emphasize rigid gender role typing, but have gendered knowledge itself: For instance, **curriculum** commonly regarded as more (masculine) has been mathematics and science whereas the humanities—gendered feminine—is considered inferior, "softer," and less empirical. The value and perceived masculinity of knowledge is a cornerstone of patriarchy.

In this context, heterosexuality and masculine dominance are presented as "normal" and "natural." The homosexual male subverts male power by challenging the normalcy of hetero-masculinity but also reinforces masculine power and reproduces patriarchy when, for instance, in male homosexual couplings, one partner assumes the feminine role. Similarly, male teachers who work within the feminine sphere of elementary school also find their sexuality and gender questioned as they undermine male status. Lesbians represent a direct challenge to patriarchy in that lesbianism presents Woman independent of Man. Subsequently, if the lesbian is also teacher she presents an opportunity for women/feminism to subvert the Institutional State Apparatus: the school.

Schools present an image of themselves as ideologically free or neutral while ideologies of dominance (patriarchy) are transmitted to school children via curricula content, school processes/procedures, and those individuals constructed as models of normativity: teachers. The lesbian teacher is an alternative model for existence, one without men as the identifiable source of power and validation.

Homosexuality and the gendered feminine have historically been hidden and characterized as weak, passive, and abnormal, diminishing lesbian and gay educators socially and lessening the threats to the status quo. The consequence of this for queer youth has been the absence of real, accomplished, and visible positive role models. The lesbian teacher suggests a woman-centered lived experience that is not in service to men. She is quite possibly for a lesbian youth the first affirmative indication that there are others like her and that she is not deviant in her sexuality.

The growing visibility of homosexuals within our schools is, however, testament to the strides made by feminists. Equally, the growing volume and visibility of profeminist men (both homosexual and heterosexual) who advocate gender equity and the revision of oppressive traditions contributes to the redress of imbalances which arise from the relegation of the feminine as inferior.

Bibliography

Cole, Elizabeth. 1993. *Philosophy and Feminist Criticism*: Paragon House: New York.
de Beauvoir, Simone. 1949. *The Second Sex* (translated edition: 1988). London: Picador.
Grosz, Elizabeth. 1994. *Volatile Bodies: Towards a Corporeal Feminism*. Sydney: Allen and Unwin.
Gunew, Sneja. 1990. *Feminist Knowledge: Critique & Construct*. London: Routledge.
Khayatt, Madiha Didi. 1990. "Legalised Invisibility." *Women's Studies International Forum* 13, no. 3: 185–193.
———. 1992. *Lesbian Teachers: An Invisible Presence*. Albany: State University of New York.
Lerner, Gerda. 1997. *Why History Matters*. New York: Oxford University Press.

Web Site

Center for Digital Discourse and Culture at Virginia Tech. University. 1999. Kristin Switala. Accessed May 31, 2005. http://www.cddc.vt.edu/feminism/enin.html.

Films, Youth and Educators in

Gilad Padva

Youth films often feature such themes as painful **adolescence**, confrontation with institutions, erotic pubescence, initial same-sex experiences, confusing infatuation, intergenerational relationships, and the formation of **sexual identity**. In particular, the cinematic representation of **queer** adolescence emphasizes and sometimes also sensationalizes these themes, as the rebellious protagonist challenges not only the

See also Asia, LGBT Youth and Issues; Australia, LGBT Youth and Issues in; Bisexuality; Camp; China, LGBT Youth in; France, LGBT Youth and Issues in; Mexico, LGBT Youth and Issues in; Popular Culture; The L Word; Queer and Queer Theory; Single-Sex Schools; Sissy Boy; Social Class; Stereotypes; Transgender Youth; Women's Studies; Youth Culture.

social order but also the sexual order and its powerful agents: parents, teachers, counselors, coaches, and popular role models in mass culture (Padva 2004). These themes are interrelated with complex power relationships among the teenagers themselves, between adolescents and parents, and between teachers and students (Foucault 1976). Alternative queer films in the mid-1990s and early twenty-first century, however, do not represent homosexuality as a perversion or abnormality, nor as a fashionable trend adopted by nonconformist juveniles. It is certainly not portrayed as "just a phase." Rather, the new progay cinema provides its young viewers with alternative role models, countercultural identifications, and a sense of social community.

In mainstream Hollywood and European cinema of the 1950s, for example, queer adolescents were often represented as confused youth who did not conform to their **gender identity**; boys who were "too feminine" and girls who were "too masculine." Consequently, these stigmatized protagonists were persecuted by their schoolmates and teachers, and they were often neglected by peers and families, being left to face exclusion and guilt (Russo 1981). These outcast characters showed the young audience what was about to happen to anyone who deviated from the conventional **gender roles**. In these conservative films, their homosexuality was never discussed. Rather, it was camouflaged as feminine masculinity or masculine femininity. For example, Vincent Minnelli's *Tea and Sympathy* (USA 1956) represents an outcast in a boarding school who is more sensitive and delicate than his schoolmates. At the "Happy End," older (and married) Tom visits his old school. His sissyness is depicted as nothing but a phase.

Likewise, "Plato" (Sal Mineo) in Nicholas Ray's *Rebel Without a Cause* (USA 1955) is a sensitive, agonized adolescent. The desperate protagonist Jimmy Stark (James Dean), despising his alienated parents, creates an alternative family with his soul mates Judy (Natalie Wood) and Plato, who is hopelessly infatuated with Jimmy. These queer protagonists embody one of the predominant gay types in twentieth century culture: the Sad Young Man. As neither androgynously in-between the genders nor playing with the signs of gender, the Sad Young Man's relationship to masculinity is more difficult. As a young man, he has not yet achieved the expected assertive, masculine hardness, representing somewhat of a martyr figure (Dyer 1993).

In the 1980s, North American and West European cinema often represented queer youth more sympathetically. Young gay and lesbian protagonists were not characterized as perverts but they were still sad young men and women, suffering persecution, isolation, and abuse. Beaten by schoolmates, punished by teachers, and mistreated by parents, these unfortunate and miserable adolescents were young martyrs who had no chance for salvation. A paradigmatic film is Marek Kanievska's *Another Country* (UK 1984), an adaptation of Julian Mitchell's novel and play about the Guy Burgess and Donald MacLean 1950s spy scandal. *Another Country* features the agonized Guy Bennett (Rupert Everett), a pupil at a prestigious and tough British boarding school, together with his best (heterosexual) Marxist friend Tommy Judd (Colin Firth). After another gay student is exposed and commits suicide, Guy is increasingly persecuted by the senior students. Later he has a secret relationship with another pupil, James Harcourt (Cary Elwes), a quiet, shy boy. A senior student discovers a love letter and sentences Guy to a savage beating. In contrast to the transformed married Tom in *Tea and Sympathy*, Guy Bennett transgresses not only the sexual but also the political systems, represented at the end of the film as an adult expatriate living in the Soviet Union.

Another melancholic portrayal of aristocratic gay love in a British educational institution appears in James Ivory's adaptation of E. M. Forster's 1914 novel *Maurice* (UK 1987). The film begins with young students at pre-World War I Cambridge University listening to an old-fashioned don lecturing on Plato's most homoerotic work–*Symposium*. The embarrassed don refers to the "Love that dare not speak its name." Maurice (James Wilby) is infatuated with his handsome classmate Clive (Hugh Grant), who eventually breaks the relationship and marries. Maurice leaves the university and develops an interclass affair with Scudder (Rupert Graves), Clive's muscular and unruly gamekeeper.

Other suffering young gay protagonists can be found in Alfred Hitchcock's *Rope* (USA 1948), focusing on a pair of gay college students (Brandon and Phillip, although never explicitly designated as such) who meet with their former professor, Rupert Cadell played by Jimmy Stewart, after they have murdered a boy. The Leopold-Loeb scandal of 1924 also inspired Tom Kalin's *Swoon* (USA 1991), highlighting the young protagonists' homosexuality. *Children* (UK 1976), the first part of *The Terence Davies Trilogy* (UK 1984), also depicts the hardships faced by a queer boy in both his violent boys' school and family.

Interestingly, there are also exceptional cinematic articulations of coming of age, characterized by vivid sexual curiosity, like the surprising homoerotic spectacle in Boaz Davidson's nostalgic comedy *Lemon Popsicle* (Israel 1978), in which Tel Aviv high school students in the 1950s catch their friend, Froyke, peeping into the girls' locker room and fully aroused. Contending that his erection is bigger than theirs, the boys hold a measuring contest where Froyke is crowned "King of the Schmocks," symbolizing the turning of the "nerd" into a "man" (Talmon 2001). In Judd Ne'eman's *Paratroopers* (Israel 1977), however, the nerd protagonist is not glorified but annihilated. In a violent nude scene, Private Weissman (Moni Moshonov) is almost raped in the communal showers by his comrades who aggressively express their anxiety about the "effeminate" male body (Yosef 2004) ; he eventually commits **suicide**.

Toward the 1990s, Western cinema had gradually changed its depiction of **lesbian, gay, bisexual,** and **transgender** (LGBT) youth, although they still experienced **discrimination**, gay bashing, and hostile parents. Queer protagonists and their queer spectators now challenged their homophobic classmates and teachers, came-out and confronted their parents, were generally accepted by their families and close friends, and celebrated their gayness (Padva 2004).

Since then, American independent film movement of mainly white queer filmmakers, known as, the New Queer Cinema, have created new narrative forms aimed primarily at gay audiences (Doty 2000; Levy 1999; Rich 1992). Hettie MacDonald's *Beautiful Thing* (UK 1995), for instance, is based on a play by Jonathan Harvey, articulating the love story of two working-class lads from East London: Jamie, a delicate boy, and Ste, the football captain who is often beaten by his drug-dealer older brother and his abusive father. Jamie's **coming out** to his mother in *Beautiful Thing* takes place after his first sexual act with Ste and certain symbolic acts of coming to terms with his sexuality: buying an issue of *Gay Times* magazine and visiting a gay bar. For better or worse, the melodramatic coming-outcoming out of such agonized protagonists, typical to new queer adolescence melodramas, strongly supports the notion of a fixed and stable **sexual orientation**. One exception to this can be found in François Ozon's short film *A Summer Dress* (France 1996), a comic tale about a handsome gay youth who experiences sexual intercourse with a mysterious woman on the beach.

Significantly, the New Queer Cinema is characterized by complex representations of the queer body and eroticization of physical inequality in same-sex relationships. Greg Araki's *Totally Fucked Up* (USA 1993) features gay and lesbian teens in alienated Los Angeles, focusing on the tragic story of Andy, a high school student who falls in love with Ian, an older and more promiscuous film student. David Moreton's *Edge of Seventeen* (USA 1998) goes back to the 1980s, portraying the coming out of Eric, a middle-class Ohio boy who falls in love with an older and more muscular, hairy, and tanned college student. Simon Shore's *Get Real* (UK/South Africa 1998) presents the complex relationship of the sensitive Steven and the athletic champion John. Asian films, influenced by the increasing gay visibility in Western cinema, also formulate physical inequality between the protagonists. Most notable are Stanley Kwan's *Lan Yu* (Hong Kong 2001), about the relationship between a Chinese businessman and a young student, and Zhang Yuan's *East Palace, West Palace* (China/France 1997), articulating the erotic tension between Shi (Yang Jian), a heterosexual Bejing police officer, and A-Lan (Ye Jing), a young gay writer, who is arrested in the Beijing cruising area and interrogated by Shi.

Several films portray gay youth as hustlers. Gus Van Sant's *My Own Private Idaho* (USA 1991) chronicles the unfulfilled love of a young **sex worker** (the late River Phoenix), a weak and sickly boy, and his more mature and masculine friend (Keanu Reeves), who protects his heterosexual image by sleeping with men only for money, and eventually returning to his forgiving well-established family. Barbet Schroeder's *Our Lady of the Assassins* (France/Columbia 2000) features the intimate relationship of Fernando (German Jaramillo), a middle-aged man who visits Medellin, the Columbian city of his birth, which has become extremely violent and dominated by the drug cartel, and Alexis (Anderson Ballesteros), a member of a youth street gang. Ruthie Schatz' and Adi Barash's documentary *Garden* (Israel 2004) follows the friendship of two hustlers in Tel Aviv, a Palestinian and an Israeli–Arab, their desperate search for a home, and their complicated relations with the Israeli and Palestinian authorities.

Lesbian adolescents' representations in New Queer Cinema highlight the diverse **discrimination** faced by the female protagonists because of the interrelations between patriarchy and heterosexuality, chauvinism and **homophobia**. Peter Jackson's *Heavenly Creatures* (New Zealand 1994) dramatizes a passionate interclass affair between two high school girls in the 1950s. When their parents decide to send Juliet (Kate Winslet) out of the country, her lover Pauline (Melanie Lynskey) commits matricide. One of the protagonists in *If These Walls Could Talk 2* (USA 2000), a lesbian feminist student attending a U.S. college during the early 1970s, is discriminated against by straight feminist activists. Lee Rose's *The Truth about Jane* (USA 2001) articulates the unbearable **bullying** of a lesbian high school student, and ends in a pride march, in which the protagonist marches together with her parents.

Bisexual adolescence has been represented in only a few films, such as Andrew Fleming's film *Threesome* (USA 1994), which portrays a problematic and passionate love triangle between young college students, including a significant homoerotic sex scene. However, the possibility of a proud bisexual identity is practically refuted as the gay protagonist concludes in the epilogue that his bisexuality was nothing but a phase.

The **childhood** and adolescence of transgender individuals is depicted in several films as especially difficult because of their sexual *and* gender transgressions. In

Richard Spence's *Different for Girls* (UK 1996), the transgender protagonist encounters her old friend from the **Catholic** boys' school, who had protected her when she was being bullied, as a queer boy. Bigoted educational establishment and pupils are also criticized in Alain Berliner's *My Life in Pink* (Belgium-France-UK 1997), a family melodrama intercut with significant surrealist scenes, focused on seven-year-old Ludovic who decides that he is a girl and falls in love with his (male) best friend. Another child who transgresses the straight dress codes and gender roles is seen in Shirley MacLaine's *Bruno* (USA 2000). An exceptional film is Kimberly Peirce's *Boys Don't Cry* (USA 1999), based on Susan Muska's documentary *The Brandon Teena Story* (USA 1998), featuring the hardship and brutal murder of a young female-to-male transgender from Nebraska.

Ethnic minorities are often misrepresented in American and West European fictional LGBT films. Stereotypically, gay and lesbian adolescents in New Queer Cinema are mostly white. When LGBT youth of color appear on screen, they are often represented as the "exotic" Other. For example, Jim Fall's *Trick* (USA 1999) celebrates the physical attraction between Gabriel (Christian Campbell), a young white musical composer, and Mark (Jean Paul Pitoc), a muscular **Latino**-looking go-go dancer whom he meets in a gay bar. The camera tilts up and down the dancer's body when he dances in tight red pants on the counter, and later, when he sits in tight jeans and T shirt on the subway. Although these arousing shots of the exotic dancer, who is more attractive than the boy, celebrate this interracial gay relationship, Gabriel's white gaze can be interpreted not only as a homoerotic objectification, but also as a sort of postcolonial look on the "exotic" Mark.

Ana Kokkinos' *Head On* (Australia 1998), focuses on the Greek community in Melbourne. The gay protagonist, nineteen-year-old Ari (Alex Dimitriades), is a degenerated sex addict and drug user and dealer. Another significant film is E. Kutlug Ataman's *Lola und Bilidikid* (Germany 1998) about the Turkish gay community in Berlin, featuring sixteen-year-old Murat (Baki Davrak), who gradually comes out and finds the murderer of his transgender brother Lola (Gandi Mukli). Nigel Finch's *Stonewall* (UK 1995) focuses on LaMiranda (Guillermo Diaz), a Hispanic transgender who falls in love with Matty Dean (Fred Weller), a young white gay man from the Midwest, who has come to the Big Apple. LaMiranda introduces him to New York's African American and Hispanic transgender communities and other regulars at the Stonewall Inn, before the infamous 1969 police confrontation (Padva 2000).

Queer adolescent melodramas in the 1990s and 2000s are largely based on the presumed distinction, perhaps even an essentialist dichotomy, between straight and gay sexualities, and that one should realize what one is to live one's true sexual identity. Characters reflect little sexual fluidity unless they are in transition from one sexual identity to another. And, like their youthful viewers, are often seen as confused queer adolescents, who suffer daily hardship in their family, school and community (Padva 2004).

In contrast to the popularity of cinematic representations of LGBT youth and students, there are fewer representations of LGBT educators. Among these, several focus on relationships—erotic or not—between students and educators. Leontine Sagan's *Mädchen in Uniform* (Germany 1931) features a lonely student at a girls' boarding school who develops a romantic relationship with her teacher. In *Hide and Seek* (Israel 1981), director Dan Wolman, featuring an adolescent boy in Jerusalem during the British Mandate in the 1940s, details the injuring of the boy's

Bad Education (2004 Spain) aka *La Mala Edu-cación*. Directed by Pedro Almodóvar. Shown from left as Father Manolo discovers them in the washroom stall: Ignacio "Nacho" Pérez (as young Ignacio), Raúl García Forneiro (as young Enrique). Showtime/Photofest

teacher and the murder of the teachers' Arab lover by a gang of Jewish nationalists. John Greyson's postmodernist **AIDS** musical *Zero Patience* (Canada 1993) includes a musical number by the HIV positive gay teacher who sings together with his students a bilingual song about his apprehensions: "I know that I don't know/*Je sais que je ne sais pas.*" A more melancholic and traumatic teacher–student relationship is depicted in Pedro Almodovar's *Bad Education* (Spain 2004), focusing on two young students at a Catholic boy's school, their reunion after many years, and their confrontation with an abusive teacher.

Homosexual panic by parents or students is a common theme. William Wyler's *The Children's Hour* (USA 1961), is about two unmarried female teachers (Audrey Hepburn and Shirley MacLaine) in a girls' high school, accused by a cruel student of having an "unnatural relationship," and Ron Peck's *Nighthawks* (UK 1978), directed as a semidocumentary, featuring a sad young teacher in London who comes out to his hostile students. Although parental panic is evident in Frank Oz's *In & Out* (USA 1997), this Hollywood mainstream romantic melodrama, focusing on high school English teacher and **sports** coach Howard Brackett (Kevin Kline), centers on the community's reactions to his outing on prime-time TV by his former student (Matt Dillon). The eventual support from his students and the community distinguishes this film from the others.

LGBT documentaries, mostly produced by queer filmmakers, reflect an independent attitude toward sexual diversity, stressing sexual tolerance, parental understanding, and self-acceptance. *Framed Youth, or Revolt of the Teenage Perverts* (UK 1983), for instance, featuring young lesbians and gay men in London, includes a youthful Jimmy Sommerville, who confronts heterosexual views on homosexuality. Vicky Seitchik's *Queer Son* (USA 1993) is a sensitive portrayal of North American fathers who often find it difficult to cope with their sons' coming out and Hrafnhildure Gunnarsdottir and Thorvaldur Kristinnson's *Straight Out* (Iceland 2003) is about Scandinavian youths' coming out. Significantly, a sort of alternative **sexuality education** is given in Christienne Clarke's *The Truth about Gay Sex* (UK 2002), first broadcast on Britain's Channel Four, which provides a sincere, erotic but non-pornographic discussion of all-male erotic practices, safe sex, love, and intimacies. In contrast, the nonerotic 1996 episode of the Israeli Educational Television's talk show *Klafim Ptuhim* (Open Cards), which featured queer youth, was banned by **Israel**'s Education Minister until the Supreme Court issued a countervailing decision (Kama 2000).

There are also specific discussions of discrimination and bullying at schools, as in Cindy Marshall's *Sticks, Stones and Stereotypes* (USA 1988), and in the documentary *I Just Want to Say* (USA 1998), in which tennis champion Martina Navratilova hosts a panel of parents, students, and teachers who discuss antigay bias in American schools. The difficulties of ethnic queer minorities, who are particularly discriminated and persecuted inside and outside their communities, are represented in documentaries such as Arlyn Gajilan's *Kim* (USA 1988), portraying a young Puerto Rican lesbian's coming out and coming of age in New York City; Jorge Lozano and Samuel Lopez's *Samuel and Samantha on "The Emancipation of All"* (El Salvador 1993), about a young transvestite's life; Mickey Chen's *Boys for Beauty* (Taiwan 1998), portraying three gay teenagers and their family relations in Confucian Chinese society; and Lora E. Branch's two-part *Kevin's Room* (USA 2001), about **African American** young gay men. And, queer filmmakers are revealing their queer adolescence and sexual emancipation as in Mitch McCabe's continuous attempts to come out to her parents in *Playing the Part* (USA 1994), Sue Friedrich's *Hide and Seek* (USA 1997), about her queer youth, and Tomer Heymann's coming out to the tough teenagers with whom he worked as a youth leader in *It Kinda Scares Me* (Israel 2001).

New Queer Cinema, a highly persuasive medium, offers a potential tool for educators at the secondary school and university levels to promote acceptance of diverse sexualities in their classes, and also to support particular queer students. It is possible to begin an effective discussion about sexuality not with a lengthy lecture but with a short introduction, followed by showing a queer melodrama, such as *Get Real* (UK 1998), in its entirety. A later discussion of Steven's difficulties, erotic experiences, his complicated relationship with his parents, and his affair with John, may serve to exemplify and elaborate primal issues: pubescence and adolescence, safe sex, homophobia, self-acceptance, coming out, human rights, pluralism. Alternatively, a teacher could show video excerpts articulating the development of Jamie and Stee's romance in *Beautiful Thing* (UK 1996) in comparison to the growing romance of other high school students, Carlos (Jay Hernandez) and Nicole (Kirsten Dunst), in John Stockwell's popular melodrama *Crazy/Beautiful* (USA 2001). Such an analogy between gay and straight relationships can pave the way for a more open-minded discussion of love, sex, and sexuality.

Bibliography

Bryant, Wayne. 1997. *Bisexual Characters in Film*. Binghamton, NY: Haworth Press.

Doty, Alexander. 2000. "Film: New Queer Cinema." Pp. 321–323 in *Gay Histories and Cultures: An Encyclopedia*. Edited by George Haggerty. New York: Garland.

Dyer, Richard. 1993. "Seen to Be Believed: Some Problems in the Representation of Gay People as Typical." Pp. 19–51 in *The Matter of Images: Essays on Representation*. Edited by Richard Dyer. London and New York: Routledge.

Foucault, Michel. 1976. *The History of Sexuality, Volume I*. Translated by Robert Hurley. Harmondsworth, Middlesex: Penguin.

Kama, Amit. 2000. "From *Terra Incognita* to *Terra Firma*: The Logbook of the Voyage of Gay Men's Community into the Israeli Public Sphere." *Journal of Homosexuality* 38, no. 4, pp. 133–162.

Levy, Emanuel. 1999. "The New Gay and Lesbian Cinema." Pp. 442–493 in *Cinema of Outsiders: The Rise of American Independent Film*. Edited by Emanuel Levy. New York and London: New York University Press.

McAfee, Lynda. 1997. "Film and Videography." Pp. 241–263 in *Between the Sheets, in the Streets: Queer, Lesbian, Gay Documentary*. Edited by Chris Holmund and Cynthia Fuchs. Minneapolis and London: University of Minnesota Press.

Padva, Gilad. 2000. "*Priscilla* Fights Back: The Politicization of Camp Subculture." *Journal of Communication Inquiry* 24, no. 2, pp. 216–243.

———. 2004. "Edge of Seventeen: Melodramatic Coming-Out in New Queer Adolescence Films." *Communication and Critical/Cultural Studies* 1, no. 4, pp. 355–372.

Rich, B. Ruby. 1992. "New Gay Cinema." *Sight and Sound* 2, no. 5: 31–34.

Rofes, Eric. 2005. "Canada: A Videotape Collection Focused on Bullying, Homophobia, and Queer Youth." *Journal of Gay and Lesbian Issues in Education* 2, no. 4.

Russo, Vito. 1987 (1981). *The Celluloid Closet: Homosexuality in the Movies*. New York: Harper and Row.

Talmon, Miri. 2001. *Israeli Graffiti: Nostalgia, Groups, and Collective Identity in Israeli Cinema* [in Hebrew]. Tel Aviv and Haifa: Open University of Israel Press and Haifa University Press.

Waugh, Thomas. 1988. "Lesbian and Gay Documentary: Minority Self-Imaging, Oppositional Film Practice, and the Question of Image Ethics." Pp. 248–272 in *Image Ethics: The Moral Rights of Subjects in Photographs, Film and Television*. Edited by Larry Gross, John Katz Stewart, and Jay Rubi. New York and Oxford: Oxford University Press.

Yosef, Raz. 2004. *Beyond Flesh: Queer Masculinities and Nationalism in Israeli Cinema*. Piscataway, NJ: Rutgers University Press.

Web Sites

Allmovie. 2005. Accessed May 31, 2005. http://www.allmovie.com. U.S. site that provides information about films' synopsis, cast, and reviews.

Frameline. 2003. Accessed May 31, 2005. http://66.39.24.176/distribution/2002FLDistCat. pdf Film+Video Catalog 2002–2003. Also, see the home page (http://www.frameline. org) where the newest catalogue can be ordered.

Imdb. 2005. Accessed May 31, 2005. http://www.imdb.com. Useful information about past and recent films.

OGLBTC Videos: Education/Youth Documentaries. April 2000. Accessed May 31, 2005. http://www.uic.edu/depts/quic/oglbc/resources/videos/video_education-youth.html. A filmography provided by the University of Illinois at Chicago.

Foucault, Michel (1926–1984)

Dennis Carlson

Michel Foucault was an influential French philosopher and historian who argued that the "truth" about sexuality is not naturally given but rather produced within a cultural and historical context, involving established power relations. Foucault's work leads us to question how Western culture has organized sexuality and what "truths" it has produced about homosexuality in various historical eras. Recent "poststructural" approaches to homosexuality and **sexual identity** have been heavily influenced by Foucault's work. In regard to the education on **lesbian, gay, bisexual,** and **transgender** (LGBT) issues and working with queer youth, his work points to the importance of understanding the historical construction of "gayness" and challenges the notion that sexual identities are naturally given and have a fixed essence or character. Instead, it suggests that homosexuality and homosexual **desire** takes on different forms in different cultures and eras. Gay identity as we know it is particular to modern, Western culture and closely tied to a normal/abnormal binary opposition. "Straightness" gets privileged and defined as "normal," and "gayness" gets marginalized and treated as deviant or "abnormal." **Queer theory**, rooted in

See also Adolescent Sexualities; Butler, Judith; Christian Moral Instruction on Homosexuality; Communication; Lacan, Jacques; Poststructuralism; Psychoanalysis and Education; Queer Pedagogy; Queer Studies.

many of Foucault's concepts, is a movement in the liberal arts academy that understands sexual identity along these lines, although it has had almost no impact to this point on **sexuality education** in K-12 public education, partially because it threatens established categories of identity, in which individuals, activist groups, and businesses now have a vested interest. Nevertheless, Foucault's work has direct implications for the study of resistance by queer youth, particularly the current generation who is more likely to resist identifying themselves as gay or lesbian, embracing instead terms like gender-queer, trans, queer. Foucault died of **AIDS** in 1984 as he was finishing work on volume three of his *History of Sexuality*.

In the introductory volume to the *History of Sexuality* (1978), Foucault challenged the so-called repressive hypothesis, according to which Victorian culture was marked by the repression of speaking or writing about anything sexual. The repressive hypothesis is related, he argued, to the modern tendency to think of sexuality as something that is either repressed or released. From Foucault's standpoint, it is not that simple. In fact, the Victorian age, the late nineteenth century, was characterized by a proliferation of discourse (writing and speaking) about sexuality and an almost obsessive concern with the "problem of sexuality." Around sexuality, Victorian society constructed an immense "apparatus" for producing truth, particularly as represented by the scientific-medical disciplines of knowledge, perhaps best represented by **Magnus Hirschfeld**'s Institute of Sexual Science in Berlin, whose motto was "per scientiam ad justitiam" (through knowledge to justice).

Foucault argued that the "the homosexual" was a creation of the psychiatric discourse of the late nineteenth century, pioneered by **Sigmund Freud**. Only when the psychiatric community "named" homosexuals as a group, a category of abnormal people who were to be treated, did the homosexual come into existence. The production of the homosexual is, in Foucault's language, part of a project of "normalization," establishing a norm of correct or healthy heterosexuality and constructing a category of abnormal sexual Others. As a sexual Other, the homosexual affirmed the normality and correctness of **compulsory heterosexuality**. Foucault observes that in Christian traditions and modern psychiatry it is possible to see continuities in the treatment of homosexuality. Both dictate laws of sexuality based on the binaries licit and illicit, permitted and forbidden, healthy and unhealthy. Christian and psychiatric discourses also establish mechanisms or apparatuses for bringing individuals under the gaze of power. "Western man has become a confessing animal" (Foucault 1978, 59); through psychiatric rituals of confession, homosexuals were made to acknowledge that they were "sick" and needed help and treatment to become "well" again.

The second volume of Foucault's *History of Sexuality*, titled *The Use of Pleasure* (1985), focused on a discussion of pederasty as it was practiced in Hellenic Greek society among upper class males, and on the ethics that regulated relationships between men and adolescent boys. Foucault locates this institutionalized practice within the historical context of patriarchal Greek culture. Since women were presumed to be inferior to men, they were not viewed as suitable objects of romantic love. The ideal of beauty, valor, and honor, and thus of romantic attachment, became the adolescent Greek male. At the same time, the inequality in age and status between the two males allowed the elder male to maintain the role of domination, which was essential to the performance of a masculine identity. The role of the youth was to resist the advances of the elder male as much as possible in order to maintain his honor and masculinity, although at some point he also was expected to submit to the proper suitor's persistent advances. The contradictions at the heart of this institutionalized form of pederasty, according to Foucault, were that it called for young males to assume a contradictory role, of submitting and not submitting, and also that it was open to the abuse of power. Nevertheless, Foucault argued that, in its idealized form, it was regulated by an ethic of care and concern for young males. This **mentoring** was associated with the development of skills of self-mastery, virtue, and honor among young men.

In education, this raises questions about the characteristics of ethical versus un-ethical relationships between LGBT youth and older men, and about the role of mentors for these youth. Foucault argued that in all of their sexual and nonsexual relations Greeks were governed not so much by moral codes or laws as by an ethic which valued individual freedom or autonomy, nonexploitive relationships, and care for the other. Within such an ethic, homosexuality and homosexual relations were not uniformly condemned. Indeed, they were often celebrated. The real issue was the ethical character of sexual relations, either homosexual or heterosexual. This, Foucault argued, was in stark contract to the growing influence of a Judeo–Christian morality and a movement in Greek culture that viewed sexuality as itself a corrupting or evil influence, and that condemned all nonprocreative sexuality, including homosexuality. This change was the result of a whole series of interrelated developments that led to a new language of sexuality that framed sexuality first in moralistic and later in medical terms. Foucault's work suggests that the liberation of homosexuality, and the homosexual, may be linked to a movement beyond both moralistic and medical models of sexuality. Indeed, the modern gay rights movement has had to fight against both the moralistic condemnation of religious dogma and the medicalization of homosexuality as a "disorder."

While the perspective on homosexuality and **sexual identity** represented by Foucault remains outside the mainstream in sexuality education, it is at the cutting-edge of thinking about education and sexuality in the liberal arts academy. There, it is associated with the growing influence of cultural studies perspectives that explore the social construction of "whiteness," and "blackness," "masculinity" and "femininity," and "straightness" and "gayness." These categories are viewed as having meaning only relationally, as part of an identity binary. Some scholars have argued that schools have been and continue to be major institutions of who Foucault called "normalization," involving the establishment of a binary that separates "normal" from "abnormal" youth (Popkewitz and Brennan 1998). Normalization, in this case, is associated with educational practices of silencing LGBT adolescents, erasing their history, representing homosexuality through oppressive **stereotypes**, establishing heterosexual privilege (as in high school proms), tolerating or condoning **homophobia** and the **harassment** of LGBT youth, and in other ways associating gay identity with an undesirable or unhealthy lifestyle (Carlson 1997; Middleton 1998). Educators seeking to empower LGBT youth challenge these normalizing practices by, among other activities, posing questions rather than affirming dominant notions of what it means to be a "normal" male or female, as well as challenging the historical and cultural production of sexual.

Bibliography

Carlson, Dennis. 1997. "Gayness, Multicultural Education, and Community." Pp. 99–118 in *Making Progress: Education and Culture in New Times*. New York: Teachers College Press.

Foucault, Michel. 1978. *The History of Sexuality Volume 1: An Introduction*. New York: Pantheon.

———. 1985. *The Use of Pleasure*. Translated by Robert Hurley. New York: Pantheon.

Middleton, Sue. 1998. *Disciplining Sexuality: Foucault, Life Histories, and Education*. New York: Teachers College Press.

Pinar, William, ed. 1998. *Queer Theory in Education*. Mahwah, NJ: Lawrence Erlbaum.

Popkewitz, Thomas, and Marie Brennan, eds. 1998. *Foucault's Challenge: Discourse, Knowledge, and Power in Education*. New York: Teachers College Press.

Web Sites

Foucault Studies. May 2005. Accessed May 31, 2005. http://www.qut.edu.au/edu/cpo1/foucst. New online journal with first issue December 2004. Also includes extensive links, bibliographies, glossary, and other useful resources.

Welcome to the World of Michel Foucault. May 2002. Zoran Jevtic. Accessed May 31, 2005. http://www.csun.edu/~hfspc002/foucault.home.html. Includes genealogy of Foucault, discussion sites, and links.

France, LGBT Youth and Issues in

Loykie Loïc Lomine

That young French people may be **lesbian, gay, bisexual** or **transgender/transsexual** (LGBT), is a notion seemingly alien to contemporary French society. France may have legalized homosexuality in the wake of its 1789 famous revolution but, as a country, it has never paid much attention to its **queer** youth and their specific needs. LGBT issues are not addressed in French schools; very few organizations and services provide LGBT youngsters with support and opportunities to explore and express their **sexual identity**. Although queer adults in France have benefited from sexual liberation and liberal legislation, **homophobia** has seemingly crystallized against queer young people.

In French schools, be they state schools or private (generally parochial) schools, sexuality and related issues, such as sexual relationships, are only tackled in terms of health education. This "medicalized" perspective is mainly concerned with contraception, HIV/**AIDS**-awareness, and the prevention of sexually transmitted diseases. There is no state-sanctioned socio-cultural discourse validating or even acknowledging the existence of a respectable plurality of sexual orientations. The 2003 legislation about **sexuality education** at school (covering both primary and secondary education) is a lengthy 4,000-word text, articulating aims and objectives, actions and their implementation, yet it does not make any reference to LGBT issues or youth. The term "homophobic" appears twice to stress the importance of education in the fight against **prejudice**, but the roots of homophobia and the importance of LGBT awareness-raising are not addressed.

Heteronormativity is also evident in the national syllabus. There is no requirement to mention LGBT issues or to address the specific needs of queer youth. Proactive pedagogy, however, is possible. Some teachers may include LGBT issues, as long as it stays in line within the boundaries of the official **curriculum**. In a citizenship class,

See also Christian Moral Instruction on Homosexuality; Coming Out, Youth; Community LGBT Youth Groups; Educational Policies; Europe, LGBT Youth and Issues in; Mental Health; School Climate, K-12; Youth, At Risk.

there may be a teacher-led discussion of the emerging types of nontraditional families; in a French class, students might be assigned to study argumentative techniques in a newspaper article about homophobia; in a literature class, a teacher and students may analyse of the works of Gide or Genet. When teachers themselves are homophobic or have no interest in LGBT issues, they are unlikely to address them at all. Thus, most French children go through primary and secondary school without hearing any reference to LGBT issues, except for playground insults such as *pédé* (poof) and *gouine* (dyke). Students questioning their sexual identity or those who are LGBT have little recourse to such **harassment** and find little support within the school. However, the inclusive notion of "queer" has entered higher education (Cusset 2002; Eribon 1998), but not primary and secondary schools in France. In the absence of official guidelines, Web sites like HomoEdu provide valuable resources and suggestions for gay-friendly teachers keen to softly integrate LGBT issues into the French curriculum and to address the needs of LGBT youth.

This may seem paradoxical. France has developed a largely liberal approach to LGBT issues, culminating in 1999 with the creation of a legal partnership framework, the *Pacte Civil de Solidarité* (literally Civil Solidarity Pact). This legal mechanism gives all adult couples (regardless of **gender identity** or **sexual orientation**) many of the same fiscal and social rights as those who are formally wedded, such as housing rights, health and welfare benefits, the right to file a joint tax return and to inheritance. Moreover, an increasing number of politicians are suggesting that it might be advisable to eventually change the law to allow gay marriage. François Hollande, the current head of the Socialist Party (Noël Mamère) and leader of a leftist Green Party, is mayor of small town near Bordeaux where he officiated at France's first gay wedding ceremony in 2004 (a very symbolic event, even if the union was annulled by a court shortly afterwards). In Paris, Mayor Bertrand Delanoë came out on prime-time television in 1998 (a couple of years before he was elected), and throughout France even right-wing politicians have supported laws to criminalize homophobia.

Nevertheless, within this liberal political context, LGBT youth have remained largely invisible, and there has been little effort to address their needs. Contemporary books, praised for their comprehensive discussion of sexual politics including LGBT issues, such as *Liberté, Égalité, Sexualités* (Fabre and Fassin 2003), fail to make any reference to young people. Even within LGBT subcultures, most support groups, debates, events, stories, statistics, and Web sites are biased toward adults.

Two of the few exceptions are the hotline telephone service, *Ligne Azur Jeunes et Sexualité*, for young people who want to talk anonymously about their sexuality, and the dynamic Paris-based association *MAG Jeunes Gais (Mouvement d'Affirmation des jeunes gais & lesbiennes)*, created in 1990 for teenagers from age sixteen upwards. There is no LGBT organization or community support group for younger people. Further, there are no college groups explicitly for queer youth and, for parents, the French version of PFLAG, named "Contact," created in 1993, is very small and little known.

There has also been an overprotective, patronizing, and ageist attitude toward sexual minority youth. Until recently, the age of consent was different for heterosexual and homosexual behavior: fifteen years for the former, twenty-one years for the latter (then eighteen years from 1974 onward). The spirit of the law was that young people could not be expected nor trusted to be knowingly able to make informed decisions about nonmainstream forms of sexuality. In 1982, this legal discrepancy was abolished (the date is sometimes misinterpreted as the landmark for the decriminalization of homosexuality but only the age of consent was a legal issue).

A key difference with some other European countries such as the **United Kingdom** and the Netherlands is that French LGBT youth often encounter hostility on the basis of religious principles. The secularization of French society (symbolized by the sharp decline of church attendance) does not mean that France is not deeply attached to its **Catholic** heritage and related values. Seventy-five percent of French people define themselves as Catholic (Mermet 2003), and the Vatican unambiguously condemns homosexual behavior. The 1992 Catechism of the Catholic Church has three paragraphs (2357–2359) explaining that "homosexual acts are intrinsically disordered," "under no circumstances can they be approved" and that "homosexual persons are called to chastity." Similar theological hostility to non-heterosexual forms of sexuality is found in Islam for 3 percent and Protestantism, which serve 3 and 1.5 percent of the population, respectively. When asked by the French Senate to comment about the PACS bill from a **Muslim** perspective, Dalil Boubakeur, rector of the Muslim Institute of the Paris Mosque, explained that Islam is theologically opposed to homosexuality. The representatives from the other faiths consulted (Catholic, Protestant, and **Jewish**) articulated similar views. LGBT adults may be able to take some distance from the official discourse of established religions or to join more inclusive religious movements. There are a few Metropolitan Community Churches (MCC) in France (especially in Paris and in the South: Aix, Montpellier), as well as cognate groups such as the "Eglise Alliance," in Lille and themed church-based organizations like "Chrétiens et SIDA," (Christians and AIDS), based in the largest towns and **urban** areas. In any case, young people often do not have the same freedom, especially when their parents hold different views.

According to the French *Ministère de l'Education Nationale* (2004) two million pupils in France (17 percent of all those in formal education) are currently educated in private, mostly Catholic schools. In such institutions, LGBT pupils are likely to get even less support if they want to come out or just to discuss sexuality with an educator, who is also subject to school authority. At best, they hear messages about their *croix* (burden) as *brebis égarée* (stray sheep), their *handicap* and their *blessure* (wound), to use the French Catholic phraseology for homosexuality. At worst, they are told that they must pray for God's forgiveness to become "normal," and that they need to be cured if not punished.

LGBT youth, growing up in religious families or semireligious environments, are most likely to encounter lack of understanding and to find little support. It is particularly difficult for queer youth from families of foreign origin who face other issues of acculturation and integration. According to the 1999 census, foreigners living in France (7.4 percent of the whole population, slightly above the average of the European Union) are of two main origins: Southern Europe (in descending numerical order: Portugal, Italy, and Spain) and North Africa (Algeria, Morocco, Tunisia). Because, culturally, southern Europe is even more Catholic than France, LGBT youth whose parents emigrate from Portugal, Italy or Spain are likely to experience greater pressure from their extended family to conform heterosexually from **dating** and marriage to demeanor and dress. Likewise, those from North African origin will often have Muslim parents who understand homosexuality as irreconcilable to Islamic principles. Young immigrants from these strictly religious backgrounds may well experience conflict between their cultural and religious identities and their sexuality, with little, if any, support group or individuals available.

For French LGBT youth—native or immigrant—the visible presence of LGBT people around them (especially adults) helps them safely come out and become proud of their sexual identity. Lacking individual, familial, or institutional support, homosexuality is only perceived as a stigma, a secret, or a shame. LGBT youth often experience emotional and psychological problems, from low self-esteem and guilt to internalized homophobia and self-hatred, sometimes leading to depression if not suicidal thoughts, even **suicide**.

In France, as in many countries, suicide rates for LGBT youth are much higher than for their heterosexual counterparts. In a substantial study on suicide risks among LGBT French youth, reported that over 1,000 young people commit suicide each year in France, and in the case of LGBT youth, homophobia was a critical factor (Firdion 2001). Building upon North American studies, suicide risks for LGBT youth were not due to homosexuality per se, but were found to be associated with surrounding problems of ridicule, harassment, and rejection. Arguing that it is everybody's responsibility, Firdion suggested a sensible plan of action for identifying key players, not just in the health sector (as too often homosexuality is only biologically mentioned with reference to **AIDS**), but also in the mass media, the education system, and the leisure industry. He also recommended that the French education system address LGBT issues, starting with appropriate training for all staff, both teachers and nonteaching staff like nurses and counselors, and both in public and private schools. Others have argued for an official requirement to include LGBT issues in teacher training programs. As of yet, this is not the case.

Mass media representations of LGBT people are often stereotypical and sources of ridicule. Typically in talk shows "the gay man" will be effeminate and promiscuous, while "the lesbian" will be masculine. Many films (such as the 1995 block-buster *Gazon Maudit*, showed in English under the title *French Twist*) humorously play with these clichés. A few recent films, however, have started problematizing gender and sexual representations, notably *Le Placard* (*The Closet* 2001) where a straight man (Daniel Auteuil) must pretend he is gay in order to keep his job while working with bigoted, rugby-playing, alpha-male, office-bully colleague, Gérard Depardieu.

One also can occasionally find positive representations of LGBT youth in cinema. A very good example is Téchiné's 1984 award-winning **film** *Les Roseaux Sauvages* (The Wild Reeds), which depicts three teenagers discovering their sexuality, one of them a gay boy. Set in a boarding school in 1962, the film has been praised for its poetry and sensitivity, and most importantly it proves that arts and culture can have a critical role to play to help LGBT youth understand and accept their sexual identity.

Young adult **literature** has been more inclusive of sexual minorities. In France, there is an increasing number of books for youngsters featuring young gays and lesbians—although none with prominent transgender characters. For example, the love story of the two teenage girls, Sarah and Colline, in Claire Mazard's *Macaron Citron* (2001), is intended for readers ages thirteen and up. *Les lettres de mon petit frère* (The Letters of My Little Brother, Donner 1992) is intended for a younger readership (eight to thirteen years old). Here a young boy fully supports his older brother's homosexuality, in sharp contrast with their mother's prejudice against the boyfriend. These relatively few texts usually depict close same-sex friendships and intimacy without necessarily any explicit reference to sexual acts. They do not reflect an essentialist understanding of sexual orientation, but one where sexuality identity and behavior are fluid. In *Les carnets de Lily B.*, (Lily B's Diaries), Lily asks herself: "*L'homme de ma vie est peut-être une femme ?*" (Maybe the man of life is a woman?). Taken-for-granted boundaries between concepts (such as masculinity/femininity and gay/straight) are occasionally challenged in youth literature, exactly in the spirit of **queer theory** (Chaimbault 2002).

Bibliography

Chaimbault, Thomas. 2002. *L'homosexualité dans la Littérature de Jeunesse*. (Homosexuality in Youth Literature). Unpublished Masters Thesis, Université de Lille. Accessed April 1, 2004. http://perso.wanadoo.fr/citrouille/articles/Lille3/HOMOSEXUALITE.html. http://www.univ-lille3.fr/jeunet/jpro/colloque/col7/chaimbault.htm.

Cusset, François. 2002. *Queer Critics*. Paris: Presses Universitaires de France Donner, Christophe. 1992. *Les Lettres de Mon Petit Frère* (*Letters from my Little Brother*). Paris: Ecole des loisirs.

Eribon, Didier. 1998. *Les Etudes Gay et Lesbiennes* (*Gay and Lesbian Studies*). Paris: Editions du Centre Pompidou.

Fabre, Clarisse, and Eric Fassin. 2003. *Liberté, Egalité, Sexualités*. (*Liberty, Equality, Sexualities*). Paris: Belfond.

Firdion, Jean-Marie. 2001. *Le risque de Suicide Chez les Jeunes à Orientation Sexuelle non Conventionnelle (Lesbiennes, Bisexuels, Gais). Rapport du Groupe de Travail pour Homosexualités et Socialisme. (Suicide Risk amongst LGBT Youth: Report from Working Group on Homosexuality and Socialism*). Paris: Montblanc H & O.

Le Normand, Véronique. 2002. *Les carnets de Lily B*. (*Lily B's Diaries*) Paris: Pocket Jeunesse.

Mazard, Claire. 2001. *Macaron Citron*. (*Lemon-Yellow Macaroon*). Paris: Syros jeunesse.

Mermet, Gerard. 2003. *Francoscopie 2003: Pour Comprendre les Français*. (*To Understand the French*). Paris: Larousse.

Web Sites

Catechism of the Catholic Church. November 2003. Accessed May 31, 2005. http://www.vatican.va/archive/ccc/index.htm. 1992 official version, full text available in several languages, including English. Homosexuality is discussed within part three, section two, chapter two, article 6, subsection 2 (entitled "the vocation to chastity").

Homo-Edu. October 2004. Accessed October 8, 2004. http://homoedu.free.fr/. Web site about homosexuality and education (in French); resources such as suggestions and recommendations for teachers keen to integrate LGBT issues into the curriculum.

Ministère de l'Education Nationale. August 2004. Accessed October 8, 2004. http://www. education.gouv.fr/index.php http://www.education.gouv.fr/botexte/bo030227/MENE0300322C.htm>. Includes the full 2003 legal text about sexual education at school.

Fraternities

Shane L. Windmeyer and George A. Miller

"Fraternities"—a term for social organizations of male students at a college or university, usually designated by Greek letters—have been a part of higher education in the United States for more than 200 years. Although there have always been gay and bisexual men in fraternities, it is only in the last decade that they have been

See also Antidiscrimination Policy; Cocurricular Activities; College Age Students; Coming Out, Youth; Compulsory Heterosexuality; Passing; Race and Racism; Residence Life in Colleges; Single-Sex Schools.

acknowledged, sometimes accepted, and often rejected. Since 1995, there has been seen a dramatic increase in the number of men coming out in the college fraternity. As a result, new fraternities have been founded which cater to gay, bisexual, and straight progressive men, and these organizations continue to flourish on campuses today.

When Phi Beta Kappa was founded at the College of William and Mary in Williamsburg, on December 5, 1776, this gave birth to one of the most storied traditions of American higher education: the college fraternity. The original members of Phi Beta Kappa were teenage men who banded together in the interest of promoting friendship, morality, and literature. In addition to choosing a name represented by Greek letters, the organization developed a motto, a handshake, and a ritual of initiation—all of which were highly secretive. Interest in fraternities soon spread to other campuses, and Phi Beta Kappa established local chapters at other institutions including Harvard and Yale Universities. Other students who were not selected to join or who had no interest in joining Phi Beta Kappa established new organizations and adopted different sets of Greek letters and secrets, distinguishing themselves from Phi Beta Kappa.

In 1776, access to higher education in the United States was limited to Caucasian, Protestant, upper-class males. Therefore, membership in early fraternities was limited to students with only these characteristics. As a more diverse population entered the classrooms, students were denied membership to the existing fraternities and often started their own. In 1851, the Adelphean Society was founded at Georgia Female College (now Georgia Wesleyan) and is considered the first fraternal organization for women (sorority), later changing its name to Alpha Delta Pi. At the City College of New York, Delta Sigma Phi was founded in 1899 in an effort to provide a brotherhood where Christian and Jewish men could coexist. Alpha Phi Alpha fraternity was founded at Cornell University in 1906 as the first fraternity for **African American** men. Some fraternities were founded for students studying specific academic disciplines whereas others were formed as honorary organizations to recognize outstanding scholarship. Fraternities also were established as coeducational organizations, offering membership to men and women. While student organizations certainly exist on campuses throughout the globe, the phenomenon of the fraternity is almost exclusively limited to the United States and Canada. Some fraternities have a huge national presence with more than 200 chapters on North American campuses whereas local fraternities exist at only one institution.

Gay and **bisexual youth** have always been a part of college fraternities, often closeted until after graduation. In 1996, Douglas N. Case published the first and only national quantitative study to date on gay and bisexual men within the college fraternity. He described these men as the "invisible membership." Case ascertained that the percentage of **gay youth** who are in fraternities is similar to the percentage of male students on campus who are gay or bisexual. On average, the male respondents were able to confirm (from knowledge received either during or after college), that 5 to 6 percent of members in their fraternity chapters were gay or bisexual. He also found that gay and bisexual members joined a fraternity for similar reasons as heterosexual members, namely to find friendship and camaraderie, as a social outlet, and to have a support group and sense of belonging. Despite the common misperception, Case concluded that sexual attraction was not a motivation for joining fraternities. He also discovered that 80 percent of the gay and bisexual men held a major executive office in their chapters such as president, vice president, secretary, treasurer, and new member educator. The tendency toward "overachievement,"

Case believes, reflected a need of gay and bisexual male students for self-validation and acceptance from the fraternity.

The Lambda 10 Project National Clearinghouse for Gay, Lesbian, Bisexual Fraternity and Sorority Issues was founded in 1995 at Indiana University to heighten the visibility of gay, lesbian, and bisexual members of the college fraternity system by serving as a clearinghouse for resources and educational materials. Three years later, *Out on Fraternity Row: Personal Accounts of Being Gay in a College Fraternity* (Windmeyer and Freeman 1998) was the first book to look closely at the collective experience of **sexual identity** and fraternity life. This anthology chronicled the positive impact of gay and bisexual brothers within fraternity life, the collective harms of **homophobia** on friendship/brotherhood, and the prevalent "denial dynamic" in joining a fraternity—the belief that somehow by joining a fraternity my "gay feelings" will subside. Men in fraternities can no longer deny that there are gay and bisexual men within their ranks or that homophobia is a pervasive problem.

The experience of gay and bisexual men varies greatly depending on the men within the chapter, the **school climate**, and the national fraternity leadership. Men who rush as openly gay or bisexual are often denied fraternity membership. The acceptance of gay and bisexual fraternity brothers is relatively greater when members join the fraternity closeted, establish a close friendship and brotherhood, and then disclose their sexual identity. The Lambda 10 Project documents cases of men who have been kicked out for being gay or bisexual as well as men who are welcomed or accepted for whom they are.

National fraternities have increasingly taken a stand on **sexual orientation** issues by adding nondiscrimination language to fraternity bylaws, by implementing chapter educational services, and by training staff members on the issue. However, according to the Lambda 10 Project, less than 10 percent of national fraternities have taken such actions. **Heterosexism** and **homophobia** are pervasive in many chapters (Windmeyer and Freeman 1998). A key to change in fraternities are the alumni. These graduated members often shape the policy and practices of the fraternity and are the most resistant to change that does not reflect their own values and college experience. For some openly gay and bisexual men wanting to join a fraternity, that may leave only one choice: a gay and bisexual sensitive fraternity. In 1986, Delta Lambda Phi became the first national social fraternity for gay, bisexual, and straight progressive men. The purpose of the fraternity is not much different than that of a traditional fraternity. Free of heterosexism and homophobia, the

Jay Larson, Phi Alpha Gamma cofounder, stands arm in arm with James Schaefer, Phi Alpha Gamma cofounder, as Greg Schwiesow, Phi Alpha Gamma member, holds a sign in support of public displays of affection for homosexuals. Phi Alpha Gamma held a kiss-in in an effort to challenge societal norms. From and courtesy of Iowa State Daily, photograph by Dan Wagner, March 29, 1991.

fraternal environment provides a safe, comfortable space for men to develop a strong sense of friendship and a balanced sexual identity—whether it be gay, bisexual, or heterosexual. Straight members do not need to conform to gender norms or be concerned about proving their heterosexuality to be accepted by the fraternity brothers. These men are able to gain the promise of fraternity life—friendship, valuable leadership skills, and a positive self-esteem without the hostility and hatred often present toward gay and bisexual men in a traditional fraternity. Delta Lambda Phi witnessed solid growth in the late 1990s and is currently the oldest and largest gay and bisexual sensitive fraternity with over twenty-five chapters and colonies. In 1999, a second gay and bisexual sensitive fraternity was founded. The emergence of Alpha Lambda Tau is further evidence that gay and bisexual men long for a fraternity experience. Many men are coming to campus openly gay and bisexual, so the need for such fraternities will only increase as more men are looking for the fraternity experience without the heterosexism and homophobia.

While gay men and bisexuals are certainly finding more opportunities to be a part of the fraternity experience, **transgender youth** will face a tougher battle, especially if they want to join existing fraternities. In addition to encountering prejudice, federal legislation may be an obstacle for these students. The U.S. Educational Amendments of 1972, commonly known as "Title IX," prohibit **discrimination** against people on the basis of gender by organizations that receive federal financial assistance from. However, fraternities have the legal right to restrict their membership to men since they are granted an exemption by the federal government. A challenge presents itself, however, when a person born as a biological female, but who lives life as a male, wants to join a fraternity. From a legal perspective, a fraternity could jeopardize its single-sex status by admitting such a student who is not biologically male into the organization.

As more and more people come out of the closet and at younger ages, fraternity members will see an increase in the number of gay and bisexual men who desire to be a part of the Greek experience (Baker 2002). This visibility, however, may result in more homophobia, biphobia, and incidents of hate directed toward gays and bisexuals. As a result, college **administrators** as well as national fraternity leaders will likely place more emphasis on creating **educational policies**, practices, and resources that affirm the presence and acceptance of gay and bisexual members. In addition, fraternities founded to provide the Greek experience to gay, bisexual, and perhaps even transgender students will continue to grow both in the number of chapters as well as the number of students per chapter.

Bibliography

Anson, Jack L., and Robert F. Marchesani, Jr., eds. 1991. *Baird's Manual of American College Fraternities*. 20th ed. Indianapolis: Baird's Manual Foundation.

Baker, Jean. 2002. *How Homophobia Hurts Children*. Binghamton, NY: Haworth Press.

Case, Douglas N. 1996, April/May. "A Glimpse of the Invisible Membership." *Perspectives: A Publication for the Members of the Association of Fraternity Advisors* 33, no. 3: 7–10.

MacGillivray, Ian. 2004. *Sexual Orientation and School Policy*. Lanham, MD: Rowman and Littlefield.

Windmeyer, Shane L., and Pamela W. Freeman, eds. 1998. *Out On Fraternity Row: Personal Accounts of Being Gay in a College Fraternity*. Los Angeles: Alyson.

———. 2002. *Fraternity & Sorority Anti-Homophobia Training Manual*. Charlotte, NC: The Lambda 10 Project.

Web Sites

Delta Lambda Phi. 2004. Accessed December 20, 2004. http://www.dlp.org/. national/
Listing of Delta Lambda Phi local fraternity chapters as well as historical background
information on the founding of the organization, it's principles and values as the first
and largest national fraternity for gay, bisexual and progressive men.

Lambda 10 Project. October 2004. Shane L. Windmeyer. Accessed December 20, 2004.
http://www.lambda10.org/. Resource clearinghouse of educational interventions, books,
articles, personal essays, and other Web links related to sexual orientation issues in
fraternity and sorority life as well as a listing of over 4,000+ openly gay men and
women in college fraternities and sororities to network for visibility and support of
coming out today on campus.

Freud, Sigmund (1856–1939)

Deborah P. Britzman

Sigmund Freud is the founder of **psychoanalysis**, a theory of human and cultural
development and a set of clinical practices. Psychoanalysis is meant to understand
and address suffering. Freud asserted that all humans begin life with a bisexual dis-
position. His views provoked moral anxiety—then and now. Just as individuals suffer from neurosis, so does culture. Individual case history contains both remnants
of social history and the personal, idiomatic history of infancy. Freud's theories understand unconscious conflicts within such phenomena as: culture, morality, artistic
creativity, jokes, social institutions, group psychology, mourning, discontentment,
aggression and war, love, hatred, education, dreams, language and constructions,
psychical reality, gender, sexuality, and the family.

Sexuality is at the center of Freud's theories. His understanding of the nature of
homosexuality and heterosexuality can seem contradictory and, for this reason, interpretations of Freud's theories range from conservative to radical. How can it be
otherwise, given Freud's "discovery" of the unconscious—a dynamic aspect of
emotional life that contains its own logic and conserves and condenses discarded,
repressed, infantile, and intolerable ideas? Indeed, psychical reality contains a veritable caldron of unacceptable and scandalously destructive impulses and incestuous
wishes, fantasies that pressure private dreams and public motivations.

Freud left behind a voluminous correspondence with his colleagues and his
writing consists of twenty-four volumes, *The Standard Edition*, 1886–1940. They
contain articles, case studies, lectures, books, and technique papers. The "early
Freud" emphasizes relations between pleasure and unpleasure and how repression
affects vitality and thinking; the "late Freud" centers on conflicts between the life
and death drives that organize psychical and cultural life. Drive theory leads Freud
to the origins and development of aggression, hatred, and love. While the early
Freud attributes neurosis to disturbances of sexual life, by around 1923 he revised
psychoanalysis to take into account the far more disturbing death drive.

See also Adolescent Sexualities; Bisexuality; Communication; Feminism; Foucault, Michel;
Gender Identity; Lacan, Jacques; Sexual Identity; Sexuality Education.

In theories of repression and drives, Freud stressed that the human is always subject to two simultaneous realities: everyday life and psychical reality. This volatile combination structures perception, ideas, judgments, projections, defenses, and thoughts. Both realities contain conscious and unconscious content; the ego's function is to perceive the difference between inner and outer worlds and defend against their respective dangers. Freud opened new understandings of objectivity and subjectivity, viewing cognition and emotion as relational and dynamic. He challenged social disparagement and moral condemnation of pathology by positing pathology and normality as a continuum. Through a study of pathology, normality can be approximated. Freud blurred the line between madness and sanity; he studied ordinary neurosis or anxiety, calling these mistakes "the psychopathology of everyday life."

Freud was condemned as perverse by social conservatives, applauded by social radicals for his advocacy of sexual information and frank discussion with children and adolescents, and welcomed by the burgeoning European and North American homophile leagues for his liberal views on homosexuality. He differed from **Magnus Hirschfeld** on the question of object choice as an inborn feature of sexuality. What was original for Freud was polymorphous perversity. He influenced artistic movements such as surrealism and literature and affected education with his enlightened views devoid of authoritarianism. With the German Nazi occupation of Austria and because Freud was Jewish, in 1939 an ailing Freud and some of his immediate family went into exile to London. Today, Freud's theories shape contemporary discussions of psychoanalysts, literary critics, queer theorists, feminists, **AIDS** researchers, educators and postcolonial critics. The work of **Judith Butler** on gender trouble is one example of Freud's influence on **queer theory**. Freud's appeal is with his great clarity, radical claims, analytical method, and an original, still unmatched openness to understanding human otherness and cultural discontentment.

Deep contention surrounds Freud's view of the human as split between conscious awareness and unconscious **desire**, his famous observation that the ego is not master of its own house, his insistence that consciousness is the exception for the human, and his placing of infantile sexuality and aggression in the center of sexuality. Freud attempted to remove superstitious thought and its moral condemnation from consideration of sexuality by defining its force widely, seeing sexuality in the infant, artistic endeavors, choices of work, thinking thoughts, and in slips of the tongue. Even those who disagree with Freud cannot avoid using the language of psychoanalysis to describe flummoxed events as a Freudian slip and difficult people as defensive, narcissistic, anal, and egotistical. Although Freud's terms have entered popular culture, there continue to be misconceptions and fears concerning his views, as well as important revisions of psychoanalysis in Europe, Latin America, North America, and Asia.

Of the psychoanalytic concepts that continue to cause controversy in such fields as **mental health**, law, religion, politics, and education, sexuality and the family romance are prominent. Freud's enduring and startling claims on these matters are found in his 1905 *Three Essays on Sexuality*. How can we know sexuality if observation is so subject to misunderstanding and to the observer's prejudices and social mores, and if a great deal of sexual development is confined to thinking and fantasy? Freud answered that understanding sexuality requires detours into language, cultural achievements, discontentment, and fantasies of being and having. Sexual instinct is tied to the drive for knowledge and mastery. He argued that from the beginning of life sexuality has internal causes. Sexuality is not reducible to genital intercourse or object choice. Our first object is our own bodily pleasures and the mother's breast. Freud placed sexuality at the center of psychical life, arguing that the baby's body is erotically affected and that its sexuality is polymorphously perverse, originally bisexual. This force of Eros leaves in its wake and colors the future of curiosity. The startling implication is that we have curiosity because we have sexuality. The paradox for educators is that without our sexuality we would not be able to think, yet sexuality is resistant to rational appeals.

Freud named children "little sex researchers" because of their fantastic theories about sexuality, how babies are made, and what the genitals of self and other mean. The child's sexual research is a precursor to intellectual development: "Sexual researches of those early years of childhood," Freud writes, "are always carried out in solitude. They constitute a first step towards taking an independent attitude in the world, and imply a high degree of alienation of the child from the people in his environment who formally engaged his complete confidence" (197). Freud critiqued: "the mental dams against sexuality—shame, disgust, and morality" (191), arguing that these social values create inhibitions and insecurity in thinking and delay the child's capacity for independence. They also cause unhappiness in civilization and a hatred of sexuality.

A second dimension of sexuality is the Oedipus complex. This cluster of libidinal experiences refers to the ways the child, between the ages of three to six, imagines sexuality and both desires one parent while hating the other as a rival. The Oedipus complex presents the child with the difficult work of individuation: to make a separate self and construct intellectual pleasures from new ideas. This emotional work occurs within the "family romance," a triangular relation of mother, father, and child. In Freud's view, the child has the painful task of accepting that the parents have a life beyond the child's, that the child cannot be the center of the parent's universe, and that the child must learn to relinquish omnipotent wishes, exchanging these for consideration of others, social consciousness and assumption of guilt, and for the promises of adulthood. When the Oedipus struggle recedes, the child moves into latency, giving her or him time to think without the pressures of deep conflictual urges. If all goes well, the child begins to learn the difference between fantasy and reality—and with this difference develops a conscience or what Freud called the "super-ego." With adolescence, the Oedipal crisis reemerges, giving passion to adolescents' yearnings and anguish, their desire for magical powers, intellectual and physical prowess, crowds, and sexual experimentation.

Freud left the fields of child analysis, education, and adolescent development to his daughter, Anna Freud (1895–1982), although his theory of mind and emotions—what he called psychical reality—continues to influence the understanding of developmental tasks and psychical conflicts of youth. In adolescence, Freud argued, what matters most is the world of ideas. Later, Anna Freud spoke of the **adolescence** large capacity for intellectualization, necessary for the dual freedoms of abstract thought and establishing one's authority to think. Freud's third essay on sexuality, titled, "The Transformations of Puberty-New Arrangements," stresses the importance of sexuality to the development of mental life. For Freud: "It is in the world of ideas, however, that the choice of an object is accomplished at first; the sexual life of maturing youth is almost entirely restricted to indulging in phantasies . . . in ideas that are not destined to be carried into effect" (225–226). The emotional world is played out in two competing levels: the having of ideas and so constructing knowledge, and the fantasies necessary for the pleasure of thinking sexuality and of experiencing one's sexual attractiveness. Contemporary educators use Freud's views to argue that sexuality and information are a human right.

When Freud speaks of object choice, sexuality has already expressed itself internally, in fantasized relations with parents of the same or the other sex, and in **childhood** theories of sexuality and gender. Freud depicted three senses of masculinity and femininity: as active/passive, as biological, and as sociological. It is the first sense that held Freud's interest and that gives his theories of gender such contradictory force and importance today. While Freud connects masculinity with activity and femininity with passivity, these qualities were neither tied to biological sex nor to moral judgments. All individuals exhibit both qualities; the dilemma is in whether these qualities inhibit a capacity for passionate engagement with life through these different yet complementary qualities.

Bibliography

Dean, Tim, and Christopher Lane, eds. 2001. *Homosexuality and Psychoanalysis*. Chicago: University of Chicago Press.

Freidman, Richard C., and Jennifer I. Downey. 2002. *Sexual Orientation and Psychoanalysis: Sexual Science and Clinical Practice*. New York: Columbia University Press.

Freud, Sigmund. 1953–1974. *The Standard Edition of the Complete Psychological Works of Sigmund Freud*. Edited and translated by James Strachey, in collaboration with Anna Freud, assisted by Alix Strachey and Alan Tyson. 24 vols. London: Hogarth Press and Institute for Psychoanalysis.

Gay, Peter. 1998. *Freud: A Life for Our Time*. New York: Norton.

Johansson, Warren. 1990. "Freudian Concepts." Pp. 432–437. In *Encyclopedia of Homosexuality*. Edited by Wayne Dynes. New York: Garland.

G

Gay, Lesbian, and Straight Education Network (GLSEN)

Kevin K. Kumashiro

Since its founding in 1990, the Gay, Lesbian, and Straight Education Network (GLSEN) has worked to end bias against **lesbian, gay, bisexual,** and **transgender** (LGBT) people in United States' schools and especially to create schools that are safe and welcoming for students of all sexual orientations and gender identities. Its mission gradually expanded from supporting lesbian and gay teachers to advocating for school reform. By 2003, GLSEN was the largest and most visible organization of its kind, with three national offices serving over thirty employees, more than eighty community-based chapters, and over 1,200 **gay–straight alliances** in schools.

GLSEN began as a support group for teachers in Boston, initially named the Gay and Lesbian Independent School Teachers' Network. Kevin Jennings, then a high school social studies teacher, formed the group to address the isolation experienced by gay and lesbian teachers. In 1991, the group renamed itself the Gay and Lesbian School Teachers Network (GLSTN), and was soon influencing statewide **educational policy**. In 1992, newly elected Governor William Weld created the Commission on Gay and Lesbian Youth to address, among other problems, the disproportionately high rates of **suicide** and harm among LGBT youth. The Education Committee of the Commission, with significant involvement of GLSTN members, produced a document, "Making Schools Safe for Gay and Lesbian Youth," and, in 1993, the Massachusetts Board of Education adopted the document's key recommendations.

In 1994, GLSTN became a nonprofit organization, opened a national office in New York City, and hired Jennings as its Executive Director. It also changed its name to the Gay, Lesbian, and Straight Teachers Network to acknowledge the involvement of heterosexual **allies**. In subsequent years, community-based chapters were formed across the United States, and GLSTN became increasingly involved in various local struggles against homophobic practices and policies. One struggle that gained national attention was that in Salt Lake City in 1996. Students were interested in forming gay–straight alliances. The school board did not support the existence of such organizations, and because it was prohibited from discriminating against them, decided to disband all extracurricular student organizations. GLSTN assisted the students in their struggle against the school board, and in 1997, continuing to draw attention to this issue, hosted its first national conference in Salt Lake City. GLSTN then became the Gay, Lesbian, and Straight Education Network (GLSEN), reflecting its ongoing mission expansion from supporting teachers to advocating for broader educational change.

During the late 1990s, GLSEN began conducting and publishing **research** on schools throughout the United States. In 1997, it released the first of its annual "Report Cards" of school districts' policies regarding protection and inclusion, and, two years later, published the results of its first "**School Climate** Survey,"

See also Agency; Curriculum, Antibias; Activism, LGBT Teachers; Professional Educational Organizations; Teachers, LGBT and History.

based on data collected from students. Both reports illustrated the lack of school safety experienced by LGBT students. The organization also coproduced the video, *Out of the Past: The Struggle for Gay and Lesbian Rights in America* (Jeffrey Dupre, director), that documented struggles throughout history against homophobia, including the struggle in Salt Lake City's schools.

In 1999, GLSEN spearheaded a coalition of ten mainstream educational and mental-health organizations—including the American Federation of Teachers and the American Psychological Association—to produce "Just the Facts about Sexual Orientation and Youth: A Primer for Principals, Educators and School Personnel" (Just the Facts Coalition 1999). Distributed to school **administrators** across the United States, it challenged the teachings of the **reparative therapies** and ministries that claimed to "repair" or "transform" a person's **sexual orientation** and that had been encouraging public schools to offer such programs to students. The following year, GLSEN worked with community-based groups to defeat a ballot initiative in Oregon that would have prohibited teaching about LGBT people and challenging **homophobia** (which critics considered to be "promoting" homosexuality) in schools. It also helped to pass legislation in eight states protecting LGBT students from **discrimination** and **harassment** as well as collaborated with its European counterpart, **GLBT Educational Equity** (GLEE) to develop leadership training courses for school teachers.

In 2001, GLSEN joined MTV to launch "Fight for Your Rights: Take a Stand against Discrimination," the largest ever campaign to educate the public about anti-LGBT bias. The next year, GLSEN worked with the National Education Association, the nation's largest professional employee association, to adopt resolutions calling for schools that are safe and hospitable for LGBT students and employees. The same year, GLSEN coordinated the seventh annual national **"Day of Silence"** in which students vowed silence to protest the silencing of LGBT people. Over 150,000 students on over 1,700 campuses participated.

GLSEN's evolution has not occurred without criticism, even from its membership. Lesbian and gay teachers who had few other places to go felt abandoned as GLSEN shifted its focus from supporting teachers to advocating for broader school change. People of color and allies wanted GLSEN to do more than merely acknowledge the harmful impact of **racism** and its intersection with homophobia, and have sparked ongoing debates on whether GLSEN should do more to address struggles that, on the surface, may not seem directly related to LGBT youth and education. Sometimes this criticism has led to substantive changes. Youth who valued GLSEN's role in developing student leaders formed a Youth Empowerment Initiative to advocate for a bigger role by young people in the organization, resulting in the addition of students to the Board of Directors and the creation of a student organizing department. **Transgender** and allied members called for more attention to the links between homophobia and **gender role** conformity, resulting in GLSEN expanding its mission statement to include "gender identity/expression," in 2000.

Bibliography

Jennings, Kevin, ed. 1994. *One Teacher in Ten: Gay and Lesbian Educators Tell Their Stories*. Boston: Alyson Publications.

Just the Facts Coalition. 1999. *Just the Facts about Sexual Orientation and Youth: A Primer for Principals, Educators and School Personnel*. Washington, DC: National Education Association.

Web Sites

Day of Silence Project. April 2005. GLSEN and the United States Student Association. Accessed June 1, 2005. http://www.dayofsilence.org/. The Day of Silence is a student-led day of action where those who support making anti-LGBT bias unacceptable in schools take a day-long vow of silence to recognize and protest the discrimination and harassment—in effect, the silencing—experienced by LGBT students and their allies.

Gay, Lesbian, and Straight Education Network. June 2005. Accessed June 1, 2005. http://www.glsen.org. This official Web site contains various information and resources for students, teachers, and advocates interested in creating safe schools for all people, regardless of sexual orientation and gender identity/expression.

Gay Youth

James T. Sears

Although "gay" has often been used synonymously with all sexual minorities, it refers specifically to homosexual men. The first known usage of the word, within a queer context, occurred in Gertrude Stein's "Miss Furr and Miss Skeene," but throughout most of the twentieth century "gay" was commonly used in mainstream advertisements and speech while the word was "queered" by sexual minorities. By the 1970s, not only had the word become widely understood for its other usage by heterosexuals, but its universality had been challenged by women who preferred "lesbian," or the more radicalized "dyke." Although concepts like "youth" and "**adolescence**" are as problematic as the category "gay," gay youth are in adolescence or in their early twenties. Most research during the past century has been on gay men with research on gay youth steadily growing from the 1970s, focusing primarily on **identity development**, **coming out**, and risk factors associated with being a sexual minority in a heterosexual culture. Since 1990, there has been more research on racial and ethnic minorities, gay youth outside of North America, and, most recently, on **resiliency** among gay youth.

Identity development for Euro-American gay youth, appropriating the theoretical ideas of Erick Erikson among others, has relied on case studies and samples of convenience to examine stages of sexual identity formation. Although the linear theories generally begin with a general sense of same-sex attraction followed by awareness of **sexual identity** and then engagement in same-sex behavior, in actuality the movement of an individual from one stage to the next is much more variable. Some gay youth first engage in same-sex behavior in **childhood**, which is then followed by feelings of attraction. Others identify themselves as gay before ever engaging in sexual behavior. Whatever the progression, identity development is associated with physical maturation from early pubescence, beginning around age thirteen, to the conclusion of physical maturation by one's very early twenties. There has been a downward drift of the onset of puberty, however, throughout the past century and, coupled to the advance of the gay rights movement, more gay youth are

See also Adolescent Sexualities; AIDS: College Campus Programming; Families, LGBT; Heteronormativity; Parents, Responses to Homosexuality; Religion and Psychological Development; White Antiracism; Youth Culture; Youth, At Risk; Youth, Homeless.

coming out at an earlier age. On average, gay males have had more sexual partners than their heterosexual peers by the time they reach age fifteen (Rotheram-Borus and Langabeer 2001), although this varies not only by individual but by racial and ethnic group. **Asian American** gay youth, for example, report not engaging in homosexual behavior for an average of three years longer (Russell and Truong 2001).

In classic identity development theory, coming out and the integration of one's sexual identity to oneself is considered the final stage of this process. As sexual maturity and activity has reached the lower end of adolescence so, too, has coming out. Scholars now estimate this occurring, on average, at about age fifteen or sixteen (Raymond 1994; Savin-Williams 2001). This presents greater problems for gay youth as they navigate through heteronormative institutions, most notably the school, family, and place of worship. Consequently, gay youth require more support systems—ranging from school and community-based groups to anti**bullying** policies and **antibias curriculum**. However, even in countries that are relatively progressive, such as the Netherlands, **Canada**, and **New Zealand**, these support systems are, at best, fragmented with particular difficulties in access by youth in **rural** areas.

Most gay youth come out first to friends since support from parents or teachers often is questionable. For a minority of gay youth, parental reactions to their son's homosexuality may result in rejection—either psychologically or physically. Additionally, the elaborate school and social system that helps heterosexual youth mature emotionally and sexually, like **dating** rituals and **proms**, are generally unavailable to gay youth. Religious institutions also are more likely to condemn their same-sex desires and behaviors than to embrace them. For all of these reasons, many gay youth are at risk.

Nearly three decades of **qualitative** and **quantitative research** has documented the myriad of pitfalls during the transition from gay youth to adulthood. Like identity development, this at-risk research is rooted in essentialism (homosexual orientation as a biological and transcultural phenomenon), has employed a "deficit" model (the focus is on the unhealthy aspects of gay youth's lives or what is missing from them), and has been largely based on Euro-American samples. Nevertheless, research has consistently found that gay youth are at greater risk than their heterosexual counterparts for: **alcoholism, drug use**, and **substance abuse; mental health** problems such as lower self-esteem and poor **body image; eating disorders**, particularly anorexia. In turn, eating disorders in males also are associated with childhood gender nonconformity, which generally results in **bullying** and **harassment**—and a tendency to attempt **suicide** (Strong, Singh, and Randall 2000).

Analyzing data from one state's **Youth Risk Behavior Survey** (Oregon Department of Human Resources 1998), for example, has found those young men who were recently (within the prior month) harassed because of perceived **sexual orientation** were six times more likely to evidence suicidality. Generally, rates of attempted and completed suicides are also two to three times higher vis-à-vis heterosexual youth (e.g., Bagely and Tremblay 1997). Gay youth, too, are disproportionately represented in the street kid population and prostitution. And, there is a greater risk for HIV infection and other sexually transmitted infections such as chlamydia and gonorrhea. For instance, the Centre for Infectious Disease Prevention and Control in Canada has found that in the twenty and older age bracket, nearly one-half of zero-positive conversions were due to same-sex behavior (Health Canada 2004).

These generalized findings have been replicated not only in North America, but in **Europe** and Oceania (e.g., Hillier et al. 2005). There has been more limited investigation in other countries such as **Israel, Japan, Brazil,** and **India**—but those few studies also follow this trend. Research into youth of color and youth outside the United States on at-risk factors is also revealing. Studies of mostly black or Hispanic youth (Rotheram-Borus et al. 1994; Rotheram-Borus et al. 1995) have found high rates of alcohol use; one study reported 76 percent lifetime use, with 22 percent acknowledging weekly alcohol consumption. In Brazil, a study of more than 100 street youth found these adolescents often engaging in high-risk sexual activity (De Sousa 2000). Sex workers who practice same-sex behavior are often poorly educated and generally deny their homosexuality. As they complete adolescence, these masculine-oriented "michê" are already past their earning prime (Mendès-Leité 1995). More than 50 percent of the new HIV positive cases in Brazil are detected among adolescents (Abramovay 2004).

In order to better understand gay youth who are not Euro-American, it is important to understand that concepts of identity development, coming out, and "gay" are culturally framed, which in turn affects intervention strategies related to health as well as education. In the United States, for example, many **African Americans** prefer terms such as "same gender loving" or "on the Down Low," in referring to their sexual activity. Gayness is equated with whiteness. This is also true in other non-Western countries, particularly those in **Africa** and the Middle East, where governmental officials have long condemned homosexuality as a disease of the colonizer. Further, in **Asia** and in most Asian American communities, the cultural importance of marriage and **desire** not to give public offense or shame to one's family, contributes to gay youth seldom being out to more than their friends and to a greater percentage of gay youth (compared to Euro-Americans) seriously contemplating or entering into heterosexual marriages.

In most contemporary societies, however, the image of the gender nonconforming gay youth remains problematic. **Gender roles** and expectations of **gender identity** result in a range of derisive words for the gender nonconforming boy or youth: "sissy boy," "girl," "poof," "maricon," "niang niang qiang" (sissy), "bakla," "tong xing lian" (homo/fag), and "jia ya tou" (fake girl). For some, proving their masculinity or, at least, disproving their homosexuality translates into a variety of counterproductive coping behaviors, from refusing to engage in sissified activities like **dance** and **art**, behaviors such as crying and crossing one's legs, or adopting gay fashions to assuming a hypermasculine role by participating in "rough" sports such as football or even engaging in homophobic-based bullying and violence. Some, like their parents, seek psychological assistance through diagnosis as **Gender Identity Disorder** or by participating in reparative therapy. Others may elect to pursue academics to the exclusion of other activities. For instance, in **China,** *Niang niang qiang* can often avoid bullying by doing very well in school, allowing the family to rationalize the lack of female interest to longer-term planning for a better family future. Adopting this "model minority" stereotype also deflects unwelcome questions from peers and teachers.

Issues of identity development and risk factors associated with gay youth are also impacted by **social class, disabilities,** geographic location, and religious beliefs. In the American South, coming from a family fully committed to the precepts of **religious fundamentalism** often contributes to these problems just as growing up in social privilege, even within a small town, can provide greater sexual elasticity and broader social leeway (Sears 1991). Those living in countries with strict **Muslim** fundamentalist teachings may also be at risk in facing the harsh penalties for sodomy meted out by Islamic countries such as **Egypt** and Afghanistan. Even in countries which have a secularized state, such as **France** and **Russia**, people prefer to adhere outwardly to **Christian** norms of gender and sexuality. And, in the most liberal country, the Netherlands, the influx of non-European families with fundamentalist religious beliefs has created strains on that country's approach to tolerance and has contributed to intergenerational conflicts.

For gay youth living in rural areas, the theme from country to country is one of isolation. In **South Africa**, despite its liberal constitution but limited progress on LGBT issues, those outside major cities are more subject to tribal customs and have little access to queer communities or support groups due to distance and financial hardship. In **Australia**, researchers have linked the isolation, loneliness, and alienation of queer youth to suicidality, finding that male youth suicide rates were twice that of male youth in urban areas (Quinn 2003). The **film** *Out in the Bush* (Australia 1997), documents the experiences of gay youth in the Outback. Given the poorer health systems in many rural areas, gay youth are at increased risk to HIV. In China, the recent influx of poor migrant youth has created a "gay underclass," many of whom engage in **sex work** or blackmail. Particularly in non-Western countries, to be a "gay youth" is to live in an urban area. In Western countries, some efforts are being made to reach out to this rural gay population of young persons such as GaBaLoT (http://gabalot.ca), which provides support for rural southern Ontario gay youth, and the Two-Spirited Youth Program, based in Vancouver, supporting **native and indigenous gay youth**.

In hearing cultures and within gay communities which prize not only youthfulness but Adonis-like bodies, gay youth who are physically or intellectually impaired face difficult and sometimes unique challenges. For example, for those youth who live in residential institutions, issues such as the absence of privacy and the antisexual attitudes of caregivers impact their abilities to express themselves sexually within safe environments. In one study, eight out of ten educators considered heterosexual expression acceptable for youth with moderate intellectual disabilities—but only one in five for same-sex expressions (Wolfe 1997). Harassment from peers or engaging in same-sex harassment as a form of passing is one strategy appropriated by disabled gay youth (Shakespeare 1999). In the United States, the Matthew Limon case, wherein an intellectually challenged gay youth who had just turned eighteen and had performed oral sex on another male teenager within the same residential institution, that resulted in seventeen-year prison sentence, evidences the discomfort of [homo]sexuality within such institutions when practiced by the disabled.

The traditional understanding has been that cultural markers add an additional burden to a gay male, such as being both African American and gay or being both from a working class background and homosexual. The notion, however, of identities as being fixed categories resulting in "double" or "triple" oppression, has been challenged lately by scholars applying queer theory as well as researchers (Davis 1999; Kumashiro 2001; Martino and Pallotta-Chiarolli 2003). Clearly, the intersections of **race, ethnicity**, and sexuality are problematic. There are difficulties with mostly white organizations, such as **gay–straight alliances** or community support groups as well as with finding support within black cultural, religious, and educational institutions (Sears 1995). For instance, of the more than 100 historically black colleges and universities, only a few host LGBT student organizations.

Despite the array of issues confronting gay youth, relatively few efforts have been forthcoming from government-supported schools. In the **curriculum**, there is little inclusion of gay issues found from teaching **literature** and **history** to **poetry** and **science**—even in **sexuality education**, which in almost every country is focused exclusively on heterosexual reproduction. Although educators, particularly school administrators, are well-positioned to offer support for gay youth, there has been, at minimum, a reluctance to engage in such **activism** and, at worst, outright **homophobia**, despite the large number of **professional educational organizations**, which have adopted such recommendations. More progress, however, has been made during the past ten years. Citing intolerance of harassment based on sexual identity, some communities have launched multiyear education initiatives to address these serious concerns. Three examples of such efforts is the curriculum developed by the Safe Schools Coalition (http://www.safeschoolscoalition.org), the antibullying programs initiated in Australia (see, for example, http://www.lawlink.nsw.gov.au/cpd.nsf/files/SkoolsOutRpt.webversion111202.pdf/$FILE/SkoolsOutRpt.webversion111202.pdf), and the recently launched school campaign, Programa Brasil Sem Homofobia http://www.mj.gov.br/sedh/ct/004_1_3.pdf). Equally importantly, there has been the development of school-based programs such as gay–straight alliances in the United States and to a lesser degree in Canada and the **United Kingdom**. In the United States, court rulings outlawing school board or administrator decisions to not recognize such student-led groups have been found to be in violation of the federal Equal Access Act. Other **legal** rights for students, particularly with reference to having a safe learning environment have resulted in substantial law suits against school districts. Both of these have served to encourage even reluctant school **administrators** to take a more proactive approach to LGBT issues and youth in their schools. A handful of school-based programs in **Mexico**, Brazil, the United States, and Canada serve gay youth who have found their school climate too difficult in which to learn. Although these initiatives have their own problems—racism, isolation of queer youth, poor funding—these are, at least in the short term, essential developments in providing **school safety**.

During the last few years, researchers on gay youth have begun to focus their attention on resilience and strengths rather than risk and deficits (Russell 2004; Savin-Williams 2001). By examining both "protective factors" (supportive families and schools, intelligence) and "developmental assets" (use of technology), gay youth who have been able to survive are now coming into focus. How specific factors and assets balance against the myriad of risk factors facing all queer youth should provide important insights into how educational policies and programs (along with other institutions such as religion, the media, the workplace, and family) can significantly contribute to resilience.

Relatedly, youth agency is represented in efforts that empower

Naithen Ritz, Mr. Teen Iowa Unltd., 2002. Courtesy of Gay Youth Unlimited, www.youth-unlimited.org

youth to assume greater responsibilities for their well-being. From **queer zines** to protests, this generation's gay youth has built on the shoulders of past band of brothers. For instance, in Paris there is *MAG Jeunes Gais (Mouvement d'Affirmation des jeunes gais & lesbiennes)*, created in 1990 for teenagers from age sixteen upwards. AQU[25] A (Asian and Pacific Islander, Queer and Questioning, Under 25 and Under, All Together)—is run by queer youth and includes a peer leadership program. "Minus18" manages dance parties for LGBT youth fourteen to seventeen years in Melbourne, and Youth Unlimited (http://www.youth-unlimited.org.) is an Iowa-based queer operated youth group offering drag pageants and a summer drag camp. Finally, the BQY: The Black Queer Youth Initiative (http://www. soytoronto.org/current.html.) in Toronto provides safe and social space for queer youth under age twenty-nine.

Efforts of gay youth who have made a difference not only in their lives but the lives of others is reflective of both agency and resiliency—as well as provide important examples for other gay youth. These include Jamie Nabozny whose landmark lawsuit against his Wisconsin school system has helped to insure that educators are liable for unsafe school environments; James Dale, an Eagle Scout and Assistant Scoutmaster from New Jersey whose unsuccessful suit against the **Boy Scouts of America** brought the needs of gay youth and the gaps in antidiscrimination policies to public light; and, Dan Bozzuto and Cory Johnson, star high school athletes, whose coming out brought a reconsideration of old prejudices held by their community, coaches, players, and fans; Pedro Zamora, whose tireless efforts in **HIV education** brought greater tolerance of and attention to the disease—as well as a human face.

Bibliography

Abramovay, Miriam. 2004. *Juventudes e Sexualidade* (Youth and Sexuality).Brasília: UNESCO, MEC, Ministério da Saúde/DST/Aids, Secretaria Especial de Políticas para as Mulheres, Instituto Ayrton Senna.

Bagley, Chris, and Pierre Tremblay. 1997. "Suicidal Behaviors on Homosexual and Bisexual Males." *Crisis* 18 no. 1: 24–34.

D'Augelli, Anthony. 1998. "Lesbian and Gay Male Development: Steps Toward an Analysis of Lesbians' and Gay Men's Lives." Pp. 118–132 in *Lesbian and Gay Psychology: Theory, Research, and Clinical Applications. Psychological Perspectives on Lesbian and Gay Issues, Vol. 1.* Edited by Beverley Greene and Gregory Herek. Thousand Oaks, CA: Sage.

Davis, James. 1999. "Forbidden Fruit: Black Males' Construction of Transgressive Sexualities in Middle School." Pp. 49–59 in *Queering Elementary Education: Advancing the Dialogue about Sexualities and Schooling.* Edited by William J. Letts IV and James T. Sears. Lanham, MD: Rowman and Littlefield Publishers.

De Sousa, Isabela Cabral Félix. 2000. "Deadly Education: The Spread of HIV/AIDS— Conceptual and Practical Approaches to HIV/AIDS: The Brazilian Experience." *Current Issues in Comparative Education* 3, no. 1. Accessed October 5, 2004. http://www. tc. columbia.edu/cice/articles/if131.htm

Health Canada: AIDS. 2004, September. Accessed November 16, 2004. http://www. he-sc.gc.ca/english/diseases/aids.html. Official Canadian source of HIV/AIDS related medical and scientific information.

Hillier, Lynne, Alina Turner, and Anne Mitchell. 2005. *Writing Themselves In Again: 6 Years On, The 2nd National Report on the Sexuality, Health and Well-Being of Same-Sex Attracted Young People in Australia*, Melbourne: Australian Research Centre in Sex, Health and Society, La Trobe University. Kumashiro, Kevin, ed. 2001. *Troubling*

Intersections of Race and Sexuality: Queer Students of Color and Anti-Oppressive Education. Lanham, MD: Rowman and Littlefield.

Martino, Wayne, and Maria Pallotta-Chiarolli. 2003. *So What's a Boy: Addressing Issues of Masculinity and Schooling.* Buckingham: Open University Press.

Mendès-Leité, Rommel. 1995. *Michê: La Masculinité au Marché ou Les Aléas de la 'Prostitution Virile' au Brésil.* (Michê: Masculinity on the Market or The Chances of "Virile Prostitution" in Brazil). Accessed October 5, 2004. http://semgai.free.fr/ contenu/textes/RML/rML_Miche.html. Originally published in *Un Sujet Inclassable? Approches Sociologiques, Littéraires et Juridiques des Homosexualités.* Edited by Rommel Mendès-Leité. Lille: Cahiers GKC.

Oregon Department of Human Resources. 1998. *Suicidal Behavior: A Survey of Oregon High School Students 1997* (prepared by David Hopkins). Portland: Author.

Quinn, Karolynne. 2003. "Establishing an Association between Rural Youth Suicide and Same-Sex Attraction." *The International Electronic Journal of Rural and Remote Health Research, Education, Practice and Policy.* Accessed December 4, 2004. http:// e-jrh.deakin.edu.au/articles/showarticlenew.asp?ArticleID=222.

Raymond, Diane. 1994. "Homophobia, Identity, and the Meanings of Desire: Reflections on the Cultural Construction of Gay and Lesbian Adolescent Sexuality." Pp. 115–150 in *Sexual Cultures and the Construction of Adolescent Identities.* Edited by Janice M. Irvine. Philadelphia: Temple University Press.

Rotheram-Borus, Mary Jane, Margaret Rosario, Heino F. L. Meyer-Bahlburg, Cheryl Koopman, Steven C. Dopkins, and Mark Davies. 1994. "Sexual and Substance Use Acts of Gay and Bisexual Male Adolescents in New York City." *Journal of Sex Research* 31: 47–57.

Rotheram-Borus, Mary Jane, Margaret Rosario, Ronan Van Rossem, Helen Reid, and Roy Gillis. 1995. "Prevalence, Course, and Predictors of Multiple Problem Behaviors among Gay and Bisexual Male Adolescents." *Developmental Psychology* 31: 75–85.

Rotheram-Borus, Mary Jane, and Kris A. Langabeer. 2001. "Developmental Trajectories of Gay, Lesbian, and Bisexual Youth." Pp. 97–128 in *Lesbian, Gay, and Bisexual Identities and Youth: Psychological Perspectives.* Edited by Anthony R. D'Augelli and Charlotte J. Patterson. New York: Oxford.

Russell, Stephen T. 2004. "Beyond Risk: Resilience in the Lives of Sexual Minority Youth." *Journal of Gay and Lesbian Issues in Education* 2, no. 3: 5–18.

Russell, Stephen T., and Nhan L. Truong. 2001. "Adolescent Sexual Orientation, Race and Ethnicity, and School Environments: A National Study of Sexual Minority Youth of Color. Pp. 113–130 in *Troubling Intersections of Race and Sexuality: Queer Students of Color and Anti-Oppressive Education.* Edited by Kevin K. Kumashiro. Lanham, MD: Rowman and Littlefield.

Ryan, Caitlin, and Donna Futterman. 1998. *Lesbian & Gay Youth: Care & Counseling.* New York: Columbia University Press.

Savin-Williams, Ritch C. 2001. "A Critique of Research on Sexual-Minority Youths." *Journal of Adolescence* 24, no. 1: 5–13.

Sears, James T. 1991. *Growing up Gay in the South.* New York: Haworth Press.

———. 1995. "Black-Gay or Gay-Black?: Choosing Identities and Identifying Choices." Pp. 135–57 in *The Gay Teen: Educational Practice and Theory for Lesbian, Gay, and Bisexual Adolescents.* Edited by Gerald Unks. New York: Routledge.

Shakespeare, Tom. 1999. "The Sexual Politics of Disabled Masculinity." *Sexuality and Disability* 17, no.1: 53–64.

Strong, Scott M., Devendra Singh, and Patrick K. Randall. 2000. "Childhood Gender Nonconformity and Body Dissatisfaction in Gay and Heterosexual Men." *Sex Roles: A Journal of Research* 43 nos. 7–8: 427–439.

Wolfe, Pamela. 1997. "The Influence of Personal Values on Issues of Sexuality and Disability." *Sexuality and Disability* 15, no. 2: 69–89.

Gay–Straight Alliances

Arthur Lipkin

A gay–straight alliance (GSA) is a middle or high school-based student association organized to advance the understanding of homosexualities, to reduce heterosexism, and to support the welfare of sexual minorities in schools and communities. Five years after Los Angeles biology teacher Virginia Uribe founded the first public high school gay support group, Project 10, at Fairfax High School in 1984, gay and heterosexual secondary school students began to organize school-based alliances in Massachusetts. By 2003, there were over 1,000 high school GSAs in 48 states in the United States, mostly on the east and west coasts and upper midwest. There are 25,000 high schools without a GSA, and middle school GSAs are rare. There are also some in Canada and the United Kingdom.

Besides bringing straight allies to the project of making schools safe for all, the GSA also encourages students who are fearful of coming out or uncertain of their sexual orientation to participate, usually without assumptions or pressure to identify. **Lesbian, gay, bisexual,** and **transgender** (LGBT) students are free to come out at their own pace or not at all.

A GSA is more likely to be an advocacy group for gay rights, school safety, and inclusion than to be a direct service provider to sexual minority youth. Students who need support with coming out, dealing with family, and other personal sexuality issues may need more than what this group provides. Some students have organized GSA subgroups for sexual minority youth only or find a community-based program for counseling, identity solidification, and socialization. The latter are often freer to discuss sex-related issues and are usually more relaxed about sexually expressive behavior.

Under its various banners (e.g., Pride Alliance, Safe Haven, Spectrum) the GSA has become a cornerstone of the antihomophobia school reform movement. It may play a number of different roles, from the confidential counseling group meeting secretly (really a "proto-GSA"), to the group that instigates and coordinates the LGBT school agenda, to the "ideal GSA" that plays a conscientious role in a broader institutional social justice project. (Griffin et al. 2004) By its very presence, the GSA may lead some students to reexamine conventional gender and sexuality frameworks they have taken for granted and perhaps to discover the inadequacies of sexuality labels. Such discourses might also prompt LGBT students to ally themselves with others who are oppressed because of race and other identity markers (Mayo 2004).

Opposition to GSAs is common. Besides frequent administrative barriers, these school-based groups also face outright hostility. Posters are routinely torn down or defaced and student organizers are sometimes harassed or physically attacked. Although a few GSAs meet off campus to protect student safety and confidentiality, most choose to meet at school both for convenience and as a public gesture for tolerance.

Opponents regularly charge that GSAs influence students to become gay, but there is no empirical evidence for that accusation. Rather, students who become less fearful of or hateful toward homosexuality may have fewer inhibitions in exploring

See also African American Youth; Antidiscrimination Policy; Educational Policies; Legal Issues, Students; White Antiracism.

the full range of their sexual interests (Mayo 2004). Some find confirmation of their gay or bisexual desires, others do not, and some become less invested in sexuality labels overall.

GSAs may also encounter challenges getting started and maintaining momentum. Some of these are common to other youth organizations. Among these challenges are:

- balancing student privacy with the need for visibility vis-à-vis other school clubs;
- developing student leadership;
- depending on overcommitted students;
- getting new members;
- reflecting the diversity of the school;
- mitigating cliques within the group;
- making the group comfortable for new, perhaps intimidated, students and still exciting the veterans;
- dealing with different levels of openness—those who come out to the advisor and some peers, but not to the group, or come out in the group but not more widely in the school;
- maintaining trust and confidentiality;
- keeping the group focused;
- harmonizing educational, activist, counseling, and social agendas;
- motivating student follow-through on projects;
- combating isolation by communicating with other GSAs;
- working out relationships with community-based youth and adult groups;
- dealing with community resistance and hostility.

Location and political demographics often determine community resistance. A GSA in an isolated conservative town may find it hard to meet at all. The federal Equal Access Act of 1984 and the 1990 U.S. Supreme Court Decision in *Board of Education v. Mergens*, however, have helped GSAs organize in recalcitrant communities like Salt Lake City and Orange County, California. For many GSAs, however, the most important challenges are leadership, diversity, goal setting, and isolation.

GSAs' enrollment often fluctuates considerably from year to year. The changes might merely reflect certain social justice issues going in and out of style, but the problem could relate more to leadership than to trendiness. Clearly, underclass students have to be prepared in advance for leadership roles. Key components of such training are power sharing, group decision-making, creative thinking, delegation of tasks, and leadership by inspiration and example. Over the long term, numbers are less important than group cohesion and effectiveness. An energetic few students with a dedicated advisor can create a distinguished record.

The question of who chooses to participate is vexing. The GSA may be a haven for alienated misfits ("freaks") or a bohemian countercultural enclave (like the prototypical drama club) or both. Moreover, its composition tends to perpetuate itself, and a disproportionate GSA membership of alienated, troubled gay and straight young students inhibits the formation of a healthy youth culture. The counseling needs of individual students can overwhelm the advisor and detract from the group's necessary focus on group needs and objectives. The tensions between individual counseling and community-building can be exhausting, especially for advisors who are not trained mental health service providers and substance abuse counselors.

As a purported safe space for sexual minority youth, it is no wonder that other nonconformists seek it out. A youth group who won't hassle its members about homosexuality is likely to be nonjudgmental about other characteristics that evoke ridicule and harassment among more conventional adolescents. Regardless of their sexuality or gender identity, teens who deviate from traditional gender role and presentation, find respite in a GSA (Griffin et al. 2004).

Sexual minority youth who cannot pass for straight, or who choose not to, are most likely to need a GSA as a support against victimization. They are already at disproportionate risk for depression, suicide, and substance abuse (Garofalo et al. 1998). Other gay youth who can remain closeted or are better supported outside school—and therefore less needy—might not associate with the GSA, if it meant "outing" themselves or being seen in "bad company."

Many GSAs are composed mostly of straight, bisexual, and nonlabeled girls (Doppler 2000). They apparently suffer fewer negative consequences in the larger school because of their GSA membership than do boys. That result is consistent with girls having greater latitude in gender expression generally and with sexual minority females being less threatening to straight people.

Because gender issues are an intrinsic part of gay, lesbian, and bisexual student concerns, some level of gender analysis and critique is assumed in a GSA. However, the conservative environment of a school community and the residual conventionality of GSA members and advisors may still discourage transgender student participation in some GSAs. A small number of transstudents have been involved in Massachusetts GSAs, for example, but more have opted for community-based support groups. Alternative academic venues, like New York's Harvey Milk School, also currently appear to better meet the needs of transadolescents. Still, in Hawaii, school groups for gender identity support have succeeded in lowering the incidence of drop-out and other risk behaviors (Bopp, Juday, and Charters 2004).

Racial and ethnic diversity is also a clear challenge. Students of color may not feel welcome in a group that does not reflect or evince an understanding of their cultural identity and experience or is composed of mostly Euro-American youth (McCready 2000). Moreover, the heteronormative pressure within their cultural peer group prevents many minority youth from entering a gay setting, especially in the school where detection is likely. To appeal to multiple minority students, the GSA could recruit adults of color as advisors, elect students of color to leadership positions, sponsor joint activities with other more diverse school groups, and bring in speakers and films to initiate discussion about nonwhite, non-European gays and lesbians. Majority-white GSAs can also develop and act on an antiracist agenda and cooperate with other school organizations in social justice projects.

Most adolescent GSA members (like their counterparts in other groups like the Latino Club, the Black Student Union) arrive with their needs paramount. Most have to be motivated and shown how to think beyond themselves and their particular experience. To spur this kind of human development, peer dialogue and mutual endeavor within and among groups are required. The objectives are for students genuinely to understand and empathize with "the other" and to commit to diversity, multiculturalism, and justice—not merely to parrot adult language.

Goal-setting can also be a challenge since there are multiple reasons students join a GSA: to learn about gay and lesbian issues; to change the school and the community through political activism; to gain support and counseling for coming out; to socialize. The difficulty often is meeting as many expectations as possible without spreading the group (or its advisors) too thin.

Whether it meets openly in the school or more privately elsewhere, it is difficult to maintain the confidentiality of those participating in GSAs. Gay students and allies also are subject to teasing and harassment. And its members can feel besieged, alone, and dispirited. GSAs can combat this isolation by reaching out to other GSAs in their area and by communicating with more through networks, or regional and national conferences. National and local conferences sponsored by GLSEN and its affiliated chapters and the California-based GSA Network represent two such opportunities.

Students often have trouble finding faculty advisors for their GSA. It can be a difficult role. Besides encountering political opposition, advisors may have their sexuality questioned and actions monitored. Advisors who themselves are gay and lesbian or bisexual face additional challenges to be "ideal" role models and all-knowing advisors. School officials may delegate to them a solitary advocacy burden. And sometimes they find their nurturing of gay students mistaken for seduction.

Despite the twenty-year history of GSAs in the United States, there is little research about them. A handful of studies published in the United States from 2000 to 2004 has only begun to investigate their function and impact on students and schools.

Bibliography

Bopp, P. Jayne, Timothy R. Juday, and Cloudia W. Charters. 2004. "A School-Based Program to Improve Life Skills and to Prevent HIV Infection in Multicultural Transgendered Youth in Hawai'i." *Journal of Gay and Lesbian Issues in Education* 1, no. 4: 3–21.

Doppler, Judith. 2000. *A Description of Gay/Straight Alliances in the Public Schools of Massachusetts.* Unpublished doctoral dissertation, University of Massachusetts, Amherst, MA.

Garofalo, Robert R. Cameron Wolf, Shari Kessel, Judith Palfrey, and Robert H. DuRant. 1998. "The Association between Health Risk Behaviors and Sexual Orientation Among a School-Based Sample or Adolescents." *Pediatrics* 101, no. 5: 900–901.

Griffin, Pat, Camille Lee, Jeffrey Waugh, and Chad Beyer. 2004. "Describing Roles that Gay–Straight Alliances Play in Schools: From Individual Support to School Change." *Journal of Gay and Lesbian Issues in Education* 1, no. 3: 7–22.

Lee, Camille. 2002. "The Impact of Belonging to a High School Gay/Straight Alliance." *The High School Journal* 85, no. 3: 14–26.

Mayo, Cris. 2004. "Queering School Communities: Ethical Curiosity and Gay Straight Alliances." *Journal of Gay and Lesbian Issues in Education* 1, no. 3: 23–36.

McCready, Lance. 2000. "When Fitting in Isn't an Option, or Why Black Queer Males at a California High School Stay Away from Project 10." Pp. 37–54 in *Troubling Intersections of Race and Sexuality.* Edited by K. Kumashiro. Lanham, MD: Rowman and Littlefield.

Web Site

Gay–Straight Alliance Network. May 2005. Accessed June 1, 2005. http://www.
gsanetwork.org. The Gay–Straight Alliance Network is a youth-led Organization that
connects school-based Gay–Straight Alliances (GSAs) to each other and to community
resources.

Gender Identity

Lynne Carroll

Gender identity refers to an individual's self-identification as a man, woman, transgender, or other identity category. Historically, Stoller (1964) introduced the term
"gender identity," in the early 1960s to refer to the early awareness of oneself as male
or female. Gender identity is believed to evolve from a complex set of socio–cultural
practices whereby human bodies are transformed on the basis of biological sex into
"men" and "women." One's gender identity is thought to be manifested through
dress, behavior, **communication**, both verbal and nonverbal, and social interests.
Once used interchangeably, the term "gender" is now favored over the term "sex," to
describe the social and cognitive dimensions of one's biologically determined sex.

Although a great majority of persons may see themselves as either male or
female a growing number of young people do not believe that sex and gender are
dichotomous. Many young persons see themselves as somewhere in the middle of
the gender continuum and some define themselves as neither male nor female but
"other." The latter are sometimes referred to as "androgyne," "ambigendered,"
"Two-Spirited," "bigendered," "transgenderist," "genderqueer," "gender variants"
and "gender outlaws."

Early attempts to explain the development of gender identity generally focused on
early **childhood**. Assuming a developmental perspective, these theorists believed that
gender identity was tentatively formed before children began schooling, at approximately two to three years of age, strengthening as they progressed through elementary
school with the roles assigned to each gender continually reinforced and enforced.
More specifically, Kohlberg (1966) proposed a cognitive developmental model of gender development that posited that gender identity couldn't be learned until children
reached a particular stage in intellectual development. He observed that most two- to
three-year-olds were able to answer correctly when asked to identify their gender as
male or female. Between the ages of three and five, children developed the cognitive realization that their gender is relatively fixed or "constant" regardless of ephemeral
changes like hairstyles and clothing. Alternately, the social learning perspective, advanced by psychologists Bandura and Mischel, theorized that children acquired their
gender identity through observing others and through their complex history of behavioral reinforcement. During middle school years, children also learned that gender
identity is closely aligned with sexuality. Children preferentially attend to same-sex
or gender-appropriate models, most of whom are heterosexual, and are either directly
or vicariously reinforced for stereotypically consistent sexual behaviors.

See also Antidiscrimination Policy; Feminism; Heteronormativity; Identity Development;
Identity Politics; Native and Indigenous LGBT Youth; Philosophy, Teaching of; Poststructuralism; Racial Identity; School Safety and Safe School Zones; Sexual Identity; Stereotypes.

As numerous writers have observed, many young people and adults have experienced the negative repercussions of how any deviation from normative **gender roles** leaves one open to accusations of homosexuality (Bem 1993). The threat of such an accusation in and of itself served to reinforce **compulsory heterosexuality** (Bohan 1996). Thus, early theoretical models of gender identity and sexuality were based upon what is currently termed an essentialist perspective, which held that gender identity and **sexual orientation** are linear, binary (either male or female, heterosexual or homosexual), relatively stable, and biologically determined (Lorber 1996).

Within the last two decades, contemporary understandings of gender identity and sexual orientation have suggested that these are multiple and fluid (Deaux and Stewart 2001). Hence, persons define themselves with regard to gender identity within historical and cultural contexts over time and as a complex of intersecting identities across multiple dimensions of gender, sexual orientation, **race**, **ethnicity**, and **social class**. Perhaps one of the most influential contemporary theoreticians is **Judith Butler**. In *Gender Trouble* (1990), she argued that feminine or masculine behaviors are performative and are the byproduct of cultural norms. Much like RuPaul's motto, "You're born naked and all the rest is drag," there is no essential woman (or man), and no deep sense of self that every woman (or man) has and influences what she (or he) does, and no fixed relationship between one's anatomy, identity, and sexuality. Butler's idea that gender is performed is a key concept in **queer theory**. From a social constructionist theoretical framework, gender identity is continually renegotiated in the context of competing messages and discourses (Butler 1990; Lorber 1996). As sexual minorities gain increasing visibility in popular culture and as younger cohorts come of age, the sense that there are more alternatives for sexual and gender identities has increased, as is evidenced by the increased acceptance of **bisexuality** among younger generations. Interestingly, in other cultures and historical contexts, gender divergence and **multiple genders** were seen as desirable. For example, in several North American Indian tribes, persons who assumed opposite gender roles, "Two-Spirit people," were revered and considered to be prophets and visionaries.

Gender dimorphism is part of the cultural infrastructure and is enforced through all of our major Western social institutions: the family, school, law, religion, and medicine. For example, psychological theory reproduces as scientific knowledge that gender categories are normal and that persons who transgress them are thought of as "objects." Within the psychiatric and medical professions, persons who present as gender dysphoric (defined as psychological discomfort with one's biological sex) are often counseled to alter their bodies and encouraged to adapt a new gender presentation so they may "pass" (conceal the fact that they are differently gendered) successfully and not be "read" or discovered. In most instances, the costs of treatment are covered only if the patient is rendered a diagnosis according to the 4th edition of the ***Diagnostic and Statistical Manual of Mental Disorders*** (DSM-IV-TR; American Psychiatric Association. Association 2000) of **Gender Identity Disorder**.

Today, as postmodern feminist, queer, and cultural academics advance increasingly complex explanations of sex and gender, transgender activists like Riki Anne Wilchings, Kate Bornstein, Pat Califa, and Holly Devor advocate for a future in which a multiplicity of genders, sexes, and sexualities might be imagined and enacted—a future already imagined in novels like the *Left Hand of Darkness* and *Riverfinger Women* a generation earlier.

Boys Don't Cry (2000). Directed by Kimberly Peirce. Shown: Chloe Sevigny, Hilary Swank. Fox Searchlight Pict/Photofest © Fox Searchlight Pictures

Such activists have criticized academicians because they write about gender identity without acknowledging the daily realities of those persons who stray from compliance with the appearance of what is considered "normal" gender expression. Although an increasing number of "gender queer" youth do not conform to conventional gender identities, they are often marginalized and experience harassment, prejudice, and discrimination. The plight of those who challenge rules of gender expression is graphically and painfully illustrated in *Boys Don't Cry* (USA 1999). This film depicted the experiences of teenager Brandon Teena, a biological female, who lived as a male and was brutally raped and murdered after two male acquaintances discovered her biological sex was female.

The emerging consciousness about the nature of gender identity and sexuality as well as the increasing visibility and political **activism** of the transgender community create challenges for educators and counselors. While many continue to struggle to make schools safe for **gay, lesbian, bisexual,** and questioning youth, the needs of gender-variant youth usually are ignored. Creating a safe, gender affirmative environment for young people means recognizing that gender orientation is often experienced by young people as more fluid than implied by contemporary or medical definitions of gender. To begin with, **administrators,** teachers, and school counselors must explore their roles as alleviators or agitators in the emotional distress of youth who challenge the binary gender system. Sensitivity training, school nondiscrimination and antiharassment policies must include a specific focus on gender identity and **transgender youth**. Safe spaces, even those that might exist for GLB students, must clearly invite, affirm, and provide inclusive services specific to the needs of gender variant and transgender persons. **Curriculum** content, from early childhood **literature** to **biology**, needs to be examined for heteronormative, essentialist, and gender biases. In social studies, for example, gender variant persons such as the Hijira of India, could be included.

Bibliography

American Psychiatric Association. 2000. *Diagnostic and Statistical Manual of Mental Disorders*, 4th ed. Washington, DC: Author.

Bem, Sandra L. 1993. *The Lenses of Gender: Transforming the Debate on Sexual Inequality*. New Haven, CT: Yale University Press.

Bohan, Janis S. 1996. *Psychology and Sexual Orientation: Coming to Terms*. New York: Routledge.

Butler, Judith. 1990. *Gender Trouble*. London: Routledge.

Deaux, Kay, and Abigail, J. Stewart. 2001. "Framing Gendered Identities." Pp. 84- 100 in *Handbook of the Psychology of Women and Gender*. Edited by Rhoda K. Unger. New York: Wiley.

Kohlberg, Lawrence. 1966. "A Cognitive-Developmental Analysis of Children's Sex-Role Concepts and Attitudes." Pp. 82–173 in *The Development of Sex Differences*. Edited by Eleanor E. Maccoby. Stanford, CA: Stanford University Press.

Lorber, Judith. 1996. *Paradoxes of Gender*. New Haven, CT: Yale University Press.

Stoller Robert J. 1964. "A Contribution to the Study of Gender Identity." *International Journal of Psycho-Analysis* 45: 220–226.

Web Sites

Gender YOUTH. December 2004. Accessed December 18, 2004. http://www.gpac.org/youth. A national campaign to start grassroots activism on college campuses to fight gender-based harassment, bullying and violence.

The International Foundation for Gender Education (IFGE). December 2004. Accessed December 18, 2004. http://www.ifge.org. An advocacy, referral, and educational organization for promoting the free expression of gender identity.

Gender Identity Disorder

Mary Lou Rasmussen

Young people who are thought to exhibit "atypical gender identifications" may be diagnosed with Gender Identity Disorder (GID) in childhood. However, there is much debate about what constitutes a "typical" **gender identity**. The criteria for the development of a GID diagnosis are laid out in the American Psychiatric Association's *Diagnostic and Statistical Manual of Mental Disorders* (DSM-IV) (APA 1994). The diagnostic classification, in **childhood**, includes two principal components. One component pertains to strong and persistent cross-gender identification, which is understood as the **desire** to *be*, or the insistence that one is of the other sex. For such a diagnosis to be verified the *DSM-IV* also calls for evidence of persistent discomfort about one's assigned sex or a sense of inappropriateness in the **gender role** of that sex. Such a classification has a potential for medical experts to pathologize young people who do not conform to societal, religious, or parental norms regarding gender appropriate behavior. The classification also ignores that many people do not regard cross-gender feelings or behaviors as a disorder and the fact that gender identity is culturally variable. People may also object to the GID classification because they believe there is a physical underlying cause. These people advocate or seek physical modifications to bring the body into harmony with one's "natural" or "essential" gender identity. Despite criticisms of the GID diagnostic classification, it is a means to obtain medical assistance to make the transition from male to female, or vice versa. As a growing number of youth are challenging gender roles or identifying themselves as **transgender**, it is important that educators have some knowledge of GID and the debates that accompany it.

Diagnosis of GID for children, as outlined in the DSM-IV (APA 1994, 302.85), occurs when at least four of these criteria are met: repeatedly stated desire to be, or insistence that he or she is, the other sex; in boys, preference for **cross-dressing** or

See also Adolescent Sexualities; Bullying; Heteronormativity; Intersex; Multiple Genders; Parents, Responses to Homosexuality; Queer and Queer Theory; Sissy Boy; Stereotypes.

simulating female attire; in girls, insistence on wearing only stereotypical masculine clothing; strong and persistent preferences for cross-sex roles in make-believe play or persistent fantasies of being the other sex; intense desire to participate in the stereotypical games and pastimes of the other sex; and/or strong preferences for playmates of the other sex.

In boys, the disturbance is manifested by any of the following: assertion that his penis or testes are disgusting or will disappear; or assertion that it would be better not to have a penis; or aversion toward rough-and-tumble play; and rejection of male stereotypical toys, games and activities. In girls, it is evident in: rejection of urinating in a sitting position; assertion that she has or will grow a penis; or assertion that she does not want to grow breasts or menstruate; or marked aversion toward normative feminine clothing.

The diagnostic classification of GID for children has been the subject of much debate in medical and queer communities. Embedded in this classification is experts' investment in the maintenance of a distinct gender binary. This classification rests on the assumptions that there is some general agreement about what constitutes appropriate masculine and feminine attire, and masculine and feminine "games and pastimes," and that the consistent desire to cross genders is psychopathological.

The GID classification is rooted in Western conceptions of gender, sex, and sexuality. Around the world, however, there are many differing interpretations of gender and sex roles. Two such cultural differences may be found among Aboriginal Sistergirls of **Australia** and **Native** Two-Spirit people in North America. Even within Western societies, what constitutes cross-gender behavior is often situational, as evident in appropriateness of Scottish lads wearing "kilts," or the general acceptance of prepubescent "**tomboys.**"

The GID classification also conflates gender and sexual identities, evidencing **compulsory heterosexuality.** Esben Benestad/Esther Pirelli (2001), a bigendered therapist from Norway, has found that a "major proportion" of GID-diagnosed children become homosexual adults with a smaller proportion identifying themselves as heterosexual and only a "very small proportion" becoming transgender.

In his study of "Sissies and Sisters," William Spurlin (1998), a queer theorist, argues that GID classification is homophobic and gender phobic with the "'treatment' of GID, usually at the behest of 'concerned' parents, . . . [and] often aimed at the prevention of gay outcome" (83). An earlier DSM classification of "atypical sexual object choice" resonates in the contemporary formation of GID; both are underpinned by the privileging of heterosexuality as the elemental form of **sexual identity.**

A major textbook for psychology students, details a psychosocial treatment for "mistaken gender identity" which the authors state they have "successfully" deployed (Barlow and Durand 1999). The treatment is designed to enable their clients to "act in a more typically masculine manner . . . avoiding ridicule by simply choosing to behave differently in some situations" (307). The treatment regime described incorporates "procedures . . . to alter . . . patterns of sexual arousal," enabling clients not only to "behave like a seventeen-year-old-boy, but also to feel like a seventeen-year-old-boy" (307). Such treatments may include a focus on modification of voice, dress, and gestures so that they conform more closely to stereotypical notions of masculinity.

There are tensions within and around the medical and transcommunities regarding whose knowledge should prevail in the determination of treatments for people who self-identify as transgender or wish to become **transsexual**. Herbert Bower (2001), an Australian medical expert on gender dysphoria, asserts trans-sexuals need to establish a long history of cross-dressing in order to be legitimated in their classification. Further, too much enjoyment of anal sex may be associated with a homosexual proclivity, cancelling out the validity of the transsexual identity. In contrast, other medical experts such as Benestad (2001) have voiced their opposition to developing medical treatments for young people who do not conform to expectations of gender appropriate behavior:

> The quest is not for the possibly transgendered child or adolescent to understand or take care of the world, but for the world to understand and take care of the transgendered. . . . [T]ransgenderedness is not a disease (and can thus not be treated) . . . the main source of pain and trouble for transgendered young people is the way they are met and perceived by the world. The main therapeutic route to a better situation for the identified transgendered is to treat their world of significant others: parents, teachers, siblings, and so on.

In a similar vein, Douglas Haldeman (2000), a clinical faculty member of the Psychology Department of the University of Washington, suggests that the legitimate goal for treatment of Gender Identity Disorder is to facilitate gender atypical youth in coming to terms with their experience, and educating the young person's family and school community about the different but equal value and potential benefits of gender atypicality. GID diagnosis, according to Haldeman, is not amenable to psychotherapeutic treatment, and it may have the effect of causing shame without changing the gender atypical behavior.

Haldeman also argues that diagnosing GID often confuses gender identity with **sexual orientation**. Such a conflation, he asserts, potentially causes further pain and confusion for the child. Thus, he recommends that those working with "gender atypical youth" in schools turn their focus from attempts to modify these children's behavior. As an alternative, he argues school psychologists adopt a strategy in which they "step back and refrain from placing a culturally designed template on gender atypical youth" (199). In addition, Haldeman suggests that treatment "might be better directed toward those who truly experience gender dysphoria in the extreme and toward the bullies who victimize them" (199). Alongside this, school counselors and psychologists might work on educating parents, students, and peers about the fluidity of gender, and maybe even consider how such fluidity can enrich the school community.

Bibliography

American Psychiatric Association. 1994. *Diagnostic and Statistical Manual of Mental Disorders*. Washington, DC: Author.

Barlow, David H., and V. Mark Durand. 1999. *Abnormal Psychology: An Integrative Approach*. 2nd ed. New York: Brooks/Cole.

Benestad, Esben/Esther Pirelli. 2001. *Options of Gender Belonging*. Live video link, viewed July 26, 2001. Adelaide, Australia.

Bower, Herbert. 2001. "The Gender Identity Disorder in the DSM-IV Classification: A Critical Evaluation." *Australian and New Zealand Journal of Psychiatry* 35: 1–8.

Green, Richard. 1987. *The "Sissy Boy Syndrome" and the Development of Homosexuality*. New Haven, CT: Yale University Press.

Haldeman, Douglas. 2000. "Gender Atypical Youth: Clinical and Social Issues." *School Psychology Review* 29. no. 2: 192–200.

Murray, Alexander S. 1998. "Objectively, Subjectively, Psychiatry and Politics." *Australasian Psychiatry* 1: 59–60.

Spurlin, William J. 1998. "Sissies and Sisters: Gender, Sexuality and the Possibilities of Coalition." Pp. 74 – 101 in *Coming Out of Feminism?* Edited by Mandy Merck, Naomi Segal, and Elizabeth Wright. Oxford: Blackwell.

Web Sites

Benestad, Esben/Esther Pirelli. 1998. Conference report, Third international congress of sex and gender, Oxford, England, Accessed December 18, 2004. http://www.cat.org.au/ultra/congress.html. Brief and easy to read introduction to some of the issues relating to young people who may be classified as GID or who have an intersex identification.

Di Ceghe, Domenico, Claire Sturge, and Adrian Sutton. The Royal College of Psychiatrists Gender Identity Disorders in Children and Adolescents Guidance for Management Council Report CR63, January 1998. Accessed December 18, 2004. http://www.symposion.com/ijt/ijtc0402.htm. Provides medical information on the diagnosis of GID and also offers a list of suggested readings pertaining to GID's history and changing treatment paradigms.

The Harry Benjamin International Gender Dysphoria Association, Inc. Standards of Care for Gender Identity Disorders. February 2001. Accessed December 18, 2004. http://www.hbigda.org/soc.cfm. A detailed discussion of the treatment of children, adolescents and adults diagnosed with GID.

Hirschfield, Scott. Defining Gender in Straight Jackets. Gay, Lesbian and Straight Education Network Education Department Resource. 2000. http://www.glsen.org/cgi-bin/iowa/all/news/record/1644.html. Accessed December 18, 2004. GLSEN article on gender identity issues in education.

Gender Roles

Karen E. Lovaas

The term "gender roles" refers both to socially defined expectations about how females and males should behave and to the public expression of **gender identity**. Gender generally refers to socially defined differences between women and men. In contrast, sex usually refers to biological differences, which many believe form the foundation for gender differences in behavior. For example, women's role in childbearing may be seen as logically leading women to play a larger role in rearing children, preparing food, and caring for the home. Beliefs about gender role differences as natural and, therefore, stable and universal, are reinforced through many social practices and institutions. Thus, departures from these roles are frequently viewed

See also Antibias Curriculum; Bullying; Camp; Compulsory Heterosexuality; Cross-dressing; Dating; Gender Identity Disorder; Heterosexism; Identity Development; Men's Studies; Multiple Genders; Queer and Queer Theory; Sexism; Stereotypes; Women's Movement.

as abnormal, unacceptable, or threatening to social order. Young people, especially **lesbian, gay, bisexual**, and **transgender youth** (LGBT), must navigate through these gender role expectations and may experience negative reactions at a critical juncture in their lives. Rigid gender roles, however, affect all young people as they delimit the range of gender behaviors and identities.

Theories from several fields offer explanations for gender role development. Biological theories attribute capabilities and personal qualities seen as masculine and feminine to the impact of chromosomes and hormones on how the body, including the brain, develops. Psychodyamic theories focus on the impact of children's internalization of their primary caretakers on the development of self-definition and gender identity. Psychological theories look at the impact of close interpersonal relationships, extending beyond parents to other family members and peers, focusing on how the child learns gender roles in interaction with others, often imitating others' behavior. Finally, cultural and anthropological theories consider the broader context of the cultural system, ranging from the arts to language, and how that shapes the individual performance of socially sanctioned norms.

Typically, gender roles, particularly when constructed as one for male children and adults and one for female children and adults, are not assigned equal value within a culture or society. However, there are great variations in gender role arrangements across cultures and historical eras. Gender roles are not universally construed. Across both time and place, there is evidence of great human plasticity in developing social systems in which groups of people have varying degrees of status and perform different kinds of functions within an established division of labor; sex generally has been a central feature of the organizational logic of these arrangements. But gender is not always linked to sexual anatomy. It is not a given across cultures or time periods either that there are only two sexes and two genders or that the roles remain the same. For example, in **Native** tribal nations of North America's Pacific Northwest, there were at least four genders until fairly recent times. Some of the anthropological research following Margaret Mead's work (O'Kelly and Carney 1986) has suggested that different types of cultures—hunter-gatherer, horticultural, agrarian, and industrial-capitalist—construct different gender role arrangements. Overall, hunter-gatherer and horticultural societies have tended to have the least division and most equality in gender roles while agrarian and industrial–capitalist societies have been most likely to create stratified gender roles emphasizing difference.

Contemporary Western societies believe that there are two sexes and a corresponding set of gender roles. In the latter half of the nineteenth century, an era sometimes referred to as the Victorian Age and the Industrial Revolution, medical and social theories flourished that asserted that men and women were best understood as physiological and psychological opposites. Separate social spheres, the public world for men and the private or domestic world for women, were seen as logical extensions or manifestations of these innate differences. The legacy of this viewpoint is still evident today. Masculinity is frequently described as manifesting itself in qualities such as, aggressiveness, dominance, rationality, objectivity, task orientation, and a propensity toward risk-taking. Conversely, femininity is widely seen as tendencies toward passivity, submission, emotionality, subjectivity, relationship orientation, and risk avoidance. These stereotypical configurations persist despite a growing recognition that most people are capable of both the instrumentality associated with masculinity and the expressivity associated with femininity and adjust their behavior in line with the specific circumstances of each situation they face, including the genders of the other people present.

In the majority of cultures where gender roles have been studied, female and male children are treated differently in significant ways from birth (given that the technology now exists to identify anatomical sex prior to birth, some would argue that this distinctive treatment can begin while the developing fetus is in the womb). These differences include: how infants are held, handled, dressed, and played with; what activities are encouraged and behaviors modeled; what verbal messages are given about who they are, how they should behave, and what kind of future lives they may expect. The implicit and explicit messages children receive regarding behaving in congruence with their gender roles, frequently pertain to the negative, that is, with whom they should *not* identify, what they should *not* do or wear or look like. LGBT youth are particularly likely to grow up feeling that many of the ways they are most drawn to expressing themselves are most likely to receive negative responses. Nonconformity to gender prescriptions of appropriate behavior are generally dealt with less harshly in **childhood** versus **adolescence**. For example, curiosity about the clothing of an older family member of a different gender may be viewed as inconsequential or amusing for a four-year-old, but sharply punished if encountered in child a few years older.

While gender role socialization begins in the family, other social institutions produce a myriad of messages about gender status and prescribed roles. These include policies and practices in the education, religion, government, media, and the **workplace**. In school settings, for example, beyond the heterosexist bias prominent in curricular materials, largely conveyed through the erasure of sexually diverse and gender transgressive individuals and groups, there are heterosexist biases in the unspoken **curriculum** of organizational structures and teachers' comments and other behaviors that privilege heterosexual students and relationships, and denigrate **queer** students and relationships. Individual boys and girls respond to and internalize these messages, in what is sometimes called a coconstruction process. That is, rather than being either a passive recipient of all cultural messages one receives, or being an entirely independent creator of one's gender role, each child interacts at interpersonal and group levels to adopt, perform, resist, and/or challenge gender, shaping a gender role that is both personal and social. Queer youth learn to take extra care in crafting gender performances that allow them to negotiate the landscape of **heteronormativity**, often by mimicking gender performances that are socially sanctioned and recognizing when they may switch style to communicate a queer identity to other LGBT youth and adults.

Historically, women have adopted masculine styles of clothing and behavior for a variety of reasons, including to pass as men in male-dominated occupations such as the military. In nineteenth century writings, there are numerous United States and British references to female couples who lived together in relationships similar to what later were referred to as butch-femme relationships, that is, one partner's behavior and appearance appeared similar to the role of a husband in a traditional heterosexual couple and the other partner's to the role of a wife. Radclyffe Hall's 1920 renowned novel, *The Well of Loneliness*, featured such a couple. Further, as women gained greater financial resources and with it, a greater sense of social independence, many "New Women" of the late nineteenth and early twentieth centuries changed to more "mannish styles of dress."

Feminists, especially those associated with the second wave of **feminism** of the 1960s and 1970s, have long argued that perceived gender differences are best understood as the result of social conditioning and political agendas rather than the expression of innate differences. The social movements of this era, including feminism and gay liberation, helped to usher in a considerable loosening of traditional gender roles. For example, the designation "androgynous" was used to refer to the presence of both feminine and masculine characteristics as youth more freely adopted dress and behaviors of the other gender.

Children and youth who resist a traditional gender role may be seen in one cultural setting, such as traditional Native American, as revealing a special and honored identity status of "Two Spirit," whereas in another it may be viewed as a "phase" or stage one is going through—although the degree of tolerance may vary by gender, a **"tomboy"** is often given greater childhood latitude than a **"sissy."** In a third culture, crossing gender boundaries may be seen as sufficiently negative as to require immediate intervention. Family members, peers, educators, and other onlookers may step in to discipline and attempt to "correct" such behaviors and attitudes. In fact, there are sometimes social movements aimed at reinforcing what are deemed correct, traditional gender roles. A contemporary example may be seen in the conservative Christian men's group, the Promise Keepers, begun in the early 1990s (Messner 1997).

If gender roles were the result of natural, innate, universal qualities, one may fairly ask whether such efforts would be required to reinforce stable gender boundaries. Likewise, if gender roles were viewed as representing a spectrum of equally valued variations in human expressiveness, rather than a limited set of hierarchically ranked positions, would so many societies suffer from misogyny and **homophobia**? Sex, gender, and sexuality have been defined in large measure in relation to one another. In the West, one is either male or female. If labeled male, one should be masculine, if labeled female, feminine. Masculine males should be attracted to feminine females. Heteronormativity assumes that sexual **desire** is based on sex and gender differences that "opposites" attract. When girls behave in ways associated with masculinity, for example, showing strong interest in participating in vigorous **sports**, or do not show interest in activities associated with femininity, these behaviors may be seen as indicators of homosexual interest. Likewise, boys who are drawn to activities associated with femininity, such as playing with dolls or dressing up in girls' or women's clothing, are likely to be perceived as gay. In heterosexist societies, individuals who identify as gay, lesbian, bisexual, queer, transgender, **transsexual**, are frequently targets of verbal and physical **harassment** and social **discrimination**. Interestingly, **research** on homophobia has repeatedly found that those most likely to harbor homophobic attitudes are people whose beliefs and behaviors are most in line with traditional, polarized notions about gender roles (Sears and Williams 1997).

How do gender roles relate to sexuality? Based on a heteronormative model, a feminine sexuality would be passively dependent on a masculine partner's more autonomous sexuality. Women defying social expectations with sexual behaviors, such as initiating and leading, are frequently viewed as a destructive force, negatively effecting men, the family, and society at large, though they are likely to be portrayed in popular media as thrilling and glamorous, as in the femme fatales in much **film** noir. Conversely, men who do not follow these guidelines are likely to be ridiculed as "unmanly" and repudiating a birthright, although they can be held up as comic relief in popular culture through film and television.

Gender role performance and gender identity are being reexamined; their reliance on the core rigidity of this dualistic system is being scrutinized. For example, those who identify as Drag King/Queen, Butch/Femme, and even terms such as top/bottom and S/M rely upon a traditional gender duality of contrasting performances and expectations. However, through the efforts of queer and feminist theories, gender is increasingly being understood as comprising more than the two options of masculine or feminine; instead it might be viewed as a spectrum of qualities, tendencies, and behaviors. We may variously see gender roles as a necessity, as rich resources of individual and cultural expression and identity, as archaic and unwarranted, as repressive and harmful mechanisms of social control. In any case, the continuing existence of gender roles in most societies tells us that structuring many social arrangements and institutions around apparent differences in anatomy between biological males and females and the largely assumed and very controversial psychological differences between women and men, continues to serve significant social functions. Educators can provide students ample evidence of alternative perspectives on gender roles and interrupt these simplistic and oppressive binaries by choice of curricular materials, use of examples, and ways of responding to students.

Bibliography

Bornstein, Kate. 1995. *Gender Outlaw: On Men, Women, and the Rest of Us*. New York: Vintage Books.

Connell, Robert W. 2002. *Gender*. Cambridge, UK: Polity.

Kessler, Suzanne, and Wendy McKenna. 1985. *Gender: An Ethnomethodological Approach*. Chicago: University of Chicago Press.

Messner, Michael. 1997. *Politics of Masculinities: Men in Movements*. Thousand Oaks, CA: Sage.

Nestle, Joan, ed. 1992. *The Persistent Desire: A Femme-Butch Reader*. Boston: Alyson.

O'Kelly, Charlotte G., and Larry S. Carney. 1986. *Women and Men in Society*. 2nd ed. Belmont, CA: Wadsworth.

Ramet, Sabrina, ed. 1996. *Gender Reversals and Gender Cultures: Anthropological and Historical Perspectives*. London and New York: Routledge.

Rottnek, Matthew, ed. 1999. *Sissies and Tomboys: Gender Nonconformity and Homosexual Childhood*. New York: New York University.

Sears, James T., and Walter L. Williams, eds. 1997. *Overcoming Heterosexism and Homophobia: Strategies That Work*. New York: Columbia University Press.

Whitehead, Stephen. 2002. *Men and Masculinities: Key Themes and New Directions*. Cambridge, UK: Polity Press.

Web Sites

About Gender. December 2004. Derby TV/TS Group. Accessed December 15, 2004. http://www.gender.org.uk/about/. This site features detailed discussions on aspects of gender from psychoanalysis to genetics.

BUBL Information Service. 2004. Andersonian Library, Strathclyde University, Glasgow, Scotland. Accessed December 15, 2004. http://bubl.ac.uk/link/g/genderstudies.htm. An excellent selection of Internet resources related to gender studies.

Gender and Sexuality. Eserver, Iowa State University. Accessed December 15, 2004. http://eserver.org/gender/. Useful collection of links on gender and sexuality.

Gender Studies. Voice of the Shuttle, Department of English at University of California at Santa Barbara. Accessed December 15, 2004. http://vos.ucsb.edu/browse.asp?id=2711.

The extensive set of links on this page are organized into categories ranging from Women's Studies to Cybergender & Techgender.

The International Foundation for Gender Education. December 2004. Accessed December 10, 2004. http://www.ifge.org/. Serves as an information provider and clearinghouse for referrals about all matters which are transgressive of established social gender norms.

Geography, Teaching of

Judy Hemingway

Although the scope of current geography goes well beyond established concerns with maps, geographical education in schools and colleges is marked by a reluctance to address "difficult" topics, especially those relating to the visceral lifeworlds of young people. This disciplinary reserve or "squeamishness" is particularly striking with regard to sex and sexuality. A survey of the contents of contemporary examination syllabi and popular high school and college geography textbooks evidences such conservatism. This denial of a vital aspect of human existence endorses sexual illiteracy and promotes intolerance and injustice. Specifically, it disenfranchises **lesbian, gay, bisexual, transgender,** and questioning youth who fall outside the heterosexual norms in which geography and society alike are embedded. The neglect of sex and sexuality in undergraduate geography, however, stands in distinct contrast to recent trends in academic branches of the discipline. Applying these developments, progressive teachers can be better equipped to identify themes and strategies for exploration in geography classrooms. Further, employing **critical social theory,** affirmative pedagogies can build upon the everyday experiences of young people whose needs, wants, and desires remain largely unvoiced, and thereby act as agents of change. By connecting recent geographical inquiry with radicalizing student-centered pedagogic practices **"compulsory heterosexuality"** can be resisted and minds opened to the possibility of diverse forms of sexual citizenship.

Pioneering **research** on the geographies of sex and sexuality emerged in the early 1980s and expanded during the 1990s. This branch of scholarship continues to burgeon as the degree to which sexuality is entwined in social imaginations, identifications, and representations is realized. These democratizing advances, achieved notably in the subdisciplinary fields of social and cultural geography, have been articulated principally by anglophone geographers in North America, Britain, **New Zealand,** and **Australia.** In providing a useful overview of intellectual shifts, the American geographers Michael Brown and Larry Knopp (2003) have recorded the growth of **"queer"** geographies, constructively outlining suggestions for future trajectories of scholastic inquiry. Similarly, the radical British geographers Alison Blunt and Jane Wills (2000) have documented, among a number of dissident geographies, the history and conceptual foundations underpinning geographies of **desire.**

See also Curriculum, Secondary; Curriculum, Higher Education; LGBT Studies; Literature, College; Queer Pedagogy; Queer Studies.

Attuned to and spurred by a general emancipatory movement across the social sciences, geographers have opposed the tyranny of silence that marginalizes those labelled as sexual nonconformists by vigorously promoting "difference" or the "right to be." At the same time, and from a disciplinary stance, they have explored how space influences myriad aspects of daily social, sexual, cultural, and economic life. Geographical investigations have highlighted how space can be used in the service of in/excluding certain groups so that while some are deemed to be "in place" others are rendered "out of place" (Cresswell 1996). Analytically, this profound modification of how it is possible to think about space foregrounds how supposedly neutral spaces are imbued with meaning and social intent. Geographers have shown, explicitly, how streets, shops, homes, communal open spaces, work places, and educational establishments are sexualized.

These environments, familiar to students, can be explored by teachers and learners for their heteronormative underpinnings: advertising images on billboards; canned **music** lyrics in malls; the use of domestic rooms for specific purposes such as bedrooms for heterosexual coupling; public signs of romantic courtship (kissing, holding of hands); and the dress codes of teaching staff. Significantly, by showing that space is socially constructed rather than fixed, geographical endeavor has also indicated how "straight" space can be contested, even momentarily "queered" by, for instance, Gay Pride marches and demonstrations, lesbian teams playing on ball fields, and gay couples dancing in "straight" nightclubs (Cresswell 1996). These events provide lesson material for interrogating **urban** space and metrocentric lifestyles. Similarly, nonmetropolitan areas such as **rural** North Dakota (Kramer 1995) can be probed for examples in which the construction of space as heterosexual is challenged since bars, bookstores, parking lots, and public restrooms can be gay as well as "straight." The singularity of space can also be contested in holiday destinations, for instance the Spanish resort of Sitges, where the "straight" daytime beach becomes gay at night.

Raising the visibility and audibility of sexual minorities, reveals rather than conceals "difference"—an aim of these unsettling geographers and geographies. The groundbreaking and theoretically-informed volume covering a diversity of sexual orientations and experiences in **Europe**, America, Australia, **Africa**, and the Pacific, edited by British geographers David Bell and Gill Valentine (1995), illustrates this point. Jon Binnie's (1995) chapter, for instance, investigates the sexualization and promotion of Amsterdam and London's Soho district as gay centers. Contrastingly, the focus of Lynda Johnston and Gill Valentine (1995) on the space of the home offers an account of lesbian identity performance and surveillance in New Zealand.

Of greater significance though, with regard to democratic potential, are the powerful theoretical frameworks, investigative tools, and politicizing strategies that have been developed by a broader spectrum of critical geographers. What has been demonstrated is that the surveying of sexualities, that is the literal and figurative plotting of lesbian, gay, bisexual, and transgender concerns on the disciplinary map, does not go far enough. To chart is not to liberate. The roots of oppression are not confronted; sexual **prejudice** is not unlearned. Arguably, the more demanding challenge tackled by radical geographers has been the development of intellectual apparatuses that assist in unpacking the mechanisms of subjugation that daily confront gender nonconformists. Critical geography teachers reject "knee-jerk inclusivism" to facilitate the rethinking of lived experience from the perspectives of peripherally-located sexual dissidents.

Thus, the disruption of naturalized heterosexuality in day-to-day **communication** presents a major task for geographers and teachers of geography. It is also one that can be tackled in classrooms by deconstructing the language used in geography texts. As a pedagogical device, teaching resources frequently refer to "typical" families as a means of introducing commonly-taught geographical themes such as employment. Characteristically, and in order to maintain economic growth, families are composed of role-defined members. "Husbands" are naturally "fathers" wedded to dutifully fertile "wives" who are the "mothers" of obligatory children. Upholding traditional "family values" and conforming to social expectations, the "father" is likely to work outside the home to support his dependents, whereas the "wife" will undertake domestic chores and possibly temporary part-time employment to facilitate the bearing and raising of offspring. It is within such conventional family units that "childlessness" tends to be negatively portrayed, not only as biologically abnormal, but also socially irresponsible. Those who have not procreated are regarded as contributing to the moral, economic, and, in times of dwindling populations, national decline. It is by interrogating the everyday language used in geographical literature that critical teachers and students can begin to queer(y) the way in which words powerfully sustain heteronormative institutions, in this case marriage.

Discriminatory processes may also be more easily observable. This is witnessed in the spatial regulation or ghettoization of homosexuality whereby certain locations, predominantly gentrified urban housing and leisure areas, become identified as "gay" or "lesbian" or read as queer texts. Such boundary-making distinctions are not, however, unproblematic since **sexual orientation** is not necessarily a marker of separateness from society. What becomes important to realize is that both invisible and readily apprehended means of repression (and resistance to that oppression), are materially enacted in everyday life and in the diverse public and private places and spaces of work, study, recreation, and repose (Pain 2001).

One of the spheres in which sexuality is least discussed, yet where the need is paramount, is formal schooling (which is not to deny the value of informal or "street" learning that takes place in schools and colleges). Yet, "the subjects of sexuality and **sexual identity** remain virtually untouched in English primary and secondary schools" (Atkinson 2002, 119). Geography is unexempt from this criticism on either side of the Atlantic.

Corrin and David Flint's (2001) nuanced reporting of homosexuality and the city offers a rare instance of curricular daring. Their account makes legible lesbian facilities in Paris, which include social centers, cinemas, and bookshops, as well as gay male social venues in the English resort of Brighton, such as cottages or tea rooms, cruising grounds, and gay saunas. Their study also highlights some of the problems associated with forms of representation, such as distribution mapping in which symbols are used to locate clusters of selected phenomena, in this case gay men and lesbian women. For not all gay people live in the clusters plotted, and neither are all those shown in a cluster necessarily lesbian, gay, bisexual, or transgender.

Developing links between progressive strands of education and professional geography, such as politicizing awareness of space, geography teachers in schools and colleges can contribute to constructive social change, including civil rights for those who enjoy nonheterosexual lifestyles and same-sex relationships. An empowering **curriculum** and "pedagogy of affirmation" (Kincheloe and Steinberg 1997, 250) would also help queer youth better recognize, express, and understand their oppressions. Although not geographical, Web sites listed at the end of this entry can suggest ideas and approaches for discussion and classroom activities.

Together, radical geographical knowledges and unauthorized educational methods hold open the potential of enfranchising students who are marginalized along diverse axes: the established categories of **race, social class,** and gender; and the newer alignments of age, **ethnicity,** and sexuality. Importantly, while making oppression and repression observable, which is to acknowledge that the peripheries which sexual dissidents often inhabit can be unbearably painful places, the greater challenge to critical pedagogic practitioners is the development of emancipatory curricula and procedures that provide operational images of better futures; that is, of making materially possible a more sexually liberal and just society where there is no place for homophobic **bullying.** An initial step toward these goals may well lie in the mobilization of approaches that reveal that curriculum subjects are not asexual.

In taking **heteronormativity** out of the realm of the assumed or naturalized commonsensical understanding, it is useful in a geographical context to reference demographic or population studies. It is possible to engage with this well-established syllabus topic in school and college geography through one of David Waugh's (1997) widely-used textbooks. The extent to which heterosexuality is privileged in geography can be demonstrated by reference to age-sex pyramids whether at the scale of continents, countries, regions, or cities. Unproblematically divided into a binary opposition of male and female, these structural representations of populations allow for no alternative sexual identities, which is to render sexual dissidents "missing subjects." In these age–sex diagrams which are concerned chiefly, for the purposes of strategic planning, with the effects of fluctuating birth and death rates and migration, heterosexuality is presented as the norm. Indeed, Waugh (1997, 94) writes that in order to maintain a stable population "each woman needs to have, on average, 2.1 children." For those women and men who resist reproduction or for whom fertility is not an issue, this heteronormative statement is one that marginalizes. Similarly, references to contraception as a means of controlling population growth estrange sexual dissidents since once again heterosexuality is presented as the norm. Criticalist geography pedagogues can work with students on an array of materials both formal (for instance textbooks, maps, and other officially-sanctioned "educational" resources) and popular (including **films,** magazines, and advertizing materials) in order to denaturalize (hetero)normativity or "what ought to be." In contesting heterosexual assumptions, decloseting strategies can work toward more inclusive versions of sexual citizenship where hitherto excluded lesbian, gay, bisexual, and transgender youth would belong. This move toward inclusivity is, nevertheless, double-edged since there are some "queers" who do not seek assimilation into society's mainstream and whose active choice is "outsiderness."

Bibliography

Atkinson, Elizabeth. 2002. "Education for Diversity in a Multisexual Society: Negotiating the Contradictions of Contemporary Discourse." *Sex Education* 2, no. 2: 119–132.

Bell, David, and Gill Valentine, eds. 1995. *Mapping Desire: Geographies of Sexualities.* London: Routledge.

Binnie, Jon. 1995. "Trading Places: Consumption, Sexuality and the Production of Queer Space." Pp. 182–199 in *Mapping Desire: Geographies of Sexualities.* Edited by David Bell and Gill Valentine. London: Routledge.

Blunt, Alison, and Jane Wills. 2000. *Dissident Geographies: An Introduction to Radical Ideas and Practice.* Harlow: Prentice Hall.

Brown, Michael, and Larry Knopp. 2003. "Queer Cultural Geographies—We're Here! We're Queer! We're Over There, Too!" Pp. 313–324 in *Handbook of Cultural Geography*. Edited by Kay Anderson, Mona Domosh, Steve Pile, and Nigel Thrift. London: Sage.

Cresswell, Tim. 1996. *In Place/Out of Place: Geography, Ideology, and Transgression*. Minneapolis: University of Minnesota Press.

Flint, Corrin, and David Flint. 2001. *Urbanisation: Changing Environments*. 2nd ed. London: Collins Educational.

Johnston, Lynda, and Gill Valentine. 1995. "Wherever I Lay My Girlfriend, That's My Home: The Performance and Surveillance of Lesbian Identities in Domestic Environments." Pp. 99–113 in *Mapping Desire: Geographies of Sexualities*. Edited by David Bell and Gill Valentine. London: Routledge.

Kincheloe, Joe L., and Shirley R. Steinberg. 1997. *Changing Multiculturalism*. Buckingham: Open University Press.

Kramer, Jerry Lee. 1995. "Bachelor Farmers and Spinsters: Gay and Lesbian Identities and Communities in Rural North Dakota." Pp. 200–213 in *Mapping Desire: Geographies of Sexualities*. Edited by David Bell and Gill Valentine. London: Routledge.

Pain, Rachel. 2001. "Geographies of Gender and Sexuality." Pp. 120–140 in *Introducing Social Geographies*. Edited by Rachel Pain, Michael Barke, Duncan Fuller, Jamie Gough, Robert MacFarlane, and Graham Mowl. London: Arnold.

Waugh, David. 1997. *The UK & Europe*. Walton-on-Thames: Thomas Nelson and Sons.

Web Sites

Schools Out! December 2004. Accessed December 15, 2004. http://www.schools-out.org.uk. Working toward multisexual equality in education, this antidiscriminatory organization provides resources and strategies for those teachers wanting to explore a range of LGBT issues. The Web site also contains innovative lesson plans for use across the full age-range of compulsory schooling.

Stonewall. November 2004. Accessed December 15, 2004. http://www.stonewall.org.uk. Premised on the conviction that every child has the right to learning environments that are safe, supportive, and respectful, *Stonewall* campaigns in support of sexual minority youth. Its information bank holds a section on education that deals with matters including the law and homophobic bullying.

Tatchell, Peter. December 2004. Accessed December 15, 2004. http://www.petertatchell.net. Among the concerns of the international "queer" rights activist Peter Tatchell, an iconic figure closely associated with the direct action group *Outrage!*, is the promotion of sexual literacy among adolescents. Contending that sexual rights are human rights, Tatchell's Web site includes publications dealing with teenage sex education.

Gifted Education, LGBT Youth in

Terence P. Friedrichs

Gifted youth, compared to same-age peers, demonstrate high potential or excellent performance on various skills highly valued by schools and communities (Hallahan and Kauffman 1994). Recently, the term "gifted" has expanded beyond its historical core of intellectual and academic competencies to encompass other school-based skills, including creativity, visual and performing arts, leadership, and, at

See also Mentoring; Resiliency.

times, athletics. Further, some theorists have attempted to broaden the definition of giftedness, so that a child's "giftedness" can be judged not only by school authorities, but also by experts from those students' racial-minority, disability, or sexual-minority communities (Davis and Rimm 1998). **Lesbian, gay, bisexual,** and **transgender** (LGBT) **youth** appear to meet federal, professional, or cultural definitions of giftedness at least as frequently as similarly-sized student populations do and have access to increasingly-available advocacy and resource options (Cohn 2002; Friedrichs 2005; Peterson and Rischar 2000).

The precise prevalence of "gifted LGBT" youth will depend on the breadth of the definitions for "gifted" and "LGBT." According to some gifted education authorities, if the definition of gifted is a traditional one—based on students' attainment of scores in the uppermost portion of the general population on intelligence or achievement tests—then the gifted population will be 1-to-2 percent (Davis and Rimm 1998; Hallahan and Kauffman 1994). If giftedness, however, is defined as participation in a school-based gifted program, then about 6 percent of youth will be considered gifted (National Center for Education Statistics 2002). And, should giftedness be viewed simply as displaying one or more school-based criteria for outstanding performance, then the percentage will be as high as 20 percent or more of the overall population (Hallahan and Kauffman 1994).

"Sexual-minority" youth also vary in prevalence, depending on whether "LGBT" students are defined by their identities, same-sex feelings, or same-sex sexual behaviors. If one uses the definitions least likely to cause confusion (i.e., "gifted," as those students in gifted programs, and "LGBT," as youth with LGBT identities), then there may be as many as 260,000 gifted LGBT students across the United States (Friedrichs 2005). Friedrichs and Etheridge (1995), in a survey of eight U.S. metropolitan LGBT social-and-support groups, found that there can be many gifted-LGBT youth in some localities. Thirty-six percent of the 53 youth in these groups (including 24 percent of the boys and 48 percent of the girls) were enrolled in programs for the gifted. Of these students, all but two had IQ scores over 130, had grade-point averages of 3.5, or had won awards for creativity, leadership, or athletics, either at school or in the community.

Only limited data exist on possible causal or correlative explanations for these and other LGBT students' excellent performance on teachers' varied gifted-assessment measures. The students' intellectual giftedness may be connected with their oral language skills. Their dedication to, and excellence in, academics and leadership may reflect, in some cases, a desire to compensate for their "second-class" LGBT status (Peterson and Rischar 2000). Their creativity, as with many students' divergent thinking, has been attributed, in part, to socialization in a creative sexual-minority community. For many types of high-potential LGBT students, their teachers may often nominate them for gifted programs because these youth may fit stereotypical notions of the well-spoken, strongly academic, and conventionally-creative pupils whom educators like to see in such programs (Davis and Rimm 1998). In **sports,** where there seem to be fewer open, excelling LGBT youth, there is uncertainty over precisely which factors most prevent LGBT youth from doing well. Friedrichs (2005) found that athletically-gifted LGBT youth vastly preferred individual to team sports, but these subjects did not specify the reason for this preference.

There are different strategies for teaching the varied groups of gifted LGBT students, depending on whether they excel in intelligence, achievement, creativity, visual or performing arts, leadership, or athletics. However, certain common instructional recommendations can be made across gifts (NAGC 2001). Gifted LGBT students, for example, can be provided with psychologically safe spaces in which to concentrate on their strengths. They should be able to engage in journal writing, class discussions, or private conversations with teachers about their same-sex feelings and **sexual identity**. They also should be able to delve into a **curriculum** that includes, for example, sexual minority **history**, **literature**, and **art**, as well as **sexuality education**, **dance**, sports, and **physical education** that are inclusive of LGBT issues and persons. Interacting, too, with LGBT peers, teachers, and counselors within school environments sensitive to LGBT culture is certainly helpful to all LGBT youth, but particularly beneficial to gifted sexual-minority students, with their early and strong interest in, and/or identification with, the LGBT community.

There are at least three support and advocacy approaches that educators can use as they work with LGBT gifted youth. First, educators can assist **gay–straight alliances** (GSAs), taking initial inventories of outstanding student strengths and subsequently finding opportunities for youth with those strengths. In GSAs, these students can develop their talents (particularly creative, artistic, and leadership skills), as they expand awareness about their LGBT identities and civil rights, through networking opportunities with other youth, at local, statewide, or regional LGBT conferences.

Educators also can provide various high-potential LGBT youth, whether they are GSA participants or not, with information about and encouragement to attend broader community activities related to their strengths. One such activity, for a promising LGBT actor, might be a tryout for a community play, whereas another opportunity, for a high-potential mathematician, might be an appropriately-challenging university math class.

Third, educators can link gifted LGBT students to intensive community mentorships in their fields of strength. Thus, a student talented in creative writing can study under a LGBT professional writer, whereas another youth with communication and organizing gifts can expand skills at a community-based **HIV education** center.

The Council for Exceptional Children's (CEC's) GLB Caucus, since 1995, has undertaken education, support, and advocacy efforts for gifted-education and special-education teachers of LGBT youth. And the National Association for Gifted Children (NAGC), since 1998, has had a LGBT Task Force (NAGC-LGBT), which studies the well-being of America's gifted LGBT youth, examines the status of LGBT issues in NAGC, and disseminates basic information on gifted LGBT youth. In 1998, NAGC passed a LGBT-inclusive nondiscrimination resolution for its members and, in 2001, approved a position paper encouraging teachers to treat sexual minorities equitably and sensitively.

Bibliography

Cohn, Sanford, 2002. "Gifted Students who are Gay, Lesbian, or Bisexual." Pp. 145–153 in *Social and Emotional Needs of Gifted Children: What Do We Know?* Edited by Maureen Neihart, Sally M. Reis, Nancy M. Robinson, and Sidney M. Moon. Washington, DC: National Association for Gifted Children.

Davis, Gary A., and Sylvia B. Rimm. 1998. *Education of the Gifted and Talented*. Needham Heights, MA: Allyn and Bacon.

Friedrichs, Terence P., and Regina L. Etheridge. 1995. "Gifted and Gay—Reasons to Help." *The Association for the Gifted (TAG) Newsletter* 17, no. 1: 4–5.

———. 2005. *Contextual Social and Emotional Needs, and Preferred Instructional Approaches for Gifted Gay-and-Bisexual Male Adolescents*. Ed.D. dissertation for University of St. Thomas, Minneapolis, MN (available through UMI, Ann Arbor, MI).

Hallahan, Daniel P., and James M. Kauffman. 1994. *Exceptional Children: Introduction to Special Education*. Boston: Allyn and Bacon.

National Association for Gifted Children. 2001. Position Paper on the Education of Gifted Students who are Gay, Lesbian, Bisexual, or Transgendered. Washington, DC: Author.

National Center for Education Statistics. 2002. *Digest of Education Statistics*. Washington, DC: U.S. Department of Education.

Peterson, Jean S., and Suzanne Rischar. 2000. "Gifted and Gay: The Adolescent Experience." *Gifted Child Quarterly* 43: 430–444.

Web Sites

Council for Exceptional Children. June 2005. Accessed May 30, 2005. http://www.cec.org. CEC's Web site refers to CEC's policy statements and its purchasable collection of articles related to equity for exceptional LGBT students.

National Association for Gifted Children. 2005. Accessed May 30, 2005. http://www. nagc. org. This site alludes to NAGC's purchasable position papers on the appropriate education of gifted LGBT youth and other underrepresented gifted populations.

GLBT Educational Equity (GLEE)

Timothy Bedford

GLBT Educational Equity (GLEE) is an action research project based at Oulu University in Finland that coempowers teachers to promote lesbian, gay, bisexual, and transgender (LGBT) equity in schools. The project, established in 1999 with funding from the European Union's (EU) Comenius programme, has developed a leadership training course to raise awareness of LGBT issues and for participating teachers to develop an action plan for their school communities. An **Internet**-based support network, GLEENET, assists teachers in carrying out these plans. This has online resources as well as communication facilities sustaining a network of educators to counter **homophobia** and **heterosexism** in European schools. Actions by participants have included teacher training, **curriculum** development, and **research** in LGBT issues.

In 1999, the European Union Treaty of Amsterdam came into force and its Article 13 gave the EU authority to adopt measures against **discrimination** based on **sexual orientation**. This marked a turning point in efforts to counter discrimination in Europe. There followed EU directives (2000/78/EC) prohibiting discrimination in employment and training on grounds of a person's religion or belief, disability, age, or sexual orientation.

August 2003 marked the elimination of the last law in Europe outlawing sexual relationships between people of the same gender. Despite this some countries still have discriminatory provisions in the criminal law, and most European countries such as Italy and Poland provide no legal recognition for same-sex partners. In a European survey, the Netherlands came out on top, closely followed by Denmark, Sweden, and **France** (The Greens/EFA in the European Parliament, 2001). In these countries there was depenalization of homosexuality and absence of other discriminatory laws, equal age of consent and freedom of association, antidiscrimination

See also Antibias Curriculum; Europe, LGBT Youth and Issues in; Professional Educational Organizations.

laws, registered partnership or marriage, and asylum laws. **Adoption** by same-sex couples, however, was only possible in the Netherlands.

Despite legal equality, discrimination continues even in countries where there are the most progressive laws. In 2002, for example, the Dutch Society for Integration of Homosexuality, COC, organized a survey of students and teachers on homosexuality in school, receiving about 500 responses. LGBT students often felt threatened by other students and they

> complained of bullying, nasty jokes and physical and mental abuse due to their sexual orientation. In a large number of schools homosexuality was a taboo subject with lacking support from teachers and school boards. Pupils feel abandoned. Homosexual teachers feel isolated. The sad conclusion is: if we don't talk about it, it doesn't exist. (ILGA-Europe 2003, 16)

In countries where the laws do not exist, there is a greater degree of **activism** to improve the situation. For example, in the **United Kingdom**, a 1988 Act, **Section 28**, prohibited local authorities from "promoting" homosexuality and led to LGBT activism by teaching unions (it was repealed in 2003). Southern European countries have made up the most applications for the GLEE Leadership Course, the lack of LGBT civil rights being their main motivation for applying.

At both the national and European levels, there is a dearth of **research** on the extent of discrimination faced by LGBT youth, and even less on these youth in schools. In general, GLEE project participants from different European countries have noted that:

- name-calling and other forms of **bullying** occur daily in schools and are often ignored by teachers;
- LGBT people are usually invisible in the curriculum and **educational policies**;
- there is a lack of accurate information on sexuality and **sexual identity**;
- LGBT youth often experience confusion, fear, alienation, and low self-esteem;
- schools are places where LGBT students experience **prejudice** and discrimination; and
- intervention programs to address LGBT issues in schools are rare

These findings tend to support the little extant data (Douglas et al. 1997; Rivers 1995). There are, however, notable differences between and within countries, especially between **urban** and **rural** areas and between regions with centralized or decentralized school systems. For example, in Berlin, the Senate has passed AV27, which is an instruction to incorporate LGBT issues into all school subject areas. This does not exist in other parts of Germany because the education system is decentralized, and in more rural Bavaria, many LGBT teachers are closeted, fear parental reactions, and have had negative experiences.

Although it is difficult to generalize across Europe, effective interventions in the schools to counter homophobia and heterosexism are rare and underresearched. There is an absence of teacher in-service education on sexual diversity. Although some counter-homophobia materials and LGBT inclusive curricula have been developed in various European countries, they have not been used extensively and effectively, as most teachers lack the skills, confidence, and support to address sexuality issues. Typically, where interventions in schools have taken place, they have been characterised by "one off" events arranged by a person or body external to the school (e.g., inviting a LGBT speaker into class or to talk to a group of teachers). In response, a team of educators from Europe and the education director from the **Gay Lesbian Straight Education Network** (GLSEN) have developed an international leadership training course for teachers to raise awareness of discrimination, coempower teachers to carry out actions in their school communities, develop international projects, and apply for funding from the EU.

GLEENET is one of the key tools in this effort. This Internet-based support network provides a resource center as well as a safe space for on-going **communication** among participating teachers to share ideas and collectively to develop materials for local action. GLEENET is a part of a new pedagogy, known as Web Assisted Transformative Pedagogy (WATP), developed for the leadership training course with GLEENET providing the Web-assisted element. WATP is based on theories on transformative learning, **multicultural education**, and discrimination, and data collected during the project on homophobia and heterosexism in schools, the transformative elements of WATP and GLEENET, and teachers' actions in schools.

There have been leadership training courses in August 2000 and July 2002, both in Oulu, Finland. Following the first course, the Inequality in School transnational project was created. The project successfully obtained EU funding and involves schools from Portugal, the United Kingdom, and **Ireland**. The project activities in Portugal, for example, have included: (1) the development of school curricula with the integration of LGBT content into **dance** classes; (2) workshops for teachers to raise awareness of LGBT issues; (3) presentations at conferences, including a video of the dance lessons and discussion of strategies to integrate these issues; (4) a teachers' survey to gauge awareness and understanding about homophobia; and (5) school projects such as art and photo exhibitions to raise awareness about **racism** and homophobia.

The activities of the Irish partner focused on giving workshops and conferences to educate teachers about LGBT issues. Activities in the United Kingdom included presenting at the National Union of Teachers' conferences and integrating LGBT content into school curricula such as children's story books. One product of this project is the "EI Pack" for training teachers that includes lesson suggestions along with resources like photographs and games. Another product is a video, *How to Prevent Homophobia in Schools*, with guidelines for implementing a school-based project and interviews conducted during dance classes with students, ages seven to twelve as well as interviews with teachers about issues of homophobia.

Following the leadership training course in 2002, participants engaged in many different actions ranging from assessment surveys of the school culture for LGBT students to the development of a teacher training curriculum. In addition, Towards an Inclusive School was created as a partnership of schools from France, Germany, Austria, and Italy and received EU funding. This transnational project's focus is on training and curriculum development to promote inclusive schools.

Bibliography

Douglas, Nicola, Ian Warwick, Sophie Kemp, and Geoff Whitty. 1997. *Playing It Safe: Responses of Secondary School Teachers to Lesbian, Gay and Bisexual Pupils, Bullying, HIV and AIDS Education and Section 28.* London: Health and Education Research Unit. Institute of Education. University of London.

The Greens/EFA in the European Parliament. 2001. *EU Enlargement: A Gay Perspective. Report on a Public Hearing on the Position of Lesbian Women and Gay Men in the EU Accession Countries.* Brussels: Laurant and Bakker.

ILGA-Europe. 1998a. *Equality for Lesbians and Gay Men. A Relevant Issue in the Civil and Social Dialogue. A Report of ILGA-Europe, the European Region of the International Lesbian and Gay Association.* Vienna: Melzer Druck Ges.m.b.H.

———. 1998b. *After Amsterdam: Sexual Orientation and the European Union. A Guide.* Vienna: Melzer Druck Ges.m.b.H.

———. 2003. *IGLA Newsletter* 3, no. 3.

Rivers, Ian. 1995. "The Victimisation of Gay Teenagers in Schools: Homophobia in Education." *Pastoral Care* 3, March: 35–41.

Sheehan, B. 2000. *Education Lesbian and Gay Students. Developing Equal Opportunities.* Dublin: Gay HIV Strategies and Nexus Research Co-Operative.

Web Sites

European Unions Community Action Programme to Combat Social Exclusion, 2003–2006. Accessed May 28, 2005. http://europa.eu.int/comm/employment_social/soc-prot/soc-incl/faq_en.htm. Details the EU Action Programmes to support activities to combat discrimination on grounds of racial or ethnic origin, religion or belief, disability, age, or sexual orientation.

GLEE. February 25, 2003. Accessed May 28, 2005. http://glee.oulu.fi. Gives general information about GLEE project activities and provides limited access to GLEENET, which contains an extensive resource center.

ILGA-Europe. May 2005. Accessed May 28, 2005. http://www.ilga-europe.org. Details of the European region of the International Lesbian and Gay Association (ILGA) work to achieve equal rights for lesbians, gay men, bisexuals and transgendered people.

Graffiti

Amardo Rodriguez

Graffiti allow for the purest kind of anonymous **communication**, providing a forum for forbidden and taboo topics. Although written in the privacy of a toilet stall, the writing of graffiti is an essentially social act, according to Bruner and Kelso (1980, 241): "To write graffiti is to communicate; one never finds graffiti where they cannot be seen by others." Sexual minority students on college/university and high school campuses encounter hostility through bathroom graffiti, which are typically derogatory and violent. They also use bathroom graffiti to challenge this hostility and to create a safe space for a variety of discourses that schools would prefer to suppress. The lack of explicit rules and protocols allow people to express themselves without the fear of social punishment that arises from any kind of violation. Graffiti, therefore, level the playing field by getting past factors such as social status, hierarchical

See also Feminism; Gender Roles; Harassment; School Safety and Safe School Zones.

position, education, access, familiarity with rules, expertise, and communication competence that privilege certain persons against others.

Gilmar and Brown (1983) allowed a class of high school students to produce graffiti on blackboards, revealing their thoughts and concerns. The exercise was conducive for discourse with other students who did not share any meaningful relationship and provided invaluable insight on the effectiveness of the curriculum:

- The world will end tomorrow.
- The world ended yesterday. You just didn't notice.
- I knew I missed something when I fell asleep in geometry.

Graffiti raise issues, subjects, and concerns that organizations would prefer remain silenced. Indeed, **college age students** often use graffiti to facilitate the communication of ideas and concerns that campuses either explicitly or implicitly discourage. Graffiti among lesbians, and between lesbians and heterosexual women, are particularly common in women's bathrooms on college campuses (Bruner and Kelso 1980; Cole 1991; Rodriguez and Clair 1999). Compared with the graffiti found in men's bathrooms on college campuses, most of these graffiti are lengthy, carefully crafted, and involve many discussants. Moreover, women's graffiti are more interactive and supportive. Women raise serious questions about such topics as love, how to handle sexual relations, and relationships. Also, they solicit advice and share experiences. For example:

- African American women. Look! Don't judge people. You don't understand homosexuality at all! If it was a choice I wouldn't choose it because of all this abuse.
- Why can't I just be myself in this world?
- Be yourself sista. I got your back.
- Goddess power Forevah!
- Dykes & Lesbians do what you please.

Graffiti fulfill an important social and psychological function. Hentschel (1987, 305) contends that women are aware that other women will respond to their graffiti: "Where direct communication is impossible or very restricted, women have discovered graffiti as an opportunity to express themselves openly, but safely. They have thereby turned graffiti into something completely different from what we have known them to be, giving them new meanings and new functions."

Many scholars posit that women use the bathrooms to build a community that is without the aggressive and hostile features that patriarchy fosters (Bruner and Kelso 1980). Similarly, Cole (1991) contends that women use graffiti to counter their subordinated position in a patriarchal society: "Because womyn are free to choose the topics [of discussion] . . . womyn are able to share interests and experiences they may not generally share with men. As a result, womyn's . . . . graffiti open avenues that call male dominance into question" (p. 403). For example:

- This has been a crazy and upsetting weekend for me. What should I do? My boyfriend didn't come home. I'm on probation. I lost my job and financial aid and can't really afford to be here without it. Should I just drop out or continue on part time until I'm off probation and get back the $$$. Help!

- You are not alone! Hang in there, that is what I am doing. Keep your health up . . . believe it or not, it has a tremendous effect on your outlook on life, Don't Give Up.

- Same here. My boyfriend came through. We both are having problems. This school is my main one. What do I do?

- I was on academic probation and they suspended me for a whole semester; my parents wouldn't speak to me and told me not to come home; for the first time I was on my own. I became pregnant and was up shits creak. I was very upset and none of my friends were able to help because it was difficult for them to relate to my problems. I found a job as a waitress at night and during the week worked a full time job, rented a room until I was able to find an apartment. Cooled out the whole semester. Now I'm back in school, have a job, my own apartment, and I'm enjoying life. Don't Give Up!

- I have my own problems which are shared by a lot of people and may seem small. Studying and tests are a bitch. They kick your ass and they slap your face. I'm looking for a good man like the one I had who can hold me; tell me it's gonna be alright. . . . When I find him my problems will be nearly solved. But until that day sisters, God be with you. Among the distressed but will survive. And I hope all of you will try.

- I hope that sister listens to all of y'all. You people are the first example of worthwhile and good bathroom communication and you show more maturity than most. All of y'all keep on keeping on and something good will come someday.

Both internationally and cross-culturally, the graffiti found in men's bathrooms are consistently different from that found in women's bathrooms (Innala and Ernulf 1992; Rodriguez and Clair 1999). These graffiti are more self-centered and competitive. Also, men make significantly more derogatory inscriptions—and homosexuals are one of the primary objects of denigration:

- Fags of [Name of school deleted] unite. If we don't AIDS will.
- So we can burn you together bitches.
- All you fags and dykes will burn for eternity.

Some scholars believe that the violent and sexually graphic nature of men's graffiti reflect the persistence of an infantile sexuality among many men. Others contend that higher authority and greater threat better explain men's graffiti. In other words, men use graffiti to intimidate groups who threaten their dominance.

The distinct differences between men's and women's graffiti continue to attract scholarly attention. Many scholars believe that sexual graffiti offer a great source of data on the extent and nature of the suppressed sexual **desires** of men and women and can even yield unique insights about sexual attraction, fantasy, behavior, and changing attitudes towards sexual minority groups.

Bibliography

Bruner, Edward M., and Jane P. Kelso. 1980. "Gender Differences in Graffiti: A Semiotic Perspective." *Women's Studies International Quarterly* 3: 239–252.

Cole, Caroline M. 1991. "Oh Wise Women of the Stalls." *Discourse & Society* 2: 401–411.

Gilmar, Sybil, and Doris Brown. 1983. "The Final Word on the Bright Adolescent or What to Do with Graffiti." *English Journal* 72: 42–46.

Hentschel, Elke. 1987. "Women's Graffiti." *Multilingual Journal of Cross-Cultural and Interlanguage Communication* 6: 287–308.

Innala, Sune M., and Kurt E. Ernulf. 1992. "Understanding Male Homosexual Attraction: An Analysis of Restroom Graffiti." *Journal of Social Behavior and Personality* 7: 503–510.

Rodriguez, Amardo, and Robin P. Clair. 1999. "Graffiti as Communication: Exploring the Discursive Tensions of Anonymous Texts." *Southern Communication Journal* 65: 1–15.

Stocker, Terrance L., Linda W. Dutcher, Stephen M. Hargrove, and Edwin A. Cook. 1972. "Social Analysis of Graffiti." *Journal of American Folklore* 85: 356–366.

Hall, G. Stanley (1844–1924)

Susan Talburt

Known as "the father of adolescence," G. Stanley Hall was born in Ashfield, Massachusetts. Hall's prolific work in child study lent scientific sanction to the cult of **childhood**, defined **adolescence** as a distinct life phase, justified reformers' programs for male youth, and formed a basis for such fields as child development, educational psychology, and mental testing. Reflecting late nineteenth-century concerns about the future of youth and society and changing gender relations, Hall's psychological and educational treatises advocated sex-segregated schooling for males in order to counter the emasculating, unnatural effects of civilization. As sexologists framed masturbation and homosexuality as effeminizing, Hall sought to cultivate masculinity through homosocial, or same-sex, bonds and to regulate male bonds through activity and adult supervision. Hall's advocacy of manly activities based on boys' natural interests in order to create disciplined young men denied the presence of the homoerotic or homosexual even as it sought to suppress it.

In 1878, Hall earned the first doctorate in psychology at Harvard University. Beginning with his early 1880s lectures on pedagogy at Harvard and his subsequent work on studying children's knowledge, beliefs, and interests in order to redirect teaching practices, Hall became a preeminent psychologist. During his appointment at Johns Hopkins University, he founded the *American Journal of Psychology* in 1887. In 1888, he assumed the first presidency of Clark University in Worcester, Massachusetts, where he founded the journal, *Pedagogical Seminary* three years later. He retired in 1920, four years before his death.

Hall worked in a time of social upheaval due to urbanization and industrialization and of scientific optimism about the progress of civilization. With social change and the rapid expansion of secondary schools, late nineteenth-century United States' education sought to inculcate self-discipline in youth in order to replace external authority with internal control. As scientists questioned the speculative nature of humanistic school curricula based on Western culture, educators were drawing on romantic ideas of European educators such as Rousseau, Pestalozzi, and Froebel to develop pedagogical methods of appealing to the natural interests of children.

Influenced by evolutionary theory as an explanation of the social order, Hall believed that heredity was more important than environment in determining individuals' traits. Believing that education should foster evolution according to natural abilities, he advocated "individualization" of educational methods and content according to sex, age, ability, and vocational possibilities. Hall also embraced romanticism's idealization of rural life, which cultivated health and vitality, as opposed to the city's unnatural diversions which endangered natural development. He promoted the protection of youths' virtue from degeneracy through elements of eugenics, including sterilization and segregation of the "unfit."

In the 1880s and 1890s Hall led the child study movement, gathering reports of children's play and physical development. He interpreted catalogs of children's

See also Gender Roles; Race and Racism; Scouting; Single-Sex Schools.

"natural" interests through an evolutionary framework to explain a natural order of development, which would offer a scientific basis for educational methods. Hall upheld the theory of recapitulation, the idea that "ontogeny recapitulates phylogeny," or that individual development follows the historical development of the race. Developing children expressed predispositions for activities that corresponded with "culture–epochs" of their races. Hall portrayed children as engaged by the imagination and impulses in a world apart from civilized adult society. Child study promoted cooperation, service to society, and sound health, a preoccupation of physicians and parents for some time. Hall worried that, like cities, schools inhibited physical vitality, which formed the basis for moral and mental development. He urged schools to undertake measurement, diagnosis, and training in muscular function in order to cultivate strong, moral young men. His work contributed to the placement of medical health officers in schools by 1910.

In his 1904 two-volume *Adolescence*, Hall formulated the modern concept of adolescence, which he called "a new birth, for the higher and more completely human traits are now born."(xiii) Adolescence was a unique phase corresponding to the race's progress from savagery to civilization. At puberty, the adolescent broke with the harmony of childhood and entered a period of upheaval during which he had to master instincts inherited from the past. Adolescence entailed possibilities of progress and dangers of degeneration. If savage instincts were not allowed a degree of expression, they might later emerge to disrupt adult life. Youth needed to pass through a period of juvenile behavior. Since only Caucasian races could evolve to the highest levels of civilization, adolescence was fundamentally a white middle-class phenomenon, dependent on adult guidance to develop self-disciplined males.

The key was to offer youth freedom while establishing order through suppression and control. **Adolescent sexuality** was at the center of Hall's concerns, which resonated with popular literature of the sexual hygiene movement by framing adolescence as a stage of storm and stress in need of protection. As sexuality entered the public sphere as an activity that included romance and pleasure, and as women's entry into the workplace eroded men and women's separate spheres, masculinity was increasingly in crisis. Closely linked to sexuality, masculinity was split between natural passions and civilized control. The late nineteenth-century male was ideally aggressive and assertive, yet able to master impulses through self-restraint. Manliness, like civilization, was a physical and moral standard to achieve. Hall favored frank **sexuality education** of youth to reduce vice and disease and to combat racial decline. Adolescent males' constant thoughts of sex meant that education should train the will and occupy youth in order to redirect sexual energy to appropriate outlets.

Hall believed that women were intrinsically different from men and that the sexes became increasingly distinguished through evolution. Some education was good preparation for her responsibilities as wife and mother. Concerned that female teachers were "feminizing" boys and neglecting to teach manly virtues, Hall advocated sex-segregated schooling and male teachers for boys, particularly during adolescence. Because Hall thought girls naturally regulated their sexual feelings, he focused on encouraging male self-control.

Although Hall praised sexual intercourse as integral to health and happiness, he considered masturbation to be an unnatural, dangerous vice that was "far more common among civilized than among savage races" (1904, 453). A particular concern in nineteenth-century America, masturbation was not only a sinful vice but a waste of nervous energy, as semen was considered a source of strength. Masturbators risked insanity, disease, weakening of mind and body, and emasculation. The too studious and unathletic were presumed to be masturbators. Puberty and schooling's indoor, sedentary nature increased temptation, leaving adolescent boys susceptible to civilization's emasculating tendencies. At the same time, overuse of the brain was thought to cause neurasthenia, a disease of middle-class men who lost their nervous force and suffered exhaustion as they competed for success. Although Hall did not address homosexuality in his writings, he surely had read European sexologists' writings about homosexuals, who, like masturbators and neurasthenics, offered another indication of feminization and mental and physical degeneration.

A virile education was needed to counteract the threats schools posed to boys by draining their nervous energies. Hall harnessed recapitulation as a means of developing savage boys into civilized, virile men. Hall came to idealize military virtues and patriotism as instilling aggressiveness and strength in young men, and advocated war games and **sports** in schools. These all-male activities would promote discipline, loyalty, service, cooperation, and solidarity among boys while discouraging unhealthy vices.

For reformers concerned with **prostitution**, gambling, smoking, and masturbation, Hall's ideas suggested that proper supervision of young men could advance the race. Halls' work justified the administration of middle-class adolescent males in gender-segregated organizations such as the Boy Scouts of America and the Young Men's Christian Association. Those "character builders" borrowed Hall's idea that boys must live out their instincts, but under adult supervision (Macleod 1983). These reformers used Hall's suggestion that gangs were intrinsic to boys' evolutionary behaviors as a scientific rationale for channeling negative group interactions into cooperative, prosocial activities. They similarly appropriated recapitulation's idea that boys were savages as a rationale for camping. Overcivilized boys could be masculinized through primitive activities that would recapitulate natural racial development and cultivate virility, willfulness, and rationality while distracting boys from unnatural sexual temptations. A perfectible manhood and civilization could be realized through regulation of male homosociality.

Bibliography

Bederman, Gail. 1995. *Manliness and Civilization: A Cultural History of Gender and Race in the United States, 1880–1917.* Chicago and London: University of Chicago Press.

Curti, Merle. 1959. *The Social Ideas of American Educators.* Paterson, NJ: Pageant.

Hall, G. Stanley. 1904. *Adolescence: Its Psychology and Its Relations to Physiology, Anthropology, Sociology, Sex, Crime, Religion and Education.* 2 vols. New York: Appleton.

Lesko, Nancy. 2001. *Act Your Age! A Cultural Construction of Adolescence.* New York and London: RoutledgeFalmer.

Macleod, David I. 1983. *Building Character in the American Boy: The Boy Scouts, YMCA, and Their Forerunners, 1870–1920.* Madison: University of Wisconsin Press.

Ross, Dorothy. 1972. *G. Stanley Hall: The Psychologist as Prophet.* Chicago: University of Chicago Press.

Harassment

Benjamin Baez

Harassment is the physical or verbal abuse of a student by other students or school officials because of the student's suspected **sexual orientation**. Most **educational policies**, following legal principles, further qualify this definition by requiring that harassment include physical and verbal conduct that (1) creates a hostile environment by interfering with a student's educational opportunities and physical and psychological well-being, or (2) is seriously threatening or intimidating. When the harassment is sexual in nature, the term "sexual harassment" is used. "Harassment by association" refers to physical or verbal abuse directed at those students considered to be associated with suspected **lesbian, gay, bisexual,** or **transgender** (LGBT) students. "Harassment" is not synonymous with a "hate crime," although very severe physical or threatening forms of harassment may also constitute hate crimes. A hate crime is a criminal act in which the victim is selected because of his or her sexual orientation and can involve attacks both on persons and property; harassment, conversely, is usually not criminal (but civil) and does not include attacks on property.

Homophobia leads to pervasive harassment and violence against LGBT persons. LGBT students are not immune from such harassment in public schools despite the fact that school officials have considerably more leeway to deal with such harassment than do other public agencies. To better understand the context of harassment in schools, it is important to attend to the general violence against LGBT persons.

The murder of **Matthew Shepard**, in 1998, highlights the issue of violence against LGBT persons. Federal Bureau of Investigation (FBI) crime statistics show a large number of hate crimes motivated by the victim's sexual orientation. The FBI reports that 1,244 of 7,462 bias-motivated incidents (or 16 percent) in 2002 were based on sexual orientation. But even such a high number belies the real story, which is likely to be one of underreporting, since in certain cities, the FBI crimes statistics reflect zero hate crimes against LGBT persons. Same-sex domestic violence and rape are likely to be underreported, most likely because of fear of public exposure (since arrest reports are public records). Additionally, victims may fear further abuse by law enforcement officials. Thus, the disparity between the reports of crimes against LGBT persons and the reality of such crimes minimizes the problem of hate violence, a problem exacerbated by the fact that LGBT status is not included in hate crimes laws in the United States.

In the United States, the extent of homophobic harassment in schools has been reported by the American Civil Liberties Union (ACLU), the **Gay, Lesbian and Straight Education Network** (GLSEN), Parents, Families, and Friends of Lesbians and Gays (PFFLAG), and the Lambda Legal Defense and Education Fund The overwhelming majority of openly (and closeted) LGBT students report hearing homophobic remarks throughout the school day; direct physical and verbal harassment is not uncommon for LGBT students. **The GLBT Educational Equity** (GLEE) Project, commissioned and funded by the European Union, reported similar findings in

See also Activism, LGBT teachers; Antidiscrimination Policy; Bullying; Educational Policies; Graffiti; Legal Issues, students; Mental Health; Race and Racism; School Safety and Safe School Zones; Workplace Issues; Youth, At Risk.

European countries. Much of this harassment is homophobic in nature, such as antigay insults and physical abuse, but LGBT students also experience sexual harassment, which they are unlikely to report. School officials often contribute to the problem by making harassing remarks themselves or by failing to address such harassment when it occurs. The ACLU reports that such harassment is particularly pervasive in underserved **rural** communities, which have been largely unaffected by gains in urban school districts. About a million LGBT youth attend schools in small towns. Furthermore, a study by the Human Rights Watch finds that harassment against LGBT students of color is prevalent and is usually combined with racial and ethnic harassment.

As a result of harassment, LGBT students are more likely than their peers to skip school because of safety concerns. The Human Rights Watch study, confirming the findings in other national studies, found that these students are also likely to perform poorly in class, abandon school activities, or even suffer physical injury. Further, many LGBT students also suffer depression and resort to alcohol and drugs to cope with this harassment. Despite this evidence, school officials often ignore homophobia, which leads to harassment and hate crimes against LGBT students and their supporters.

Given the extent of the harassment of LGBT students, the physical and psychological problems it creates, and the inadequate responses from school officials, LGBT students have looked to the courts for a solution. In **Canada** and in many countries in **Europe**, for example, LGBT students are able to seek legal protection under national laws prohibiting sexual-orientation discrimination. The International Lesbian and Gay Association's survey of actual and proposed international policies indicates increased protection of LGBT individuals, including students. LGBT students in the United States, however, have few legal remedies. They can recover damages under Title IX of the Educational Amendments of 1972 from schools that *deliberately* fail to protect them from sexual harassment creating a hostile environment. The Office of Civil Rights of the Department of Education (OCR), which enforces Title IX, proposes that Title IX will not apply to mere heckling, suggesting that the severity and pervasiveness of the harassment will be important considerations. Nevertheless, courts have allowed LGBT students (and those perceived to be) to recover damages under Title IX from schools that fail to prevent their harassment by other students. In 2001, for example, a federal court held in *Henkle v. Gregory* that students can recover damages under Title IX from schools that fail to control severe and pervasive same-sex harassment.

When the harassment is pervasive and severe, LGBT students may recover damages under the United States Constitution's Fourteenth Amendment. In an important 1996 case, a federal court held in *Nabozny v. Podlesny* that a school that failed to protect a gay student from pervasive and extensive physical and verbal harassment violated his constitutional rights. This case seems an anomaly with regard to the support of constitutional rights for LGBT students, but it does support a general pattern of courts' intolerance for the failure of school officials to protect LGBT students from severe harassment by other students.

More likely, the systemic harassment and violence against LGBT students is addressed through hate speech/**hate crime** policies and laws at the local, national, state, and international levels. Courts, however, have turned down, under freedom-of-speech principles, codes and statutes that appear solely to get at the underlying message (i.e., codes prohibiting homophobic insults), but they have upheld codes and legislation that increase the punishment for bias-motivated crimes and conduct. But even those policies allowing for increased penalties still are vulnerable to legal challenges.

With regard to LGBT students, the free-speech issues associated with hate-speech codes create an important paradox. Hate-speech codes and antiharassment policies addressing verbal conduct have not only provided some protection against the harassment of LGBT students, but they also have contributed a tone of intolerance for homophobia. LGBT students, however, have gained more substantive rights under the freedom-of-expression principles than others. These freedoms have allowed LGBT students to express their progay perspectives and to organize with others to promote positive views of LGBT students. Thus, to argue for too great a prohibition of homophobic expression runs the risk of rolling back gains made by LGBT students under freedom-of-expression principles. Furthermore, many supportive groups argue that the best practice for eliminating homophobia, and thus harassment, is for schools to encourage honest and open discussion of homosexuality.

Indeed, the ACLU and other supportive groups report that hate speech/crimes policies are often advanced as *the* answers to bias-motivated violence, but that increased penalties is not enough. Although such policies set a general tone of tolerance, they do not deter hate violence against LGBT individuals. It must be remembered that the acts covered by such policies is already criminal (or in violation of campus policies), and the threat of increased punishment will not deter homophobic individuals. Thus, the best course for preventing harassment is addressing the attitudes that support it.

Since not all harassment can be addressed through legal means, it is important to look at how such harassment is addressed through nonlegal means. There has been a concerted attempt by local, national, and international organizations, such as the ACLU and the GLEE Project, to work with schools and other agencies to use education as a form of prevention. The ACLU, through its *Making Schools Safe Program*, and the GLEE Project offer training and information about harassment to schools.

To combat homophobic attitudes, antibigotry programs in all schools are crucial, as is curricula that include accurate information about sexual orientation, the history of the gay-rights movement, and sexual minority role models. In addition to targeting schools, antidiscrimination laws and policies are necessary to prevent sexual orientation **discrimination**. Furthermore, school and other officials must set a tone of intolerance for bigotry, condemning every instance of homophobic behavior.

In addition to combating homophobia in schools, LGBT students must have the right and support to express themselves in schools, and teachers must encourage all students to discuss homosexuality honestly and openly, while being careful to ensure that such discussion does not become harassing. Not all antigay expression is harassing and not all antigay harassment needs to be responded to by punishment. Educators engaging students in these discussions may be a better way to prevent future harassment than waiting for harassment to actually take place or to escalate further.

Harassment of LGBT students by teachers is less rare than that committed by their peers, although harassment by teachers may be more difficult for students because it involves a violation of trust. The legal remedies against teachers are similar to those of other school officials. LGBT students also may sue teachers and school officials individually, often under the state or provincial law of torts or applicable human rights legislation.

390

LGBT teachers are not immune from harassment, which can be perpetuated by colleagues or students, but they often have fewer rights than do students. Employment is often considered a privilege, not a right (unlike school attendance), and local and national legislation often do not protect teachers from harassment. Title IX offers protection against school officials for sexual harassment, and few human rights protect teachers and other employees from other forms of discrimination by school officials. Also the hate crime policies discussed before also offer teachers protection. But LGBT teachers have very little remedy against harassment by students, especially if the school **administrators** refuse to take action against those students.

Bibliography

Baker, Jean M. 2002. *How Homophobia Hurts Children: Nurturing Diversity at Home, at School, and in the Community.* Binghamton, NY: Harrington Park Press.

Department of Education. 1999. *Protecting Students from Harassment and Hate Crimes: A Guide for Schools.* Washington, D.C.: Office of Civil Rights, Department of Education.

Human Rights Watch. 2001, May. *Hatred in the Hallways: Violence and Discrimination Against Lesbian, Gay, Bisexual, and Transgender Students in U.S. Schools.* New York: Human Rights Watch.

Perrotti, Jeff, and Kim Westheimer. 2002. *When the Drama Club is Not Enough: Lessons from the Safe Schools Program for Gay and Lesbian Students.* Boston, MA: Beacon Press.

Web Sites

Crime in the United States 2002. December 2003. Federal Bureau of Investigation. Accessed December 5, 2004. http://www.fbi.gov/ucr/cius_02/html/web/offreported/offreported.html. Reports on the hate crimes motivated by, among other factors, sexual orientation.

Making Schools Safe for Gay Youth. June 2003. American Civil Liberties Union. Accessed December 4, 2004. http://www.aclu.org/safeschools/safe_schools.html. Comprehensive site includes information not only about the legal rights of LGBT youths but provides support for creating safe school environments for LGBT students.

World Legal Survey. May 2004. International Lesbian and Gay Association. Accessed December 5, 2004. http://www.ilga.org/files_target.asp?FileCategoryID=42. Provides information about progay activities in all countries. ILGA conducts a survey of international policies affecting LGBT individuals.

Hate Crimes

Penny J. Rice, Jeremy P. Hayes and Todd K. Herriott

Hate crimes are acts of violence, property damage, or the threat of such crimes, which are motivated in whole or part by the offender's bias based on **race**, religion, **ethnicity**, national origin, gender, physical or mental **disability**, or **sexual orientation** (United States Department of Justice 2001). A hate crime is meant to send a message

See also Antibias Curriculum; Antidiscrimination Policy; Bullying; Community LGBT Youth Groups; Harassment; Prejudice; School Safety and Safe School Zones; Sexual Abuse and Assault; Shephard, Matthew; Youth, At Risk.

to an entire community or group of people. Youth, in their formative years, are frequently the victims and perpetrators of hate crimes. Of the LGBT-related hate crimes reported to the National Coalition of Anti-Violence Programs (2004) in the United States, in 2003, 43 percent of offenders and more than one-fourth of victims were under the age of twenty-nine. Between 1990 and 1999, reports on hate crimes increased each year, with crimes perpetrated against **lesbian, gay, bisexual**, or **transgender** (LGBT) individuals increasing 328 percent during a time when serious crime continued to decrease nationally (Anti-Defamation League 2001).

The definition of a hate crime, and which categories of difference are included in the definition, vary internationally. The Hate Crimes Statistics Act of 1990 legally formalized the definition of hate crimes in the United States, and bias on the basis of sexual orientation is included. However, defining and reporting hate crimes is fraught with difficulties. First, the general public tends to believe that all violent crimes committed are "about hate" (Perry 2003, 2). Second, law enforcement agencies may lack the knowledge and understanding to recognize, report, and investigate hate crimes. Data collection, comparison, and even reporting are hampered by a lack of agreed upon terminology or understanding of what constitutes a hate crime. Additionally, the degree to which individual law enforcement agencies understand and address issues of sexual orientation varies.

There are also international concerns. Each country has different policies and practices in acknowledging or defining a hate crime. Countries emphasize different aspects of hate crimes, include different descriptors, and designate different populations as potential victims. Finally, what was once seen as culturally acceptable during one time period might be considered a hate crime during a different period. Although an increasing number of countries include sexual orientation in nondiscrimination laws, few countries include sexual orientation in their hate crime definitions. The United States and **Canada** include acts against religion, ethnicity, sexual orientation, age, and disability in defining hate crimes. Germany uses the terms politically-motivated violence, xenophobic criminality, and right-wing or left-wing extremism. Racial vilification is the term used in **Australia**. Hate crimes in **Africa, Asia**, and **South America** tend to be closely connected to large-scale terrorism or political instability. England, and Wales define hate crimes primarily as motivated by racism and also include hate speech. **France** includes racism, intolerance, and xenophobia.

The United States was one of the first countries to begin collecting data on hate crimes. As global attention to human rights has increased, other countries have begun data collection. However, the differences in the definition of a hate crime and data collection methods create a challenge for comparison between countries and regions. In a 1996 survey of 4,000 lesbian, gay, and bisexual people in the **United Kingdom**, 34 percent of the men and 24 percent of the women reported being victimized in the previous five years (Mason and Palmer 1996). Similarly, in Sweden, a survey showed that 23 percent of the 600 lesbian and gay respondents were victimized (ILGA-Europe 2000).

Perpetrators of hate crimes may find support for their actions through cultural socialization. Cues received from family, friends, neighbors, media, church, school, and many other sources guide an individual's understanding of self and others while encouraging and proscribing discriminatory acts. Harro (2000) describes this socialization cycle that systematically promotes specific approved behaviors and reactions to specific vilified behaviors. When such socialization occurs, reacting negatively to those who transgress societal expectations is seen as part of a moral or civic duty. The impact of this socialization cycle on LGBT and questioning youth can be quite detrimental to their physical and **mental health**. Internalizing society's ideology of sex and gender, they can experience a great deal of negative feelings toward themselves when dealing with their sexual identities (Herek 2000).

While Harro's socialization cycle illustrates the cultural mechanism for the continuation of oppressive systems and ideas, other scholars hypothesize that hate crimes on the basis of sexual orientation are rooted in an individual's psychology. **Homophobia** can be traced to an individual's struggle with his **sexual identity**. By violently rejecting sexual feelings, the perpetrator internalizes homophobic attitudes and self-hatred. This internal dissonance could result in violence against an LGBT individual to prove "heterosexual manhood" to himself and to his peers, suggesting that the norms and taboos of a society, as they relate to sex, gender, and sexuality, might well be rooted in the construct of masculinity. This internalized homophobia can result in severe self-hatred, fear of discovery, extreme isolation, high risk for **suicide,** as well as acts of violence toward out LGBT individuals.

Proactive interventions to prevent hate crimes on the basis of sexual orientation are being initiated around the world. Norway responded to the active recruitment of their youth into hate groups with extreme right-wing ideologies, including homophobia, racism, xenophobia, and anti-Semitism. Children as young as twelve years were being influenced by these groups. EXIT-Leaving Violent Youth Groups helps children and young adults who want to leave hate groups temporarily move away from their neighborhoods, connecting with social resources and therapy. In addition, the youth's family receives support and a network of resources for assistance. Results have shown a decrease in hate crimes and a reduction of the impact of hate groups in several Norwegian towns.

The most effective interventions increase awareness of sexuality issues. Self-directed readings, attendance at educational speakers and rallies, and taking courses on gender or **queer studies** are all ways people have responded proactively when hate crimes occur. Individuals, communities, and institutions also expand their awareness of hate crimes through learning about the local and federal laws and policies impacting LGBT individuals and couples, and learning about local and national LGBT organizations. Furthermore, when **allies** speak out publicly that they want the hate to stop, more people listen and hear the message that hate crimes are not tolerated. Law enforcement agencies, however, are only beginning to educate their investigative officers on LGBT-related hate crimes and working with victims.

Herek (Herrick and Berrill 1992) recommends that reactive measures to hate crimes must first begin with a caring for and supporting of the victim. Caring communities connect resources and support systems to victims and the LGBT community. Family, friends, and allies of the victims encourage and support them as they report the incident to the appropriate channels. Activists and allies of the LGBT community take action when authorities fail to respond to hate crimes by initiating telephone calls, e-mails, faxes, letters, petitions, and media coverage.

Bibliography

Anti-Defamation League. 2001. "Hate Crime Laws." Accessed June 7, 2005. http://www. adl.org/99hatecrime/intro.asp.

Harro, Bobbie. 2000. "The Cycle of Liberation." Pp. 463–469 in *Readings for Diversity and Social Justice: An Anthology on Racism, Antisemitism, Sexism, Heterosexism,*

Ableism, and Classism. Edited by Maurianne Adams, Warren J. Blumenfeld, Rosie Castaneda, Heather W. Hackman, Madeline L. Peters, and Ximena Zuniga. New York: Routledge.

Herek, Gregory M. 2000. "Internalized Homophobia Among Gay Men, Lesbians, and Bisexuals." Pp. 281–282 in *Readings for Diversity and Social Justice: An Anthology on Racism, Antisemitism, Sexism, Heterosexism, Ableism, and Classism.* Edited by Maurianne Adams, Warren J. Blumenfeld, Rosie Castaneda, Heather W. Hackman, Madeline L. Peters, and Ximena Zuniga. New York: Routledge.

Herek, Gregory M., and Kevin T. Berrill. 1992. *Hate Crimes: Confronting Violence against Lesbians and Gay Men.* Thousand Oaks, CA: Sage.

ILGA-Europe. 2000. *Discrimination against Lesbian, Gay and Bisexual Persons in Europe.* Accessed June 7, 2005. http://www.ilga-europe.org/m3/council_of_europe/coe_submission_sept00.html.

Mason, Angela, and Anya Palmer. 1996. *Queer Bashing: A National Survey of Hate Crimes against Lesbians and Gay Men.* London: Stonewall.

National Coalition of Anti-Violence Programs. 2004. *Anti-Lesbian, Gay, Bisexual and Transgender Violence in 2003.* Accessed May 30, 2005. http://www.avp.org/publications/reports/2003NCAVP_HV_Report.pdf.

Perry, Barbara. 2003. "Where Do We Go From Here? Researching Hate Crime." *Internet Journal of Criminology.* Accessed June 7, 2005. http://www.internetjournalofcriminology.com/Where%20Do%20We%20Go%20From%20Here.%20Researching%20Hate%20Crime.pdf.

Shaw, Margaret, and Olivier Barchechat. 2002. *Preventing Hate Crimes: International Strategies and Practice.* International Centre for the Prevention of Crime. Accessed June 7, 2005. http://www.crime-prevention-intl.org/publications/pub_3_1.pdf.

United States Department of Justice. 2001, October. Stephen Wessler and Margaret Moss. *Hate Crimes on Campus: The Problem and Efforts To Confront It.* Accessed June 7, 2005. http://www.ncjrs.org/pdffiles1/bja/187249.pdf.

Web Sites

Hate Crimes Research Network. March 2004. Accessed June 7, 2005. http://www.hatecrime.net/. Links academic research being conducted on bias-motivated crime. Includes research by sociologists, criminologists, psychologists, and other academics including graduate students.

HateCrime.org March 2005. Accessed May 30, 2005. http://www.hatecrime.org/. Provides extensive educational, historic, and legislative resources. Includes listing of hate crime victims.

Human Rights Campaign. May 2005. Accessed May 30, 2005. http://www.hrc.org/. Provides a national voice for gay, lesbian, bisexual, and transgender issues. Includes a listing of hate crimes collected primarily through media and police reports.

Intelligence Project. 2005. Southern Poverty Law Center. Accessed May 30, 2005. http://www.splcenter.org/intel/history.jsp. Monitors, investigates, and reports on groups and extremist activity in the United States. A quarterly magazine updates and informs interested parties on the latest hate crimes and activities being investigated and provides training for law enforcement professionals.

U.S. Map of Hate Groups. April 2005. Accessed May 30, 2005. Tolerance.Org. http://www.tolerance.org/maps/hate/incidents.jsp. A Web project of the Southern Poverty Law Center provides a wealth of educational resources for community and individual education and descriptive data on hate crimes.

Heteronormativity

Gust A. Yep

"Heteronormativity"—a powerful form of social regulation and control—is a term used to expose and highlight how institutionalized heterosexuality is consciously and unconsciously accepted and reproduced. In education as well as mainstream society, heterosexuality is simply presented as "the way people naturally are"—an unquestionable emblem of normality (Kumashiro 2002; Letts and Sears 1999). Heteronormativity points to how heterosexuality is viewed and accepted as *the* standard for legitimate, authentic, prescriptive, and ruling social, cultural, and sexual arrangements in modern Western societies. Heteronormativity is everywhere: It is always already present in our individual psyches (e.g., our thinking), collective consciousness (e.g., community values), social institutions (e.g., marriage), cultural practices (e.g., wedding rituals), and knowledge systems (e.g., education). In spite of its prevalence, heteronormativity remains largely invisible and elusive to most people by presenting heterosexuality as a natural state and a social "given" with a sense of rightness, moral rectitude, and a projected cultural ideal. For example, **"coming out"** for **lesbian, gay, bisexual, transgender,** and questioning (LGBTQ) youth is typically a life-defining event (Baker 2002; Gray 1999). It is a public declaration of their sexuality. On the other hand, heterosexual students rarely need to come out to proclaim their **sexual identity**.

This sense of heterosexual moral superiority, cultural accomplishment, and social privilege permeates all aspects of social life. It systematically creates and perpetuates a social hierarchy with heterosexuals holding most of the power, including legal protection, cultural endorsement, political access, and control over ideology and knowledge systems. In the process, it creates abject and abominable bodies, souls, persons, and life forms. For example, homosexuality, as a deviation from the standard of "normal" heterosexuality, has been treated as a mental illness, immorality, or weakness of the soul, and in some instances, a crime punishable by law. In other words, heteronormativity creates the conditions for the oppression, suffering, annihilation, and erasure of individuals who do not conform to or are perceived to deviate from the heterosexual mandate. As such, heteronormativity is a site of symbolic, psychic, and material violence that deeply affects individuals across the spectrum of sexualities.

Heteronormativity affects everyone, but in different ways and to different degrees. Because heterosexuality is a patriarchal institution, women living inside the heteronormative borders (i.e., heterosexually-identified women) are subordinated through culturally idealized conceptions of marriage and motherhood. These conceptions propel women to enter into relationships with unequal power and to engage in unpaid labor in the service of men. Heteronormativity also affects men who are heterosexually-identified. Heterosexuality constitutes men as "real" men (i.e., "real" men are aggressively heterosexual). As such, it keeps men living inside the heteronormative borders fearful of being emasculated and deprived from a range of

See also Adoption; Discrimination; Feminism; Gender Roles; Heterosexism; Men's Studies; Mental Health; Queer and Queer Theory; Sexism; School Climate, College; School Climate, K-12; Women's Studies.

gender performances, sexual possibilities, and life pleasures through a lifelong labor of "proving" their manhood. For example, most straight men are afraid to be sensitive, tender, and emotional because of the fear of being perceived or labeled "sissy" or "faggot"—an ever-present threat to their manhood.

The violence and harm of heteronormativity on individuals living outside the heteronormative mandate are more obvious. Focusing on heteronormativity as a foundational source of human oppression and suffering, Yep (2002; 2003) identified four domains of violence: (1) soul murder and internalized **homophobia**, (2) **hate crimes** and externalized homophobia, (3) discursive violence against nonheteronormative individuals, and (4) institutional violence against nonheteronormative individuals.

Soul murder and internalized homophobia are the psychic and psychological injuries that individuals inflict upon themselves. Very early in life children learn from interpersonal contacts, media messages, and educational institutions that deviations from the heteronormative standard, such as homosexuality, are anxiety-ridden, fear-inducing, guilt-producing, shame-provoking, hate-deserving, psychologically-blemishing, and physically-threatening. Children learn that homosexuality is "bad." Internalized homophobia, in the form of self-hatred and self-destructive thoughts and behavioral patterns, become firmly ingrained in the lives and psyches of individuals in heteronormative society. Because of this, it is hardly surprising that LGBTQ youth and young adults experience depression, **alcoholism, drug use**, social isolation and rejection, alienation, and higher rates of **suicide** than their non-LGBTQ counterparts (Fenaughty and Harré 2003). Soul murder, or the deliberate attempt to eradicate or compromise the identity of an individual in order to force him or her to fit the heterosexual mandate, is a powerfully insidious and culturally accepted form of psychological abuse (Yep 2002, 2003). In classrooms, this routinely occurs when teachers and the educational systems unrelentingly communicate to LGBTQ students that their sexuality is abnormal and unnatural. In this **communication** process, these students learn that their selfhood and identity are wrong, bad, or downright evil.

Hate crimes and externalized homophobia are injuries inflicted on others. Fueled by heteronormativity, externalized homophobia is commonplace. It can be directed to any person who is perceived or assumed to be a "sexual other"—someone who is viewed as deviating from the heterosexual norm. It can be manifested in multiple ways: **harassment**, avoidance, verbal abuse, differential treatment and discriminatory behavior, and physical violence. The use of name-calling toward individuals who are perceived to be outside the boundaries of heteronormativity (e.g., "faggot," "dyke") is common in everyday interaction. In U.S. middle and high schools, for example, verbal harassment is a pervasive problem, and teachers, **administrators**, and other fellow students rarely step in to stop it (Human Rights Watch 2001). When these individuals overlook and disregard such situations, they provide a clear message that it is permissible to hate those who are perceived to be sexual others, thus, the cycle of homophobia gets perpetuated in society. In addition, verbal harassment, if allowed to persist, can lead to an overall hostile environment and other forms of violence, including **bullying**, physical violence, and **sexual abuse or assault**. The most extreme expression of externalized homophobia is hate crimes.

Discursive violence refers to words, images, gestures, tones, presentations, and omissions used to treat differentially, degrade, disparage, and represent LGBTQ people and their experiences (Yep 2003). In everyday discourse, they are not only treated differently, but also talked about differently. From everyday conversation to media images, LGBT experiences are represented differently from the heteronormative standard. In everyday conversations, for example, it is not considered socially peculiar for people to closely scrutinize and make the most intimate, intrusive, and personal inquiries about the lives of people living outside of the boundaries of **compulsory heterosexuality**. In schools and elsewhere, comments and questions such as "what do lesbians do in bed anyway?" or "how does a female-to-male (FTM) transgender have sex?" directed at lesbians and FTMs, respectively, are not unusual. While these invasive inquiries into the lives of lesbian, gay, or transgender people are deemed as demonstrations of interest in "their lifestyle," such scrutiny of sexually unmarked individuals (e.g., heterosexuals) is often considered inappropriate, offensive, and in bad taste. Similarly, references to a lesbian or gay partner as a "friend" when their heterosexual counterparts are routinely referred to as "spouse," "wife," or "husband," though not necessarily ill intentioned, are symbolically violent acts that reaffirm and reproduce the lower status of the lesbian and gay person in current social and sexual hierarchies. In the media, individuals and groups living outside of the heteronormative order are also represented differently. Although lesbians, gays, and transgender individuals have gone from complete invisibility to greater visibility in many societies, this is not necessarily unproblematic. LGBTQ people in television talk shows, such as *The Jerry Springer Show*, are generally presented as "social issues," "spectacles," or "freaks" for the amusement, entertainment, and consumption by presumably straight audiences.

Institutional violence refers to systematic and socially accepted injuries inflicted upon individuals outside of the heteronormative mandate (Yep 2003). Institutional violence is widespread for LGBTQ individuals and communities. Undergirding all social institutions is heteronormativity. Heteronormative thinking is deeply ingrained and strategically invisible in education, social policy, the family, domestic and intimate life, the mass media and **popular culture**, and every social institution. Heteronormativity actively and methodically subordinates, disempowers, denies, and rejects individuals who do not conform to the heterosexual mandate by criminalizing them, denying them protection against discrimination, refusing them basic rights and recognition, or all of the above. For example, there are numerous basic rights that heterosexual individuals take for granted which LGBTQ children and adults are categorically denied: marry a person of the same sex, gain custody of their children, become foster and adoptive parents, visit one's same-sex partner in the hospital, obtain bereavement leave when one's partner passes away, file joint income tax returns with one's partner. For an LGBTQ student, even **dating** someone of the same sex or escorting that person to the school **prom** cannot be readily exercised without some school or community controversy.

Educators have generally been complicit in perpetuating heteronormativity. Although this process is not always conscious (which makes it even more insidious), heteronormativity has been maintained in classroom practices (e.g., treating nonheteronormative identities differently), **curriculum** (e.g., the absence of LGBTQ persons in textbooks), and disciplinary knowledge systems (e.g., most theories of human behavior and models of human relationships presume heterosexuality). By becoming more aware of how heteronormativity deeply affects individuals with different sexual identities (for a classroom exercise, see Yep 2002), students, educators, administrators, and other school personnel can think about, discuss, engage, and relate to each other in more humane, compassionate and inclusive ways.

Bibliography

Baker, Jean M. 2002. *How Homophobia Hurts Children: Nurturing Diversity at Home, at School, and in the Community*. Binghamton, NY: Harrington Park Press.

Fenaughty, John, and Niki Harré. 2003. "Life on the Seesaw: A Qualitative Study of Suicide Resiliency Factors for Young Gay Men." *Journal of Homosexuality* 45, no. 1: 1–22.

Gray, Mary L. 1999. *In Your Face: Stories from the Lives of Queer Youth*. Binghamton, NY: Harrington Park Press.

Human Rights Watch. 2001. *Hatred in the Hallways: Violence and Discrimination against Lesbian, Gay, Bisexual, and Transgender Students in U.S. Schools*. New York: Author.

Katz, Jonathan N. 1995. *The Invention of Heterosexuality*. New York: Dutton.

Kumashiro, Kevin. 2002. *Troubling Education: Queer Activism and Antioppressive Pedagogy*. New York: RoutledgeFalmer.

Letts, William J., and James T. Sears, eds. 1999. *Queering Elementary Education: Advancing the Dialogue about Sexualities and Schooling*. Lanham, MD: Rowman and Littlefield.

Rubin, Gayle S. 1993. "Thinking Sex: Notes for a Radical Theory of the Politics of Sexuality." Pp. 3–44 in *The Gay and Lesbian Studies Reader*. Edited by Henry Abelove, Michèlle Barale, and David Halperin. New York: Routledge.

Sedgwick, Eve K. 1990. *Epistemology of the Closet*. Berkeley: University of California Press.

Warner, Michael. 1993. "Introduction." Pp. vii–xxxi in *Fear of a Queer Planet: Queer Politics and Social Theory*. Edited by Michael Warner. Minneapolis: University of Minnesota Press.

———. 2002. *Publics and Counterpublics*. New York: Zone.

Yep, Gust A. 2002. "From Homophobia and Heterosexism to Heteronormativity: Toward the Development of a Model of Queer Interventions in the University Classroom." *Journal of Lesbian Studies* 6, nos. 3/4: 163–176.

———. 2003. "The Violence of Heteronormativity in Communication Studies: Notes on Injury, Healing, and Queer-World Making." Pp. 11–59 in *Queer Theory and Communication: From Disciplining Queers to Queering the Discipline(s)*. Edited by Gust A. Yep, Karen E. Lovaas, and John P. Elia. Binghamton, NY: Harrington Park Press.

Web Site

Introductory Guide to Critical Theory. November 2003. Dino Felluga. Purdue University. Accessed June 1, 2005. http://www.sla.purdue.edu/academic/engl/theory/genderandsex. This extensive site covers many subjects, including gender and sex. Sample applications, lesson plans, modules, and links are included.

Heterosexism

John E. Petrovic

Heterosexism is a form of oppression based on **sexual identity** that casts nonheterosexuality as abnormal, deviant, or immoral. In presuming the superiority of heterosexuality, heterosexism assumes that everyone is or should be heterosexual. In this definition, "nonheterosexuality" is meant to include all sexual minorities including **lesbian, gay, bisexual,** and **transgender** (LGBT) people. Like all forms of oppression, heterosexism creates and supports certain privileges for those in power. In

See also Antibias Curriculum; Communication; Educational Policies; Tomboy.

schools, heterosexism is evident in curricula and teaching practices that are silent about LGBT issues or raise them only in negative associations such as in discussions about **AIDS**. Heterosexism is also evident in many school policies. For example, some schools disallow same-sex couples from attending the **prom** or **gay–straight alliances** from meeting on campus.

The term heterosexism came into use during the 1970s as the LGBT community added its voice to the civil rights movement. The term avoids the rhetorical weakness of "**homophobia**," since most people who support the more prevalent and pernicious forms of **prejudice** against LGBT people can legitimately claim that they do not "fear" nonheterosexual people. The term heterosexism encapsulates the idea that prejudice against LGBT people is comprised of a constellation of normative beliefs around sexuality, sex, and **gender roles**. A normative belief indicates that "this is the norm" and/or "this is how things should be." Historically, for example, it was "normal" that men went out to work while women stayed home to maintain the household. Similarly, boys in school "normally" play football or baseball and take shop. By not engaging in normative gender roles, the masculinity and sexuality of boys who take **dance**, sing in the choir, or study home economics are often questioned. One way of thinking about oppression then is that it involves taking the normative beliefs of a society and imposing them on everyone. In this sense, prejudice against LGBT people is much more akin to other sorts of oppression such as **racism** and **sexism**. The term "heterosexism" captures the sources of this oppression more accurately than other terms such as "homophobia."

"Heterosexism" is closely related in meaning to the term "**heteronormativity**." "Heterosexism" signals an emphasis on the characteristics of individual acts, beliefs, or attitudes. Heteronormativity, in contrast, is a characteristic possessed by an entire culture or discourse community and refers to the way heterosexuality is taken for granted as the "normal" form of sexual **desire** and sexual practice in that culture or community. Heterosexism and heteronormativity form opposite sides of a cycle of oppression. Heteronormative cultural values inspire and enable heterosexist practices. Heterosexist practices, in turn, reinforce heteronormative values such as in the case of the school prom. Here the exclusionary policy is inspired by the heteronormative discourses that say the only normal form of romance is between persons of other genders. It may also stem from the false assumption that everyone is heterosexual. The heterosexist policy of exclusion set by a principal or school board, in turn, reinforces this norm by communicating to students that only heterosexual relationships are acceptable. Heterosexism, therefore, can be said to be caused by heteronormativity, and that in turn heteronormativity is perpetuated by heterosexist acts (Petrovic and Rosiek 2003).

The resultant assumptions made about sexuality generally, and the belief that one sexuality is "right" and all others are "wrong," are perpetuated by privilege. These assumptions are enforced through the punishment of those who break the mold, including exclusionary rules and policies, physical abuse, social isolation, and verbal abuse.

Some people dismiss words such as "heterosexism" or "heteronormativity" as political correctness. But what people believe and how they view the world are shaped by the language used to describe the world. The use of different terms and language helps people to see the world differently. "Heterosexism," as a word and concept, provides some of the language necessary for discussions around nonheterosexuality to shift from being about "abnormality" to being about "oppression."

This provides the opportunity to analyze more critically the effects of **compulsory heterosexuality** (the idea that everyone must be heterosexual). Compulsory heterosexuality, as an effect of the oppression of heterosexism, not only affects lesbian, gay, bisexual, or transgender youth but also people who identify as heterosexual. In this vein, heterosexism affects these youth by forcing them to hide their true identities. Hiding one's identity, referred to as "closeting" "**passing**," "on the Down Low," or "being in the closet," includes a host of behaviors that heterosexual people might not think twice about and other forms of self-censorship that heterosexual people do not have to think about at all. For example, LGBT students do not feel the same freedom that heterosexual students do to hold hands in the hallway. Often times, LGBT people censor their speech to speak in gender neutral language, using, for example, "they" instead of "he" or "she" to refer to intimate friends. Such self-censorship even affects what students wear, especially transgender students. Using language or engaging in behaviors that make it known one is nonheterosexual require assuring it is safe to do so considering the context and people.

Heterosexism affects the behaviors and choices of people who identify as heterosexual as well. In these effects the overlap between sexism and heterosexism is further revealed. For example, men might choose not to sit with legs crossed at the knee since this is considered a "feminine" position. Boys in school who choose to play house instead of football are likely to have to endure taunts of "fag" or "**sissy**." This is because heterosexism serves the purpose of defining masculinity and what it means to be a "real" man. Expressing hostility toward gay people serves the psychological function of enhancing one's "masculine" identity (Herek 1986) and the "homophobic stigma is a powerful enforcer of conventional gender behavior" (Lipkin 1999, 55). Similarly, girls who choose to play a **sport** such as softball instead of trying out for cheerleading face taunts of "dyke." In short, heterosexism affects everyone (Blumenfeld 1992).

The fear of being thought to be sexually different is one of the other effects of heterosexism. This affects the actions of closeted people and of heterosexual people. People who choose to ignore slurs against LGBT people, for example, may do so out of fear of being called gay themselves. This may partly explain the results of one study which demonstrated that, when faced with derogatory comments about LGBT people in class discussion, most teachers chose not to respond, even after most had previously indicated they would discipline students for making such comments (Sears 1992).

Although heterosexism indeed affects everyone, it is clear that heterosexual people are not affected in the same violent (be it physical, emotional, or spiritual violence) ways. In fact, heterosexually-identified people enjoy a fairly lengthy list of privileges in a heterosexist society. They can let their sexuality be known even if they serve in the armed forces or choose to adopt children. They can be sure they will not be denied a place to live, employment, or health insurance because of their sexuality. Heterosexual children need not fear being disowned by their parents because of their sexuality. Children of heterosexual parents can expect to see their family represented in their school curriculum and **children of LGBT parents** need not be silent in the classroom.

Although individual attitudes against LGBT people reflect heterosexism, the examples of heterosexism above represent the rules, laws, and procedures of societal institutions. This is what is termed "institutionalized heterosexism." A principal way of combating the institutionalized heterosexism in schools is to raise awareness among individual teachers. In **Europe**, the **GLBT Educational Equity** (GLEE) Project, funded by the European Commission, represents one such endeavor. This project is an interactive network of teacher training, **curriculum** development, and **research** interventions to counter homophobia and heterosexism in schools. Through teachers and direct curricular intervention, schools can help to reduce individually held heterosexist attitudes. Care must be taken, however. Although silence around LGBT issues or misinformation can be countered in schools, without authentic discussion about the topic, heterosexist attitudes are less likely to change. But as Lipkin (1999, 338) points out, "The possibility that inclusive curriculum by itself is an unproven agent for reducing prejudice does not diminish its positive influence on [sexual] minorities or the intellectual desirability of complete and accurate instruction."

Confronting heterosexism in schools through direct curricular intervention, however, cannot occur without confronting societal heterosexism. Having themselves been socialized into a heterosexist society, the reactions of individual school leaders, as well as members of the community and school board members, against dealing in a socially just way with the issue of homosexuality in schools can be quite virulent. Thus, the fight against heterosexism must be multipronged.

There have been few evaluations of the effectiveness of particular strategies in reducing heterosexism (Sears 1997). Individual heterosexism, however, can be reduced through intervention, particularly through discussion and reading. Communication strategies address the functions that heterosexism serves for the attitude holder. They "create specific cognitive inconsistencies in the mind of the receiver and ways to reduce the dissonance in the direction of lessening their negative attitudes" (Yep 1997, 61). In this vein, Petrovic and Rosiek (2003) highlight the cognitive inconsistencies, which they call "hitches," present in the thinking of some teachers. Understanding the heterosexist assumptions that some people make allows us to identify the cognitive inconsistencies.

Bibliography

Blumenfeld, Warren J. 1992. *Homophobia: How We All Pay the Price*. Boston: Beacon Press.

Friend, Richard A. 1993. "Choices, Not Closets: Heterosexism and Homophobia in Schools." Pp. 209–235 in *Beyond Silenced Voices: Class, Race, and Gender in United States Schools*. Edited by Lois Weis and Michelle Fine. Albany: State University of New York Press.

Herek, Gregory M. 1986. "On Heterosexual Masculinity: Some Psychical Consequences of the Social Construction of Gender." *American Behavioral Scientist* 29, no. 5: 563–577.

Jung, Patricia B., and Ralph F. Smith. 1993. *Heterosexism: An Ethical Challenge*. Albany: State University of New York Press.

Lipkin, Arthur. 1999. *Understanding Homosexuality, Changing Schools*. Boulder, CO: Westview Press.

Petrovic, John E., and Jerry Rosiek. 2003. "Disrupting the Heteronormative Subjectivities of Christian Pre-Service Teachers: A Deweyan Prolegomenon." *Equity & Excellence in Education* 36, no. 2: 161–169.

Sears, James T. 1992. "Educators, Homosexuality, and Homosexual Students: Are Personal Feelings Related to Professional Beliefs?" *Journal of Homosexuality* 22, nos. 3/4: 29–79.

———. 1997. "Thinking Critically/Intervening Effectively about Heterosexism and Homophobia: A Twenty-Five-Year Research Retrospective." Pp.13–48 in *Overcoming*

Heterosexism and Homophobia. Edited by James T. Sears and Walter L. Williams. New York: Columbia University Press.

Yep, Gust A. 1997. "Changing Homophobic and Heterosexist Attitudes: An Overview of Persuasive Communication Approaches." Pp. 49–64 in *Overcoming Heterosexism and Homophobia*. Edited by James T. Sears and Walter L. Williams. New York: Columbia University Press.

Web Sites

The Heterosexism Inquirer. November 2003. Leslie Bella. Accessed June 8, 2005. http://www.mun.ca/the/themain.html. Canadian-based site with lots of information, including research, personal stories, and other links, that increase awareness of the existence and impact of heterosexism, through curriculum and educational materials as well as through promotion and evaluation of strategies to challenge heterosexism.

Sexual Orientation: Science, Education, and Policy. March 2005. Gregory M. Herek. Accessed June 8, 2005. http://psychology.ucdavis.edu/rainbow/index.html. Provides a wealth of factual and scientific knowledge for education and enlightened public policy related to sexual orientation. Definitions, scientific research reports, public opinion polls, policy reports, and commentaries are all easily accessed through clearly labeled links and an alphabetized listing of the site contents.

Hirschfeld, Magnus (1868–1935)

Susan Birden

Magnus Hirschfeld, the great German sexologist, was a socialist, a Jew, a homosexual, a physician, and a pioneer in sociology and education about human sexuality in all its forms, but especially homosexuality and transvestism. Hirschfeld, who possessed enormous energy, imagination, and ambition, organized numerous international psychological and medical congresses dedicated to **research** on sexual matters, tirelessly advocated policies for societal acceptance of homosexuals, and profoundly affected the vigorous homosexual rights movement in pre-Nazi Germany. He also founded the first institute for sexual research, which provided facilities for hundreds of international researchers, as well as therapy and **sexuality education** for the general public. His belief in the power of scientific knowledge to change public opinion resulted in his motto: *"per scientiam ad justitiam,"* justice through knowledge. Hirschfeld authored nearly two hundred titles, including articles, pamphlets, book reviews, and several lengthy books that addressed legal, historical, medical, and anthropological aspects of homosexuality and transvestism. Hirschfeld's commitment to informing the public about scientific advances in sexuality led him to write several of these books with popular readers in mind.

Sexology, from its inception, critiqued prevailing sexual attitudes and traditional assumptions about sex. Hirschfeld contended that homosexuality was an inborn mental and physical condition of a specific biological phenomenon, which he theorized constituted a "third sex"—a human being between male and female. Hirschfeld believed, as did an earlier researcher Karl Heinrich Ulrich, that homosexuality was a psychic **bisexuality**, a woman's mind in a man's body, or vice versa.

See also Cross-Dressing; Identity Politics; Sexual Orientation.

Many of Hirschfeld's colleagues adamantly disagreed with him. Benedict Friedländer and Adolf Brand, for instance, rejected a biological explanation for homosexuality and maintained that homoerotic relations between older and younger men had contributed to the glory of Greece and was the basis for the modern state. They sought to refashion the image of homosexual men as even more masculine and athletic than the heterosexual man. However, Hirschfeld's theories became far better known and relatively more accepted by the public.

Hirschfeld repeatedly tried to reform Germany's notorious law, Paragraph 175, which stipulated that, "A male who indulges in criminally indecent activities with another male or who allows himself to participate in such activities will be punished with jail." In the 1903 attempt at repeal, Hirschfeld and his Scientific-Humanitarian Committee initiated the unprecedented distribution of over 6,000 questionnaires to Berlin factory workers and university students, asking about contemporary sex habits and attitudes. Based on these data, Hirschfeld concluded that about 2.2 percent of German males were homosexual. (These data must be regarded with some suspicion given that they were collected in Berlin, which had long been much more sexually progressive and somewhat of a haven for homosexuals.) Although the data failed to persuade lawmakers, Hirschfeld's methods and analyses influenced scientific and activist communities.

While convictions of male homosexuality in Germany carried a prison sentence, the average lesbian enjoyed a kind of legal immunity. During the Weimar Republic (1919–1933) luxurious lesbian bars and nightclubs flourished. Lesbian magazines enjoyed healthy circulations, and a few lesbian plays achieved wide-spread popularity. All of this was possible because neither the Second German Empire nor the Weimar Republic had promulgated laws forbidding or punishing sexual acts between women. When the political reform movement tried to include sexual relations between women in Paragraph 175, Hirschfeld threw his support behind Germany's **women's movement,** guided by Helene Stöcker, successfully stalling these efforts.

Hirschfeld was also a sociological pioneer. During the first years of the twentieth century, he visited pubs, hotels, and private houses of homosexuals and transvestites, often with medical colleagues, to see and to learn about their lifestyles. Hirschfeld not only studied these hundreds of individuals, he greatly enjoyed their company. In fact, he befriended transvestites to such a degree that he came under suspicion of being one himself.

Hirschfeld wrote several books based upon his sociological research. In *Berlin's Third Sex*, he depicted not only the outstanding characteristics of homosexuals, but also the milieu in which they lived and loved, providing a picture of Berlin unlike anything Germany had ever seen. *Transvestites*, a book praised almost universally by scientists, was one of the highlights of his career. In it, Hirschfeld made the case that transvestism was a sexual variation in itself, not due to underlying homosexuality. These theories left an indelible mark on psychological history. Finally, *The Homosexuality of Men and Women* was based on his observation and knowledge of over 10,000 men and women he had studied, not only in Germany but also in Paris, London, the United States, North Africa, and some Asian countries.

Hirschfeld's major achievement was the establishment of the Institute for Sexual Research, in 1919. In it he amassed a library of over 30,000 rare anthropological, medical, legal, and social documents about sexuality. The archives contained an extensive collection of sexual instruments and other items, including sado-masochistic whips, chains and torture instruments, lacey undergarments worn by Prussian officers beneath their uniforms, and fantasy paintings drawn by Hirschfeld's patients. The archives also included more than 6,000 case histories, several thousand photographs of transvestites and other sexual variants, collections of fetishes, 3,000 microscopic slides of brain tissue, and thousands of psychobiological questionnaires.

The Institute employed physicians and provided research facilities where scientists from all over the world were welcome to work. Attending physicians at the Institute offered medical care and sexual **counseling**—a practice considered radically reformist. Moreover, Hirschfeld insisted that physicians and researchers provide sex education to the public in the form of lectures followed by question-and-answer sessions. This form of popular teaching, which reached massive audiences from all walks of life, was a breakthrough in sex education.

Hirschfeld's innovations in sex education included films about homosexuality. Hirschfeld acted as an advisor for *Anders als die Andern (Different from the Others)*, a **film** that told the story of a young homosexual man who had committed suicide when a blackmailer tried to extort money from him. When the young man's lover contemplates suicide in the film, Hirschfeld, playing himself, saves the youth's life through empathetic therapy. The film made dramatic history as a breakthrough in the presentation of unorthodox love and served to enlighten the general public about this misunderstood subject.

Despite Hirschfeld's international fame and contributions to science and education, he became a much-despised figure in Germany. He was ostracized by Albert Moll and other scientists who claimed that Hirschfeld's activism confused science with propaganda and a pragmatic agenda. Hirschfeld's ceaseless campaign for the repeal of Paragraph 175 also made him the object of Nazi loathing.

When Hitler became Chancellor of Germany, in 1933, homosexual-rights organizations were banned. Within four months the Nazis descended upon Hirschfeld's Institute, confiscating over 12,000 books and 34,000 photographs. These were burned in a public ceremony four days later. Ludwig L. Lenz, a gynecologist who worked at the Institute, claimed that part of the Nazi's keen interest in the Institute was because Hirschfeld had treated many high ranking Nazi officials for perversions and sexually transmitted diseases. They feared that their intimate secrets, confessions, and medical records would be exposed. Some evidence even suggests that Hirschfeld's 40,000 case histories were not destroyed, but used as evidence to send homosexuals to concentration camps.

Following the destruction of his Institute, Hirschfeld fled to France. Only after the Nazis had destroyed his lifework did Hirschfeld concede that much of his research had unwittingly deepened popular prejudices by defining homosexuals as medically deviant. When Hirschfeld died suddenly on his sixty-seventh birthday, in 1935, he had been working to reestablish his Institute of Sexology in France.

Bibliography

Blasius, Mark, and Shane Phelan, eds. 1997. *We are Everywhere: A Historical Sourcebook of Gay and Lesbian Politics*. New York: Routledge.

Fademan, Lillian, and Brigitte Ericksson. 1990. *Lesbians in Germany: 1890's-1920's*. Tallahassee, FL: Naiad Press.

Friedman, Jeffrey, and Rob Epstein. 2002. *Paragraph 175* [Videotape]. New York: New Yorker Video.

Hirschfeld, Magnus. 2000, original published 1920. *The Homosexuality of Men and Women*. Translated by Michael A. Lombardi-Nash. New York: Prometheus.

Isherwood, Christopher. 2001. *Christopher and His Kind*. Minneapolis: University of Minnesota Press.

Oosterhuis, Harry, and Hubert Kennedy, eds. 1991. *Homosexuality and Male Bonding in Pre-Nazi Germany*. New York: Harrington Park Press.

Steakley, James D. 1993. *Homosexual Emancipation Movement in Germany*. North Stratford, NH: Ayer.

Wolff, Charlotte. 1986. *Magnus Hirschfeld: A Portrait of a Pioneer in Sexology*. London: Quartet Books.

Web Site

Magnus-Hirschfeld-Gesellschaft e.V. December 2003. Accessed December 15, 2004. http://www.hirschfeld.in-berlin.de/index.html. Dedicated to explaining the work of Hirschfeld's Institute (in German).

History, Teaching of

Margaret Smith Crocco

Over the last thirty years, the field of history has begun to reflect the fact that sexuality is a topic with a history. Changes in the nature of this discipline and changes in society have helped support inclusion of sexuality in **curriculum** and **research** in history. Nevertheless, gay and lesbian studies and attention to the history of **bisexuality** and transgender issues have all found greater visibility at the college level than at the precollegiate level. Only in recent years have a few teachers in K-12 schools broken the silence about sexuality in teaching history. But in approaching this topic, educators at all levels can now draw upon an expanded body of literature, videos, and other resources that make it possible to introduce the history of gays, lesbians, transgender persons, and bisexuals at a variety of grade levels and in both American and world history courses.

In addressing the changes of the last two decades, it is important to consider briefly the nature of the historical enterprise. Writing history is a highly selective process. Differences exist between what is called "History," that is, the chronicling of past events for students and other audiences, and the totality of past human experience, or "history." Professional historians strive for objectivity in their recreation of the past; nevertheless, the selection of events for historical scrutiny is always governed by a set of standards for determining "historical significance." Traditionally, historians focused on politics and economics because these arenas were considered the most significant stages of human action. Historical accounts focused on those with power in these domains, typically men of the dominant culture. It was assumed that the lives of these "great men" had played the greatest role in shaping the past and were, thus, most worthy of historical scrutiny.

Over the last one hundred years, standards of significance in history have shifted. These changes have come about slowly, due to trends both inside and outside the profession.

See also Antibias Curriculum; Identity Politics; Johns Committee; LGBT Studies; Multicultural Education; Multiple Genders; Political Science, Teaching of; Rainbow Flag and Other Pride Symbols; Secondary Schools, LGBT; Teachers, LGBT and History; Women's Movement.

Two parallel movements within the field of history—one of the 1920s and another of the 1970s—opened historical inquiry up to what came to be known as "social history," that is, the lives of ordinary men and women. In the first "new social history" movement of the 1920s, some historians turned their attention to labor, as well as **race** and gender, to a more limited extent. In the second "new social history" movement of the 1970s, which championed "history from the bottom up," many more historians took up the topics of race, **ethnicity**, and gender, so much so that one traditional historian lamented that the "margins had become the center, and the center the margins." Fresh historical scholarship began to uncover the pasts of those who had remained "hidden from history" (Duberman, Vicinus, and Chauncey 1990). Since then, gay and lesbian history, dealing primarily with Western societies, has grown substantially.

An additional influence creating change within the historical profession came from society at large. Progress in the human rights movement, especially in Western democracies, provided impetus for rewriting national histories. The gains of the United States' civil rights movement for **African Americans** from the 1940s through the 1960s influenced women and gays to press their own movements more vigorously. In New York City, the **Stonewall** riots of 1969 signaled a watershed moment in the U.S. gay movement. This event produced more militant efforts on behalf of gays, lesbians, and bisexuals for equality in American life, which contributed in turn to an explosion in gay and lesbian history.

New scholarship has emphasized the fluid and constructed nature of gender and sexual identity in history. One of the key moments in the timeline of gay and lesbian history in the United States came in the early part of the twentieth century. **Sigmund Freud**'s views on **sexual identity** brought about the pathologizing of same-sex attraction. New labels such as "lesbian" and "homosexual" came into widespread use, changing the categorization and signification of same-sex attraction in the West. Dichotomous thinking in Western thinking reduced the range of possibilities within human sexuality to two options: homosexual and heterosexual. As a result, historians—even gay and lesbian historians—have often overlooked evidence of bisexuality in literary and historical figures presumed to be gay or lesbian, for example, those of the Harlem Renaissance (Black 2001). Throughout the twentieth century, Freud's ideas precipitated much new research about sexuality and heavily influenced views on what constitutes "normal" sexual behavior. Not until 1973 would the American Psychiatric Association remove homosexuality from its *Diagnostic & Statistical Manual of Mental Disorders.*

Great sensitivity to time, place, and culture is demanded in teaching about the history of sexuality. For example, societies as distinct as ancient **Egypt** and modern **India** have recognized what has been called the "third gender." The labels, "berdache" and "Two-Spirit" people, which have been applied to **Native** American and Latin American cultures, extend the range of options beyond "homosexual" and "heterosexual." Use of the term "transgendered" in relation to these categories fails to capture the ways in which this identity has been constructed in these societies.

Lesbianism, a term dating to the early twentieth century, provides another example of the socially constructed nature of same-sex relationships. Throughout the nineteenth century, American women created communities of mutual support, such as **women's colleges**, and often passionate, lifelong attachment sometimes referred to as "Boston marriages." Historians today differ about whether the term "lesbian" should be applied to such relationships.

What progress has been made in introducing topics such as these into the teaching of history? At the college level, academic courses focused on the history of sexuality are fairly common. Research, dissertations, and books on gay and lesbian history are in widespread circulation; there is considerably less scholarship on bisexual and transgender history. In short, the history of sexuality has found academic legitimacy within higher education.

By contrast, teaching this history remains uncommon at the precollegiate level. In recent years, a growing number of voices have been raised to support inclusion of gay and lesbian history in schools (Jennings 1994). Likewise, documentary **films** appropriate for high school use are also widely available, including *Out of the Past* (1998), a seventy-minute documentary about the gay rights movement for which a teaching guide is available, *Common Threads: Stories from the Quilt* (1990), about the **AIDS** epidemic, *Before Stonewall* (1984), a chronicle of gay life prior to the late 1960s, and *Brother Outsider* (2003), a documentary on the life of Bayard Rustin.

These resources can be used in conjunction with various pedagogical strategies. Some teachers introduce human sexuality into their curriculum in a token fashion, simply by naming the **sexual orientation** of prominent figures in American history, such as James Baldwin. A more in-depth approach might consider landmark events in the civil rights movements for gays and lesbians, especially the Stonewall riots and the U.S. Supreme Court's overturning *Bowers v. Hardwick* (1986) with *Lawrence & Garner v. Texas* (2003).

Other significant topics in gay and lesbian history that could be linked to themes taught in U.S. history courses include: the Harlem Renaissance, **discrimination** against gays in the military, civil rights leader Bayard Rustin, the women's rights movement of the past two centuries, the 1950s founding of the Mattachine Society (the first major gay organization in the United States), and the 2003 opening of the first gay public high school, the Harvey Milk High School in New York City.

March on Washington, 1979, marked the first large-scale demonstration for LGBT rights in the United States and was modeled after the 1963 Civil Rights March on Washington organized by Bayard Rustin. One hundred thousand persons from every state and territory marched on the nation's capital—a product of two years of planning and three decades of activism. Courtesy of Marge "Clearwater" Reed.

The U.S. Holocaust Museum in Washington, D.C. includes an exhibit on imprisonment of homosexuals in concentration camps during the Second World War. Teaching about the Nazi use of "**pink triangles**" to label and persecute lesbian, gays, bisexuals, and transgender people (including the use of films such as *Pink Triangles*, *Paragraph 175*, and *Bent*) can lead to discussion of the Universal Declaration of Human Rights (1949), and other United Nations' efforts to expand human rights to gays and lesbians. (In 1995, for the first time, abuses of gay and lesbian rights were adjudicated at the United Nation's International Tribunal on Human Rights Violations against Sexual Minorities.)

In 1994, Rodney Wilson led a movement to establish October as "Gay and Lesbian Pride Month." As a Missouri social studies teacher, Wilson was shocked by the lack of attention to lesbian, gay, bisexual, and transgender issues and history in social studies textbooks. The support Wilson received for his efforts from community groups reflects the influence of historical developments since Stonewall and the event's subsequent annual commemoration in New York City and Los Angeles. In 2000, the Stonewall Inn was declared a national historical landmark as the birthplace of the modern gay and lesbian civil rights movement. One way to celebrate the month is by making use of the hidden curriculum potential of the classroom, in this case, the bulletin boards. Teaching for Change, an organization promoting educational materials for equity and diversity, publishes a poster about gays in history headlined "Unfortunately, history has set the record a little too straight." Organizations such as the **Gay, Lesbian, and Straight Educators Network** (GLSEN) include a range of materials on its Web site for addressing the silence about gay and lesbian history in school curricula.

Teaching inclusive history can take many forms, from tokenism to thorough analysis. At the very least, examining topics such as "The Modern Gay Rights Movement" will provide students with a deeper understanding of the challenges faced by gays and lesbians up to the present day. In teaching such a unit, high school and **college age students** can research laws in their states and their school's **educational policies** and practices related to gay rights. Invited guest speakers and videos can offer personal recollections of the gay and lesbian struggle. As part of this effort, students can also critique textbook silence and other "official" historical representations about this and other topics deemed "dangerous" to the adolescent mind.

Bibliography

Black, Allida, ed. 2001. *Modern American Queer History*. Philadelphia: Temple University.

Blasius, Mark, and Shane Phelan, eds. 1997. *We Are Everywhere: A Historical Sourcebook of Gay and Lesbian Politics*. New York: Routledge.

Duberman, Martin, Martha Vicinus, and George Chauncey, eds. 1990. *Hidden from History: Reclaiming the Gay and Lesbian Past*. New York: Meridian.

Faderman, Lillian. 1981. *Surpassing the Love of Men: Romantic Friendship and Love between Women from the Renaissance to the Present*. New York: Morrow.

Jennings, Kevin. 1994. *Becoming Visible: A Reader in Gay and Lesbian History for High School and College Students*. New York: Alyson.

Katz, Jonathan Ned. 1992. *Gay American History: Lesbians and Gay Men in the USA: A Documentary History*. New York: Plume.

National Museum and Archive of Gay and Lesbian History. 1996. *The Gay Almanac*. New York: Berkley.

Web Sites

The Gay, Lesbian, and Straight Network. May 2005. GLSEN. Accessed May 31, 2005. http://www.glsen.org. Includes a resource center with ideas, books, and videos for incorporating gay and lesbian history into precollegiate education. The site hosts a variety of curriculum materials related to teaching history in its educators' section.

The Human Rights Education Association. May 2005. HREA. Accessed May 31, 2005. http://www.hrea.org. A study guide on the topic of "Sexual Orientation and Human Rights" provides a cross-national perspective on this subject. This site will provide an entry point into the consideration of efforts to protect the rights of gays, lesbians, bisexuals, and transgender individuals worldwide.

The Lesbian Herstory Archives. May 2005. Lesbian Herstory Educational Foundation, Inc. Accessed May 31, 2005. http://www.lesbianherstoryarchives.org. Documents and preserves historical information about the lives of lesbians. This is an excellent repository of primary sources related to teaching about lesbian history.

The National Women's History Project. May 2005. NWHP. Accessed May 31, 2005. http://www.nwhp.org. A clearinghouse and promoter of inclusion of women's history, including that of lesbians, into school curriculum. Although the site includes some historical content, it is most useful for finding books and materials related to the teaching of gay and lesbian history.

Teaching for Change. April 2005. Teaching for Change, Building Social Justice, Starting in the Classroom. Accessed May 31, 2005. http://www.teachingforchange.org. Offers a variety of materials for the school curriculum, including resources which link to teaching about the history of sexuality.

HIV Education

Michael Gard

Education about the human immunodeficiency virus (HIV) or, more correctly, viruses, which leads to **Acquired Immune Deficiency Syndrome (AIDS)**, is of particular relevance to queer youth since they may be at particular risk of infection, although this varies within and between countries. HIV education generally focuses on those areas of conduct seen as most likely to result in person-to-person transmission of the virus—sexual activity and intravenous (IV) drug use. HIV education is not synonymous with **sexuality education,** but rather is connected to a wide range of medical, social, and ethical issues. For example, while we may immediately associate HIV education with safe-sex practices, education for people of any age living with HIV and education designed to combat **discrimination** against HIV positive people are also legitimate concerns. Programs take a variety of forms and are conducted by schools through officially sanctioned curricula or informal networks such as universities, community groups, government agencies, national and international nongovernment organizations (NGOs), the United Nations, and others. HIV education explicitly for queer young people, however, has often been the province of grass-roots community groups, which have been at the forefront of developing innovative educational interventions. "Best practice" in HIV education has moved well beyond the simple provision of information

See also Adolescent Sexualities; Agency; AIDS; Australia, Sexualities Curriculum in; Brazil, LGBT Youth and Issues in; Canada, HIV/AIDS Education in; Identity Politics; Japan, HIV/AIDS Education in.

to consider and factor in the complex social and cultural contexts in which sex and IV drugs are used and negotiated by queer youth. Initiatives which seek to "empower" and connect queer youth are currently popular.

The degree to which HIV-AIDS has been seen primarily as a gay male concern is the source of considerable debate among queer groups. This, in part, has been a function of how "community" has been defined, which until recently has been a central site for HIV education campaigns. For example, it remains the case that HIV research and education programs for and about young **lesbians** are far less common than for **gay youth**.

Educating young people about sex and drug use remains deeply controversial. As Silin (1995) argues, a "passion for ignorance" is likely to remain a powerful force as policy makers, teachers, parents, and others make decisions about what young people should know and how they should conduct themselves. In countries with conservative "abstinence" agendas for school HIV and general sexuality education, particularly but not only the United States, queer youth are often portrayed as either "sick," sinners, or simply invisible. There, too, is some evidence that the numbers of teachers teaching "abstinence only" programs in the United States has risen sharply in the last five years (Hanssens 2001). When sexuality is discussed, much school-based sex education focuses on the mechanics of "safe" heterosexual sex. Within an Australian context, Harrison and Hillier (1999) write of the "critical turn" in HIV education, which seeks not only to acknowledge that other kinds of sex exist, but foregrounds the issues of power, which are often central to the decisions young people make about sex.

A more socially critical approach to HIV education is supported by researchers who question the effectiveness of abstinence-only approaches, which ignore ethnic and cultural issues (Irvine 1995). This is particularly critical given that, in the United States, the Centers for Disease Control and Prevention (CDC) reports that HIV infection is high among **transgender, African American, Latino**, and mixed race males (National Center for HIV, STD and TB Prevention 2005). It has also been estimated that people between the ages of thirteen and twenty-four account for about half of all new infections (Hanssens 2001). Australian statistics estimate that, at the end of 2002, people under thirty years of age made up approximately 57 percent of all people living with HIV-AIDS (7,577 out of a total of 13,422) and about 13 percent of all recorded AIDS deaths (790 out of total of 6,258). People under age 30 made up one-quarter of new HIV diagnoses in 2002 (75 men and 32 women out of a total of 815) (Access Information Centre 2004).

The association of HIV with queer groups can be seen as having both positive and negative consequences for queer youth. For example, there are those who argue that the HIV-AIDS epidemic has generated an invigorated sense of community among queer people, whereas others see a deadly disease as a most unfortunate and ultimately futile rallying point. Rasmussen (2002), among others, has noted the way a preoccupation with HIV/AIDS may simply exacerbate problems with otherwise well-meaning school health education programs. They argue that young queer people have tended to be constructed as "wounded identities," their lives filled with discrimination, abuse and, now, the ever-present risk of life-threatening disease.

Either way, HIV education directed at young people has tended both to rely on and, in the process, to perpetuate the idea of a "gay community." This tendency has its roots in a predominantly epidemiological approach to health promotion which first attempts to identify its target group and then provide this group with the information it is thought to need. Therefore, in the midst of wider "social marketing" campaigns during the 1980s, which sought to educate Western societies *en masse*, the idea that people simply need to be informed dominated programs directed at queer groups. This approach was evident through the recycling of condom-based "safe-sex" messages aimed at young people and the "gay community."

These approaches have played a role in slowing infection rates in the West, although this has varied across social groups. These differences, as well as the more general and enduring divide between people's knowledge and behavior, brought about a questioning of information-driven approaches and a call for more focus on the social and cultural contexts in which sex and drug use happen. Reviewing the first decade of HIV education in the United States, Freudenberg (1990) stresses that people actively construct their health knowledge rather than being passive knowledge receivers. The initial success of information-based approaches, he asserts, has had the negative effect of making HIV-AIDS and intravenous drug use look like isolated issues, existing within social vacuums and unrelated to wider questions of power, disadvantage, poverty, and discrimination.

HIV education has changed over the last ten to fifteen years. The Mpowerment Project, originally based in California employs teams of young gay men to plan and implement a variety of discussion and publicity based strategies, each specifically embedded in the places and events at which gay people meet. This intervention has reported significant reductions in unprotected anal sex (Hays, Rebchook, and Kegeles 2003). In the United Kingdom, London's youth group, *Outzone* (http://www. outzone.org/outzone/safersex/axis.htm) provides gay and bisexual youth with a free and confidential health clinic, which connects to social events and facilitates new spaces for young gay males to meet, talk, and discuss their experiences. The AIDS Council of New South Wales in Australia runs programs such as "Stir it Up" and other lesbian health projects (ACON 2005a) and "The Fun & Esteem Project" (ACON 2005b) for young queer people. These aim at tapping into and creating community-based dialogues and networks. While important, HIV education is just one part of these initiatives, a point which recognizes that young people make decisions about sex and drugs in the context of their social and cultural lives rather than being robots which need only to be "programmed" with the right information.

Some researchers have problematized the idea of a "gay community," pointing out that many queer youth do not identify as "gay" or do not see themselves as part of it. This may be because of geographical isolation, particularly in rural areas, where a well-developed network of gay identifying people and organizations may not exist or for other reasons such as **ethnic identity** and **social class**. McInnes, Bollen, and Race's (2002) research in the outer suburbs of Adelaide and Sydney in Australia, for example, shows that "gayness" can be something that people move fluidly into and out of as they negotiate their school, work, family and social lives, each with their different levels of acceptance of nonnormative sexualities.

Nevertheless, there are more "holistic" programs which claim to deal with questions of isolation, self-esteem, fatalism, and social connectedness that embrace the concept of community. Here the language of "capacity building" and "empowerment" has replaced that of "risk prevention" as it tackles issues of self-esteem, isolation, and fatalism, which often shape the sexual decisions of young people. For example, the Utah AIDS Foundation's "The Village" (2005) program seeks to make connections between existing gay organizations and to connect with young gay males who live in rural and regional parts of the state. Its slogan, "It's not just about sex, it's about life!" moves away from the disease model to the idea of community.

With the idea of "holistic" HIV education in mind, scholars have highlighted the contradictions within approaches attempting to prescribe safe-sex behaviors (such as insisting on condom use) and, at the same time, trying to "empower" young people (Rofes 1996). This tension between *telling* young people what to do while expecting them to make *their* decisions has produced education programs such as Mpowerment, which focus more on informal gatherings of young people, dialogue, and the exchange of ideas and feelings. These approaches signify a greater concern with the experiences and knowledge of the "learner" and, perhaps more importantly, a realization that many queer young people will practice "unsafe" sex at least some of the time.

In a more general sense, HIV educators have challenged formal and mechanistic ideas that "education" is something which happens in classrooms or via explicit public information-driven programs. McInnes, Bollen and Race (2002) have argued that people are "educated" about sex and, in particular, new and adventurous kinds of gay sex, within sexual episodes themselves. And while it is true for all young people, their research shows that the decisions gay males make about how they will do sex are not simply matters of what they "know." Indeed, they argue that some gay sexual practices derive their value precisely because they are "risky," "on the edge," and at odds with "rational" knowledge.

Outside of the English-speaking West, the situation is hugely varied and rapidly changing. Sub-Saharan Africa and the Asia/Pacific regions remain the areas in which HIV infection rates among the young appear to be highest and, for the most part, are still rising. HIV data are notoriously imprecise and controversial, particularly in countries where both the virus itself and homosexuality carry heavy stigma. UNAIDS estimates that 26.6 million people live with HIV/AIDS in Sub-Saharan Africa and that there were 3.2 million new infections in 2003. They also estimate that about 10 million Africans aged between fifteen and twenty-four and 3 million under fifteen live with HIV/AIDS. Hardest hit appear to be Botswana, Swaziland, and Zimbabwe all with adult infection rates (age fifteen and older) above 30 percent.

A wide variety of governmental and nongovernmental organizations (NGOs) are working to alleviate the African situation. For example, the United Nations UNAIDS and CDC assist individual African governments to produce **curriculum** materials for schools. In Botswana for example, the CDC supports the *Youth Health Organization*, a local NGO which seeks to create and involve young people in HIV initiatives such as HIV testing, reducing HIV stigma, and challenging traditional patriarchal beliefs about sexual conduct. Nongovernmental organizations such as the United Kingdom-based *Avert* and PLAN International are also active in Africa. In Mali, PLAN coordinates youth-specific programs including group discussions, home visits, school presentations, live theater, and electronic media announcements. It is noticeable that, unlike some other parts of the non-Western world where queer **activism** has a longer tradition, HIV education specifically for queer young people appears to be rare.

In China, a mixture of a gradually (albeit unevenly) liberalizing cultural environment and the expanding reach of information technology has meant that unofficial queer organizations are now actively raising awareness about HIV-AIDS and making connections between queer people. Chinese resources such as the Shanghai Hotline for Sexual Minorities (a telephone counseling service) and Roger Meng's *Guangzou Comrade* Internet site are instructive because, by necessity, HIV education in this context does not stand alone. Instead, it is connected to "outreach" programs (newsletters, social gatherings, public seminars), which are designed to raise self-esteem, fight **prejudice**, and place queer issues within a broader political and human rights context.

Bibliography

Access Information Centre. 2005. Accessed May 31, 2005. http://www.accessinfo.org.au/hiv_stats.htm

ACON. 2005a. AIDS Council of New South Wales. Accessed May 31, 2005. http://www.acon.org.au/community/index.cfm?cat_id=72.

ACON. 2005b. AIDS Council of New South Wales. Accessed May 31, 2005. http://www.acon.org.au/community/index.cfm?doc_id=1030&subcat=67&cat_id=66.

Freudenberg, Nicholas. 1990. "AIDS Prevention in the United States: Lessons from the First Decade." *International Journal of Health Services* 20, no. 4: 589–599.

Hanssens, Catherine. 2001. Lambda Legal. Accessed May 31, 2005. http://www.thebody.com/lambda/youth.html.

Harrison, Lyn, and Lynne Hillier. 1999. "What Should be the 'Subject' of Sex Education." *Discourse: Studies in the Cultural Politics of Education* 20, no. 2: 279–288.

Hays, Robert B., Gregory M. Rebchook, and Susan M. Kegeles. 2003. "The Mpowerment Project: Community-Building with Young Gay and Bisexual Men to Prevent HIV1." *American Journal of Community Psychology* 31, no. 3–4: 301–312.

Irvine, Janice. 1995. *Sexuality Education across Cultures*. San Francisco: Jossey-Bass.

McInnes, David, Jonathan Bollen, and Kane Race. 2002. *Sexual Learning and Adventurous Sex*. Sydney: School of Humanities, University of Western Sydney.

National Center for HIV, STD and TB Prevention. 2005, January. Centers for Disease Control and Prevention. Accessed May 31, 2005. http://www.cdc.gov/hiv/stat-trends.htm#atrisk

Rasmussen, Mary Lou. 2002. *Safety and Subversion and the Role of Agency in the Production of Sexualities in School Spaces*. Paper presented at the American Educational Research Association Annual Meeting, New Orleans, April 1–5.

Rofes, Eric. 1996. *Reviving the Tribe: Regenerating Gay Men's Sexuality and Culture in the Ongoing Epidemic*. Binghamton, NY: Haworth Press.

Silin, Jonathan G. 1995. *Sex, Death, and the Education of Children: Our Passion for Ignorance in the Age of* AIDS. New York: Teachers College Press.

The Village. 2005. UTAH AIDS Foundation. Accessed May 31, 2005. http://www.utahaids.org/index.php?id=MTUx.

Web Sites

Guangzhou Comrade. 2004. Accessed February 1, 2004. http://www.gztz.org. is perhaps the best known of China-based HIV education sites.

YouthCo. 2004. Accessed October 15, 2004. http://www.youthco.org. Canadian based "nonprofit organization working to involve youth ages 15–29 from all communities in addressing HIV/AIDS, Hepatitis C and related issues," featuring newsletters, statistics, information on HIV testing, and volunteer work opportunities.

Homophobia

John P. Elia

The term homophobia—heterosexuals' discomfort of being in close proximity to homosexuals and homosexuals' self-hatred and self-denigration—was introduced into the American English lexicon by psychologist George Weinberg, in the late 1960s. Although widely used—from chants among LGBT marchers to explanations for antigay

See also Antibias Curriculum; College Campus Programming; School Safety and Safe School Zones; Youth, At Risk; Youth, Homeless.

legislation—its usage has come under increased criticism by scholars and researchers. First, phobia, in the psychological sense, is a fear suffered by a relatively small percentage of the population. However, it extends well beyond the individual to encompass society's antihomosexual views, which manifest themselves in individual actions, ranging from name calling to murder. Further, those who display antihomosexual **prejudice** do not exhibit the physiological responses that are often associated with phobias (Shields and Harriman 1984). Nevertheless, the phenomenon of antihomosexual prejudice, rooted in societal norms and evidenced in individual actions, has a negative impact on the physical and **mental health** of sexual minority youth. This may include low self-esteem, poor academic performance, suicidal thoughts, **substance abuse**, and **eating disorders**. Additionally, thinking about the functions that homophobia serves allows more specific educational interventions to occur.

Social psychologist Gregory Herek (1984) has contributed to our understanding homophobia, identifying various psychological functions it serves for heterosexuals. Herek empirically found four chief psychological functions of homophobia: the experiential, value expressive, social expressive, and ego defensive. The experiential function determines attitudes in terms of the kinds of experiences heterosexuals have had with sexual minorities. For instance, if a heterosexual student experiences positive relationships with a gay or lesbian peer, he or she may not hold gays or lesbians in contempt and, therefore, would likely feel positively about such associations. Conversely, if a heterosexual student had negative experiences with her or his gay or lesbian schoolmates, then a negative attitude about homosexuality would likely result. The consistent strong correlation between someone knowing a gay or lesbian person and not expressing homophobic views, attitudes, or behaviors supports this explanation (Sears 1997).

The value-expressive function serves to make heterosexually-identified individuals feel more secure about their **sexual identity** by expressing values from religious doctrine or political ideology, which, in turn, justifies homophobic attitudes and behaviors. Yelling down gay rights marchers or expressing hatred toward "fags" destined to "burn in hell" outwardly manifest at this psychological function. Moving from expressing values to winning approval and acceptance from significant others leads to the third function of homophobia: social expressive. For instance, in an effort to win peer approval, a youth might verbally or physically threaten those believed to be lesbian, gay, bisexual, transgender, or queer. Asserting his masculinity and heterosexuality, the boy may solidify his social position in the school. Finally, ego defense functions to prevent anxieties, insecurities, or troubling thoughts about one's sexuality or gender. For example, a high school female student might express disdain for sexual minorities, or an adolescent youth may attack a "queer" walking home, allowing each to shore up (consciously or subconsciously) their heterosexuality and, thereby, avoid the potential distress of discovering a less-than-heterosexual side of oneself.

Historically, interventions have mostly focused on stopping outward manifestations of homophobia such as name-calling, taunting, and physical assault of **lesbian, gay, bisexual, transgender**, or **queer** (LGBTQ) youth. For example, some schools in the United States have adopted antislur and zero-tolerance policies that target these **bullying** behaviors. Although these **educational policies** are well intended, they fail to address the underlying, structural causes of this form of prejudice.

Using Herek's four functions of homophobia, we can consider more effective pedagogical interventions in the schools. Employing the four-function model as a hub, prejudice reduction can be integrated throughout the curriculum, from health education to literature. Often, a **sexuality education** teacher is charged with the responsibility of dealing with issues of homosexuality in more progressive schools. In these schools, where there is discussion of homosexuality, lessons and activities that address homophobia directly are important. Providing a thoughtful and an effective educational experience to overcome homophobia throughout the **curriculum**, and not just in any one particular class, is important. However, in many schools, teachers are prohibited from discussing this topic, even in sexuality education classes, either by the school district or by state law. Here, teaching students about the deleterious effects of prejudice, in general, is a viable option. Students, then, can extrapolate to more specific forms of prejudice.

Another pedagogical strategy is to de-center **heteronormativity**, encouraging teachers to be more inclusive of nonnormative sexualities and gender expressions when teachers plan and present educational activities. This can be accomplished subtly or more directly, again depending on school policy. Further, given how **sexism** is inextricably linked to homophobia, a focus on sexism and **gender role** expectations can readily be addressed.

Whatever specific pedagogical strategies are used, focusing solely on behavioral manifestations of homophobia, as has been traditionally the case, is not the most effective approach. Addressing behavior through adoption and enforcement of educational policies combined with a focus on the various functions which homophobia serves is essential.

Homophobia contributes to a plethora of problems for LGBT youth. Certainly, at the very least, the self-esteem and perceived self-worth of gay and lesbian youth are compromised due to the ubiquitous negative attitudes and prejudice against homosexuality. Among some of the more serious by-products of homophobia on youth include **drug use**, school failure, being thrown out of home, loss of family and friendships, and **suicide**. In fact, data from the United States National Institutes of Mental Health (NIMH) indicate that youth suicides and attempted suicides are often associated with distress about sexual identity.

A common assumption is that homophobia only affects gays, lesbians, and bisexuals, or that transphobia is only a problem for transgender persons. All youth are harmed as a result of these prejudices. Often it is the presumption of one's sexual minority or **gender identity** status, along with heterosexism and pervasive heteronormativity, which triggers these phobias in others. For example, an individual who does not enact the socially expected gender roles, such as a "**sissy boy**" acting in an effeminate manner, is socially unacceptable no matter what his actual sexual identity. The inability, particularly among Western men, to express their feminine qualities is related to a fear of social ostracism. Similarly, overt male-bonding found in all-male military schools or contact **sports** allows for the expression of affection only within the context of hypermasculinity. Finally, because transgressive sexual and gender behaviors are generally despised and stigmatized, heterosexual youth who might otherwise want to pursue friendships with nonheterosexual peers might not do so due to the notion of "guilt by association."

Although homophobia is widespread, there are numerous studies on adult attitudes toward homosexuality that show a strong correlation between antihomosexual prejudice and demographics and personality traits (Sears 1997). For instance, some general characteristics of those who express homophobia are: males, older, not well educated, and residing in the Midwest, South or in rural areas. In terms of personality traits, those who express homophobia are more likely to hold conservative religious views, express authoritarian beliefs, have guilt and shame about sexuality, and subscribe to traditional gender roles.

Because nearly all youth attend schools, it is important that curricular and cocurricular interventions occur. For instance, the teaching of **history** can be vastly improved by including the historical contributions that sexual minorities have made. Similarly, literature teachers can question the absence or masking of same-sex love in **poetry** filled with heterosexual references. Finally, in teaching sexuality education, teachers can encourage students to interrogate and challenge heterosexist ideologies and heteronormative assumptions. Full integration—as opposed to tokenism and further marginalization—of gays, bisexuals, transgender persons, and lesbians throughout most if not all subjects can help to erode the harmful effects of homophobia by reducing heteronormativity and **heterosexism**.

Cocurricular activities are also important in the continued efforts to abate homophobia. **Gay–straight alliances**, for example, facilitate not only an understanding of homosexuality, but also structure an environment in schools whereby sexual minority youth and heterosexual youth work together to create a **school climate** imbued with social justice, not to mention one more hospitable to queer students.

As educators and others work with youth to impart knowledge about homosexuality and to curb antihomosexual prejudice, it is important to consider the intersections of cognition with affect and behavior. Teaching *about* the negative impact of such attitudes and behavior or providing information *about* the contributions of sexual minorities is less likely to affect a decline in homophobia, than focusing also on the affective and behavioral domains. Paul Van de Ven (1997) summarizes various considerations for having a comprehensive antihomophobia program, based on his research integrating the cognitive, behavioral, and affective domains. He notes that not only do most educators have little knowledge about gay and lesbian youth, these professionals could gain considerable skills and attitudinal changes by informal discussions, in-service trainings, and conferences. Additionally, realistic and enforceable **antidiscrimination policies** that enjoy widespread and vocal support by school **administrators** and the community are necessary complements to curriculum and cocurriculum inclusion. Finally, linking antigay prejudice to forms of masculinity undergirding homophobia, challenging sexism, and deconstructing sexual and gender hierarchies are essential components of a comprehensive antihomophobia program.

Bibliography

Blumenfeld, Warren J., ed. 1992. *Homophobia: How We All Pay the Price.* Boston: Beacon Press.

Herek, Gregory M. 1984. Attitudes Toward Lesbians and Gay Men: A Factor-Analytic Study. *Journal of Homosexuality,* 10, nos. 1 & 2: 39–51.

———, ed. 1998. *Stigma and Sexual Orientation: Understanding Prejudice against Lesbians, Gay Men, and Bisexuals.* Thousand Oaks, CA: Sage.

Herek, Gregory M., and Kevin T. Berrill, eds. 1992. *Hate Crimes: Confronting Violence against Lesbians and Gay Men.* Thousand Oaks, CA: Sage.

Rothblum, Esther D., and Lynn A. Bond, eds. 1996. *Preventing Heterosexism and Homophobia.* Thousand Oaks, CA: Sage.

Sears, James T. 1997. "Thinking Critically/ Intervening Effectively about Heterosexism and Homophobia: A Twenty-Five Year Research Retrospective." Pp. 13–48 in *Overcoming*

Heterosexism and Homophobia: Strategies That Work. Edited by James T. Sears and Walter L. Williams. New York: Columbia University Press.

Shields, S. A., and R. E. Harriman. 1984. "Fear of Male Homosexuality: Cardiac Responses of Low and High Homonegative Males. *Journal of Homosexuality,* 10, nos.1 & 2: 53–67.

Van de Ven, Paul. 1997. "Promoting Respect for Different Viewpoints and Ways of Living to Australian High School Students." Pp. 218–232 in *Overcoming Heterosexism and Homophobia: Strategies That Work.* Edited by James T. Sears and Walter L. Williams. New York: Columbia University Press.

Weinberg, George. 1972. *Society and the Healthy Homosexual.* New York: Anchor.

Web Sites

QueerTheory.com. 2004. Accessed December 5, 2004. http://www.queertheory.com/theories/sexuality/homophobia.htm. Links to a several online resources on homophobia.

Sexual Prejudice: Understanding Homophobia and Heterosexism. 2004. Greg Herek. Accessed December 5, 2004. http://psychology.ucdavis.edu/rainbow/html/prej_defn.html. Offers the historical context of homophobia and sexual prejudice, as well as defines key terms. Additionally, it provides a critique of the concept homophobia and offers the concept of sexual prejudice as a useful alternative and provides three key features of it.

I

Identity Development

Allison J. Kelaher Young

Identity development is an ongoing process of answering the questions, "Who am I?" and "Where do I belong?" In general, this is a process by which an individual perceives him or herself in relation to others. In terms of **sexual identity**, this psychological and sociological process involves assessing one's sexual attitudes and behaviors in relation to heterosexual norms. With respect to **gender identity** and **sexual orientation**, identity development refers more specifically to the evolution of a gay, lesbian, bisexual, and/or transgender identity. Historically, the process of identity development is framed in terms of attitudes (i.e., attractions, beliefs) and behaviors. **Research** has identified a number of identity development milestones in **childhood** and **adolescence** related to both attitudes and behaviors. For instance, attitudes include awareness of same-sex attraction, self-disclosure, self-labeling, and internalized **homophobia**. Likewise, behaviors involve disclosure of identity to others, sexual activity with same-sex partners, and engagement in intimate relationships. This approach, however, has been criticized as essentialist by some scholars of **feminism** and **poststructuralism** who understand identity construction in more flexible, dynamic ways.

Early models of sexual identity development focused on stages of the identification process. One example is Cass' (1984) six-stage model, which uses a psychological framework:

1. *Identity confusion*—initial questioning of sexual identity. At this point, an individual can choose to continue to explore sexual minority identity or reject the possibility, thereby foreclosing development.

2. *Identity comparison*—examination of the differences between self and heterosexual others. This may involve initial contacts with sexual minority individuals or groups.

3. *Identity tolerance*—increasing contact with other sexual minority individuals or groups, though this contact is not yet public. These contacts are selective and their quality influences behavior.

4. *Identity acceptance*—increased commitment to the sexual minority identity. Here, an individual may begin to disclose his or her identity to others, while beginning to consider how to maintain a presence in the dominant society as a sexual minority individual.

5. *Identity pride*—identification becomes more public, with loyalty to sexual minorities as a group. There may be feelings of frustration and anger at the social injustice experienced by sexual minorities.

See also Adolescent Sexualities; Australia, Research on Sexual Identities; College Age Students; Queer and Queer Theory; Racial Identity; Religion and Psychological Development.

6. *Identity synthesis* — a sexual minority identity has been integrated into the individual's overall identity. View of self and view of perception of others is consistent so that private and public selves are united.

Researchers using this model have found that the stages generally followed the order in the model, though there appears to be some overlap in the earlier (1 and 2) and later (5 and 6) stages. Thus, a four-stage model might be a more parsimonious depiction of sexual identity development.

Thus, for Cass, youth begin the process of identification with a period of comparison and confusion. One might think "I'm not like others . . . why?" Exposure to sexual minorities through interpersonal relationships and cultural events would help young people to contextualize these feelings of difference. As one begins to adopt a sexual identity, one internalizes the various meanings of his or her minority identity.

In contrast, Troiden's (1989) four-stage sociological model of identity development, focusing on the role of the social context on self-definition. Troiden argues that the process begins before puberty and ends in adulthood, encapsulating a wide spectrum of youth. Beginning with a period of confusion similar to that proposed by Cass, Troiden argues that youth identify as gay or lesbian, by adolescence and that this identification solidifies by adulthood. At that point, the individual has incorporated a sexual minority identity into one's overall identity:

1. *Sensitization*—prepubertal stage where the individual perceives self as different from same-sex peers (marginalization). This stage essentially sets the tone for later sexual identity development.

2. *Identity confusion*—adolescence; individual begins to question sexual identity. Early adolescents consider the *possibility* of minority sexuality, questioning who they are and where they belong. By mid- to late adolescence, the individual considers the *probability* of sexual minority status.

3. *Identity assumption*—during or later in adolescence; individual adopts a sexual minority identity, accompanied by a sexual minority presentation of self. This would be considered the "coming out" stage.

4. *Identity commitment*—early adulthood; internal and external dimensions of sexual identity are consistent, emotionally and sexually. Identity as a sexual minority is legitimized and the individual is comfortable with both the identity and the role. Engagement in a same-sex intimate relationship demarcates this stage.

Troiden acknowledged the wide range of timing and sequence of developmental milestones, as well as characteristics that influence an individual's development of sexual identity while accounting for historical (cohort) effects. These include the influence of individual characteristics (i.e., gender, **ethnicity**, educational level), interpersonal contexts (i.e., family and peer support), and social organizational contexts (i.e., school, **workplace**).

A third model describes identity both as an intrapersonal (psychological) process and an interpersonal (sociological) process. McCarn and Fassinger's (1996) model of lesbian identity development accounts for the interaction between individual sexual identity as well as group membership identity. This model has four phases:

1. *Awareness*—the individual acknowledges feelings of difference, as well as the existence of difference in others' sexual identities.

2. *Exploration*—the individual begins to examine feelings of same-sex attraction, as well as her/his attitudes and relation to gays and lesbians as a group.

3. *Deepening/Commitment*—the individual incorporates choices about sexuality as part of self, as well as becomes more involved with sexual minority reference groups. She also is aware of the consequences of her choices and the existence of oppression around those choices.

4. *Internalization/Synthesis*—the individual experiences self-acceptance and internal consistency, as well as openly identifies as a member of a sexual minority group.

Stage models of identity development share an essentialist philosophy. That is, all offer a universal or generalizable idea of the sequence and timing of sexual identity milestones. For instance, it is generally accepted that between the ages of eight and eleven there is a development of awareness of same-sex attractions; between the ages of twelve and fifteen, same-sex sexual behaviors emerge; between the ages of fifteen and eighteen there is an identification of sexual minority status; between the ages of seventeen and nineteen an individual begins to disclose his or her identity to others; and between the ages eighteen and twenty the individual would begin to focus on the development of same-sex intimate relationships (Dubé and Savin-Williams 1999).

Although stage models offer useful heuristics for understanding a process as complex as sexual identity development, they are not without criticism. Social constructionists and those operating from a postmodernist perspective challenge the essentialist assumptions underlying these models as well as the absence of cross-cultural and non-Western research. In contrast, they argue that identity is a process of continual negotiation between the individual and her or his social contexts (Talburt 2000).

In addition, these stage models are largely predicated on a homosexual orientation. Historically, bisexual identity has been viewed as sexual identity development arrested in the confusion stage. It was seen more as a strategy for dealing with identity conflict, as a transitional period before the individual identified as gay or lesbian, or as a way to maintain heterosexual privilege. Many people equated **bisexuality** with ambivalence. Because of these views, bisexuals may experience a "double closet," invalidated by both the gay and lesbian community and the heterosexual community.

More current models have framed bisexuality in a nonlinear fashion and as a flexible and adaptive approach to sexuality (Blumstein and Schwartz 2000). Three major themes arise for bisexuals:

1. *Labeling*—perception of self as different. The individual acknowledges the perceptions of others.

2. *Conflicting events*—experience in heterosexual and homosexual relationships. The individual seeks to resolve this seeming dualistic conflict.

3. *Reference group contact*—choice of social group to refer to either heterosexuals, homosexuals, or both. The individual gains or loses validation from his or her social group.

Although these themes can be related to stages within the linear models, they do not appear in any given order. Indeed, **bisexual youth** would negotiate and renegotiate these themes throughout the lifespan. In addition, this negotiation process is dependent upon various social contexts within which youth live and work.

Rust (2000) argues that there is greater variability in sexual self-identification with multiple changes in sexual identity spread across the lifespan. Conceptualizing such nonlinear models as the creation and recreation of sexual essence (i.e., attractions and behaviors) with respect to the social and political contexts, she believes that bisexuality identity development may be better served by defining with an event or task model rather than a stage model. Here the object of attraction is a particular person not a specific gender.

The contexts of ethnicity and gender have also been shown to affect the process of sexual identity development. Diamond (2000), for instance, has confirmed the fluidity of women's sexual identities described by Rust. Across a two-year study, half of the participants experienced multiple changes in identity as sexual minorities. Although most sexual behavior was consistent with their attractions, one fourth of the lesbians had engaged sexually with men within this two-year period. Thus, bisexual and **lesbian youth** might experience a variety of shifts in sexual identity, based upon attraction rather than on their sexual identity.

Similarly, recent research comparing gay and bisexual men of various ethnic groups has found that the timing and sequence of development milestones such as same-sex attractions, engagement in same-sex sexual activity, identity labeling, and identity disclosure differ (Dubé and Savin-Williams 1999). For example, identity disclosure to family, and other gender romantic and sexual involvement were found to be different among Euro-American, **African American, Latino,** and **Asian American** males. African American youth were more likely to have a longer period of time between same-sex sexual activity and identifying as gay or bisexual whereas Asian-American youth were more likely to identify as gay or bisexual before becoming involved in same-sex sexual activity. Thus, the white, Western notion of "**coming out**" may not have the same meaning across racial and ethnic groups and, in fact, may not prove useful in understanding the sexualities cross-culturally.

Bibliography

Blumstein, Philip C., and Pepper Schwartz. 2000. "Bisexuality: Some Social Psychology Issues." Pp. 339–351 in *Bisexuality in the United States: A Social Science Reader.* Edited by Paula C. Rodríguez Rust. New York: Columbia University Press.

Cass, Vivienne C. 1984. "Homosexual Identity Formation: Testing a Theoretical Model." *Journal of Sex Research* 20, no. 2: 143–167.

Diamond, Lisa M. 2000. "Sexual Identity, Attractions, and Behavior among Young Sexual-Minority Women Over a 2-Year Period." *Developmental Psychology* 36, no. 2: 241–250.

Dubé, Eric M., and Ritch C. Savin-Williams. 1999. "Sexual Identity Development among Ethnic Sexual-Minority Male Youths." *Developmental Psychology* 35, no. 6: 1389–1398.

McCarn, Susan R., and Ruth E. Fassinger. 1996. "Revisioning Sexual Minority Identity Formation: A New Model of Lesbian Identity and its Implications." *Counseling Psychologist* 24, no. 3: 508–534.

Rodríguez Rust, Paula C. 2000. "The Biology, Psychology, Sociology and Sexuality of Bisexuality." Pp. 403–470 in *Bisexuality in the United States: A Social Science Reader*. Edited by Paula C. Rodríguez Rust. New York: Columbia University Press.

Talburt, Susan. 2000. *Subject to Identity: Knowledge, Sexuality, and Academic Practices in Higher Education*. Albany: State University of New York Press.

Troiden, Richard R. 1989. "The Formation of Homosexual Identities." *Journal of Homosexuality* 17, nos. 1–2: 43–73.

Zinik, Gary. 2000. "Identity Conflict or Adaptive Flexibility? Bisexuality Reconsidered." Pp. 55–60 in *Bisexuality in the United States: A Social Science Reader*. Edited by Paula C. Rodríguez Rust. New York: Columbia University Press.

Identity Politics

John E. Petrovic and **Jerry Rosiek**

Oftentimes people unite around some aspect of their identity, such as **race**, gender, or **sexual orientation**. If this group has experienced **discrimination** or feels discriminated against in some way because of this aspect of its collective identity, it may begin to engage politically to challenge the sources of such discrimination. "Identity politics" refers to this process. The 1950s and 1960s witnessed the rise of the civil rights movement with its appeal that universal ideals (e.g., life, liberty, equality, and justice) be applied to all. Since the 1970s, the appeal has been to identify these ideals as an important resource among oppressed and marginalized groups in challenging inequitable social relations. Deeper consideration of these universal ideals began to shed light on the specific circumstances of different groups. Soon universalist appeals gave way to more specific struggles based on the creation of a common group identity. **African Americans**, Native Americans, women, gays and lesbians, the disabled, and other groups have engaged in identity politics to leverage social change. In schools, identity politics is applied through policy and curricular efforts to overcome **heteronormativity** and to provide LGBT youth with educational environments that recognize their particular needs and interests. Such actions have included student demands to form **gay–straight alliance** clubs, petitions to add "sexual orientation" to school **antidiscrimination** statements, and efforts to include gay and lesbian issues in all school **curricula**.

The modern gay movement or gay identity politics began in the 1950s with organizations such as the Daughters of Bilitis and the Mattachine Society. Both groups, the former strictly women, formed to help individuals cope with problems relating to their homosexuality, to create a sense of community, and to challenge antigay discrimination. In their efforts to challenge discrimination, these early organizations typically engaged in what is called "identity politics of assimilation." Much like the civil rights appeal to universal ideals, identity politics of assimilation emphasize identification with the dominant group, saying in a sense, "We are the same as you. As such, we would like to be included and be accorded the same rights

See also Asian American Youth; Colonialism and Homosexuality; Ethnic Identity; Native and Indigenous LGBT Youth; Racial Identity; White Antiracism.

and responsibilities as you." Critics of this strategy argue that by focusing on universal notions of human sameness, the politics of assimilation have rendered the gay community invisible.

After the **Stonewall** riots in 1969, the Gay Liberation Front (GLF) was formed, breaking ranks with the more conservative groups and assimilationist practices of the prior decades. This more radical approach to identity politics, the politics of recognition, is evident in the introduction of the GLF Manifesto:

> Throughout recorded history, oppressed groups have organized to claim their rights and obtain their needs. Homosexuals, who have been oppressed by physical violence and by ideological and psychological attacks at every level of social interaction, are at last becoming angry. To you, our gay sisters and brothers, we say that you are oppressed; we intend to show you examples of the hatred and fear with which straight society relegates us to the position and treatment of subhumans, and to explain their basis. We will show you how we can use our righteous anger to uproot the present oppressive system with its decaying and constricting ideology, and how we, together with other oppressed groups, can start to form a new order, and a liberated life-style, from the alternatives which we offer. (Equality Alliance 2004)

In challenging the "constricting ideology," engagement in politics of recognition says, "We are different from you, and we want you to recognize and respect that difference. Regardless, we take pride in our gay identities." (Some groups take this last sentiment of pride in the identity politics of recognition to another level by proposing separate, autonomous spheres of action for oppressed groups, e.g., Pan-Africanists.) Thus, the politics of recognition required the development of a gay identity, of a gay culture to be recognized and liberated.

Although engagement in identity politics of recognition has brought about significant changes by forcing heterosexuals to face the issue of homosexuality, it is not without its critics. The primary criticism is that defining a particular identity as X also tends to limit the boundaries of the identity, making it very rigid (Dean 1996). In other words, providing a definition of what it means to be "gay" will certainly exclude some people who identify as gay but who do not fit the definition exactly. Defining groups of people serves to police the borders of the identity of the group—keeping some in and others out. The idea that an identity can be defined by seeking some "true," invariable, or fixed nature of being X is called "essentialism;" it raises a lot of questions. Should only those people who hold the same views or ideals about their identity be able to participate in solidarity with that group? To what extent is it possible or even desirable to rule out within-group variation?

Essentialism and a rigid construction of identity also lead us to ignore the possibility and need for deeper analyses of the many factors and circumstances that influence our identities. It is not the same, for example, to be an upper middle class, white, gay student as it is to attend school as a lower middle class, African American, lesbian. The interaction of race, gender, **social class**, and **sexual identity** lead to very different life experiences. Thus, there is a need to consider the idea of making spaces for differences within difference (Kopelson 2002). A rigid conception of identity also reinforces the group's minority status and, consequently, all of the negative baggage and assumptions of inferiority that that might entail.

Given this critique, gay identity politics is giving way to queer politics. Unlike identity politics in which a primary goal is to organize around an essential identity, queer politics questions all identities. In this view, identities are seen not as essential or something that occurs naturally, but as being formed by the culture, institutions, and language around us. These social forces box us into specific identities. Basically, we are "told" how to act, behave, dress, and talk. Typically these "boxes" are presented as binary opposites. One is male or female, straight or gay, black or white. But human identity and being are much more complex than this. The focus of queer politics is to unite people in opposition to the forces that put us all into identity boxes.

By not essentializing identities, the queer politics movement theoretically allows progress beyond the "us vs. them" worldview. It also helps to refocus on the real sources of human oppression maintained by differences in political power. Under identity politics, for example, the **women's movement** attempted to break the glass ceiling, and the **Latino** and African American movements sought integration (assimilation) into mainstream society. But what were they fighting for? Women were essentially fighting to be more like men, whereas Latinos and African Americans were fighting for equal access to jobs in, say, the Border Patrol or the FBI. In other words, the movements driven by identity politics of assimilation failed to question the paradoxes of these groups' struggle. They failed to see that those in power also engage in identity politics. For example, heterosexuality is not only taken for granted as being upstanding and morally correct, but also it is state-authorized (e.g., through the institution of marriage) as such. Nonheterosexuality and other nonmainstream identities are simultaneously presented as opposite to these "upstanding" identities (Cohen 2001). Nevertheless, such identity politics of power are not recognized as such. They are "just the way it is."

Queer politics and **queer pedagogy**, guided by **queer theory** and **poststructuralism**, endeavor to expose such assumptions. It is not about *being* "queer"; it is a way of *thinking* about the world, presenting a far more complex and nuanced understanding of power. For the dominant codes of power do not adversely affect only those persons who happen to identify as gay, lesbian, bisexual, or transgender. Essentializing heterosexuality limits the ways that those individuals who are "straight" may "choose" to lead their lives. For example, heterosexuality is often defined by courtship and marriage. People reaching a certain age without having married or young people not involved in heterosexual dating often come under suspicion.

On the one hand, as per queer politics, it is argued that a person's identity is not static. It is in constant flux and is not one-dimensional. On the other hand, as per identity politics of recognition, the construction of identity may be necessary to overcome oppression and to arrive at political consciousness. Identity politics of recognition helps to expose the hidden assumptions of universality and the cultural biases smuggled into supposedly neutral institutions like school and **educational policies** and practices. Despite the claim that curricular content is or should be neutral, heterosexuality is privileged, making the hidden curriculum *anti* other sexualities. For example, in elementary school curricula, social studies consist, in part, of discussions about "family." While some nontraditional family units (single parent households or biracial families) are increasingly presented, a vast majority of schools exclude any discussion of children in families of same-sex parents.

The politics of recognition demands that such discussions take place in schools, perhaps even at the risk of essentialism. This demand further requires that policies be put into place that support and reinforce this curriculum. Encouraging, or at the least, not disallowing gay–straight alliances would be one such policy. Some other specific examples of policies that would promote recognition of LGBT students and their needs in schools include providing gender-neutral bathrooms, adding sexual orientation and **gender identity** to nondiscrimination clauses, and hiring openly gay or lesbian faculty and staff.

Bibliography

Anner, John. 1996. *Beyond Identity Politics: Emerging Social Justice Movements in Communities of Color*. Boston: South End Press.

Cohen, Cathy J. 2001. "Punks, Bulldaggers, and Welfare Queens: The Radical Potential of Queer Politics?" Pp. 200–227 in *Sexual Identities, Queer Politics*. Edited by Mark Blasius. Princeton, NJ: Princeton University Press.

Dean, Jodi. 1996. *Solidarity of Strangers: Feminism after Identity Politics*. Berkeley: University of California Press.

Kopelson, Karen. 2002. "Dis/Integrating the Gay/Queer Binary: 'Reconstructed Identity Politics' for a Performative Pedagogy." *College English* 65, no. 1: 17–35.

Petrovic, John E. 1999. "Moral Democratic Education and Homosexuality: Censoring Morality." *Journal of Moral Education* 28, no. 2: 201–209.

Sears, James T., and William Letts, eds. 1999. *Queering Elementary Education*. Lanham, MD: Rowman & Littlefield.

Web Site

Equality Alliance. November 2004. Accessed December 19, 2004. http://www.pfc.org.uk. In 1998, eighty organizations from across the United Kingdom met and formed the Equality Alliance. The aim was to create a democratic membership organization that would unite LGBT activists and groups behind common demands. These organizations wanted to share their ideas, experiences, and resources to maximize their campaigning.

India, LGBT Youth and Issues in

Suresh Parekh

For the ten to fifty million lesbian, gay, bisexual, and transgender (LGBT) Indians it is not easy to be a sexual minority within a society where cultural and religious misconceptions, immense social stigma, and an outdated penal code exist. Historically, normal variants of human sexuality—homosexuality, **bisexuality**, and **transsexuality**—were tolerated and valued in Indian society. The Hindu civilization was the first to give all forms of human sexuality, sexual activities, and sexual pleasures a highly respectable and dignified place in every aspect of life, art, literature, and even religion. However, today, more than half of India's population lives in small towns and villages with very restricted and nonliberated social, ethical, and religious environments. All nonprocreative sexual practices—between men or women—are considered as unnatural, inhuman, grotesque, and unlawful. Section 377 of Indian Penal Code (IPC), a law, enacted by the British colonizers nearly 150 years ago, criminalizes homosexual intimacy. Nevertheless, an emerging gay rights movement since the 1980s has made some inroads into Indian society. There is, however, little research in this area and slight preparation of teachers and counselors to work with LGBT youth.

See also Asia, LGBT Youth and Issues in; Colonialism and Homosexuality; Community LGBT Youth Groups; Educational Policies; Gender Roles; Identity Politics; Intersex; Multiple Genders; Parents, Responses to Homosexuality; Reparative Therapy; Social Class.

Since the known history of Hindu civilization, at least half of the population of one billion people of India worship with devotion and ardor the God Shiva or Shankar, symbolized as an erected penis or lingum based in or coming out from an open vagina or *yoni* (the main deity in any Shiv temple is the Shivling, a black stone carved in the shape of an erected penis based on a vagina-shaped stone foundation). The seers and sages of ancient India accepted and recognized Kama (sexual pleasure, sexual fulfillment) as one of the four prime and principal aims of whole life of a human being. The walls and the pillars of hundreds of not so famous and world-famous temples or religious places like Khajuraho, Konark, and Modhera, built between the sixth and twelfth centuries, depict love scenes, sexual intercourse, sexual postures, and love making with ultimate, unparalleled, and supreme artistic skills. The *Kama Sutra*, *Anang Ranga*, *Ratti Rahasya*, *Shringar Shatak* and the *Sanskrit* epics and dramas are among the world's first authoritative and monumental literary works, written by Hindu saints and religious scholars. There are references of same-sex love and stories of bisexual and transgender persons in the greatest epics, *Ramayan* and *Mahabharat*. There, too, are Hindu festivals and sects that celebrate homosexual acts. There are descriptions of Tantric initiation rites, which evoked the idea of universal bisexuality.

Tolerance toward different sexual practices changed with many invasions from ancient to colonial times. From **Muslim** Mughal invaders to **Christian** British colonialists, cultural and social beliefs, traditions, and ideologies on every aspect of human life, including sexuality, were brought to India. These have profoundly impacted Indian understanding of gender, sexuality, and sexual practices. For example, the Judeo–Christian moral and religious values, which prevailed throughout the British Empire, maintained that any nonprocreative sexual act was sinful and against nature. Consequently, sodomy was criminalized in the Indian Penal Code, which remains in force.

What is it to be a gay or a lesbian or a bisexual or a hijra in India? On the evening of August 15, 2004, the Delhi police found the murdered bodies of two youth from a house in the posh area of South Delhi. While searching the residence, authorities discovered homosexual photographs, CDs, and other literature; there were no signs of theft or burglary. Some sections of the media decried the rise in homosexual activities; few protested the apparent crime of homophobic violence. The following month, Delhi High Court dismissed a writ petition challenging the constitutional validity of Section 377 of Indian Penal Code.

Not only within the traditional family and social environment of the **rural** areas, but also in the highly-educated urban communities, marriage and procreation are central to a man or woman's status in the family and to their social identity. Thus, family and societal pressures become unavoidable and increasingly intense as LGBT youth enter adulthood. Scolding, surveillance, restrictions on movement, beatings, treatment by physicians, psychiatrists or even quacks, and referral to religious leaders are common family responses. For most sexual minority youth, it is difficult to withstand such persuasive opposition. Most ultimately surrender to these pressures to please the family, to save it from social dishonor, or to retain the security of the family. However, many who marry heterosexually become bisexual or remain closeted homosexuals.

In many cases, Indian bisexuality is situational. Prison guards, teachers, or wardens in boarding schools and orphan houses—due to their job situations, lack of enough money, authoritative positions, and nonavailability of heterosexual partners— engage in same-sex behaviors. There, too, are some Indian bisexual women and men who continue to feel the need for the social recognition and financial support coming from their family and married life. Thus, some socially, professionally, or politically active married women engage in lesbianism.

The case of the hijra is different. This Indian transgender—an institutionalized third gender, neither male nor female—has a long history. Numerous stories and anecdotes are found in all types of India literary works, including the greatest epics of *Ramayan* and *Mahabharat*, in the *Kama Sutra*, and throughout travelogues of visitors to India during ancient and middle ages.

No serious attempts have been made to know the number or percentage of hijras in Indian population; estimates range from 50,000 to 500,000. Although hijras are found in every village, town, and city, the greater number live in metropolitan areas like Mumbai, Delhi, Calcutta, Ahmedabad, and Hydrabad where they easily find more opportunities to perform their traditional roles.

Generally, five to fifteen hijras share a house. One of the reasons hijras live communally is the Hindu belief that, in a past life, he spoiled the life of a woman because in marriage he was incapable of satisfying the wife's sexual and maternal wishes. For this sin, he must live the next seven lives as hijra. Hijra communities are so accessible and accommodating in nature and in structure that they attract persons with diverse personalities, sexual needs, and gender identities. In older times, it was a common belief that older hijras kidnapped effeminate or normal boys in order to nurture them as hijras. However, no substantial evidence supports this belief, as most hijras join of their own volition during their adolescence or adulthood. In some cases, more in the lower castes, parents willfully leave their effeminate or physiologically impotent child with the hijra community, believing the child will devote his life to the religious service of the Mother Goddess and receive blessings to be born as a "normal" male or female in the next life.

Individuals who join the hijra community are hermaphrodites, physiologically impotent and behaviorally effeminate. Hijras engage in sexual relations with males, and homosexual prostitution is widespread (Nanda 1986). Due to having a defective sexual organ or lacking a complete reproductive system, they are considered neither fully male nor female. These individuals show more effeminacy in their behavioral patterns. During childhood, these boys prefer to dress in girl's clothes, to play with girls, to engage in feminine household duties, and to stay away from boyhood games. In many cases, these individuals are persuaded and encouraged by older men to engage in homosexual activities. These activities strain relations in the family, neighborhood, and school. Ultimately, there remains no option for the youth but to enter the hijra community:

> When an individual decides to formally join the hijra community, he is taken to Bombay to visit one of the seven major gurus, usually the guru of the person who has brought him there. At the initiation ritual, the guru gives the novice a new, female name. The novice vows to obey the guru and the rules of the community. The guru then presents the new chela with some gifts . . . This guru–chela relationship is a lifelong bond of reciprocity in which the guru is obligated to help the chela and the chela is obligated to be loyal and obedient to the guru. (Nanda 1986, 36).

Emasculation or the castration of the male organ, performed before the picture of the Mother Goddess, is one of the most important rituals within the hijra community.

During earlier eras, hijras earned their living by serving the aristocracy as slaves or servants. Renowned for their loyalty, they were "confidants of their masters and mistresses" often gaining "an elevated social position and have had many honors and distinctions bestowed upon them" (Jaffrey 1997, 25, 189). In contemporary India, their only major traditional role is conferring well wishes and blessings at occasions such as engagements, marriages, and childbirths. Here, they sometimes sing and dance before receiving charity. Once or twice a year hijras also visit every merchant establishment and each residence to collect alms. In the last decade, many hijras, particularly

Three hijras conferring blessings on a new-born child in Junagadh City, India. © 2004 Suresh C. Parekh

in the states of Uttar Pradesh, Madhya Pradesh, and Gujarat, have sought election in local, municipal, district, and assembly contests, and some have won.

From the later part of the 1970s, some Indian gay and lesbian individuals started "coming out." During the next decade, many Indians, living in North America and **Europe** who had already "come out" in the West, explored homosexuality within the Indian context. This corresponded with the rapid spread of **AIDS/HIV** infections in India and the urgent need to create proper sexual health services, appropriate guidance for safer sexual practices, and emotional support accessible to **lesbian, gay, bisexual**, and **transgender** youth. India has the second largest HIV-positive population in the world and the fastest growing infection rate. The emergence of Indian (and South Asian) gay and lesbian organizations such as Trikone and Samakami in the United States, Khush in **Canada**, Naz Foundation International, Shakti, and Dost in the **United Kingdom,** and publications such as *Khush Khayal, Shakti Khabar*, and *Pukar* proved instrumental in the emergence of the lesbian and gay movement in India.

A host of Indian-based organizations have emerged: Naz Foundation India Trust (Calcutta and New Delhi); Hum Safar Trust and Khush Club (Mumbai); Counsel Club, Fun Club (Calcutta); Sakhi, Sathi, AIDS Bhedbhav Virodhi Andolan (ABVA) in New Delhi; Good As You (GAY) in Bangalore; Gay Information Centre (Secunderabad); Lakshya Trust (Vadodara). There, too, are the exclusively lesbian organizations Sakhi Lesbian Resource Centre (New Delhi), Sisters (Chennai), and Stree Sangama (Mumbai). These organizations provide various types of support to LGBT youth, facilitating regular meetings where they can meet, gain information, and support each other, and helping to develop a sense of identity as well as a feeling of togetherness. They arrange parties and social gatherings and celebrate festivals and special occasions as well as accommodations and employment. These groups provide support systems related to sexual health, such as information on various facts of HIV transmission and testing facilities for HIV and other sexually transmitted infections (STI). Some organizations have also recruited trained counselors and social workers in their projects and even organized training programs by which young gays and lesbians are trained in counseling techniques.

Such organizations have successfully organized major seminars in India. In December 1993, Sakhi, a lesbian resource center, presented a workshop on "Gender

Constructions and History of Alternate Sexualities in South Asia." The Delhi seminar aimed at reviving the alternate historical and mythological traditions and delved deeply into diverse issues related to gays, lesbians, and bisexuals. One year later, the second major seminar, "Gay Men and Men Who Have Sex With Men," was organized in Mumbai. This was a consultation meeting on sexual health for gays and MSMs and the issues related to sexual identities. Sponsored by the Hum Safar Trust and The Naz Project, this seminar became the first South Asian Gay Conference. The Lakshya Trust, established in 2000, successfully organized the first state level gay conference in Gujarat in 2001, with gay youth from all over Gujarat participating in this three-day conference. These major conferences followed a decade of activism.

In the last quarter of 1991, AIDS Bhedbhav Virodhi Andolan (ABVA) in New Delhi, published, *Less Than Gay: A Citizen's Report on the Status of Homosexuality in India*. Its Charter of Demands called for the fundamental constitutional rights of the LGBT population of India for freedom and equality in all respects of social, professional, and political life. The Demands included repeal of IPC Section 377 and other discrimination laws, legalization of same-sex marriages, enactment of civil rights legislation, establishment of a commission to deal with and document human rights violations against LGBT individuals, and reformation of police policy to end harassment (Parekh 2003).

In August 1992, ABVA organized a protest demonstration against the unwarranted and illegal arrest of some individuals suspected to be homosexuals. Many social and human rights organizations also participated in this protest before a police headquarters in New Delhi, which received wide publicity and became one of the most significant events in the history of the gay and lesbian movement in India (Joseph 1996). This was followed, in 1994, by a Public Interest Litigation filed by ABVA in the Delhi High Court to consider the constitutional validity of IPC Section 377 and to abolish it because it violated privacy rights. This Section, enacted by the British colonial government in the 1860s, outlaws sodomy and other "unnatural offences" such as oral sex. It has created an environment in which MSMs have become most vulnerable to HIV/AIDS and STIs while prohibiting the Indian Government from educating people on HIV/AIDS transmission through homosexual sex.

The Indian education system requires an adolescent to spend five years in high school and higher secondary (junior college) education, beginning at about the age of thirteen. Mainly there are three types of schools: government schools (funded by either central or state governments), schools managed by private educational trusts but government-funded, and self-finance schools managed by trusts. Although there is no **discrimination** in admissions, examinations, or any other school activities on the basis of **sexual orientation** (due to the rights to equal opportunity in education granted by the Constitution of India), in many cases, effeminate boys become targets for various types of bullying, including abuse, harassment, or homophobic physical violence from fellow students, school employees, and sometimes teachers. Due to this, many LGBT youth experience guilt, fear, helplessness, and humiliation; most do not disclose their sexual identity. Emotional support and psychological assistance from trained counselors to LGBT students is almost nonexistent. Most schools do not have school counselors and even those working in expensive schools in cities lack sensitivity and knowledge about LGBT youth.

The National Human Rights Commission of India is active in violations related to women, children, and other minorities, but it has not involved itself significantly on LGBT issues. For example, in 2001, The Naz Foundation India Trust filed a complaint on behalf of a young boy who was forced to receive almost four years of **counseling** and drug treatment aimed at the conversion of his homosexuality. The case was taken up twice for a hearing but ultimately the Commission failed to take action, in part because of Section 377 of the IPC.

The **curriculum**, too, remains heterosexual. Lately, the educational policy to include subjects of sex education at different school levels has, in principal, been accepted. However, it is not fully implemented in every school, normal variants of human sexuality are not included, and teachers are not being trained on issues and problems of LGBT students.

The **Internet** has helped the LGBT population, especially queer youth, in many ways. Most gay and lesbian organizations have Web sites, and privileged LGBT youth living in **urban** areas are savvy in accessing these online resources. In a socially and religiously stigmatized society, it has become very easy for these youth to arrange meetings and parties, share their experiences and feelings, and connect to the LGBT world. However, poor and uneducated youth, particularly those living in rural areas, lack this resource, as do many schools, which cannot provide computer education to their students.

Access to research on LGBT issues is also severely limited. Indian academicians, working in the behavioral sciences, have avoided undertaking research and writing on this subject. Almost no empirical research has been undertaken on the issues and problems confronting LGBT youth. For example, in the twenty-seven volumes of *The Indian Journal of Clinical Psychology* (1974–2000), only 2 of the 829 research papers published were on the subject of homosexuality (Parekh, 2003).

Bibliography

AIDS Bhedbhav Virodhi Andolan (ABVA). 1991. *Less Than Gay: A Citizen's Report on the Status of Homosexuality in India*. New Delhi: Author.

Asthana, Sheena, and Robert Oostvogels. 2001. "The Social Construction of Male Homosexuality in India: Implications for HIV Transmission and Prevention." *Social Science & Medicine* 52: 707–721.

Jaffray, Zia. 1997. *The Invisibles: A Tale of the Eunuchs of India*. London: Weidenfeld & Nicolson.

Joseph, Sherry. 1996. "Gay and Lesbian Movement in India." *Economic and Political Weekly,* August 17: 2228–2233.

Nanda, Serena. 1986. "The Hijras of India: Cultural and Individual Dimensions of an Institutionalized Third Gender Role." *Journal of Homosexuality* 2, nos. 3/4: 35–54.

Parekh, Suresh. 2003. "Homosexuality in India: The Light at the End of the Tunnel." *Journal of Gay and Lesbian Psychotherapy* 7, nos. 1/2: 145–163.

Internet, Gay Men and the

Rodney Jones

The Internet has had a dramatic impact on the lives of **gay youth** worldwide, changing the way they meet friends and form relationships, maintaining and expanding communities, engaging in political activism, sharing information about

See also Asia, LGBT Youth and Issues in; Colonialism and Homosexuality; Internet, Lesbians and the; Queer Zines; Youth Culture.

important issues like HIV/**AIDS**, and defining what it means to be gay. The Internet has been a particularly important medium for those whom expression of **sexual identity** is constrained in real life contexts, such as younger men, men who do not identify themselves as exclusively gay, and men who live in homophobic societies or in **rural** areas. While the Internet has changed the way gay men interact, they have also changed the Internet. They were among the first to colonize "cyberspace" and studies have shown that more gay men regularly use the Internet and have used it longer than heterosexual men (Kolko 2003). Gay men have also played an important role in the development of Internet culture and have been at the forefront of movements to preserve online free speech and diversity.

Perhaps the first organized presence of gay men in cyberspace was in the USENET group soc.motts, founded by Steve Dyer in 1983 as an outgrowth of the group net.singles. Soon it became one of the most popular and well-respected USENET groups. Since then literally thousands of gay newsgroups (e.g., alt.politics.homosexuality, soc.support.youth.gaylesbian-bi), Web sites, bulletin boards, e-mail discussion lists (listserves), chat rooms and IRC channels, multiple user virtual role-playing environments (MUDS and MOOS)—including a significant area in the first and most well-established MOO, LambdaMOO—and online **dating** services have been established. Large Internet Service Providers (ISPs) such as America Online and Microsoft Network provide community forums and chat areas for gay men. In addition, a number of directories and "meta-Web sites" exist to help gay men navigate the complex terrain of gay cyberspace, the most notable being the Queer Resources Directory, started in 1991 by Ron Buckmire. Many gay Web sites like Queer Planet, Planet Out, and Gay.com, offer links to information about news and politics, entertainment, activism, travel, dating and romance, online chat rooms as well as erotic images.

One of the most important contributions of the Internet is that it provides "safe spaces" for the discussion of sexuality and the building of gay communities, compensating for the social isolation many gay men experience in physical spaces. This is particularly true for young gay men who do not have access to bars, clubs, and school or community support groups. The relative anonymity of the Internet can provide nonthreatening ways for young people to make contact with others and to explore issues of sexuality. It also allows them to safely access support and educational materials, meet friends, and express themselves through online discussions, and more recently, Weblogs (online journals). One of the earliest examples of a gay youth Weblog was the online diary of "JohnTeen Ø" published in America Online's Gay and Lesbian Community Forum in 1994 (Silberman 1994), which was instrumental in bringing the issues of gay youth into the mainstream of the digital discussion. Today, thousands of gay youth are "blogging," and many of these sites are consolidated in "Weblog communities" like Xanga.com.

The Web has played an important role in disseminating information about HIV/AIDS to gay youth. Sites such as YouthHIV.org provide access to detailed and accurate information about this disease and about safer sex for youth whose families, schools, or communities have not done as well in providing networks of support for HIV-positive gay youth.

The Internet has also been a powerful medium for gay **activism** and political action. It facilitates external and internal communication by small, grassroots, or student organizations as well as by major national or international groups such as the Human Rights Campaign, the Gay and Lesbian Alliance Against Defamation, the National Gay and Lesbian Task Force, and the International Gay and Lesbian Human Rights Commission. In 1999, for example, Eagle Scout Steven Cozza, then age fourteen, used a personal Webpage (scoutingforall.org) to promote and attract volunteers for his campaign to force the **Boy Scouts of America** to end its discriminatory policies against gay youth. Cozza's organization has members from every region of the United States.

Despite the relative freedom of speech gay men enjoy in cyberspace, censorship has always been an important issue. From gay men's first steps into cyberspace, there have been forces bent on silencing their voices. The establishment of soc.motts, for example, suffered extreme resistance from USENET administrators, and, in the mid 1990s, efforts by Compuserve in Germany to ban pornographic materials on the Web threatened to make gay political and educational Web sites (including those for **AIDS/HIV education**) inaccessible. In the United States, the Communications Decency Act (passed by the U.S. Congress in 1996, but later struck down by the courts) and similar laws passed by states have threatened free speech by gay men in cyberspace. United States federal law requires that software be installed on computers with Internet access in public libraries and schools receiving federal funding to block users from accessing pornographic Web sites, but these filters also block many sites dealing with gay political, social and health issues, including information on HIV/AIDS. In a recent case, the U.S. Supreme Court upheld this policy.

Many believe that the Internet has had a profound impact on the way men define gay identity and gay community (Woodland 2000). The relative anonymity of the medium allows users to experiment with different identities and sexualities, and the diversity of Web sites, newsgroups, and other online spaces provides an opportunity for youth with special interests or concerns to make contact with like-minded individuals.

The Internet has also been instrumental in the formation of gay communities in conservative societies and those with authoritarian governments. One dramatic example of this is Singapore, a society in which homosexuality is outlawed and made socially invisible by a conservative, paternalistic state. Here the Internet has provided spaces for building a gay community, developing gay activism, educating and networking gay youth, and integrating Singapore into the larger gay culture of the Asian region centered in places like Hong Kong, Taipei, and Bangkok. Much of this has occurred through the personal homepages of individual Singaporean gay men, such as Alex Au's *Yawning Bread* (http://www.yawningbread.org/index2.htm). This site has become such a focus for gay political discussion that it has influenced reporting in mainstream media. A survey conducted on the site showing that most Singaporeans hold tolerant opinions of gays and lesbians, for example, was reported in the nation's largest newspaper, *The Straits Times* (Offord 2003).

Commercial sites have also been influential. Most notably, Fridae.com, a popular gay dating service Web site has been instrumental in sponsoring and promoting the annual "Nation" parties, pan-Asian gay parties held on Singapore's national day that, for the past few years, have given "repressive" Singapore the reputation as one of Asia's rising gay social centers.

While the Internet creates opportunities for the development of local gay cultures, some have also noted that it has contributed to the "globalization of gay identities" based on the North American model of gay liberation and **identity politics** (Cate 2000). In most countries, gay youth generally learn about gay identity from North American and European Internet sites, which may marginalize local issues and indigenous gay identities.

The Internet, however, also poses risks. The explosive popularity of gay chat rooms and online dating services is one example. Several researchers have found a greater tendency to engage in unsafe sex among men who meet sexual partners online (McFarlane, Bull, and Rietmeijer 2000). In one high-profile case, a 1999 outbreak of syphilis in San Francisco was linked to a popular gay chat room. The relative anonymity afforded by the medium also increases opportunities for deception and homophobic activities. In 2003, for example, it was reported that police in **Egypt** were using a chat room to pose as potential sexual partners to entrap gay men (http://www.q.co.za/2001/2003/01/10-egypt.html).

Just as the Internet has facilitated gay activism, it has also been used by conservative political and **religious fundamentalist** organizations such as the United States-based Web site God Hates Fags (http://www.godhatesfags.com) and Canada's Family Action Coalition (http://www.familyaction.org). **Homophobia** also enters chat rooms, USNET groups, and listservs sometimes as verbal **harassment**.

Internet users still remain primarily young, white, European or North American men living in developed nations—as are those who maintain program and control most Internet sites. In 1999, it was estimated that, in 2005, there would be more than 10 million gay and lesbian Internet users in North America, whereas estimates for Africa and the Middle East were less than 100,000 and 20,000, respectively (Nua 1999). Two years later there were already 13.5 million global Internet users and *Computer Economics* projected the worldwide gay Internet population would exceed 22 million by 2005 (http://whorlpool.905host.net/files/edarchive13. htm; http://flashcommerce.com/articles/00/04/23/094150930.html).

The digital divide does not just separate developed and developing nations, but also different populations within developed countries. Although gay youth have, in general, more access to, and are savvier about, new communication technology than older generations, the access and skills they have varies greatly based on factors such as **social class**, quality of education, and the availability of computers in schools, community centers and homes. United States' minority gay youth generally have less access to the resources and support the Internet provides.

Bibliography

Berry, Chris, and Fran Martin, eds. 2003. *Mobile Cultures: New Media in Queer Asia.* Durham, NC: Duke University Press.

Cate, Paul Louis. 2000. *Out of the Closets and into the World: The Nationalization and Globalization of American Gay Identity.* Unpublished PhD. Dissertation. Georgetown University, Washington, DC.

Dawson, Jeff. 1997. *Gay and Lesbian On-line.* Berkeley: Peachpit Press.

Kolko, Jed. 2003, June. "Gays Are the Technology Early Adopters You Want." http://www.forrester.com/ER/Research/Brief/Excerpt/0,1317,17004,00.html. Accessed June 9, 2005.

McFarlane M., Sheana S. Bull, and Cornelis Rietmeijer. 2000. "The Internet as a Newly Emerging Risk Environment for Sexually Transmitted Diseases." *Journal of the American Medical Association* 284: 443–446.

Nua Surveys. 1999, July. "Over 17 Million Gay and Lesbian Internet Users by 2005." http://www.nua.ie/surveys/index.cgi?f=VS&art_id=905355025&rel=true. Accessed June 9, 2005.

Offord, Baden. 2003. "Singaporean Queering of the Internet: Toward a New Form of Cultural Transmission of Rights Discourse." Pp. 133–157 in *Mobile Cultures: New Media in Queer Asia*. Edited by Chris Berry and Fran Martin. Durham, NC: Duke University Press.

Silberman, Steve. 1994. "We're Teen, We're Queer and We've Got Email." *Wired* 2, no. 11. http://www.wired.com/wired/archive/2.11/gay.teen_pr.html. Accessed June 9, 2005.

Wakeford, Nina. 2000. "Cyberqueer." Pp. 403–415 in *The Cybercultures Reader*. Edited by David Bell and Barbara Kennedy. London: Routledge.

Woodland, Randal. 2000. "Queer Spaces, Modem Boys and Pagan Statues: Gay/Lesbian Identity and the Construction of Cyberspace." Pp. 416–431 in *The Cybercultures Reader*. Edited by David Bell and Barbara Kennedy. London: Routledge.

Web Sites

Digital Queers. Accessed June 9, 2005. http://www.lib.usc.edu/~mchugh/projects/DQ/home.html. An organization that promotes technology in LGBT communities and provides technical support to activist organizations.

Fridae.com: Asia's Gay + Lesbian Network. June 2005. Accessed June 9, 2005. http://www.fridae.com. One of the most popular Web sites in East Asian for gays and lesbians. It includes political and entertainment news as well as a **dating** service for members.

Gay.com. June 2005. Accessed June 9, 2005. http://gay.com/index.html. One of the most popular Internet Web sites for gay men with a very active international chatroom.

GAYNET. Roger B. A. Klorese. Accessed June 9, 2005. http://www.ibiblio.org/usenet-i/groups-html/bit.listserv.gaynet.html. The oldest and most active e-mail discussion list for gay men with a focus on collage campuses and gay politics.

Gay Youth: A Xanga Blogring. June 2005. Accessed June 9, 2005. http://www.xanga.com/blogrings/blogring.asp?id=2066. A good source of links to the thousands of Weblogs operated by queer youth.

Queer Resources Directory. June 2005. Accessed June 9, 2005. http://www.qrd.org/qrd. One of the largest and most comprehensive Internet gateways for gay men and lesbians, providing links to pages on queer culture, activism, history, health, and other issues.

soc.support.youth.gay.gay-lesbian-bi. 2005. Accessed June 9, 2005. http://groups-beta.google.com/group/soc.support.youth.gay-lesbian-bi. A moderated usenet news group providing support for gay, lesbian and bisexual youth.

Youth.org. April 2001. Accessed June 9, 2005. http://www.youth.org. A Web site offering advice, support, and useful links for gay youth.

YouthHIV.org: A Project of Advocates for Youth. June 2005. Accessed June 9, 2005. http://www.youthhiv.org. A Web site providing support for HIV-positive youth.

Internet, Lesbians and the

Mary Bryson and *Mary L. Gray*

Research concerning queer, lesbian, bisexual, and/or transgender (QLBT) young women and the Internet is scarce, and has focused almost exclusively on English-speaking and North American women, despite a proliferation of studies on related topics, such as "women and the Internet" or "sexuality and cyberculture." Published scholarship on adult QLBT women and the Internet has focused on (a) *online*

See also Colonialism and Homosexuality; Internet, Gay Men and the; Youth Culture.

public knowledge spaces (e.g., Web sites) and (b) perceptions of and experiences in *cyberspace locations, communities, and spaces* (e.g., e-mail lists, chat rooms etc.). **Lesbian youth** are members of a stigmatized and vulnerable subculture. The Internet can potentially provide these young women with access both to knowledge and to community and is, therefore, educationally and culturally significant.

In *public knowledge* spaces, users typically access an Internet location, such as a Web site, where the primary mode of **communication** is asynchronous and non-interactive. Users locate information and occasionally have access to a space for reading and posting messages. As Internet search engines improve, it becomes easier to find QLBT information sources online. However, portal sites (e.g., lesbian.com, lesbian.org) and resource sites (e.g., Queer Resources Directory, Planetout.com, Gayzoo.com), where a wide variety of knowledge and links are collected in one place, continue to serve an important function—ease of access to culturally relevant content. Cyberspace "travel guides," such as Jeff Dawson's (2003) *Gay and Lesbian Online*, provide the cyber-newbie with annotated and categorized collections of QLBT links. Although most Web sites identified as "gay" or "queer" are designed to appeal specifically to white gay men, it is important, as Wakeford (1997) argues, to take into account the radical potential of Web sites created by and for "grrls" and women (e.g., GeekGirl, Techno-Dyke). Web sites *can* provide QLBT women with culturally appropriate and specific knowledge that would otherwise be either inaccessible or very difficult to locate. As such, Web sites serve a very important educational function. Despite the male focus of most queer Web sites, with concerted digging QLBT women and grrls can find leads and links to content produced for and by women like them. QLBT women and grrls may begin by sifting through male-dominated public knowledge spaces, but with persistence, these Web sites can lead to women's online interactive spaces.

In *interactive spaces*, participants typically make use of a variety of tools, both asynchronous (e.g., e-mail) and synchronous (e.g., chat) in order to participate in an online community (e.g., Gay.com's "Women's Floor"). Bryson's (in press) **research** on QLBT women and Internet communities suggests that cyberculture serves a variety of functions that are relevant to the lives of queer women. These include: interaction with other queer women in a space that is relatively safe; opportunities to experiment with **sexual identity** and practice/s; entry into a cultural context within which to learn *how to be queer* through immersion and participation in a sexually-specific subculture; and access to cultural knowledge.

Correll's (1995) ethnography of the Lesbian Café, an Internet bulletin board system (BBS), provides an elaborate account of the negotiation of individual and community identities in the ongoing construction of, and participation in a lesbian bar existing wholly online. Her research provides ample evidence of the positive significance of online interactive spaces to a diverse group of women at risk of stigmatization and isolation. Cyberspaces are not, however, digital utopias for Sapphic community formation and interaction. Wincapaw's (2000) study of QLBT women's experiences in lesbian e-mail lists suggests that many of the exclusionary forces that divide and prevent access to embodied queer communities (e.g., **racism**, ableism) are reproduced in online interactions.

Although adult QLBT women can expect to find resources and communities geared towards their interests, young QLBT women face different barriers to accessing information intended for them. Web sites produced for QLBT youth reproduce the same biases toward white, gay, and male-identifying audiences. These sites rarely offer content specifically for young women. Commercial portals presume women—young or old—are a less lucrative advertising market. Funding available to build nonprofit organizational Web sites comes from **HIV education** programs and funds that target young men having or interested in having sex with men. These knowledge spaces implicitly—and, at times, explicitly—exclude young women.

QLBT youth more broadly find themselves locked out of the eighteen and older interactive spaces of commercially-produced chat rooms and lists created for their older counterparts. The nonprofit or community-based lists, arguably more central to QLBT women, are also often limited to those over eighteen. As a result, younger women have to hunt harder online to find opportunities to connect with other women. QLBT youth may seek community in the online fan sites of feminist singers like Ani Difranco or search through the regional chat rooms and groups of a large commercial portal like Yahoo for clues left by other young women possibly like them.

Youth generally have fewer resources to create their own knowledge or interactive spaces. In response, QLBT young people have collectively created online **queer zines** and Web log communities that bring young women and young men together. Addison and Comstock (1998, 367) quote a young person describing how she used the Internet to explore her sexuality: "I would go to the library and look up stuff on les-bi-gay issues, then I would go to the Internet and look it up. So, it turned from just wanting to escape . . . to becoming a place where I found knowledge . . . and it was a safe way to do it too."

While examining Internet zines found on one queer youth Web site as spaces for such exploration, Addison and Comstock also note that the opportunity for voice and political change is tempered by gender and **social class** inequalities. Gray (1999) found a similar discrepancy between the liberating potential of the Internet. Young men were far more likely to talk about their uses of this medium as a means to find community and relevant information than the young women in her study. It is impossible to determine whether this gap is due to the limited sample of youth involved or the historical moment of the mid-1990s when fewer young women were reportedly involved in computer use. A more recent study (Gray 2004) suggests young QLBT women are as heavily involved in using the Internet as their male peers. They use the personal ads and resource listings of larger, commercial sites to find out about groups and people already in their area that may have Web sites or information of their own linked to these larger listings. Although more young queer men report use of the Internet to solicit casual sexual encounters, young women were just as likely to acknowledge the importance of interactive spaces in finding new acquaintances and arranging romantic liaisons through Internet contacts. For young QLBT women, the most pressing issue is no longer how to get online (if technological know-how was ever the underlying problem). Today, there are tougher burdens to bear. After finding a secure and confidential link to the Internet, young women must still make their way through complicated layers of less-than-relevant commercially and individually created spaces to find connections to other QLBT women.

Bibliography

Addison, Joanne, and Michelle Comstock. 1998. "Virtually Out: The Emergence of a Lesbian, Bisexual and Gay Youth Cyberculture." Pp. 367–378 in *Generations of Youth*. Edited by Joe Austin & Michael Willard. New York: New York University Press.

Bryson, Mary. In Press. "When Jill Jacks In: Queer Women and The Net." *Feminist Media Studies*.

439

Correll, Shelley. 1995. "The Ethnography of an Electronic Bar." *Journal of Contemporary Ethnography* 24, no. 3: 270–298.

Dawson, Jeff. 2003. *Gay and Lesbian Online*. 5th ed. Los Angeles: Advocate Books.

Gray, Mary. 1999. *In Your Face: Stories from the Lives of Queer Youth*. Binghamton, NY: Haworth Press.

———. 2004. *Coming of Age in a Digital Era: Youth Queering Technologies in Small Town, USA*. Unpublished PhD. Dissertation. University of California, San Diego.

Nakamura, Lisa. 2000. "'Where Do You Want to Go Today?': Cybernetic Tourism, the Internet, and Transnationality." Pp. 15–26 in *Race in Cyberspace*. Edited by Beth Kolko, Lisa Nakamura, and Gilbert Rodman. New York: Routledge.

Wakeford, Nina. 1996. "Sexualized Bodies in Cyberspace." Pp. 93–104 in *Beyond the Book: Theory, Culture, and the Politics of Cyberspace*. Edited by Warren Chernaik, Marilyn Deegan, and Andrew Gibson. London: Centre for English Studies, University of London.

———. 1997. "Networking Women and Grrls with Information/Communication Technology." Pp. 51–66 in *Processed Lives: Gender and Technology in Everyday Life*. Edited by Jennifer Terry and Melodie Calvert. New York: Routledge.

Wincapaw, Celeste. 2000. "The Virtual Spaces of Lesbian and Bisexual Women's Electronic Mailing Lists." *Journal of Lesbian Studies* 4, no. 1: 45–59.

Web Sites

Lesbian.com. August 2004. Accessed June 9, 2005. http://www.lesbian.com. Dyke culture portal intended to facilitate networking and access to culturally relevant knowledge and sites.

Lesbian.org. 1999. Accessed June 9, 2005. http://www.lesbian.org. Resource site with links to a wide array of queer women's culture and communities.

OutProud. 2005. Accessed June 9, 2005. http://www.outproud.org. National Coalition for Gay, Lesbian, Bisexual & Transgender Youth.

Queer Youth TV. Accessed June 9, 2005. http://www.queeryouthtv.org. Provides information for the LGBT youth audience and the general public through original Internet video content that promotes a critical understanding of LGBT culture, institutions, topics, and issues.

Youth Resource: A Project of Advocates for Youth. June 2005. Accessed June 9, 2005. http://www.youthresource.com. Organization that provides useful information that appeals directly to youth regardless of location.

Intersex

Lynne Carroll

Formally termed "hermaphrodites," intersex people are born with some combination of ambiguous genitalia. Goldschmidt first introduced the term "intersex" in 1923 to describe a broad range of medical conditions characterized by anomalies of sexual anatomies. Today, the word "intersex" continues to be used as an umbrella term to denote many different types of medical syndromes. Intersex persons are also commonly referred to as "transgendered," another umbrella term that includes a

See also Adolescent Sexualities; Heterosexism; Multiple Genders; Sexism; Sexual Identity; Transsexuality; Youth, At Risk; Youth, Homelessness.

vast array of differing identity categories such as transsexual, drag queen, drag king, cross-dresser, and bigendered. While many parents and school personnel including teachers, **administrators**, and counselors, are beginning to recognize the needs of gay, lesbian, bisexual, and questioning youth (GLBQ), intersex youth continue to be ignored and rendered invisible in schools and universities. Consequently, many intersex and sex-reassigned youth live in fear and isolation, hiding their bodies and concealing their identities from others. Traditional **biology** curricula found in most high schools make understanding and acceptance of intersex persons more difficult.

The prevalence of intersexuality is estimated to be 1.7 percent of all live births (Fausto-Sterling 2000). According to Fausto-Sterling (2000), the most common forms of intersexuality are genetic females who are born with enlarged clitorises or with male genitals (congenital adrenal hyperplasia), genetic males born with feminized genitalia (androgen insensitivity syndrome), individuals whose gonads do not develop (gonadal dysgensesis), a condition in genetic males in which the penile urethra exits other than at the tip of the penis (hypospadias), unusual chromosome compositions such as XXY (Klinefelter Syndrome) or XO (Turner Syndrome), and "true hermaphrodites" (infants born with a combination of ovaries and testes). Recent scientific evidence suggests that several factors must be taken into account in determination of sex beyond the external genitalia of newborns: chromosomal, gonadal, hormonal, internal reproductive structures, external sex organs, sex of assignment and rearing, and sexual self-identification. Intersex persons typically experience incongruities between one or more factors. The sexual differentiation process begins after fertilization with different chromosomal complexes. While the sex chromosome in the maternal ovum is always an X, the sperm contains either an X or Y chromosome. In the initial stages of fetal development, the fetus is female. Sex differentiation occurs at about the third month with the presence of a Y or X chromosome. The sex chromosome complex for males is XY and for females XX. In the case of intersex births, there are a number of possible chromosomal variations.

The practice of interceding at birth through reconstructive surgeries on the genitals of intersex infants began in the 1950s with the advent of refinements in surgical technology. Sexologist, John Money, developed the standard medical protocol for the treatment of infants born with ambiguous genitalia. Money (1985) proposed that children develop a **gender identity** during the first two years of life through interaction with their parents, their perception of their genitals, and biological influences originating in utero. His protocol required that infants with obviously ambiguous genitals undergo chromosomal and hormonal tests by a multidisciplinary team of medical specialists such as geneticists, endocrinologists, and pediatric urologists in order to make a determination as to which sex the informant will be assigned. Gender reassignment was usually made within 48 hours of birth, and determined by the potential to surgically create nonambiguous, functioning genitals. The determining factor in many cases has been the actual size of the penis. In cases where the penis was adequate in size, chromosomal tests are performed. In genetic males (babies with a Y chromosome), phalluses of 2.5 centimeters or less (about an inch) in length are considered to be inadequate. In the case of genetic females (babies lacking a Y chromosome), those who are born with ambiguous genitalia are assigned as girls. Surgeons consider "enlarged" clitorises to be "cosmetically offensive" in girls and surgical reduction is performed (Dreger 1998).

In the past ten years, the convergence of several factors—including the influence of the gay liberation movement, the personal stories of adults who rejected initial sex/gender assignment, and those who experienced genital scarring, infection, orgasmic incapacity and emotional trauma—have led many to call for a moratorium on genital surgeries. In perhaps the most widely publicized case, entitled "John/Joan," John's penis was destroyed accidentally during a circumcision at eight months old (Colapinto 1997). Money and colleagues at Johns Hopkins University surgically removed his testes and performed cosmetic surgery. They claimed that efforts to raise John as Joan were successful. However, in 1997, Colapinto revealed that John never adjusted to his assigned sex; today he lives as man.

Currently, the medical treatment of the intersex is in a state of flux. No uniform standards that govern the medical management of intersexuality. Intersex persons have begun to speak out against genital surgeries and to organize politically. For example, in 1993, Cheryl Chase, an intersex person, founded the Intersex Society of North American. In 1996, twenty-six members of the Intersex Society of North America (ISNA) picketed the annual meeting of the American Academy of Pediatrics. Two years later, a special issue of the *Journal of Clinical Ethics* called for drastic changes in medical practices (Dreger 1998). Many within the medical and psychiatric establishment now believe that traditional medical practices performed on intersex infants were done more for the benefit of their parents and doctors. According to intersex activist Suzanne Kessler (1998), such surgeries are performed because infants born with ambiguous genitalia are a "threat" to the binary gender system and thus, ultimately to our culture. Intersex and gender variant persons challenge traditional heterosexist assumptions and constitute role models for a future world in which multiple identities and sexualities are not only possible but also desirable.

Researchers also have also begun to criticize the lack of scientific studies including long-term follow-up after surgery of intersex persons (Zucker 2001). Although it was assumed that there were psychological risks for intersex children who did not undergo sex reassignment, researchers are only just beginning to explore possible risks associated with the trauma of surgery, medical and parental withholding of information, and family attitudes. For example, in cases where clitoroplasty (enlarged tissue is trimmed and the nerve-rich glans area is retained to preserve sensation in the clitoris) is performed, patients may have difficulties in achieving orgasm (Minto et al. 2003). Similarly, the psychological and emotional consequence in cases where children are reassigned as female and the vagina is surgically recreated (necessitating a lifelong process of "vaginal dilation") has only begun to be studied (Hird 2003).

Today, the intersex movement seeks to halt pediatric surgery and hormone treatments that attempt to normalize infants into the dominant "male" and "female" roles. The ISNA is devoted, for example, to increasing the rights of intersexed persons to define themselves without doctor or parental interference. Many are of the opinion that sex assignment and genital surgery should at least be delayed until the child can make an informed decision. Thus, children might be raised as neither boy nor girl, but as "intersex." The ISNA also demands that **counseling** be more readily available since most of the limited counseling now available is provided by the consulting physician rather than by a trained therapist (Hird 2003).

As the issue of intersexuality gains increasing public attention and as more and more persons resist traditional medical procedures that aim to preserve the gender binary, the needs of intersex and **transgender youth** will become more apparent to the educator. They are frequently more easily identified or "read," by virtue of their nonconforming physical appearances and are consequently more vulnerable to verbal and physical **harassment** and acts of hate (GLSEN 2001).

Challenges that gender variant youth, including the intersexed, experience in our current transphobic culture are numerous, including verbal and physical harassment and physical assaults in schools and increased risk for homelessness, **substance abuse**, HIV infection and other sexually transmitted diseases, **prostitution**, and **suicide**. Additionally, the traditional biology **curriculum** of most high schools reflects an essentialist understanding about gender and sexuality. Information about the nature of sexuality and about the process of sexual differentiation is presented from the perspective of heterosexuality/reproduction. The process of sexual differentiation is presented as clear-cut (versus multilayered and diverse) under the guise of scientific "neutrality." Cast in this perspective, intersexuality is considered a biological accident and "correctable" through medical intervention. To present such an account only serves to maintain traditional gender divisions and to obscure the notion that masculinity and femininity are cultural constructs (Fausto-Sterling 2000). An intellectually honest biology curriculum which includes complete information and current research about the nature of sexual differentiation and the multideterminer nature of gender identity represents one step in the process of making schools more affirming of intersex and gender variant youth.

Bibliography

Colapinto, Joseph. 1997. "The True Story of John/Joan." *Rolling Stone*, (December): 54–58+.

Dreger, Alice E. 1998. "A History of Intersexuality: From the Age of Gonads to the Age of Consent." *Journal of Clinical Ethics* 9, no. 4: 345–355.

Fausto-Sterling, Anne. 2000. *Sexing the Body: Gender Politics and the Construction of Sexuality*. New York: Basic.

GLSEN. 2001, October. "National School Climate Survey." Accessed June 9, 2005. http://www.glsen.org/cgi-bin/iowa/all/library/record/827.html.

Hird, Miriam J. 2003. "Considerations for Psychoanalytic Theory of Gender Identities and Sexual Desire: The Case of Intersex." *Signs* 28: 1067–1092.

Kessler, Suzanne. 1998. *Lessons from the Intersexed*. New Brunswick, NJ: Rutgers University Press.

Minto, Catherine L., Lihe-Mei Liao, Christopher R. Woodhouse, Phillip G. Ransley, and Sarah M. Creighton. 2003. "The Effect of Clitoral Surgery on Sexual Outcome in Individuals Who Have Intersex Conditions with Ambiguous Gentialia: A Cross-Sectional Study." *The Lancet* 361: 9356.

Money, John. 1985. "The Conceptual Neutering of Gender and the Criminalization of Sex." *Archives of Sexual Behavior* 14: 279–290.

———. 1994. *Sex Errors of the Body and Related Syndromes. A Guide to Counseling Children, Adolsecents, and Their Families*. Baltimore: Paul H. Brookes.

Zucker, Kenneth J. 2001. "Biological Influences on Psychosexual Differentiation." Pp. 101–115 in *Handbook of the Psychology of Women and Gender*. Edited by Rhonda K. Unger. New York: Wiley.

Web Sites

Intersex Society of North America. December 2004. Accessed December 20, 2004. http://www.isna.org. A policy and advocacy organization whose mission is to end the secrecy, shame, and unwanted genital surgery for people born with atypical reproductive anatomies.

Queerbodies. 2003. Accessed December 20, 2004. http://www.queerbodies.org. A youth outreach project of bodieslikeours.org intended to provide education and information to the intersexed and their loved ones.

Ireland, LGBT Youth and Issues in

Michael Barron

Lesbian, gay, bisexual, and **transgender youth** (LGBT) are becoming more visible in Irish society. This is due, in part, to the work of LGBT community projects, particularly in larger **urban** areas such as Cork and Dublin as well as by LGBT visibility in the media and the implementation of equality legislation. In recent years, there have been a number of **curriculum** developments, allowing students to receive positive information about LGBT issues. These evidence the growing diversity of Irish society. The Catholic Church has, however, until recently played a powerful role in shaping Irish opinion towards LGBT people. This continues to be an issue within formal education as the Church maintains just over half of postprimary schools (students ages 12–18) in the Republic of Ireland. The experiences of LGBT young people in Northern Ireland (The North) and in The Republic (The South) differ in significant ways, particularly because just over half of the population in The North are members of one of the Protestant religions, whereas 92 percent of The South's population identify as Catholic. The school system in both areas is also different, with schools in The North using the British education system. This entry focuses on LGBT youth in The South with some reference to the situation in The North.

Ireland has seen a number of progressive changes over the past twenty years. For LGBT Irish, the single most significant event was the decriminalization of male same-sex sexual behavior, in 1993 (the age of consent was also equalized at seventeen). This event was the fruit of decades of work by lesbian and gay rights activists and allowed for LGBT rights to be protected in a series of progressive legislation which was to follow. Decriminalization also allowed the "gay scene" to move above-ground and for gay bars and clubs to visibly occupy social space in the larger cities.

LGBT community centers, all located in major coastal urban areas, are more visible and active in community development. Although continuing to struggle with limited state funding, six of the seven centers presently accommodate **LGBT community youth groups**, offering café and social space and providing information services. Telephone supports, which are operated on a voluntary basis, are among the oldest LGBT resources in Ireland. Ten Gay Helplines (four specifically supporting women) throughout the island offer important support to **rural youth**. Gay Switchboard Dublin, for instance, has reported a significant number of calls from young people in rural areas who find it very difficult to access additional support services. There has been no **research** into the lives of rural LGBT young people in Ireland, but the experiences of LGBT community groups in Limerick, Cork, and Dublin suggest they experience greater isolation than their urban counterparts.

See also Antidiscrimination Policy; Catholic Education; Coming Out, Youth; Counseling; Educational Policy; Europe, LGBT Youth and Issues in; Legal Issues, Students; Sissy Boy; United Kingdom, LGBT Youth and Issues in; Youth, At Risk; Youth, Homeless.

One service that regularly welcomes LGBT young people from rural areas is the BeLonG To Youth Project. Ireland's only designated LGBT youth service is based in OUThouse, Dublin's LGBT community center. It is also the only LGBT support service funded by The Department of Education and Science, permitting BeLonG To to focus on social and developmental education for youth, ages fourteen to twenty-three (prior state funding to LGBT organizations was almost exclusively granted by the Department of Health for **HIV education**). LGBT youth often travel to Dublin to access the projects services due to the lack of equivalent services elsewhere.

BeLonG To Youth Project, Gay Pride Parade, Dublin, July 2004. Courtesy of BeLonG To Youth Project.

BeLonG To Youth Project has reported that young people it works with have disclosed acts of self-harm and suicidal thoughts and that accessing appropriate counseling services for these young people, who are often not "out" to their parents, is a considerable problem (Gay Community News May 2004). Despite the fact that international research (Bontempo & D'Augelli 2002 Remafedi, Farrow, and Deisher 1991, and Northern Irish research (YouthNet 2004) has indicated that LGBT young people are more likely to attempt and complete **suicide** than their heterosexual counterparts, the Irish government has failed to protect this vulnerable population from this threat. A report by the National Task Force on Suicide, in 1998, failed to include LGBT youth as an at-risk group, despite recommendations by lesbian and gay community groups. In 2004, the government allocated an additional €13.65 million to suicide prevention measures. With the exception of providing part funding to one report, none of this money was assigned to LGBT **mental health** services.

School continues to be a site of alienation and marginalization for Irish LGBT young people. Homophobic **harassment** causes them to be disproportionately likely to leave school early (Combat Poverty Agency 1995; Gay HIV Strategies, 2000). Fifty-seven percent of lesbians and gay men surveyed experienced problems in school due to their **sexual identity** (Combat Poverty Agency 1995). This report further found that 8 percent left school early, one-in-four were physically assaulted because of their sexuality, and one-third were homeless at some stage in their lives. Another study of LGBT youth attending BeLonG To Youth Service found that 73 percent of respondents experienced problems (including verbal and physical **bullying**, damage to property, and alienation) in their schools in reaction to their **sexual orientation** or **gender identity** (MacManus 2004). Most (98 percent) had no access to information about LGBT life in their schools, and one-half reported that a negative image of LGBT people prevailed. **Homophobia** negatively impacted the studies of 42 percent, and one-fifth of the respondents left school early, primarily due to negative reactions to their sexual orientation.

These negative experiences occur in spite of the Education Act (1998) and the Equal Status Act (2000). The latter specifically outlaws **discrimination** by schools on the basis of a student's sexual orientation or gender (including transgender), as well as on seven other grounds such as **race**, religion, and disability. A school discriminates *directly* (if someone is treated less favorably specifically on one of the nine grounds; *indirectly* (if a person from one of the groups outlined in the nine grounds cannot comply with a policy or requirement); and *by association*, (if someone is discriminated against because of their association with members of a group outlined in the nine grounds). Further, Section 11(2), dealing with student **sexual harassment** or other harassment by other students, can be used to protect LGBT students.

In order for a student to seek protection under the Equal Status Act, a (free) legal case must be filed against the school. However, the potential personal cost for an LGBT young person to publicly charge their school with discrimination on the basis of their sexual identity is very high. Additionally, religious schools, which are in most cases publicly funded but privately governed, are allowed to uphold their religious beliefs, further complicating how LGBT issues are treated.

A recent Irish study found that experiences of bullying and **stereotyping** in school had a very negative impact on **body image** among gay and bisexual young men, ages fifteen to twenty-five (Barron 2004). This qualitative study (one-third of the participants had left school early due to homophobia) found that they were exposed to extremely negative messages about the appearance of gay men. These messages indicated that gay men were weak, **camp**, and feminine. Consequently, these men consciously altered their appearance and reported a high level of "internalized homophobia." Further, harassment of these men was largely premised on them being "effeminized" by others who used language degrading to women to describe them and who mimicked their "feminine" body movements. This feminization was systematic and closely aligned to traditional **gender roles**. Participants were isolated, bullied, and physically assaulted largely because they did not play or watch sports or behave aggressively like other "normal" young men.

In Northern Ireland, YouthNet (2004) carried out the most substantial study of Irish LGBT young people's needs and experiences. Two-thirds of the 362 respondents experienced verbal abuse, one-in-three had experienced at least one physical assault, and 29 percent had attempted suicide. Levels of **eating disorders** and unsafe sexual practices were also high and they were five times more likely than heterosexual youth to be medicated for depression.

In the postprimary school curriculum, there are two areas where LGBT issues can be discussed. The "Civic, Social and Political Education" (CSPE) program focuses on citizenship based on human rights. CSPE encourages young people to engage in action projects to promote understanding of the marginalization and discrimination experienced by minorities. Additionally, the "Social Personal and Health Education" (SPHE) program, specifically its "Relationships and Sexuality Education" component, includes sections on "human sexuality" and "information on and sensitivity to sexual orientation." Although these programs provide significant opportunities to discuss LGBT issues, their delivery is at the discretion of individual school policy. In the case of the SPHE program, each school maintains a committee of parents, teachers, and members of the school board who decide the programmatic details. The result is uneven inclusion of LGBT issues.

An All-Ireland gay men's sex survey found that two-thirds of the respondents between the ages of sixteen and nineteen had never tested for HIV (Carrol et al. 2001). This age group displayed significantly less knowledge about HIV risks than older gay men, also found it more difficult to acquire and use condoms, and were more likely to "sometimes feel lonely" than older men. Although there is a sizeable unmet need for HIV preventive work among young men (Sigma Research/Gay Health Network 2002), HIV testing and community outreach services for gay and bisexual men are well-developed in the country's largest urban centers of Dublin, Belfast, and Cork. In Dublin, the high-profile Gay Men's Health Project (GMHP), as part of The East Coast Area Health Board, operates a clinic for HIV and STI testing. GMHP also provides a full-time counseling service for men and women, a well-established personal development course (which many young men have participated in), and an active and well-respected Outreach Service to bars, clubs, and public sex sites. The Southern Gay Men's Health Project in Cork and Rainbow Services in Belfast provide similar services.

As has been reported in other countries, bisexual and transgender youth experience marginalization from both mainstream Irish society and from lesbians and gay men. In 2002, Bi-Irish, a Dublin-based political, social, and support group for bisexual people, surveyed the Irish queer community about attitudes towards bisexuality and the needs of bisexual people. This survey found considerable misunderstandings about, and mistrust toward, bisexuals among lesbians and gay men coupled to the belief among bisexuals that their social space, mental health, political, and parenting needs were unmet (Bi-Irish 2002).

Transgender people in Ireland have recently gained greater visibility. The highly publicized case of Lydia Foy who is suing the state for the right to change her name on her birth certificate, and the decline in emigration, as reported by the Irish transgender support group, Si, has increased their visibility. The Transgender Equality Network lobbies for civil rights for transgender people, and community projects such as OUThouse in Dublin and Lesbians in Cork are welcoming more transgender people to their services. Transgender youth continue, however, to be more marginalized than their gay and lesbian counterparts as is evidenced by twice as high rate of self-harm (50 percent vs. 26 percent) reported by respondents to the YouthNet study.

LGBT youth have only recently been featured in Irish **popular culture**. *Cowboys and Angels* (2004) and *Goldfish Memory* (2003) cinematically represent lesbian and gay youth experience, while *The Crying Game* (1994) centrally featured a transgender character. Colin Farrell, a very popular Irish actor, played a bisexual character in the Hollywood **films** *A Home at the End of the World* (2004) and *Alexander* (2003). OUTlook, the annual Dublin-based international lesbian and gay film festival, features short films by LGBT young people. On television, the two most popular Irish soap operas, *Fair City* and *Rus na Run,* have had positive gay characters. British television (which is very popular in Ireland) has featured high profile Irish LGBT personalities, most notably chat show host and comedian Graham Norton and *Big Brother* winner and TV presenter Brian Dowling.

Bibliography

Barron, Michael. 2004. *You're Meant to be a Man! Why Are You Girlie? Be a Man! Gay and Bisexual Young Men—Body Image: Stereotyping, Bullying and Body Image.* Unpublished Masters Thesis. London: Brunel University.

Bi-Irish. 2002. *Bisexuality: A Survey of Attitudes, Needs and Definitions amongst the Irish Queer Community.* Dublin: Author.

Bontempo, Daniel E., and Anthony R. D'Augelli. 2002. "Effects of At-School Victimisation and Sexual Orientation on Lesbian, Gay, or Bisexual Youths' Health Risk Behaviour." *Journal of Adolescent Health* 30: 364–374.

Carrol, Davis, Bill Foley, Brian Sheenan, Mick Quinlan, and Ronan Watters, eds. 2001. *Vital Statistics 2000: An All Ireland Gay Men's Sex Survey.* Dublin: East Coast Area Health Board Publishing.

Combat Poverty Agency. 1995. *Poverty-Lesbians and Gay Men: The Economic and Social Effects of Discrimination*. Dublin: Author.

Cosgrove, Judith. 2002. *Bisexuality: A Survey of Attitudes, Needs and Definitions amongst the Irish Queer Community*. Dublin: Bi Irish.

Equality Authority. 2002. *Implementing Equality for Lesbians, Gays and Bisexuals* Dublin: Equality Authority.

———. 2004. *Schools and the Equal Status Act*. Dublin: Equality Authority.

Gay HIV Strategies/Nexus Research. 2000. *Education: Lesbians and Gay Men: Developing Equal Opportunities*. Dublin: Gay HIV Strategies.

GLEN/Nexus. 1995. *Poverty-Lesbians and Gay Men: The Economic and Social Effects of Discrimination*. Dublin: Combat Poverty Agency.

MacManus, Edward. 2004. *The School-Based Lives of Lesbian, Gay, Bisexual and Transgender (LGBT) Youth*. Unpublished Masters Thesis Dublin: University College Dublin.

Remafedi, G., J. Farrow, and R. Deisher. 1991. "Risk Factors for Attempted Suicide in Gay and Bisexual Youth. Pediatrics" 87, no. 6: 869–876.

Sigma Research/Gay Health Network. 2002. *Vital Statistics 2000: An All Ireland Gay Men's Sex Survey*. Dublin: East Coast Area Health Board Publishing.

YouthNet. 2004. *ShOut: Research into the Needs of Young People in Northern Ireland who Identify as Lesbian, Gay, Bisexual and/or Transgender*. Belfast: YouthNet.

Web Sites

BeLonG To Youth Project, September 2004. Accessed June 7, 2005. http://www.belongto.org. This Dublin-based LGBT youth project site provides information about LGBT issues such as bullying and coming out and contains personal stories from Irish LGBT young people. It also contains a message board which is accessed by both members of BeLonG To and young people from rural areas.

Gay Community News, June 2005. Accessed June 7, 2005. http://www.gcn.ie/newgcn/home.asp. Ireland's main monthly LGBT magazine, which has traditionally focused on social and political issues and carries frequent features about young people.

Lesbians in Cork, June 2005. Accessed June 7, 2005. http://www.linc.ie. Ireland's only exclusively queer women's project. The site is primarily for women who identify as lesbian or bisexual; this may include transgender people (or those in transition) who identify as lesbian or bisexual.

OUThouse Community Centre, June 2005. Accessed June 7, 2005. http://www.outhouse.ie. Information about the LGBT community, events, and ongoing groups.

Si, Transgender support group, April 2005. Accessed June 7, 2005. http://www.transgender.org/si/. Provides information on transgender supports and social spaces in Ireland.

Israel, LGBT Issues in

Amit Kama

By and large, two main eras can be demarcated in charting Israeli lesbian, gay, bisexual, and transgender (LGBT) history: the current period beginning in the early 1990s, when LGBTs have begun to be dynamic actors within the public sphere,

See also Antidiscrimination Policy; Colonialism and Homosexuality; Heteronormativity; Intersex; Israel, LGBT Youth in; Jewish Moral Instruction on Homosexuality; Lesbian Feminism; Parents, LGBT; Popular Culture; Sexual Identity; Transsexuality.

politics, and media discourses; and, the remainder of history, so to speak, when LGBT identities were polluted, transparent, and symbolically annihilated and their images were severely stigmatized. The present situation is complex and mixed. The overall ease to come out, the intense media attention, as well as past achievements are to be commended, yet LGBTs are still, in many respects, second-class citizens with limited rights. Nevertheless, thanks to recent developments and processes, the younger LGBT generation faces less formal restrictions and societal sanctions, and benefits from a more welcoming atmosphere than its predecessors. To be sure, even when young people do encounter hardships, they have many resources, such as support groups across the country, to assist them in their struggles to become fully functional adults.

A remnant of British rule (1917–1948), the sodomy law was incorporated into the Israeli legal code after the British Mandate ended and the State of Israel was founded in 1948. In practice, the penalty of up to ten years of imprisonment was rarely enforced, and guidelines written by Israel's Attorney General in the early 1960s, asserted that sexual behavior between two adults in privacy need not be a matter for police prosecution. However, the inherent threat of legal sanctions reinforced invisibility and social marginality. Several other factors colluded in this process: (1) The Zionist ethos accentuating the precedence of a collective and united body of Israelis over personal needs and identities, especially in the face of an enduring sense of immanent threat from the Arab neighbors; (2) Zionism saw the apotheosis of the masculinity embodied in the new Jew's virile ideal, thereby precluding and repressing any signs of femininity; and, (3) Israeli citizens were supposed to bear as many progeny as possible in order to strengthen the nation. It is perhaps redundant to conclude that Israeli society, by and large, expressed intolerant attitudes toward "sexual deviants," who egotistically broke the cherished ethos, and, therefore, might contribute to the dissolution of the country. In this ideological, legal, and social climate, LGBT identity formation and **coming out** were neither feasible nor desired.

During the latter stages of this era, an LGBT community developed. In 1975, the Society for the Protection of Personal Rights (SPPR) was founded by a small group of gay men. They sought to provide a support network, constitute a hub of social activities, and furnish a focus of communal identification for a heterogeneous amalgam of disjointed individuals. But, for roughly the next thirteen years, its impact on both the public sphere and the LGBT community was quite negligible. SPPR activists were still in the closet, and their peers dreaded joining the organization due to the overall homophobic atmosphere prevalent at the time. The organization has grown dramatically in the years after 1993 and became an umbrella association for various groups around the country. Among its many activities and contributions, five are pivotal: organizing the annual Gay Pride Parade in Tel Aviv, which attracts some 20,000 people from many walks of life; publishing a monthly called *Zman Varod* (Pink Time); founding youth groups; running a telephone helpline; and, establishing a community center in Tel Aviv.

Following the footsteps of the SPPR, several other Israeli organizations have been founded. This includes the Community of Lesbian Feminists (CLAF), a nationwide political and social organization (established in 1987) led by and oriented to feminist lesbians. CLAF publishes *Pandora*, a lesbian journal. Another group, the Jerusalem Open House, is an independent organization intended to create a tolerant and pluralistic city where sexual and other minorities can live equally and openly. It runs a community center in down-town Jerusalem and organizes an annual parade. Belah Do'eget is the only association dedicated to furthering **AIDS** awareness within the LGBT community. It was established in 1994 after prolonged debates as to whether there should be such a group within LGBT community, possibly reinforcing societal **stereotypes** concerning gay men. Belah Do'eget organizes educational campaigns and Wigstock, an annual fund-raising event. Ge'ut is a unique Israeli phenomenon in which an LGBT caucus operates within a national political party (left-wing MERETZ). Ge'ut enjoys a full statutory position among other party bodies, and its head is automatically a member of MERETZ governing council. Ge'ut has successfully promoted several gay and lesbian candidates, among them the first openly gay Member of Knesset (Israeli Parliament) Prof. Uzi Even, members of the Tel Aviv city hall Etai Pinkas and Michal Eden, and member of the Jerusalem city hall Sa'ar Netan'el.

One all-inclusive generalization is that Israeli society has been less homophobic than many other societies. For instance, **hate crimes**, on the basis of **sexual orientation** and/or gender nonconformity, are virtually unknown. Being a socially and geographically small country, Israel exhibits a very tight web of interpersonal relationships. Israelis are likely to enact various roles with the same persons in different contexts. For instance, one's colleague may be her uncle's best friend; one's neighbor may be his military commander. Therefore, the anonymity sought by LGBTs and found in **urban** centers in other countries cannot be achieved here. As a result, being out to some people is, as a matter of fact, being out to many others.

Family ties and the family institution itself seem to be one of Israel's most fundamental value and norm. Doubtlessly, the entire social fabric is based on the crucial importance of having and raising a family—and safekeeping its cohesion. Israeli individuals are socialized to be loyal and devoted family members, hence, familial rejection on the basis of sexuality is quite rare. Consequently, as the general cultural climate is more conducive to being homosexual, coming out in both private realms and the public spheres grows in number and scope. This is not to be construed as if LGBTs face no—real or perceived—threats or that there is no sense of apprehension and anxiety surrounding the act of coming out.

The sodomy clause was removed from the Israeli legal code when the law was amended on March 22, 1988. Many legal, political, cultural, and social changes have since occurred. One legal measure was the addition of sexual orientation to the Law of Equal Rights at the Workplace, in 1992. Employees cannot be discriminated against on the basis of sexual orientation in any aspect of their employment. This law is universally enforced, thus school teachers who come out cannot be fired. A few gay men have reaped the fruits of this legal gain. The first was Jonathan Danilowitz whose partner was acknowledged by the Supreme Court, in November 1994, to be entitled to receive full spousal benefits by the former's employer. Another case was Adir Steiner's successful struggle to be acknowledged by the military authorities as the late Colonel Doron Meisel's widower in order to receive various rights.

In late 1992, Member of Knesset, Ya'el Dayan, formed a parliamentary subcommittee for the prevention of **discrimination** on the basis of sexual orientation. On February 2, 1993, it had its first meeting, which proved to be the second crucial turning point in the history of the Israeli LGBT community. Among the speakers at the event was Prof. Uzi Even, who demanded the abolition of the discriminatory policy of the Israel Defense Forces (IDF), listing all homosexual soldiers as mentally disturbed, automatically assigning them to psychiatric examination, and barring them from security "sensitive" positions. This demand to share in the burden of the military service with the rest of society prompted cabinet ministers and military officers to amend the discriminatory military policy, which was shortly thereafter revised. As of June 1993, soldiers are recruited, placed, and advanced regardless of their sexual orientation. The IDF is also tolerant toward **transgender** soldiers.

Indeed, by the mid-1990s, the era of LGBT symbolic annihilation was replaced by a more tolerant reception and participation thanks to several concurrent shifts within Israel. Among these changes, some were particularly vital such as depathologizing of homosexuality, which was largely incorporated by local professional communities of psychologists and psychiatrists who no longer view homosexuality as a mental disorder. Moreover, **identity politics** infiltrated into the local arena, as evidenced by the fact that dispersed individuals had begun perceiving themselves as part of a "gay community." Due to transformations in ideology and social practices, especially a decline of the Zionist ethos, assuming a LGB or T identity is now an acceptable and desired goal.

It seems as if the tremendously remarkable steps of the 1990s have come to a standstill, as almost no further legal achievements of any consequential impact have been accomplished. For instance, in 2000, the Supreme Court acknowledged the right of two lesbian women—Ruth and Nicole Brener-Kadish—to be registered as mothers for one's child. This decision, however, was contested by the State and has not been implemented, yet (and it does not seem likely to be in the foreseeable future). Any other vital measures needed in order for Israeli LGBTs to become full-fledged citizens (e.g., marriage, child **adoption**) cannot be implemented due to the current political constellation. The very presence of gay and lesbian representatives in the parliament and city halls does not and cannot in itself overcome persistent obstacles that are grounded in Israel's political map. The Orthodox Jewish sector, which comprises about 20 percent of the Jewish population, holds a larger share in the Knesset where it has an overwhelming power. As long as the basic political structure does not set apart religion and its institutions from the civil establishment, LGBT nondiscrimination demands—and of other minorities as well—will be hard to fulfill.

On the other hand, there have actually been some striking changes within other institutions; paramount among them are the media. Since 1993, there has been a practically continuous and rather sympathetic coverage of LGBTs and relevant issues by various media. LGBTs now constitute a vital part of public discourses and increasingly populate mainstream newspapers articles and magazine stories as well as various television genres; especially, talk shows, soap operas and other dramatic programs, game shows, and, recently, reality television. However, gay men are undeniably the most visible and active actors on the public stage; lesbians lag far behind with only a few and far between representations; the transgender group is represented by two or three male-to-female persons; **bisexual**s are completely invisible. Indeed, most popular texts produced in recent years revolve around gay men's experiences: the internationally acclaimed **films** *Yossi and Jagger* (2002) and *Walk on Water* (2004), TV series *Florentene* (1997–2000), and musical drama *Ba'al Ba'al Lev* (Gotta Have Heart 1998)—all directed by Eytan Fox who wants "to do for Israeli culture what Ang Lee did to Taiwanese culture with films like *The Wedding Banquet* and *Eat, Drink, Man, Woman*" (Curiel 1998).

The transgender singer Dana International was popular in the LGBT cultural circuit in the early 1990s, becoming central in the mainstream musicscape by mid-decade. In 1998, she represented Israel in the annual Eurovision Song Contest and won the first prize. Upon returning to Israel, Dana International was welcomed by tens of thousands of fans and was ceremoniously received at the Knesset. This event does not imply that transgender people enjoy an equal place at the Israeli table; most of them are situated at the very margins of Israel's society. However, the Ministry of Health assists in operations and postoperational persons can update their identity documents.

Generally speaking, two subpopulations maintain a separate existence alongside the mainstream Israeli society. One is the Ultra-Orthodox Jewish minority; Israeli-Arabs (Moslems, Christians, Druze, and Bedouins) compose the other. Neither group shares mainstream cultural and social arenas. For example, they use different languages (Yiddish and Arabic, respectively), hold a differentiated set of values and behavioral norms, keep autonomous schooling systems, and do not join the army. They, too, hold traditional, conservative views of sexuality and mostly deny the existence of homosexuality within their people. There is no readily available documented information about LGBT within these groups.

Bibliography

Curiel, D. 1998, July 18. Film Festival Showing Sexy Israeli Drama. *San Francisco Chronicle*. Accessed June 9, 2005. http://www.sfgate.com/cgi-bin/article.cgi?file=/chronicle/archive/1998/07/18/DD1760.DTL.

Gross, Aeyal M. 2001. "Challenges to Compulsory Heterosexuality: Recognition and Non-Recognition of Same-Sex Couples in Israeli Law." Pp. 391–414 in *Legal Recognition of Same-Sex Partnerships: A Study of National, European and International Law*. Edited by Robert Wintemute and Mads Andenas. Oxford: Hart Publishing.

Harel, Alon. 2000. "The Rise and Fall of the Israeli Gay Legal Revolution." *Columbia Human Rights Law Review* 31, no. 2: 443–471.

Kama, Amit. 2000. "From *Terra Incognita* to *Terra Firma*: The Logbook of the Voyage of the Gay Community into the Israeli Public Sphere." *Journal of Homosexuality* 38, no. 4: 133–162.

———. 2003. "Negation and Validation of Self via the Media: Israeli Gay Men's (Dis)Engagement Patterns with Their Representations." *The Communication Review* 6, no. 1: 71–94.

Lemish, Dafna. 2004. "'My Kind of Campfire?': The Eurovision Song Contest and Israeli Gay Men." *Popular Communications* 2, no. 1: 41–63.

Moore, Tracy. 1999. *Lesbiot: Israeli Lesbians Talk about Sexuality, Feminism, Judaism and Their Lives*. London: Cassell.

Shokeid, Moshe. 2003. "Closeted Cosmopolitans: Israeli Gays between Center and Periphery." *Global Networks* 3, no. 3: 387–399.

Sumakai-Fink, Amir, and Jacob Press. 1999. *Independence Park: The Lives of Gay Men in Israel*. Stanford, CA: Stanford University Press.

Walzer, Lee. 2000. *Between Sodom and Eden: A Gay Journey Through Today's Changing Israel*. New York: Columbia University Press.

Weishut, Daniel J. N. 2000. "Attitudes toward Homosexuality: An Overview." *Israel Journal of Psychiatry and Related Sciences* 37, no. 4: 308–319.

Web Sites

The Aguda, the association of GLBT in Israel (formerly the SPPR). Daniel Berkovich. Accessed December 2, 2004. http://www.aguda-ta.org.il/content/english.asp.

CLAF: Community of Feminist Lesbians. Accessed December 2, 2004. http://www.gay.org.il/claf.

The Haifa Forum. February 2003. Accessed December 2, 2004. http://gay.org.il/haifa/
index-e.htm. Serves the LGBT community in Haifa and northern Israel. Site includes
links, activities, and events.

Israel, LGBT Youth in

Amit Kama

The current situation in Israel is rather favorable for **lesbian, gay, bisexual,** and
transgender youth (LGBT), particularly compared to previous generations. Political, judicial, cultural, ideological, and social developments of the past decade mean
these youth face less formal restrictions and societal sanctions as well as benefit
from a more welcoming atmosphere. When Israeli Jewish non-Orthodox LGBT
youth do encounter hardships, there are many resources, such as the **Internet** and
support groups to assist them. By and large, Israeli LGBT youth face similar or
even identical problems and issues like their contemporaries in other industrialized
countries. Their life experiences—including psychological and social aspects like
identity development, coming out, dealing with both internalized and external
homophobia—are certainly not unique. On the contrary, it may be argued that
these very terms and conceptions are imported into the indigenous "cultural psy-
che" from the West, that is, the United States of America. Ideas of "identity,"
"community," and "coming out" have influenced Israeli culture in the past three
decades. It is plausible that outside of a globalized, postmodern, media-saturated
world, these concepts would have never materialized.

Israel's political structure does not separate religious from state apparatuses. In
this sense Israel is somewhat clerical. Several domains are exclusively controlled by
Jewish law. Marriage, divorce, and death, for instance, are performed by rabbis and
according to Halachaic regulations. This phenomenon constitutes a grave obstacle
for implementing full civil rights for the LGBT community; nevertheless, on the
personal, individual level it does not seem to bear any conspicuous influence.

Although no rigorous, large-scale **research** has been hitherto conducted about
Israeli LGBT youth, the overall impression is that there are no strikingly different
types of experiences or challenges faced by Israeli Jewish non-Orthodox LGBT
youth based on such sociodemographic variables as religiosity, **ethnicity,** or socio-
economic status. Israel's two subpopulations—Ultra-Orthodox Jews and Israeli-
Arabs (Moslems, Christians, Druze, and Bedouins)—maintain a separate existence
alongside the mainstream Israeli society and there is no readily available documented information about LGBT youth within these groups.

There are some distinctive aspects that impact LGBT (and all) Israeli youth.
One is paramount in the present context: mandatory military service for all Jewish
citizens at the age of eighteen (males for three years, females for two). The military
is a cultural crucible, where young adults from all walks of life (except for Arabs
and Orthodox Jews) blend. The army is perceived to be an organic and indispensable

See also Activism, LGBT Youth; Adolescence; Agency; College Campus Organizing;
Community LGBT Youth Groups; Educational Policies; Israel, LGBT Issues in; Jewish
Moral Instruction on Homosexuality; Youth, At Risk.

body; its roles are military and social. A feeling of imminent threat of their very existence causes most Israelis to realize that universal and obligatory conscription is necessary, and to acknowledge that being a soldier is a civil duty as well as a social and personal privilege. Additionally, serving in the army is considered to be an "entrance ticket" into the social fabric and is the abrupt psychosocial adolescent transformation from being "youth" to being "adults." Once teenagers join the army, they are no longer considered by themselves or by society as youth, but responsible, accountable, and to some degree, independent adults.

Men who leave the army at the age of twenty-one (and women a year earlier) are now supposed to be and act as full citizens. However, most enter a period of "moratorium" (in Eric Erikson's theory of psychosocial development, this is a period of delay before an adolescent's final commitment to a mature adult identity), lasting one to two years. During this stage, many travel abroad. Only afterward do young Israeli adults attend higher education and/or find a job at which point, unlike other countries, they cannot be easily categorized as youth.

From 1948, when the Israel Defense Forces were formed, LGBT adolescents were mostly recruited automatically, unless they explicitly disclosed their **sexual orientation**. In such cases, they were usually dismissed. LGBT soldiers who came out during their service were either discharged, deprived of certain "sensitive" positions (intelligence and reconnaissance tasks), or denied promotion. This military policy was harmful on many levels. LGBTs felt inferior, inadequate, and had trouble finding certain jobs and faced other state discriminations. Most critically, they were excluded from the Israeli social framework.

On February 2, 1993, a rapid chain of events, initiated by Prof. Uzi Even's speech at the Israeli parliament (Knesset), brought the annulment of this **discrimination,** and the military policy was officially changed that June. Since then, recruitment, positioning, and advancement have been uniform regardless of sexual orientation. Transgender soldiers are also to some extent embraced by the military: At least one male-to-female and one female-to-male soldier were allowed to serve.

This event evidences the Israeli LGBT's community entrenched need to be included within the large society. However, this change of policy did not end all manifestations of **homophobia.** Unquestionably, the army is an acutely homosocial world, in which close male bonding is highly encouraged, yet homosexuality *per se* is still very much the object of ridicule and shame. In other words, even though they face no formal discrimination, LGBT soldiers may nonetheless endure **harassment** and **prejudice** from peers and/or commanders.

This momentous change, coupled with several other legal and judicial advancements, brought burgeoning visibility, communal political mobilization, and an increasing trend of coming out. One result was a younger generation insisting its needs be met within the existing LGBT community. In 1994, young LGBTs stepped forward within The Society for the Protection of Personal Rights (the national gay organization formed in 1975) to demand formal attention and recognition. The principal objection to forming youth groups was grounded in the deep-rooted stereotype of the voracious homosexual as corruptor of youth, which could be used by authorities to harm the entire organization and community. In spite of these anxieties, a youth social and counseling support group was established in Tel Aviv. Psychologists and other experts served as the group's counselors, while young adults functioned as guides. Similar groups have since formed under the same auspices across the country, even in remote **rural** towns.

Other youth organizations have followed. TZAHAL BET—derived from the Hebrew name of the Israeli army but actually an acronym of Young Gay, Lesbian, and Bisexual People—was basically a social gathering with no "adult supervision." Its various groups gradually lost momentum and dissolved during the second half of the 1990s.

In 2002, No'ar Ge'eh (Youth Pride) was initiated by an adult gay man. Active in more than a dozen locations throughout Israel, over a thousand members take part in weekly activities with one hundred volunteers, providing guidance and assistance. Through an affiliation with the adult LGBT community, youth are assumed to be better able to participate in society with confidence and pride. The organized activities vary for two cohort groups: middle- and high-school students and soldiers between the ages of eighteen through twenty-one. As a result of a survey of participants' requirements, the older-age groups were divided between genders. However, all young gay men, lesbians, and bisexuals are embraced as equals Youth Pride offers a wide range of social activities as well as furnishing aids to combat homophobia and facilitate a healthy identity formation. Two boards of professionals—one is a supervisory committee, the other conducts research and is responsible for collecting and disseminating information concerning LGBT youth—maintain standards of operation. Since all these endeavors have been accomplished outside of the national education system, no groups have been established within schools.

2002 saw another crucial development with the founding of Beth Dror (House of Freedom). This is a halfway house—established, operated, supervised, and funded by the Tel Aviv city hall, the National Insurance Institute, and various nongovernmental organizations—for LGBT youth who are rejected from their families or feel unwanted because of their sexuality. Its main objectives are to assist these teenagers and to facilitate their prompt return to their homes and schools. Beth Dror offers rooms, meals, and shelter for eight people simultaneously for the shortest period possible. Other homes for unwanted youth exist in Israel, but Beth Dror caters only to LGBTs.

A LGBT youth official caucus, constituting an organic section of a national political party (left-wing MERETZ) is run autonomously and led by elected young adults. Hatzva'im Shelanu (Our Colors) was established, in 2003, to politically empower LGBT youth and organize demonstrations, petitions, and the like. Other vital developments during the last decade were the publication of two handbooks by the Ministry of Education, Culture, and Sport: One is for teachers and school advisors, entitled *Homosexual Orientation*, the other, *AIDS: A Question of Life*, is an AIDS prevention educational program for seventh to twelfth grade pupils. The former includes chapters such as a theoretical background, review of legal aspects, some life stories, and suggestions for in-class activities; the latter consists of statistical and medical data, safe-sex guidelines, policies concerning pupils with AIDS, and in-class activities. Although both issues are supposed to be integrated within the **sexuality education** curriculum, most schools seem not to do so.

Seeking to change the attitudes and improve the climate in high schools around Israel, Hoshen (Hebrew acronym for Education and Change), sends a gay man and a lesbian who unfold their life stories and hold question and answer sessions with students in the classroom. The situation is vastly better in universities and colleges, where many LGBT/Queer-related courses are regularly offered by openly gay and lesbian professors, and LGBT student groups exist. "The Other Ten Percent" at the Hebrew University in Jerusalem, "TQ/Techno Queers" at the Israel Institute of

Technology in Haifa, and "B-Gay" at the Tel Aviv University are basically social groups. There are a couple of scholarly discussion groups of which "The Gay & Lesbian Studies/Queer Theory Reading Group at Tel-Aviv University" is the premier and organizes an annual Homo-Lesbian and Queer Theory conference entitled Sex Akher (Different Sex), under the auspices of the Tel Aviv University.

In spite of these strides, findings from several studies suggest that heterosexual Israeli university students are little acquainted with homosexuality. For instance, Lieblich and Friedman (1985) found that Israeli students held more negative attitudes toward homosexuals than American students who studied in Israel, though the difference in attitudes was less toward lesbians than toward gay men. Ben-Ari (1998) studied the attitude change of **social work** students enrolled in a course on homosexuality at an Israeli university. At the start of the course, students' associations to the word "homosexuality" were predominantly stigmatized and negative. A positive change in attitudes during the course was attributed by the subjects to both its experiential and theoretical ingredients. Another study of Israeli students shows that prejudice and verbal abuse of others based on perceived homosexuality is common (Weishut 2000). Prejudice was reported to be higher among religious than among secular students and more pronounced toward gay men than lesbians. As in many studies in the West, acquaintance with homosexuals was found to be related to more positive attitudes. Presently the No'ar Ge'eh research board is conducting a survey on high school students' experiences within their schools, exploring issues of acceptance, tolerance, and violence (both verbal and physical) exhibited by peers and teachers.

As in other cultural arenas, Israeli media offer but a few images and representations of LGBT youth (unlike the recent trend of unprecedented numbers of gay adults who regularly inhabit Israeli media). One youth-oriented (with their parents being another target audience) book was published in 2000: *Mom, I've Got Something to Tell You* by Dvora Luz and Sarah Avni. The book is based on personal accounts such as Yosi Even-Kama's life story. He narrates his biography from being thrown out of his home upon coming out to his parents until he was embraced by a gay couple, who were promptly recognized by the Ministry of Social Affairs to be his foster parents. This recognition constituted a legal precedent in which a same-sex couple was allowed to become a foster family. Sadly, this case is unique and did not recur.

Although Israeli television has undergone a transformation in recent years and although LGBTs and their images are more visible in the public sphere, Education Minister Zvulun Hamer reconsigned homosexuality to the closet. In September 1996, Hamer banned Klafim Ptuhim (Open Cards), the first (and only) TV program about LGBT adolescents. Public demonstrations were followed by an appeal to the Supreme Court. On September 21, 1997, the Court required the minister to broadcast the program at the scheduled time (the afternoon "educational slot"). The one-hour program was later aired and quite sympathetically received.

The Internet serves as an indispensable and essential tool for LGBT adolescents who either live far away from the **urban** center of Tel Aviv or are too apprehensive to come out. Several forums and chat programs enable these and other youth to communicate and overcome a sense of isolation or loneliness.

By and large, based on developing evidence (which has not been systematically studied or documented) and personal experiences of people working with LGBT youth, we can surmise that the age of coming out is getting increasingly lower. Furthermore, it seems that disclosure of one's homosexuality triggers less homophobic reactions than in the past. This does not necessarily mean that all **queer** youth who come out are fully embraced by their families and/or other social circles; yet, animosity and hostility levels are certainly lesser than for previous generations. Finally, in 2000, the Knesset changed the age of consent for homosexual intercourse from eighteen to sixteen (as is the case for heterosexual acts).

Bibliography

Ben-Ari, Adital T. 1998. "An Experiential Attitude Change: Social Work Students and Homosexuality." *Journal of Homosexuality* 36, no. 2: 59–71.

Kama, Amit. 2005. "An Unrelenting Mental Press: Israeli Gay Men's Ontological Duality and Its Discontent." *The Journal of Men's Studies* 13, no. 2: 169–184.

Kaplan, Danny. 2002. *Brothers and Others in Arms: The Making of Love and War in Israeli Combat Units*. Binghamton, NY: Harrington Park Press.

Lieblich, Amia, and Gitza Friedman. 1985. "Attitudes toward Male and Female Homosexuality and Sex-Role Stereotypes in Israeli and American Students." *Sex Roles* 12, nos. 5/6: 561–570.

Weishut, Daniel J. N. 2000. "Attitudes toward Homosexuality: An Overview." *Israel Journal of Psychiatry and Related Sciences* 37, no. 4: 308–319.

Web Sites

The Gay & Lesbian Studies / Queer Theory Reading Group at Tel-Aviv University. April 2003. Accessed December 2, 2004. http://www.gay.org.il/qttau/index.html.

The Other Ten Percent. August 2003. Accessed December 2, 2004. http://planet.nana.co.il/asiron/emain.html. The GLBT students' union of the Hebrew University in Jerusalem.

J

Japan, Gay and Transgender Youth in

Takashi Sugiyama and *Keiko Ofuji*

Since the 1990s, the gay movement in Japan has produced youth support groups, circles at universities, changes in gay culture, positive changes in the media, and support of the gay and transgender communities. Although no overt **harassment** or **discrimination** against gay and transgender youth exist in Japan, homosexuality often is a target of ridicule on television. Transgender people have begun to gain more attention because of the influence of television shows and social activist movements. However, there remains a general ignorance of and indifference to the human and civil rights of sexual minorities. The **Internet** has had both positive and negative impact.

A number of support groups that serve gay and transgender youth have been established recently. The first umbrella organization for high school students was *Aka* (OCCUR, the Gay & Lesbian Action Association), founded in 1986. OCCUR has established queer youth networks, offered **counseling** services and events for **AIDS**, investigated problems related to human and civil rights, recommended changes in social policy, as well as worked with foreign organizations. For example, in 1988, it fought against the opponents of the "AIDS Prevention Law" and succeeded in changing the definition of homosexuality from "abnormal sexual love" to "one of sexual orientations" in the *Japanese Language Dictionary*. Youth activists in OCCUR also successfully sued the Tokyo Metropolitan Board of Education (TMBE), in 1994 and 1997. Earlier TMBE had denied OCCUR members the use of the "Fuchu Youth House," social or educational activities. In ruling in favor of OCCUR, the judge ruled that, "The administrative authorities need to be more careful when considering situations concerning homosexuals and other minority groups, and they need to consider the homosexuals' rights and well-being" (Hanrei Times Company 1999, 214).

Another support group, the VSG (Various Sexuality Group), was established in 1998 for Osaka youth. Recruiting members through local magazines, these youth activists have published and circulated newsletters, as well as organized meetings and social events where they talk about their school lives, self-acceptance, **coming out**, and family relationships.

There are many sexual minority groups organized at universities, but there is no school support. Early ones were *GLOW* at Waseda University, *Chu-dai Hilltop* at Chuo University, and *VIVID* at Toyo University. Initially, the goal of most groups was to socialize. *VIVID* was the first to study sexuality and has published a booklet of sexuality terms.

Transgender (TG) and transsexual (TS) youth support groups also have been widely established. The most prominent one, TNJ (Trans-Net Japan) created in 1996, includes TG and TS people, partners, counselors, medical associates, and

See also Activism, LGBT Youth; Asia, LGBT Youth and Issues in; College Campus Organizing; Community LGBT Youth Groups; Japan, HIV/AIDS Education in; Japan, LGBT Issues in; Japan, Lesbian and Bisexual Youth in; Popular Culture; Social Class; Transsexuality; Youth, At Risk.

supporters. TNJ provides symposia and workshops that include discussions about the **Gender Identity Disorder** (GID) Special Law passed by the Japanese Diet in July 2003, lectures by guest speakers, and an annual report meeting. TNJ arranges events such as an appreciation of cherry blossom celebration, transgender children and parents get-together, and an exchange with self-help groups throughout the country. Trans-Net Japan occasionally makes public comments, requests, or protests to national and local governments and to the media. For example, since 1994, TNJ has gained support for a "Transgender Day" (April 4), protesting against the expression *Okama-no Hi* (Fagot's Day) by *Nikkan Sport* (a sport newspaper). TNJ supports a performing arts group, Trans-Project Group, based on TG themes and its self-help groups are located in middle-sized cities such as Kita-Kyushu, Okayama, and Akita, with other events held in larger cities such as Hiroshima and Sendai.

G-Front Kansai is another support group, established in 1994, for TG/TS and other sexual minority groups in the Kansai area (around Osaka). The group publishes a monthly newsletter, as well as an annual news booklet and a personal voice-letter, and it also sponsors unique discussions groups, Trans Salon and Men's Salon, and offers workshops on sexuality and aging. Their meetings include book readings, discussions, films, and orientation for newcomers. Some members give lectures at schools and public meetings. Another group, K-Fun, was started by male-to-female **college students** in the Kansai area. Today, many members are female-to-male youth who hold monthly meetings and enjoy talking, drinking, and singing karaoke.

In 1999, Kyoto students founded ACDC Children. Members provide a variety of events such as monthly meetings and parties, workshops (sharing stories, reading books, and holding discussions), and films. In order to interest and educate the heterosexual society about sexual diversity, they provide newsletters and publications at universities, coffee shops, and institutions in Kyoto City. The group produces and sells T-shirts and stickers and participates in university festivals.

At present, **queer** students from more than fifty national and private colleges, universities, and vocational schools, mostly in the Tokyo area, participate in "University Students' Night." Sponsors include gay magazine publishers, video makers, owners of "*hatten-ba*" (sexual meeting places), and sake makers. Aside from being a popular social event, this provides an opportunity to learn about safe sex and AIDS (some profits are donated to AIDS prevention), and helps students realize the importance of the gay community.

Some Japanese gay male youth frequent meeting places (*hatten-ba*) or engage in gay **prostitution** (*urisen*). In metropolitan areas, *hatten-ba* may require a fee, such as hotels and gay saunas, whereas others places such as public parks and movie theaters do not. Male prostitutes may work as "hosts" at gay bars or clubs or freelance in more public places, and transgender youth may work as *urisen* where customers are usually heterosexual men. Gay prostitution is also used by some youth to meet same-sex friends among the hosts. The **film**, *Hatachi no Binetsu* ("A Touch of Fever," literally, the little fever of a 20-year-old), directed by Ryosuke Hashiguchi in 1993, portrays a university student who works part time as an *urisen* and follows his search for gay identity.

Since the 1990s, public attitudes have been positively influenced by the gay and mainstream media. *Badi*, a magazine for young gay men, began publishing in 1993. This monthly publication, which is readily available in **urban** as well as **rural** bookstores, introduces life styles of gays with photographs, stories, and personal columns. Gay books also are easily found in the sections for homosexual and/or gender issues in libraries or bookstores. *Doseiai Nyumon* (Welcome to the Gay Community), a complete guide to gay life for young gay men featuring photographs from the Tokyo Lesbian and Gay parade, sold 2500 copies in its first edition.

Gay and transgender youth also have been portrayed as main characters in **literature**, magazines, and **film**. *Yaoi* is a genre in girls' books and magazines about the love story between two boys. Nine short novelmagazines, twelve comic magazines, and thirty comic books in this genre are published every month. Popular *Yaoi* **comics**, which treat gays positively are *Trip* (1998) and *Boku-no Sukina Sensei* (My Favorite Teacher, 1998). A controversial comic with a gay theme is *Hi-izuru-tokoro-no Tenshi* (Prince in a Country of Rising Sun, 1994), in which Prince Shotoku (574–622) is portrayed as gay. The patterns of transgender comics are either transforming from male-to-female (and to male) or **cross-dressing**. Typical of these comics are *Ranma 1/2* (1988, English), *Hen* (Queer, 1990), *Stop!! Hibarikun* (1990), and *Onnanoko-de Seikai* (It is Right to be a Girl, 1996).

The first popular television drama in which the complicated loves and lives of young gay people were openly described as ordinary, conveying the theme that love is love regardless of the person's sexuality, was *Dosokai* (Class Reunion). Shown during ten Wednesday nights in 1993, the bars and clubs in Shinjuku-Nichome (Tokyo's gay district) were nearly empty. This 55-minute series featured the love relationship among three young gay men (Atari, Fuma, Ushio), one bisexual teenager (Arashi), and two straight women (Natsuki, Yui—Arashi's sister). Atari dates Natsuki, Yui, and Fuma. He does not realize that he is **bisexual** until later. Breaking up with Atari, Natsuki marries Fuma who tries to forget Atari. Arashi is attracted to Fuma but he has a sexual relationship with Natsuki. In the end, Ushio becomes transsexual and marries Atari. Natsuki tells Fuma that she is pregnant, but Arashi is accidentally killed before learning about it.

During the 2002 television season, another popular TV drama series, *Kinpachi-Sensei* (teacher) *in* (homeroom) *3-B*, introduced Nao, a student who was transitioning from female-to-male. The difficulties of becoming transgender in a typical middle school were described realistically. His voice did not change; his breasts grew bigger; nobody treated him as a man; he could not make friends. The story begins when a health teacher chooses a transgender issue as a topic for her lesson in a classroom in middle school, where Nao is present. She explains that a TG person is a person who thinks she or he is a man or woman, but her or his body is not. As the story progresses, the health teacher introduces Kinpachi to the Sexual Minority Teachers Network. Nao is eventually accepted by his peers.

Transgenderism in Japan, however, begins well before the television era. *Kabuki* plays were very popular in the Genroku period (1688–1703) after women were forbidden to perform in *kabuki* in 1629 due to moral issues. With the advent of men's *kabuki*, young men with long hair over their faces dressed as *o-kosho* (page) or as women (*oyama*), fascinating the audience. This *kabuki* style, called *wakshu* ("adolescent") *kabuki*, was forbidden in 1652 because of the corruption of public morals. Those young *kabuki* actors were also prostitutes, and *kagema-chaya*, originally an anteroom for actors, became a place for male prostitution. However, *kabuki* came back the following year as *yaro* ("rough man") *kabuki*, in which these young actors were forced to cut their hair by the authorities. To keep their charm, they used a *yaro* hat—a tie.

Some same-sex lovers were also prominent. During the Genroku period they "swore eternal love, tattooing or cutting each other's arms or thighs so as to mix their blood." (Watanabe and Iwata 1987, 91). And the writer, Saikaku Ihara (1642–1693), created many love stories between young men in his books including *Nanshoku O-kagami* (The Great Mirror of Male Love) in 1687. *Nanshoku* was accepted and flourished as a popular subculture with rigid **gender roles** of the couple as a man and a woman being the norm.

Given this rich transgender history, the greater tolerance for transgender persons—considered a biological fact of life—should not be surprising in contemporary Japanese society. After the broadcasting of the Nao's story and at the request of transgender people, the GID Special Law was implemented. This law allows transgender people, who are older than twenty, unmarried, and without children, to undergo gender reassignment surgery and legally to change their names after two medical doctors approve their condition. However, there are only a few medical institutes where this kind of the operation is performed in Japan. Well before adulthood, **gender identity** becomes a problem for some children when they are forced to wear uniforms in middle school that obviously identify them as either girls or boys. A few schools have begun to consider the difficulties of TG students and changed **educational policies** for them. Traditional families pose another problem for both transgender males and gay youth who face difficulties as sons who are expected to keep and carry on the family name by marrying and siring children.

In Japan, students do not learn much about sexuality and safe sex. Homosexuality is usually not a topic in the school curriculum because it is not listed in the governmental guidelines which schools and teachers must follow. Therefore, knowledge about sexual diversity is gleaned mainly through the media, friends, and the Internet. The Internet has made it easier for transgender as well as gay youth, especially in rural areas, to access information and to network. However, this requires some money and always presents the problem for "closeted" youth that their sexuality might be accidentally discovered or disclosed.

HIV/AIDS is another major problem facing sexual minority youth. Infection of HIV among young people has exploded in Japan. The gay community is concerned about the situation and does provide opportunities where gay youth can improve their knowledge and decision-making abilities. In many schools, despite national guidelines, **HIV education** is limited and has not had significant impact on safe sex behavior.

Bibliography

"Cho-Danshi-no Real-Life (Real Life of Super Men)." 2004. *Badi*, August: 60–70.
Fushimi Noriaki. 2002. *Gay toiu Keiken* (The Gay Experience). Tokyo: Pott Shuppan.
Hanrei Times. 1999. *Hanrei Times No. 986* (Case File No. 986). Tokyo: Author.
Ihara Saikaku. 1990. *Nanshoku O-kagami* (The Great Mirror of Male Love). Translated by Paul Gordon Schalow. Stanford: Stanford University Press.
Ito Satoru, and Yanase Ryuta. 2001. *Coming Out in Japan*. Translated by F. Conlan. Melbourne: Trans Pacific Press.
Komiya Akihiko. 2004. "Difficulties Japanese Gay Youth Encounter." Translated by Keiko Ofuji. *Journal of Gay and Lesbian Issues in Education* 1, no. 2: 29–34.
Leupp, Gary P. 1995. *Male Colors: The Construction of Homosexuality in Tokugawa Japan*. Berkeley: University of California Press.

McLelland, Mark J. 2000. *Male Homosexuality in Modern Japan: Cultural Myths and Social Realities*. Surrey: Curzon Press.

———. 2005. *Queer Japan from the Pacific War to the Internet Age*. Lanham, MD: Rowman and Littlefield.

Mizoguchi Akiko. 2000. "Homophobic Homos, Rapes of Love, and Queer Lesbians: An Analysis of Recent *Yaoi* Texts." *Queer Japan* 2 (April): 193–211.

Sugiyama Takashi, Komiya Akihiko, Watanabe Daisuke, and M. Tsuzuki, eds. 2002. *Doseiai: Tayoona Sexuality* (Homosexuality and Other Sexualities: How to Teach about Human Rights and Living Together). Tokyo: Kodomo-no-mirai-sha (Japan Institute for Research in the Education and Culture of Human Sexuality)

Watanabe Tsuneo, and Iwata Jun'ichi. 1987. *The Love of the Samurai: A Thousand Years of Japanese Homosexuality*. Translated by D. R. Roberts. London: GMP Publishers.

Web Sites

Ono Yumiko. November 4, 1991. Gay Rights Emergence Forces Issues Japan Has Avoided. *The Wall Street Journal*. Accessed June 9, 2005. http://www.aidsinfobbs.org/articles/wallstj/91/297. Describes the emergence of the gay rights movement in Japan as the Association for the Gay and Lesbian Movement (Occur) sued the Tokyo Metropolitan Government's Board of Education.

Queer Samurai Japan for Gay Youth. June 2004. Accessed December 4, 2004. http://www.geocities.co.jp/Berkeley/3508/start.html. Detailed site that provides an extraordinarily wide range of history and culture, bibliographies, and links for queer youth on Japan.

Japan, HIV/AIDS Education in

Akihiko Komiya

The advent of **AIDS** in Japan, beginning in the mid-1980s, politicized **gay youth** who tried to educate their peers on AIDS. When AIDS cases were first reported, in 1985, it was often connected with gay men. As of 2003, there were 6,500 case of persons with HIV (PWH) and another 3,000 persons with AIDS (PWA). Except for the cases from contaminated blood, more than 70 percent of PWH are in their twenties and thirties, most of whom contracted the disease through sexual behavior (AIDS Report 2003). Japanese educational efforts, through the Ministry of Education and Science, has had limited impact.

The efforts to educate Japanese citizens on HIV/AIDS have been complicated by political as well as educational obstacles, rooted in homophobic **prejudice** as much as bureaucratic slowness. Although the first AIDS patient in Japan was a hemophiliac, the Ministry of Health and Welfare falsely reported, in 1985, that the first patient was a homosexual. Three years later, the "AIDS Prevention Law" was proposed, discriminating against PWA/PWH—including homosexuals and sex workers.

As a response, community-conscious gay activists assumed responsibility for HIV education among gay men. Minami Teishirou founded AIDS Action, a peer support group on AIDS that took actions such as providing a hotline service in the late 1980s. OCCUR (The Association for the Lesbian and Gay Movement), consisting

See also Adolescent Sexualities, Canada, LGBT Youth in; Community LGBT Youth Groups; HIV Education; Homophobia; Japan, LGBT Issues in; Mental Health; Prostitution or Sex Work; Sexuality Education; Urban Youth and Schools; Youth, At Risk.

of gay and **lesbian youth,** raised objections at press conferences, and edited *AIDS Information,* which was distributed in gay bars and bathhouses. These community-based AIDS efforts, in turn, fostered many activists. Promoting AIDS education empowered Japanese **queer** youth and facilitated gay **activism,** which reinforced AIDS activism. In 1991, the number of PWH/A contracted through heterosexual behavior had risen 350 percent, which resulted in the School Association for Student Health, an extra-governmental organization, to fully revise its guidelines for AIDS education, recommending inclusion of condom information.

In school settings, progress has been slow. HIV/AIDS are not necessarily addressed in Japanese schools, despite guidelines issued by the Ministry of Education and Science (MES), which has recommended its inclusion in health and **physical education.** MES provides national guidelines for teaching. For example, in junior high school, teachers should stress the effectiveness of abstinence to prevent HIV infection and mention condom usage. For children with intellectual **disabilities,** teachers may deal with AIDS/sexual health in their classrooms. In one such class, intellectually disabled students compare HIV to a familiar villain from a popular TV show and learn how to prevent HIV by using condoms through the dialogue with their teacher (Watanabe 1999).

In Japan's "model school program," the Education and Science Ministry assigns motivated teachers within some outstanding schools to **research** and develop certain themes such as moral education and environmental education. Those schools then become models for other schools in particular subjects. At Misato Senior High School, in Okinawa Prefecture, various aspects of AIDS are taught in many subjects (http://www.misato-h.open.ed.jp/kenkyu/kenkyu-m.htm). During the first year, students read an English story about a singer who donates money to people with AIDS in English classes, learn immunology in **biology,** and, in social studies classes, study how to live her or his own life. Second year students learn preventive measures in physical and health education, gather information on AIDS from the **Internet** and make posters on AIDS in information technology, and learn how to prevent AIDS in domestic science. All students study **discrimination** and prejudice for the World's AIDS Day in their homerooms, attend a lecture on AIDS/sexuality, and hold exhibitions on AIDS/sexuality at the school festival. The PTA also writes articles in its newspaper, giving parents AIDS information.

Misato Senior High School is not typical. In many school settings, despite national guidelines, only a limited number of teachers educate their students about HIV and AIDS. According to one study carried out by the Health and Welfare Ministry, about one-third of university students report being taught about AIDS in junior high school and slightly less than one-half received instruction at the senior high level (Ushitora 2001). Although the number of people with HIV or AIDS is increasing through both heterosexual and homosexual contacts (AIDS Report 2003), particularly in the younger generation, teachers who address this issue are a minority. Further, teachers willing to talk about human rights issues for people with HIV/AIDS often don't know how to deal with sexuality issues in their classrooms. The cumulative result is limited exposure and ever more restricted content.

Nevertheless, there is some evidence to suggest that even these limited efforts have had some impact. Since 2001, socioepidemiological studies on HIV/AIDS prevention among high school students in Kyushu, the southern part of Japan, have found that their intervention has brought changes in students' attitudes and behaviors toward HIV prevention (Kihara 2004).

Much of HIV/AIDS education continues outside of Japanese schools. PLACE (Positive Living And Community Empowerment) Tokyo provides counseling and information services to PWH/A and their families, a hotline, and a speakers service (http://www.ptokyo.com/). A yearly **camp** performance event, the "Voice," promotes understanding about HIV/AIDS issues. OCCUR, now subsidized by the Health and Welfare Ministry, holds a "Dating Party" where the participants meet during the day to chat and attend brief lectures on safer sex at a community center. OCCUR also delivers small seminars on safer sex in gay bars. The great majority of participants are youth. Rainbow Ring is an organic network of people committed to "life with sex, HIV, and a condom." Sponsored by the Tokyo Metropolitan Government, go-com. is a monthly peer-organized workshop on safer sex. Both organizers and participants are youth in their teens and early twenties who meet in a drop-in center, set up by the Japanese Foundation for AIDS Prevention, in Shinjuku 2-Chome, the largest gay community in Japan.

Bibliography

AIDS Report. 2003. "Report on PWH/PWA" no. 62: 4. Tokyo: AIDS Yobou Zaidan (Japanese Foundation for AIDS Prevention).

Gun Yoshinori. 2000. "Shingakushuushidouyouryouwo-misuete-seikyouikunojugyouwo-doukumitateruka" (How to Develop a Teaching Plan in the New Guidelines). Pp.62–78 in *Chuugakuseino-seikyouiku* (Sex Education for Junior High Schoolers). Edited by Nogami Kazuhiko. Tokyo: Shougaku-kan.

Kazama Takashi. 1997. "Eizu-no-geika-to-douseiaisha-no-seijika" (Homosexualizing the AIDS and Politicizing Gays). *Gendai-Shisou* (Philosopher) 25, no. 6: 405–421.

Kihara Masahiro. 2004. *Socio-Epidemiological Studies on Monitoring and Prevention of HIV/AIDS.* Tokyo: Health and Welfare Ministry.

Komiya Akihiko. 2002. "Seikyouikuga-miotoshiteirumono." (Some Thoughts on AIDS-What We Have Overlooked). *Gendai-seikyouiku-kenkyu-geppou* (Monthly Report Sex Education Today) 20, no. 8: 1–6.

Kondou Masanobu. 1994. "From Kondou's Remarks on the Symposium Held by the Education Ministry for AIDS Education." Accessed June 3, 2005. http://www.hokenkai.or.jp/2/2-6/2-61/2-61-4.html.

Ono-Kihara Masako, Kihara Masahiko, and Yamazaki Hiroshi. 2002. "Sexual Practice and the Risk for HIV/STI Infection of Youth in Japan." *Japan Medical Association Journal* 45: 520–525.

Ushitora Kaori. 2001. "Deeta- wo-yomu" (Data Analysis). *Sexuality* 4: 111–119.

Watanabe, Takeko. 1999. "Eizuwo-utsusanaihouhouwo-kangaete-tameshitemiyou." (Let's Learn AIDS and Live with PWA). *Sei-to-sei-no-kyouiku* (Human Sexuality and Education) 24: 76–79.

Web Sites

AIDS Yobou Zaidan (Japanese Foundation for AIDS Prevention). Accessed June 3, 2005. http://www.jfap.or.jp. This Foundation disseminates knowledge on the prevention of AIDS to assist studies for the prevention and treatment of AIDS and to conduct international exchanges of information on AIDS so as to contribute to enhance health and welfare of the people.

JASE (The Japanese Association for Sex Education). 2005. Accessed June 3, 2005. http://www.jase.or.jp/. This corporation for public welfare, established with the approval of the Ministry of Education, provides many kinds of projects, services and seminars.

LAP (Life Aids Project). May 2005. Accessed June 3, 2005. http://www.lap.jp/. This non-governmental organization aims to support PWH/A as constructing mutually supportive relationships and care between PWH/A and People Without HIV/AIDS. Its Web site is famous for both quality and quantity.

Ningen-to-Sei-Kyouiku-Kenkyuu-Kyougikai (The Council for Education and Study on Human Sexuality). 2005. Accessed June 3, 2005. http://www.seikyokyo.org/. A non-governmental organization well-known for its liberal and enterprising teaching practices and theories. It started to tackle the lesbian and gay human rights issues as early as 1980s.

Japan, Lesbian and Bisexual Youth in

Keiko Ofuji

Lesbian and bisexual youth have long been invisible in Japanese society, that is, until some lesbians went public during the 1990s. Hiroko Kakefuda's 1992 autobiography, *Lesbian-de Aru-toiu-koto* (Being Lesbian) was followed three years later by Michiru Sasano's *Coming Out* and then *Onana-kara-Otoko-ni Natta Watashi* (I, Who Became a Man from a Woman), by Masae Torai, in 1996, and Kumiko Ikeda's *Sensei no Lesbian Sengen* (A Teacher's Lesbian Declaration) the next year. Their stories encouraged **lesbian youth,** but they remained largely ignored by mainstream Japanese society due to women's status, social and familial expectations, poor education, plus an indifference to and ignorance of sexual minorities in Japan. *Rezu* ("lez") is one of the derogatory words used by others. Nevertheless, lesbians have developed a distinctive Japanese community and culture. Japanese lesbians call themselves *bian*.

The possibilities for young women have improved as some old customs that enforced the preferential treatment of boys have been eliminated. However, lesbian and **bisexual youth** face difficulties, particularly as they enter adulthood. Social expectations and familial expectations of marriage limit career independence for women. Although many parents encourage their daughters to have a career, it is also more difficult for a young woman with a degree from a four-year college to get a full-time position at a company when competing with similarly qualified young men. Other parents simply discourage their daughters from getting a higher education so that they will remain submissive, marry, and have children. Conservative Japanese politicians encourage women to stay at home to be good wives and wise mothers (*ryosai-kenbo*), especially because fewer young people are marrying, the Japanese birth rate is low (1.29 in 2003), and the rate of divorce is increasing. Lesbians, therefore, are often forced to marry for purely economic reasons. Due to the Japanese Civil Law and its registration system, divorce is socially and financially disadvantageous for women.

Some women start careers late in life, often after they have recognized their **sexual orientation** in their twenties. The average salary of women (except for those

See also Activism, LGBT Teachers; Asia, LGBT Youth and Issues in; Community LGBT Youth Groups; Compulsory Heterosexuality; Crush; Feminism; Japan, HIV/AIDS Education in; Japan, LGBT Issues in; Japan, Gay and Transgender Youth in; Parents, LGBT; Sexism; Single-Sex Schools; Social Class.

of public servants) is 60 percent of a man's salary, and women are most often employed as office workers with no possibilities for promotion.

A woman's rights to make decisions concerning her sexuality and reproduction are ignored socially and politically in Japan. Single people and single parents are sometimes not accepted as fully adult persons (*ichininmae*). Single mothers are worried that their children will be treated differently, and there is no law guaranteeing that "illegitimate children" will inherit their father's property. Lesbians who want to have a child get married and remain in their marriages because **pregnancy** and **adoption** are almost impossible for single women in Japan. Those lesbian couples who have children prefer to live separately because it is more practical for a single mother family to get a social welfare support.

These social and political limitations notwithstanding, single lesbian mothers or lesbian mothers who live with another lesbian mother or partner have increased in Japan. However, there are no laws governing domestic partnerships. Many teachers do not acknowledge or talk about lesbian mothers with children, and the topic is not included in the governmental educational guidelines.

There are two large organizations that support lesbians and bisexual women of any age. *OLP* (Organization for Lesbian Power) with its 200 members was originally started in Osaka, in 1994. *OLP* organizes meetings and workshops, including lectures and seminars on sexuality, gender, and partner relationships, and sponsors social events. Kansai Weekend is an organized overnight event that encourages small group discussion. OLP publishes a newsletter and works together with organizations such as *WRAP UP*, a group researching women's sexually transmitted infections (STIs). Within a community space, called *QRWC*, *OLP* members meet and maintain a small lending library. Young members tend to remain in the organization until they find friends and/or a partner; some go on to organize smaller groups.

LOUD (Lesbians of Undeniable Drive, 113 individual and 14 group members) has operated a private community center for lesbians and bisexual people in Tokyo since 1995. The space is used for meetings, seminars, events, and printing the writings of lesbian and bisexual women and their supporters. *LOUD* also holds an open house event and sponsors a youth-oriented Candle (Light) Night party every month for women. Like OLP, this organization publishes a newsletter and operates a library. It also offers a discrete post office box service and sells products such as T-shirts and stickers. OLP members make plans and organize activities collectively, while LOUD encourages other groups to make plans and organize events and use the center. Bisexual young women are welcome to participate in these support groups. However, some lesbians avoid a bisexual partner due to the fear that she might leave the relationship for a man.

Today, lesbian youth, learning from the new feminist ideas, are freer from gender **stereotypes** and masculine and feminine role-playing. Many lesbian youth in Japan find friends, partners, and information through the **Internet** as well as through events sponsored by clubs, bars, and other organizations. Traditionally, magazines have been the primary mode of **communication**. Until 1992, the "Yuri-Corner" (*Yuri* literally means lily, but it implies platonic female bonding) was the only written means of communication among lesbians—and this column was within a gay magazine, *Bara-zoku*. From 1992 to 1995, *Labrys*, a small community magazine, offered lesbians a means to contact other lesbians. Ten issues were published, readership reached 2,300 and *Labrys* readers established small, local, lesbian and bisexual groups throughout Japan. More commercial magazines, *Phryne*, (1995) *Anise*

(1996–97, 2001–03), and *Carmilla* (2002–present), followed and were available in some bookshops, stores in gay districts, community centers, or by mail order.

The ages of *Anise* readers vary from teens to seventies, but it is most popular among lesbians in their twenties. *Anise* includes a variety of sections. A feature article in each volume may be about lesbian history and statistics on sexual orientation, partners, and so forth. The magazine includes interviews, biographical stories of lesbian singles and couples, an advice column, readers' column, lesbian sex, STIs and occasional lists of words and terms. Some partners of the couples introduced in *Anise* are lesbian, bisexual, **transgender**, or questioning persons. *Anise* offers short novels and **comics**, information about circles, organizations, events, bars, publications, movies, and videos.

According to the members of *OLP* and *LOUD*, inconsistent publication of lesbian magazines is due to the lack of financial power of lesbians; that is, many of them are students, part-time employees, or housewives. The lack of economic resources is also reflected in the low number of lesbian bars compared to the hundreds of small men's bars found in popular gay districts. Even though some young women go to bars, many young lesbian women cannot afford it.

Japanese comics are another educational medium that features lesbians and bisexual women as main characters, although they are much less popular than gay and transgender characters. One of the most popular comics was *Versailles no Bara* (A Rose of Versailles), especially because the traditional all-female *Takarazuka Review* produced a stage version in the mid- to late 1970s. It tells a story of the beautiful, strong-willed, bisexual or transgender (it is not exactly indicated in the comic) girl, Oscar, who was raised and educated as a boy by her noble father, because she was the only child.

One of the most recent popular comics is *Maria-sama-ga Miteru* (Maria is Watching), which is based on a novel of the same name by Oyuki Konno. The storyline centers on the "sister system" among select girls at a private, female **Catholic** high school. This genre, known as *Yuri* (girls bonding at school), depicts the close platonic relationships among girls long considered part of the growing up process in Japanese society. Here, the *senpai* (senior) and *kohai* (junior) relationship among students is sometimes close, distant, or powerful (in a way that seniors are dominant). Other very popular comics among lesbians are *Love My Life* and *Indigo Blue* by Ebine Yamaji. The main character of *Indigo Blue* is a twenty-nine-year-old bisexual woman, Rutsu, who loves a heterosexual man sexually and a lesbian woman emotionally and sexually. Her complex feelings and search for her identity are poignantly described. *Love My Life* follows the personal growth of a lesbian couple, Ichiko (age eighteen) and Eri (age twenty-two) as they enter society. These fictional characters serve as role models for some young lesbians who try to establish careers and relationships like Ichiko and Eri. In 2003, the *Show-Gun Theater* group performed *Love My Life* in two versions, one with the original lesbian couple and a second version in which the couple was gay.

Love My Life Book Cover.
© Evine Yamaji, 2001. Originally published in Japan in 2001 by SHODENSHA Publishing Co., Ltd.,Tokyo.

Leupp, Gary P. 1995. *Male Colors: The Construction of Homosexuality in Tokugawa Japan*. Berkeley: University of California Press.

Ministry of Education. 1979. *Seito-no Mondai-kodo-no Kiso-shiryo*. (Basic Data Relating to Student Problem Behavior). Tokyo: Author.

Pflugfelder, Gregory. 1999. *Cartographies of Desire: Male-Male Sexuality in Japanese Discourse, 1600–1950*. Berkeley: University of California Press.

Sei-Kyo-Kyo, ed. 1991. *Doseiai Project: Atarashii Fukei — Seikyoiku to Doseiai* (Homosexuality Project: New Developments in Sexuality Education Including Homosexuality). Tokyo: Author.

Sugiyama Takashi. 2001. *Gakko ni Okeru Doseiai no Seito-tachi e no Shien & Enjo no Kanosei* (Possibilities for Support and Help for Gay Youth: Educational Environments of Gay Students in High Schools). Kyoto: Kyoto Seika University.

———. 2002. "Doseiai Kyoiku (Homosexuality Education)." Pp. 139–144 in *Doseiai Nyumon* (Welcome to the Gay Community). Edited by Noriaki Fushimi. Tokyo: Potto Shuppan.

Sugiyama Takashi, Komiya Akihiko, Watanabe Daisuke, and M. Tsuzuki, eds. 2002. *Doseiai: Tayoona Sexuality* (Homosexuality and Other Sexualities: How to Teach about Human Rights and Living Together). Tokyo: Kodomo-no-mirai-sha (Japan Institute for Research in the Education and Culture of Human Sexuality). Translated, in part, by Keiko Ofuji in *Journal of Gay and Lesbian Issues in Education* 1, no. 1: 73–94.

Summerhawk, Barbara, Chiron McMahill, and Darren McDonald, eds. 1998. *Queer Japan: Personal Stories of Japanese Lesbians, Gays, Transsexuals and Bisexuals*. Norwich, VT: New Victoria.

Torai Masae. 1997. *Onna kara Otoko ni natta Watashi* (I, Who Became a Man from a Woman). Tokyo: Seikyu-sha.

Watanabe Tsuneo, and Iwata Jun'ichi. 1989. *The Love of the Samurai: A Thousand Years of Japanese Homosexuality*. Translated by D. R. Roberts. London: GMP Publishers.

Web Sites

Japan's First Gay Lawsuit Wins. September 24, 1997. Accessed June 9, 2005. http://gaytoday.badpuppy.com/garchive/world/092497wo.htm. Details on the Tokyo High Court ruling against the city Board of Education for discriminating against OCCUR in 1990 by refusing to let its members hold an overnight study meeting at a city-run youth hostel.

Sexuality Education Being Censorsed in Japan. August 2003. Ofuji, Keiko. Accessed June 9, 2005. http://www.bates.edu/~kofuji/humanrights/release.html. Media release on Japanese governmental intervention on sexuality education in schools in Tokyo, with related articles in English and links.

Jewish Moral Instruction and Homosexuality

Madelaine Imber

There are many different perspectives within Judaism relating to homosexuality; they are often contradictory. Given that there is no overarching governing of the different branches of the faith within Judaism, including Conservative, Orthodox

See also Community LGBT Youth Groups; Muslim Moral Instruction on Homosexuality; Parents, LGBT; Parents, Responses to Homosexuality; Religion and Psychological Development; Religious Fundamentalism; Spirituality; Transsexuality.

475

and Reform, there is no singular moral position on homosexuality and many different beliefs around sexuality and gender. Additionally, many people view Judaism as a cultural identity that may be distinct from religious beliefs as in the case of non-practicing Jews who identify as Jewish. The extent to which Jews follow the Scriptures depends upon their level of religiousness and their strand of Judaism. Jewish texts are always open to interpretation and study, so there is often more than one answer to any question. This, naturally, can be very confusing for **lesbian, gay, bisexual,** and **transgender youth** who seek to understand their **sexual identity** and often attempt to marry it to their faith.

The Jewish Scriptures consist of the Torah (first five books of the Old Testament) and the *Halakhah*, which are the Jewish laws; both of these are used in the Jewish understanding of sexuality. The more religious branches of Judaism follow these laws more closely (along with other laws, such as those governing diet) and thus have a greater aversion to homosexuality. As the faith is not centralized, each branch, country, and even congregation can have slightly different perspectives and levels of acceptance. Jews and Christians share the Old Testament, which includes the most well-known rejection of homosexuality as an "abomination" (Leviticus 18: 22). As a patriarchal religion, much of Judaic commentary on sexual prohibitions revolves around male homosexuality; however, in modern times, there have been restrictions put forward in rabbinical law around lesbianism (Greenberg 2004). **Bisexuality** is not dealt with individually—it is only considered when the individual is engaged in same-sex relations. Similarly, transgender is not mentioned, although it could fall under homosexuality due to the decreased likelihood of procreation. A "third sex," or what we might now call **intersex,** is mentioned in Jewish law (*Halakhah*), but there is limited discussion about it (Unterman in Magonet 1995).

Orthodox (*frum*), the most devout form of Judaism, including Hasidism and ultra-Orthodox groups, follows the laws of the *Halakhah* and the Torah that can be applied to modern times. The main aim is to serve G-d as a good Jew—the core of this is to marry and procreate. Thus, homosexuality's standing is on par with adultery, bestiality, and incest in the Torah and *Halakhah* (Eron in Swindler, 1993). Homosexuality is understood as anal sex between men, which is strictly prohibited. Some scholars and even some Orthodox rabbis confine the sin to this act; other sexual behaviors between men are, therefore, permissible. Although there are contradictions, the main school of thought, nevertheless, is that same-gender attraction and behavior are wrong. Lesbianism is not as strictly prohibited as male homosexuality, but, since women in Orthodoxy are seen in relation to men (daughters, wives, mothers), it is unacceptable within any of these roles.

The difficulties facing Orthodox women are different from those of the men. By the time many lesbians or bisexual women have come to terms with their sexuality, they could already be married and have children (Manning 1999). This marital dependence coupled with the lack of community status should they separate from their husbands to live as lesbians is why there appears to be more Orthodox gay men coming out than lesbians (Greenberg 2004).

There are gay rabbis (women cannot assume this role within Orthodoxy) who find a path within Orthodoxy and homosexuality (Greenberg 2004). Homosexuality is seen by some as a choice, as G-d would not create it, and celibacy is offered as one option (as within the **Catholic** faith), yet rabbis disagree on this solution. According to proponents of Orthodox Judaism, homosexuality is G-d's test to you in this lifetime, and the challenge is to live a good Jewish life, despite attractions to people of the same sex, in a heterosexual marital relationship. Transgender and intersex are not discussed in the *Halakhah*, given that these terms are relatively new. Presumably, Orthodoxy would struggle with the body modification of transgender, as it alters G-d's gifts, but intersex would not be as big an issue since it is the body provided by G-d.

Conservative Jews observe many of the laws in the Torah and *Halakhah*, but not as stringently as Orthodox Jews. There is still a focus on reproducing and serving G-d, which makes homosexuality be seen as incompatible. As with other issues, this is open for discussion and possible negotiation. Nonetheless, Conservative Judaism rejects **discrimination** against lesbians, gays, and bisexuals and accepts them into many congregations (again, depending on the individual stances of the specific congregations and rabbis). Like many **Christian** faiths, the behavior is seen as sinful, but the sinner is still welcome (Zelizer 1995). There are gay Conservative rabbis (again, this is restricted to men) who have come out subsequent to their ordination. Placing these gay men in congregations has caused concern in the Rabbinical Assembly, which is responsible for such placement, and there is always the risk that such placement will not be made (Zelizer 1995). There also is ongoing debate around other LGBT issues such as the place of gay or lesbian parents, young Jewish people in their coming of age ritual (*Bnei Mitzvah*), and death of a same-sex partner. The *Bnei Mitzvah* is an important ritual; however, it is gendered and heteronormative: Boys become men, girls become women, and both are expected to fit into their respective **gender roles**. For young queers this ritual is a privilege and a curse, representing a move to an adulthood not of their design.

Reform Jews are arguably the most liberal and progressive followers of the Jewish faith, and their interpretations of Jewish law are far more varied and open. As early as 1990, the American Hebrew Congregations began ordaining openly gay and lesbian rabbis. There are a growing number of LGBT Reform congregations. The first, Beth Chayim Chadashim in Los Angles, was established in 1972, closely followed by New York City's Congregation Beth Simchat Torah, in 1973. A large support group in London, the Jewish Gay and Lesbian Group, evolved at the same time. Subsequently, other congregations have sprung up in smaller cities, with at least twelve in the United States and other countries with a visible queer community. Since 2000, there have been commitment ceremonies for same-gender couples which, at times, even contravene civil law. However, few rabbis outside of these congregations would perform such ceremonies.

Within mainstream Reform congregations, levels of acceptance vary, and **heteronormativity** is still very much entrenched, with the focus remaining on the conventional ideas of family and traditional values. As a result, queer youth may still feel marginalized within this strand of Judaism and become more likely to move away from the faith as they come to terms with their sexual or **gender identity**. However, in terms of community participation, the main message is one of understanding and inclusion. As Reform Jews are often more progressive than other branches of Judaism, there is discussion and debate in many congregations around queer issues. Although many congregation members may be homophobic, the issue is still discussed, and there are avenues for young queers to speak to leaders within the community who are accepting.

There are many queer Jews who feel a strong connection to their faith regardless of its moral instruction on homosexuality. Some of these Jews who may have been brought up in Orthodox or Conservative households have come back to the faith though Reform Judaism. This demonstrates the depth of faith and community that reside within many people brought up within the Jewish faith—even if they have been rejected by one section; many wish to find their way back to the fold in some form. The feeling of being an outsider, as a Jew, also dovetails with the "otherness" of nonnormative sexuality—"to be a Jew is to have a history and to be queer is to have a history" (Nestle in Shneer and Aviv 2002, 24). For many youth, queer or not, being raised Jewish gives them an understanding of living outside the "norm." For LGBT youth this may increase their **resilience** as they come to understand and accept their sexual identity. For heterosexual youth, being Jewish may give them a window of understanding for being a minority and, thus, greater empathy toward sexual minority individuals and support on related issues as an **ally.**

There are diverse support networks for queer Jewish youth, regardless of their religious branch. Generally, where there is a LGBT community and a Jewish community, there will be a supportive network for those who are Jewish and queer, and even specific Jewish LGBT youth groups. Many act as surrogate families, conducting religious services together and celebrating festivals and other rituals. In **Australia,** there are groups for men and women, open to LGBT Jews and their partners. Within these, if there are enough young people, a subgroup exists for queer youth. If there is not a specific youth group, these youth can find an open and accepting community in these support groups and congregations, even if they are alienated from their branch of faith and/or their families.

There are Web sites, too, that act as a focal point for young LGBT Orthodox Jews. For many queer youth, the **Internet** provides an easy and anonymous access point, especially for those who may be Orthodox, married, closeted, or questioning their identity. In these spaces, there are opportunities for young people to join their faith with their sexual identity safely and within a community; often seen as impossible through other more traditional forms of **communication.**

Famous LGBT people have or still do identify as Jewish. Writers Gertrude Stein and Adrianne Rich are renowned within and outside of the queer community. Leslie Feinberg, who was brought up Jewish, is at the forefront of the transgender movement. Tony Kushner and George Cukor are just a few of many other people who have found a bridge between their queer identity and their Jewish faith. And, **Magnus Hirschfeld** led the first modern homosexual movement in early twentieth-century Germany.

Almost every branch of Judaism has links to **Israel**, strongly identifying with a Jewish homeland. However, given that the most immediate issue for Israeli Jews is the tension between Jews and Arabs, sexuality or divisions within the Jewish community are subordinated to the larger political issues.

Bibliography

Greenberg, Steven. 2004. *Wrestling with God and Men.* Madison: University of Wisconsin Press.

Magonet, Johnathan, ed. 1995. *Jewish Explorations of Sexuality.* Providence, RI: Berghahn.

Manning, Christel J. 1999. *God Gave us the Right.* News Brunswick, NJ: Rutgers University Press.

Shneer, David, and Caryn Aviv, eds. 2002. *Queer Jews.* New York: Routledge.

Swindler, Arlene, ed. 1993. *Homosexuality and World Religions.* Valley Forge, PA: Trinity Press.

Zelizer, Gerald L. 1995. "Conservative Rabbis, Their Movement and American Judaism." *Judaism: A Quarterly Journal on Jewish Life and Thought* 3, no. 44: 292–304.

Web Sites

Congregation Beth Simchat Torah. December 2004. Sharon Kleinbaum. Accessed December 18, 2004. http://www.cbst.org. This Web site of New York's first GLBT Reform congregation has information about Judaism, GLBTI issues, and as well as links to other congregations in the United States.

Dina's List. Accessed December 18, 2004. http://www.starways.net/beth/dina.html. An e-mail group especially for transgender Orthodox Jews—a space for discussion and support for transgender people at all stages (or none) of surgery.

Jqyouth.org. 2003. Newboy. Accessed December 18, 2004. http://www.jqyouth.org. Resource for young gay, lesbian, bisexual, and transgendered Jews with mailing lists and contact info for local groups, and helpful links.

The Orthodykes Home Page. Accessed December 18, 2004. http://www.orthodykes.org. and A Community of Frum Gay Jews. 2004. Accessed December 18, 2004. http://members. aol.com/gayjews/. Both include information and support for gay men and lesbians coming from an Orthodox Jewish background. Sites also have e-mail lists, meetings, and biblical analysis of GLBTI issues, and options for personal posting about being gay/lesbian and Jewish.

Trembling before G-d. 2003. Accessed December 18, 2004. http://www.tremblingbeforegd. com. Web site discusses the film with links to a range of Web sites around GLBTI and Jewish issues.

Twice Bless Archives. Johnny Abush. November 2004. Accessed December 18, 2004. http://www.usc.edu/isd/archives/oneigla/tb/. Links and information for GLBTI Jews around the globe.

Johns Committee

Ronni Sanlo

The Florida Legislative Investigative Committee, known as the Johns Committee for its first chair, Senator Charley Johns, was created by the Florida legislature in 1956. Originally investigating the National Association for the Advancement of Colored People (NAACP), the Committee turned to lesbian and gay citizens when the NAACP refused to cooperate. Hundreds of college professors and students, as well as public school teachers, left education either by coercion or humiliation, or, for some, by suicide (Sears 1997). Several of Florida's school districts and universities, including the University of Florida, fully cooperated as teachers, professors, and **college students** were interrogated, threatened, and intimidated. The Johns Committee released its report to the legislature in 1964. It contained information about homosexuality coupled to graphic language and photographs. Embarrassed and embattled, the Florida legislature disbanded the Committee and rescinded the report, which sold well on the black market as state-supported pornography (Beutke 1999). But the effects of the intolerance live on.

Charley Johns had been the acting governor of Florida before losing the gubernatorial Democratic primary race in 1954. Believing that civil rights work and the

See also Educational Policies; Licensure; Teachers, LGBT and History.

NAACP were infiltrated by communists and seeking an opportunity to return to the governorship, Johns convinced the legislature to form and fund the seven-person committee that was principally charged to investigate NAACP activities in Florida in hopes of dismantling the organization and dismissing all educators who supported it. Like similar state-sanctioned groups in other southern states, the Committee "trivialized civil rights, compromised academic freedom, and threatened the constitutional protection supposedly afforded to all Floridians" (Schnur 1997, 132).

The Johns Committee began by investigating the Tallahassee bus boycotts. When it demanded that the NAACP turn over its membership rolls presumably to establish a link to Communism (Pope 2003), the civil rights organization refused, and the United States Supreme Court prohibited the Committee from obtaining the membership lists (Beutke 1999).

In 1959, the Committee report "insinuated that homosexual behavior tended to increase with educational attainment" (Schnur 1997, 138). Investigators identified homosexuals on campus through various undercover operations and through the assistance of those apprehended. College professors and students, as well as public school teachers, were harshly interrogated under oath and without aid of legal counsel (Sears 1997). The coerced information obtained during those horrific sessions was used either to pressure the professor to leave the university, to have teaching certificates revoked, or to pressure presidents of universities to dismiss professors and expel students (Pope 2003).

Florida State University and the University of South Florida had tried, albeit unsuccessfully, to stop the investigations. University of Florida president, J. Wayne Reitz, cooperated with the Committee, fearing decreased funding from the legislature (Beutke 1999). Hundreds of professors and students were fired or expelled. The Board of Control, the governing body of the state's universities, "ceded its authority to the committee by sanctioning abuses in the investigation" (Schnur 1997, 137). Although Committee tactics violated Florida law, in 1958 alone, fifteen professors and over fifty students left the University of Florida (Beutke 1999).

Homosexuality and Citizenship in Florida, January 1964.

The report of the Johns Committee, released May 17, 1964, was entitled "Homosexuality and Citizenship in Florida," but because of the abstract purple cover, it was called the Purple Pamphlet (Sanlo 1999; Sears 1997). It contained ways in which homosexuals could be identified, suggestive photos of young men and boys, a glossary of terms, and a bibliography. Because of the large number of graphic photos, the report was called "disturbing," "in bad taste," and "crude" (Sears 1997). State Attorney Richard E. Gerstein branded it "obscene and pornographic and demanded that distribution be" stopped (Schnur 1997, 149).

In disgust, the legislature threw out the report. Charley Johns resigned from the Committee in 1964, and the legislature disbanded it in 1965 (Pope 2003; Schnur 1997). Although the thousands of pages of interrogations and notes amassed by the Johns Committee were to be sealed well into the twenty-first century, Florida was compelled to open them to the public, serving as the basis for a number of documentary histories (Beutke 1999; Schnur 1997; Sears 1997). Neither the state of Florida nor Charlie Johns ever apologized for their actions; their victims were never compensated.

Bibliography

Beutke, Allyson A. 1999. *Behind Closed Doors: The Dark Legacy of the Johns Committee.* University of Florida film documentary.

Pope, M. 2003, May 11. Red Scare, White Supremacy, Purple Haze: Joe McCarthy, Charley Johns and the Ripples of Fanaticism. *Tallahassee Democrat*, E1. Sanlo, Ronni L. 1999. *Unheard Voices: The Effects of Silence on Lesbian and Gay Educators.* Westport, CT: Bergin and Garvey.

Schnur, James A. 1997. "Closet Crusaders: The Johns Committee and Homophobia, 1956–1965." Pp. 132–163 in *Carryin' On in the Lesbian and Gay South.* Edited by John Howard. New York: New York University Press.

Sears, James T. 1997. *Lonely Hunters: An Oral History of Lesbian and Gay Southern Life, 1948–1968.* New York: HarperCollins/Westview.

Web Sites

Behind Closed Doors: The Dark Legacy of the Johns Committee 1999. Allyson A. Beutke. Accessed December 20, 2004. http://www.behindcloseddoorsfilm.com. Describes the documentary *Behind Closed Doors* and contains much of the content of the film with descriptions, commentary, and production notes.

Florida Legislative Investigation Committee 2001. June 2005. James T. Sears. Accessed June 9, 2005. http://www.jtsears.com/johnsmain. Accompanies Sears' *Lonely Hunters: An Oral History of Lesbian and Gay Southern Life, 1948–1968* and contains stories that were not included in the book but are important to the understanding of the work and devastation of the Johns Committee and its impact on gay and lesbian teachers and educators.